Accession no.
36185768

D1757533

THE ROUTLEDGE HANDBOOK OF LANGUAGE AND CULTURE

The Routledge Handbook of Language and Culture presents the first comprehensive survey of research on the relationship between language and culture. It provides readers with a clear and accessible introduction to both interdisciplinary and multidisciplinary studies of language and culture, and addresses key issues of language and culturally based linguistic research from a variety of perspectives and theoretical frameworks.

This Handbook features thirty-three newly commissioned chapters which:

- cover key areas such as cognitive psychology, cognitive linguistics, cognitive anthropology, linguistic anthropology, cultural anthropology, and sociolinguistics
- offer insights into the historical development, contemporary theory, research, and practice of each topic, and explore the potential future directions of the field
- show readers how language and culture research can be of practical benefit to applied areas of research and practice, such as intercultural communication and second language teaching and learning.

Written by a group of prominent scholars from around the globe, *The Routledge Handbook of Language and Culture* provides a vital resource for scholars and students working in this area.

Farzad Sharifian is a Professor within the School of Languages, Literatures, Cultures, and Linguistics, and the Director of Language and Society Centre at Monash University, Australia.

Routledge Handbooks in Linguistics

Routledge Handbooks in Linguistics provide overviews of a whole subject area or sub-discipline in linguistics, and survey the state of the discipline, including emerging and cutting-edge areas. Edited by leading scholars, these volumes include contributions from key academics from around the world and are essential reading for both advanced undergraduate and postgraduate students.

The Routledge Handbook of Syntax
Edited by Andrew Carnie, Yosuke Sato and Daniel Siddiqi

The Routledge Handbook of Historical Linguistics
Edited by Claire Bowern and Bethwyn Evans

The Routledge Handbook of Semantics
Edited by Nick Riemer

The Routledge Handbook of Linguistics
Edited by Keith Allan

THE ROUTLEDGE
HANDBOOK OF LANGUAGE
AND CULTURE

Edited by
Farzad Sharifian

LIS - LIBRARY

Date	Fund
26/6/15	1-Che

Order No.
263630x

University of Chester

Routledge
Taylor & Francis Group

LONDON AND NEW YORK

First published 2015
by Routledge
2 Park Square, Milton Park, Abingdon, Oxon OX14 4RN

and by Routledge
711 Third Avenue, New York, NY 10017

Routledge is an imprint of the Taylor & Francis Group, an informa business

© 2015 Selection and editorial matter, Farzad Sharifian; individual chapters, the contributors

The right of the editor to be identified as the author of the editorial material, and of the authors for their individual chapters, has been asserted in accordance with sections 77 and 78 of the Copyright, Designs and Patents Act 1988.

All rights reserved. No part of this book may be reprinted or reproduced or utilised in any form or by any electronic, mechanical, or other means, now known or hereafter invented, including photocopying and recording, or in any information storage or retrieval system, without permission in writing from the publishers.

Trademark notice: Product or corporate names may be trademarks or registered trademarks, and are used only for identification and explanation without intent to infringe.

British Library Cataloguing-in-Publication Data
A catalogue record for this book is available from the British Library

Library of Congress Cataloging in Publication Data
The Routledge Handbook of language and culture / edited by Farzad Sharifian.
1. Language and culture--Handbooks, manuals, etc. 2. Linguistics--Handbooks, manuals, etc.
I. Sharifian, Farzad, editor.
P35.R68 2014
306.44--dc23
2014016038

ISBN: 978-0-415-52701-9 (hbk)
ISBN: 978-1-315-79399-3 (ebk)

Typeset in Bembo
by Taylor and Francis Books

MIX
Paper from
responsible sources
FSC   FSC® C013056
www.fsc.org

Printed and bound in Great Britain by
TJ International Ltd, Padstow, Cornwall

CONTENTS

Contents

Contents

FIGURES AND TABLES

Figures

Tables

CONTRIBUTORS

Jeanette Altarriba is a professor of psychology and Vice Provost and Dean for Undergraduate Education at the University at Albany, State University of New York, as well as the Director of the Cognition and Language Laboratory at SUNY-Albany. Her research interests include psychology of language, psycholinguistics, second language acquisition, bilingualism, knowledge representation, eye movements and reading, concept and category formation, and cognition and emotion.

Dwight Atkinson is Associate Professor of English at Purdue University, Indiana, USA. His primary research interests are second language writing, second language acquisition, qualitative research methods, theories of culture, and English language education in the lives of first-generation learners in India. Recent publications include articles in *TESOL Quarterly*, *Language Teaching*, *Encyclopedia of Second Language Acquisition* (Routledge), and the edited volume, *Alternative Approaches to Second Language Acquisition* (Routledge).

Nigel Armstrong is senior lecturer in French at the University of Leeds, UK. His current teaching and research focus on two related subject areas: sociolinguistic variation in contemporary spoken French; and the study, from a translation perspective, of how language is used in popular culture. Previous publications include *Translation, Linguistics, Culture* and (with Ian Mackenzie) *Standardization, Ideology and Linguistics*.

Enrique Bernárdez is Professor of Linguistics at the Complutense University, Madrid. His main areas of research are the relations between language and culture, cognitive linguistics, Modern Icelandic, and Amerindian languages. He has published several books, among them: *Introducción a la Lingüística del Texto* (Madrid, 1982); *¿Qué son las lenguas?* (1999, 2004); *El lenguaje como cultura* (2008).

Penelope Brown is a linguistic anthropologist affiliated with the Max Planck Institute for Psycholinguistics in the Netherlands. She has worked for many years in the Mexican Tzeltal Maya community of Tenejapa, focusing on the study of adult language use in its sociocultural context and on Tzeltal child language acquisition and socialization.

Don Dedrick is an associate professor at the University of Guelph, Ontario, Canada, where he teaches in the Department of Psychology and the Department of Philosophy. He has a Ph.D. in philosophy from the University of Toronto. He has written about colour and cognition, as well as the metaphysics of colour.

Jean-Marc Dewaele is Professor of Applied Linguistics and Multilingualism at Birkbeck, University of London. His areas of research include individual differences in second language acquisition and multilingualism. He is editor of the *International Journal of Bilingual Education and Bilingualism*, former president of the *European Second Language Association*, and executive committee member of the *International Association of Multilingualism*.

Peter Eglin is Professor of Sociology at Wilfrid Laurier University, Waterloo, Canada. His academic interests are ethnomethodology and conversation analysis, philosophy of social science, human rights, and the responsibility of intellectuals. He is author of *Talk and Taxonomy: A Methodological Comparison of Ethnosemantics and Ethnomethodology* (1980) and *Intellectual Citizenship and the Problem of Incarnation* (2013).

Roslyn M. Frank is Professor Emeritus at the University of Iowa, co-editor of *Body, Language and Mind, Vol. 1 Embodiment* and *Vol. 2 Sociocultural Situatedness* (2008). Her research areas are cognitive linguistics, ethnography, and anthropological linguistics with a special emphasis on the Basque language and culture.

Anna Gladkova is an adjunct lecturer in linguistics at the School of Behavioural, Cognitive and Social Sciences, University of New England, Australia. Her research interests are in the areas of semantics, ethnopragmatics, linguistic anthropology, and intercultural communication.

Cliff Goddard is Professor of Linguistics at Griffith University, Brisbane, Australia. He is a leading proponent of the Natural Semantic Metalanguage approach to semantics and its sister theory, the cultural scripts approach to pragmatics. His major publications include the edited volumes *Ethnopragmatics* (2006), *Cross-Linguistic Semantics* (2008), and *Semantics and/in Social Cognition* (2013, special issue of *Australian Journal of Linguistics*), the textbook *Semantic Analysis* (2nd edn, 2011), and *Words and Meanings: Lexical Semantics across Domains, Languages and Cultures* (co-authored with Anna Wierzbicka, 2014).

Istvan Kecskes is Professor of Linguistics and Education at the State University of New York, Albany, USA where he teaches graduate courses in pragmatics, second language acquisition and bilingualism, and directs the English as a Second Language Ph.D. and MA programmes. Professor Kecskes is the President of the American Pragmatics Association, and the founding editor of several international journals, including *Intercultural Pragmatics*.

Andy Kirkpatrick is Professor in the Department of Languages and Linguistics at Griffith University, Brisbane Australia. He is the author of *World Englishes: Implications for International Communication and English Language Teaching* (2007), and the editor of *The Routledge Handbook of World Englishes*. His most recent book is *English as an International Language in Asia: Implications for Language Education* (2012, co-edited with Roly Sussex).

Claire Kramsch is Professor of German and Affiliate Professor of Education at the University of California at Berkeley, US. Her research interests are foreign language learning and teaching, discourse analysis and the relation of language and culture. Her recent books include *Language and Culture* (1998) and *The Multilingual Subject* (2009). She is guest editor of a 2014 special issue of the *Modern Language Journal* (on teaching foreign languages in an era of globalization), and is currently editing with Ulrike Jessner *Multilingualism: The Challenges*, to be published in 2015.

David B. Kronenfeld is Professor Emeritus of Cognitive Anthropology at the University of California/Riverside. He has published several books on kinship, semantics, and pragmatics, as well as articles addressing social organization, agent-based simulation, ethnicity, and the relationship among language, culture, and thought.

Paul F. Lai teaches Issues in English Teaching and Language Study for Educators at the University of California, Berkeley, Graduate School of Education. His areas of research include language, learning, and civic socialization among diverse youth. He has conducted practitioner inquiry, discourse analysis, and case study research projects on US immigrant youth, foreign language classes, and youth action research.

John Leavitt is Professor in the Department of Anthropology at the Université de Montréal, Canada, specializing in linguistic anthropology. His areas of research include comparative mythology, spirit possession and its relation to language, and the history of ideas about language diversity, with field research in the Central Himalayan region of northern India. He is the author of *Linguistic Relativities: Language Diversity and Modern Thought* (2011).

Ian G. Malcolm is Emeritus Professor of Applied Linguistics at Edith Cowan University in Perth, Western Australia. He has carried out research and published extensively on Aboriginal English and, with the help of Aboriginal and non-Aboriginal colleagues, has contributed to the development of the 'two-way bidialectal education' approach which is widely recognized and practised in Australia.

Meredith Marra is a senior lecturer at Victoria University of Wellington, New Zealand, where she teaches sociolinguistics at all levels. Meredith's core research interest is workplace discourse, especially the language of business meetings and the role of humour, gender, and most recently ethnicity at work.

Patrick McConvell is a Discovery Outstanding Research Award (DORA) Fellow of the Australian Research Council at the Australian National University, working on the AustKin kinship project, and on linguistic evidence for prehistoric groupings and migrations in Australia.

Sara Mills is Research Professor in Linguistics at Sheffield Hallam University. She researches feminist linguistics and politeness theory. She has published books, including *Gender and Politeness* (2003), *Language and Sexism* (2009), and is currently working on a book on gender and representation with Abolaji, and a book on indirectness with Grainger. She is also working on a project aiming to challenge the status of what we think we know about English politeness.

Frank Polzenhagen teaches English linguistics at the University of Heidelberg, Germany. The main concern of his work has been to develop a synthesis of cognitive linguistics and variationist sociolinguistics, with a focus on second-language varieties of English. His publications in this field include *Cultural Conceptualisations in West African English* (2007) and *World Englishes: A Cognitive Sociolinguistic Approach* (2009, co-authored with Hans-Georg Wolf).

Karen Risager is Professor Emerita in Cultural Encounters, Roskilde University, Denmark. Her main research area is the structure of the relationship between language and culture in a global and transnational perspective, including the concept of linguaculture, especially related to the educational field and to the field of research itself (the multilingual research process). Her books include *Language and Culture: Global Flows and Local Complexity* (2006) and *Language and Culture Pedagogy: From a National to a Transnational Paradigm* (2007).

Crystal J. Robinson is a member of the Cognition and Language Laboratory at the University at Albany, State University of New York. Her research includes investigating a potential adaptive component in bilingual memory. She is also working on a collaborative project investigating creative perception and production across cultures.

Sandra R. Schecter is Professor of Education and Applied and Theoretical Linguistics at York University, Ontario, Canada. Her research and publications focus on language policy and planning, language socialization, language and cultural identity, and bilingual and multilingual language acquisition and learning.

Farzad Sharifian is Professor and the Director of Language and Society Centre at Monash University, Australia. He is the author of *Cultural Conceptualisations and Language* (2011), the founding editor of the *International Journal of Language and Culture*, and editor (with Ning Yu) of the book series *Cognitive Linguistic Studies in Cultural Contexts*.

Chris Sinha is Distinguished Professor of Cognitive Science at Hunan University. He is Past President (2005–7) of the UK Cognitive Linguistics Association, Past President (2011–13) of the International Cognitive Linguistics Association, and General Editor of the journal *Language and Cognition*. Chris's central research interest is in the relations between language, cognition, and culture. A main aim of his research is to integrate cognitive linguistic with sociocultural approaches to language, communication, and human development. He has published widely in disciplines including anthropology, linguistics, education, evolutionary biology, connection science, as well as developmental and cultural psychology.

Laura Sterponi is Associate Professor of Language Literacy and Culture at the University of California, Berkeley Graduate School of Education. Merging her training in developmental psychology (Ph.D., 2002) and applied linguistics (Ph.D., 2004), she has developed a research programme that is centrally concerned with the role of language and literacy practices in children's development and education. Her studies have examined communicative practices in both typical and atypical children (specifically children with autism). Her work has been published in *Human Development*, *Discourse Studies*, *Linguistics & Education*, and *Journal of Child Language*.

Claudia Strauss is Professor of Anthropology at Pitzer College, California. She is the author of *Making Sense of Public Opinion: American Discourses about Immigration and Social Programs*, co-author (with Naomi Quinn) of *A Cognitive Theory of Cultural Meaning*, and co-editor (with Roy D'Andrade) of *Human Motives and Cultural Models*. Her current research examines personal narratives of unemployed Americans.

Lidia Tanaka is a senior lecturer in the Japanese and Asian Studies Program at La Trobe University. Her research interests are in language and gender, and language in communicative interactions. Her publications include a number of journal articles and the book *Gender,*

Language and Culture: A Study of Japanese Television Interview Discourse (2004). She is currently involved in a collaborative project looking at language changes in the speech of working-class women in the Kobe area from 1989 to 2000.

Peeter Torop is Professor of Cultural Semiotics at the Department of Semiotics and the head of the Institute of Philosophy and Semiotics at the University of Tartu, Estonia. He is also co-editor of the journal of *Sign Systems Studies* and a co-editor of the book series *Tartu Semiotics Library*. His latest books are: *La traduzione totale. Tipi di processo traduttivo nella cultura* (2010); *Tõlge ja kultuur* [Translation and culture] (2011); (as co-editor, with Katalin Kroó) *Text within Text – Culture within Culture* (2014).

Anna Wierzbicka is a professor of linguistics at the Australian National University. She is the author of more than twenty books, spanning many disciplines across the humanities, all underpinned by the conviction that an innate 'alphabet of human thoughts' is the key to all human understanding and to the diversity of languages and cultures. She is originator of the Natural Semantic Metalanguage approach to language, thought, and culture. Her latest books are *Imprisoned in English: The Hazards of English as a Default Language* (2013) and *Words and Meanings: Lexical Semantics across Domains, Languages, and Cultures* (co-authored with Cliff Goddard, 2013).

Hans–Georg Wolf is Chair Professor for the Development and Variation of the English Language at Potsdam University, Germany. His research interests include world Englishes, cognitive linguistics (including cognitive sociolinguistics and cultural linguistics), corpus linguistics, pragmatics, colonial language policy, and lexicography. His most recent books are *A Dictionary of Hong Kong English: Words from the Fragrant Harbor* (2011, with Patrick J. Cummings), and *World Englishes: A Cognitive Sociolinguistic Approach* (2009, with Frank Polzenhagen).

Xiaoyan Xia is a lecturer at the School of Foreign Languages and Literature, Beijing Normal University, Beijing, China. Her research interest is in applied cognitive linguistics, second language acquisition and foreign language teaching. Current research topics include cognitive approaches to second language acquisition, cognitive approaches to contrastive written discourse analysis, and the influence of differences in thinking modes on foreign language writing.

Zhengdao Ye is a Lecturer in Linguistics and Translation Studies at the School of Literature, Languages, and Linguistics, The Australian National University. Her teaching and research interests intersect meaning, culture, and translation. She has lectured and published extensively in these areas.

Ning Yu is Professor of Applied Linguistics and co-director of the Confucius Institute at Pennsylvania State University. His research focuses on the relationship between language, culture, and cognition. His publications include two monographs, *The Contemporary Theory of Metaphor: A Perspective from Chinese* (1998) and *The Chinese* HEART *in a Cognitive Perspective: Culture, Body, and Language* (2009).

ACKNOWLEDGEMENTS

The editor wishes to thank the authors of the chapters in the *Handbook* not only for their valuable contributions, but also for their help in serving as internal reviewers of other contributions. The external reviewers also deserve a special word of thanks for their helpful comments, especially on the initial proposal for the *Handbook*. I am also grateful to Nadia Seemungal, Rachel Daw, and Helen Tredget at Routledge for their help and support during the preparation of the book. A special word of thanks goes to Professor Roslyn M. Frank for generously offering to read and comment on all the chapters that were submitted for the *Handbook*. I am also grateful to Amanda Young for her very helpful editorial assistance. I received financial support from Australian Research Council twice throughout the process of editing this book (ARC DP [project number DP0877310] and ARC DP [DP140100353]). I also received financial support from the Alexander von Humboldt Foundation (through a Humboldt Fellowship for Experienced Researchers, based at the University of Potsdam, Germany) for part of the period during which I edited the *Handbook*.

A shorter version of Chapter 32 was published in M. Yamaguchi, D. Tay, and B. Blount (eds), *Approaches to Language, Culture, and Cognition: The Intersection of Cognitive Linguistics and Linguistic Anthropology*, Basingstoke, UK: Palgrave Macmillan, 2014. [www.palgrave.com/page/detail/?sf1=id_product&st1=634057]

The author wishes to thank Palgrave Macmillan for granting the permission to publish an expanded version of the chapter in this volume.

PART I

Overview and
historical background

1

LANGUAGE AND CULTURE: OVERVIEW

Farzad Sharifian

Interest in studying the relationship between language and culture can be traced back at least to the eighteenth century. Wilhelm Von Humboldt (1767–1835), Franz Boas (1858 –1942), Edward Sapir (1884–1939), and Benjamin Whorf (1897–1941) are prominent scholars who all emphasized the relationship between language, thought, and culture. However, a unified sub-discipline focusing on the relationship between language and culture has never been fully developed. Taking the US alone, Duranti (2003) distinguishes between three different paradigms in the history of the study of language as culture, which is summarized in Table 1.1.

Although Duranti associates the development of each paradigm with a certain period in history, he maintains that all three paradigms persist today. As for the labels, Duranti (2009: 33) notes that the term 'ethnolinguistics' has been a popular term in Europe for studies of language and culture (see Underhill, 2012). No matter which label or which theoretical orientation is adopted to study the relationship between language and culture, the difficulty in defining both terms has partly contributed to the immature development of a unified sub-discipline for the study of language and culture. Views of language have in the past century ranged from language as a cognitive system/faculty of the mind, to language as action, language as social practice, language as a complex adaptive system, etc. Culture has similarly been viewed differently by different schools of thought. It has been seen, for example, as a cognitive system, as a symbolic system, as social practice, or as a construct (see Foley, 1997; and Chapters 10 and 28 this volume). Furthermore, the relations between language, culture, and thought provoke different questions in different disciplines and are treated variously by the scholars within each field.

The challenge that has faced studies of language and culture, due to the complexity of the two notions, has been reflected in the absence of a handbook dedicated to language and culture.[1] While numerous handbooks have been published on areas such as pragmatics, sociolinguistics, and historical linguistics, no handbook has ever been dedicated to studies of language and culture. The aim of this *Handbook* is, therefore, to bring together a comprehensive and historical survey of studies of language and culture.

The chapters in this *Handbook* represent various approaches, interdisciplinary and multi-disciplinary theoretical orientations, analytical frameworks, analytical tools, and constructs associated with studies of language and culture. This introductory chapter provides an overview of how each chapter contributes to the general theme of language and culture from a particular focus or sub-theme/sub-discipline. There is no doubt the reader will notice a certain degree

Table 1.1 Three different paradigms in the history of the study of language as culture (Duranti, 2003)

Focus	View of language	Associated labels
Documentation, description, and classification of indigenous languages	Language as lexicon and grammar	Anthropological linguistics
Language use in context	Language as a culturally organized and culturally organizing domain	Linguistic anthropology, ethnography of speaking
Identity formation, narrative, and ideology	Language as an interactional achievement filled with indexical values	Social constructivism

of overlap between some chapters. It is both inevitable and in most cases beneficial to discussions of how certain constructs, such as 'Community of Practice' (Lave and Wenger, 1991), have been helpful for scholars interested in studying language and culture in various disciplines/sub-disciplines.

Overall, the *Handbook*, with its many diverse contributory chapters, set out to achieve the following aims:

to provide readers with a clear and accessible introduction to the interdisciplinary and multi-disciplinary scope of studies of language and culture, offering insights into their historical development, contemporary theory, research, and practice, and potential future directions;

to familiarize readers with various approaches to language and culturally based linguistic research, and key issues from a variety of perspectives/disciplines/sub-disciplines;

to help readers develop a critical awareness of the strengths and limitations of different or competing theories and approaches to language and culture research;

to raise readers' awareness of the contested nature of culture and language and the complex connections between the two;

to show readers how language and culture research can be of practical benefit to applied areas of research and practice, including intercultural communication and second-language teaching/learning;

to draw attention to the potential for new, deeper understandings of language and culture through increased dialogue and collaboration between scholars/theorists from various disciplines and sub-disciplines, including cognitive psychology, cognitive linguistics, cognitive anthropology, linguistic anthropology, cultural anthropology, and sociolinguistics.

In terms of structure, Part I presents an overview of the *Handbook* and a historical account of research on the relationship between language and culture, in particular on the thesis of 'linguistic relativity'. The next set of chapters (Part II) explores research in those areas of language and culture that are united by their use of the prefix 'ethno' plus an aspect of language (e.g. ethnosyntax). In Part III, the chapters survey research on language and culture with a more specialized focus, such as gender or kinship. Part IV includes chapters that present research on various aspects of the relationship between language, culture, and cognition. The chapters in Part V review research on language and culture according to particular sub-disciplines, such as sociolinguistics. Part VI includes chapters that survey research on language and culture in applied domains such as in intercultural communication and second-language learning. Part VII is dedicated to chapters that engage with the field of Cultural Linguistics, including future research on language and culture. What follows summarizes each chapter in some detail.

In Chapter 2 Leavitt engages with the history of research on language and culture, in particular the historical development of the thesis of linguistic relativity, the most influential theoretical framework in studies of language and culture. Due to its significant impact, many scholars simply equate studies of language and culture with linguistic relativity, as well as controversies surrounding its correct interpretation. Leavitt traces the roots of studies of language and culture back to the sixteenth century and discusses the philosophical views that each subsequent school of thought held in relation to language and culture. He then focuses on common misrepresentations of the views held by Boas, Sapir, and Whorf, collectively referred to as 'linguistic relativity' and the causes of such misrepresentations. He argues that the view of language as determining and limiting speakers' world-view was never held by scholars such as Boas, Sapir, and Whorf. Rather, they emphasized that particular language patterns tend to guide habitual patterns of conceptualization. For Boas, different languages categorize and carve up experience differently, and words of human languages reflect cultural interests. Different languages may require different aspects of experience to be *attended* to. Whorf made a distinction between habitual thought, which tends to follow the ready-made paths made available to it by language, and the limitless potentialities of thought. Leavitt notes that the 1990s witnessed a shift in research on linguistic relativity. For example, empirical research, particularly in cognitive science, has been focusing on, and revealing, the influence of language specifics on patterns of conceptualization, sometimes termed 'Whorf effects'. He argues that '[g]iven that human beings are using specific languages, with all of the peculiarities of each, as tools to help think and communicate about the world and themselves thousands of times a day, this [Whorf effect] is hardly surprising – it is simply a case of the tools used having some influence on the final product'.

In Chapter 3, Gladkova provides an account of research on ethnosyntax, the study of how syntax, including morphology, encodes culture. Maintaining that the theoretical foundations of ethnosyntax were laid by Sapir and Whorf, Gladkova makes a distinction between a narrow and a broad sense of ethnosyntax. Ethnosyntax in the narrow sense explores cultural meanings of particular grammatical structures whereas ethnosyntax in the broad sense examines how pragmatic and cultural norms influence the choice of grammatical structures. Gladkova provides several examples for each approach. As an example of morpho-syntax encoding cultural meaning, she presents the case of Russian, where an attitude of endearment and intimacy is encoded by a diminutive. As an example of the second broader sense, she compares request speech acts in Russian and English, and examines how these languages employ different grammatical structures to perform the same speech act and how this usage is compatible with broader cultural norms.

In Chapter 4, Leavitt presents a history of research on ethnosemantics, the study of meaning across cultures, observing that '[t]he key question in putting an ethno- before semantics is whether meanings are universal, either innate in the mind or given by the world, or whether they vary from language to language, society to society'. He presents an account of the three traditions of Boasian cultural semantics, Neohumboldtian comparative semantics, and 'classical' ethnosemantics. He notes that the ethnosemantics practised by Boas and his students sought to identify semantic differences at all levels of language beyond the phoneme. The Neohumboldtian school of ethnosemantics maintained that 'each language could be studied as a coherent system, and that the meanings carried in the language, its "contents", formed a whole that could be identified with the world-orientation or world-view of its speakers'. That is, each language formed a coherent system that 'determined the range of people's thought'. Leavitt observes that 'classical' ethnosemantics, also known as ethnographic semantics or, often, cognitive anthropology, explored culture as knowledge and sought to identify how cultural knowledge was organized. This tradition focused on studies of vocabulary related to domains such as kinship, plants, animals, or disease. Here vocabulary is viewed hierarchically as a window onto the organization of particular knowledge domains in the minds of speakers in a given speech community. Leavitt notes that ethnosemantics fell into disfavour during the 1970s as universalistic theories of language began to emerge in linguistics. Finally, he notes that it has recently been revived in the work of the school of Natural Semantic Metalanguage (NSM) (see Chapters 3, 5, and 23 this volume) and in other research that examines the relationship between language and cultural conceptualizations (Sharifian, 2011).

In Chapter 5, Goddard focuses on ethnopragmatics, one approach to the study of the links between language in use and culture. Ethnopragmatics explores emic (or culture-internal) perspectives upon the use of various speech practices across different languages of the world. This approach is based on the premise that there is an explanatory link between the cultural values/ norms and the speech practices specific to a speech community. Goddard maintains that the NSM serves as a rigorous tool for ethnopragmatics to decompose cultural norms and notions in terms of simple meanings that appear to be shared by all languages. Since ethnopragmatics relies on linguistic evidence and ethnographic data from insiders to the culture, one of its central objectives is to explore 'cultural key words', or words that capture culturally constructed concepts which are pivotal to the ways of thinking, feeling, behaving, and speaking of a speech community. As examples of ethnopragmatic research, the chapter presents two ethnographic sketches from Anglo English and Chinese culture (the latter contributed by Zhengdao Ye).

In Chapter 6, Risager focuses on the notion of 'linguaculture' (or languaculture) and traces its roots in the works of American scholars, in particular Paul Friedrich and Michael Agar. For Friedrich, language and culture constitute a single domain (linguaculture) where verbal aspects of culture merge with semantic meanings. Agar uses the term 'languaculture' and regards culture as residing in language, and language as being loaded with culture. Risager (2006) introduces a new transnational and global perspective onto the notion of linguaculture. According to this perspective the use of language (linguistic practice) is viewed as flows in social networks of people and speech communities. These networks develop further when people migrate or learn additional languages. For Risager, linguistic practice is the external locus of language, which exists alongside an internal one; that is, linguistic resources in the individual. She also identifies a third locus, that is, the language system, which has a more deliberately constructed or 'artificial' nature, representing a reification of the language conceived as a coherent whole, or maybe an object, or even an organism or a person. For Risager, people carry their linguistic resources with them from one cultural context to the next as they move around the world. Overall, Risager reveals how the concept of 'linguaculture' can be productively used in a whole range of areas of study of language and culture, particularly if it is interpreted in a dynamic sense that is sensitive to transnational and global flows of people and languages.

In Chapter 7, Tanaka focuses on research on language, gender, and culture. She notes that the relationship between language and gender has been of interest to scholars from several fields of inquiry, including psychology, linguistics, and anthropology and that many of these scholars view gender as a construct that, among other things, maintains inequalities in society. Language is one of the tools used to construct gendered identities and characteristics associated with men and women, a function that is observed in cultures as diverse as Arabic, Japanese, American, or Thai. In her historical survey of the research on language and gender across different languages, Tanaka focuses on three specific approaches. The first approach relies on a textual analysis of linguistic resources that reflect gender stereotypes, for example, those portraying female speakers as emotional. The second approach explores features of human languages that 'have designated semantic, pragmatic or lexical elements for the exclusive use of female and male speakers'. This approach has shown, among other things, that in some languages different registers are used by men and women. The third approach analyses spoken discourse to find gendered differences in discourse strategies. For example, when it comes to turn taking, some studies have shown that male speakers have a tendency to dominate the interaction by more frequent interruption and other strategies. The differences between the use of language by male and female speakers has led some scholars to view gender as a 'culture' on its own and some others to argue that language is used to create differences and control less powerful groups. Tanaka also discusses the emergence of what she refers to as 'third wave' theory of the relationship between language, gender, and culture. This theory subscribes to the notion of a Community of Practice (see Chapters 25 and 26 this volume) and focuses on how language is understood in every community of practice. This theory rejects a binary construct of gender and includes less studied LGBT perspectives.

In Chapter 8, Kecskes explores the relationship between language, culture, and context. Adopting a socio-cognitive perspective, he views culture as a set of shared knowledge structures that capture the norms, values, and customs to which the members of a society have access. For Kecskes, both language and context 'are rooted in culture, and they both are "carriers" of culture and both reflect culture but in a different way. A part of culture is encoded in the language. What is encoded in language is past experience with different contexts while the actual situational context represents actual, present experience.' Thus, Kecskes regards context as a dynamic construct that captures both prior contexts of experience and the actual situational context. Prior context is in the mind of the speaker while the actual situational context exists in the external world as a field of action. Within the framework of the socio-cognitive approach, meaning is the result of the interplay between these two forms of context. Kecskes elaborates on this framework and provides several examples which reveal how the interpretation of formulaic language draws on both forms of context. The examples provided demonstrate a strong link between language, culture, and context.

In Chapter 9, Mills argues that although language and culture are often used synonymously in politeness research, a distinction should be made between the two. She presents a survey of traditional approaches to politeness research, highlighting shortcomings, such as the fact that traditional approaches to politeness research attempted to formulate global models that would apply to all languages. However, some empirical research has shown the incommensurability of politeness across languages. Mills also elaborates on the 'discursive approach' to politeness and observes that this approach explores the ways in which context, resources, and social forces/ideologies shape the potential interpretations of (im)politeness. Similar to the socio-cognitive approach captured in Kecskes's chapter, the discursive approach to politeness focuses on the role of context in judgements of (im)polite language. Within this approach, (im)politeness is not necessarily inherent in the meanings of utterances since various other factors can influence the hearer's judgement of politeness/impoliteness. The discursive approach, in general, questions the tendency of traditional approaches to present an essentialist picture of cultures and speakers. The reality of languages and cultures is much more heterogeneous and distributed than is assumed under the traditional approaches. Mills argues that individuals are active agents who negotiate and contest cultural and linguistic norms in real communicative contexts.

In Chapter 10, Eglin critically reviews the field of language, culture, and interaction in terms of the persistence of the correspondence theory of meaning. He argues this theory compromises the professed focus on the uses to which language and culture are put by members of society in the course of social interaction. He argues that abstracting language and culture from their uses as if they were independent, substantive things confounds the understanding of how words come to mean what they do. Such a theoretical step entails a failure to appreciate that social interaction alone provide sense and reference for language, culture and society. Measured against this Wittgensteinian position that the concepts of language are instruments, the various schools of thought gathered under the title of Language and Social Interaction (Leeds–Hurwitz, 2010: 6–8) are shown to remain susceptible to reified concepts of language and culture, residual positivism, metaphysical social constructionism, or identity politics reflective of the interests of analysts rather than those of the actors. Eglin illustrates his argument by critically contrasting ethnosemantic and ethnomethodological (conversation–analytic) analyses of the same naturally occurring data, and by debating Kitzinger's claim that Conversation Analysis's classical corpus of data displays undisclosed heteronormativity.

In Chapter 11, Kronenfeld presents an account of research on culture and kinship language. He notes that in linguistic anthropology, the focus of culture and kinship language has been on formal semantic analysis and also on the usage of kinship terminologies. Kinship language serves as 'a useful laboratory for studying the relationship between language and culture'. Kronenfeld elaborates on the two formal analytic definitional systems of kin terms: the semantic and pragmatic. The semantic approach examines the distinctions between kin categories, such as the sex-of-referent difference between 'father' and 'mother'. The pragmatic approach focuses on how referents of kin terms interrelate, such as the definition of 'nephew' as 'child of a sibling'. Another area of relevance here is the examination of the relationship between kin categories and their cultural and communicative uses; examples include, how terminologies relate to kin groups and rules of succession; how one behaves towards one's father and to whom else do such behaviours go; what non-kin does one address as, for example, 'uncle' – for what reasons and under what conditions? Throughout this chapter, Kronenfeld presents a detailed discussion of the formal systems that anthropologists have developed to study kinship across different languages and cultures.

In Chapter 12, Torop provides an account of the area of research known as 'cultural semiotics', also known as 'semiotics of culture'. Torop notes that cultural semiotics can refer to a methodological tool, a diversity of methods, or a sub-discipline of general semiotics. Cultural semiotics, in the sense of a sub-discipline, explores cultures as a type of human symbolic activity and as a system of cultural languages (sign systems). Language, and the analysis of language, is an important component of cultural semiotics as it is a major sign system. Language 'is the preserver of the culture's collective experience and the reflector of its creativity'. From a semiotic point of view, every culture has tools for self-description and every culture is a metasystem of object and metalanguages: verbal, visual, audiovisual, etc. Noting that the notion of 'text' is the principal concept in cultural semiotics, Torop points out that it is used both a manifestation of a language while at the same time texts are thought to create languages. In this broad sense of the term, text can refer to natural 'textual' objects (e.g., a book or a picture), or to 'textualizable' objects (e.g., culture as text, an event, a behaviour, etc.). It can also refer to abstract an invisible abstract whole, such as a mental text in collective consciousness. Each 'text' is interrelated, implicitly or explicitly, with many different texts, in a phenomenon referred to as 'intertextuality'. Cultures are describable on the static level as collection or system of texts and on the dynamic level as an intertextual mental whole. The value of cultural semiotics is in the development of methodo-logical and empirical principles of dynamic holistic analysis of culture and in interdisciplinary collaboration between different disciplines and theories in cultural research.

In Chapter 13, Armstrong explores the topic of language, culture, and translation focusing on the difficulties faced by translators when rendering aspects of language that are closely associated with culture. He refers to two senses of the term 'culture': the anthropological sense, which refers to practices and traditions that characterize a community, and the narrower sense, which refers to artistic enterprises. Armstrong maintains that in both these senses examples of culture pervade language at all levels. He argues that the challenges facing a translator relate to two aspects of the relationship between language and culture, both part of the Sapir–Whorf hypothesis. First, language encodes culturally significant elements and events. Second, language has a bearing on culture in that every language focuses the attention of speakers on certain aspects of experience at the expense of others, a thesis that is referred to as 'thinking for speaking' (Slobin, 1996). Armstrong observes that, although the problems for translators created by the first one are more common, both these directions of influence create challenges for translators when rendering from a source language to a target language. He also discusses a range of views concerning the relationship between language and culture as they are captured in metaphorical expressions such as 'culture has its root in language' and 'culture is infused in language'. The first statement suggests 'culture' can be 'transplanted' into another language but the second statement does not. These reflect the range of views that exists regarding the 'translatability of language and culture'. Finally Armstrong discusses the cultural shifts that have been taking place since the 1960s in the direction of 'informalization', which has reduced, among other things, the distinction between low and high culture.

Chapter 14 by Schecter focuses on research on language, culture, and identity. She notes three distinct approaches: a social anthropology approach, a sociocultural approach, and a participatory/relational approach. The social anthropological approach is concerned with the boundaries involved in the social construction of differences between different groups of people. According to this approach, culture is associated with ethnicity/national borders such that being a 'native speaker' of a language is determined through birth. The sociocultural approach explores the interaction between an individual's multiple identities, which are both externally and internally constructed, in sociocultural contexts. This approach views language as having a mediating role in the construction of individual and sociocultural identities. The participatory/relational approach moves away from the notions of 'family' and 'community' as the units of analysis for examining the ways in which individuals construct their social–linguistic identities. Under this approach, identity construction, particularly as it relates to language, relies more on the resources that people have access to, rather than who they are or what they own. What a person does, or can do, with language is more relevant to their identity than where they come from, for example. Identities, according to this view, are negotiated, multidimensional, dynamic, relational, and complex, rather than fixed and attached to those units of society with which individuals are affiliated.

In Chapter 15, McConvell presents an account of the research on language and culture history in which historical linguistic evidence is used in the reconstruction of prehistoric cultures. The chapter presents a survey of linguistic prehistory research on proto- and early Indo-European culture, on some North American language families, on Africa, Austronesian, and Australian Aboriginal languages. The fields of vocabulary that are used in this kind of research include material culture, technology, religious belief systems and practices, and social organization, including kinship. An important aim of linguistic prehistory research is to provide a chronological account of cultural changes. McConvell maintains that linguistic prehistory research often benefits from findings from other disciplines, in particular archaeology, palaeobiology, and biological genetics. These disciplines similarly benefit from linguistic prehistory research. He also notes that '[l]inguistic prehistory adds a time dimension to our general appreciation of the links between culture and language by showing how these aspects influence each other over time and the mechanisms which produce change in either or both together'.

In Chapter 16, Yu presents a survey of research and theory on the relationship between language, culture, and body, from the perspective of Cultural Linguistics (Sharifian, Chapter 32 this volume). A major strand of research within cognitive linguistics has explored conceptual metaphors that use the human body as their source domain (e.g., THE HEART AS THE SEAT OF

EMOTIONS, reflected in sentences such as *You broke my heart*). Philosophically this school of thought subscribes to the 'embodiment' strand in cognitive science, the view that the body shapes the mind (the mind is in the body), which rejects Cartesian body–mind dualism. As Yu puts it, 'the mind emerges and takes shape from the body with which we interact with our environment'. This approach to the study of human cognition is also known as *embodied cognition*. Yu presents a historical survey of research on embodiment from a multidisciplinary perspective, including a discussion of various interpretations of the term 'embodiment'. While early work on embodied language (known as Conceptual Metaphor Theory) within the paradigm of cognitive linguistics had a universalistic undertone, Cultural Linguistics has focused on the role of culture in shaping embodied language. Yu argues that different cultures conceptualize body and bodily experience differently, 'attributing different values and significances to various body parts and organs and their functions'. In his many publications Yu has revealed, for example, how certain linguistic expressions in Chinese reflect the conceptualization of THE HEART IS THE RULER OF THE BODY. He maintains (Yu, 2007: 27) that the 'target-domain concept here is an important one because the heart organ is regarded as the central faculty of cognition and the site of both affective and cognitive activities in ancient Chinese philosophy' – hence the role of culture in embodied metaphor.

In Chapter 17, Robinson and Altarriba focus on research on the relationship between culture and language processing. Research in this area has mainly explored the influence of cultural factors on the development of cognitive abilities in bilinguals. In general, research findings show that language and culture are central to cognitive processing. Robinson and Altarriba review several strands of research, including work on bilingualism and emotion as well as that on language and memory, where the findings strongly suggest that 'behaviour that is guided by linguistic processing is in most cases also regulated by the cultural context of the speaker'. Also, research suggests that with an increase in the number of languages a person speaks comes a widening of their conceptual horizon. Similarly, exposure to and interaction with a new cultural environment modifies certain aspects of cognition such as cognitive categorization. This research makes it clear that the linguistic and cultural nature of each individual's background needs to be included as a variable in studies of cognition and cognitive processing.

In Chapter 18, Polzenhagen and Xia present an overview of research on language, culture and prototypicality. Prototype theory argues that form–meaning pairings create/form categories which are organized in terms of a centre–periphery, where the prototype is the best, most typical, or most central member of a particular category. Objects and entities belong to the category by virtue of their sharing of common features with this prototype. Polzenhagen and Xia survey theoretical work on prototypicality across various disciplines, including cognitive psychology and cognitive linguistics. They maintain that the role of culture and context on categorization has always been the focus of those scholars interested in prototype theory with a background in cultural anthropology. In Cognitive Linguistics, conceptual categories are viewed as shaped by individuals' interactions with and perception of the world including the cultural environment and their bodily experience. Conceptual categories are both embodied and culturally constructed. Words of human languages index conceptual categories and, as such, reveal how different cultures categorize the world. That is, certain vocabulary items reflect world-views held collectively by speakers of the language. Furthermore, linguistic prototypes fulfil a crucial role in social (re-)cognition in that they are socially diagnostic and serve as linguistic identity markers. Polzenhagen and Xia also discuss how in language-contact and culture-contact situations, such as L2 learning, individuals can develop 'culturally blended concepts' due to exposure to more than one system of conceptual categorization.

In Chapter 19, Dedrick reviews research on colour language, thought, and culture. The questions addressed in this area of research include whether or not differences in the colour words one finds in different languages mean that speakers think differently about colour and whether colour language influences cognition. This question has been of interest to many researchers across a number of disciplines including anthropology, linguistics, cognitive psychology, and neuroscience. Dedrick presents a historical survey of research on colour naming and discusses its implications for the relationship between language, mind, biology, and culture. In general, he notes that views concerning this relationship range from a so-called 'universalist' position, which considers colour names and corresponding colour categories (or at least basic sets of them) to be universal, to a view that considers colour categories to be primarily determined by their cultural significance. The earliest empirically supported relativist hypotheses claimed that culturally significant colours are more codable in language and hence more memorable. Dedrick observes that some scholars have argued for a reverse effect, that is, 'it is memorability that determines codability and that what is assumed to be "culturally significant" is more of an *outcome* of this biologically grounded psychological salience'. Overall, Dedrick notes that research on colour language, cognition, and culture is characterized by mixed results and mixed interpretations. Despite ongoing controversy, he defers to a contemporary consensus: colour language sometimes demonstrates an effect of language on thought and, in other respects, is resistant to such an effect.

In Chapter 20, Brown focuses on research on the interface between language, culture, and spatial cognition. She notes that conceptualizing space is central to human cognition and provides a framework for thinking and talking about objects and events, as well as more abstract notions like time, number, and kinship. Observing that languages vary widely in the resources they provide for talking about space, Brown raises the so-called Whorfian question of whether the language of space might influence the way speakers *think* about spatial relations even when they are not talking. Scholars of spatial language and cognition have identified three basic frames of reference that languages use to refer to spatial relations: (1) an 'absolute' coordinate system, such as north, south, east, west; (2) a 'relative' coordinate system projected from the body's viewpoint (e.g., left of the house); and (3) an intrinsic, object-centred coordinate system (e.g., at the back of the house). Brown notes that languages vary radically not only in terms of their lexical resources for spatial description and their spatial semantics but also in their preferred choice of coordinate system. She surveys significant empirical research that has shown that the language that one speaks correlates with the way one calculates spatial relations in non-linguistic tasks. These results are also supported by studies of the gestural accompaniments to spatial talk, as well as by research on children's acquisition and use of spatial language in different speech communities. Brown concludes by observing that the evidence for whether speakers' use of frames of spatial reference influences their thinking would be strengthened by more careful embedding of language use in ethnography, and especially by detailed studies of the use of spatial language in natural contexts.

In Chapter 21, Sinha and Bernárdez present a survey of research on cultural and linguistic concepts of time and space. They review recent research that has shown significant cross-linguistic variation in the language of space and time. An influential strand of research in this area has focused on the analysis of space–time metaphors, or the conceptualization of *time as space*, from the perspective of Conceptual Metaphor Theory (CMT). Sinha and Bernárdez criticize this line of research for its failure to situate space–time mapping within the broader patterns of culture and worldview. Based on a survey of empirical research, they argue that while the temporal aspect of our life experiences may be transcultural, conceptualizations of time are to a large extent culturally constructed. The experience of time has two aspects: duration and succession. Sinha and Bernárdez maintain that while it is likely that in all cultures, individuals experience and talk about events in terms of duration and succession, the particular words and concepts that they use to refer to temporal duration and temporal landmarks are often language and culture specific. They also refer to research that shows that the conceptualization and linguistic expression of time intervals are widely variable culturally. The cultural structuring of time intervals is in large part achieved by the invention and use of artefacts such as clocks and calendars. Sinha and Bernárdez propose a general theoretical perspective of extended material–symbolic cultural embodiment, consistent with a 'post-Whorfian' perspective on the interrelations between language, cognition and culture, and their covariation. They conclude by addressing questions such as whether or not space is the only source domain for the conceptualization of time, and whether all linguistic space–time correspondences should be regarded as space–time metaphorical mappings.

In Chapter 22, Sterponi and Lai present a survey of major theoretical frameworks addressing the relationship between culture and language acquisition. To begin with, they note that in this area of research the notion of 'culture' is used in two different senses: one as a developmental mechanism in human beings, and the other as the specific social contexts in which a child is 'initiated' into the cultural systems of meaning. Collectively, these two senses define culture as 'both related to the psychological make-up of the individual and to the socio-historical contexts in which s/he is born and develops'. Sterponi and Lai distinguish between two major approaches that explore the role of culture in language acquisition: the usage-based approach, from developmental psychology, and the language socialization approach, from linguistic anthropology. The usage-based approach holds the view that children's general cognitive capabilities provide them with the means to learn language. The language socialization approach examines language development in terms of the processes that children undergo as they become competent members of a sociocultural group. Sterponi and Lai argue that these two approaches are compatible as well as complementary, since according to the first approach culture is a species-specific resource for ontogenetic development and, for the second approach, cultures are instantiated in their own places and times.

In Chapter 23, Wierzbicka elaborates on research in the area of language and cultural scripts, or representations of cultural norms that are encoded in language. Wierzbicka argues that the system of meaning analysis she and colleagues have developed, called the Natural Semantic Metalanguage (NSM), can readily be used to capture and articulate cultural scripts (see also Chapter 5 this volume). She observes that many bilingual speakers whose lives are characterized by cross-cultural experiences often navigate between two systems of cultural scripts, embedded in their use of lexical items, grammar, and speech acts. She argues that the approach of NSM can best capture such experiences in a rigorous manner by using a limited number of conceptual primes that appear to exist in all languages. Wierzbicka presents examples of the use of NSM to explicate certain cultural scripts from Russian, Anglo English, and a number of Australian Aboriginal languages. Thereby, Wierzbicka reveals how languages can differ from each other in terms of their speakers' norms about how much to reveal to other people, or certain people, about what one thinks, for example. She makes similar observations about individuals' expression of emotions towards others.

In Chapter 24, Dewaele surveys research on culture and emotional language. He observes that there are cultural differences in linguistic expressions of emotions. He notes that research on the relationship between language, culture, and emotion has typically been carried out by cultural and cognitive psychologists as well as by applied linguists. Applied linguists have also been interested in possible differences in expressions/perceptions of emotions across L1 and L2 in bilinguals/multilinguals. Cultural psychologists have explored differences in expressions of emotions across collectivist and individualistic cultures. Cognitive psychologists have, on the other hand, examined processing of emotion words by bilinguals/multilinguals. A relevant question in this area is whether the same emotion concepts exist in a person's L1 and L2.

Empirical research has revealed that bilinguals often express differences between their L1 and L2 in terms of the intensity or the absence or presence of certain emotion concepts, for example. Such differences may, among other things, lead to different perceptions of the self by bilinguals, depending on which language can be chosen in a particular context for emotional expression. In general, research in this area has revealed that culture flows through the experience and communication of emotions, mediated by linguistic expression.

In Chapter 25, Marra provides an account of research on culture in the area of sociolinguistics. She notes that culture is a fundamental concept in Interactional Sociolinguistics, according to which language is viewed as social interaction. Within the approach of Interactional Sociolinguistics, culture, and cultural differences in particular are seen as a source of potential miscommunication during linguistic interaction. Marra refers to a wealth of studies where scholars have attributed instances of miscommunication to cultural differences in the use of language. During the 1990s, Interactional Sociolinguists began to define culture in a broader sense, combining ethnicity and its associated culture(s) with variables such as gender (or gender groups). Marra observes that the paradigm shift in sociolinguistics, from Interactional Sociolinguistics to social constructionism, redefined 'culture' so that it was more dynamic and less rigid than before. The focus of the social constructionist paradigm is on how people employ language to construct and negotiate social identities during interaction. Rather than being predefined, culture and cultural identity are therefore emergent properties arising from the context of interaction. Marra also discusses how the notion of a 'Community of Practice' (see for example Chapter 26 this volume) has become useful within the framework of social constructionism. Based on this notion, '[t]hrough participation we can begin as peripheral members of a group and through shared practices built up over time in the form of an apprenticeship we can progress to core members of a community'. This concept has proved to be beneficial in several other areas of research on language and culture too, as is reflected in several chapters in the *Handbook*.

In Chapter 26, Strauss focuses on language and culture research in cognitive anthropology, the sub-field that studies the interrelationship between human society and human thought/ thinking. She notes that cognitive anthropologists can be divided into two groups according to their object of study: some are interested in exploring the process of thinking, others in examining the product of thinking (thoughts). Strauss observes that the notion of 'culture' is more relevant to those who study thoughts, as they are interested in shared cultural understandings. Cognitive anthropologists who explore the process of thinking (cognition-in-practice researchers) view language primarily as a tool or resource, whereas those who are interested in thoughts (e.g., cultural models and consensus analysis researchers) consider language as *data* from which they can deduce shared cultural understandings. Strauss also notes that the scholars who founded cognitive anthropology 'were inspired both by rigorous descriptions of linguistic knowledge and by various theories of how linguistic knowledge is mentally represented'. She further elaborates on how various approaches to cognitive anthropology have relied on units of language, such as lexical items and their meanings, as well as larger stretches of discourse, as data, which, for example, instantiate learned cultural schemas. In terms of contributions made by cognitive anthropologists to linguistic anthropology, Strauss refers to the notion of a 'Community of Practice', developed by cognition-in-practice researchers, and which is used by scholars across several areas of research on language and culture (see for example Chapter 25 this volume). Strauss also notes that cognitive anthropologists' study of implicit assumptions has contributed to the study of communicative competence and that these concepts can be usefully applied to indexical associations and language ideologies.

In Chapter 27, Kramsch focuses on language and culture in foreign language (FL) learning/ teaching. She first presents a historical account of the definition of 'culture' in FL teaching and notes, for example, that prior to the 1960s, the notion of 'culture' when applied to language referred to literature and the arts. After the 1960s, the notion captured culturally appropriate use of language, including the appropriate use of pragmalinguistic and sociopragmatic norms. In recent years, globalization, including the proliferation of global media and electronic social networks, has given new meaning to the notions of 'communication', 'language', and 'culture'. Communication in what Kramsch calls the 'postmodern' era is not just about the transmission of information, but also the construction and positioning of the self and self-identity. In addition, she notes that the increasing diversification of learners' needs and interests has led to multiple definitions and interpretations of the notion of 'language', depending on the context and the content of learning and use. Language could be framed, for example as a commodity or as a marker of self-identity. Culture in the new era is viewed mainly in terms of the subjective meanings that speakers associate with experience. As Kramsch puts it, 'Cultures are portable schemas of interpretation of actions and events that people have acquired through primary socialization and which change over time as people migrate or enter into contact with people who have been socialized differently'. In many cases, national cultures have become hybrid and fragmented, with meanings of words becoming subjectively dependent on the context of their use. She argues that '[i]f culture is redefined as a meaning-making process, then it has to be seen as constructed by the speech acts and discursive practices of individual speakers and writers as they use the language and other symbolic systems for communicative purposes. For language teachers, who have to teach this meaning making process, the challenge is how to seize the moment to move the students beyond cultural stereotypes and engage them with the differences in attitudes and world-views indexed by variations in discourse.'

In Chapter 28, Atkinson surveys research on whether the notion of culture is useful in the field of second-language writing (SLW), a sub-field of applied linguistics and composition. One approach, known as *contrastive rhetoric*, explores the influence of first-language patterns of text organization on writers writing in a second language. For example, second-language writers from certain backgrounds writing in English for academic purposes may delay their thesis or main claim until late in their text. Other work on culture in SLW has dealt with the possible cultural particularity of such concepts as critical thinking, plagiarism, and written voice. Much of this work has more recently been criticized by neo-Marxist and poststructuralist/postmodernist scholars, who find the notion of 'culture' as used in SLW problematic. Their critique is not unique to SLW, however, having prevailed, for example, in anthropology to the point that as Atkinson puts it '[i]n the very field which innovated the concept in fact – anthropology – culture has been "half-abandoned"'. SLW scholars who repudiate the notion of culture, propose alternative notions, such as 'cosmopolitanism', 'critical multiculturalism', and hybridity, suggesting that one's natal culture is becoming irrelevant or at least far less influential (if it ever was at all) over individual values and behaviour in a globalized world. But, as Atkinson notes, 'today's world is hardly dissolving into a cultureless mass, but rather that a dialectic is at work – cultural conventions and hybridity are co-constructive, working hand in hand'. Atkinson ends by suggesting a return to understanding the term culture as an anthropological concept, as its inventors (e.g., Lowie, 1920) understood it.

In Chapter 29, Malcolm engages with the topic of language and culture in second-dialect learning. He notes that the global spread of international languages such as English has led to the development of new varieties of these languages, whereby many speech communities for which the language was not an L1 now use English to express their own cultural norms. Malcolm focuses on the case of minority students who are required by the educational systems in countries such as the US and Australia to learn so-called 'standard' Englishes (e.g., Standard American English, Standard Australian English) at school. He notes that the literature on the learning of 'standard' Englishes by 'non-standard' speakers in the US has often associated speaking the 'non-standard' variety with cognitive, cultural, and linguistic deficit. Other scholars, however, have shown empirically that these 'non-standard' varieties are just as highly structured and systematic as the standard variety. This group of scholars has called for the introduction of 'bi-dialectal' programmes at school where the speakers of vernacular varieties can maintain their vernacular variety while developing competence in the variety spoken by the 'mainstream' speakers in the society. Malcolm notes that debates surrounding the notion of 'standard/non-standard' use of language by minority speakers have largely ignored the relevance of culture. However the students' home dialect encodes their cultural conceptualizations and for this reason carries their cultural identity. Malcolm refers to his own recent research in cognitive linguistics and Cultural Linguistics, and that of his associates, analysing the speech of Aboriginal English-speaking students in Australia in terms of Aboriginal cultural conceptualizations. Often unfamiliarity with such conceptualizations by non-Aboriginal educators has led to mis-communication between the educators and students, disadvantaging the students throughout their journey at school.

In Chapter 30, Wolf provides a survey of research on language and culture in the field of intercultural communication. He refers to three paradigms that focus on intercultural commu-nication research: the dominant paradigm exploring *successful functioning* in intercultural encounters; a minority group of scholars focusing on intercultural *understanding*; and a third school that he refers to as 'deconstructionist, and or postmodernist' scholarship. Wolf presents an account of the historical development of the field of intercultural communication, and discusses different interpretations of the terms associated with intercultural communication. He notes that the functionalist school of the study of intercultural communication views intercultural encounters as 'problem situations' that require certain 'skills' in order to 'manage' such encounters successfully. The intercultural understanding approach, with its hermeneutic orientation, puts human beings at the centre, and focuses on differences at the level of conceptualizations and their realizations in language. The third school of thought in intercultural communication research moves away from cultural differences and focuses on socio-political inequalities, situa-tionality, fluidity, and negotiability. As Wolf states, this group almost eliminates the term 'culture' from intercultural communication research. He argues that a fear of essentialism is responsible. A similar observation can, of course, be made about avoiding the concept of culture across several disciplines including anthropology and applied linguistics. Finally, Wolf discusses how research in the areas of cognitive linguistics and Cultural Linguistics has significantly contributed to our understanding of the role of cultural conceptualizations in intercultural communication. These sub-disciplines provide robust analytical tools that avoid essentializing speech commu-nities and speakers, such as the notion of 'cultural schema', and allow for a better understanding of how speakers draw on deeper levels of culturally constructed conceptualizations during intercultural communication.

In Chapter 31, Kirkpatrick presents an account of research on culture in World Englishes, a research paradigm in applied linguistics that explores the development of varieties of English around the globe, through processes such as indigenization or nativization of the language. He maintains that studies of these varieties provide us with significant clues about the inter-relationship between language and culture, since new varieties of English emerge in various speech communities around the world to express culturally motivated needs and norms in English, as a language of both intra- and inter-national communication. Kirkpatrick elaborates on various processes through which new varieties of English accommodate the culture of the speech community that develops them. For example, a new variety may adopt lexical items from local languages or translate from local languages into English to express culture-specific concepts. These new varieties may give new cultural meanings to already existing English words. For instance, Kirkpatrick notes that speakers of new varieties may use pragmatic norms that are rooted in cultural norms and values of the new speech community that have not hitherto been associated with English. New varieties are also used in writing local literatures, often involving drawing on local and culturally preferred rhetorical norms. In addition, Kirkpatrick examines how in some cases new varieties are used by the speakers to display and construct certain identities, including local cultural identities. He argues that an understanding of the ways in which the new varieties encode cultural norms and concepts is crucial to successful intercultural communication, particularly in an age of globalization where intercultural communication is becoming more and more the default form of everyday communication for many speakers across the world.

Chapter 32 presents an overview of the recently developed multidisciplinary research area of Cultural Linguistics. Cultural Linguistics examines the relationship between language and cultural cognition, and in particular cultural conceptualizations. It draws on the theoretical and analytical advancements from several disciplines including cognitive linguistics and cognitive anthropology. In fact, Cultural Linguistics initially grew out of an interest in integrating cognitive linguistics with the three traditions within linguistic anthropology of Boasian linguistics, ethnosemantics, and the ethnography of speaking. The major assumption underlying the approach of Cultural Linguistics is that many features of language encode cultural–conceptual structures such as cultural schemas, cultural categories, and cultural metaphors. In particular, the semantic and pragmatic meanings that underlie the use of language largely dwell in cultural conceptualizations. The chapter elaborates on these observations and provides examples of how cultural conceptualizations may be linguistically encoded. Applications of Cultural Linguistics have enabled fruitful investigations of the cultural grounding of language in several applied domains such as World Englishes, intercultural communication, and political discourse analysis.

In Chapter 33, Frank presents an assessment of Cultural Linguistics as a future direction for research on language and culture. She notes that 'Cultural Linguistics has the potential to bring forth a model that successfully melds together complementary approaches, e.g., viewing language as "a complex adaptive system" and bringing to bear upon it concepts drawn from cognitive science such as "distributed cognition" and "multi-agent dynamic systems theory".' Frank observes that the framework of Cultural Linguistics is compatible with the major paradigm shift in cognitive science, from 'between-the-ears', 'classic cognitivism' to 'enactive cognitivism'. She also elaborates on the premise of Cultural Linguistics that views the construction, emergence, and perpetuation of cultural conceptualizations as a case of the emergence of a complex adaptive system (CAS), which runs counter to the essentialist views of language and culture. She further notes that Cultural Linguistics views cultural cognition as socially situated action, which is again congruent with enactive cognitivism and the dynamic systems approach. In addition, Frank reviews the approach of socially distributed cognition, noting that it moves beyond the level of the individual to explore 'interactions between people and their environment, in addition to phenomena that emerge in social interactions'. She argues that the tenets and the theoretical framework of Cultural Linguistics closely match those of this approach. Frank maintains that the openness of Cultural linguistics to boundary crossing and its multidisciplinary scope establishes it as 'a flexible transdisciplinary umbrella for future work on language and culture'. She concludes by stating that 'Cultural Linguistics promises to serve as a bridge that brings together researchers from a variety of fields, allowing them to focus on problems of mutual concern from a new perspective and in all likelihood discover new problems (and solutions) that until now have not been visible'.

Concluding remarks

By way of appraisal, it is clear that the chapters included in the *Handbook*, taken collectively, represent a major step forward, as they bring together and elaborate upon methodological approaches as well as conceptual and analytical frameworks that are central to studies of language and culture. The range of contributions to the *Handbook* reflects the multidisciplinary and transdisciplinary scope of the questions, methodologies, and theoretical orientations that characterize research on language and culture. The contributions also highlight the challenges that scholars interested in the relationship between language and culture have faced in their scholarly pursuits due to the ontological and epistemological complexity of this relationship. The chapters of the *Handbook* also bring into focus promising new directions for the future of research on language and culture. They reveal, for example, that recent advancements in various disciplines related to studies of language, culture, and cognition provide exciting opportunities for the development of novel approaches that could shed significant light on the complex nature of the cognitive nexus between language and culture. It is hoped that the *Handbook* will serve as a clear and coherent blueprint for scholarly thinking and research on language and culture, and also generate further research in each of the areas represented in the *Handbook*.

Note

1 An exception to this would be the publication of 'readers', such as Hymes (1964), Blount (1995), and Duranti (2009).

References

Blount, B. G. (ed.) (1995) *Language, Culture, and Society: A Book of Readings*, Prospect Heights, IL: Waveland Press. [expanded reissue of the 1974 book]

Duranti, A. (2003) 'Language as Culture in U.S. Anthropology: Three Paradigms', *Current Anthropology* 44: 323–47.

——(ed.) (2009) *Linguistic Anthropology: A Reader*, 2nd edn, Malden, MA: Wiley-Blackwell.

Foley, W. A. (1997) *Anthropological Linguistics: An Introduction*, Oxford: Basil Blackwell.

Hymes, D. (1964) *Language in Culture and Society: A Reader in Linguistics and Anthropology*, New York: Harper & Row.

Lave, J. and E. Wenger (1991) *Situated Learning: Legitimate Peripheral Participation*, Cambridge: Cambridge University Press.

Leeds-Hurwitz, W. (ed.) (2010) *The Social History of Language and Social Interaction: People, Places, Ideas*, Cresskill, NJ: Hampton Press.

Risager, K. (2006) *Language and Culture: Global Flows and Local Complexity*, Clevedon, UK: Multilingual Matters.

Sharifian, F. (2011) *Cultural Conceptualisations and Language: Theoretical Framework and Applications*, Amsterdam/Philadelphia, PA: John Benjamins.

Slobin, D. I. (1996) 'From 'Thought and Language' to 'Thinking for Speaking'', in J. J. Gumperz and S. C. Levinson (eds), *Rethinking Linguistic Relativity*, Cambridge: Cambridge University Press, pp. 70–96.

Underhill, J. W. (2012) *Ethnolinguistics and Cultural Concepts: Truth, Love, Hate and War*. Cambridge: Cambridge University Press.

Yu, N. (2007) 'Heart and Cognition in Ancient Chinese Philosophy', *Journal of Cognition and Culture* 7(1/2), 27–47.

2

LINGUISTIC RELATIVITY: PRECURSORS AND TRANSFORMATIONS

John Leavitt

Introduction

The term and the notion of 'linguistic relativity' are usually associated with the names of the American linguist Edward Sapir (1884–1939) and his student Benjamin Lee Whorf (1897–1941), who developed the ideas of Sapir's teacher Franz Boas (1858–1942), one of the founders of North American anthropology and linguistics. For these scholars, the diversity of languages was one of the central facts about human beings and potentially, at least, had implications for conceptualization of natural and social situations. In the 1920s and 1930s Sapir and Whorf both proposed a 'principle of linguistic relativity' with an explicit reference to Einstein's theory of relativity: this amounted to maintaining that differences between the languages of speaker and analyst constituted a factor that had to be taken explicitly into account in any analysis of social and cultural life – just as in Einstein's relativity the velocity and direction of the measurer him- or herself had to figure in the determination of those of any other entity. In neither case was there a privileged fixed point or centre from which everything else could be judged.

For Boas and his students, each language constituted a system organized at several levels, each of which had its own kind of coherence. For each language, the level of sounds, of phonology, was evidently structured and obviously different from the sound organization of other languages: this is what produced the phenomenon of accent. With the level of lexicon one arrived at units of meaning, which divided the world in unique ways for each language and for its speakers, largely correlated with the speakers' way of life – if the way of life changed, then lexicon was likely to change along with it. It was at the 'higher' level of grammatical categories – e.g., tense, gender, number in Western languages, data source or shape in some others – that one found organizations of meaning and orientations towards some aspects of experience rather than others, organizations and orientations that were pervasive and relatively inaccessible to conscious manipulation. A speaker of English must, through the use of tense, specify the relationship between the time of the event spoken about and the time of speaking, and must do so hundreds of times every day; a speaker of Aymara need only specify this relationship when it is pertinent to do so, but must specify how she knows what she's talking about, again (at least) hundreds of times every day. Without claiming that language determines culture or thought, the linguistic relativity principle says that such differences are real, are potentially important, and deserve to be attended to.

This kind of a principle faces immediate opposition from one well-established school of thought, and risks being identified with another. Since Aristotle, the view has been widespread in the West that all humans think in the same way, and that language merely serves to code and communicate already-formed thoughts. Such a view is basic to such philosophical monuments as Cartesian rationalism, Locke's empiricism, and Kant's transcendentalism; and this kind of universalism is carried on today by the dominant mode of cognitive science. If the basis of a whole discipline is that the speaker of any language is merely translating from a universal 'mentalese' (see, for instance, Pinker, 1994), then *any* claims of the importance of the specifics of a given language are highly troublesome.

The strategy most commonly used to overcome or avoid this issue has been to identify linguistic relativity with the *other* great Western view of the relationship among language, thought, and culture, which identifies these as aspects of a single national or ethnic whole, varying from people to people. This kind of view goes back to the Romantics in the early nineteenth century and remains powerful in nationalist and ethnic affirmation movements today. It holds that every language is a natural part of a unique national or cultural totality; in other words, that the human world is made up of a number of national or ethnic essences. The language one speaks, in this view, reflects – or indeed determines – one's mode of thought, in a way that is distinct for each nation. In some of these models, one's language in fact *limits* what it is possible to think.

The difference between such essentialism and the much more open principle of linguistic relativity should be clear. But for decades the two have been identified, especially by schools of thought that seek or assume a single universal human mode of thinking or knowing the world. This convenient straw man can be disposed of even more easily if, unlike Boas and company, we eliminate some aspects of language – sounds, which obviously differ from language to language in ways of which speakers are only partly conscious; or grammatical structures, which oblige speakers to attend to certain aspects of reality whether these are relevant or not – leaving only isolated words to represent 'language'.

The whole combination – the claim that the *words* your language gives you determine and *limit* what it is possible for you to think – while evidently false (or because it is evidently false) has come to be the most common definition given of 'linguistic relativity', even by authors who are striving to be fair and balanced. In the succinct formulation of John I. Saeed in his textbook on *Semantics* (second edition, 2003: 40, third edition, 2009: 41), linguistic relativity is the view that 'lexicalized concepts impose restrictions on possible ways of thinking'. In fact, as is clear in the definition given above, none of the actual proponents of linguistic relativity made any such claim (on page 43 of his book (third edn.), Saeed himself notes the importance of grammatical categories, as opposed to words, for Whorf); on the contrary, no language, they insisted, puts limits on what it is possible to conceptualize – while they continued to demonstrate a seductive power of established language patterns to offer easy-to-follow mental paths. This becomes particularly clear in Whorf's distinction between least-effort 'habitual thinking', largely guided by a received language and culture, and what it is *possible* for a person to conceive, in particular by becoming familiar with languages and cultures very different from his or her own.

Here I will lay out some of the elements of linguistic relativity as presented by the Boasians. To understand why Boas came to his formulation of this theory, this presentation will be preceded by a brief history of major Western approaches to language diversity before Boas, laying out the sources of both universalist and pluralist options. After the discussion of Boasian linguistic relativity I will give brief presentations of an alternative pluralist option contemporary with his, that of the 'neo-Humboldtian' school of linguistics in Germany; and I will follow this with a discussion of developments since the deaths of the idea's original proponents: the virtual suppression of serious consideration of language diversity in the decades of the rise and hegemony of cognitive psychology and Chomskyan linguistics, and the recent rise of interest in linguistic relativity in a number of fields.

Major reactions to linguistic diversity

One of the striking things about human languages is that there are many of them. In the West, this has generally been presented either as a curse, as in the Tower of Babel story or Mallarmé's line *les langues imparfaites en cela que plusieurs*; or as a blessing, an enrichment of human life. While it is certainly an oversimplification, it is still possible to see much of Western thinking about language diversity as tending toward an opposition of two poles. The majority view has been to see language differences as a practical problem, insignificant compared to the universality of human thought, of human experience of the world, or both. Explicitly against such universalism, tendencies have continued to arise defending and indeed glorifying diversity as an inherent good, usually as part of projects of national and ethnic self-promotion.

Beginning in the sixteenth century, but finding their full formulation in the seventeenth, practitioners and theorists of three major Western European philosophical and scientific languages – French, English, and German – took distinctive tacks in facing diversity and claiming their own particular strengths, propounding three distinct linguistic ideologies.

The French tendency, which was greatly strengthened with the rise of Cartesian rationalism in the seventeenth century, was to valorize French for its relatively rigid syntax, said to be natural and to follow the order of reason, particularly as opposed to the free word order of Latin. The idea of a single 'natural' or 'direct' order of thought had come from some Hellenistic philosophers, and their model was expressed in sentences in the order subject, verb, object, with adjectives after their nouns and adverbs after verbs. As it happens, this fit closely with the baseline order of the French sentence (Scaglione, 1972: 74–6, 105–121). Already in the sixteenth century, Louis Meigret wrote that

> the French style fits it (the order of nature) much better than does the Latin ... (French follows) the order that nature holds to in her works, and which the usage of speech has tended to follow.
>
> *(1550 [1880]: 195–6)*

The English tendency was to see English as a particularly useful and simple language, or indeed (in the seventeenth century) to invent new languages that reflected the real world with even greater faithfulness. Again, already in the sixteenth century, Richard Mulcaster wrote

> I do not think that anie language, be it whatsoever, is better able to utter all arguments, either with more pith, or greater planeness, than our English tung is.
>
> *(1582; cited in Baugh and Cable, 1978: 202)*

Where each of these lauded their language because of its supposed superiority in terms of an external ideal, defenders of German praised it for its very distinctiveness, its particular music, the aptness of its words, and the flexibility of its word order. Again, the full development of this position would come in the seventeenth and eighteenth centuries, but already in 1573 Laurentius Albertus would praise German for its purity and distinctiveness; the purpose of his grammar is to show 'the abundance and marvellous variation of combining words in our language' (cited in McLelland, 2001: 15).

All of these tendencies received their clearest expressions in the 1660s. In France, Cartesian theorists claimed the universality of French word order as a direct restatement of the natural and universal order of reason: 'la raison est de tout pays', wrote Louis Le Laboureur (1669), arguing that everyone in the world thought like Frenchmen, and that 'inverting' languages such as Latin required an additional step in order to scramble their sentences.

In England, the Royal Society encouraged a simple and direct style, with 'so many words standing for as many things' and no superfluous verbosity (Thomas Sprat, 1667; see Vickers 1987). But the quest for words standing directly for things went much farther in the numerous English and Scottish schemes for new languages that would directly reflect knowledge of the world of things, culminating in Bishop John Wilkins's great 'Real Character' (1668) in which the world was divided into categories, sub-categories, and sub-sub-categories, each of which was figured with a distinctive line and subordinate squiggles to form a universal ideography which could also be expressed in syllables (see J. L. Borges's essay 'The Analytical Language of John Wilkins' in Borges, 1952 [1968]).

These approaches to language diversity fit well, in both French and English cases, with wider philosophical tendencies: French rationalism and British empiricism and what might already be called a British proto-utilitarianist tendency. In France, in particular, the view that reason was 'de tout pays' and that language differences were secondary also led to a distinctive theory of translation in which any text, from any period of history and showing no matter what peculiarities of form or content, was to be translated into standard respectable seventeenth-century French and standard French style. This transformation was often seen as an improvement on the original, giving it a balance and an elegance that it lacked. Both because of their elegance and because of the freedom they took with their originals, these translations came to be called 'les Belles Infidèles' (Zuber, 1968).

In Germany, on the other hand, there was a developing strain of the defence and admiration of German for its own characteristics, for its German-ness, rather than as an exemplar of universal reason or a handy way of handling empirical evidence. This tendency was exemplified in Schottelius's work, again in the 1660s. Schottelius wrote that the strength of German lay in its body of roots, which

> are made up of their own natural letters and not foreign ones ... [and] have an
> appealing sound and fully express their object.
>
> *(1663, cited in Faust, 1981: 51)*

This appeal to the Germanness of German was developed as part of G. W. Leibniz's philosophy of a multiple and diverse universe. Here each language has its unique part to play in the whole. In particular, Leibniz insists that thinking itself is not a pre-semiotic, already-there activity which is only externalized by language – the assumption of both French rationalists and British empiricists – but that thought and reason are themselves processes carried out through the use of signs, especially but not exclusively linguistic signs. This philosophical position carries the clear implication that differing systems of signs will have an impact on thinking itself.

The relatively clear seventeenth-century positions would be challenged in the eighteenth century, particularly in Britain and France. Debates between rationalists and progressives in France culminated in Condillac's defence of free word order and his claim that thinking itself required the use of distinctive signs – an idea he had acquired from Leibniz's follower Christian Wolff. Reactionaries like the self-styled Comte de Rivarol (1784) reiterated the arguments about the superiority of French rigidity – 'la syntaxe du français est incorruptible' – while revolutionaries proclaimed liberty in the choice of word order. The Reaction of the early nineteenth century brought claims (by the reactionary thinkers De Maistre and Bonald) that the Revolution itself was the predictable result of the corruption of language. Eighteenth-century Britain, for its part, saw battles between French-influenced neo-rationalists (James Harris, Monboddo) and resurgent empiricists (Horne Tooke).

In Germany, again, linguistic and cultural diversity was praised as a good in itself in the pre-Romanticism of J. G. Hamann (1730–88) and J. G. Herder (1744–1803). The attack on universalism was heightened after Herder's teacher Immanuel Kant (*Critique of Pure Reason*, 1781) came to maintain that all human thought has the same form. In their two metacritiques of Kant's *Critique*, both Hamann and Herder claimed that forms of thought come from already-given languages and so are as diverse as the languages themselves.

This view came into its own with the German Romantics early in the nineteenth century. The Romantics fully valorized diversity and cultural and linguistic specificity. Following on Herder, they felt that the highly distinctive productions of rural, illiterate people – their stories, songs, dances, costumes – represented the true and authentic soul of each nation (*Volksgeist*) and as such merited devoted study. Romantic translation practice, the reverse of the *Belles Infidèles*, sought to capture the distinctive, even disturbing, tone of the original in order to enlarge the taste of the target readership and, in this case, German literature (Berman, 1984 [1992]). Romantic projects of national self-exploration were exemplified in the work of the brothers Jakob (1785–1863) and Wilhelm Grimm (1786–1859), who compiled not only their collection of folktales, but also the German grammar, German dictionary, and the main collections of medieval German laws and legends, and Germanic (i.e., Scandinavian) myths. Similar projects were undertaken in most European countries and with most European ethnic groups in the nineteenth century, and continued to be carried out throughout the world as an integral part of nationalist and ethnicist movements. The assumption in every case seems to be that of a plurality of essences: each 'national spirit' is carried by a traditional way of living that includes language, literature, but particularly rural and oral literature, traditional dress, ways of living the land, folk ecology and a distinctive landscape.

Even as one Romantic project was the valorization of one's own language and culture, another was the vast comparative study of all languages and cultures. Perhaps the heroes of this kind of effort were the brothers Wilhelm (1767–1835) and Alexander von Humboldt (1769–1859), respectively the founders of linguistics as the comparative study of forms of language and of geography as the comparative study of modes of natural life. For Wilhelm von Humboldt

> The *mental individuality* of a people and the *shape of its language* are so intimately fused with one another, that if one were given, the other would have to be completely derivable from it. Language is, as it were, the outer appearance of the spirit of a people; the language is their spirit and the spirit their language; we can never think of them sufficiently as identical.
>
> *(Humboldt, 1836 [1999]: 46)*

The later nineteenth century

The latter part of the nineteenth century was marked by the rise in prestige of the natural sciences and of corresponding universalistic ideologies of science. In Germany, as a way of defending humanist diversity, a clear distinction was made between the universalist law-seeking methods of the natural sciences (*Naturwissenschaften*) and the particularist interpretative methods of what came to be called historical or spiritual sciences (*Geisteswissenschaften*).

The study of language throughout the century was dominated by the discovery of the genetic relationships among languages, particularly those of the Indo-European language family.

Practitioners of this new science, which was particularly developed in Germany, focused primarily on the Indo-European languages, with other languages serving almost as foils. Towards the end of the century, with the rise of the Neogrammarian school, historical linguistics came to identify itself as a natural science seeking universal laws of the transformation of isolated sounds, with little interest in particular languages as systems or in the relationship of language to other aspects of life.

Even as historical linguistics, clearly the dominant school in language study throughout the century, became more and more narrowly natural–scientific, a small number of scholars (a 'Humboldtian stream') maintained a very different kind of linguistics, one concerned with the structure of distinct languages as systems, with all the languages of the world in their diversity, and with the relationship of language structure to literary creation and other social practices. This kind of linguistics, primarily part of the cultural rather than the natural sciences, was championed above all by Heymann Steinthal (1823–99), whose overall view would be cited as a model by Boas.

But the great European intellectual development of the second half of the nineteenth century was that of cultural evolutionism, which sought to understand all of human history as a progress from uniform savagery and lack of organization to a state of highly organized civilization typical of modern Western societies. Holding that history recapitulates phylogeny, small-scale non-Western societies, peasant beliefs and superstitions, children, were all held to represent survivals of earlier, more primitive stages.

Both historical linguistics and evolutionism shared models that recognized the existence of diversity but valorized it differently. In both cases there was a single superior mode – modern European societies and ideas on the one hand, Indo-European languages on the other – which set a yardstick for measuring a range of inferior societies, modes of thought, or languages. With a fair deal of difficulty, evolutionists tried to show how languages spoken by 'primitive' people were themselves primitive. They found themselves focusing particularly on limited areas of the lexicon, such as numbers, in which modern Western languages have more terms than do the languages spoken by small-scale societies; or, for instance, the presence or absence of gestures – the less gesturing, the more civilized the people, to the point that a number of evolutionists maintained the fiction that there were people whose spoken languages were so scanty that they could not communicate at night (Tylor, 1871: 164; Morgan 1877: 37; Starr 1895: 170).

Boas, Sapir, Whorf, and their contemporaries

At the end of the nineteenth century, then, a young scholar like Boas, with an interest in the interaction of perception and reality, would have faced a number of theoretical options. At this point, both historical linguistics and evolutionist anthropology were squarely on the side of the natural sciences: the first limited its interest to transformations, especially laws of sound transformation most particularly within languages of the Indo-European family, considered the most advanced type of language; the latter judged all human activity as leading up to the modern West.

Boas rejected both of these positions. Born, raised, and trained in Germany, his central initial interest was in the relationship between the physical world as measured by modern science and the world as perceived by human subjects. He began his education in physics and moved by gradual degrees towards perception, then on to the collective perception of the environment, i.e., to geography. Boas passed through some of the most developed branches of German science, from physics to psychophysics to psychology and then to geography and finally to ethnology, with what appears to have been a fairly late discovery of the implications of linguistics (on Boas's training, see Stocking, 1968).

In the early 1880s Boas undertook field research on the way the Inuit of Baffin Island perceive and conceive their geographical surroundings. Upon his return to Germany, Boas worked in Berlin with German ethnologists and linguists, including Steinthal, who were resisting both evolutionism and the atomism of historical linguistics. As a geographer-cum-ethnologist, Boas identified with the work of Alexander von Humboldt (Boas, 1887a) and so placed himself on the side of the spiritual sciences. But the spiritual sciences themselves, as practised in nineteenth-century Germany, maintained the Romantic identification of each culture with a single given language, social order, set of customs, religion, and mode of thinking – while Boas's increasing knowledge of history and ethnology, and particularly his exposure to the indigenous languages and cultures of Canada and the Pacific Northwest, his next field area, would show this unity of language/thought/culture to be only a sometime thing, itself a historical artefact, and by no means a necessary condition for human life.

Boas's training was thus on the cusp of the natural and spiritual sciences, putting him in a position to rethink the presuppositions of both camps. The model Boas came to was of a world made up of culture areas – not as a necessary and pregiven expression of the soul of a people, as for the Romantics, but as distinctive historical formations that in some cases, and for some period of time, achieved particular coherence. In a radical decentration of human history, Boas rejected the idea of a single fixed measure for all cultures, instead seeing every human historical formations as offering potential points of view on all the others. As George Stocking has noted (1968), Boas was the first to write in English using the term cultures in the plural (it had been used in this way earlier in German by Steinthal and the *Völkerpsychologie* school).

When a culture area had a high degree of coherence, it meant that many borrowed or diffused traits would be transformed as they passed an areal boundary. And this was as true of languages as of any other cultural materials. The North Pacific Coast is not only a culture area, but also represents a linguistic area (Beck, 2000). Here languages of a number of different families, coming from different sources, had cohabited long enough to exchange important traits and so form a recognizable unity. Here, even more than in cultural traits, one could trace the origins and observe the transformations of linguistic structures across areal boundaries.

Boas moved to the United States in 1887. His early publications show a constant concern to shift away from the evolutionist focus on single traits, in language or culture, developing through time, towards an interest in each language as a system: he says, using Humboldt's formula, that we should seek the 'inner form' of each language and language type (1911: 81); and each culture area as a unique expression of human: he writes of the 'peculiar style of each group' (1887b) and later of the 'genius of a people' (1934). Boas instantiated this view of human history and culture first in his work at the American Museum of Natural History, then as the founder of the first academic anthropology department in North America, at Columbia University.

As Boas would insist over and over again, while there is no necessary correlation between language, culture, and thinking (in the sense of thinking processes, as in superior and inferior thinking), a well-established culture area will tend to inflect material coming into it in a distinctive direction.[1] It is at the boundaries of such areas that we can observe transformations in material – and conversely, the observance of such transformations provides the best evidence for the existence of linguistic, or cultural, areas (Darnell, 1998).

Boas's linguistics connected explicitly back through Steinthal to the nineteenth-century 'Humboldtian stream'. His interest was in all the languages of the world, their internal structuring, their implied distinctive points of view on the world (*Weltansicht*).

Boas presents his overall picture of language as structured on several levels in the 'Introduction' to the *Handbook of American Indian Languages* (1911).

As against the evolutionist view that 'primitive' languages have fluid and ill-defined sounds, Boas sees the sound system of each language as a coherent whole largely determining the subject's perception of sounds in other languages. On the level of words, he points out, as indeed many had before him, that the semantic boundaries of given words rarely overlap exactly from language to language, meaning that different languages will carve experience up differently. On the other hand, he points out, individual words are relatively easily produced, easily lost, and will tend to map cultural interests.

The case is very different with pervasive, especially obligatory, grammatical categories, such as tense or number in modern Western European languages, or the obligatory marking of physical shape or source of knowledge in some others. Such categories tend to remain unconscious and to orient the speaker's attention to certain aspects of lived experience. Note that this is in no way a limiting of thought, but rather a requirement that certain aspects of experience be attended to, whether they are relevant to the immediate situation or not. For Roman Jakobson, this discovery of the implications of obligatory grammatical categories was Boas's greatest contribution to linguistics (1959a): as he summed it up, 'languages differ essentially in what they must convey, not in what they can convey' (Jakobson, 1959b). Right here we have a clear exemplification of what Sapir would call linguistic relativity. It in no way limits or restricts or determines what can be thought: but an English speaker is required to refer constantly to the temporal relationship between the event spoken of and the moment of speaking, and in cases where this is unreal or irrelevant some available category must be imposed. An Aymara speaker, on the other hand, faces no such temporal imperative, but must choose among forms that specify how he or she knows what is being spoken about (Hardman, 1986). It is certainly possible for a speaker of English to use English to understand the Aymara categories, and vice versa, and such understanding opens up the possibility of attending to the world in new and unfamiliar ways: but to use evidentiality in English in an obligatory way – always to have to specify how you know what you are saying – or obligatory tense in Aymara would be, to say the least, burdensome, and produce highly abnormal forms of language for each.

The development of the idea of linguistic relativity by Sapir and Whorf can be seen as an explicit rendering of the implications of the Boasian model.

Unlike Boas, Sapir was trained in the humanities, and, like Humboldt, one of his central interests was in the poetic use of language. Sapir was the most brilliant exponent of Boas's programme of language description using tools forged for the languages themselves, rather than imposing standard Western grammatical categories. And it was Sapir who first proposed the idea of a linguistic relativity in parallel with the relativity of Einstein. Whorf, for his part, was not a professional academic but a chemical engineer and fire insurance inspector with a fascination for languages in their variety. A student of Sapir's, an excellent descriptive linguist, particularly of Uto-Aztecan languages, and an active member of Sapir's group of linguists at Yale, Whorf made a number of important contributions to the developing relativity model. He made the clear distinction between habitual thought, which tends to be lazy and follow the easiest paths available – those offered by language and culture – and the potentialities of thought, which are unlimited. Whorf also recognized that much grammatical patterning, while exerting real effects, lacks explicit marking as such, and developed the idea of the cryptotype to account for such patterning. And in a series of published papers and manuscripts on the Hopi language of Arizona, Whorf offered an extensive treatment of the categories of a single non-Western language (on Whorf, see P. Lee, 1996).

Both Whorf and Sapir indulged in some language that sounds highly deterministic, and it is these passages that are the most frequently quoted. In a short chapter like this one I cannot try to take these passages apart and put them back into context. I will just say that the analogy both authors use constantly for the influence of language on conceptualization is one of roads: familiar paths, tracks, ruts, which are temptingly easy to follow but which the energetic walker can always leave behind to explore less familiar territory.

Within the Americanist domain, some younger contemporaries of these scholars continued to work into the 1950s and after. Essential work included Dorothy Demetrocopoulou Lee's analyses of the Wintu language of northern California and Harry Hoijer's of Navajo.

We should also note a major linguistic movement that ran chronologically parallel to that of the Boasians and which has often been seen as propounding the same ideas. Starting in the 1920s, a number of German linguists and literary historians argued for the centrality of linguistic content and the uniqueness of each language. In particular, Leo Weisgerber (1899–1985) showed how sensory domains were organized differently by different languages, and Jost Trier (1894–1970) developed the notion that vocabularies were made up of fields of association, which he called 'word-fields', in which each element set boundaries to the others to form a kind of mosaic: this led to the notion of semantic fields, which was a major force in semantic theory for many years (Öhman, 1953). This movement, which looked explicitly to Wilhelm von Humboldt for its inspiration, came to be called neo-Humboldtian or neo-Romantic, or content-oriented analysis (Basilius, 1952). In marked contrast to the basic ideas of the Boasians, however, neo-Humboldtian linguists maintained that one's first language, the mother tongue, constitutes a horizon beyond which it is impossible to go: even the learning of other languages proceeds through the mother tongue. Given this view, it is not surprising that the major works of neo-Humboldtian linguistics are analyses of various aspects of German; nor that it was not difficult for the movement as a whole to be incorporated into the National Socialist project in the 1930s, with most of the major non-Jewish Neo-Humboldtians participating more or less enthusiastically. After the war, both Weisgerber and Trier continued their careers, and the neo-Humboldtian perspective remained dominant in West German linguistics until the 1970s.

Many of the hostile characterizations of linguistic relativity, and particularly of Whorf's ideas (most recently in Deutscher, 2010), in fact fit those of the Neo-Humboldtians. Here it is indeed said that language determines and limits what it is possible to think, that outside language no thought is possible, and that the absence of a word means the absence of a corresponding concept.

After Boas

Sapir, Whorf, and Boas all died between 1939 and 1942. By the early 1950s, psychologists and linguists were wanting to operationalize investigation of the question of the importance of differences among languages, and they required a hypothesis for testing. In a 1951conference, Hoijer first proposed a 'Sapir–Whorf hypothesis'. The phrase was soon picked up by philosophers and psychologists as meaning that one's language determines one's thought and limits what it is possible to think. This was a model that philosophers had no trouble demolishing (Black, 1962; Davidson, 1974). Psychologists saw the issue as a question of testing two variables, language and thought. They reduced language to vocabulary sets, since these were easy to test for – where the Boasians had always insisted on the systematicity of sounds and the pervasiveness of grammatical categories; and by 'thought' they meant not the construal of the world, as had the Boasians, but psychological processes such as memory and recognition. Not terribly surprisingly, the findings of most psychologists in this domain in the 1950s and 1960s were either ambiguous or clearly negative. These findings were taken up in the rising tide of innatist Chomskyan linguistics and universalist cognitive science effectively to dismiss the possibility of any important or interesting diversity of culture or language. By the 1970s and 1980s, the universality of the calculating human mind was looking like received truth, and the 'Sapir–Whorf hypothesis' was raised in psychological, philosophical, and most linguistic milieux only as a kind of sad ghost of errors past.

Yet during this very period there were important rethinkings of linguistic relativity going on in anthropology, particularly in linguistic anthropology, and to some extent in literary studies. Here I will only mention the work of Dell Hymes (1966), who raised the possibility of a relativity of the use of language, and not only of its structure; Paul Friedrich, who extended Sapir's views of the centrality of poetic language and the interaction of language structure and aesthetics (e.g., 1986); Michael Silverstein and his collaborators, who sought to replace specific questions of 'influence' of language on conceptualization into a wider semiotic frame (e.g., 1977); and James Fernandez, who has spearheaded the specifically tropological analysis of cultural forms (e.g., 1986).

The 1990s and after

The ground began to shift in the 1990s. In 1992, John Lucy, a psychologist with training in anthropology and linguistics, published twin volumes on linguistic relativity. In the first he re-presented the history of ideas, cutting through decades of misrepresentation to give a far more realistic picture of the Sapir–Whorf project than had until then been available. In particular, Lucy insisted on the importance of testing for pervasive grammatical categories rather than merely for vocabulary items. In the second volume, he presented his own series of experiments comparing English- and Mayan-speaking subjects on the categories of number and animacy and finding significant differences between the two on psychological tasks specifically involving these categories. Lucy had found what were coming to be called 'Whorf effects'. The two projects offered in these books, one historical, one experimental, have continued with increasing importance from that point on. In 1996, Penny Lee published *The Whorf Theory Complex*, still the major study of what Whorf was really about; and new work continues to reread Boas and company in light of the influences upon them and their influence on others (e.g. Bunzl, 1996; Leavitt, 2011).

But the real explosion has come in work in experimental psychology. 'Whorf effects' are being found in the conception of space (Levinson, 2003), time (Boroditsky, 2001), gender (Boroditsky, Schmidt, and Phillips 2003), colour (Roberson and Hanley, 2010). While the debate is still hot, there is a growing mass of research supporting some kind of influence of language specifics on conceptualization. Given that human beings are using specific languages, with all of the peculiarities of each, as tools to help think and communicate about the world and themselves thousands of times a day, this is hardly surprising – it is simply a case of the tools used having some influence on the final product.

Future directions

The sudden and widespread development of apparently successful experimental paradigms for testing the effects of linguistic differences has been called a 'Whorfian Renaissance'. But the Renaissance is potentially much broader than that. Anthropologists and culturally minded linguists continue to look into the role of language in conceptualization in the case of particular societies (Regna Darnell, Sean O'Neill, A. L. Becker). The idea that each language is a distinctive raw material that inflects the very products that it enables pervades the work of new generations of ethnopoeticians (e.g., Bernard Bate, Anthony Webster). And translation theory, which has always had to take language differences seriously, continues to offer models of workable linguistic relativity.

Psychology has made its point, and we can certainly expect greater refinement, new discoveries, and perhaps the proposal of overarching theories as more information comes in about the language–thought interface in particular situations.

Within linguistics itself we see a rediscovery of a range of grammatical categories, from aspect to data source.

A key area, as Friedrich, has pointed out, is that of poetics, which brings together literary scholars, linguists, folklorists, and field anthropologists. Since all aspects of a language become significant, become 'charged', when it is being used to aesthetic effect (Jakobson, 1960), here is where we will find a heightening of the qualities of each language as material. Language is used around the world to move people to tears, to evoke gods, to set political transformations in motion: how is this done in a material as varied as that of human languages?

Finally, if we take the differences among languages seriously, as having real effects on people's conception of the world, then the practice of translation can be seen as a crossing between worlds. The vast mass of translation as now practised is between pairs drawn from a tiny number of the world's languages (Bellos, 2011). The considerations advanced here urge the possibility of a multilateral world of translation, since we simply do not know what kinds of ways of organizing reality are out there. Translation becomes the frontline practice in the exploration of the linguistic multiverse. To actually do a translation requires a kind of practical, modest acceptance of linguistic relativity: a recognition of difference at many levels, a recognition that we simply do not know what these differences are or far they might go (Evans and Levinson, 2009), and a willingness to explore them.

Related topics

language and culture: an overview; the linguistic relativity hypothesis revisited; linguaculture; language, culture and colour; language, culture and spatial cognition; culture and semiotics; culture and translation; language and culture in sociocultural anthropology; cultural linguistics; a future agenda

Note

1 This model of an oriented field of force that inflects incoming elements and at the same time is transformed by them seems to have first been developed by the philosopher J. F. Herbart (1776–1841) to explain the distinctiveness and transformation of each human mind. The model was centrally influential in the late nineteenth-century 'psychology of peoples' (*Völkerpsychologie*) of Moritz Lazarus and Heymann Steinthal, the latter the direct inspiration for Boasian linguistics.

Further reading

Evans, Nicholas (2010) *Dying Words: Endangered Languages and What They Have to Teach Us*, Chichester, UK: Wiley-Blackwell. (An overview of the enormous diversity of the world's languages.)

Gumperz, John and Stephen Levinson (eds) (1996) *Rethinking Linguistic Relativity*, Cambridge: Cambridge University Press. (The first major collection of essays on the topic.)

Leavitt, John (2011) *Linguistic Relativities: Language Diversity and Modern Thought*, Cambridge: Cambridge University Press. (An attempt to give an overall history of Western ideas about language diversity, with a focus on linguistic relativity.)

Lee, Penny (1996) *The Whorf Theory Complex*, Amsterdam: John Benjamins. (The most accurate and thorough reconstruction of linguistic relativity as a mature theory.)

Sapir, Edward (1921) *Language: The Study of Speech*, Boston, MA: Houghton Mifflin. (Still in print. The best presentation of Boasian linguistics.)

Whorf, Benjamin Lee (2010) *Language, Thought, and Reality: Selected Writings of Benjamin Lee Whorf*, 2nd edn, Cambridge, MA: MIT Press. (First published 1956. The standard collection of Whorf's writings on linguistics, now in a new edition with introduction by Stephen Levinson.)

References

Basilius, Harold (1952) 'Neo-Humboldtian Ethnolinguistics', *Word* 8: 95–105.

Baugh, Albert Croll and Thomas Cable (1978) *A History of the English Language*, 3rd edn, Englewood Cliffs, NJ: Prentice-Hall.

Beck, David (2000) 'Grammatical Convergence and the Genesis of Diversity in the Northwest Coast Sprachbund', *Anthropological Linguistics* 42: 147–213.

Bellos, David (2011) *Is That a Fish in Your Ear? The Amazing Adventure of Translation*, London: Allen Lane.

Berman, Antoine (1984 [1992]) *The Experience of the Foreign: Culture and Translation in Romantic Germany*, trans. Stefan Heyvaert, Albany, NY: SUNY Press.

Black, Max (1962) *Models and Metaphors*, Ithaca, NY: Cornell University Press.

Boas, Franz (1887a) 'The Study of Geography', *Science* 9: 137–41.

——(1887b) 'The Occurrence of Similar Inventions in Areas Widely Apart', *Science* 9: 485–6.

——(1889) 'On Alternating Sounds', *American Anthropologist* 2: 47–53.

——(1911) 'Introduction', in Franz Boas (ed.), *Handbook of American Indian Languages*, Washington, DC: Government Printing Office, pp. 1–83.

Borges, Jorge Luis (1952 [1984]) *Other Inquisitions*, trans. Ruth L. C. Simms, Austin, TX: University of Texas Press.

Boroditsky, Lera (2001) 'Does Language Shape Thought? Mandarin and English Speakers' Conceptions of Time', *Cognitive Psychology* 43: 1–22.

——, Lauren A. Schmidt and Webb Phillips (2003) 'Sex, Syntax, and Semantics', in Dedre Gentner and Susan Goldin-Meadow (eds), *Language in Mind: Advances in the Study of Language and Thought*, Cambridge, MA: MIT Press, pp. 61–79.

Bunzl, Matti (1996) 'Franz Boas and the Humboldtian Tradition: From *Volksgeist* and *Nationalcharakter* to an Anthropological Concept of Culture', in George W. Stocking, Jr. (ed.), *Volksgeist as Method and Ethic*, Madison, WI: University of Wisconsin Press, pp. 17–78.

Darnell, Regna (1998) *And Along Came Boas: Continuity and Revolution in American Anthropology*, Amsterdam: Benjamins.

Davidson, Donald (1974) 'On the Very Idea of a Conceptual Scheme', *Proceedings and Addresses of the American Philosophical Association* 47: 5–20.

Deutscher, Guy (2010) *Through the Language Glass*, London: Heinemann.

Evans, Nicholas and Stephen C. Levinson (2009) 'The Myth of Language Universals: Language Diversity and Its Importance for Cognitive Science', *Behavioral and Brain Sciences* 32: 429–48.

Faust, Manfred (1981) 'Schottelius' Concept of Word Formation', in Jürgen Trabant (ed.), *Logos Semantikos*, I. Madrid: Gredos, pp. 359–70.

Fernandez, James W. (1986) *Persuasions and Performances: The Play of Tropes in Culture*, Bloomington, IN: Indiana University Press.

Friedrich, Paul (1986) *The Language Parallax*, Austin, TX: University of Texas Press.

Hardman, Martha James (1986) 'Data-Source Marking in the Jaqi Languages', in Wallace Chafe and Johanna Nichols (eds), *Evidentiality: The Linguistic Coding of Epistemology*. Norwood, NJ: Ablex, pp. 113–36.

Humboldt, Wilhelm von (1836 [1999]) *On Language: The Diversity of Human Language-Structure and Its Influence on the Development of Mankind*, trans. Peter Heath, 2nd edn, Cambridge: Cambridge University Press.

Hymes, Dell (1966) 'Two Types of Linguistic Relativity', in William Bright (ed.), *Sociolinguistics*, The Hague: Mouton, pp. 131–56.

Jakobson, Roman (1959a) 'Boas' View of Grammatical Meaning', in Walter Goldschmidt (ed.), *The Anthropology of Franz Boas: Essays on the Centennial of His Birth*, Washington, DC: American Anthropological Association, pp. 139–45.

——(1959b) 'Linguistic Aspects of Translation'. In Reuben A. Brower, ed., *On Translation*. Cambridge, MA: Harvard University Press, pp. 232–8.

Leavitt, John (2011) *Linguistic Relativities: Language Diversity and Modern Thought*, Cambridge: Cambridge University Press.

Lee, Penny (1996) *The Whorf Theory Complex*, Amsterdam: John Benjamins.

Le Laboureur, Louis (1669) *Les avantages de la langue française sur la langue latine*, 2nd edn, Paris: Guillaume de Luynes.

Levinson, Stephen C. (2003) *Space in Language and Cognition: Explorations in Cognitive Diversity*, Cambridge: Cambridge University Press.

Lucy, John A. (1992a) *Language Diversity and Thought*, Cambridge: Cambridge University Press.

——(1992b) *Grammatical Categories and Cognition*, Cambridge: Cambridge University Press.

McLelland, Nicola (2001) 'Albertus (1573) and Ölinger (1574): Creating the First Grammars of German', *Historiographia Linguistica* 28: 2–38.

Meigret, Louis (1550 [1880]) *Tretté de la gramere françoèze*, ed. Wendelin Foerster, Heilbron: Henninger.

Morgan, Lewis Henry (1877) *Ancient Society*, Chicago, IL: C. H. Kerr.

Öhman, Suzanne (1953) 'Theories of the 'Linguistic Field'', *Word* 9: 123–34.

Pinker, Steven (1994) *The Language Instinct*, New York: William Morrow.

Rivarol, Antoine de (1784) *De l'universalité de la langue française*, Berlin: Académie Royale.

Roberson, Debi and J. Richard Hanley (2010) 'Relatively Speaking: An Account of the Relationship between Language and Thought in the Color Domain', in Barbara C. Malt and Phillip Wolff (eds), *Words and the Mind: How Words Can Capture Human Experience*, New York: Oxford University Press, pp. 183–98.

Sapir, Edward (1921) *Language: An Introduction to the Study of Speech*, Boston, MA: Houghton Mifflin.

Scaglione, Aldo D. (1972) *The Classical Theory of Composition from Its Origins to the Present*, Chapel Hill, NC: University of North Carolina Press.

Silverstein, Michael (1976) 'Shifters, Linguistic Categories, and Cultural Description', in Keith H. Basso and Henry A. Selby (eds), *Meaning in Anthropology*. Albuquerque, NM: University of New Mexico Press, pp. 11–55.

Starr, Frederick (1895) *Some First Steps in Human Progress*, Meadville, PA: Chatauqua.

Stocking, George W., Jr. (1968) *Race, Culture, and Evolution*, New York: Free Press.

Tylor, Edward Burnett (1871) *Primitive Culture*, London: John Murray.

Vickers, Brian (ed.) (1987) *English Science: Bacon to Newton*, Cambridge: Cambridge University Press.

Whorf, Benjamin Lee (1956) *Language, Thought, and Reality*, Cambridge, MA: MIT Press.

Wilkins, John (1668) *An Essay towards a Real Character and a Philosophical Language*, London: Gellibrand and the Royal Society.

Zuber, Roger (1968) *Les 'Belles infidèles' et la formation du goût classique*, Paris: Armand Colin.

PART II

Ethnolinguistics

3
ETHNOSYNTAX

Anna Gladkova

1 Introduction

Ethnosyntax is an approach to studying grammar as a vehicle of culture. The term 'ethnosyntax' was introduced by Wierzbicka (1979) to reflect a new perspective on grammatical studies with a particular focus on cultural meaning. She advocated the view that grammatical constructions are not semantically arbitrary and their meanings are related to broader cultural understandings.

Since the idea of cultural meaning is important in the ethnosyntax approach, the understanding of 'culture' must be identified. 'Culture' here means people's shared ideas, meanings and understandings. The most relevant interpretation of 'culture' in this regard has been offered by the anthropologist Clifford Geertz. In his view, the concept of culture denotes 'a historically transmitted pattern of meanings embodied in symbols, a system of inherited conceptions expressed in symbolic forms by means of which men communicate, perpetuate, and develop their knowledge about and attitudes towards life' (Geertz, 1973: 89). This interpretation of culture is sometimes labelled as 'semiotic' (Sarangi, 2009).

Although the development of ethnosyntax as an approach in linguistics is relatively recent, its ideological and theoretical foundations were laid in the works by Sapir and Whorf (Chapter 2 this volume). Sapir (1949) argued that language and thought are in a relationship of mutual dependence. Whorf (1956) formulated the 'linguistic relativity principle', which postulates that conceptual systems are relative and dependent on language; that is, speakers of a particular language share a certain world-view because their language determines the way they 'see' the world. Speakers of another language 'see' the world through the prism of this other language and, therefore, their linguistic view is different (Chapter 2 this volume). Whorf's observations applied to lexicon and grammar.

Two senses of ethnosyntax can be distinguished – a 'narrow' and a 'broad' one (Enfield, 2002; Goddard, 2002). Ethnosyntax in a 'narrow' sense aims to locate and articulate cultural understandings that are embedded in the meanings of particular grammatical structures. Ethnosyntax in a broad sense studies how pragmatic and cultural rules affect the use of grammatical structures. Ethnosyntax in this sense overlaps with some studies in the area of pragmatics, such as ethnopragmatics (Goddard 2002, 2006; Chapter 5 this volume) and ethnography of speaking (e.g., Gumperz and Hymes, 1972).

The following discussion provides examples of studies in ethnosyntax in its broad and narrow senses. It also focuses on two traditionally distinguished components of grammar – morphology (inflection and word formation) and syntax (a system of rules which describe how all well-formed sentences of a language can be derived from basic elements).

The accumulated experience of research into ethnosyntax allowed researchers to formulate methodological requirements to this kind of linguistic investigations. There is a degree of unanimity among scholars that research into cultural element of grammatical constructions involves the analysis of their meaning (e.g., Wierzbicka 1979, 1989, 2002; Enfield, 2002; Goddard, 2002; Simpson, 2002). As emphasized by Wierzbicka (1979), a key to decoding cultural meanings embedded in grammatical structures lies in a semantic approach to studying grammar. Conducting an ethnosyntactic analysis involves identifying a construction in question, investigating its meaning, and establishing connections between this meaning and some wider shared cultural assumptions or understandings (Wierzbicka, 1979, 1988; Goddard, 2002; Simpson, 2002: 291–2). Some scholars also argue for the importance of a comparative cross-linguistic and cross-cultural analysis of grammatical constructions and associated cultural understandings (Simpson, 2002; Enfield, 2002).

A significant view in ethnosyntax is that cultural specificity of grammatical structures needs to be studied with a culture-neutral methodology to avoid a lingua- and ethnocentric bias in research (e.g., Wierzbicka, 1979, 1989, 2002; Chapter 23 this volume; Goddard, 2002). Such metalanguage can be found in the Natural Semantic Metalanguage (NSM). NSM comprises 65 empirically identified universal meanings (along with a limited number of more complex meanings known as semantic molecules) which combine with each other in certain ways to form a mini-language. This metalanguage lies at the core of every language (e.g., Goddard and Wierzbicka, 2002, 2014; Chapter 23 this volume). NSM is applied in semantic studies of words and grammatical constructions to formulate explications, as well as in studies of cultural and pragmatic factors underlying language use to formulate cultural scripts. Several of the examples provided in this chapter represent studies which rely on the use of NSM as a methodological tool.

This chapter is structured as follows. Section 2 provides examples of cultural meaning embedded at the level of morphology and syntax relying on examples from English, Russian, and Spanish. Section 3 illustrates variation in the use of grammatical structures due to the influence of cultural factors on the basis of ways of wording 'requests' in English and Russian. Section 4 concludes. Section 5 sets future directions for research in ethnosyntax.

2 Cultural meaning at the level of morphology and syntax

2.1 Morphology

Diminutives are an interesting example of a linguistic phenomenon encoding cultural meaning at the level of morphology. The term 'diminutive' refers to a formation of a word that conveys the idea of 'smallness' of the object or quality named, generally, in conjunction with an attitude of intimacy or endearment towards it. This phenomenon is found in many languages, but its scope and exact semantic content vary from language to language. Here this variation will be demonstrated using Russian, Columbian Spanish, and Australian English.

Russian has a highly developed system of expressive derivation. It applies to nouns, adjectives, and adverbs, for example:

nos 'nose.NOUN.MASC.SG' – *nosik* 'nose.DIM',

solnce 'sun.NOUN.NEUT.SG' – *solnyško* 'sun.DIM',

krasivyj 'beautiful.ADJ.MASC.SG' – *krasiven'kij* 'beautiful.DIM',

bystro 'quickly.ADV' – *bystren'ko* 'quickly.DIM'.

The system of expressive derivation in personal names is also extremely rich and is largely consistent with the one for nouns. For example, a feminine name *Ljudmila* has the following derivatives: *Ljuda, Ljudočka, Ljudka, Ljudok, Ljudusik, Ljudasik, Ljudaša, Ljusja, Ljus'ka, Ljusik, Ljusenok, Mila, Miločka*. A masculine name *Jurij* has the derivatives *Jura, Juročka, Jurik, Juron'ka, Juranja, Juraša, Jurčik, Jurasja* (among others). A list of comparable length can be produced for almost any Russian personal name. Each form conveys a different meaning, and the choice of the form depends on the attitude the speaker wants to express towards the addressee. The nuances of these meaning, however, are difficult for cultural outsiders and learners of a language to decipher (Gladkova, 2007). There is a strong association between diminutives and small children (as diminutives are used to talk about and to children), but they are also used among adults in colloquial speech.

Wierzbicka (1992) argues that with a meaning-based approach to grammar one can unravel cultural information embedded in the derivative forms of personal name. She proposes semantic formulae as representations of meanings of models of expressive derivation. We will illustrate her studies on the basis of two forms in Russian, the suffixes *-očka* and *-ik*.

The suffix *-očka* is a relatively common way of forming diminutive forms for nouns of feminine gender. As a way of generalization, it can be said that it is used as either a diminutive-forming suffix in nouns containing a cluster of consonants or long consonants or it can be added to words already containing another diminutive suffix *-k(a)*. The former case can be illustrated with the following examples:

vaza 'vase' – *vazočka* 'vase.DIM'

zvezda 'star' – *zvezdočka* 'star.DIM'

kofta 'cardigan' – *koftočka* 'cardigan.DIM'

vanna 'bathtub' – *vannočka* 'bathtub.DIM'.

In the latter case *-očka* constitutes a 'double diminutive' and its formation can be demonstrated as follows:

poljana 'clearing' – *poljanka* 'clearing.DIM' – *poljanočka* 'clearing.DIM'

lošad' 'horse' – *lošadka* 'horse.DIM' – *lošadočka* 'horse.DIM'

krovat' 'bed' – *krovatka* 'bed.DIM' – *krovatočka* 'bed.DIM'.

According to the Russian Grammar of the Russian Academy of Sciences (Švedova, 1980), *-očka* is a highly emotive formation expressing endearment and as a 'double diminutive' it expresses an increased degree of endearment.

The use of the forms with *-očka* evoke the idea of 'smallness' and are often used in contexts associated with children. They convey affection, love, and protection, that is attitudes associated with and directed towards children. Wierzbicka (1992: 246–7) argues that *-očka* has an association not just with children, but with small children and it is consistent with its function as a 'double diminutive'.

This attitude also extends to diminutive forms with *-očka* in personal names. Such forms (e.g., *Juročka, Ljubočka*) suggest a particularly small size and very good feelings associated with small children. Such forms are commonly used in interaction with children, however, they can also be used to address adults. As a way of illustration, the following cases from the oral subcorpus of the *Russian National Corpus* can be quoted. In example (1) a 30-year-old mother addresses her 5-year-old daughter using the name form with -*očka* while giving her a bath:

(1) Female, 5-year-old: *Xolodnaja*. 'Cold.'
     Female, 30-year-old: *Kak raz, kak raz. Ne xolodnaja? Govori, Svetočka. Ja mogu pogorjačee.*
     'It's all right, it's all right. Not cold? Say, Sveta-DIM. I can make it warmer.'

The following example is taken form a database recorded at a GP practice. In it a 50-year-old male doctor addresses a younger female nurse as *Iročka*:

(2) *Iročka, vy svobodny? Sxodite v registraturu za kartočkoj.*
     'Ira-DIM, are you free? Go to the registration office to pick up the patient's records.'

The invariant of meaning of this form can be represented in universal human concepts as they are identified in NSM as follows (Wierzbicka, 1992: 247):

[A] *Ljudočka, Juročka*

     (a) I feel something very good towards you
     (b) like people can feel when they say things to small children

Another group of words to be considered in this discussion are those with the suffix -*ik*. According to the Russian Grammar (Švedova, 1980), words with the suffix -*ik* express the idea of 'smallness', which can often be accompanied by an affectionate attitude. This observation applies to -*ik* as a diminutive suffix which is added to masculine nouns ending in consonants (another variant of -*ik* is used to form nouns from adjectives):

lob – *lobik* 'forehead'

sad – *sadik* 'garden'

xvost – *xvostik* 'tail'

dom – *domik* 'house'

slon – *slonik* 'elephant'

Some words ending in -*ik* can express disparagement (e.g., *tipčik* < *tip* 'type', *xozjajčik* < *xozjain* 'host/owner').

Unlike the suffix -*očka*, the suffix -*ik* is not a 'double diminutive' (Wierzbicka, 1992: 250). While both suffixes denote the idea of 'smallness', -*ik* expresses less affectionate attitude than -*očka* and it also does not necessarily evoke an association with small children.

The suffix -*ik* can be used to form affectionate forms for masculine and feminine names:

Mark – *Marik* (m.)

Jura – *Jurik* (m.)

Sveta – *Svetik* (f.)

Ljusja – *Ljusik* (f.).

This suffix has boyish associations, in both masculine and feminine forms, which is consistent with the fact that *-ik* originally is a masculine form and it is used to form nouns of masculine gender. Masculine forms in *-ik*, compared to forms in *-očka*, are less affectionate and express a 'boyish attitude'. The invariant of this meaning is as follows (Wierzbicka, 1992: 251):

[B] *Jurik, Marik* (masculine names)

  (a) I feel something good towards you
  (b) like people can feel towards small boys

Feminine forms in *-ik* are less common than masculine forms. They are playful and very informal. For example, while feminine forms in *-očka* can be used in the workplace context between people who know each other well (as in example 2), feminine forms in *-ik* can only be used among friends. Some examples from the oral subcorpus of the *Russian National Corpus* indicate that feminine forms in *-ik* are often used along with other colloquial expressions:

(3) Female, 18-year-old: *Privet!* 'Hi!'
  Male, 23-year-old: *Privetik, Svetik! A gde vse?* 'Hi, Sveta-DIM! Where's everyone?'
  Female, 18-year-old: *Ne znaj, ja toka nedavno vstala.* 'Dunno, I just got up.'

In this exchange between an 18-year-old female Sveta (Svetik) and a 23-year-old male (Sasha), both interlocutors use elements of colloquial speech: *privetik* 'hi-DIM' (also rhyming with *Svetik*), *ne znaj* 'not know.2SG' (rather than first-person singular form), and a reduced form *toka* (from *tol'ko* 'just'). Similar features are observed in an exchange between two teenagers:

(4) Female 1, 15-year-old: *Da už! Nu ladnen'ko, Svetik! Pokedova!* 'Well. OK, Svetik! Bye!'
  Female 2, 15-year-old: *Poka.* 'Bye!'

In this example the female addressing Sveta as *Svetik* also uses colloquial forms *ladnen'ko* (a diminutive from of *ladno* 'OK') and *pokedova* (from *poka* 'buye').

The invariant of meaning for feminine forms with *-ik* is as follows (Wierzbicka, 1992: 251):

[C] *Ljusik, Svetik* (feminine forms)

  (a) I feel something good towards you
  (b) I feel something good when I say things to you
  (c) I want to say things to you like people can say something to a small boy, not to a small girl

Formulae of this kind allow us to show overlapping components of meaning in the structures under investigation as well as their differences. Explications [A], [B], and [C] have similar components (a). Their differences lie in the fact that explication [A] has reference to 'small children', while explications [B] and [C] have reference to 'small boys' with [C] also containing reference to 'small girls'. Explication [A] also shows that a more affectionate attitude expressed by forms with *-očka* can be rendered by the use of the prime VERY. Therefore, the attitudinal component in [A] is expressed as 'feel something very good', while in [B] and [C] it is expressed as 'feel something good'.

  Reference to small children has not been shown to apply to all forms of expressive derivation in Russian as it is not relevant in the forms with the suffix *-en'ka* (e.g. *Katen'ka, Miten'ka*) and with the suffix *-uška* (e.g. *Nikituška, Annuška*) (Wierzbicka, 1992). This fact suggests that reference to children cannot be claimed to be an invariant of meaning for all forms of diminutives in Russian.

Linguistic elaboration in the domain of expressive derivation in Russian has a significant cultural importance. In particular, this elaboration can be related to two important cultural themes of Russian. First, it is reflective of a general cultural value placed on open and spontaneous display of emotions. Second, it relates to the value of displaying affectionate feelings in intimate personal relations (Gladkova 2013a, 2013b). These cultural rules can be formulated in the form of cultural scripts as follows (Wierzbicka, 1999):

[D]   [many people think like this at many times:]
      it is good if other people can know what someone feels

[E]   [many people think like this at many times:]
      if I know someone well
      when I feel something good towards this someone
      it is good if this someone can know it when I say something to this someone

[F]   [many people think like this at many times:]
      if I know someone well
      when I say something to this someone
      it is good if this someone can know what I feel towards this someone
      when I think about this someone

Spanish, like Russian, is also rich in expressive derivation. However, there is no complete overlap between the two systems. Travis (2004) employs Wierzbicka's approach in analysing a diminutive suffix *-ito/-ita* in Columbian Spanish using spoken data of Colombian Spanish. According to Travis's data, this suffix is much more frequent and productive than other diminutive suffixes in Spanish *-illo/a* and *-in/a*. Travis identifies several uses of the suffix *-ito/-ita* on the basis of a corpus study and demonstrates that this suffix serves several functions – from its core uses in relation to children to expressing affection, contempt, and hedging speech acts. For each of the uses Travis proposes a semantic formula in universal concepts. Travis argues that the use of diminutives in Colombian Spanish is based on the prototype of using a diminutive when speaking to children and, therefore, implies feelings of the kind that can be felt when speaking to children. However, she also notes that the meaning of the suffix is generalized in situations when contempt is expressed or when someone expresses requests or offers and reference to children is lost.

The use of *-ito/-ita* is very common in expressing affection when speaking to and about adults. Such uses can be demonstrated with the following examples from Travis' data (2004: 259):

(5)   – *Cómase una arepa también, oyó?* 'Have an arepa [Colombian pancake] too, you hear?'
      – *Bueno, mijita. Gracias.* 'OK, my daughter-DIM. Thank you.'

In this example *mijita* 'my daughter-DIM' is used as a diminutive fictive kin term by a cleaning lady to the owner of the house (who is her boss). In example (6) a phonological variant of the suffix *-ito* (that is *-ico*) is used jokingly by a woman when addressing her husband (Travis, 2004: 260):

(6)   *tú eres un monstrico … Un monstruo come pancakes.*
      'You are a monster-DIM. A pancake-eating monster.'

The prototype of use of *-ito* to express affection when talking about an adult can be formulated in the form of a cultural script as follows (Travis, 2004: 261):

[G]   [many people think like this at many times when they say something about someone:]

when I say this about this someone, I feel something good towards this someone
like people can feel towards a child when they are saying something to this child

The Spanish script [G] can be compared to the Russian explication [A] in that both contain reference to children. However, there are also differences in that Russian forms with *-očka* make reference to small children and also express a greater degree of affection ('feel something very good') than the Spanish forms with *-ito*. Moreover, explications [B] and [C] contain reference to small boy and small girls, but not small children. Travis notes that semantic and pragmatic functions of the diminutive in Spanish differ from those in Russian in that a Spanish prototype of a diminutive is child focused, while Russian is not.

English also has diminutive forms, but their use is much more rare and less versatile than the use of diminutive forms in Russian and Spanish. Australian English has a distinctive diminutive form, such as *Chrissy prezzies* (Christmas presents), *barbie* (barbeque), *salties* (salt-water crocodiles), *freshies* (fresh-water crocodiles), *Brissie* (Brisbane), *Tassie* (Tasmania). The following are some examples from the Australian subcorpus of *Collins Wordbanks Online*:

(7)   *What Chrissie presents did you give your loved ones last year? More CDs?*

(8)   *Captain Jason chucked a few steaks on the barbie and opened a cask or three.*

(9)   *A billabong cruise is just one of the many things a visitor to Darwin can do in a day, with most tour companies including sightings of crocodiles (both 'freshie' and 'salty') on their itineraries.*

Goddard and Wierzbicka (2008) argue that the use of this kind of 'diminutive' is different from the use of a 'regular' diminutive (e.g., *birdie*, *horsie*) in that it involves abbreviation and it does not convey a 'childish effect'. The Australian forms reflect a 'familiarity' effect (they apply to objects or phenomena well familiar to people in Australia) and the 'unimpressed' or 'undaunted' attitude that 'it is not a big thing' (as a shortened form of the word indicates). Goddard and Wierzbicka (2008) propose the following explication for these forms:

[H]   barbie, freshies
(a) something
(b) when I say this about it, I think about it like this:
(c)   "it is not something big
(d)   when I say something about it, I don't want to say it with a big word
(e)   people here don't have to think much about things like this
(f)   because they know things like this well"
(g) when I think about it like this, I feel something good

This explication demonstrates differences in meaning between the Australian forms and Russian and Spanish forms. It also shows differences at underlying cultural values in that rules of 'emotion expression' in Russian (scripts D–F) are not applicable to the Australian context where the expression of emotions is toned down.

Thus, with the help of a refined methodology of semantic analysis it can be demonstrated that 'diminutive' forms in Russian, Columbian Spanish, and Australian English convey cultural attitudes and that these attitudes differ across these languages. Other well-researched examples of culturally salient morphology are honorifics in Japanese (e.g., Prideaux, 1970; Loveday, 1986), Korean honorifics and cultural scripts (Yoon, 2004), case in Polish (Wierzbicka, 2008), and reciprocal constructions (Nedjalkov, 2007; Wierzbicka 2009).

2.2 Syntax

We will now turn our attention to examples of culture-specific information embedded at the level of syntax. As an illustration, we will consider a link between dative impersonal constructions in Russian and the cultural themes of 'fatalism', 'irrationality', and 'unpredictability'. We will rely on Wierzbicka's (1992) and Goddard's (2003) work. Examples will be sourced from the *Russian National Corpus*.

Russian is rich in impersonal constructions. Malchukov and Ogawa (2011: 20) define impersonal constructions as 'constructions lacking a referential subject'. In this chapter we will consider Russian constructions of the type where the notional subject lacks typical subject properties. They are also called 'dative reflexive' constructions because the nominal subject occurs in the dative case and the verb is in the reflexive form. We will consider two types of constructions – with mental verbs and with other intransitive verbs.

The first construction combines a dative human subject and a mental verb in the third-person neuter reflexive form. Some mental state verbs occur in this construction – *xotet'sja* 'to want itself', *dumat'sja* 'to think itself', *verit'sja* 'to believe itself', *pomnit'sja* 'to remember itself':

(10) *Kogda ja vpervye popal na stanciju, mne ne verilos', čto ja smogu vynesti zdes' i nedelju.*

'When I first came to the station I-DAT didn't believe-REF that I would be able to stay there for even a week.'

(11) *Pokidat' stolicu emu ne xotelos', no on ponimal: moskovskoj konkurencii emu ne vyderžat'.*

'He-DAT didn't want-REF to leave the capital, but he understood that he couldn't withstand the competition in Moscow.'

(12) *Mne dumaetsja, takie materialy budut interesny dlja čitatelej vašego žurnala.*

'I-DAT think-REF that such material would be interesting for the readers of your journal.'

(13) *Mne jasno pomnitsja letnee utro i skameečka na dorožke, iduščej ot kalitki k terrase.*

'I-DAT clearly remember-REF the summer morning and the bench on the path leading from the gate to the terrace.'

Speakers of Russian also have an option of using nominative constructions with the verb in the active voice, such as *ja dumaju* 'I think', *on xočet* 'he wants', *ja pomnju* 'I remember'. However, in certain contexts it is preferred to use dative constructions. Overall, dative constructions are less frequent than nominal constructions, but their use is still quite significant. For example, according to the *Russian National Corpus* data, the form *on xočet* 'he.NOM.SG want.3SG.PRES' is about three times more frequent than the form *emu xočetsja* 'he.DAT.SG. want.REF.PRES' (10,824 uses vs. 3,293 uses) and the form *ja xoču* 'I.NOM.SG want.1SG. PRES' is about four times more frequent than *mne xočetsja* 'I.DAT.SG want.REF.PRES' (21,318 uses vs. 5,366 uses).

Goddard (2003: 416) comments that this structure 'implies that for some unknown reason the mental event simply 'happens' inside us' and it suggests 'a spontaneous and involuntary' mental state. The choice of the dative construction over the nominative one suggests the denial of responsibility over the action and at the same time submission to it. The reflexive form of the verb, the absence of the nominative subject and the presentation of the experiencer in the dative case as a recipient of the state contribute these semantic elements to the structure.

In contemporary English there is no exact equivalent of such construction. English has a clear preference towards 'active' constructions, such as *I want, I believe, I think*, etc. The closest equivalent of the Russian construction would be the expressions *It seems to me* and *It occurs to me*. However, their frequency is significantly lower than the frequency of the active construction. For example, in the 550-million-word *Collins Wordbanks Online* corpus there are 232,607 occurrences of *I think* and only 2,245 occurrences of *it seems to me*, and 133 occurrences of *it occurs to me* (that is, respectively, 103 and 1749 times fewer). In the past, English also employed dative constructions, such as *methinks* (Bromhead, 2009), but they fell out of use.

The meaning of the Russian construction is represented in universal human concepts as follows (after Goddard 2003: 417):

[I] *Mne xočetsja/veritsja* (lit. 'it doesn't want/believe itself to me')

something happens inside me
because of this, I want/believe this
I don't know why

[J] *Mne ne xočetsja/veritsja* (lit. 'it doesn't want/believe itself to me')

something happens inside me
because of this, I cannot not want/believe this
I don't know why

Besides mental acts, numerous other verbs can occur in impersonal dative constructions in Russian. There is a range of verbs that are used in impersonal constructions either in negation or with evaluative adverbs. Below are some examples of such construction in negation:

(14) *Prosto im čego-to ne spitsja.*

'They-DAT simply don't sleep-REF.'

(15) *Nado otsypat'sja, a kak-to ne spitsja.*

'I need to sleep, but I-DAT somewhat don't sleep-REF.'

(16) *Čeloveka po-svoemu neordinarnogo, ee tomila 'oxota k peremene mest' – ej počemu-to ne rabotalos' v odnom i tom že teatre.*

'As a rather unusual person, she was driven by the desire for change; for some reason she-DAT didn't work-REF in one and the same theatre.'

(17) *Tolstoj pisal pis'ma, pisal dnevnik, no nad čem-to drugim v te nedeli počti ne rabotalos'.*

'Tolstoy wrote letters and the diary but he-DAT didn't work-REF on anything else in those weeks for some reason.'

This construction can also be used with adverbs of manner:

(18)   *Emu ploxo rabotalos' v ètot den'.*

'He-DAT worked-REF badly that day.'

(19)   *Nam interesno rabotalos' s togdašnim zamestitelem direktora.*

'We-DAT worked-REF with the deputy director of that time with enthusiasm.'

(20)   *– A doma vam ploxo žilos'? – Ja ne skazal by, čto ploxo, udovletvoritel'no.*

'– Did you-DAT live-REF badly at home? – I wouldn't say badly, but satisfactory.'

(21)   *Ot nego vsegda isxodila kakaja-to radost' […] S nim legko žilos'.*

'He always radiated joy. It was easy to live-REF with him.'

The construction with negation expresses inexplicable state when something that one wants or needs to do does not happen. It mainly occurs with verbs expressing an action one wants or is expected to do at a particular time (*spat'* 'sleep', *rabotat'* 'work', *pet'* 'sing'). The 'inexplicable' attitude embedded in this construction is supported by a common use of indefinite pronominal adverbs *počemu-to* 'for some reason', *kak-to* 'somewhat', *čto-to* 'for some reason/somewhat'. Its explication is as follows (after Wierzbicka 1992: 425–6):

[K]   *Mne ne spitsja/rabotaetsja* ('to me it doesn't sleep/work')
      I want to do something Y
      because of this, I am doing it
      at the same time I feel something because I think like this:
            I can't do it
            I don't know why
            it is not because I don't want to do it

The construction using evaluative adverbs is explicated as follows:

[L]   *Mne xorošo/ploxo/interesno živetsja/rabotaetsja* 'to me it well/badly/interestingly lives/works'

      I am doing something now
      it happens in some way, not in another way
      I don't know why it is like this
      it's not because I want it to be like this

These constructions embed in their meaning the ideas of 'not being in control' and 'irrationality'. More impersonal constructions in Russian reflect similar ideas or even something akin to 'fatalism' (Wierzbicka, 1992; Goddard, 2003). These ideas penetrate Russian lexicon at different levels. At the level of lexicon they are evident in the words *sud'ba* 'fate', *rok* 'fate', *avos'* 'perhaps/maybe', among which *sud'ba* is most culturally significant. *Sud'ba* refers to an imaginary force which determines the course of a person's life and to which a person must submit. These ideas also have been shown to be integrated in the meaning of some Russian emotion terms (Wierzbicka, 1999) as well as temporal terms and constructions (Apresjan, 2012; Gladkova, 2012). At the level of syntax it appears in impersonal constructions discussed in this chapter as well as in some passive constructions.

There is considerable variation in impersonal constructions across languages (Malchukov and Ogawa, 2012). Their meanings can be studied and compared across languages using the same set of linguistic universals embedded in NSM.

3 Grammatical structures and cultural influence on their use

In this section we provide an illustration of variation in the use of grammatical structures due to the influence of cultural factors. As a case study we will consider ways of wording 'requests' in English and Russian. Requests are a type of speech act. As a part of the speech act theory, Austin (1962) distinguished between statements (that is, utterances that may be assigned a truth value) and performatives (that is, utterances that perform some actions whose successful completion rests on felicity conditions). Searle (1979) proposed a further classification of performatives and, according to his classification, requests (along with commands) belong to the group of directives.

It is important to note that the word 'request' is used as a technical label and it is erroneous to equate all speech of this type in different languages with the English word *request*. While other languages might have a term close to 'request' it might not necessarily fully overlap in meaning with the English term. For examples, the closest term in Russian is *pros'ba*. According to Zalizniak (2005: 283–4), the Russian word differs from its English equivalent and implies the idea of inequality between the speaker and the hearer; the hearer is perceived as someone being above the speaker in status. At the same time, Zalizniak argues, *pros'ba* implies an establishment of some sort of a relationship between two people in that the speaker expects the hearer to do something for him or her out of good attitude towards the speaker. Therefore, the Russian word *pros'ba* presupposes a certain intrusion into a private sphere of the hearer not only in the way that certain actions are expected from him or her, but also some feelings. The difference between the Russian and English terms well highlights the danger of ethnocentrism in linguistic analysis when terms of one language are used to analyse speech practices in another language.

We will use the term 'request' as a label due to existing conventions, but it should be borne in mind that the aspects of meaning of the English terms are not meant to represent the semantic and pragmatic reality of other languages. 'Request' as a technical term stands for a speech act in which the speaker expresses his or her want for the hearer to do something. At the same time, it is not obvious to both the speaker and the hearer that the hearer will perform this act under normal circumstances (Searle, 1969).

In this section, on the basis of English and Russian we will demonstrate how different languages employ different grammatical structures to express requests and how this choice is consistent with broader cultural ideas and understandings.

English employs a variety of ways for expressing 'request'. One of the ways, often considered as most common, is to use an interrogative or interrogative-cum-conditional form, as in the following examples from *Collins Wordbanks Online* (Wierzbicka, 1991: 32):

(22)   *Will you give mother and father my love?*

(23)   *Look, will you please stop it!*

(24)   *Will you tell the court, please.*

(25)   *Would you mind moving on, please?*

(26)   *Captain Paterson, would you please come with me.*

(27)   *Would you be so kind as escort Commandant Warner to the First Sister's quarters?*

(28)   *Please would you come with me.*

(29)   *Would you mind telling me what you're doing here?*

(30)   *Would you care to join me for a drink?*

(31)   *Why don't you do one of your funny voices and cheer the kid up?*

(32)   *Could you be a little more specific?*

(33)   *Could you give me some guidance please?*

(34)   *Can you get in the front please?*

(35)   *Can you pass me a towel?*

The use of an imperative form is also a possible way of wording a request (e.g., *Shut up!*), but using a bare infinitive form is considered rude and the imperative is often 'softened' by the use of modifiers, that is words like *please, just, dear.*

(36)   *Hang on a minute, please.*

(37)   *Pass my monocle, dear boy, I'll need a view of this.*

(38)   *Just be on your guard.*

In English requests are also expressed by tag questions:

(39)   *Meet him here, will you?*

(40)   *Cut it out, would you please.*

(41)   *You couldn't possibly come back, could you?*

(42)   *You couldn't give me his name, could you?*

(43)   *You can explain, can you?*

Other ways to express requests is to employ speaker-oriented utterances which contain an indirect question:

(44)   *Actually I wonder if you could excuse me for a moment.*

(45)   *Yes, but I wonder if you can tell me something else.*

(46)   *I wondered if you'd care to meet me for a drink or something.*

One could employ declarative utterances expressing a hypothetical wish of the speaker:

(47)   *I would like to ask you to sing one for me.*

Utterances where the speaker expresses his or her gratitude to the hearer in case the request is performed are also possible:

(48)   *I'd appreciate it if you'd be careful with her.*

(49)   *I would appreciate it if you made no mention of my existence.*

Bowe and Martin (2009: 20) report on a survey of middle managers in business in the eastern area of Melbourne conducted in 1995. The aim was to find out which of the following forms are most commonly used in requests:

(a) Pass the salt (please).
(b) Can you pass the salt?
(c) Can you reach the salt?
(d) Would you mind passing the salt?
(e) I would appreciate if you would pass the salt.
(f) Would you pass the salt?

Their findings suggest that the most frequently used request forms were variants of (b) and (f) with the addition of the word *please*, that is, forms like *Can you pass the salt please* and *Would you please pass the salt*.

Russian also employs a variety of linguistic structures to express request, but their choice and distribution differs from English. The most commonly used structure is that of imperative (Larina, 2009). The following examples are taken from the *Russian National Corpus*:

(50)   *Rasskažite, kak èto proizošlo.*

'Tell, how it happened.'

(51)   *Prideš', pozvoni.*

'(When you) come, call.'

(52)   *Devuška, skažite, novyx pravil uličnogo dviženija net?*

'Girl, say, are there new road rules?'

(53)   *Peredaj salfetku.*

'Pass the napkin.'

(54)   *Daj kakoe-nibud' bljudečko?*

'Give any saucer?'

Unlike in English, this structure is considered neutral and not rude. However, it can also be 'softened' by the use of the following devices: the word *požalujsta* 'please' (example 55), the use of diminutive forms in the forms of address (names or kin terms) (examples 56, 57) and the use of minimizers or diminutive forms (examples 58, 59):

(55)   *Skažite požalujsta, a cvety č'i?*

'Tell, please, whose are the flowers?'

(56)   *Babul', otkroj, èto ja.*

'Grandma-DIM, open, it's me.'

(57)   *Lenočka, skaži tete, v kakom ty klasse?*

'Lena-DIM, tell aunty what grade you are in?'

LIBRARY, UNIVERSITY CHESTER

(58)   *Čerez časik podojdite.*

'Come in an hour-DIM.'

(59)   *Daj-ka mne žurnal'čik, ja gljanu.*

'Give-INT me the magazine-DIM, I'll have a look.'

Requests in the form of imperatives can also be intensified by the use of intensifying particles (as in 59 and 60), 'double' (or even 'triple') imperative (examples 61 and 62), and repetition (example 63):

(60)   *Nu pozovi-ka ego.*

'Well, call-INT him.'

(61)   *Slušaj, starik. Sgonjaj na Smolenku, a?*

'Listen, old man. Drive to Smolenka, ah?'

(62)   *Slušaj, bud' drugom, pomogi matanaliz sdat'.*

'Listen, be a friend, help me to pass mathematical analysis.'

(63)   *Rasskazyvaj-rasskazyvaj.*

'Tell, tell.'

The use of a 'double imperative' in requests is characteristic of a 'camaraderie' attitude (Larina, 2009; Gladkova, 2013b).

Interrogative forms are also possible in the expression of requests in Russian, but their scope and frequency is much smaller than it is in English. Examples (22–30), if translated into Russian, would simply not be possible as an expression of request. In Russian the interrogative forms are used in the future (as in 64). Moreover, the use of negation can be regarded as a more polite form because it implies a possibility of a negative response:

(64)   *Vy ne podskažite, pjatnovyvoditel' "Boss" u vas est'?*

'Won't you tell if you have "Boss" stain remover?'

Like English, Russian also uses speaker-oriented utterances in question and statement forms.

Larina (2009) conducted a study in which Russian and English native speakers performed a discourse completion task to several 'request' situations. According to this data, Russians speakers use imperative three times more often than English speakers, while English speakers use interrogative forms four times more often than Russians speakers (Larina 2009: 450).

From the point of view of ethnosyntax, the difference in preference towards different grammatical structures in the expression of 'request' can be explained by prevalence of different cultural values. Wierzbicka (2006) relates a common use of whimperatives for wording requests, the cultural rules of using *thank you* and the avoidance of phrases like *you must* in suggestions in English, with the prevalence of the value of 'personal autonomy'. She argues that the idea that 'it is not good to impose and force other people to do certain things' is a cultural idea shared by English speakers and that it finds its realization in language. Wierzbicka (2006: 52) formulates this cultural rule as follows:[1]

[M]   [people think like this:]
    no one can say to another person:
        "I want you to do this
        you have to do it because of this"

[N]   [people think like this:]
    no one can say to another person:
        "I don't want you to do this
        you can't do it because of this"

She comments on these scripts as follows: 'These scripts don't say that people can do anything they want to do or that there can be no rules legitimately preventing people from doing what they want to do. Rather, they say that it cannot be another person's expression of will that prevents me from doing what I want to do or forces me to do what I don't want to do' (Wierzbicka, 2006: 52).

In Russian 'personal autonomy' and 'privacy' are not regarded as important cultural values. In fact, Russian does not have a word that fully corresponds to the English word *privacy*. Therefore, the idea of 'distancing' in a speech act like 'request' is not realized in Russian to the same degree as it is in English. In certain forms of Russian requests, particularly when diminutive forms are used, it is the idea of 'expressing good feelings', that is script [E], that becomes dominant.

4 Conclusions

Language is highly sensitive to cultural and societal processes. Grammatically elaborated areas of a language commonly embed meanings or ideas that are particularly salient in the collective psyche of a people. Knowledge of these meanings or ideas can equip cultural outsiders with more effective and successful tools of communication with the representatives of the culture.

This chapter has provided some examples of studies illustrating cultural significance of grammar within the ethnosyntax approach. These investigations can be of particular importance to other areas of linguistics, including language teaching. The proposed formulae can be applied in language teaching to explain meanings and use of grammatical constructions. Moreover, appellation to broader cultural rules can explain to learners why there exists variation in grammatical constructions across languages. The use of universal human concepts makes it possible to translate these formulae into any language without any change in meaning.

5 Future directions

Despite the fact that ethnosyntax was established as a new direction of research in linguistics more than thirty years ago, it remains an area that has received limited attention. While detailed studies of grammatical phenomena are common, only few studies attempt to establish connections between grammar and culture. This calls for the following directions in future research.

Broader investigations of language and culture are required. Ethnosyntax studies are closely linked with and will benefit from other investigations of lexicon and grammar that aim to establish connections between language and cultural values.

Language-specific studies of grammatical structures at different levels in relation to culture are needed.

Cross-linguistic and cross-cultural studies of grammatical structures will shed further light on the issues of cultural specificity.

Methodological aspects of ethnosyntax studies need to be developed and universal metalanguage needs to be employed in such studies to avoid ethnocentrism.

Studies in ethnosyntax in a historical perspective can contribute to the research on the issues of grammatical variation and change in relation to cultural values.

The results of ethnosyntax studies have enormous potential for language pedagogy and cross-cultural training as they can make language-specific structures more clear and accessible to language and culture learners.

Related topics

the linguistic relativity hypothesis revisited; ethnosemantics; ethnopragmatics; language, culture, and politeness; cultural semiotics; language and cultural scripts

Further reading

Enfield, N. J. (ed.) (2002) *Ethnosyntax: Explorations in Grammar and Culture*, Oxford: Oxford University Press. (Includes several studies on ethnosyntax on a broad variety of languages employing diverse methodologies as well as a good theoretical explanation of the approach.)
Goddard, C. (ed.) (2006) *Ethnopragmatics: Understanding Discourse in Cultural Context*, Berlin: Mouton de Gruyter. (A collection of studies that represent ethnosyntax in a broad sense.)
NSM homepage, www.griffith.edu.au/humanities-languages/school-languages-linguistics/research/natural-semantic-metalanguage-homepage (Online resource on the NSM approach with a basic explanation of it, an exhaustive list of publications, and several downloadable papers.)
Whorf, B. (1956) *Language, Thought and Reality: Selected Writings of Benjamin Lee Whorf*, ed. J. Carroll, Cambridge, MA: MIT Press. (A must-read classics on the relationship between language and thought.)
Wierzbicka, A. (1988) *The Semantics of Grammar*, Amsterdam: John Benjamins. (A pioneering study in ethnosyntax with illustrations from different languages.)

Note

1 In more recent NSM scripts, scripts of this kind are usually formulated as 'many people think like this' (see Chapters 5 and 23 this volume).

References

Apresjan, V. (2012) 'The "Russian" Attitude to Time', in L. Filipovic and K. Jaszczolt (eds), *Space and Time across Languages and Cultures. Vol. II: Language, Culture and Cognition*, Amsterdam: John Benjamins, pp. 103–120.
Austin, J. L. (1962) *How to Do Things with Words*, Oxford: Oxford University Press.
Bowe, H. and K. Martin (2009) *Communication across Cultures: Mutual Understanding in a Global World*, Cambridge: Cambridge University Press.
Bromhead, H. (2009) *The Reign of Truth and Faith: Epistemic expressions in 16th and 17th century English*, Berlin: Mouton de Gruyter.
Cobuild Wordbanks Online, www.collinslanguage.com/content-solutions/wordbanks (accessed December 2012).
Enfield, N. J. (2002) 'Ethnosyntax: Introduction', in N. J. Enfield (ed.), *Ethnosyntax: Explorations in Grammar and Culture*, Oxford: Oxford University Press, pp. 3–30.
——(ed.) (2002) *Ethnosyntax: Explorations in Grammar and Culture*, Oxford: Oxford University Press.
Geertz, C. (1973) *The Interpretation of Cultures: Selected Essays by Clifford Geertz*, London: Hutchinson.
Gladkova, A. (2007) 'The Journey of Self-discovery in Another Language', in M. Besemeres and A. Wierzbicka (eds), *Translating Lives: Living with Two Languages and Cultures*, St. Lucia: University of Queensland Press, pp. 139–49.
——(2012) 'Universals and Specifics of "Time" in Russian', in L. Filipovic and K. Jaszczolt (eds), *Space and Time across Languages and Cultures. Vol. II: Language, Culture and Cognition*, Amsterdam: John Benjamins, pp. 167–88.

——(2013a) '"Is He One of Ours?" The Cultural Semantics and Ethnopragmatics of Social Categories in Russian', *Journal of Pragmatics*, 55: 180–94.

——(2013b) '"Intimate" Talk in Russian: Human Relationships and Folk Psychotherapy', *Australian Journal of Linguistics*, special issue, semantics and/in social cognition, ed. C. Goddard, 33(3): 322–44.

Goddard, C. (2002) 'Ethnosyntax, Ethnopragmatics, Sign–Function, and Culture', in N. J. Enfield (ed.), *Ethnosyntax: Explorations in Grammar and Culture*, Oxford: Oxford University Press, pp. 52–73.

——(2003) 'Whorf Meets Wierzbicka: Variation and Universals in Language and Thinking', *Language Sciences*, 25: 393–432.

——(2006) 'Ethnopragmatics: A New Paradigm', in C. Goddard (ed.), *Ethnopragmatics: Understanding Discourse in Cultural Context*, Berlin: Mouton de Gruyter, pp. 1–30.

——(ed.) (2006) *Ethnopragmatics: Understanding Discourse in Cultural Context*, Berlin: Mouton de Gruyter.

Goddard, C. and A. Wierzbicka (2008) 'Universal Human Concepts as a Basis for Contrastive Linguistic Semantics', in M. Gómez-Gonzáles, L. Mackenzie, A.-M. Simon-Vandenbergen, and E. Gonzáles Álvarez (eds), *Current Trends in Contrastive Linguistics: Functional and Cognitive Perspectives*, Amsterdam: John Benjamins, pp. 205–26.

Goddard, C. and A. Wierzbicka (eds) (2002) *Meaning and Universal Grammar: Theory and Empirical Findings*, vols I, II, Amsterdam: John Benjamins.

Goddard, C. and A. Wierzbicka (2014) *Words and Meanings: Lexical Semantics across Domains, Languages and Cultures*, Oxford: Oxford University Press.

Gumperz, J. and D. Hymes (1972) *Directions in Sociolinguistics: The Ethnography of Communication*, New York: Holt, Rinehart and Winston.

Larina, T. (2009) *Kategorija vežlivosti i stil' kommunikacii* [Category of politeness and styles of communication], Moscow: Jazyki slavjanskix kul'tur.

Loveday, L. (1986) *Explorations in Japanese Sociolinguistics*, Amsterdam: John Benjamins.

Malchukov, A. and A. Ogawa (2011) 'Towards a Typology of Impersonal Constructions: A Semantic Map Approach', in A. Malchukov and A. Siewierska (eds), *Impersonal Constructions: A Cross-linguistic Perspective*, Amsterdam: John Benjamins, pp. 17–54.

Nedjalkov, V. P. (ed.) (2007) *Reciprocal Constructions*, Amsterdam: John Benjamins.

Prideaux, G. (1970) *The Syntax of Japanese Honorifics*, The Hague: Mouton.

Russian National Corpus, www.ruscorpora.ru (accessed December 2012).

Sapir, E. (1949) *Selected Writings of Edward Sapir in Language, Culture and Personality*, ed. D. Mandelbaum, Berkeley, CA: University of California Press.

Sarangi, S. (2009) 'Culture', in G. Senft, J. Östman, and J. Verschueren (eds), *Culture and Language Use*, Amsterdam: John Benjamins, pp. 81–104.

Searle, J. R. (1969) *Speech Acts*, Cambridge: Cambridge University Press.

——(1979) *Expression and Meaning: Studies in the Theory of Speech Acts*, Cambridge: Cambridge University Press.

Simpson, J. (2002) 'From Common Ground to Syntactic Construction: Associated Path in Warlpiri', in N. J. Enfield (ed.), *Ethnosyntax: Explorations in Grammar and Culture*, Oxford: Oxford University Press, pp. 287–307.

Švedova, N. (ed.) (1980) *Russkaja grammatika [Russian grammar]*, Moscow: Nauka (http://rusgram.narod.ru/index1.html, accessed 15 December 2012).

Travis, C. (2004) 'The Ethnopragmatics of the Diminutive in Conversational Colombian Spanish', *Intercultural Pragmatics*, 1(2): 249–74.

Whorf, B. (1956) *Language, Thought and Reality: Selected Writings of Benjamin Lee Whorf*, ed. J. Carroll, Cambridge, MA: MIT Press.

Wierzbicka, A. (1979) 'Ethnosyntax and the Philosophy of Grammar', *Studies in Language*, 3(3): 313–83.

——(1988) *The Semantics of Grammar*, Amsterdam: John Benjamins.

——(1992) *Semantics, Culture, and Cognition: Universal Human Concepts in Culture-Specific Configurations*, Oxford: Oxford University Press.

——(1999) *Emotions across Languages and Cultures: Diversity and Universals*, Cambridge: Cambridge University Press.

——(2002) 'English Causative Constructions in an Ethnosyntactic Perspective: Focusing on LET', in N. J Enfield (ed.), *Ethnosyntax: Explorations in Grammar and Culture*, Oxford: Oxford University Press, pp. 162–203.

——(2006) *English: Meaning and Culture*, Oxford: Oxford University Press.

——(2008) 'Case in NSM: A Reanalysis of the Polish Dative', in A. Malchukov and A. Spencer (eds), *The Oxford Handbook of Case*, Oxford: Oxford University Press, pp. 151–69.

——(2009) '"Reciprocity": An NSM Approach to Linguistic Typology and Social Universals', *Studies in Language*, 33(1): 103–74.

Yoon, K.-J. (2004) 'Not Just Words: Korean Social Models and the Use of Honorifics', *Intercultural Pragmatics*, 1(2): 189–210.

Zalianiak, Anna (2005) 'Zametki o slovax *obščenie, otnošenie, pros'ba, čuvstva, èmocii*' [Notes about the words *obščenie, otnošenie, pros'ba, čuvstva, èmocii*], in A. Zalizniak *et al. Ključevye idei russkoj jazykovoj kartiny mira.* Moscow: Jazyki slavjanskoj kul'tury.

4

ETHNOSEMANTICS

John Leavitt

Introduction

What is meaning? And, more specifically, do all humans *mean* the same things by words that can be used successfully to point to the same thing?

There is an urban legend that says that when Captain Cook first visited Australia, he saw an animal he had never seen before hopping along. He asked one of the locals what the animal was called, and the answer was 'kangaroo'. Turns out that 'kangaroo' in the Australian language means 'I don't know'.[1]

This is, apparently, a completely false story. The word would indeed seem to come from Captain Cook's first encounters with Australian native people, but *gaɲurru* in Guugu Yimidhirr turns out to mean – a kangaroo, 'a large black or grey kangaroo, probably specifically the male *Macropus robustus*' (Dixon *et al.*, 1990: 67–8), also known as a wallaroo. But this real history illustrates the point better than the false one. The source word for 'kangaroo' was in fact an adequate indicator of the animal that went hopping by that day. This still tells us very little about what the word *gaɲurru*, or indeed what a male *Macropus robustus*, *meant* to the people Cook met. We have some idea of what it means to English-speaking North Americans: a kangaroo is an amusing animal with a funny name. You can go see it in person in a zoo, and it's often to be seen on television nature programmes; it hops, carries its babies in a pouch – making stuffed kangaroos a double gift for children: you get a big one and a little one for the price of one – and boxes ferociously, always beating Bugs Bunny in cartoons. It is very likely, to say the least, that the kangaroo, and the word *gaɲurru*, *meant* something very different to the people who gave it that name – and who, for instance, hunted and ate them. But it depends on what you mean by 'mean'.

In the history of Western theories of the meaning of meaning we see a kind of pendulum swing between, on the one hand, approaches that assume or seek to discover what 'meaning' means in general for human beings, and on the other, those that take as central the diversity of human languages and cultures and try to discover the patterning of meaning in each case. Hence the difference between *semantics* as a general science of meaning and *ethnosemantics* as the exploration of particular meaningful universes.

Ethnosemantics

Most textbooks on semantics begin by defining the field as the study or science of meaning (Ullmann, 1957: 1; Palmer, 1976: 1; Lyons, 1977: 1; Saeed, 2003: 3; Goddard, 2011: 1;

cf. Tamba, 2007: 7) – some of them put the definition in the title (Ullmann, 1962); it has come to constitute an important aspect of linguistics, philosophy, and other disciplines. This inter-disciplinarity is reflective of the many meanings of the word 'meaning' and other words that are its semantic neighbours, to use the metaphor of the semantic field that was popular for a time (see below). For while everybody feels that they know what meaning means, its many partial synonyms in fact cover a lot of semantic ground. In English, meaning is not quite the same thing as sense, signification, significance, or import; in French one has *sens* (which also means 'direction'), *signification, signifiance, acception*; the colloquial usage translating 'to mean', as in 'What does X mean?', is *vouloir dire* 'to want to say'. In German, the division between *Sinn*, often translated meaning or sense or, more technically, intension, and *Bedeutung*, often translated as meaning or reference or extension, has been the source of over a century of philosophical discussion since Frege.

The word semantics, first used in the late nineteenth century, derives from the Greek *semainein* 'to say, indicate', itself from *séma* 'sign'. These are also the sources of the term semiotics, the science of signs. Semantics translates the French *sémantique*, introduced in 1883 by Michel Bréal as a name for a postulated linguistic science that would study the transformations of meaning along with the transformations of sounds and words. A parallel project, but much more closely tied to classical atomistic historical linguistics, had existed in Germany since the beginning of the century under the name semasiology (history of German *Semasiologie* and French *sémantique* in Nerlich, 1992).

For its part, the addition of the prefix ethno-, from the Greek *éthnos*, a people or a nation, to a field of study indicates a comparative, cross-cultural extension of the field, with the implied or explicit criticism that the discipline as constituted without the prefix does not truly live up to a claim of universality, but in fact represents the unchallenged formalization of modern Western assumptions. Thus ethnosemantics would be the study of meaning across cultures, whether by looking at differences in what is meant by words with the same apparent referent (e.g., a grey kangaroo), by discovering ways of organizing knowledge or theories about the attribution of meaning, and/or by seeking to identify universals in what people signify and the ways they do so. In this broad sense, ethnosemantics covers much of what is studied in cultural and social anthropology, linguistics, history, and comparative religion.

In spite of this vastness of potential reference, the term ethnosemantics is most commonly used to label a primarily North American intellectual movement, also called ethnoscience or cognitive anthropology (although 'cognitive anthropology' has come to designate a much wider field: see Chapter 26 this volume), that played an important role in the interface between linguistics and anthropology particularly from the mid 1950s into the 1970s. More recently, the term has been revived in the attempt to locate universal semantic primitives and map their deployment in different languages and societies (e.g., Wierzbicka, 1996).

Here I would like to use 'ethnosemantics' in a somewhat wider sense, given both the potential breadth of meaning of the term itself and the historical links of 'classical ethnosemantics' with what went earlier, as well as its contrast with what came later. I will enlarge the discussion to include two other major intellectual movements: the linguistically inspired anthropology developed by Franz Boas and his students during the first four decades of the twentieth century; and the parallel and largely contemporary school in German linguistics and literary studies called, variously, neo-Humboldtian, neo-Romantic, word-field theory, or content-oriented linguistics.

The key question in putting an ethno- before semantics is whether meanings are universal, either innate in the mind or given by the world, or whether they vary from language to language, society to society. In the first view, ethnosemantics would be a way to verify and specify general semantics; in the second, each 'semantic system' (Goodenough, 1956: 195) requires independent analysis, and all universal bets are off. In this, the questions behind ethnosemantics, and its different formulations, reconnect with some of the fundamental questions of Western thought since the Renaissance, pitting universalists against pluralists of various stripes (Leavitt, 2011). And semantics as a field, at least as it is practised in anthropology and linguistics, has continued to veer between accepting and neglecting or rejecting the importance – or existence – of a plurality of diverse systems of meaning. Here, of course, I will be making no attempt at a history of semantic theory (but see Ullmann, 1962; Nerlich, 1992; Larrivée, 2008) or a general presentation of the field, but looking at the rise, fall, and arguments of some schools that can properly be called *ethno*semantic.

Let us note that the disappearance of these schools does not result from their having been proved mistaken, but from broader shifts of intellectual trends of the kind Roy D'Andrade (1995: 3) has called 'agenda hopping'.

Boasian cultural semantics

In his introduction to the major collection of articles from the ethnosemantics movement of the 1960s, Stephen Tyler (1969) notes that 'most' earlier anthropology had presumed the universality of our categories and simply sought to map other people's categories onto these. The one great exception that he recognizes is Franz Boas (1969: 6, 20 n. 6). In fact, the general thrust of the comparative cultural linguistics practised by Boas (1858–1942) from the late 1880s, and by his students Edward Sapir, Dorothy Demetracopoulou Lee, and Benjamin Lee Whorf, was clearly ethnosemantic in that it sought to identify differences in meaning at all levels of language beyond the phoneme: among lexemes, and especially among differing grammatical categories.

Boas, like the neo-Humboldtians in Germany (see below), drew on a series of primarily German precursors – Herder, Wilhelm von Humboldt, the Romantics – who had both conceived languages as distinctive coherent systems and had held that formulation in signs was a necessary part of human conceptualization. These views contrasted with the main traditions in Western philosophy (Descartes, Locke, Kant), which saw thought and conceptualization as preceding their formulation in words, and in language study, which saw sounds and words as isolated units changing through time. The systemic view of distinct languages and the requirement that concepts be conceived through such systems meant that for Herder *et al.*, the world was seen as a multitude of worlds, each people/nation/culture/language as an indivisible whole expressing a unique spirit. This multitudinous view of the universe was particularly operationalized in the work of Humboldt, who maintained that each language or language type organized meaning in its own ways and sought to document these ways, analysing dozens of languages that were as different as possible from each other.

The 'Humboldtian stream' in linguistics (Koerner, 1977) was carried on as a minority tendency through the nineteenth century, as against the majority of practitioners of Indo-European-based historical linguistics. It was maintained particularly in the linguistics of Heymann Steinthal and the cultural psychology of his collaborator Moritz Lazarus, who together edited the *Zeitschrift für Völkerpsychologie*, 'Journal of the Psychology of Peoples', starting in 1859 (Trautmann-Waller, 2004, 2006). Boas, trained in Germany before going to the United States, came out of this cultural and scientific milieu (Bunzl, 1996).

Boas, who was at once an ethnologist, a linguist, and a physical anthropologist, held that languages are systems, and that human cultures are semantic wholes, internally integrated to some degree. The existence of such wholes is revealed geographically by the transformations that given cultural elements undergo when crossing a cultural boundary (hence Boas's often misunderstood interest in diffusion); the existence of linguistic systems is revealed in exactly the same way, by border phenomena, predictable mishearings and misunderstandings, which can be understood as mutual interference between systems (see, for instance, Chapter 32 this volume). This is the model Boas laid out for phonology and phonetics in his paper 'On Alternating Sounds' (1889).

Now the level of sounds, however systemic Boas maintains that it is, does not, in itself, involve meaning. But exactly the same model of internal organization which becomes perceptible when violated is extended to meaning, whether of lexical items or grammatical patterns, in the major statement of Boas's linguistics, his introduction to the *Handbook of American Indian Languages* (1911).

Here he discusses the different levels of language. First, the organization of sounds. But then he goes on to words: since it is impossible to have a separate word for every experience, any division of the world into words requires the constitution of categories, and to some degree these categories, their extensions and groupings, can differ from language to language.

> Since the total range of personal experience which language serves to express is infinitely varied, and its whole scope must be expressed by a limited number of phonetic groups, it is obvious that an extended classification of experiences must underlie all articulate speech.
>
> *(Boas, 1911: 24)*

Boas's examples again draw on the contrast between systems, giving examples of how concepts that are identified or grouped together in modern Western languages are divided up in others, and conversely how those that modern Western languages treat as unrelated may be grouped together. This is a point that has raised great contention in the literature, so I will dwell on two of his examples a bit here, beginning with the second. The Dakota language draws on a single root, *xtaka*, glossed 'to grip', to produce words for concepts which it would not occur to a speaker of a modern Western language to group together: *naxta'ka* 'to kick', *paxta'ka* 'to bind in bundles', *yaxta'ka* 'to bite', *ic'axta'ka* 'to be near to', *boxta'ka* 'to pound' (Boas, 1911: 26). The point here is that while it is perfectly possible for the reader to recognize the justification of this grouping, to see what these all have in common, it is simply not something that is evident or obvious to speakers of a modern Western language.

It is the converse example, that of snow, that has produced heated debate. As an example of experiences that modern Western languages group together in a single term, and by immediate implication a single concept, but which another tradition divides up (just as we separate 'to kick', 'to bind in bundles', etc.), Boas offers the example of Inuktitut words for snow. There are, he says, four (Boas, 1911: 25–6): *aput*, glossed 'snow on the ground'; *qana* 'falling snow'; *piqsirpoq* 'drifting snow'; and *qimuqsuq* 'a snowdrift'.

This example was picked up by other authors and rapidly became the urban legend that the Inuit have hundreds of words for snow, used sometimes as an example of the wondrous variety of conceptualizations of the world, at other times as an example of the inability of the primitive mind to generalize or abstract. The debunking of the legend (Martin, 1986), and the fact that avid skiers, for example, have an elaborate vocabulary of snow in English, were used for general attacks against any argument that differences in lexicon matter at all (Pullum, 1991).

To understand what Boas was arguing it is helpful to go back to the text itself. The Inuktitut snow example comes immediately after a brief discussion of the fact that English has different words for what we can also conceive as different forms of water: water, lake, river, brook, rain, dew, wave, foam. 'It is perfectly conceivable that this variety of ideas, each of which is expressed by a single independent term in English, might be expressed in other languages by derivations from the same term' (Boas, 1911: 25).

So the whole argument, with its counterpunching examples, is serving to say that 'each language, from the point of view of another language, may be arbitrary in its classifications; that which appears as a single simple idea in one language may be characterized by a series of distinct phonetic groups in another' (Boas, 1911: 26).

Boas recognized that there is nothing surprising about an important part of the environment or a crucial aspect of a people's life receiving a richer and more specific vocabulary than might be expected among people in other circumstances.

> It seems fairly evident that the selection of such simple terms must to a certain extent depend upon the chief interests of a people; and where it is necessary to distinguish a certain phenomenon in many aspects, which in the life of the people play each an entirely independent rôle, many independent words may develop, while in other cases modifications of a single term may suffice.
>
> *(Boas, 1911: 26)*

This suggests that single lexemes are likely to change fairly easily if the 'interests of a people' change. This is not the case when one goes up a level to that of grammatical patterns, which are farther from active awareness (Silverstein, 1981 [2001]). Boas divides his presentation between 'grammatical processes' and a long discussion of grammatical categories. Again, his focus here is on the interference between systems. Boas presumes that grammatical categories have meaning – they are as semantic as any other part of language (Jakobson, 1959); and that, in particular, obligatory grammatical categories operate as largely unconscious frames for organizing ideational content. He goes through the obligatory categories of modern Western languages – noun and verb, tense, gender, number – and shows how these cannot be assumed to operate for all languages, many of which presume very different underlying forms. In each case, contrast of different languages is what serves to bring out underlying patterns in each. His conclusion:

> The few examples that I have given here illustrate that many of the categories which we are inclined to consider as essential may be absent in foreign languages, and that other categories may occur as substitutes.
>
> *(Boas, 1911: 42)*

Boas follows this section with a one-page 'interpretation of grammatical categories' in which he sums up his whole procedure:

> We conclude from the examples here given that in a discussion of the characteristics of various languages different fundamental categories will be found, and that in a comparison of different languages it will be necessary to compare as well the phonetic characteristics as the characteristics of the vocabulary and those of the grammatical concepts in order to give each language its proper place.
>
> *(1911: 43)*

This kind of a view is profoundly ethnosemantic; and it motivates the mode of description of languages in the rest of the volume and in the whole 'Boas project' for language description (Stocking, 1974):

> In accordance with the general views expressed in the introductory chapters, the method of treatment has been throughout an analytical one. No attempt has been

made to compare the forms of the Indian grammars with the grammars of English, Latin, or even among themselves; but in each case the psychological groupings which are given depend entirely upon the inner form of each language. In other words, the grammar has been treated as though an intelligent Indian was going to develop the forms of his own thoughts by an analysis of his own form of speech.

(p. 81)

The idea of an 'inner form of each language' comes straight from Humboldt and, as we will see, will motivate the neo-Humboldtians in Germany.

Some of Boas's students and students' students continued to develop these ideas. His most brilliant linguistic student was Edward Sapir (1884–1939), who organized his 1921 book *Language* by dividing chapters on the formal patterning of grammar and the conceptual patterning of grammar. Boas's student Dorothy D. Lee (1905–75) and Sapir's student B. L. Whorf (1897–1941) spent much of their careers exploring the semantic implications of grammatical forms in, respectively, the Wintu language of northern California and the Hopi language of Arizona. In both cases, the working assumption is that linguistic form implies meaning – it is what Dell Hymes would later call form-meaning covariation (e.g., 1981: 333) – and that one must not assume that one already controls the world of meaning, or that meaning worlds are all the same. Instead, one must begin with the actual forms, ideally forms that are obligatory or widespread in the language, follow their usage, and map out their implications – which can, and often does, lead to surprises. This as opposed to presuming the universality of meanings and mapping the forms onto what we think we already know (see Chapter 2 this volume).

For the Boasians, meaning is everywhere, at all levels of language. As Whorf wrote in a manuscript found after his death (1956: 73)

> What needs to be seen by anthropologists, who to a large extent may have gotten the idea that linguistics is merely a highly specialised and tediously technical pigeonhole in a far corner of the anthropological workshop, is that linguistics is essentially the quest of MEANING … the simple fact is that its real concern is to light up the thick darkness of the language, and thereby of much of the thought, the culture, and outlook upon life of a given community, with the light of this 'golden something,' as I have heard it called, this transmuting principle of meaning.

Given that the Boasians noted the parallel of diversity in systems of meaning ('thought') to that among phonological systems, one can appreciate John Lucy's characterization of Whorf's claim of a relationship between language patterning and thought patterning as 'semantic accent' (2003: 5).

Neo-Humboldtian comparative semantics

Equally ethnosemantic was the 'content analysis' or 'neo-Humboldtian' school that dominated German linguistics and literary history from the 1920s into the 1970s.

By the 1920s a number of German philologists and literary scholars were looking back to Humboldt's arguments, maintained through the nineteenth century by a small group of scholars, notably Steinthal, that each language could be studied as a coherent system, and that the meanings carried in the language, its 'contents', formed a whole that could be identified with the world orientation or world-view of its speakers. This conception of languages, and indeed cultures, as multiple systems was directly opposed to that which came to dominate historical linguistics, which sought to isolate each sound or word as a single unit whose transformations were to be explained by the operation of a single set of universal natural-scientific-type laws. Ferdinand de Saussure's posthumous *Course in General Linguistics* (1916) was drawn on to support a systemic view of each language as a coherent whole with all of its elements conditioning each other; and certain parts of the *Course*, particularly the discussion of linguistic value, was taken as an argument for the determination of a people's categories of thought by its linguistic categories.

Programmatic statements calling for a new linguistics of the 'inner form of speech' (a phrase of Humboldt's) were offered by Walter Porzig and Leo Weisgerber in the early and mid 1920s, with Weisgerber setting out a programme of research on how different languages organized different sensory domains. In 1927, Weisgerber published a denunciation of traditional sema-siology (*Bedeutungslehre*) for its atomism and its assumption of a given world of 'things' out there (Nerlich, 1992: 116–18).

But what solidified the movement was Jost Trier's book *The German Vocabulary in the Semantic Domain of Understanding* of 1931. Trier, a specialist in medieval German literature, analysed the vocabulary of the domain of knowledge as it changed through time, arguing that lexical sets form structured wholes in which each term sets semantic limits to the others: this is the idea of a semantic field, or *Wortfeld*, introduced here. Using the available texts, Trier sought to determine the meanings and semantic boundaries of words for intellectual activity in the High German literature of around 1200 CE and again around 1300 CE. What he found are two coherent synchronic systems, between which there occurred a major shift.

In the first period the intellectual lexicon was organized around three terms distinguished along two semantic dimensions: that of feudal social relations, whereby *kunst* indicated courtly intelligence and skills, *list* a lower and more popular kind of intelligence; and while both of these were marked as belonging to the secular world, *wîsheit*, distinguished by its universality, denoted a general wisdom that could be religious as well. By 1300, this terminological economy had changed entirely. *List*, now taking on its modern sense of 'cunning, trick', was no longer used for legitimate intellectual activity. And both dimensions that had structured the earlier field, that of feudal hierarchy and that of universality, had disappeared. Instead, *wîsheit* now meant only theological and mystical experience; *kunst* was already taking on the meaning of art, while the word *wizzen* came to designate non-artistic forms of knowing.

Trier's work was taken to have proved the usefulness of the idea of semantic field, and specifically to have revealed a hitherto unsuspected way of constructing ideas about conceptual life, one that had been hidden under the apparent familiarity of the vocabulary. The idea of semantic fields was picked up outside Germany and became a major theme in semantics in English-language (e.g., Ullmann, 1957) and, for instance, Eastern European scholarship (Schaff, 1964 [1973]). In a frequently quoted passage, Trier locates the semantic field between individual words and the total vocabulary of a language:

> Fields are living realities intermediate between individual words and the totality of the vocabulary; as parts of a whole they share with words the property of being integrated in a larger structure (*sich ergliedern*) and with the vocabulary the property of being structured in terms of smaller units (*sich ausgliedern*).
> *(1934: 430, cited in Ullmann, 1957: 157; this translation from Lyons, 1977: 253)*

The assumption and growing conviction behind neo-Humboldtian linguistics was that each language, particularly its vocabulary, formed a closed and coherent set that determined the range of a people's thought. This is precisely the kind of linguistic solipsism of which the Boasians, particularly Whorf, would be accused from the 1950s on; but whereas the Boasians never assumed that there was a natural fit between a given language, culture, and mode of thought, and sought the widest possible linguistic knowledge as a means of circumventing the effects of linguistic habit on conceptualization, the neo-Humboldtians did assume a natural unity of people and language, seeing one's first language as defining a horizon from which one could never really escape. It was perfectly logical, then, that most of the work done by the school concentrated on the history and structure of the German language and, by close implication, of a German world-view. Indeed, in 1927 Weisgerber urged training German primary school students not to think in abstract critical terms, but to master typically German modes of thought as these were implicit in the German language.[2] Most of the major practitioners were participants in the National Socialist project before and during the Second World War (Hutton, 1999).

Both Trier and Weisgerber were exonerated after the war, and Weisgerber, in particular, became the leading figure in a renewed neo-Humboldtian linguistics that lasted well into the 1970s. In the 1950s and 1960s, he published several editions of a multivolume opus entitled *The Powers of the German Language*. Stephen Ullmann (1957: 310) characterizes this work as showing

> the fruitfulness of the new technique by applying it in detail to the structure of Modern German ... Weisgerber's investigations transcend the field of semantics proper: the vocabulary and the grammatical system are both probed for the ways in which they organize experience and interpose a 'sprachliche Zwischenwelt', a kind of linguistic screen, between us and the non-linguistic world.

All of the neo-Humboldtians tended to formulate their positions in absolutist ways. These hark back to Herder and the Romantics: each period or nation or language is a closed universe, a horizon that one cannot get across. By the late 1970s the movement was apparently fading out as German linguists connected with international trends in the field.

'Classical' ethnosemantics

The most common use of the term ethnosemantics, certainly among anthropologists, is to designate a movement, also known as 'ethnographic semantics', 'ethnoscience', 'cognitive anthropology', and often 'the new ethnography', that was centred in North America and practised, as an explicit method and school of thought, primarily in the 1950s and 1960s. Growing out of the Boasian tradition (see above) and the discovery methods of descriptive linguistics, it sought to identify patterns of meaning underlying domains of explicit knowledge in different societies.

The key idea motivating 'the new ethnography' was that to understand a people's culture it was necessary to reproduce their knowledge: culture was knowledge. This came after a long history of studying domains of cultural knowledge of the natural world, as well as a great debate on the appropriate way to study the social world, particularly kinship organization, between (mostly British) proponents of the study of attitudes and behaviour and (mostly American) proponents of the study of knowledge of social organization, largely through linguistic usage (Zimmermann, 2002). To redefine culture not as behaviour or sentiments or attitudes, but as knowledge, was a radical move that seemed to put it into the realm of what an outside observer could also know. The question came to be how various peoples' knowledge was organized.

Here the initial inspiration came from linguistics, from a movement in semantics called componential analysis, spearheaded by Eugene Nida (the full theory is laid out in Nida, 1975), which sought a rigorous empirical method for discovering the dimensions of organization of minimal traits, distinctive features – the idea comes from Roman Jakobson's identification of a limited set of distinctive features in phonology (Jakobson and Halle, 1956) – on which meanings were based (Barnard, 1996). This inspiration is clear in the opening manifestos of the movement, Ward Goodenough's paper 'Componential Analysis and the Study of Meaning' and Floyd Lounsbury's 'Semantic Analysis of the Pawnee Kinship Usage', both published in the same issue of the journal *Language* in 1956. As Lounsbury puts it

> It is asserted that both grammar and vocabulary hold clues to a people's world view. This, of course, amounts only to saying that language is meaningful, but that the meanings involved, and their classification, differ from one society to another; or that language is used in relating to the natural and social environment, but that different peoples experience differently and find varying significances in their environments. Of particular interest in this connection are the so-called obligatory categories in language – those features of meanings or of situations, real or imputed, of which the structure and usage of a language force recognition. It is with these that we shall be concerned in this paper. They are to be regarded as distinctive features of meaning.
>
> *(1956: 159)*

The quest will be for elementary particles or dimensions of meaning, atoms of meaning, or components. But unlike Jakobson's distinctive features in phonology, which form a limited universal set, usable for all languages, the components of meanings are not asserted to be universal – that question is left open. The work to be done is one of discovery and the elaboration of discovery procedures. As Goodenough puts it

> I have sought to avoid entanglement in general semantic theory. Adequate theory can develop, it seems to me, only as we seek seriously to describe real systems of meaning as manifest in the contexts of linguistic utterances.
>
> *(1956: 203)*

As it happened, both of these articles dealt with kinship. Goodenough's was presented as a theoretical piece, but it is mostly made up of an analysis of kinship on the island of Truk in the Pacific. Lounsbury's is presented as an analysis of kinship terminology, but in fact it is full of theoretical and methodological innovations. It is impossible here to reproduce the arguments of these two papers. Suffice it to say that each discovered principles that made these extremely complex systems make coherent sense.

Now of course kinship had always been one of the great issues, or rather was the great issue, in social anthropology in its British mode: after Lévi-Strauss's 1949 *tour de force* in the *Elementary Structures of Kinship* (see 1967 [1969]), to have these two Americans apparently offering underlying cognitive, rather than behavioural, patterns that explained overt systems was impressive, to say the least.

Roy D'Andrade (1995: 30) gives a vivid, and somewhat wistful, portrayal of the early impact of 'the new ethnography':

> It is difficult to explain the beauty which a semantic analysis of kinship terminology held for some anthropologists in 1960 ... [S]uch an analysis was experienced as a nearly magical process of discovery in which elegant simple patterns emerged from an initial jumble of kin terms and kin types. The patterns came out of the data, and, once seen, were unforgettable.

Goodenough's 1957 paper 'Cultural Anthropology and Language' sets the tone for the whole movement. It defines cultures as systems of knowledge:

> As I see it, a society's culture consists of whatever it is one has to know or believe in order to operate in a manner acceptable to its members, and do so in any role that they accept for any one of themselves.
>
> *(1957 [1964]: 36)*

Goodenough's definition explicitly excludes behaviour, emotion, and material things from culture, leaving a domain that, it is hoped, will be amenable to rigorous mapping. The way to map it is through vocabulary, and as for the neo-Humboldtians, this is to be approached through what are initially treated as recognizable domains.

One particularly impressive working out of unexpected patterns was carried out by Harold Conklin (1962) on the pronouns of Hanunóo, a language of the Philippines. The Hanunóo have what to us looks like a bizarre organization of pronouns, which give the translation equivalents 'I', 'you (singular)', 'he or she', 'we two (i.e., you and I)', 'we (exclusive of hearer)', 'we all', 'you all', and 'they'. This is a system of eight terms. The translation glosses use criteria that determine Western pronominal systems: person, number, and gender. But Conklin finds an organization based on three quite different dimensions: inclusion or exclusion of the speaker; inclusion or exclusion of the hearer; and minimal or non-minimal membership. This is presented in Figure 4.1, in which the three dimensions are marked respectively as S, H, and M:

This is a perfectly coherent and usable system, but one that depends on entirely different criteria than those we are used to.

Primarily using exhaustive studies of vocabulary in relation to realia or social relations, this kind of ethnosemantics reconstructed the knowledge of a given group of people, sometimes of a presumptively representative individual, about a relatively easy-to-define domain such as that of kinship, plants, animals, or diseases (i.e., ethnobotany, ethnozoology, ethnomedicine, whence the common rubric 'ethnoscience') or, as an illustrative example, American lunch counter foods

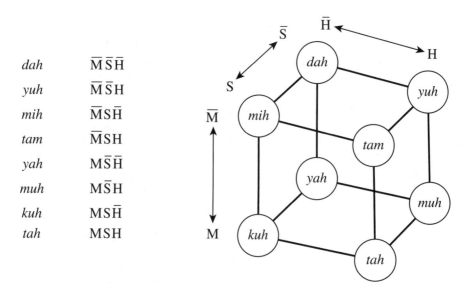

Figure 4.1 Pronominal dimensions

(Frake, 1962). In each case, the researcher sought to use the lexicon as a key to uncover the organization of that knowledge in the minds of its bearers.

Closely related to this 'new ethnography' was the appearance of a school in descriptive linguistics and translation practice that came to be known as tagmemics. Initially developed by Kenneth Pike of the Summer Institute of Linguistics as a way of improving Bible translation, tagmemics insisted on the difference between the points of view of external, objective observation (labelled 'etic', from 'phonetic') and of system-internal analysis (labelled 'emic', from 'phonemic'; Pike 1957–70). An 'emic' approach would, then, require a focus on the specific organization of meanings in particular social contexts. It was Pike's colleague Eugene Nida who developed the kind of componential analysis that would be foundational for ethnosemantics (Nida, 1975). Tagmemic analysis seeks to capture the specifics of any text in any language as a way of formalizing what is actually there without prejudgment, and with the assumption that meaning goes all the way up and down the levels of language. Coming out of this tradition, scholars such as A. L. Becker (1995) have used tagmemics to analyse the play of meaning in linguistic forms in a wide range of languages.

These approaches raise an immediate problem for anthropological method. If vocabulary is the magic key to culture as knowledge, then it is not clear why there is any need to spend actual time with the people involved other than in collecting and analysing vocabulary. The ideas that culture equals knowledge and that knowledge is verbally based ideation (rather than, say, internalized bodily habits) directly challenge the traditional anthropological practice of participant observation. Mary Black (1969), pushing the argument to its logical end, worked out many aspects of the Ojibwa knowledge of the world by sitting and eliciting, primarily with individual informants in a basement. Surely the issue is what kind of thing you are trying to learn.

From the 1970s: downfall of ethnosemantics

Ethnosemantics and semantic field theory continue to be used, notably in medical anthropology (Good, 1977, 1994 for semantic networks), where they have proved their utility. In fact, it is hard to do any kind of serious field research in anthropology without carrying out some form of ethnosemantics, whether or not this is explicitly acknowledged. The principle of seeking patterns of ideation through the use of language cannot be denied.

But by the early 1970s, critiques of ethnosemantics were arising from two opposed sides. From the side of cultural anthropology came an attack on the idea that culture is purely knowledge, and that knowledge can be presented as organized as a kind of taxonomy. Michelle Rosaldo (1972) pointed out that among the Ilongot of the Philippines, relations among plants often involved cross-cutting categories and metaphorical associations. Clifford Geertz (1974) argued that culture could not be enclosed in the head, and David Schneider (e.g., 1968, 1984) challenged the very existence of domains such as kinship as universally recognizable aspects of experience.

More devastatingly, the idea that each culture constituted its own domains of knowledge was being left behind by the explosion of universalist theorizing in linguistics, psychology, and philosophy. The year of publication of the major collection of essays from the tradition (Tyler, 1969) was also that of Berlin and Kay's *Basic Color Terms*. This comparative study of terms for colours in many languages showed first that there was a universal hierarchy of naming colours, second that this hierarchy seemed to follow an evolutionary pattern, with the smallest-scale societies having the smallest number of basic colour terms. From this point on, those who were interested in cognition turned to the experiment-based universal explanations that were coming out of linguistics and psychology; languages, with their peculiarities, came to be seen not as guides to speakers' knowledge, but as surface manifestations of universal deep structures and of non-linguistic knowledge. Roger Keesing called explicitly for a shift (an 'agenda hop'?) from structural linguistics as a model, as in ethnosemantics, to Chomskyan transformational grammar (1972).

To get an idea of the completeness of classical ethnosemantics' fall from grace, one can look, for instance, at Penelope Brown's excellent 2006 overview of 'cognitive anthropology': classic ethnoscience, while recognized as classic, gets a mere paragraph explaining its theory and practice before we are told how it 'lost its impact'; at least as much space is spent on what people said was wrong with it as on what it actually did (2006: 98–9).

Meanwhile, the field of semantics, too, was moving rapidly away from an interest in how particular communities construct the world (the ethno- part) and towards a reinforcement of universalist, cognitivist, and mathematical models of 'meaning' as such. This is clear if one looks at changes of emphasis in the standard semantics textbooks: Ullmann (1957, 1962) gives enormous space to Trier and semantic fields; this discussion, while still present, is greatly reduced in Palmer (1976); Lyons's (1977) wide-ranging and compendious two volumes give a good description of semantic field theory, but with no endorsement, and mere mention of the birth of American componential analysis in anthropological descriptions of kinship (267, 317). Steinberg and Jakobovitz's standard collection (1971) is divided into essays on linguistics, philosophy, and psychology, with nary a nod towards cultural or even major linguistic differences. Both the German semantic field tradition and that of American ethnosemantics have completely disappeared from recent textbooks, such as Saeed (2003) and Cruse (2010); these, in addition, give virtually no examples of differences among real languages – all examples come from English. And the back cover of what looks like a basic reader on semantics (Davis and Gillon, 2004) advertises the volume as follows:

> Comprehensive in its variety and breadth of theoretical frameworks and topics that it covers, it includes articles representative of the major theoretical frameworks within semantics, including: discourse representation theory, dynamic predicate logic, truth theoretic semantics, situation semantics, and cognitive semantics.

Current and future approaches

The term ethnosemantics has been revived in the school of Natural Semantic Metalanguage (NSM). NSM comes out of the work of the linguist Anna Wierzbicka (e.g., 1996), who has considered many and varied languages in an attempt to find universal basic elements of meaning, 'semantic primitives'. Wierzbicka and her followers feel that they have identified such primitives (currently there are sixty-two). Unlike other universal schemes, this one is empirically based, deriving its basic elements from what is actually there in all the languages so far examined. The theory itself insists on the enormous diversity of semantic systems, but holds that all are constructed from the same building blocks. This is generally shown by being able to paraphrase any statement in any language as a series of semantic primitives.

NSM derives explicitly from the work of the Polish linguist Andrzej Bogusławski and, before him, from Leibniz's proposal for a universal alphabet of human thought. But it also recalls Max Müller's proposal (1887: 59–63) that the roots of Indo-European form a universal set of primes from which all language and thought can be derived.

The problem with an assertion of semantic primes, whether deductively or inductively derived, is precisely that meaning is systemic, and we simply do not know how far a given semantic context will contribute to defining a given concept. And paraphrasing remains a kind of translation from one system into another, however reduced.

At the same time, the much broader Boasian ethnosemantics has been revived in recent work in a number of fields.

In cognitive psychology there has been an explosion of experimental work on such topics as time, space, colour, and gender that suggests a much more direct relationship between language and conceptualization than has been recognized for some time (see Chapter 2 this volume).

In more classical linguistic–anthropological mode, there is a return to work on the relationship between language specifics and cultural patterns (e.g., O'Neill, 2008). At the same time, linguistics in a broader sense is once again recognizing the vast diversity of language and its likely connection with cultural conceptualizations (Sharifian, 2011). Sustained discussion of such grammatical categories as evidentiality (e.g., Aikhenvald, 2004) cannot avoid engaging with the actual role of such pervasive categories as data-source marking in patterns of meaning. What has been called a 'Neo-Whorfian Renaissance' may be upon us, with its concomitant paradigm hop.

Related topics

ethnopragmatics; language, culture, and prototypes; culture and kinship language; language and cultural scripts.

Further reading

Becker, A. L. (1995) *Beyond Translation: Essays toward a Modern Philology*, Ann Arbor, MI: University of Michigan Press. Collection of essays that seeks to uncover the actual functioning of meaning in a number of Southeast Asian languages.

D'Andrade, Roy (1995) *The Development of Cognitive Anthropology*, Cambridge: Cambridge University Press. History of the development and transformation of cognitive anthropology, including 'classical' ethnosemantics.

Pike, Kenneth L. (1967) *Language in Relation to a Unified Theory of the Structure of Human Behavior*, 2nd edn, The Hague: Mouton. Classic discussion of the implications of linguistic description for other areas of human activity. Introduces the emi–etic distinction.

Tyler, Stephen A. (ed.) (1969) *Cognitive Anthropology*, New York: Holt, Rinehart, and Winston. Standard collection of important documents in 'classical ethnosemantics'.

Ullmann, Stephen (1962) *Semantics: An Introduction to the Science of Meaning*, Oxford: Blackwell. Excellent for the period, and because it is of its period gives excellent coverage to semantic field theory and other approaches.

Notes

1 See Quine's famous example (1960: ch. 2): a linguist encounters speakers of a language unknown to him. A rabbit runs by, and one of the speakers says 'Gavagai'. Quine discusses the difficulty of knowing that 'Gavagai' means more or less 'rabbit'. It's an illustration of what he calls the inscrutability or indeterminacy of reference.

2 Weisgerber's major papers from the 1920s and early 1930s are reprinted in Weisgerber (1964).

References

Aikhenvald, Alexandra Y. (2004) *Evidentiality*, Oxford: Oxford University Press.

Barnard, Alan (1996) 'Componential Analysis' and 'Ethnoscience', in Alan Barnard and Jonathan Spencer (eds), *Encyclopedia of Cultural and Social Anthropology*, London: Routledge, pp. 125–6, 202–3.

Becker, A. L. (1995) *Beyond Translation: Essays toward a Modern Philology*, Ann Arbor, MI: University of Michigan Press.

Berlin, Brent and Paul Kay (1969) *Basic Color Terms: Their Universality and Evolution*, Berkeley, CA: University of California Press.

Boas, Franz (1889) 'On Alternating Sounds', *American Anthropologist* 2: 47–53.

——(1911) 'Introduction', in Franz Boas (ed.), *Handbook of American Indian Languages*, Washington, DC: Government Printing Office, pp. 1–83. [Bulletin of the Bureau of American Ethnology, Smithsonian Institution, 40]

Brown, Penelope (2006) 'Cognitive Anthropology', in Christine Jourdan and Kevin Tuite (eds), *Language, Culture and Society*, Cambridge: Cambridge University Press, pp. 96–114.

Bunzl, Matti (1996) 'Franz Boas and the Humboldtian Tradition: From *Volksgeist* and *Nationalcharakter* to an Anthropological Concept of Culture', in George W. Stocking, Jr. (ed.), *Volksgeist as Method and Ethic*, pp. 17–78. Madison, WI: University of Wisconsin Press.

Conklin, Harold C. (1962) 'Lexicographical Treatment of Folk Taxonomies', in Fred W. Householder and Sol Saporta (eds), *Problems in Lexicography*, Bloomington, IN: Indiana University Research Center in Anthropology, Folklore, and Linguistics, pp. 119–52.

Cruse, Alan (2010) *Meaning in Language: An Introduction to Semantics and Pragmatics*, Oxford: Oxford University Press.

D'Andrade, Roy (1995) *The Development of Cognitive Anthropology*, Cambridge: Cambridge University Press.

Davis, Steven and Brendan S. Gillon (eds) (2004) *Semantics: A Reader*, Oxford: Oxford University Press.

Dixon, R. M. W., W. S. Ramson, and Mandy Thomas (1990) *Australian Aboriginal Words in English*, Melbourne: Oxford University Press.

Frake, Charles O. (1962) 'The Ethnographic Study of Cognitive Systems', in *Anthropology and Human Behavior*, Washington, DC: Anthropological Society of Washington, pp. 72–93.

Geertz, Clifford (1974) "From the Native's Point of View': On the Nature of Anthropological Understanding', *Bulletin of the American Academy of Arts and Sciences* 28: 26–45.

Goddard, Cliff (2011) *Semantic Analysis: A Practical Introduction*, 2nd edn (1st edn 1998), Oxford: Oxford University Press.

Good, Byron J. (1977) 'The Heart of What's the Matter: The Semantics of Illness in Iran', *Culture, Medicine and Psychiatry* 1: 25–58.

——(1994) *Medicine, Rationality, and Experience: An Anthropological Perspective*, Cambridge: Cambridge University Press.

Goodenough, Ward A. (1956) 'Componential Analysis and the Study of Meaning', *Language* 32: 195–216.

——(1957 [1964]) 'Cultural Anthropology and Linguistics', in Dell Hymes (ed.), *Language in Culture and Society*, New York: Harper & Row, pp. 36–9.

Hutton, Christopher M. (1999) *Linguistics and the Third Reich*, London: Routledge.

Hymes, Dell (1981) *'In Vain I Tried to Tell You': Essays in Native American Ethnopoetics*, Philadelphia, PA: University of Pennsylvania Press.

Jakobson, Roman (1959) 'Boas' View of Grammatical Meaning', in Walter Goldschmidt (ed.), *The Anthropology of Franz Boas: Essays on the Centennial of His Birth*, Washington, DC: American Anthropological Association, pp. 139–45.

Jakobson, Roman and Morris Halle (1956) *Fundamentals of Language*, The Hague: Mouton. [Janua Linguarum, Series Minor, 1]

Keesing, Roger M. (1972) 'Paradigms Lost: The New Ethnography and the New Linguistics', *Southwestern Journal of Anthropology* 28: 299–332.

Koerner, E. F. Konrad (1977) 'The Humboldtian Trend in Linguistics', in Paul J. Hopper (ed.), *Studies in Descriptive and Historical Linguistics: Festschrift for Winfred P. Lehmann*, Amsterdam: John Benjamins [Current Issues in Linguistic Theory, 4], pp. 145–58.

Larrivée, Pierre (2008) *Une histoire du sens: Panorama de la sémantique linguistique depuis Bréal*, Brussels: P. I. E. Peter Lang. [GRAMM-R. Etudes de linguistique française, 1]

Leavitt, John (2011) *Linguistic Relativities: Language Diversity and Modern Thought*, Cambridge: Cambridge University Press.

Lévi-Strauss, Claude (1967 [1969]) *The Elementary Structure of Kinship*, 2nd edn (1st edn 1949), trans. James Harle Bell and John Richard Von Sturmer, Boston, MA: Beacon Press.

Lounsbury, Floyd G. (1956) 'A Semantic Analysis of Pawnee Kinship Usage', *Language* 32: 158–94.

Lucy, John A. (2003) 'Semantic accent and linguistic relativity', paper presented at the Conference on Cross-Linguistic Data and Theories of Meaning, Max Planck Institute, Nijmegen, the Netherlands.

Lyons, John (1977) *Semantics*, Cambridge: Cambridge University Press.

Martin, Laura (1986) 'Eskimo Words for Snow: A Case Study in the Genesis and Decay of an Anthropological Example', *American Anthropologist* 88: 418–23.

Nerlich, Brigitte (1992) *Semantic Theories in Europe 1830–1930: From Etymology to Contextuality*, Amsterdam: John Benjamins. [Studies in the History of the Language Sciences, 59]

Nida, Eugene A. (1975) *Componential Analysis of Meaning: An Introduction to Semantic Structures*, The Hague: Mouton. [Approaches to Semiotics, 57]

O'Neill, Sean (2008) *Cultural Contact and Linguistic Relativity among the Indians of Northwestern California*, Norman, OK: University of Oklahoma Press.

Palmer, F. R. (1976) *Semantics: A New Outline*, Cambridge: Cambridge University Press.

Pike, Kenneth L. (1954–60) *Language in Relation to a Unified Theory of the Structure of Human Behavior*, Glendale, CA: Summer Institute of Linguistics.

Pullum, Geoffrey (1991) *The Great Eskimo Vocabulary Hoax*, Chicago, IL: University of Chicago Press.

Quine, Willard Van Orman (1960) *Word and Object*, Cambridge, MA: MIT Press.

Rosaldo, Michelle Zimbalist (1972) 'Metaphors and Folk Classification', *Southwestern Journal of Anthropology* 28: 83–99.

Saeed, John I. (2003) *Semantics*. Second edition (1st edn 1997), Malden, MA: Blackwell.

Sapir, Edward (1921) *Language: An Introduction to the Study of Speech*, Boston, MA: Houghton Mifflin.

Schaff, Adam (1964 [1973]) *Language and Cognition*, trans. Olgierd Wojtasiewicz, New York: McGraw-Hill.

Schneider, David M. (1968) *American Kinship: A Cultural Account*, Chicago, IL: University of Chicago Press.

——(1984) *Critique of the Study of Kinship*, Ann Arbor, MI: University of Michigan Press.

Sharifian, Farzad (2011) *Cultural Conceptualisations and Language: Theoretical Framework and Applications*, Amsterdam: John Benjamins.

Silverstein, Michael (1981 [2001]) 'The Limits of Awareness', in Alessandro Duranh (ed.), *Linguistic Anthropology: A Reader*, Malden, MA: Blackwell, pp. 382–401.

Steinberg, Danny D. and Leon A. Jakobovitz (eds) (1971) *Semantics: An Interdisciplinary Reader in Philosophy, Linguistics and Psychology*, Cambridge: Cambridge University Press.

Stocking, George W., Jr. (1974) 'The Boas Plan for the Study of American Indian Languages', in Dell H. Hymes (ed.), *Studies in the History of Linguistics*, Bloomington, IN: Indiana University Press, pp. 454–84.

Tamba, Irène (2007) *La sémantique*, 5th edn (1st edn 1998), Paris: PUF. [Que sais-je?, 655]

Trautmann-Waller, Céline (2006) *Aux origines d'une science allemande de la culture: Linguistique et psychologie des peuples chez Heymann Steinthal*, Paris: CNRS.

Trautmann-Waller, Céline (ed.) (2004) *Quand Berlin pensait les peuples: Anthropologie, ethnologie et psychologie (1850–1890)*, Paris: CNRS.

Trier, Jost (1931) *Der deutsche Wortschatz im Sinnbezirk des Verstandes*, Heidelberg: Carl Winter.

——(1934) 'Das sprachliche Feld. Eine Auseindandersetzung'. *Neue Jahrbücher für Wissenschaft und Jugendbildung* 10: 428–49.

Tyler, Stephen A. (ed.) (1969) *Cognitive Anthropology*, New York: Holt, Rinehart, and Winston.

Ullmann, Stephen (1957) *The Principles of Semantics*, 2nd edn (1st edn 1951), Oxford: Blackwell. [Glasgow University Publications, 84]

——(1962) *Semantics: An Introduction to the Science of Meaning*, Oxford: Blackwell.

Weisgerber, Leo (1964) *Zur Grundlegung der ganzheitlichen Sprachauffassung*, ed. Helmut Gipper, Dusseldorf: Schwann.

Whorf, Benjamin Lee (1956) *Language, Thought, and Reality*, Cambridge, MA: MIT Press.

Wierzbicka, Anna (1996) *Semantics, Primes and Universals*, New York: Oxford University Press.

Zimmermann, Francis (2002) *Enquête sur la parenté*, Paris: Gallimard.

5

ETHNOPRAGMATICS

Cliff Goddard, with Zhengdao Ye

1 Introduction

The term 'ethnopragmatics' designates an approach to language in use that sees culture as playing a central explanatory role, and at the same time opens the way for links to be drawn between language and other cultural phenomena. This approach involves a threefold alignment of objectives, methodological tools, and evidence base (Goddard, 2006).

- The *objective* of ethnopragmatics is to articulate culture-internal perspectives on the 'how and why' of speech practices in the diverse languages of the world. It is the quest to describe and explain people's ways of speaking in terms which make sense to the people concerned, i.e., in terms of indigenous values, beliefs and attitudes, social categories, emotions, and so on.
- Its *methodological tools* are based on decomposing cultural notions and capturing cultural norms in terms of simple meanings that appear to be shared between all languages. The methodology rests on a decades-long programme of semantic research by linguists in the Natural Semantic Metalanguage (NSM) programme (see Chapter 23 this volume); see Goddard (2011), Wierzbicka (1996a). Using the NSM metalanguage wards off implicit Anglocentrism and standardizes the terms of description.
- Ethnopragmatics pays particular attention to *linguistic evidence*, e.g. usage patterns discoverable using corpus techniques, interactional routines, language-specific lexicogrammatical constructions, and the like. Linguistic usage functions as an index of routine ways of thinking, and, appropriately analysed, allows us to stay close to an insider perspective. Ethnopragmatics also takes heed of the 'soft data' of anecdotal accounts, life writing, etc. of cultural insiders themselves.

Ethnopragmatics is a reconceptualization of the approach to 'cross-cultural pragmatics' inaugurated by Anna Wierzbicka's (2003[1991]) ground-breaking volume of this name. Ethnopragmatics is a more appropriate designation because it highlights the claim that there is an explanatory link between indigenous values and social models, on the one hand, and indigenous speech practices, on the other.

A key goal of ethnopragmatics is to access 'insider perspectives' of the participants. This means working through and with local categories and local ways of speaking – not in terms of sophisticated

Table 5.1 Semantic primes (English exponents)

I~ME, YOU, SOMEONE, SOMETHING~THING, PEOPLE, BODY	Substantives
KIND, PARTS	Relational substantives
THIS, THE SAME, OTHER~ELSE	Determiners
ONE, TWO, MUCH~MANY, LITTLE~FEW, SOME, ALL	Quantifiers
GOOD, BAD	Evaluators
BIG, SMALL	Descriptors
THINK, KNOW, WANT, DON'T WANT, FEEL, SEE, HEAR	Mental predicates
SAY, WORDS, TRUE	Speech
DO, HAPPEN, MOVE, TOUCH	Actions, events, movement, contact
BE (SOMEWHERE), THERE IS, BE (SOMEONE/ SOMETHING), BE (SOMEONES')	Location, existence, specification, possession
LIVE, DIE	Life and death
WHEN~TIME, NOW, BEFORE, AFTER, A LONG TIME, A SHORT TIME, FOR SOME TIME, MOMENT	Time
WHERE~PLACE, HERE, ABOVE, BELOW, FAR, NEAR, SIDE, INSIDE	Space
NOT, MAYBE, CAN, BECAUSE, IF	Logical concepts
VERY, MORE	Augmentor, intensifier
LIKE	Similarity

Note: Primes exist as the meanings of lexical units (not at the level of lexemes); exponents of primes may be words, bound morphemes, or phrasemes. They can be formally, i.e., morphologically, complex, and can have combinatorial variants or allolexes (indicated with ~). Each prime has well-specified syntactic (combinatorial) properties.

academic English and technical concepts, but in terms that are recognizable and accessible to the people concerned. This might sound paradoxical. How can one model the perspectives of cultural insiders and at the same time make oneself understood by cultural outsiders? This objective can (and can only) be achieved by framing the description in words and phrases whose meanings are shared between the languages concerned, such as universal semantic primes and molecules. Describing cultural concepts and cultural norms in this way brings other important benefits as well: it eliminates the danger of definitional circularity and allows for a very fine-grained resolution of meaning.

Table 5.1 lists the inventory of sixty-five semantic primes, using English exponents. Comparable tables have been drawn up for over thirty languages. NSM also makes use of a small set of non-primitive lexical meanings (termed 'semantic molecules') that function as building blocks, alongside semantic primes, in explications for many concepts. Some semantic molecules, such as 'man', 'woman', 'child', 'be born', 'mother', 'father', 'hands', 'mouth', 'long', and 'sharp' appear to be universal or near universal, once language-specific polysemic extensions are taken into account. To the extent that the ethnopragmatic researcher can formulate analyses in terms of this small 'intersection of all languages', the resulting analyses will be equally well expressible in any language. Even when the English version of the metalanguage is used, the analysis is not tied to English, lexically or conceptually.

2 Historical perspectives

Before the rise of generative linguistics in the 1960s, the study of languages was integrally connected with the humanistic tradition and with cultural and historical studies. Linguistics (as we see it now) was part of philology and anthropology. Under the influence of Chomsky, however, mainstream linguistics, especially in North America, disavowed its links with culture studies and sought to define itself first as a part of cognitive psychology and later as a branch of biology (biolinguistics). Interest in cultural aspects of language survived in anthropological linguistics and in the newer field of ethnography of communication, but it would be fair to characterize late twentieth-century linguistics as largely culture-blind.

This was the context into which ethnopragmatics emerged, in the late 1980s, in a series of studies by Anna Wierzbicka. These were later brought together and augmented in her landmark volume *Cross-Cultural Pragmatics* (first published 1991, reissued 2003). Wierzbicka argued, with unprecedented attention to matters of linguistic detail, that the then-prevailing universalist approaches to pragmatics, especially Grice's account of conversational implicature (Grice, 1975), Brown and Levinson's (1978) Politeness Theory, and aspects of speech-act theory (Searle, 1975), were both descriptively inadequate and profoundly Anglocentric. She called for a new approach, one that would ground conversational practices in cultural values: 'interpersonal interaction is governed, to a large extent, by norms which are culture-specific and which reflect cultural values cherished by a particular society' (Wierzbicka, 2003: v). She further insisted that cultural values should be accessed via semantic analysis of actual words in the language of the people concerned.

From the beginning, one of the cultures which Wierzbicka set out to problematize and describe was Anglo culture. Having migrated to Australia in the early 1970s from Poland, she was able to bring to this task the perspective of a bilingual, bicultural observer. In the 1980s, such a perspective was far from the norm. For many years she was almost a lone voice in her attempts to denaturalize Anglo culture and to criticize the leading anglophone writers in pragmatics. Gradually other voices began to make themselves heard, with perspectives from Korea, Japan, and other East Asian countries, e.g. Ide (1989), Matsumoto (1989), Sohn (1983), and from adjacent fields such as anthropology and cultural psychology. Nonetheless, anglophone pragmatics, especially in the Gricean line of descent, continued to be remarkably culture-blind. The 32-chapter *Handbook of Pragmatics* (Horn and Ward, 2006) did not include so much as an index entry for 'culture'.

A major advance in the development of ethnopragmatics occurred in the mid 1990s, when Wierzbicka articulated what became known as the theory of cultural scripts (Wierzbicka, 1994, 1996b; Goddard and Wierzbicka, 1997). These papers drew on contrastive examples from English, Japanese, Polish, Malay, and Russian. Others followed on a variety of other languages, by a growing community of researchers. The year 2004 saw the publication of the edited collection *Cultural Scripts* (Goddard and Wierzbicka, 2004), followed by *Ethnopragmatics* (Goddard, 2006), and *Semantics in/and Social Cognition* (Goddard, 2013).

With the decline of Chomskyan hegemony, culture and cultural issues are now back on the agenda of many linguists. Notable trends include cultural discourse analysis (Carbaugh, 2005), bilingualism studies (Pavlenko, 2006; Kecskes and Albertazzi, 2007), intercultural and contrastive pragmatics (e.g. Pütz and Neff-van Aertselaer, 2008), interactional pragmatics (Haugh and Culpeper, 2014), and the more 'culture-aware' forms of cognitive linguistics (e.g. Sharifian and

Palmer, 2007; Sharifian, 2011). To this day, however, many heavyweight scholars in linguistics still have a blind spot about Anglocentrism.

3 Critical issues

In this section, I identify three critical issues that pertain not only to ethnopragmatics but to studies of language and culture broadly. The *first* and most important is the continuing need to combat Anglocentrism in its various modes (Wierzbicka, 2014); and perhaps most urgently, the 'crypto-Anglocentrism' that is inherent when supposedly universal models are constructed from English-specific materials. It is important to be clear that this problem is not a matter of the conscious intentions of the researchers concerned (no one sets out deliberately to construct an Anglocentric model). It is about researchers taking for granted the interpretive resources of the English language (concepts such as 'imposition', 'politeness', 'tact', 'directness', 'face', 'relevance', 'interaction') and about how these assumed concepts influence the content of the models. One of the most exciting things about Brown and Levinson (1978), for example, was its cross-linguistic ambitiousness, and in particular, its use of Tamil as an extended counterpoint to English. And yet, by basing the dimensions of the model on concepts such as 'imposition' and on individualistic 'face needs',[1] it presupposed an Anglo code of communication. Defenders of Politeness Theory may dismiss the idea that everyday English concepts like *politeness* and *imposition* played any significant role in shaping the theory, but it is hard to believe that the outcome would have been the same if the starting point had been Japanese *wakimae* 'discernment' (Ide, 1989) or Chinese *hé* 'harmony, non-conflict' (see section 5.1). More recently, Enfield and Levinson (2006: 9; emphasis added) have attempted to define a new field as follows: 'a multidisciplinary approach to human *interaction*. The project asserts the centrality of social *interaction* in the organization of human societies'. Harmless enough, one might think, but on taking a cross-cultural perspective it becomes clear that the English '*interaction* concept' evokes free-standing individuals doing things with one another but remaining separate, much like the ideal of the 'free market' of rational economic actors. From a Russian point of view, one might consider founding a theory of human society in terms of the key Russian concept *obščenie* (roughly, 'communion of selves'). This would invoke very different cultural assumptions.[2]

It might be objected that Anglocentrism can be avoided by giving an English folk term a technical definition, but in practice this seldom works out. Sperber and Wilson, for example, employed the English word *relevance* to reconceptualize Grice (1975) but their attempts to clarify the meaning of 'relevance' have only led to definitions such as: 'an input is relevant to an individual when its processing in the context of available assumptions leads to a positive cognitive effect. A positive cognitive effect is a worthwhile difference to the individual's representation of the world – a true conclusion, for example' (Sperber and Wilson, 2004). This is inadequate for two reasons. First, it is so vague and abstract that both the producers and consumers of Relevance Theory are, in my opinion, still trading on their intuitive access to the meaning of the English word *relevance*. Second, key words in the definition, such as 'cognitive', 'representation', and 'processing', remain locked into Anglo English conceptual models.

A *second* critical issue is the need to denaturalize Anglo English concepts and pragmatic norms. We review aspects of Anglo ethnopragmatics in section 5.1. For the moment, consider the list of fifty Anglo English cultural key words presented in Table 5.2. According to Wierzbicka (forthcoming), none of these words has exact equivalents even in most other European languages, let alone in most other languages of the world. The listing was not devised with a view to ethnopragmatics, but it includes many terms that are directly relevant to Anglo ways of speaking, including social categories such as *friend*, social descriptors such as *reasonable* and *rude*,

Table 5.2 Fifty Anglo English cultural keywords (Wierzbicka 2014)

behaviour, business, challenge, commitment, common sense, communication, competition, control, culture, deadline, depression, efficiency, emotion, empirical, enjoy, entitled, evidence, experience, facts, fair, freedom, friend, frustration, fulfilment, fun, happy, humour, information, kindness, mind, opportunity, options, personal, privacy, rational, reality, reasonable, relationship, rights, rude, rule, science, security, self, sense, sex, story, suggestion, tolerance, work.

value-related terms such as *freedom*, *rights*, *entitled*, *personal*, and *privacy*, speech-act and genre words such as *suggestion*, *story*, and *humour*. Abstract Anglo key words such as *communication*, *information*, and *rational* have figured prominently in anglophone pragmatic theorizing.

To see how Anglo cultural key words can find their way into models of communicative behaviour in general, consider the following superbly Anglo English quotation from Spencer-Oatey's (2008) introduction to intercultural pragmatics (italics highlight words that appear in Table 5.2).

> [O]rders and requests can easily threaten rapport, because they can affect our autonomy, *freedom* of choice and *freedom* from *imposition*, and thus can threaten our *sense* of equity *rights* (our *entitlement* to considerate treatment). They need to be worded, therefore, in such a way that we feel that our *rights* to *fair* treatment have been adequately addressed.
>
> *(19; italics added)*

Just to be clear, I am not disputing the relevance of the italicized words/concepts to *Anglo* ethnopragmatics. My objection is to extending them to human beings generally.

A *third* critical issue is the need to break down the compartmentalization of pragmatics, and language-and-culture studies generally. Within linguistics, there is a need to integrate pragmatics with lexical and grammatical semantics. Despite ongoing talk about the semantics–pragmatics interface, and the like, few practitioners in either field are interested in showing how meaning is constructed by real people in real communication, subjectively in a seamless fashion. The NSM approach uses a common metalanguage for semantics and for pragmatics, thereby opening the way for an easier integration of meaning from both sources, but even the NSM research community has yet to produce well-worked accounts of meaning construction in real time, in real interactions. Equally, there is a need to integrate linguistic pragmatics with other scholarly discourses and traditions. Considering that pragmatics is supposed to be about meaning in context, it is paradoxical that most approaches to pragmatics exist in specialized academic niches and have minimal engagement with adjacent fields and disciplines such as ethnolinguistics, cultural anthropology, hermeneutics, literary studies, translation studies, philosophy, cognitive, social, and cultural psychology.

4 Main methodological tools: semantic explications, cultural scripts

This section describes the two main methodological tools of ethnopragmatics, namely: semantic explications and cultural scripts. It also introduces the notion of cultural key words.

4.1 Semantic explications for lexical–semantic analysis

A semantic explication is a reductive paraphrase of the meaning of a word, phrase, or lexico-grammatical construction. That is, it is an attempt to say in other, simpler words (the metalanguage of semantic primes and molecules) what a speaker is saying when he or she utters the expression being explicated.

Explications range in length from a few lines of semantic text to a dozen lines or more. A good explication satisfies three conditions. The first is substitutability in a broad sense: explications have to make intuitive sense to native speakers when substituted into their contexts of use, and to generate the appropriate entailments and implications. The second condition is well formedness: they have to be framed entirely in semantic primes or molecules, and conform to the syntax of the natural semantic metalanguage. The third, more difficult to evaluate, concerns coherence and logical structure; minimally, an explication has to make sense as a whole, with appropriate chains of anaphora, co-reference, causal links, etc. Often, the textual structure of explications turns out to include parallelism and counterpoint.

Most words are culture specific and culture related to some extent (Goddard, in press), but experience has shown that certain areas of the lexicon are particularly important for ethnopragmatics. By definition, this applies to cultural key words. This concept is explained below, followed by some other priority targets for lexical–semantics analysis.

(1) *Cultural key words*. This term refers to culture-rich and translation-resistant words that occupy focal points in cultural ways of thinking, acting, feeling, and speaking. Typical examples include words for values and ideals, social categories, emotions, sociality concepts, personhood constructs, and ethnophilosophical concepts. Key words and concepts do not, of course, operate in isolation. One usually finds a cluster of related key words, each with its own range of derivatives, fixed phrases and common collocations. (2) *Proverbs and common sayings*. These often tap into the same layer of 'cultural common sense' as key words. (3) *Words for social and biosocial categories* involved in social cognition in the culture concerned, e.g. 'friend', kinship terms. (4) *Words for speech acts and genres*. These represent a cultural catalogue of interaction types. (5) *Terms of address*, such as various pronouns, titles, quasi-kin terms, designations by profession or role, terms of endearment or familiarity, etc. (6) *Interactional routines*; such as greetings and partings, appropriate things to say (if anything) when good things happen, when bad things happen, when someone does something good for one, etc. (7) *Derivational morphology expressive of social meanings*; such as diminutives for expressing interpersonal 'warmth', honorifics for expressing 'respect', etc. (8) *Specialized lexicogrammatical constructions*, which may be fine-tuned to express meanings connected with, for example, emotional spontaneity, social reciprocity, or the dynamics of interpersonal causation. (9) *Discourse particles and interjections*; devices to express a speaker's feelings, intentions, and attitudes in the act of speaking or to express reactions to one's interlocutors.

4.2 Cultural scripts for capturing cultural norms, attitudes, and beliefs

Although they are written in the metalanguage of semantic primes, cultural scripts are not paraphrases of word meanings: they are 'representations of cultural norms which are widely held in a given society and are reflected in the language' (Wierzbicka, 2007: 56; see also Chapter 23 this volume). Cultural scripts exist at different levels of generality and may relate to different aspects of speaking, thinking, feeling, and acting. Some scripts capture cultural beliefs that are relevant to ways of speaking (Goddard and Wierzbicka, 2004; Goddard 2009).

High-level scripts are typically hinged around evaluational components such as 'it is good if … ' and 'it is bad if … ', or variants such as 'it can be good if … .' and 'it can be bad if … '. Another kind of framing component concerns people's perceptions of what they can and can't do, e.g. 'I can/can't say (think, do, etc.) … '. Belief scripts often begin with the framing component: 'it is like this: … '. High-level scripts, sometimes termed 'master scripts', are analogous to what are known in the ethnography of communication tradition as norms of interpretation. They explain 'why'. They often share components with cultural key words.

Lower-level scripts are more specific. They are often introduced by 'when'-components and 'if'-components, representing relevant aspects of social context. Scripts of this kind can be quite procedural. They are analogous to norms of interaction. They may be connected with broad communicative styles, with patterns of 'turn taking' and other conversational management strategies (e.g. preferences for non-interruption, for overlap, for incomplete or elliptical expressions), with specific speech practices (e.g. joking, teasing, self-promotion), with rhetorical modes of expression (e.g. active metaphorizing, hyperbole, sarcasm), with conversational routines and formulas, or go right down to matters of individual word usage.

Importantly, cultural scripts are not about actual behaviours but about participants' shared understandings and expectations, i.e. about social cognition (cf. Goddard 2013). Obviously, not everyone in a given speech community necessarily agrees with or conforms to such shared understandings. Indeed, speakers are not necessarily consciously aware of them in normal interaction. Nevertheless, the claim is that the content which can be captured cultural scripts forms a kind of interpretive backdrop to everyday interaction.

The number of scripts at play in any culture is not known, but it is safe to say that the number must be large. Cultural scripts can be interconnected in various ways, sometimes cross-cutting, sometimes reinforcing, sometimes competing, with each other. Individual scripts are not necessarily unique to a particular language; see Ameka and Breeveld (2004) and Ameka (2009) on areal cultural scripts in West Africa.

5 Two ethnopragmatic sketches: Anglo English and Chinese

This section illustrates current research by providing ethnopragmatic sketches of two cultures, based on recent work. Each sketch is highly selective, combining summary accounts of cultural key words with outlines of some cultural scripts associated with distinctive ways of speaking. Some other language varieties and cultures whose ethnopragmatics have been described include the following (the references are non-exhaustive): Ewe (Ameka and Breeveld, 2004; Ameka, 2009); French (Peeters, 2000, 2013), Danish (Levisen, 2012), Spanish (Travis, 2006), Malay (Goddard, 2000, 2004), Russian (Gladkova, 2010, 2013; Wierzbicka, 2007, 2012; Chapter 23 this volume), Singapore English (Wong, 2005, 2006, 2008, 2014), and Australian English (Wierzbicka, 1997: ch. 2, 2002; Goddard 2006, 2009, 2012).

5.1 An ethnopragmatic sketch of Chinese

In this sketch we pursue three themes: the core cultural value of *hé* 'harmony, non-conflict', the importance of *hányǎng* 'self restraint' in emotional matters, and the social dichotomies of *shēngrén* vs. *shúrén* ('stranger' vs. 'familiar person/old acquaintance') and *wàirén* vs. *zìjǐrén* ('insider' vs. 'outsider').

A core value and presiding concern in Chinese interpersonal relations is the Confucian ideal *hé* 'harmony, non-conflict' (Gao, Ting-Toomey, and Gudykunst 1996). The common saying *Hé wéi guì* '*Hé* is of utmost importance' has its origin in the *Analects*. Importantly, *hé* does not simply entail uniformity; on the contrary, the concept anticipates the existence of profound individual differences, cf. the set phrase *Hé ér bù tóng* '*Hé* but not the same', i.e. 'in harmony without being the same'. Different individual needs and interests always have the potential to lead to conflict. Conflict is destructive for everyone, whereas harmonious relations are in everyone's common interest. The overwhelming emphasis in Chinese social and interpersonal relations is therefore *not* to make one's needs and wants explicit in any situation where conflict could arise.

To understand this and other core Chinese values, norms, and expectations, the best starting point is actually the *jiā* 'family, household' and its people *jiārén* 'extended family, kin'. *Jiā* is seen as the archetypal group in Chinese culture and the feelings and behaviours codified and inculcated there are exemplars for how people should behave outside. Traditionally, several generations live under one roof and it is easy to appreciate that in such a context, conflicting interests, wants and needs would arise, both across and within generation levels. Not surprisingly, all family members aspire to *hé*, as reflected in sayings such as *Jiā hé wànshì xìng* 'A family is prosperous when it is in harmony'.

Although there is wide scholarly consensus that *hé* is of paramount importance in Chinese interpersonal relations, there is less agreement on its optimal translation. Glosses range from 'harmony', 'peace,' and 'unity', to 'kindness' and 'amiableness'. The exact cultural value embodied in *hé* is complex, but can be explicated as follows:[3]

Semantic explication for hé 和 [Chinese]

a. everyone can think about some people like this:

   "these people live in one place, they do many things in this place"

b. it is good if one of these people thinks like this about the other people:

   "if I know that one of these people wants me not to do something, I won't do it
   if I know that one of these people wants to do something, I won't say: "I don't want you to do this"
   if I feel something bad because one of these people does something, I won't do something bad to this someone because of this
   I want these people to know that I feel something good towards them"

c. it is good if all these people can think like this

   it is good if all these people can live like this

d. if they can live like this, other people can think like this about these people:

   "these people are like one thing"

e. if they can live like this, these people can live well in one place

   if they can live well like this, good things can happen to these people this is good for all these people

f. when someone has to be in one place with some other people for some time,
   it is good if this someone can think about these other people in the same way
   if they can all think like this, they can do many things well in one place because of it
   this is good for all of these people

Implicit in the explication is that *hé* has its model in a family-like situation, where many people are living in one place and doing many things together. In such a group, antagonistic behaviour should be avoided. The implication is that when faced with conflicting wills and behaviour, one should *rén* 'endure, forebear' and *ràng* 'let do, give way'. The components in (e) show the communal benefits of *hé*, as mentioned above. And, as reflected in (f), the social environment of *hé* can be extended to one's neighbours, to the work place, and indeed to any social sphere where one coexists with others.

If *hé* is the ideal, then the inculcated values of *rén* 'to endure, forebear' and *ràng* 'to let do, to give way' are instrumental in achieving the goal. The two terms have different emphases (*rén* is

73

chiefly about attitude and *ràng* chiefly about behaviour), but both are about 'holding back' what one wants to say or do. The meaning of *rěn* is explicated below (Ye, 2006; Goddard, 2011). Space prevents us exploring *ràng* here.

Semantic explication for *rěn* 忍 [Chinese]

a. everyone can think like this about some things:

"I want these things to happen
I know that they can't happen if I don't do some things
I want to do these things because of this
if I have to do these things for a long time, I don't want not to do them because of this
if I feel something bad because of this, I don't want not to do these things because of this"

b. it is good if someone always thinks like this
c. it is good if someone thinks about this when this someone feels something bad
d. it is good if someone thinks about this when someone else does something bad to this someone
e. it is good if someone does many things because this someone thinks like this
f. it is good if someone can be like this

In general, *rěn* indicates an attitude that one should uphold in the interests of one's long-term goals or 'great plans'. As an adage from the Analects has it: *Xiǎo bù rěn zé luàn dà mó* 'Lack of forbearance (*rěn*) will frustrate one's great plans'. As reflected in the final component of the explication ('it is good if someone can be like this'), *rěn* is considered a virtue and a source of inner strength pertinent to the Chinese idea of a moral person. In the context of social interaction, however, *rěn* is an assurance to achieve the ideal of *hé*. Being able to 'put up with others', so to speak, fosters peaceful coexistence among the family and the group.[4]

Rěn is an important aspect of the 'self-cultivation' ideal embodied in another Chinese cultural key word – *hányǎng* 'the ability to contain oneself'. To be *méi hányǎng* 'lack *hányǎng*' is tantamount to 'being uncouth' and 'uncivilized'. This ideal discourages overt and excessive expressions of one's emotions. It can be captured in the first instance by the master script below, which in turn predicts and spawns the following pair of scripts applying to 'feeling good' and 'feeling bad' situations.

A Chinese master script for *hányǎng* 涵养 [Chinese]

when someone feels something, it is not good if other people can know this when they see this someone's *liǎn* ('face') [m]

Chinese cultural scripts for concealing displays of 'feeling good' and 'feeling bad'

often when someone feels something very good because something very good happens to this someone, it is not good if other people can know this when they see this someone's *liǎn* ('face') [m]

often when someone feels something very bad because something very bad happens to this someone, it is not good if other people can know this when they see this someone's *liǎn* ('face') [m]

From a European point of view, it is striking to see from these scripts that in the Chinese value system, expression of one's true feelings does not count for much. Much more important is holding back visible signs of one's emotions, in the interest of values such as *hé* and *hányǎng*. This largely accounts for the Western stereotype of the Chinese 'inscrutable face' (Ye, 2006).

To complete this short overview of Chinese ethnopragmatics, we turn to key social categories, and once again, we find the prototype for these categories in *jiā* 'family, household'. For the Chinese speaker, the *jiā* sets a defining line between the interior and exterior spheres in human relationships. *Jiārén* 'family members' are thought of as 'insiders', known in Mandarin Chinese as *zìjǐrén* 'oneself person' or *zìjiārén* 'one's family person'. Non-kin, by contrast, are *wàirén* 'outsiders'. Among the non-kin, Chinese speakers make a sharp and important distinction between *shúrén* 'familiar person/old acquaintance' and *shēngrén* 'strangers'. The precise semantics of these concepts has been dealt with in detail in Ye (2004) and will not be rehearsed here. What we emphasize here is the way in which these paired social categories provide coordinates for Chinese social interaction. Their overriding social importance reflects a master cultural script associated with the adage *nèiwàiyǒubié* 'insiders and outsiders should be differentiated'. The presence of the social category words in the script itself embodies the claim they are integral to Chinese social cognition.

A Chinese master script for *nèiwàiyǒubié* 内外有别 ('insiders and outsiders should be differentiated')

> I can't think about all people in the same way
>
> I can think about *shúrén* [m] in some ways, I can't think about *shēngrén* [m] in the same ways
>
> I can think about *zìjǐrén* [m] in some ways, I can't think about *wàirén* [m] in the same ways
>
> because of this, I can't do things with all people in the same way
>
> because of this, I can't say things to all people in the same way

From this master script it follows, of course, that one communicates and interacts differently with the different categories of people. The key categories unlock a web of localized, specific 'rules of speaking' that are widely adhered to by the Chinese speakers. For example, one enacts the *dǎzhāohu* ('greeting') script only with *shúrén*, but not with *shēngrén*, and says to a guest something like 'since we are insiders, do not regard any formalities'.

It is obvious that with increasing personal contact over time, a *shēngrén* 'stranger' automatically moves to become a *shúrén* 'familiar person/old acquaintance'. Once a person becomes a *shúrén*, however, it is not so easy to move along the *wàirén/zìjǐrén* continuum, because the boundary is set by subjective criteria and is more resistant to change. This means that interactants may need to do more work in order to move across that boundary.

This brings us to a second master script in Chinese social interaction. It encourages people to think of 'pulling' relationships closer to oneself – seeking to move oneself from being *shū* 'distant' from one's interlocutors to being *qīn* 'close/intimate'[5] – and it prescribes a particular conversational strategy to achieve this end, i.e. speaking to someone in a similar fashion to how one speaks to a family member, i.e. 'like I say something to a *zìjǐrén*'.

A Chinese master script for *yóushūzhìqīn* 由疏至亲 ('from being distant to being close')

> it is good if some people think about me like this:
>
> "this someone is a *zìjǐrén* [m]

because of this, when I say something to these people,
it is good if I say it like I say something to a *zìjǐrén* [m]"

In this way, the idealized model of social interaction within the family exerts a pervasive influence on Chinese communicative style in general.

5.2 An ethnopragmatic sketch of Anglo English

For the sake of exposition we can identify three important themes in Anglo English ethno-pragmatics: the '*opinion* complex', the 'personal autonomy complex', and the 'social consensus complex'.

Wierzbicka (e.g. 2003[1991], 2006a, 2006b, 2010) has argued that the speech ways of contemporary Anglo culture have been heavily influenced by the British Enlightenment, especially as promulgated through the works of John Locke (1690, and subsequent multiple editions). One key aspect is the emphasis on distinguishing between 'expressing *opinions*', on the one hand, and 'stating *facts*', on the other. Both the key categories, i.e. *opinion* and *fact*, are cultural key words of English. Opinions are *personal* (another Anglo key word)[6] and (ideally, at least) grounded in rational thinking. The cultural orthodoxy insists that 'everyone has a right to express their opinion' but that opinions should not be held out as knowledge or as fact. One shouldn't try to 'impose' one's opinions on others (*ram them down other people's throats*, as the saying goes). One should acknowledge and leave room for other people's differing opinions.

What exactly is an *opinion?*, it may be asked – especially by speakers of the many languages of the world which lack any comparable word. Rather than take on this question here, the explication below applies to the most common conversational formula involving the word, namely, *in my opinion*. Other similar formulas include *as I see it* and *in my view*.

Semantic explication for *in my opinion*.

I want to say now:
    'I think about it like this: it is like this…'
I don't say: I know it
I know that some other people can think about it not like this
I think like this because I know some things about it
I thought about it for some time before

According to this explication, the formula *in my opinion* allows a speaker to express his or her thinking, while disclaiming certainty and acknowledging the possibility of divergent ways of thinking. Along with these allowances, however, the speaker also conveys an implicit claim to having some knowledge base and to having spent some time considering the matter.[7] (It takes some time to 'form' an *opinion*; compare: *considered opinion*, *?hasty opinion*, *?immediate opinion*.) (The raised question marks indicate odd or anomalous combinations.)

Another manifestation of the cultural priority accorded to 'not claiming too much in the way of knowledge' is the parenthetical formula *I think* (used without the complementizer *that*) in contexts like *I think Bill wrote it*, *I think it's raining*, etc. Many scholars have noted the high frequency and multifunctionality of this English formula, which conveys something like 'tentativeness', 'epistemic reserve', the 'softening' of assertion, or the like. Arguably, the *I think* formula has the effect of mitigating or cancelling the implication that 'I know this', which would normally be conveyed by a non-modal declarative sentence (Wierzbicka, 2006a). For example:

Semantic explication for *I think Bill wrote it.*

I say: I think like this – 'Bill wrote it'
I don't say more
I don't say: I know it

A third characteristic of Anglo English associated with the same complex of cultural values concerns tag questions, specifically their high frequency and high degree of grammatical elaboration (Wierzbicka, 2003[1991]; Wong, 2014). Tag questions can serve multiple functions, but a common theme is to register 'openness' to others' points of views and to seek (or appear to seek) confirmation that one's own expressed view is shared.

Key aspects of the '*opinion* complex' can be summed up in the following pair of cultural scripts. The first spells out the cultural premise of 'freedom of expression', while the second counsels epistemic reserve and openness.

Two Anglo cultural scripts connected with 'expressing opinions'

if someone wants to say about something: "when I think about it, I think like this",
    it is good if this someone can say it, it is bad if someone can't say it

when someone says about something "I think about it like this",
    it is good if this someone says at the same time:
      "I don't say: I know this
      I know that someone else can think not like this"

Associated aspects of Anglo communicative style that cannot be pursued here, for reasons of space, are the penchant for 'hedges' and down toners such as *kind of* and *a bit* (that provide safeguards against seeming to claim too much) and its dispreference for 'emotive' modes of expression (that would express conviction based on feeling, rather than on thinking and knowing).

Our second theme in this short tour of Anglo ethnopragmatics is the 'personal autonomy complex'. It is supported by a cluster of value-related key words, including *free, right,* and *entitled,* and by a brace of 'quasi-directive' conversational formulas that enable people to avoid directly expressing the message 'I want you to do this'. A useful point of entry is the following partial explication for the Anglo key word *freedom*. As discussed by Wierzbicka (1997), English *freedom* is not semantically equivalent to, for example, Latin *libertas* or Russian *svoboda*. What is distinctive about English *free* and *freedom* is their concern with being able to do things that one wants without compulsion or interference from other people. Berlin (1969: 126–7) quoted Hobbes in this connection: 'A free man is he that … is not hindered to do what he hath the will to do', and attributed the same conception to other classical English political thinkers such as Bentham, Locke, Adam Smith, and John Stuart Mill.

Partial semantic explication for *freedom* ⇒

it can be like this:

    someone can think like this about many things:
      "if I want to do it, I can do it
      other people can't say to me: "I don't want you to do it, because of this you can't do it"

if I don't want to do something, I cannot do it
other people can't say to me: "I want you to do it, because of this you can't not do it"
this is good for this someone
it is bad if someone can't think like this about many things

In support of this explication one can adduce some syntactic facts. In contemporary English, one can speak both of *freedom of X* or *freedom to X* (e.g., *freedom of action, speech,* etc.; *freedom to choose, emigrate,* etc.) and equally of *freedom from X* (e.g., *freedom from persecution, harassment, interference,* etc.).

A key part of the *freedom* ideal is, then, something like 'non-imposition', which is not seen just as a privilege for certain individuals, but as a general right ('it is bad if someone can't think like this about many things'). This, furthermore, applies not only in the political realm but right down to the level of interpersonal interaction, at least, between adults. A wide range of evidence can be adduced in favour of the following cultural script (Wierzbicka, 2006a, 2006b).

An Anglo cultural script for 'personal autonomy'

when someone does something, it is good if this someone can think about it like this:
"I am doing this because I want to do it"

Consistent with this script is the well-known fact that in most social situations Anglo English speakers prefer not to frame directive messages using the bare imperative, thereby expressing the unmitigated message 'I want you to do this'. To do so would invite perceptions that one was 'putting pressure' on the addressee (Wierzbicka, 2006b). Instead, speakers typically draw on a wide range of 'interrogative directive' constructions, such as: *Will you … ? Would you … ? Can you … ? Could you … ? Would you mind … ?* and the like. Although these constructions clearly convey a directive message, they acknowledge the addressee's autonomy by embedding the potentially confronting message into a question form, as if inviting the addressee to say whether or not he or she will comply. Another favoured strategy is the use of 'suggestive formulas', such as: *Perhaps you could … , You might like to … , I would suggest … , Can I suggest … ?, You could consider … , How about … ?, Why not … ?* (Wierzbicka, 2006b: 51f.).

Further support for the 'personal autonomy complex' in Anglo English ethnopragmatics comes from two sources, one lexical and one grammatical. The lexical source is speech-act verbs. English has a large number of directive and quasi-directive speech-act verbs, allowing an exquisite sensitivity to fine details of interpersonal dynamics (consider: *request, tell, suggest, advise, recommend, propose*). Wierzbicka (2006b) goes so far as to suggest that *suggest* is a cultural key word of Anglo English. In the grammatical area, English is graced with no fewer than three periphrastic causative constructions (with *make, get,* and *have*), and the choice enables fine distinctions to be made in respect of interpersonal causation (consider the difference between *making someone do something, getting someone to do something,* and *having someone do something*).

A third Anglo ethnopragmatic theme can be termed the 'social consensus complex'. The basic idea is that a number of key Anglo cultural concepts – including *rudeness, fairness, common sense,* and the idea of *being reasonable* – incorporate the assumption or expectation of agreement between people. Consider first the conceptual semantics of *rude* and its interactional consequences. Though many languages have words for undesirable or disapproved social behaviours, the precise semantics of *rude* are highly culture specific. As noted by Waters (2012), the nearest French equivalent is *mal élevé* ['badly raised/brought up'] but, unlike *rude,* this reflects directly on one's upbringing. The nearest Polish equivalent is *cham* [lit. 'boor'] but, unlike *rude,* it implicitly compares a person's behaviour with that of the uncouth lower classes. Both French *mal élevé* and Polish *cham* presuppose that certain well-known rules or protocols have been violated. The semantics of *rude* is much more open-ended: it depends on the idea that there can be social consensus on what kinds of behaviour are likely to cause 'offence' (i.e. 'someone else can feel something bad because of it') and 'disapproval'. Waters (2012) proposes the following explication (the abbreviation VP stands for 'verb phrase').

Semantic explication for *It's rude to VP* (e.g. *It's rude to stare, to interrupt*).

it is like this:

> it is bad if someone does something like this (VP), people can know this
> it is bad because if someone does this, someone else can feel something bad because of it
> this someone else can think something bad about this someone because of it
> other people can think the same

Waters (2012) provides evidence that although there are many standard and known *rude* behaviours, indicated by the stereotyped status of expressions such as *It's rude to interrupt (to point (at someone), to stare, to eat with one's mouth open*, etc.), the word *rude* is also used to describe interpersonal behaviours across a wide spectrum. Indeed, it is possible to discuss and seek consensus about what is or isn't *rude* in 'new' situations (for example, whether it is *rude* to break up with your girlfriend via text message). What makes *rude* elusive from the point of view of a cultural outsider or newcomer is the presumed knowledge about what kind of behaviours are likely to make someone else 'feel something bad'. In the light of the 'personal autonomy complex', it is not surprising that people who address bare imperatives to others are open to criticism not only as *pushy*, *demanding*, and *bossy*, but also as *rude*.

Now consider *fair* and *fairness*. As noted by Wierzbicka (2006a), appeals to *fairness* and expressions such as *That's not fair!* are commonly heard in daily life from both children and adults, and across informal and formal registers, e.g. in scholarly works, government publications, public administration, business, trade, and law. Yet unlike the word *just*, which arguably represents a pan-European concept, *fair* lacks precise equivalents even in other European languages. Notable aspects of English *fair* include its relational character: one is *fair* or *unfair* to someone while having 'dealings', so to speak, with the affected person. Importantly, however, *fairness* does not necessarily involve directly doing something bad to someone else, but turns on whether one's action is bad *for* someone else. In these respects, it differs markedly from *justice*. One can easily describe a teacher, for example, as *fair* or *unfair*, but hardly as *just* or *unjust*. Likewise, *rules* can be *fair* or *unfair* (and *rules* apply in situations in which people want to do things together). The link between *fairness* and *rules* highlights the fact that the idea of *fairness* implies a potential consensus about what can and can't be done within the 'rules of the game', so to speak. The following explication is adapted from Wierzbicka (2006a).

Semantic explication for *That's not fair*.

I say: "people can't do things like this

> if someone does something like this, he/she does something bad"
> if other people know about it, they can't not say the same
> when people want to do things of some kinds with other people, it is like this:

> > they can do many things as they want
> > the same time they can't do some things,
> > > because if they do things like this, it is very bad for these other people

Although *fairness* is often used in contexts that imply equality of treatment, for example, in expressions like *fair share*, this is not always or necessarily the case. Consider, for example, the expressions *fair comment* and *fair criticism*. The focus is not on the comment or criticism being the same for everyone but on whether it could be judged as justifiable by the general consensus. A similar argument can be made for other quintessentially Anglo cultural concepts, such as *common sense* and *reasonableness* (Wierzbicka, 2006a, 2010).

There are of course many different varieties of Anglo English. The three themes sketched out here are held in common between all varieties, and indeed, are partially constitutive of the notion of Anglo English in general. Each sub-variety of Anglo English, however, has its own motifs and themes; for example, the positivity and competitiveness of American English, the lingering class consciousness and high concern with *privacy* of English English, the 'low key' tone and easy familiarity of Australian English (Wierzbicka, 2002, 2006b; Goddard 2009, 2012).

6 Future directions

A great deal remains to be done in ethnopragmatics: documenting and exploring more and more languages, experimenting with new formats of cultural scripts and explications, discovering more about the intertextuality between cultural scripts, accommodating situational and interpersonal factors in greater detail.

There are practical applications for ethnopragmatics too. Because cultural scripts and explications are expressed in non-technical ordinary language, they have the potential to be readily applied to real-world needs in many situations; for example, to assist with cultural induction of immigrants and refugees, to develop the intercultural competence component of language courses, to assist governmental and international agencies to communicate more effectively with cultural minorities, to help bridge cultural gaps in international negotiations. To translate this potential into effective applications, however, requires collaboration with experts and practitioners across many fields (Goddard and Wierzbicka, 2007). Ethnopragmatics also has an important contribution to make at this time of language endangerment, by providing techniques for capturing indigenous concepts and describing indigenous speech practices in an authentic fashion, free from Anglocentrism (Goddard and Wierzbicka, 2013; Nicholls, 2013; Priestley, 2013; Wierzbicka, 2013).

In time, one may hope, continuing progress in ethnopragmatics will help overturn the hegemony of Anglo concepts in pragmatics and in language-and-culture studies generally.

Related topics

cultural linguistics; ethnosyntax; ethnosemantics; language and cultural scripts; language and culture in cognitive anthropology

Further reading

Goddard, Cliff (ed.) (2013) 'Semantics and/in Social Cognition', special issue, *Australian Journal of Linguistics* 33(3). (These seven studies show how with NSM semantic explications and cultural scripts we can circumvent Anglocentrism and tap into the social cognition of people from diverse cultures: Chinese, Russian, Danish, Koromu, Kayardild, Pitjantjatjara, Roper Kriol.)

Goddard, Cliff and Anna Wierzbicka (2014) *Words and Meanings: Lexical Semantics across Domains, Languages and Cultures*, Oxford: Oxford University Press. (Presents systematic empirically based studies of key words from different lexical domains – concrete, abstract, physical, sensory, emotional, social – in a range of languages and cultures: English, Russian, Polish, French, Warlpiri, and Malay.)

Notes

1 Ironically 'face' started its career as a loan translation from Chinese (see expressions such as *to lose face*, and *to save face*), but in Politeness Theory the concept of 'negative face' has morphed into a classically Anglo meme, 'the desire to be free from imposition' (see Matsumoto, 1988).

2 *Obščenie* (often misleadingly rendered, in this context, as 'dialogue') was crucial to Bakhtin's influential theory of what it is to be human. The word is directly related to the Russian noun *obščestvo* 'society'.

3 The explication shows that *hé* is different from Japanese *wa* ('unity'), a cognate written using the same character (Wierzbicka, 1997). Unlike Japanese *wa*, *hé* does not require group members to do the same things, or to think or feel the same way; rather, it is about maintaining good relations in the common interest.

4 This applies particularly to 'horizontal' relations. In the vertical order, the paradigm for children's behaviour is built on the notion of *xiào* ('filial duty'), known as 'filial piety' among China specialists. This uniquely Confucian concept has no counterpart in English. Though one of the preeminent Chinese values, it cannot be dealt with here (see Goddard, in press).

5 Note that *shū* and *qīn* are terms that specifically describe *relational* distance.

6 The word *personal* evokes modern Anglo ideas about the rights of the individual. The same applies even to the English *person*, unlike comparable words such as German *Mensch* or Russian *čelovek*, which simply refer to a single human being.

7 Expressions of *opinions* frequently include evaluative or modal words, e.g. *good, best, worst, should, possible, impossible*. The content of an opinion as such cannot be checked or verified, but because it supposedly rests on some knowledge base, the factual basis behind an opinion can be contested.

References

Ameka, Felix K. (2009) 'Access Rituals in West African communities: An Ethnopragmatic Perspective', in Gunter Senft and Ellen B. Basso (eds), *Ritual Communication*, New York: Berg, pp. 127–52.

Ameka, Felix K. and A. O. Breedveld (2004) 'Areal Cultural Scripts for Social Interaction in West African Communities', *Intercultural Pragmatics* 1(2): 167–87.

Berlin, Isaiah. (1969) *Four Essays on Liberty*, Oxford: Clarendon Press.

Brown, Penelope and Stephen C. Levinson (1978) 'Universals in Language Usage: Politeness Phenomena', in E. N. Goody (ed.), *Questions and Politeness*, Cambridge: Cambridge University Press, pp. 56–290.

Carbaugh, Donal (2005) *Cultures in Conversation*, Mahwah, NJ: Erlbaum.

Enfield, N. J. (2006) 'Introduction: Human Sociality as a New Interdisciplinary Field', in N. J. Enfield and S. C. Levinson (eds), *Roots of Human Sociality?: Culture, Cognition and Interaction*, New York: Berg, pp. 1–35.

Gao, G., S. Ting-Toomey, and W. Gudykunst (1996) 'Chinese Communication Process', in M. H. Bond (ed.), *Handbook of Chinese Psychology*, Hong Kong: Oxford University Press, pp. 290–3.

Gladkova, Anna (2010) *Russkaja kul'turnaja semantika: emocii, cennosti, zhiznennye ustanovki* [Russian cultural semantics: Emotions, values, attitudes], Moscow: Languages of Slavonic Cultures.

——(2013) '"Is He One of Ours?" The Cultural Semantics and Ethnopragmatics of Social Categories in Russian', *Journal of Pragmatics*, 55: 180–94.

Goddard, Cliff (2000) 'Communicative Style and Cultural Values – Cultural Scripts of Malay (Bahasa Melayu)', *Anthropological Linguistics* 42(1): 81–106.

——(2004) 'The Ethnopragmatics and Semantics of "Active" Metaphors', *Journal of Pragmatics* 36: 1211–30.

——(ed.) (2006) *Ethnopragmatics: Understanding Discourse in Cultural Context*, Berlin: Mouton de Gruyter.

——(2006) '"Lift Your Game, Martina!" – Deadpan Jocular Irony and the Ethnopragmatics of Australian English', in Cliff Goddard (ed.), *Ethnopragmatics: Understanding Discourse in Cultural Context*, Berlin: Mouton de Gruyter, pp. 65–97.

——(2009) 'Not Taking Yourself Too Seriously in Australian English: Semantic Explications, Cultural Scripts, Corpus Evidence', *Intercultural Pragmatics* 6(1): 29–53.

——(2011) *Semantic Analysis: A Practical Introduction*, rev. 2nd edn, Oxford: Oxford University Press.

——(2012) "'Early Interactions' in Australian English, American English, and English English: Cultural Differences and Cultural Scripts', *Journal of Pragmatics* 44, 1038–50.

——(2013) *Semantics and/in Social Cognition*, special issue, *Australian Journal of Linguistics*, 33(3).

——(2014) 'Words as Carriers of Cultural Meaning', in John R. Taylor (ed.), *The Oxford Handbook of the Word*, Oxford: Oxford University Press.

Goddard, Cliff and Wierzbicka, Anna (1997) 'Discourse and Culture', in Teun van Dijk (ed.), *Discourse as Social Interaction*, London: Sage Publications, pp. 231–57.

——(eds) (2004) 'Cultural Scripts', special issue, *Intercultural Pragmatics* 1(2).

——(2007) 'Semantic Primes and Cultural Scripts in Language Teaching and Intercultural Communication', in F. Sharifian and G. Palmer (eds), *Applied Cultural Linguistics: Second Language Learning/Teaching and Intercultural Communication*, Philadelphia, PA and Amsterdam: John Benjamins.

——(2014) *Words and Meanings: Lexical Semantics across Domains, Languages and Cultures*, Oxford: Oxford University Press.

Grice, H. P. (1975) 'Logic and Conversation', in P. Cole and J. L. Morgan (eds), *Syntax and Semantics 3: Speech Acts*, New York: Academic Press, pp. 41–58.

Haugh, Michael and Jonathan Culpeper (2014) *Pragmatics and the English Language*, Basingstoke, Hants.: Palgrave Macmillan.

Horn, Laurence R. and G. Ward (eds) (2006) *The Handbook of Pragmatics*, Oxford: Blackwell.

Ide, Sachiko (1989) 'Formal Forms and Discernment: Two Neglected Aspects of Universals of Linguistic Politeness', *Multilingua* 8(2/3): 223–48.

Kecskes, Istvan and Liliana Albertazzi (eds) (2007) *Cognitive Aspects of Bilingualism*, Heidelberg and London: Springer.

Locke, John (1959 [1690]) *An Essay Concerning Human Understanding*. Oxford: Clarendon Press.

Levisen, Carsten (2012) *Cultural Semantics and Social Cognition: A Case Study on the Danish Universe of Meaning*, Berlin: Mouton de Gruyter.

Matsumoto, Yoshiko (1989) 'Reexaminations of the Universality of Face', *Journal of Pragmatics* 12 (4): 403–26.

Nicholls, Sophie (2013) 'Cultural Scripts, Social Cognition and Social Interaction in Roper Kriol', *Australian Journal of Linguistics*, 33(3): 282–381.

Pavlenko, Anna (ed.) (2006) *Bilingual Minds: Emotional Experiences, Expressions, and Representation*, Clevedon, UK: Multilingual Matters.

Peeters, Bert (2000) '"S'engager" vs "to Show Restraint": Linguistic and Cultural Relativity in Discourse Management', in Susanne Niemeier and René Dirven (eds), *Evidence for Linguistic Relativity*, Amsterdam: John Benjamins, pp. 193–222.

——(ed.) (2006) *Semantic Primes and Universal Grammar: Evidence from the Romance Languages*, Amsterdam: John Benjamins.

——(2013) '*Râler, râleur, râlite: discours*, langue et valeurs culturelles', in C. Claudel, P. von Münchow, M. Pordeus, F. Pugnière-Saavedra, and G. Tréguer-Felten (eds), Cultures, discours, langues: Nouveaux abordages, Limoges: Lambert-Lucas, pp. 117–44.

Priestley, Carol (2013) 'Social Categories, Shared Experience, Reciprocity and Endangered Meanings: Examples from Koromu (PNG)', *Australian Journal of Linguistics*, 33(3): 257–81.

Pütz, Martin and JoAnne Neff-van Aertselaer (eds) (2008) *Developing Contrastive Pragmatics: Interlanguage and Cross-Cultural Perspectives*, Berlin: Mouton de Gruyter.

Searle, John (1975) 'Indirect Speech Acts', in Peter Cole and Jerry Morgan (eds) *Syntax and Semantics 3: Speech Acts*, New York: Academic Press.

Sharifian, Farzad (2011) *Cultural Conceptualisations and Language: Theoretical Framework and Applications*, Amsterdam: John Benjamins.

Sharifian, Farzad and Gary Palmer (eds) (2007) *Applied Cultural Linguistics: Implications for Second Language Learning and Intercultural Communication*, Amsterdam: John Benjamins.

Sohn, Ho-min (1983) 'Intercultural Communication in Cognitive Values: Americans and Koreans', *Language and Linguistics*, 93–136.

Spencer-Oatey, Helen (ed.) (2008) *Culturally Speaking: Culture, Communication and Politeness Theory*, 2nd edn, London: Continuum.

Travis, Catherine E. (2006) 'The Communicative Realization of *confianza* and *calor humano* in Colombian Spanish', in Cliff Goddard (ed.), *Ethnopragmatics: Understanding Discourse in Cultural Context*, Berlin: Mouton de Gruyter, pp. 199–230.

Waters, Sophia (2012) '"It's Rude to VP": The Cultural Semantics of Rudeness', *Journal of Pragmatics* 44: 1051–62.

Wierzbicka, Anna (1994) 'Cultural Scripts: A New Approach to the Study of Cross-cultural Communication', in M. Pütz (ed.), *Language Contact and Language Conflict*, Amsterdam: John Benjamins, pp. 69–88.

——(1996a) *Semantics: Primes and Universals*, New York: Oxford University Press

——(1996b) 'Japanese Cultural Scripts: Cultural Psychology and "Cultural Grammar"', *Ethos* 24(3): 527–55.

——(1997) *Understanding Cultures through Their Key Words: English, Russian, Polish, German, Japanese*, New York: Oxford University Press.

——(2002) 'Australian Cultural Scripts – *Bloody* Revisited', *Journal of Pragmatics* 34(9): 1167–1209.

——(2003[1991]) *Cross-Cultural Pragmatics: The Semantics of Social Interaction*, 2nd edn, Berlin: Mouton de Gruyter.

——(2006a) *English: Meaning and Culture*, New York: Oxford University Press.

——(2006b) 'Anglo Scripts against 'Putting Pressure' on Other People and Their Linguistic Manifestations', in Cliff Goddard (ed.), *Ethnopragmatics: Understanding Discourse in Cultural Context*, Berlin: Mouton de Gruyter, pp. 31–63.

——(2007) 'Russian Cultural Scripts: The Theory of Cultural Scripts and Its Applications', *Ethos* 30(4): 401–32.

——(2010) *Experience, Evidence and Sense: The Hidden Cultural Legacy of English*, New York: Oxford University Press.

——(2012) ''Advice' in English and in Russian: A Contrastive and Cross-cultural Perspective', in Holger Limberg and Miriam A. Locher (eds), *Advice in Discourse*, Amsterdam: John Benjamins, pp. 309–32.

——(2013) 'Translatability and the Scripting of Other Peoples' Souls', *Australian Journal of Anthropology* 24: 1–21.

——(2014) *Imprisoned in English: The Hazards of English as a Default Language*, New York: Oxford University Press.

——[forthcoming] 'Fifty Key Words of 'Anglo' Culture'.

Wilson, Deidre and Dan Sperber (2006) 'Relevance Theory', in Laurence R. Horn and Gregory Ward (eds), *The Handbook of Pragmatics*, Oxford: Blackwell, pp. 605–32.

Wong, Jock (2005) '"Why You So Singlish One?" A Semantic and Cultural Interpretation of the Singapore English Particle *One*', *Language in Society* 34(2): 239–75.

——(2006) 'Contextualizing *Aunty* in Singaporean English', *World Englishes* 25: 451–66.

——(2014) *The Culture of Singapore English*. Cambridge: Cambridge University Press.

Ye, Zhengdao (2004) 'Chinese Categorization of Interpersonal Relationships and the Cultural Logic of Chinese Social Interaction: An Indigenous Perspective', Intercultural Pragmatics 1(2): 211–30.

——(2006) 'Why the "Inscrutable" Chinese Face? Emotionality and Facial Expression in Chinese', in Cliff Goddard (ed.) *Ethnopragmatics: Understanding Discourse in Cultural Context*, Berlin: Mouton de Gruyter, pp. 127–70.

PART III

Studies of language and culture

6

LINGUACULTURE

The language–culture nexus in transnational perspective

Karen Risager

1 Introduction

People trained in language studies tend to see culture through the lens of language. Culture is typically seen as a kind of extension of language: you study language and 'its associated culture' – a very frequent phrase in the parts of linguistics that are interested in the relationship between language and culture (Risager, 2006). Among people trained in fields like anthropology or cultural studies this language-bound view of culture is not normally seen. The conceptualizations of culture in these fields may be very diverse, conflictual, and contested, but the point of departure would seldom be that 'culture' is coterminous with 'language' – unless perhaps when we are dealing with an interdisciplinary field like linguistic anthropology.

In my view, an examination of the relationship between language and culture must combine perspectives from both linguistics and anthropology (or other fields dealing with culture, such as cultural studies or postcolonial studies). If only approaches from linguistics are involved, the risk is that the understanding of culture is, from a culture–theoretical point of view, unsatisfactory and perhaps outdated. Therefore, this chapter will present a conceptualization of the language–culture relation in a combined anthropological–linguistic perspective. The primary perspective is anthropological and draws on theories of culture and globalization, especially that of the social anthropologist Ulf Hannerz (1992), who has developed the idea of transnational cultural flows (flows of lifestyles, musical genres, food and drink, pictures and films, etc. in social networks across the world). The secondary perspective is linguistic in the sense that I focus on transnational linguistic flows (also known as language spread) as cultural flows among others in the world, and then direct the attention to the culturality of language in the midst of these flows. In my view, the concept of linguaculture is useful when we are dealing with the multiple dimensions of the culturality of language in complex and fluid societies (Risager, 2006, 2012).

2 Historical perspectives

The concept of linguaculture (or languaculture, see below) is a recent offshoot of the cultural movement originating in the German-speaking areas of Europe at the end of the eighteenth century, mainly represented by the works of Johann Gottfried von Herder and Wilhelm von Humboldt. This movement introduced the idea that language should be seen as related to nation, people, and culture.

Herder, a central figure in connection with the emerging German national consciousness in the period known as the *Sturm-und-Drang* period (1765–85) was the first to formulate this idea (Herder, 1952 [1782]). His thoughts were further developed by Humboldt (Humboldt, 1907 [1836]) (see Chapter 2 this volume), a politician/diplomat and academic, who was strongly influenced by the ideas of neo-humanism concerning the value of clarity and harmony in spiritual cultivation. Humboldt was particularly interested in language as a creative activity that was made possible because of the power of the human mind. He was, then, most interested in the psychological aspect of language, especially in the role of language for thought: 'Language is the formative organ of thought' (Humboldt, 1907: 53) and for the world-view (*Weltansicht*): 'so there lies in every language a particular world-view' (60). Thus he was the first to formulate the basic idea of linguistic relativity. Furthermore he was interested in what happens to one's world-view when one learns a foreign language, as he thought that the new language marks a new standpoint or a different approach to an understanding of the world: 'one always transfers into a foreign language, more or less, one's own world-view' (60) – a thought I will come back to below.

During the nineteenth century the idea of correlation between language and people gained a national–romantic form, so that one now spoke of a mysterious, intimate connection between language, people, and national soul. This romantic idea of a fusion between language and people/nation gained considerable general support in connection with the nationalist tendencies that became increasingly strong and widespread in the course of nineteenth-century Europe, first as a progressive liberal movement, later on in various right-wing nationalist and socialist versions (Hobsbawm, 1990; Risager, 2006). Even today, the national paradigm and its insistence on the inseparability of language and culture is quite strong, especially in popular discourse in certain parts of the world such as Europe, China, and Japan. It is also quite widespread in general and applied linguistics, for example in the field of language teaching (Risager, 2007). However, it should be noted that the idea of inseparability of language and culture may not refer to the 'national' in the political sense (for example: French language and French culture in the nation state of France), but may rest more on ideas of ethnic or social groups (for example: the language and culture of the Sami people, or the language and culture of drug users).

As is well known, in the first decades of the twentieth century the German tradition of culture studies, and studies of language as part of culture, was introduced to the USA by Franz Boas and his followers in anthropology, primarily Edward Sapir and Benjamin Lee Whorf (see Chapter 2 this volume). Sapir was active in many parts of anthropology, including the study of language (Sapir, 1921). However, it should be noted that although he was very interested in the relationship between language and culture, he was not an adherent of the national paradigm and its insistence on the inseparability of language and culture. Actually, he emphasized that languages can spread across cultural areas:

> Languages may spread far beyond their original home, invading the territory of new races and of new culture spheres. A language may even die out in its primary area and live on among people violently hostile to the persons of its original speakers. Further, the accidents of history are constantly rearranging the borders of cultural areas without necessarily effacing the existing linguistic cleavages.
>
> *(Sapir, 1921: 208)*

Later in this chapter, Sapir's view will be further elaborated in a rethinking of the concepts of language and linguaculture in the context of transnational migrations.

3 Current contributions and research

3.1 Origins of the concept of 'linguaculture' in anthropology: Paul Friedrich and Michael Agar

Whereas the idea of intimate connection between language and culture is an old one, it was not until 1989 that the term linguaculture was introduced, namely by the linguistic anthropologist Paul Friedrich in an article on the relationship between political economy, ideology, and language (Friedrich, 1989). (He also used the term in a manuscript from 1988.) In the article he writes that 'the many sounds and meanings of what we conventionally call "language" and "culture" constitute a single universe of its own kind' (Friedrich, 1989: 306), and he describes the concept of linguaculture with these words: 'a domain of experience that fuses and intermingles the vocabulary, many semantic aspects of grammar, and the verbal aspects of culture' (1989: 306)

Thus the concept of linguaculture does not encompass all of culture, but only 'the verbal aspects of culture'. Friedrich adds that this terminological innovation can 'help to get rid of the decades-long balancing act between "language *and* culture" ("how much of each?"), "language *in* culture" ("culture *in* language?")' (1989: 307; italics in the original). Friedrich is the first to emphasize that there are dimensions of culture that are not related to language. At the same time he also indirectly says that there are dimensions of language that are not culture. He tries to carve out a concept that lies in the interface of language and culture.

The linguistic anthropologist Michael Agar borrows the concept from Friedrich, but changes it to 'languaculture'. He justifies his alteration of the term as follows: 'I modified it to "langua" to bring it in line with the more commonly used "language"' (Agar, 1994: 265). In his book *Language Shock: Understanding the Culture of Conversation* (1994) Agar presents, in a metaphoric style and with many anecdotal illustrations, the linguistic and anthropological basis for ideas about the interrelation between language and culture, and here he refers repeatedly to the Sapir–Whorf discussion of linguistic relativity. He deals with the misunderstandings and cultural awareness that can arise in connection with conversations, both when it is a question of 'different languages', and when it is a question of 'the same language'. Whereas Friedrich refers to locally defined variation such as southern Vermont linguaculture, Agar expands the range of languacultural variation to all social groups.

Agar introduces the concept of languaculture in order to be able to sum up culture and language in one word:

> Language, in all its varieties, in all the ways it appears in everyday life, builds a world of meanings. When you run into different meanings, when you become aware of your own and work to build a bridge to the others, 'culture' is what you're up to. Language fills the spaces between us with sound; culture forges the human connection through them. Culture is in language, and language is loaded with culture.
>
> *(Agar, 1994: 28)*

The term languaculture, then, stresses two relations: 'The *langua* in languaculture is about discourse, not just about words and sentences. And the *culture* in languaculture is about meanings that include, but go well beyond, what the dictionary and the grammar offer' (Agar, 1994: 96, italics in the original). Thus Agar focuses on meaning in discourse, particularly in conversation. But he is not as clear as Friedrich about the idea that there are dimensions of culture that are not related to language (or discourse).

Agar spends some time explaining what the Whorfian discussion is about. As so many people within modern linguistic anthropology and socio and psycholinguistics he is in favour of the weak version of the Whorfian hypothesis, with such formulations as: 'Language carries with it patterns of seeing, knowing, talking, and acting. Not patterns that imprison you, but patterns that mark the easier trails for thought and perception and action' (Agar, 1994: 71). Agar proposes that what Whorf was really talking about was 'languaculture'.

Agar also introduces the concept of 'rich points', meaning the places in conversation where people misunderstand one another. It is in this that there is the opportunity to glimpse 'culture', to become conscious of cultural differences. He writes about 'the Whorfian Alps' in linguistic communication in the sense that between people who have different languacultures (which ultimately everyone has) a number of cultural differences rise up – some small, some large – and that it is a question of bringing these out into the open and trying to go beyond them.

The concept of languaculture is developed in several of Agar's publications (see, e.g. Agar, 2008). In this article he argues that one should think of ethnography as second languaculture learning and translation. He suggests that the usual abbreviation L2 be replaced by LC2 (second languaculture), and similarly that translation should be seen as a relation between LC1 and LC2. He argues that ethnographic work is both a process where the ethnographer learns a second languaculture, including experiences with significant rich points, and a product where the ethnographer struggles with communicating his/her interpretation of LC2 in a translation to an LC1 public.

3.2 Further developments of the concept of 'linguaculture' in linguistics: Karen Risager

Whereas Agar focuses on ethnographic studies of languaculture in local settings, the author of this chapter introduces a transnational perspective in the book *Language and Culture: Global Flows and Local Complexity* (2006). The main disciplinary backgrounds for my work are sociolinguistics/the sociology of language and cultural and social anthropology, and in this interdisciplinary perspective 'languaculture' is an important interface concept. (I have used the term 'languaculture', but in my recent writings I prefer 'linguaculture' as a perhaps more straightforward term for linguists.)

As I basically see human language as a part of human culture in general, I take my point of departure in a theory of culture, particularly a theory that departs from the national paradigm and takes a transnational and global perspective, namely that of the anthropologist Ulf Hannerz. In his book *Cultural Complexity: Studies in the Social Organization of Meaning* (1992) Hannerz describes his theory of the social organization of meaning, with particular reference to cultural flows and cultural complexity. He begins by giving the following summary of his understanding of culture:

> The three dimensions of culture, to be understood in their interrelations, are thus:
>
> 1 *ideas and modes of thought* as entities and processes of the mind – the entire array of concepts, propositions, values, and the like which people within some social unit carry together, as well as their various ways of handling their ideas in characteristic modes of mental operation;
> 2 *forms of externalization*, the different ways in which meaning is made accessible to the senses, made public; and
> 3 *social distribution*, the ways in which the collective cultural inventory of meanings and meaningful external forms – that is, (1) and (2) together – is spread over a population and its social relationships.
>
> *(Hannerz, 1992: 7, italics in the original)*

In Hannerz's opinion, then, culture has two loci, an external and an internal: the external locus is meaningful, externalized forms such as speech, gestures, song, dance, and decoration. The internal locus of culture is meaning in consciousness – not perceived as an idealized consciousness but as that of concrete human beings. The individual's share in culture he mainly describes with the aid of the hermeneutical concepts perspective and horizon: each human being is unique in his or her experience-based, socially influenced perspective on the outside world, and his or her horizon is reflected by personal life experiences and education. At the individual level, society is thus seen as a network of perspectives. The two loci of culture are each other's prerequisites, and the cultural process takes place in the interaction between them. Finally, meaning in consciousness and the externalized forms of this find themselves in a constant distribution process and this means that 'people must deal with other people's meanings' (Hannerz, 1992: 14).

Thus Hannerz takes interaction at the micro level as his point of departure, describing cultural flow as a constant alternation between externalization and interpretation, with the flow passing from person to person in a constant process of distribution and transformation. But he also takes a bird's-eye perspective, stating that the cultural process takes place at both the societal micro and macro level. It occurs partly in the concrete interaction between people in interpersonal situations, but also at higher levels, right up to the highest level: the global level, i.e. via the distribution of goods and mass communication. Hannerz, then, adopts a macro-anthropological perspective. He studies, among other things, how cultural distribution processes of various, possibly global, extent result in local mixes. Thus he contributes to current critiques of essentialist and static notions of culture.

3.3 Transnational view of language: linguistic flows and linguistic complexity

Hannerz only deals with language in passing, but his model is very useful for the development of a transnational view of language that foregrounds global linguistic flows and linguistic complexity, and also contributes to current critiques of essentialist notions of language.

Referring to Hannerz's two loci for culture, an external and an internal, I would also consider language as a two-sided phenomenon: the external locus is linguistic practice, oral or written (or some kind of a mixture), and the internal locus is linguistic resources in the subject, developed during his or her socialization and total life history. But in addition to this, I would include a third locus that has a more deliberately constructed or 'artificial' nature, namely the idea of 'the language' or 'the language system' conceived as a coherent whole, or maybe an object, or even an organism or a person.

The two first-mentioned loci of language presuppose each other: linguistic practice cannot be produced and received without linguistic resources carried by individual people, and the linguistic resources of the individual cannot be developed without the experience of linguistic practice. Whereas these two loci of language are both natural and necessary, the idea of the 'language system' is not. We have to deconstruct the idea that there is a language 'out there' that we can use and study as a natural object. The 'language system' is a construct or, in other words, a family of historically and discursively constructed notions ('French', 'Arabic', etc.). At the same time it is important to note that this construct has consequences for linguistic practice and linguistic resources. The idea of the language system interacts with both linguistic practice and linguistic resources, being a kind of – more or less conscious – normative factor.

The use (linguistic practice) of a specific language may be seen as flows (and change) in social networks of people and groups of people. These networks may be located physically in individuals acting together, or they may be located in virtual space as communication networks made possible by information technologies such as telephone, the Internet, etc. These networks develop further through migration and language learning. Danish language, for example, spreads in social networks all over the world where there are Danish-speaking people as settlers, tourists, sojourners, students, soldiers, sports people, etc. People carry their Danish-language resources with them into new cultural contexts and put them to use in perhaps new ways under the new circumstances. People around the world are learning Danish as a foreign language for instance in Scandinavian departments, and thus the Danish language has spread to new individuals and new social networks. It has also spread to new users via the learning of Danish as a second language in Denmark. Seen in this perspective, quite a large number of the world's languages are spreading in large global networks and can indeed be said to be world languages – not on the basis of their numbers of speakers, but on the basis of the extent of the networks using them.

These transnational linguistic flows of a large number of different languages create local multilingual situations of great complexity, characterized by language hierarchies and struggles among language users for power and recognition. Almost every country (state) in the world is multilingual in some sense. In a small country like Denmark, for instance, over 120 languages are spoken as first languages (Risager, 2006). (For the sake of simplicity, I will not deal with the issues of language alternation and language mixing in this chapter although this is clearly also relevant for the question concerning the relationship between language and culture.)

The transnational view of language makes it possible to describe how language and culture can be separated: linguistic practice flows in social networks that may reach from one cultural context to another across the world. Or in other words – focusing on the internal locus: when people move around in the world, they carry their linguistic resources with them from one cultural context to another (see Sapir's position quoted above).

3.4 Linguaculture: three interrelated dimensions

The description of linguistic flows has implicitly focused on language codes: it is codes that are seen as flowing and intermingling in social networks – irrespective of the meanings to which they give rise. With the concept of linguaculture, the focus switches to the content or meaning side of language.

In relation to Agar's (1994) concept of languaculture, which focuses on the semantics and pragmatics of language (in discourse), I expand the concept to include two other dimensions as well: the poetics of language and the identity dimension of language. Together they are meant to encompass the full range of culturality of a language.

The semantics and pragmatics of language is the dimension specifically explored by Agar and his antecedents in linguistic anthropology represented by Sapir and Whorf, as well as by many linguists and language specialists interested in contrastive and intercultural semantics and pragmatics, both at sentence, discourse, and text levels. This dimension is about the interplay of constancy and variability in the semantic and pragmatic potentials and practices of specific languages as opposed to other languages: as regards constancy; it could be more or less obligatory distinctions between (in English) 'sister' and 'brother', between 'he' and 'she', between 'red' and 'orange', between 'hello' and 'how are you', and the denotative (dictionary) meanings of culturally specific words like 'Christmas', 'race', 'lecturer', 'done'. As regards variability, it could be the social and personal variability that is found in concrete situations of use in different parts of the world. This is a vast and well-explored field of study, including for example culturally oriented conversation analysis and (linguistic) discourse analysis.

The poetics of language is the dimension related to the kinds of meaning created in the exploitation of the interplay between form and content in the language in question – different kinds of rhymes, puns based on the relationship between speech and writing, etc. – areas that have interested literary theorists focusing on literary poetics, style and the like, as for example Roman Jakobson, and also Paul Friedrich (1986). The poetic potentials and practices of particular languages can be very different, basically because of the arbitrary–conventional relationship between form and content, as illustrated by the challenges of translating poetry from one language to another. Metaphor studies may be said to be an example of a field that intimately relates the semantic/pragmatic and the poetic dimensions of linguaculture.

The identity dimension is also called social meaning by some sociolinguists, for example Dell Hymes. It is related to the social and personal variation of the language in question, not least its pronunciation: with a specific accent, for instance, you identify yourself and make it possible for others to identify you according to their background knowledge and attitudes. Like Le Page and Tabouret-Keller (1985) I see linguistic practice as a continuing series of 'acts of identity' where people by their choice of language variety (dialectal form, code alternation, etc.) project their own understanding of the world onto the interlocutors and consciously or unconsciously invite them to react. The identity dimension has generally been explored by those scholars within sociolinguistics that are interested in the relationship between language and identity in multilingual society.

3.5 Linguaculture in first, second, and foreign language use

A language can be used as both a first, second, and foreign language, and in all its different uses it is cultural. Using a language always involves linguaculture for the simple reason that linguistic practice produces and reproduces meaning.

Traditionally the inseparability of language and culture refers to the language used as a first language, even if this is rarely explicitly stated. The national–romantic idea of an inner association between the language and the people (the nation) is in fact about people who have from childhood grown up with the first language and its culture (cf. the German expression: *die muttersprachliche Kultur*, i.e. mother tongue culture). We probably see examples of this use among researchers in the field of English as a lingua franca, who sometimes refer to people's 'linguacultural background'. Jenkins, Cogo, and Dewey, for example, writing about features that occur in lingua franca interactions, say that these features 'have been found to occur frequently and extensively with features most often being produced by numerous speakers from a wide variety of *linguacultural backgrounds*' (2011: 289, emphasis in the original). Consider also this quote from Hülmbauer: 'A *lingua franca* is a shared means of intercultural communication between speakers with different *primary lingua*–cultural backgrounds' (2012, emphasis in the original).

However when a language is used as a second or foreign language, it still produces and reproduces meaning, although the relationship between language and culture is of a different nature. A Dane who is learning German as a foreign language, for instance, especially in the first stages of learning, must draw on his/her cultural and social experiences related to the Danish language (see Humboldt's position cited above: 'one always transfers into a foreign language, more or less, one's own world-view'). There are some semantic/pragmatic distinctions that are obligatory in using German, such as an appropriate distribution of 'du' and 'Sie'. But besides such clear-cut distinctions it will be natural to build on the linguaculture developed in relation to the first language. Personal connotations to words and phrases will be transferred, and a kind of language mixture will result, where the foreign language is supplied with linguacultural matter from the first language (and possibly other languages learned). From the learner's perspective, the alleged intimate association between German language and culture is normative, not descriptive. The learner's task is to establish an association between his/her new language and his/her life experiences and cultural knowledge, and this task has to be accomplished on the basis of a growing understanding of some of the life experiences and cultural knowledge common among first language speakers. But even when the learner reaches a high level of competence, his/her linguaculture will always be the result of an accumulation of experiences during his/her entire life history, some of which may have taken place outside the target language community.

The linguaculture concept makes it possible to describe how languages are never culturally neutral. Any language (and language variety and language mixture) carries meaning potentials that are to some extent specific for this language. This also applies to English, of course, a language that carries a wealth of meaning from its diverse and conflictual histories in colonial expansion, in postcolonial settings, and in the more or less global spread of domains of use such as commercial and scientific communication. When we distinguish between language used as first, second or foreign language, it becomes clear that linguacultural flows do not follow exactly the same routes as linguistic flows. For example, when I as a Dane move around in the world, I tend to build on my Danish linguaculture, both when I speak English, French, and German. I thereby contribute to the flow of Danish linguaculture across languages.

3.6 Discursive flows – translingual and intralingual

Linguaculture in the sense presented above cannot stand alone when we want to consider all meaning carried by human language. The linguaculture concept in my perspective is bound to specific languages (mainly, but not only, in their use as first languages). But language also carries and forms discourses.

In this context, I propose to draw on the concept of discourse that has been developed by critical discourse analysts such as Fairclough (1992). This concept is content oriented: discourses are characterized by topics constructed in relation to perspectives, and more specifically ideological positions. They are mainly linguistically formed (though often incorporated in wider semiotic practices), but they are in principle not restricted to any specific language or language community. This means that discourses may transmit content from one language community or network to another. Discourses may spread from language community to language community by processes of translation and other kinds of transformation. Thus discourses (non-fictional or fictional) on nationalism, on agriculture, on Islam, on education, on democracy, on culture, on health, on language, etc. spread translingually all over the world. But any discourse is at any time embodied in a specific language, and consequently formed by the linguacultural potential of that language. In the translation process, what one tries to keep constant, is the discourse, while the linguaculture changes.

While the main point here is that the world is marked by translingual discursive flows, we may also observe that some discursive flows are strictly intralingual in the sense that they only circulate in a particular language community and never get out. This might be the case, for example, with certain discourses of opposition in dominated (language) groups. But it must be emphasized that these discourses are not bound to that particular language, they can, in principle, be translated into other languages if needed or allowed.

3.7 The language–culture nexus in transnational perspective

Whereas Agar uses linguaculture as an umbrella term for the unity of language and (parts of) culture, I propose to analyse the language–culture nexus into a range of interface concepts: language, linguaculture, and discourse. The concepts of linguaculture and discourse are meant to represent two different layers of meaning in language. Apart from these language-related forms of culture we have of course all the other forms of culture treated by for example Hannerz (1992): visual culture, architectural, musical, behavioural culture, etc., forms of culture that we, in the present linguistic perspective, could refer to as non-verbal culture.

The language–culture nexus can be seen both as a communicative event in practice (the external locus) or as a constellation in the resources of the subject (the internal locus). The language–culture nexus as a communicative event has been defined in Risager (2006) as follows:

- it is a local integration of linguistic, languacultural, discursive and other cultural flows in more or less differing social networks;
- in written language it is normally divided into a production and reception phase that can be more or less staggered in time and/or place;
- it takes place in a complex micro- and macro-context (or in several, in the case of written language);
- it is characterized by a discursive content of more or less cohesive nature, possibly including references and representations, internal or external;
- it can be multilingual, i.e. characterized by diverse forms of code-switching;
- it has place in each of the entire life-contexts of the participants (subs. producers and receivers) and it is interpreted by each of them in the light of this life context.

(186f.)

In the language–culture nexus, language, and culture can blend in a great variety of ways, and this mix can be described as relatively convergent or relatively divergent: a fairly convergent language–culture nexus could be the following: a conversation at Rønne Tourist Office (Rønne is the main town on the small Danish island of Bornholm). Those engaged in conversation were born in Rønne and speak modern Rønne dialect with Rønne linguaculture, and the discourse has to do with summer tourism in Rønne. A fairly divergent language–culture nexus could be the following: a telephone conversation between an office employee at the Berlin Zoo and an employee at the Aalborg Zoo (Aalborg is a city in Northern Jutland in Denmark). The person talking in Berlin speaks German with a tinge of Hungarian linguaculture because this person is a Hungarian immigrant. The person talking in Aalborg speaks German with some Aalborg linguaculture. They discuss a project involving an exchange of lions. In this last example the identities 'point in different directions', so to speak. They exemplify (electronically mediated) local complexity as a result of transnational processes (the examples are taken from Risager, 2006).

If one investigates only convergent situations, one can easily come to the conclusion that there is, generally speaking, a close connection or coherence between language and culture. Agar's approach is a good example of the search for coherence in the study of the role of linguaculture in situated intercultural communication, and that is clearly a fruitful approach. But if one turns one's gaze to divergent situations, exhibiting greater cultural complexity, as in the Berlin Zoo example, such a conclusion is less likely. So you cannot take the relationship between language and culture for granted. The specific blend or integration of language, linguaculture, discourse, and other culture in a given situation is always an empirical question. The methods of investigation of the language–culture nexus have to be sensitive to this complexity.

This also applies to studies of the language–culture nexus in the subject (the internal locus), i.e. the changing constellation of language(s), linguaculture(s), discourses, and other cultural meanings constructed as part of the life history of the subject. This calls for more qualitative research into subjects' complex personal language histories over time (see for example Kramsch, 2009).

4 Related research

Among other researchers who use the term linguaculture (or languaculture), one can mention Mackerras (2007), who includes the concept of linguaculture in a discussion of how a socio-cultural approach can help students become intercultural learners who can weave together everyday and scholarly concepts.

Sometimes an expression is used that serves as an alternative to linguaculture, namely 'culture-in-language', for example in Crozet and Liddicoat (2000), who deal with the teaching of culture as an integrated part of language. The expression 'culture-in-language' may be used in opposition to another expression: 'language-in-culture', which focuses on the role of language in the wider culture. A third kind of expression is 'language-and-culture' (also with an adjectival form: 'language-and-cultural'). This term emphasizes the general inseparability of language and culture, irrespective of the specific part–whole relationship. This term has for example been used in Byram *et al.* (1994) on the learning of (foreign) language and culture as an integrated whole. In the French context, the expression 'langue-culture' is often used, for instance, by Galisson (1991), who focuses on cross-cultural lexical semantics with reference to French. In the German context, the most usual (near-) equivalent for linguaculture would be 'Kultur in der Sprache', or alternatively 'Sprachkultur', but 'Sprachkultur' traditionally has another meaning, namely the cultivation of the language.

In continuation of the Sapir–Whorf tradition we find the neo-Whorfians conducting experimental and theoretical investigations on the relationships between linguistic categories and cognition, among them Lucy (1992). Gumperz and Levinson (1996) provides a comprehensive overview of different approaches to linguistic relativity at the time, including sociolinguistic studies of the production of meaning in context and critiques of idealizations such as 'language', 'culture', and 'community'.

Many other linguists and language specialists are working with linguaculture without using any of the expressions mentioned above, including the term linguaculture. Among these the following can be mentioned: Wierzbicka (1997) on cross-cultural semantics, Blum-Kulka *et al.* (1989) on cross-cultural pragmatics, Dovring (1997) on the political consequences of semantic diversity in the English language, Ochs (1988) on language socialization in culture, Lantolf (1999) on second culture acquisition in a sociocultural perspective, Sharifian and Palmer (2007) on cultural models, Kramsch (1993) on the teaching of language and culture as discourse, and Müller-Jacquier (2000) on intercultural teaching. In Stubbs (1997) one can find a sociolinguistic interpretation of linguistic relativity, focusing on relations between language use in discourse and stereotypical thinking, as can be seen for example in racist and sexist discourse. Further-more, a book on the cultural and intercultural dimensions of English as a lingua franca is being edited by Holmes and Dervin (in press). Thus quite a large number of different issues and approaches can be described as linguacultural studies.

5 Research methods

We are dealing here with a vast field characterized by a large number of research methods, and I will just mention three methods: an ethnographic approach to the study of linguacultural practices, a sociocultural approach to the study of linguacultural resources, and a semiotic/symbolic and biographic approach to practices and resources of the multilingual subject.

Agar's work can be described as a highly language-sensitive and also practically oriented approach to intercultural communication. In his 1994 book he provides an introduction to ethnographic studies of linguacultural and discursive practices (in my terms) in everyday con-versation. The focus is on how as a layperson one can build up one's cultural awareness by collecting rich points and investigating whether they form patterns, by investigating linguistic practice in certain situations in order to define frames (the typical example is what are also referred to as 'scripts', e.g. concerning typical sequences of acts when visiting a restaurant): 'Frames take language and culture and make them inseparable. The "and" disappears, and we're left with *linguaculture*' (Agar 1994: 132, italics in the original). His opinion, then, is that one ought to work inductively and empirically to build up an increasingly comprehensive set of interrelationships between frames. This is an approach that underscores the search for coherence between language and culture in different settings.

The linguacultural resources of individuals have been investigated (without using terms like linguaculture or culture-in-language) in a number of cognitive studies inspired by sociocultural and sociohistorical theory (the Vygotskyan tradition). Lantolf (1999) gives an overview of such studies in the context of second language acquisition, where a number of researchers have conducted experimental studies in order to examine what they call 'second culture acquisition', mainly by comparing word association or the use of metaphors in groups varying according to language use (use of the language in question as first or second/foreign language) and according to contexts of learning (the language learned in school in their own country or by immersion in a target language country). These approaches, in their focus on 'second language and culture acquisition', also tend to underscore the intimate relationship between language and culture, but at the same time some of the studies show that learners of a second language tend *not* to learn the second culture unless they are immersed in it, i.e. are living in a target language country (Lantolf, 1999). This is an approach that primarily looks for similarities and differences between groups of language learners/users.

Another kind of approach is represented by Kramsch (2009), which deals with the subjective aspects of language learning. It focuses on the multilingual subject and his/her language learning biography and practices in a semiotic/symbolic perspective, including links with identity, memory, emotion, and imagination. The data are mainly spoken and written data from individual language learners, including online data from for example electronic chatrooms, and published testimonies and memoirs of former language learners.

6 Future directions

Until now the concept of linguaculture seems to be used primarily in fields where there is a special emphasis on dealing with both language and culture, for instance in language teaching and learning. But the concept has something to offer for the whole range of language and culture studies. It can be used for highlighting that some forms of culture are related to language, while others are not. Thus it can prevent us from jumping into a narrow, language-bound view of culture. It can also be used to stress that languages and linguacultures (i.e. their users) may spread all over the world across diverse cultural contexts. And above all, it can be useful for the further development of methodology and empirical methods in the field: a fundamental methodological issue in relation to the analysis of the language–culture nexus is data construction and generation itself: what configurations of language–culture nexus do we traditionally focus on, and what configurations do we tend not to include in our studies? What configurations lead us to reaffirm the idea of inseparability of language and culture, and what configurations lead us to formulate ideas of complexity, mixing, and change?

Related topics

research on language and culture: a historical account; the linguistic relativity hypothesis revisited; ethnosemantics; ethnopragmatics; language, culture and context; language culture and identity; language and culture in second dialect learning; world Englishes and local cultures

Further reading

Kramsch, C. (1998) *Language and Culture*, Oxford: Oxford University Press. (An introduction to the complex relationship between language and culture.)

Risager, K. (2006) 'Culture in Language: A Transnational View', in H. L. Andersen, K. Lund, and K. Risager (eds) *Culture in Language Learning*, Aarhus: Aarhus University Press. (A presentation of the two levels of meaning in language: linguaculture and discourse.)

References

Agar, M. (1994) *Language Shock: Understanding the Culture of Conversation*, New York: William Morrow.

——(2008) 'A Linguistics for Ethnography: Why Not Second Languaculture Learning and Translation?', *Journal of Intercultural Communication*, 16. Online.

Blum-Kulka, S., J. House, and G. Kasper (eds) (1989), *Cross-cultural Pragmatics*, Norwood, NJ: Ablex.

Byram, M., C. Morgan *et al.* (1994) *Teaching-and-Learning Language-and-Culture*, Clevedon, UK: Multilingual Matters.

Crozet, C. and A. J. Liddicoat (2000) 'Teaching Culture as an Integrated Part of Language', in A. J. Liddicoat and C. Crozet (eds), *Teaching Languages, Teaching Cultures*, Applied linguistics association of Australia, Melbourne, Vic.: Language Australia.

Dovring, K. (1997) *English as lingua franca: Double Talk in Global Persuasion*, Westport, CT: Praeger.

Fairclough, N. (1992) *Discourse and Social Change*, Cambridge: Polity Press.

Friedrich, P. (1986) *The Language Parallax: Linguistic Relativism and Poetic Indeterminacy*, Austin, TX: University of Texas Press.

——(1989) 'Language, Ideology, and Political Economy', *American Anthropologist* 91: 295–312.

Galisson, R. (1991) *De la langue à la culture par les mots* [From language to culture via words], Paris: CLE International.

Gumperz, J. J. and S. C. Levinson (eds) (1996) *Rethinking Linguistic Relativity*, Cambridge: Cambridge University Press.

Hannerz, U. (1992) *Cultural Complexity: Studies in the Social Organization of Meaning*, New York: Columbia University Press.

Herder, J. G. (1952) (1st edn 1782–91) 'Ideen zur Philosophie der Geschichte der Menschheit', in J. G. Herder, *Zur Philosophie der Geschichte. Eine Auswahl in Zwei Bänden*, Berlin: Aufbau-Verlag.

Hobsbawm, E. J. (1990). *Nations and Nationalism since 1780: Programme, Myth, Reality*, Cambridge: Cambridge University Press.

Holmes, P. and F. Dervin (eds) [in press] *The Cultural and Intercultural Dimensions of English as a Lingua Franca*, Clevedon, UK: Multilingual Matters.

Hülmbauer, C. (2012). 'Lingua franca'. Online. Available www.toolkit-online.eu/docs/franca.html (accessed 24 April 2013).

Humboldt, W. von (1907) (1st edn 1836) 'Über die Verschiedenheit des menschlichen Sprachbaues und ihren Einfluss auf die geistige Entwicklung des Menschengeschlechts', in *Wilhelm von Humboldts Gesammelte Schriften*, Band VII, Berlin: B. Behr's Verlag.

Jenkins, J., A. Cogo, and M. Dewey (2011) 'State-of-the-art Article: Review of Developments in Research into English as a lingua franca', *Language Teaching* 44 (3): 281–315.

Kramsch, C. (1993) *Context and Culture in Language Teaching*, Oxford: Oxford University Press.

——(2009) *The Multilingual Subject*, Oxford: Oxford University Press.

Lantolf, J. P. (1999) 'Second Culture Acquisition: Cognitive Considerations', in E. Hinkel (ed.), *Culture in Second Language Teaching and Learning*, Cambridge: Cambridge University Press.

Le Page, R. and A. Tabouret-Keller (1985) *Acts of Identity: Creole-based Approaches to Language and Ethnicity*, Cambridge: Cambridge University Press.

Lucy, J. (1992) *Language Diversity and Thought: A Reformulation of the Linguistic Relativity Hypothesis*, Cambridge: Cambridge University Press.

Mackerras, S. (2007) 'Linguaculture in the Language Classroom: A Sociocultural Approach', *Babel* 42(2). Online.

Müller-Jacquier, B. (2000) 'Interkulturelle Didaktik' [Intercultural Didactics], in M. Byram (ed.), *Routledge Encyclopedia of Language Teaching and Learning*, London and New York: Routledge.

Ochs, E. (1988) *Culture and Language Development: Language Acquisition and Language Socialization in a Samoan Village*, Cambridge: Cambridge University Press.

Risager, K. (2006) *Language and Culture: Global Flows and Local Complexity*, Clevedon, UK: Multilingual Matters.

——(2007) *Language and Culture Pedagogy: From a National to a Transnational Paradigm*, Clevedon, UK: Multilingual Matters.

——(2012) 'Linguaculture and Transnationality: The Cultural Dimensions of Language', in J. Jackson (ed.), *The Routledge Handbook of Language and Intercultural Communication*, London and New York: Routledge.

——(2013) 'Linguaculture', in C. Chapelle (ed.), *Encyclopedia of Applied Linguistics*, Oxford: Wiley-Blackwell.

Sapir, E. (1921) *Language: An Introduction to the Study of Speech*, New York: Harvest Books.

Sharifian, F. and G. B. Palmer (2007) *Applied Cultural Linguistics*, Amsterdam: Benjamins.

Stubbs, M. (1997) 'Language and the Mediation of Experience: Linguistic Representation and Cognitive Orientation', in F. Coulmas (ed.), *The Handbook of Sociolinguistics*, Oxford: Blackwell.

Wierzbicka, A. (1997) *Understanding Cultures through Their Key Words*, New York: Oxford University Press.

7

LANGUAGE, GENDER, AND CULTURE

Lidia Tanaka[1]

1 Introduction/definitions

The relationship between language and gender has been the focus of interest in a number of disciplines such as linguistics, sociology, psychology, anthropology, philosophy, biology, and so on. Each discipline has explored a particular aspect pertaining to this topic: biology and psychology-based studies have explored the brains of males and females, examining how language is processed and learned, sociology has looked into gender and socialization, anthropology has focused on how gender roles in different cultures are defined, while the perspective found in the field of linguistics has been on differences in language use by men and women.

Aside from research solely motivated by intellectual curiosity or the linguistic and cognitive aspects of research on gender and language, one of the fundamental issues, in particular from the viewpoint of feminist linguistics, has been the question of 'power' inequality. As we will see in this chapter, one of the most powerful driving forces in this area of research is the fact that language cannot be disassociated from society. The way people use language creates and reflects inequalities in societies through what Bourdieu calls 'habitus'. Socialized norms and thinking are produced through the interplay of past events and current structures (Bourdieu 1977). Therefore, it has been argued that metaphors and other terms that denigrate women create negative concepts associated with femininity and these concepts become the norm through the unconscious use of those linguistic conventions (Bodine 1975). This phenomenon is also seen when people use language defining social status differences including gender, further aggravating and reinforcing inequalities (see e.g. Kramarae 1981; Spender 1980).

Furthermore, there is a general perception in most societies that women are more cooperative, polite and caring while men are more aggressive and competitive (see e.g. Ibraham 1986; Tannen 1993; Horie 1994; Ide 2005; Talbot 2010). These characterizations of men and women extend not only to their behaviour but also to their language. Despite the fact that research has shown that there are many other factors in the way people communicate (see e.g. Eckert and McConnell-Ginet 1998, 2003; Holmes and Meyerhoff 2003; Okamoto and Shibamoto 2004) these associations are automatic and deeply ingrained in many cultures and it is only through more research that such stereotypes can be destroyed and a deeper understanding of how people really use language to 'construct gender' can be achieved. It should be also noted that much of the research that has been carried out over the years has adopted a Western perspective leading some researchers to question its applicability to other cultures (see e.g. Ide 2005).

A similarly important concern of researchers about the relationship between language and gender is that the characteristics of men and women can be 'constructed', 'maintained', and 'reinforced' together with the concepts of 'femininity' and 'masculinity' and that they can be manipulated by a heteronormative ideology (see e.g. Butler 1990). Not only do these dichotomous categories restrain behaviours, they also offer no alternatives for people who do not fit the binary model. As a result, the notion that sexuality can be categorized as a simple dichotomous system is being challenged through new research that brings into view many variables other than gender. Progress has been made though. First, there has been the recognition that many variables which stereotypically pertain to one gender are not gendered in their actual distribution in populations; second, the reappraisal of non-binary sexual categorizations has taken place; and, third, there is the progress that has been achieved through socio-political changes in some societies where legal recognition of gays' and lesbians' rights has been gained (see e.g. Simon and Brooks 2009).

In particular, there has been an increased emphasis on the importance of analysing language and gender within the community or society where it is spoken as each language has particular conventions, expectations and rules to which every speaker is expected to adhere. The inclusion of the concepts of 'culture' or 'communities of practice' in the research is one of the most important developments in the last years. It is particularly important to acknowledge that gender cannot be analysed as an independent factor (see e.g. Okamoto and Shibamoto-Smith 2004). Similarly significant is that gender might not have the same meaning in different communities (Eckert and McConnell-Ginet 1998). This shift is particularly important as it promises to change the prevailing Western bias often found in such research.

2 Different approaches

Research on language, gender, and culture takes three broad approaches. One is the text analysis of linguistic resources such as the use of metaphors that reflect how men and women are portrayed (e.g. Hegstrom and McCarl-Nielsen 2002). It includes the study of, for example, terms of address, professions, and metaphors that show gender stereotypes. In general, it appears that in most cultures men are presented positively or as the norm, whereas females are represented negatively (see e.g. Spender 1980; Nakamura 2004). Horie (1994), for example, reports that in the Thai and Japanese languages women are portrayed as weak, emotional, and stupid (Horie 1994: 320). On the other hand, Hiraga writes that women in metaphors are regarded as a 'commodity' and dehumanized (1991: 55).

The second approach focuses on the linguistic features of many languages in the world that have designated semantic, pragmatic, or lexical elements for the exclusive use of female or male speakers. These languages include Japanese, Thai, Atayal, a number of Australian Aboriginal languages and some American languages, e.g. Karajá–Macro-Je language family, Coasati (Sherzer 1987). Other anthropological–linguistic studies focus on the relationship between language and roles. In some societies, there is a diglossic or bilingual situation where men and women use different language registers while in others, separate languages are used by men and women according to the role they are performing (Kuna (Sherzer 1987)).

The third approach has focused on how conversation or oral communication is conducted with a focus on turn-taking in same and mixed gender conversations. Some of the most influential works are those of Fishman (1978), West (1984), West and Zimmerman (1983), and Zimmerman and West (1975), who argued that women send more backchannels, known as minimal responses, and are more cooperative than men, while men use interruptions and other features to dominate the interaction. Similar studies seem to confirm this trend in other languages (see e.g. Yoshii 1996). It was concluded that women are politer than men, and consequently many studies on women's language are specifically engaged in the area of politeness. These studies have generated three different theories that are used to explain the relationship between gender and language that will be discussed later.

The next sections will examine in detail how these studies have shaped our perception of the link between gender, language, and culture. The first section introduces the various approaches taken by researchers in this area including the ground-breaking paper by Lakoff (1975) and works by other non-Anglo Saxon researchers with similar views on the inequalities created by language. The approaches of language and gender are introduced through a discussion of representative works on various languages and cultures.

The chapter also covers research that has explored the intersection between multilingualism and gender. The concluding section includes a list of unresolved problems and issues that need to be addressed in future research.

3 Historical perspectives

In this section, we will look at the earliest research, all conducted around the same time, on language and gender. Two types of research were conducted. One has a sociolinguistic/ anthropological linguistics base and the other is from a feminist perspective (that developed into three different theories). One of the first published reports available on the English language and gender is that of Jespersen (1922) who wrote that women 'talk too much' and that their sentences are unfinished, thus reinforcing the stereotype of women's language and behaviour as illogical and gossipy. During the years that followed, due to a lack of translations and other limitations in accessing material written in languages other than English, it is difficult to find similar research based on texts from other societies and languages except for some in Japanese. 'Genderlects' in Japanese has generated an enormous interest by linguists since early times; however, these studies have been mostly descriptive in nature (e.g. Kikuzawa 1929; Mashimo 1969) and they have contained evaluative comments that are very similar to Jespersen's. Most importantly, many scholars and educators stipulated how 'women should speak and behave' as early as the seventeenth century (Endo 1997). What is interesting is that despite different ideologies the patriarchally framed results are similar for different cultures.

The work that created the basis for current research directions was Lakoff's (1975) seminal paper, based on observations, which characterizes the language used by women as consultative and cooperative. Women's language, she writes, exhibits a number of features such as the high frequency of hedges, tag questions, modal constructions, qualifiers, and final intonation in statements that indicate lack of confidence. The use of empty adjectives and intensifiers is abundant, but the use of expletives is very low. These observations reinforced the stereotype about women's behaviour, but at the same time it triggered an interest in the actual use of language by women.

It is interesting that a similar work was published in Japan by Akiko Jugaku in 1979. She writes about the close relationship between the Japanese language and the inequalities in a society based on gender stereotypes, which she admits even influence her. By looking at a variety of texts, Jugaku deftly demonstrates the influence of a patriarchal system in Japan and how this system is embodied in almost all aspects of language. She includes modern magazines, songs, television programmes, classical literature, and other forms of Japanese art to show how language 'creates' the concept of 'femininity' (Jugaku 1979). Naturally, it is difficult to know whether Jugaku was influenced by Lakoff's work as it is not acknowledged as a source. However, Jugaku's 1966 publication 'Retorikku: Nihonjin no Hyoogen', with several chapters dedicated to women and language, suggests that her ideas were developed independently. It should be stressed that women's language research in Japan has a very long history even though the earlier focus was on the lexicon or syntax and ignored the social aspects of language use (see e.g. Endo 1997; Reynolds-Akiba 1993; Nakamura 2004).

Lakkof's work in many ways is the foundation of present day research on language and gender. Although Jugaku's work is not known in the West, it is fair to say that at least in Japan, her influence can be strongly felt in feminist research. While it is not the goal of this chapter to discuss the universality of gender differences in language, the fact that these two important works were published on two opposite sides of the Pacific suggests that women's social status in most countries of the world faces similar challenges (see e.g. Atanga *et al.* 2012).

Around the same time, studies that took a sociolinguistic/anthropological linguistic approach were conducted by Labov, Trudgill, and Sherzer. Labov ([1966] 1998) and Trudgill (1972) carried out major projects, looking at differences in speakers' pronunciation. What they found was that women use 'standard' pronunciation more frequently than men regardless of social class. These results further helped to spread the perception that women are more conservative and politer than men as can be seen in the studies of Trudgill (1972), Abu-haidar (1989), etc. It is interesting that a comparable study in Amsterdam yielded similar results (Brouwer 1989); however, the addition of more variables such as education and having children showed that demographic factors do affect the choice of standard language use. Nonetheless, Labov's and Trudgill's studies have been influential in creating the perception that women are more conservative and are conscious of prestige language (although Arabic presents a different case because it is a diglossic society. This will be discussed more in detail below). This phenomenon has been explained in terms of women's lower status in society whereby it is usually women who are in disadvantaged social positions and so they see language as a way to achieve higher status (Brouwer 1989).

The influence of Labov's work can also be observed in research that looked at the use of different languages or varieties of language (High and Low) in different societies. Arabic speaking countries are known for their diglossic situation with the existence of Classic Arabic or Standard Arabic (H) and also colloquial varieties (L) that are all used concurrently. Early studies on Standard Arabic and Colloquial Arabic suggest, contrary to the results by Labov and Trudgill, that men's pronunciation is closer to the more prestigious Standard Arabic (Bakir 1986). Similar studies in other countries where Arabic is spoken seem to confirm this observation (e.g. Egypt, Jordan, Iraqi (Abu-haidar 1989)); however, Ibrahim (1986) contends that it is not possible to compare Classic Arabic to English because Classic Arabic is only acquired through education. Similarly, there are many prestigious colloquial varieties, therefore, to exclusively associate prestige and H variety is untenable. Due to their social situation women in these countries consciously choose the L variety because it carries the most appropriate social connotations. Although these studies were done more than forty years ago, they are an important reminder of the danger for researchers that transferring concepts applicable in one culture or society to another can yield inaccurate results.

A different diglossic situation exists where a different language is used by men and women. This circumstance is closely related to geographical position and intrinsically tied to political and historic developments. In many countries or regions in the world, particularly those that were colonized, more than one language is spoken. One of these languages is considered H (usually the language of the colonizers) and the local language or languages are regarded as L. For example, in many South American countries, Spanish is the H language and Aymara, Quechua, and many other languages are the L language. However, the relative status of these languages is not as clearly demarcated as in other cases because speakers feel a strong sense of identity towards Quechua or Aymara despite the fact that they are aware that knowing and speaking the H language is the key towards social mobility (Howard-Malverde, 1995). Although she mentions it only briefly, Howard-Malverde acknowledges that the diglossic situation of women is closely tied to economic and cultural factors.

Sherzer (1987) reports that in some societies (Kuna Indians of Panama) where gender distinctions are clearly demarcated, verbal genre, speaking roles and patterns of speaking are similarly defined. He stresses the importance of avoiding the ethnocentric view of labelling women's speech as inferior, and that 'gender distinctions in language must be seen in the context of sociological differentiation and cultural framing of which they constitute an integral aspect' (Sherzer 1987: 119). A similar separation of language and gender can be observed in the case of the use of Hungarian and German in a small peasant community in Austria (Gal 1998) where there is a difference between the language used by young women and that used by the rest of the population. Regardless of their networks, it appears that young women prefer to use German as they see their life in the countryside as less attractive than living in the cities. This is in contrast to the young men who prefer to use Hungarian despite the relatively negative evaluation attached to the image of this language. Gal argues that the linguistic choices women make are closely related to their ability to participate in social change.

As noted previously, in some languages the gender of the speaker, or the listener, or both affect the employment of lexicon, syntax, or pragmatic elements. For example, Coasati or Thai speakers will choose a set of words, particles, etc. according to the speaker's gender; while in Arabic the choice will depend on the listener's gender. In Japanese, on the other hand, choices will depend on the gender of both the speaker and the listener. This contrasts with languages such as English, German, or French where neither the speaker's or listener's genders entail obligatory choices (Sherzer 1987). This aspect is of crucial importance in understanding how different cultures and languages perceive the relationship between gender and language (see e.g. Ide 2005).

4 Critical issues and topics

One of the main issues in the present research on language and gender is distribution of power. The focus on gender differences in society originated because of the fact that, almost universally, women have been and are socially disadvantaged. That inequality, many scholars argue, is manifested in language use, whether that is in the way that women are represented; how women speak; or the choices that they make from among many varieties of the language that are available to them.

Another central issue besides power in the research on language, gender and culture, is that language is used to 'construct' and 'reinforce' a hegemonic femininity and masculinity. Three areas are discussed in this section. First, we will look at the linguistic association of particular characteristics in relation to attributes associated with gender. The second area is the speech of men and women in languages that exhibit clear gender differences according to the speaker's or listener's gender. The third concerns the way in which men and women use language to dominate or to show cooperation.

4.1 Linguistic associations with gender

Many scholars agree that a society's language(s) contain(s) key concepts that construct prescriptive models, including gender (Kramarae 1981; Kristeva 1981; Spender 1980). Most languages exhibit gender differences in the lexicon, particularly in the use of metaphors and sayings that associate negative images with women. In languages as diverse as French, Thai, and Chinese, many sayings and metaphors present women in a negative light (Fan 1996; Hiraga 1991). For example, in Thai and Japanese women are usually referred to negatively, in particular, when talking about their unmarried status ('unsetting star' in Thai, 'old miss' in Japanese), or related to virtue and modesty (Horie 1994). Similarly, in character-based languages such as Chinese and Japanese, many stereotypical negative semantic terms are expressed with the character that represents a 'woman' (女) such as jealousy (嫉妬), noisy (姦しい) in Japanese, cunning (ning), wicked, and evil (jian) in Chinese (Fan 1996). Women in metaphors are referred to as 'food' to be consumed, 'objects' to be traded or bought (Hiraga 1997). The fact that similar expressions or metaphors can be found in various languages is a strong indication that many sociocultural values and concepts are alike.

Most importantly, the norm for titles and professional terms are those that apply to men. These terms are another way in which females are discriminated against across cultures. For example, the term minister in French is masculine and only the addition of *madame* renders it acceptable for use in addressing female ministers (van Compernolle 2009). A similar phenomenon is observed in Japanese for job titles like doctor (医師) and painter (画家) an extra character is added in order to refer to female professionals. Accordingly, a female doctor will be referred to as joi (女医) and a painter as joryuugaka (女流画家). The problem with terms and other linguistic issues in which male terms are used as the default is that 'feminization' of these titles is ideologically determined. Thus, it will also influence the particular socio-political and cultural perceptions of men and women.

4.2 Languages with gender differences

Many countries in the world possess lexical, semantic, and pragmatic linguistic choices for men and women. Although some features such as the complex pronominal and honorific systems (Japanese, Javanese, Korean, etc.) might be similar across many Asian languages, it is not possible to say that there is a particular linguistic feature that is common to all of the languages and cultures of the region. Despite some significant linguistic similarities, the languages of each of these countries have developed within divergent political, historical, and social contexts. For example, one of the most famous and most studied languages is Japanese where lexical, grammatical, and semantic choices are determined by the speaker's gender. Speakers can choose personal pronouns, verb ending, sentence final particles, and lexicon according to whether they denote 'masculinity' or 'femininity' (see e.g. Shibamoto 1985). Recent research does, however, point out there is some discrepancy between prescriptive language and real speech (see next section). Thai, Atayal, a number of Australian Aboriginal languages and some South American languages (e.g. the Karajá–Macro-Je language family) also share similar characteristics. Unfortunately, with the exception of the Thai language where a limited number of studies have been done, little is known about them due to the paucity of studies that go beyond descriptive grammars (Horie 1994; Iwasaki and Ingkaphirom 2005).

4.3 Difference or dominance or 'the third wave'

One of the most obvious ways to look at the issue of power in language is through how communication is accomplished. Recall Lakoff's work on the ways 'women speak'. She wrote that women use linguistic strategies such as hedges, that denote insecurity, and also backchannels, that demonstrate a collaborative style. Although these attributes seem to be unrelated, they are often associated with female communicative style. Hedges are used to soften a statement and thus have less imposition whereas the use of backchannels or questions shows the collaborative stance of the listener. How women and men communicate has been the focus of research resulting in three major theories, each with very strong arguments backed by research. The theory of 'difference' has taken hold as central to the disparities between male and female communication. Scholars such as Tannen (1990), Holmes (1995), and Coates (1996) have argued that women and men belong to 'different' cultures and their communication styles are not the same. Therefore, how men and women interpret particular speech acts such as compliments or interruptions or the use of backchannels, for example, are quite different. For women, a compliment exchange is a way of nurturing the friendship and the same is true with the use of backchannels. Men, on the other hand, do not consider using compliments as a way to reinforce a relationship and they do not see interrupting someone as an aggressive act (Maltz and Borker 1982).

The 'dominance' theory represented by Cameron (1992, 1996) and Spender (1980) disagrees with the 'difference' theory which argues that men and women belong to 'different' cultures, and instead, explains language as projecting social inequalities along gender lines. In other words, the way in which language is used reflects the fact that women are subjugated in society. Many studies have shown that women backchannel more often than men (Fishman 1978), that they are interrupted more frequently by men (West and Zimmerman 1983; Zimmerman and West 1984) and that language is used as a tool to subjugate women. The display of control and power in the way that conversation is managed was also demonstrated by this research.

However, many researchers have disputed both theories on the grounds that first, there are many other variables than gender that affect language use and that second, there is a problem in trying to transpose Anglo-centric concepts to other cultures. This movement gave rise to the 'third wave' theory in which the focus of research is on how language is used in every each community. The theory employed by researchers subscribing to the 'third wave' theory has introduced the concept of 'communities of practice'. It also challenges the dichotomous concept of gender, arguing that differences cannot be captured in simple binary terms (see e.g. Bing and Bergvall 1996; Freed and Greenwood 1996; Cameron 1997; Eckert and McConnell-Ginet 1998; Goodwin 1990; Weatherall 2002; Mills 2003; Mendoza-Denton 2008). In recent years, some researchers have started to look at the relevance of gender in interactions. The proponents of this new feminist Conversation Analysis (CA) share the view with 'third wave' scholars that gender is constructed and that it can be observed in social interaction. CA methodology is used to analyse talk and observe how and whether gender is relevant for interlocutors in a given interaction (Stokoe 2000; Kitzinger 2002). Feminist CA makes no assumptions or correlations between gender and the individual. Rather, they aim to discover interlocutors 'doing gender' situationally and interactionally (Stokoe 2000).

5 Current contributions and research

Research on language and gender has continued to develop and grow with many researchers including factors such as class or culture in their analysis. Embracing the 'third wave' theory has resulted in focusing on neglected settings, other languages of the world, men, lesbians, gays, and transsexuals. The great majority of past studies were based on urban middle-class women's language in America and Europe. However, after the 'third wave' theory, researchers have re-focused their studies on women from other social classes, from non-urban areas, from minorities and in different types of interactions. To cite a few examples, even in Japanese, characterized by clear gender differences, women in rural areas, where many dialects do not have honorifics, speak quite differently when compared to those who speak the official national language and therefore they do not follow the prescriptive model of 'women's language' (Sunaoshi 2004; Kumagai 2011).

Other studies analyse the speech of women at work presenting a fascinating array of findings. In 'institutional' settings, the language of women and men has been analysed yielding interesting and conflicting results, but most reveal that being female does not guarantee a 'cooperative' style of communication. On the one hand, the works of Winter (1993) and Kottoff (1997) suggest that women's stance is more cooperative on Australian television (Winter 1993) and that the dominance of males in debates on German television reinforce the asymmetry of power (Kottoff 1997). On the other hand, Johnson's (1996) study on New Zealand television and Tanaka's (2004, 2006) on Japanese television suggest that women's interviewing styles cannot always be automatically associated with a particular stance. Holmes and her associates (Holmes and Meyerhoff 2003; Holmes and Stubbe 2003; Holmes and Marra 2004) have looked at the language used in New Zealand workplaces focusing on what they call relational practice, a way of communication that looks for the 'face' needs of participants, serves to achieve workplace goals, and is regarded as dispensable. This practice, expressed in linguistic acts such as small talk, humour, and other moves that denote a collaborative stance, is closely associated with a female style of communication but is also used by men. However, because it is not the 'official' talk and because it is associated with female talk, it tends to be 'erased'. These researchers warn that their findings are from a particular community of practice and so may not be transferable.

Another area which has been closely related to gender and language is the study of politeness. Due to the association of women's language with cooperation and cooperativeness, there has been a quasi-automatic focus on politeness. In particular, this phenomenon has been observed in Japanese, a language that is renowned for its complex system of honorifics and different speech levels (Ide 1982; Endo 1997). However, recent studies demonstrate that linguistic politeness is more closely related to occupational roles than to biological gender (Takano 2000) and the relationship between politeness and gender is much more complicated than a simple equation of politeness and women's language would suggest (Mills 2003; Okamoto 2004).

Female minorities have also been studied in the last years, in particular in relation to transnational migration. Studies in relation to the gender roles of immigrant communities and their language acquisition and maintenance are abundant. To illustrate, Gordon's study of Lao women in the United States encapsulates the numerous issues with which many scholars deal. These are not only related to ESL learning and language resources, but also to the various challenges that migrants and educators face because of Lao men's loss of traditional roles and women's new-found independence (Gordon 2004). Other studies look at migrants in America, including work by Mendoza-Denton (2008) who focuses on Latina youth gangs. This is an ethnographic study of a group of school students in San Francisco that reveals how different and diverse the subcultures are in one single school. It also shows how the dynamics of the relations between the students within their communities are affected by many factors, which will eventually determine how these students identify themselves using English or Spanish. In particular, it is interesting to see that the female youth gang members in this school use a number of innovative discourse markers in their speech.

Research on language and gender has also started to incorporate the language of men and how masculinity is created. Topics related to men tend to involve talking about sports as it is one of the most visible ways in which hegemonic masculinity is constructed. The earliest works on male language were written by Johnson and Meinhoff (1997) Cameron (1998), and Kuiper (1998). Cameron (1998) demonstrates that male communicative styles do not conform to a stereotypical 'competitive' and 'aggressive' stance but rather exhibit many of the features characterized as feminine. Part of Kuiper's study (1998) is based on men's talk in a rugby football players' locker room which describes how solidarity is constructed through the use of sexually degrading language about women. The use of 'offensive' language or swearing and boasting is also shown in the work of Coates (2003) on men's language who argues that 'hegemonic' masculinity is recreated in all-male conversations. A similar study on Japanese male language is reported by SturtzSreetharan (2004) who examined the speech of men from two different regions. She writes that although the men in her study do not use the conventional 'male' linguistic particles, they do use language to create camaraderie, authority, vulgarity and male linguistic forms 'beyond and within their ideological uses' (SturtzSreetharan 2004: 286). Her research is one of the few linguistic studies that focuses on the speech of Japanese men who use a regional language.

Other works have started to look at the language of other sex groups, or queer language, including gays, lesbians, transgenders, and transsexuals. One of the earliest works on queer language is the volume edited by Livia and Hall (1997), spanning contemporary practices to historical texts, which contains chapters on the language of lesbians and gays from countries as diverse as France, Japan, India, and America. The constraints of space in this chapter do not allow for a detailed description of this material; however, it should be stressed that this volume was revolutionary in that it promoted a 'queer theory' that could account for the linguistic practices of those who do not fit the hegemonic dichotomy that associates sex and gender. The fact that the binary gender model has always been transgressed can be seen in many of the terms that exist in some of the Asian countries such as Thai (*kathoey* for drag queen), India (*hijra* male of female gender), and Japan (e.g. *okama* for gays).

Maree's (2003) study is based on a documentary on Japanese *onabe* (transsexuals) studies and their language choices stressing the importance of context in the analysis of gender indexing, such as in the use of personal pronouns and other linguistic elements. More recently, Abe (2010) has published a volume on Japanese queer language based on a variety of texts such as advice columns, talk in lesbian bars, and discourse in the media and theatre. *Oneekotoba* (gay speech) used by gays in Tokyo functions not only as an in-group marker, but, depending on each speaker's circumstances, might also be used as a means of learning standard Japanese, in particular by regional dialect speakers who have a strong accent. Others use *oneekotoba* to criticize or admonish because it has some 'traditionally feminine' linguistic items, and therefore sounds softer and more polite. Similarly, it is used in combination with very rough words, where its use is playful in manner. In contrast, studies by Hall and O'Donnovan (1996) illustrate a very different picture of the Indian *hijra*, who are sexually considered as transgendered but are brought up as men. Due to a strong bias against them, they are forced to join the *hijra* community where they opt to wear a sari and learn to speak women's language. It is interesting that *hijras* comment that using female indexed words becomes a habit (Hall and O'Donnovan 1996: 243). It is also interesting that *hijra* can switch to male or female speech and do this strategically.

There are also a number of scholars who have critically analysed written texts in light of how gender stereotypes are reproduced – for instance, analysis of magazines for young women demonstrates how images of 'femininity' and 'masculinity' are presented in ways that reinforce stereotypes (e.g. Goffman 1979; Grant and Millard 2006; Santaemilia 2009). Other texts such as newspapers, articles in news magazines, or legal documents are a powerful medium where language is used to directly or indirectly to create expectations and socially accepted behaviour and identities (including gender). For example, Santaemilia (2009) has analysed Spanish newspapers, pastoral documents and other texts to show there is a tension between the majority's acceptance of gay marriage and the conservatism of the clergy and political movements on the right. On the other hand, Inoue's (2006) book explores the complex relationship between the ideologies of the state and the construction of 'women's language'. Inoue uses diverse texts from the beginning of the twentieth century and shows how many linguistic items in Japanese 'women's language' were part of the speech style of a particular group of high school girls. Though presently their speech is considered feminine, their language at that time was considered vulgar and criticized by scholars and the media.

6 Future directions

This chapter has presented diverse studies on language, gender, and culture. While the studies considered are only a selection from the vast available literature, they serve to give an overview of the field and introduce concepts pertinent to future discussions. The research demonstrates that as researchers we should not make automatic associations of particular linguistic styles with either females or males without taking into account the context where that language is used. Similarly, the traditional dichotomous categories of 'men' and 'women' are untenable for analysing language and gender. For example, we must be aware of the fluidity of gender established by the many studies on queer language.

Despite of the sheer number of studies on this topic, it is clear that many cultures and languages are under-represented. In particular, research needs to be carried out in communities where gender differences are embedded in formal elements of the language such as Thai, or Aboriginal languages. In the case of Aboriginal languages, factors such as influence of the mainstream Australian perceptions of sexuality would need to be considered. Due to more pressing problems in relation to language such as the future of endangered languages, their survival, language planning, and so on, research on language and gender in South America, Africa, and parts of Asia is as yet extremely limited. Not knowing if, and how, gender differences are shared by all cultures and languages limits our understanding and knowledge about ourselves.

Related topics

language, culture and politeness; language, culture, and sociolinguistics

Further reading

Holmes, J. and Meyerhoff, M. (2003) *The Handbook of Language and Gender*, Oxford: Blackwell. (This edited volume covers essential theoretical works on language and gender and feminist literature. For methodologies, see Bucholtz, 'Theories of discourse as theories of gender: Discourse analysis in language and gender studies', pp. 43–68.)

Inoue, Miyako (2006) *Vicarious Language: Gender and Linguistic Modernity in Japan*, Berkeley, CA: University of California Press. (An excellent book on the complex relationship between language, gender and ideology in modern Japan.)

Livia, Anna and Hall, Kira (1997) *Queerly Phrased: Language, Gender and Sexuality*, Oxford: Oxford University Press. (This edited book contains chapters as diverse as from lesbian language to Internet communication.)

Mendoza-Denton, Norma (2008) *Homegirls: Language and Cultural Practice among Latina Youth Gangs*, Oxford: Blackwell. (An ethnographic study of Mexican/American young girls, their language choices, identity and gender.)

Note

I would like to thank Prof. Farzad Sharifian, Dr Peter Eglin, and an anonymous reviewer for their comments and suggestions that have greatly improved this chapter.

References

Abe, H. (2010) *Queer Japanese: Gender and Sexual Identities through Linguistic Practices*, New York: Palgrave Macmillan.

Abu-haidar, F. (1989) 'Are Iraqi women more prestige conscious than men? Sex differentiation in Baghdadi Arabic', *Language in Society* 18: 471–81.

Atanga, L., S. E. Ellece, L. Litosseliti, and J. Sunderland (2012) 'Gender and language in sub-Saharan African contexts: Issues and challenges', *Gender and Language* 6(1): 1–20.

Bakir, M. (1986) 'Sex differences in the approximation to standard Arabic: A case study', *Anthropological Linguistics* 28(1): 3–9.

Bing, J. and V. Bergvall (1996) 'The question of questions: Beyond binary thinking', in V. Bergvall, J. Bing, and A. Freed (eds), *Rethinking Language and Gender Research: Theory and Practice*, London: Longman, pp. 1–29.

Bodine, A. (1975) 'Androcentrism in prescriptive grammar: Singular "they", sex-indefinite "he", and "he or she"', *Language in Society* 4: 129–46.

Bourdieu, P. (1977) 'The economics of linguistic exchanges', *Social Science Information* 16(6): 648–68.

Brouwer, D. (1989) *Gender Variation in Dutch: A Sociolinguistic Study of Amsterdam Speech*, Dordrecht/Providence: Foris.

Butler, J. (1990) *Gender Trouble*, New York: Routledge.

Cameron, D. (1992) *Feminism and Linguistic Theory*, London: Macmillan Press.

——(1996) 'The language–gender interface: Challenging co-optation', in V. Bergvall, J. Bing, and A. Freed (eds), *Rethinking Language and Gender Research: Theory and Practice*, London: Longman, pp. 31–53.

——(1997) 'Theoretical debates in feminist linguistics: Questions of sex and gender', in R. Wodak (ed.), *Gender and Discourse*, Thousand Oaks, CA: Sage, pp. 21–36.

——(1998) 'Performing gender identity: Young men's talk and the construction of heterosexual masculinity', in J. Coates (ed.), *Language and Gender: A Reader*, Oxford: Blackwell, pp. 270–84.

Coates, J. (1996) *Women Talk*, Oxford: Blackwell.

——(2003) *Men Talk*, Oxford: Blackwell.

Eckert, P. and S. McConnell-Ginet (2003) *Language and Gender*, Cambridge: Cambridge University Press.

——(1998) 'Communities of practice: Where language, gender, and power all live', in J. Coates (ed.), *Language and Gender*, Oxford: Blackwell, pp. 484–94.

Endo, O. (1997) *Onna no kotoba no bunkashi*, Tokyo: Gakuyoo Shobo.

Fan, C. (1996) 'Language, gender and Chinese culture', *International Journal of Politics, Culture and Society* 10(1): 95–114.

Fishman, P. (1978) 'Interaction: The work women do', *Social Problems* 258: 397–406.

Freed, A. and A. Greenwood (1996) 'Women, men, and type of talk: What makes the difference?' *Language in Society* 25: 1–26.

Gal, S. (1998) 'Peasant men can't get wives: Language change and sex roles in a bilingual community', in J. Coates (ed.), *Language and Gender: A Reader*, Oxford: Blackwell, pp. 147–60.

Goffman, E. (1979) *Gender Advertisements*, New York: Harper & Row.

Goodwin, M. (1990) *He Said She Said: Talk as Social Interaction among Black Children*, Bloomington, IN: Indiana University Press.

Gordon, D. (2004) '"I'm tired. You clean and cook": Shifting gender identities and second language socialization', *TESOL Quarterly* 38(3): 437–57.

Grant, P. and E. J. Millard (2006) 'The stereotypes of black and white women in fashion magazine photographs: The pose of the model and the impression she creates', *Sex Roles* 54 (9–10): 659–73.

Hall, K. and V. O'Donnovan (1996) 'Shifting gender positions among Hindi-speaking Hijras', in V. Bergvall, J. Bing, and A. Freed (eds), *Rethinking Language and Gender Research: Theory and Practice*, London: Longman, pp. 228–66.

Hegstrom, J. L. and J. McCarl-Nielsen (2002) 'Gender and metaphor: Descriptions of familiar persons', *Discourse Processes* 3(3): 219–34

Hiraga, M. (1991) 'Metaphors Japanese women live by', *Working Papers on Language, Gender and Sexism* 1(1): 38–57.

Holmes, J. (1995) *Women, Men and Politeness*, London and New York: Longman.

Holmes, J. and M. Marra (2004) 'Relational practice in the workplace: Women's talk or gendered discourse?', *Language in Society* 33(3): 377–98.

Holmes, J. and M. Meyerhoff (2003) 'Different voices, different view: An introduction', in J. Holmes and M. Meyerhoff (eds), *The Handbook of Language and Gender*, Oxford: Blackwell, pp.1–18.

Holmes, J. and M. Stubbe (2003) '"Feminine" workplaces: Stereotypes and reality', in J. Holmes and M. Meyerhoff (eds), *The Handbook of Language and Gender*, Oxford: Blackwell, pp. 573–99.

Horie, P. (1994) 'How language reflects the status of women in the Thai and Japanese societies', in M. Bucholtz, A. C. Ling, J. Sutton, and C. Hines (eds), *Cultural Performances. Proceedings 3rd Berkeley Women and Language Conference*, pp. 313–21.

Howard-Malverde, R. (1995) 'Pachamama is a Spanish word: Linguistic tension between Quechua, Aymara and Spanish in Northern Potosi (Bolivia)', *Anthropological Linguistics* 37(2): 141–68.

Ibrahim, M. H. (1986) 'Standard and prestige language: A problem in Arabian sociolinguistics', *Anthropological Linguistics* 28(1): 115–26.

Ide, S. (1982) 'Japanese sociolinguistics: Politeness and women's language', *Lingua* 57: 357–85.

——(2005) 'How and why honorifics can signify dignity and elegance: The indexicality and reflexivity of linguistic rituals', in R. T. Lakoff and S. Ide (eds), *Broadening the Horizon of Linguistic Politeness*, Amsterdam: John Benjamins, pp. 45–64.

Inoue, M. (2006) *Vicarious Language*, Berkeley, CA: University of California Press.

Iwasaki, S. and P. Ingkaphirom (2005) *A Reference Grammar of Thai*, Cambridge: Cambridge University Press.

Jespersen, O. (1922) *Language: Its Nature, Development and Origin*, London: Allen and Unwin, pp. 237–54.

Johnson, G. (1996) 'The management of interaction in the television interviews of Maggie Barry', *Wellington Working Papers in Linguistics* 8: 25–53.

Johnson, S. and U. Meinhoff (1997) *Language and Masculinity*, Oxford: Blackwell.

Jugaku, A. (1966) *Retorikku: Nihonjin no Hyoogen*, Tokyo, Kyobunsha.

——(1979) *Nihongo to onna*, Tokyo: Iwanami.

Kikuzawa, S. (1929) 'Fujin no kotoba no tokuchoo ni tsuite', *Kokugo Kyoiku*, pp. 14(3): 66–75.

Kitzinger, C. (2002) 'Doing feminist conversation analysis', in P. McIlvenny (ed.), *Talking Gender and Sexuality*, Amsterdam: John Benjamins, pp. 49–77.

Kramarae, C. (1981) *Women and Men Speaking: Frameworks for Analysis*, Rowley, MA: Newbury House.

Kottoff, H. (1997) 'The interactional achievement of expert status', in H. Kottoff and R. Wodak (eds), *Communicating Gender in Context*, Amsterdam: John Benjamins, pp. 139–78.

Kristeva, J. (1981) 'Women's time', *Signs* 7(1): 13–35.

Kuiper, K. (1998) 'Sporting formulae in New Zealand English: Two models of male solidarity', in J. Coates (ed.), *Language and Gender: A Reader*, Oxford: Blackwell, pp. 285–93.

Kumagai, S. (2011) 'Tohoku dialects as a speech of rednecks: Language crossing in Japanese TV programs', *Studies in Humanities* 61(1–2): 153–69.

Labov, W. ([1966]1998), 'The interaction of sex and social class in the course of linguistic change', *Language Variation and Change* 2: 205–54. Reprinted in J. Cheshire and P. Trudgill (eds), *The Sociolinguistics Reader, Volume 2: Gender and Discourse*, London: Arnold, pp. 7–52.

Lakoff, R. (1975) *Language and Woman's Place*, New York: Harper and Row.

Livia, A. and K. Hall (1997) *Queerly Phrased: Language, Gender and Sexuality*, New York and Oxford: Oxford University Press.

Maltz, D. and R. Borker (1982) 'A cultural approach to male–female miscommunication', in J. Gumperz (ed.), *Language and Social Identity*, Cambridge: Cambridge University Press, pp. 196–216.

Maree, C. (2003) 'Ore wa ore dakara: A study of gender and language in the documentary *Shinjuku Boys*', *Intersections: Gender, History and Culture in the Asian Context*, 9.

Mashimo, S. (1969) *Fujingo no kenkyuu*, Tokyo: Tokyodo Shuppan.

Mendoza-Denton, N. (2008) *Homegirls: Language and Cultural Practice among Latina Youth Gangs*, Oxford: Blackwell.

Mills, S. (2003) *Gender and Politeness*, Cambridge: Cambridge University Press.

Nakamura, M. (2004) *Kotoba to fueminizumu*, Tokyo: Keiso Shobo.

Okamoto, S. and J. Shibamoto-Smith (2004) *Japanese Language, Gender and Ideology*, Oxford: Oxford University Press.

Okamoto, S. (2004) 'Ideology in linguistic practice and analysis: gender and politeness in Japanese revisited', in S. Okamoto and J. Shibamoto-Smith (eds), *Japanese Language, Gender and Ideology*, Oxford: Oxford University Press, pp. 38–56.

Reynolds-Akiba, K. (ed.), (1993) *Onna to Nihongo*, Tokyo: Yuushindo.

Romaine, S. (2003) 'Variation in language and gender', in J. Holmes and M. Meyerhoff (eds), *The Handbook of Language and Gender*, Oxford: Blackwell, pp. 98–118.

Santaemilia, J. (2009) '"It's unfair to be a second-class citizen because of love": The legal, sexual, discursive struggles over "gay" marriages in Spain', in J. de Bres, J. Holmes, and M. Marra (eds), *Proceedings of the 5th Biennial IGALA Conference*, pp. 317–28.

Shibamoto, J. (1985) *Japanese Women's Language*, New York: Academic Press.

Sherzer, J. (1987) 'A diversity of voices: men's and women's speech in ethnographic perspective', in S. Philips, S. Steele and C. Tang (eds), *Language, Gender and Sex in Comparative Perspective*, Cambridge: Cambridge University Press, pp. 95–120.

Simon, R. and A. Brooks (2009) *Gay and Lesbian Communities the World Over*, Plymouth: Lexington Books.

Spender, D. (1980) *Man Made Language*, London: Routledge and Kegan Paul.

Stokoe, E. (2000) 'Toward a conversation analylitic approach to gender and discourse', *Feminism and Psychology* 10: 552–63.

StrutzSreetharan, C. (2004) 'Japanese men's linguistic stereotypes and realities: Conversations from the Kansai and Kanto regions', in S. Okamoto and J. Shimaboto-Smith (eds), *Japanese Language, Gender and Ideology*, Oxford: Oxford University Press, pp. 275–289.

Sunaoshi, Y. (2004) 'Farm women's professional discourse in Ibaraki', in S. Okamoto and J. Shimaboto-Smith (eds), *Japanese Language, Gender and Ideology*, Oxford: Oxford University Press, pp.187–204.

Takano, S. (2005) 'Re-examining linguistic power: Strategic uses of directives by professional Japanese women in positions of authority and leadership', *Journal of Pragmatics* 37: 633–66.

Talbot, M. (2010) *Language and Gender*, Cambridge, MA: Polity.

Tanaka, L. (2004) *Gender, Language and Culture: A Study of Japanese Television Interview Discourse*, Amsterdam: John Benjamins.

——(2009) 'Communicative stances in Japanese interviews: Gender differences in formal interactions', *Language and Communication* 9(4): 207–404.

Tannen, D. (1990) *You Just Don't Understand*, New York: Morrow.

——(ed.) (1993) *Gender and Conversational Interaction*, Oxford: Oxford University Press.

Trudgill, P. (1972) 'Sex, covert prestige, and linguistic change in the urban British English of Norwich', *Language in Society* 1: 179–95.

van Compernolle, R. (2009) 'What do women want? Linguistic equality and the feminization of job titles in contemporary France', *Gender and Language* 3(1): 33–52.

Weatherall, A. (2002) *Gender, Language and Discourse*, London, Routledge.

West, C. (1984) 'When the doctor is a "lady": Power, status and gender in physician–patient encounters', *Symbolic Interaction* 7: 87–106.

West, C. and D. Zimmerman (1983) 'Small insults: A study of interruptions in cross-sex conversations between unacquainted persons', in B Thorne, C. Kramarae, and N. Henley (eds), *Language, Gender and Society*, Rowley, MA: Newbury House, pp. 86–111.

Winter, J. (1993) 'Gender and the political interview in an Australian context', *Journal of Pragmatics* 20: 117–39.

Yoshii, H. (1996) 'Otoko ga onna o saegiru toki: Nichijoo kaiwa no kenryoku soochi', in T. Yamada and H. Yoshii (eds), *Haijoo to sabetsu no esunomesodorojii*, Tokyo: Shinyoosha, pp. 213–50.

Zimmerman, D. and C. West (1975) 'Sex roles, interruptions and silences in conversation', in B. Thorne and N. Henley (eds), *Language and Sex: Difference and Dominance*, Rowley, MA: Newbury House, pp. 105–29.

8

LANGUAGE, CULTURE, AND CONTEXT

Istvan Kecskes

1 Introduction

This chapter aims to discuss the relationship between language and culture from the perspective of context. In my research I have argued that native-like knowledge of language can be determined as knowing preferred ways of saying things and preferred ways of organizing thoughts (Kecskes 2007a, 2010, 2013, see also Wray 2002). How do these 'preferred ways' come about? Speech community members develop unique ways of using the linguistic code with other members of the same community. In this system the selection of certain words or expressions are preferable when expressing certain phenomena like 'shoot a film', 'dust the furniture', 'make love', and so on. It is also desirable to say certain things in particular speech situations such as 'help yourself' at the table, 'welcome aboard' when greeting a new employee, 'be my guest' when answering a request, 'stick around' when asking someone to stay and the like. We also feel that we need to mitigate our criticism toward someone so we start the conversation like 'not that I cannot understand your act, but … '. If we ask for clarification we often say 'what's your point? … ', 'please make your point … why don't you make clear what your point is?' And so on and so forth, we could continue to demonstrate how conventionalized language use is.

Let me make clear what my point is. I think these 'preferred ways' are culture and language specific. They reflect the ways of thinking of speech community members about the world, their environment and their contexts. This is why it is difficult to learn another language.

That language also reflects the ways members of another speech community think about the world, their environment and their contexts. However, that is another speech community, not ours. Even if reoccurring contexts are similar, the way we lexicalize them differs to a great extent. For instance, in American English we usually ask someone to dance saying 'Would you like to dance?' or even 'Wanna dance?'. In Hungarian culture in the same situation we ask 'Szabad?' ['free'], which is a word that functions as a marker to ask for permission in the sense 'are you free to dance?'. Guests are equally valued in American, French, and Hungarian society. But lexical expressions that are used to welcome them demonstrate interesting differences:

(1)   English: Make yourself at home.
   French: Faites comme chez vous. ('Do as [you do] at home'.)
   Hungarian: Érezze magat otthon. ('Feel yourself at home'.)

Although these expressions can be considered as functional equivalents, the use of different verbs (French 'faites' is the imperative of the French equivalent of 'to do', and the Hungarian 'érezd' is the imperative of the Hungarian equivalent of 'feel') shows that each language highlights something else as important in one and the same situation. As Sapir wrote in 1929: 'No two languages are ever sufficiently similar to be considered as representing the same social reality' (Mandelbaum 1949: 162).

   These examples demonstrate very well how language, culture, and context are intertwined. Culture is the originator. Both language and context are rooted in culture, and they both are 'carriers' of culture and both reflect culture but in a different way. A part of culture is encoded in the language. What is encoded in language is past experience with different contexts while actual situational context represents actual, present experience. Gumperz (1982) said that utterances somehow carry with them their own context or project a context. Referring to Gumperz's work, Levinson (2003) claimed that the message-versus-context opposition is misleading because the message can carry with it or forecast the context. So language and context are inseparable. They are each other's contexts. The only question is which side (coded or actual) becomes dominant in a particular segment of speech, conversation, or dialogue. When getting into a speech scenario or situation (context) members of a speech community are usually able to anticipate the kinds of meaning that will be exchanged. Based on their prior experience in similar situations (contexts) they will, to some extent, be able to predict what their communicative partners are going to say (Halliday and Hasan 1985). Scollon and Scollon (2001) were right when they said that people who share the same background knowledge will have better chances of understanding one another than interlocutors who do not. Living in the same speech community enables members to share preferred ways of saying things and organizing thoughts. In what follows I will examine this complex relationship of culture, language, and context.

2 Culture

Culture in intercultural pragmatics (Kecskes 2013) is seen as a socially constituted set of various kinds of knowledge structures that individuals turn to as relevant situations permit, enable, and usually encourage. It is a system of shared beliefs, norms, values, customs, behaviours, and artefacts that the members of society use to cope with their world and with one another (Bates and Plog 1980: 6). It is an important characteristic of culture that it is differentially distributed, and that not all the members of a given social and/or cultural group adopt, live, or reflect their relatively common culture in a similar way in every moment and every life circumstance, nor do all members of the same social and/or cultural group demonstrate the same feeling of identification (see Benedict 1967; Durkheim 1982). Culture has fuzzy boundaries, and it is considered neither relatively static nor ever-changing, but both. It has both a priori and emergent features. Culture changes both diachronically (slowly through decades) and synchronically (emerges on the spot, in the moment of speech). This is where my approach may differ from the (current) mainstream way of thinking about culture, which insists on the contingent, situational, and emergent nature of cultural phenomena in speech and emphasizes that culture in no way imposes ethnic or cultural characteristics onto the communicative behaviour a priori (e.g. Blommaert 1991; Gumperz 1982, Gumperz and Roberts 1991; Rampton 1995). I argue that this approach is just as one-sided as the one that considers culture relatively static and sees a linear connection between 'culture' and 'communication' (see Knapp and Knapp-Potthoff 1987: 3). The nationality or ethnic membership of people may suggest the possibility of ethnic or cultural marking in communicative behaviour. However, in the actual situational context intercultures are co-constructed, and this process may contain elements from the participants' existing cultural background and ad hoc created elements as well. This dialectical and dynamic approach to culture is what intercultural pragmatics promotes (Kecskes 2012, 2013).

Bi and multilingual speakers have two or more languages in their mind. Whichever language channel they use for expressing their thoughts they experience both constraints and triggers originating in two or more languages. Language functions not only as a restrictive device but also as an initiator and supporter of idea/thought formulation. It channels thoughts into linguistic signs by formulating utterances, and at the same time helps the speaker shape his/her thoughts by 'offering' several linguistic options. Slobin (1996) argued that language is a transmitter of real-world experiences, and that these experiences are filtered through language into verbalized events. A bi or multilingual speaker has two or more transmitters. Why is this important?

Croft and Woods argued that 'it is not the case that any time we think we must conceptualize our experience the way that our language requires us to. But it is the case that any time we express our thoughts in language, we must conceptualize our experience in the way that our language requires us to. Cognition may be linguistically neutral, but language is not semantically neutral' (2000: 55). Slobin (1991) also made a similar point when he described 'thinking for speaking' as the appropriate domain for the influence of language on thought. Here it is important to emphasize the difference between *what we do* and *how we do it*. *What we do* may have more universal features than *how we do it*. For instance, I can be polite both in English and German but the linguistic means each language allows me to use differ to a great extent. If one language has fewer tools to express certain functions and features than another one, this does not mean that speakers of that language are less developed in any way. It is just that, for instance, Germans are polite in a different way than Americans are. But they have all the means they need to be polite the way their communalities require them to. If societal, communal needs change their language will adjust to the new circumstances and develop new or different means to express politeness.

Life and interaction with the world shapes our thoughts and language. What people of a language community find important to be expressed in their life will definitely be expressed in that language. However, this is a two-way street because the ever-changing code will also impose some requirements on us as speakers. Language is like a channel through which you must pull your ideas. Nobody denies that there is thinking without language. However, the developmental span through which an infant can get access to a huge amount of knowledge is, to a great extent, facilitated by mechanisms through which language helps us construct the incredibly complex knowledge systems we have. Consequently, a weak version of Whorfianism is in place when we talk about intercultural interaction.

Cultural expectations and phenomena that members of a speech community attend to are the main variables that motivate the use of available linguistic means. Roman Jakobson (1959: 236) pointed out a crucial fact about differences between languages in a pithy maxim: 'Languages differ essentially in what they must convey and not in what they may convey.' This claim offers us the key to unlocking the real force of language. If different languages affect our minds in different ways, it is not because of what our language allows us to think but rather because of what that language habitually obliges us to think about. *It is the 'habitual' (or better to say customary) that culture builds into language use.* This 'habitual' and/or 'customary' is what connects language and context through culture. 'Habitual and/or customary' can be a scenario, an actual situational context, and 'habitual and/or customary' is also encoded in the lexical items, which gives their dictionary meaning based on their general use in a given speech community. This is why we need to pay special attention to prior context (encoded in language) and actual situational context specifying meaning of linguistic signs used in that context.

3 How does context relate to language and culture?

The term 'context' is used in many different ways. The *Concise Oxford English Dictionary* defines context in the following way:

- the circumstances that form the setting for an event, statement, or idea,
- the parts that immediately precede and follow a word or passage and clarify its meaning

The first part of the definition refers to what we can call scenario or extra-linguistic context, while the second part refers to the linguistic context, that is to say, elements of language that either precede or follow a word, expression, or larger lexical unit. However, this is only one side of context. I usually refer to this side of context as 'actual situational context' that combines linguistic and extra-linguistic factors. This is basically similar to the definition that is used in linguistics: context usually refers to any factor – linguistic, epistemic, physical, social, etc. – that affects the actual interpretation of signs and expressions. My problem with this definition is that it refers only to 'actual situational context' and there is no mention about 'prior context' encoded in the lexical items that we use in communication.

3.1 Context as declarative and procedural knowledge

The socio-cognitive approach (Kecskes 2008, 2010, 2013) argues that context is a dynamic construct that appears in different formats in language use both as a repository and/or trigger of knowledge. Consequently, it has both a selective and a constitutive role. Several current theories of meaning (e.g. Coulson 2000; Croft 2000; Evans 2006) claim that meaning construction is primarily dependent on actual situational contexts. The socio-cognitive approach (SCA), however, claims that the meaning values of linguistic expressions, encapsulating prior contexts of experience, play as important a role in meaning construction and comprehension as actual situational context. What SCA attempts to do is to bring together individual cognition with situated cognition. It recognizes the importance of an individual's background and biases (prior context) in information processing (Finkelstein, Hambrick, and Cannella, 2008; Starbuck and Milliken 1988), but at the same time it also suggests that the context in which individuals are situated is equally strong enough to direct attention and shape interpretation (Elsbach *et al.* 2005; Ocasio 1997). In other words, the context in which individuals are located has a major effect on what they notice and interpret as well as the actions they take.

Context represents two sides of world knowledge: one that is in our mind (prior context) and the other (actual situational context) that is out there in the world (Kecskes 2008). These two sides are interwoven and inseparable. Actual situational context is viewed through prior context, and vice versa, prior context is viewed through actual situational context when communication occurs. Their encounter creates a third space. According to this approach, meaning is the result of the interplay of prior experience and current, actual situational experience. Prior experience that becomes declarative knowledge is tied to the meaning values of lexical units constituting utterances produced by interlocutors, while current experience is represented in the actual situational context (procedural knowledge) in which communication takes place, and which is interpreted (often differently) by interlocutors. Meaning formally expressed in the utterance is co-constructed online as a result of the interaction and mutual influence of the private contexts represented in the language of interlocutors and the actual situational context interpreted by interlocutors.

According to the traditional view truth conditions may be ascribed to a sentence (of an idealized language), independently of any contextual considerations. The opposing pragmatic view says that a sentence has complete truth conditions only in context. The semantic interpretation of utterances, in other words the propositions they express, their truth conditions, is the result of *pragmatic processes of expansion and contextual enrichment*. The followers of the semantic view may not be right when they think that any linguistic sign can be independent of any contextual considerations. No linguistic sign or expression can be independent of context because they carry context (prior context), they encode the history of their prior use (prior context) in a speech community. The supporters of the pragmatic view may be wrong when they do not emphasize that expansion and contextual enrichment are the results of the individual's prior experience. Suffice it to say that both sides appear to be mistaken to some extent because they talk about *context* without making a distinction between its two sides: *prior context* and *actual situational context*. The proposition literally expressed (sentence meaning) is the result of collective prior experience of speakers of a given speech community. This is expanded and/or enriched by prior experience, present situational experience and/or need of a concrete speaker when s/he uses that utterance (speaker's meaning). The speaker privatizes the collective experience by enhancing/enriching the content with his private experience. Inferred meaning (implicature) is the reflection of the interplay between prior experience of the speaker and prior experience of the hearer in an actual situational context. Prior context as understood in the socio-cognitive paradigm is declarative knowledge while actual situational context represents procedural knowledge. Anne Bezuidenhout (2004) claimed that parallels exist between the declarative–procedural divide, the semantics–pragmatics interface and the competence–performance distinction. She proposed that a clear-cut distinction must be made between procedural knowledge, which belongs to the performance system and is pragmatic, on one hand, and lexical conceptual knowledge, which belongs to the competence system and is semantic, on the other. This is in line with what the SCA claims: lexical conceptual knowledge is the basis for prior context that is encapsulated in the lexical items while procedural knowledge, which is pragmatic, is triggered by the actual situational context. Example (4) demonstrates how context (in the traditional sense of the term) makes up for the missing elements of the proposition.

(4) Bob and Mary are engaged (to each other).
     Some (not all) girls like dancing.
     I need to change (clothes).

However, the SCA claims that all of those sentences are complete without the parentheticals, and express a truth conditional, actual situational context-independent, proposition. I want to emphasize *actual situational context-independent* because what those sentences are not independent of is prior context. Prior context, reoccurring use (without the elements in parenthesis) makes their meaning clear even without actual situational context. The speaker can say Bob and Mary are engaged true or false without concern for 'to whom'. The speaker can say some girls like dancing true or false without concern for whether all do, and can say she needs to change true or false without considering in what way (clothes? diet? priorities? career?). The parentheticals add what that speaker was talking about specifically, an added propositional element based on actual situational context. But it's a new proposition. The one it supplants is still adequate in itself as the expression of a proposition, so I argue that *it is a mistake to claim that no sentence is complete without context*. It is more the case that speakers can mean more than the sentence itself means, because context supplies the rest. But the sentence does say something, completely, and sometimes it is exactly what the speaker means too.

3.2 The dynamic model of meaning (DMM) and context

The dynamic model of meaning (DMM) proposed by Kecskes (2008) argues for a broad understanding of context that includes both prior and present experience with the world. According to the DMM both sides of world knowledge (encoded private context and actual situational context) participate in meaning construction and comprehension. The degree of their respective contributions keeps changing, depending on which stage of a concrete speech situation the interlocutors happen to be in. The DMM is built on two assertions (Kecskes 2004, 2008).

(1)   The dynamic behaviour of human speech implies a reciprocal process between language and actual situational context as demonstrated in Figure 8.1.

Language encodes prior contexts and is used to make sense of actual situational contexts, so *language is never context free.* There are no meanings that are context-free because each lexical item is a repository of context(s) itself; that is to say, it is always implicitly indexed to a prior recurring context(s) of reference. Even when an explicit context (actual situational context) is not available, one is constructed from stored knowledge originating in prior experience during the process of comprehension (see Katz 2005). Suppose we hear or read the sentence 'I want to sleep with you' without any actual situational context. With no difficulty at all can we create a

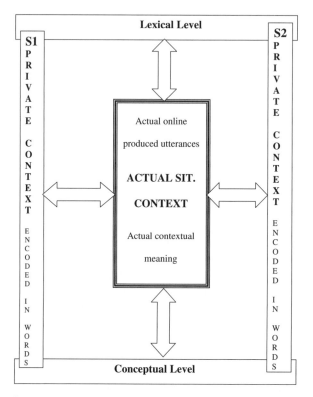

Figure 8.1 Understanding context

context based on the meaning of the words in the sentence. The interesting thing is that we all will probably make up the same context that is based on the figurative rather than the literal meaning of 'sleep'. This is how powerful salience encoded in lexical units can be.

(2)   The fact that communication is increasingly intercultural (see Blommaert 1998; Kecskes 2004; Rampton 1995) requires the development of a theory of meaning that can explain not only unilingual processing but also bi and multilingual meaning construction and comprehension. Fauconnier (1997: 188) argued that when we deal with a single language the complexities of modelling meaning do not necessarily stand out. However, when we compare two or more languages, or translate something from one language to the other, we realize that different languages have developed different ways of prompting the required cognitive constructions. Furthermore, different cultures organize their background knowledge differently. Translating from one language to another requires a reconstruction of cognitive and cultural configurations that were prompted by one language and a determination of how another language would set up similar configurations with an entirely different meaning-prompting system and pre-structured, pre-wired background.

Processing contexts and establishing repositories of contexts in the mind have both individual-specific elements and common, collective elements. That is why communication is full of misunderstandings. In Rapaport's words 'We almost always fail … Yet we almost always nearly succeed: This is the paradox of communication (2003: 402).' Why do we both fail and succeed? We have difficulties in speech communication because individual sociocultural experience with lexical items and actual situational contexts may be different even within one speech community. Prior experience creates private context that gets encapsulated in lexical items in the mind of speakers of a particular speech community. This private context incorporates core knowledge (tied to the prior experience), which is the public part of the private context, and individual-specific knowledge that may not be shared by the other members of the speech community because it is the individualized reflection of the sociocultural context. The public context, that is to say, the public part of the private context, however, is available to each speaker of that speech community because it refers to relatively similar conceptual content that is conventionalized. The paradox of communication is caused by the fact that private and public are both present all the time. However, people must be relying on communally shared rather than individual knowledge and experience. Even when a person has quite personal experiences with something (an alcoholic with drinking liquor) so that an utterance can have a private meaning ('let's have a drink'), the person knows the difference between what people generally mean by that and what it means to him/her personally (and perhaps to other alcoholics). The important point here is that the meaning value of a lexical unit refers to both relatively static and dynamic elements that are the results of actual use of the given lexical unit in different actual situational contexts. Political correctness is a matter of the private becoming public – some faction's sensitivity or private meaning brought to the awareness of the larger speech community. The 'language police' capitalize on this to impose their political vision.

Figure 8.1 demonstrates the different ways context is understood in the DMM. Speaker's private context encoded in lexical units and formulated in an utterance (actual linguistic context) is uttered (or written) 'out there' in the world by a speaker in a situation (actual situational context), and is matched ('internalized') to the private cognitive contexts 'inside' the head of the hearer (prior knowledge). Meaning is the result of interplay between the speaker's private context and the hearer's private context in the actual situational context as understood by the interlocutors.

Istvan Kecskes

3.3 Two sides of word meaning

According to the DMM (see Figure 8.2) there are two facets of the meaning value of a word (lexical unit): coresense and consense (actual contextual sense). Coresense is a denotational, diachronic, relatively constant (for a period of time), and objective feature that reflects changes in the given speech community, while consense is actual, subjective, referential, and connotational, and changed by actual situational context (see Kecskes 2004). In the DMM, a lexical item represents world knowledge based on prior contextual experience. Figure 8.2 shows how 'privatized' world knowledge may be represented in a lexical unit as a blend of coresense (general world knowledge tied to the given concept), word-specific semantic properties (lexicalized part of world knowledge), and culture-specific conceptual properties (culture-specific part of world knowledge). The dynamism of language use may result in changes in the relationship of these constituents of the blend.

Coresense is abstracted from prior contextual occurrences of a word. It is neither conceptual nor lexical, but the interface between the two linguistic and conceptual levels. Coresense is not the sum of the most essential properties of the given category, but a summary of the most familiar, regular, typical, and (generally, but not always) frequent uses of a word. It reflects the history of use of the word. It is the common core information that was called *public context* above, and is usually shared by members of a speech community. Coresense is not a pure linguistic phenomenon because it depends on extralinguistic factors such as familiarity, conventionality, and frequency. It is an essential feature of the word that pulls together conceptual semantic and lexical semantic information when a word is uttered. Coresense grows as a generalization from the most

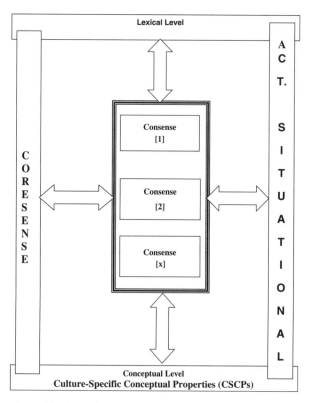

Figure 8.2 The dynamic model of meaning

120

common conceptual features of contexts the word has been used in through various interactions. This set of core features is abstracted from speakers' usage of the given lexical item. It changes in time by losing some features and/or adding new ones. Just think about the historical change in the coresense of words such as 'candy', 'kidnap', 'school', 'snack', etc.

Kecskes (2004, 2008) argued that coresense has a unique relationship with the *word-specific semantic properties* (WSSP) and *culture-specific conceptual properties* (CSCP). Word-specific semantic properties link the coresense to the lexical level while culture-specific conceptual properties tie it to the conceptual level. Culture-specific conceptual properties belong to conceptual pragmatics, while word-specific semantic properties are features of the word itself, hence are a matter of lexico-semantics. It is within these two types of properties where individual differences occur, where individual speakers' private contexts tied to a particular word may differ.

As noted above, culture-specific conceptual properties tie coresense to the conceptual level. They are the basis for figurative, metaphorical meaning and the development of word-specific semantic properties. Culture-specific conceptual properties can be revealed relatively easily if we compare words from different languages that show lexical equivalency but differ as to their culture-specific conceptual properties. For instance, let us take the concept denoted by the word 'lunch' in English and '午饭 [wǔfàn] ' in Chinese. 'Lunch' for a native speaker of American-English refers to a light meal consisting of a sandwich, soup and salad, or something else that is consumed in a 30 to 60 minute break. 'Wǔfàn' for a Chinese, denotes the meal at noon (usually consisting of several courses) that s/he consumes between 11:30 and 2 o'clock. The coresense of the two words is relatively the same; there is no word-specific semantic property attached to either, however, they differ in culture-specific conceptual properties. Bilingual people will have the same coresense for each word with different culture-specific conceptual properties, which will result in a synergic concept whose content may change depending on the extent of exposure to the two languages and cultures (see Kecskes 2007b).

Not all concepts have culture-specific conceptual properties. For instance, the concept denoted by the English word 'salt' as a noun has hardly any culture-specific conceptual property, nor does its lexical equivalents in other languages. However, a derivative of 'salt', the adjective 'salty' can have culture-specific conceptual property. Swearing is sometimes called 'salty' language, I think as a reference to sailors (on the salty sea). This is related to 'swear like a sailor'. Or again, there's the expression 'not worth his salt' meaning worthless. The word 'pumpkin', however, is different. It has a culture-specific conceptual property that usually has a positive value in American culture: a pumpkin is a popular symbol of autumn and Halloween, and parents often use the word as a nickname for their children:

(5) Father: Listen Pumpkin, how about going for ice cream?
Margie: Cool, let's go.

As seen also in the English–Chinese example ('lunch' versus 'wufan'), these culture-specific conceptual properties do not apply across cultures. An exchange like the one in (5) could hardly take place in Hungarian, where the lexical equivalent of the English word 'pumpkin' is 'tök', which carries a culture-specific conceptual property with a negative value. Hungarian children would not be happy if addressed by the word 'tök', which has the connotation of 'stupid'.

Culture-specific conceptual properties are very dynamic features of words and keep changing all the time. They are sensitive to sociocultural changes in the given language community. Culture-specific conceptual properties represent the cognitive base for word-meaning value, and are responsible for changes in the coresense of a word and its word-specific semantic properties. *When culture-specific conceptual properties get fully lexicalized they may turn into word-specific semantic properties.* This is why native speakers of English do not have to check with the conceptual system when they use words such as 'chicken out', 'kidnap', 'blackmail', etc.

On the linguistic side we have word-specific semantic properties. The term 'word-specific semantic properties' (WSSP) was coined by Cruse (1992) to denote specific semantic properties that belong to the lexical rather than the conceptual level. Word-specific semantic properties make it possible for speakers to have alternative lexical access routes to a single concept: for instance, 'run', 'dash', and 'rush'; or 'sleep', 'doze', and 'nap'. Cruse (1992: 291) argued that cognitive synonyms map onto identical concepts. The meaning properties that differentiate such cognitive synonyms as 'die', or 'pass away', can be viewed as properties of the individual lexical units, as distinct from properties of the common concept. Word-specific semantic properties are the result of the recurrent use of words in particular contexts. Originally word-specific semantic properties derive from the interplay of the given lexical unit and actual situational contexts, and they are the best evidence for category stability and variability. They usually develop from metaphors or other figures of speech, and over time they become lexicalized and conventionalized. *These words demonstrate very well how culture gets encoded in language.* Cruse (1992) argued that words with word-specific semantic properties can create a more emotive, more 'colourful' context than words without word-specific semantic properties. Compare the following sentences:

(6) John Sampton died. ————————————— John Sampton passed away
Sally disappeared in the crowd. ————————————— Sally vanished in the crowd.

It should be emphasized that word-specific semantic properties (that is, 'semantic loads'), just like culture-specific conceptual properties, are not mandatory features that are attached to each lexical unit in use. There are lexical units that have neither word-specific semantic properties, nor culture-specific conceptual properties (such as 'division', 'example', 'depart', etc.) no matter what actual situation context they are used in. Actual situational context can suppress culture-specific conceptual properties. This is, however, hardly the case with word-specific semantic properties encoded in the word, such as 'pass away', 'chicken out', 'dash', and so forth. Actual situational context cannot cancel word-specific semantic properties.

The process of diachronic development of culture-specific conceptual property into word-specific semantic property can be well demonstrated through the word 'patronize'. The primary dictionary meaning of 'patronize' is 'to act as patron of: provide aid or support for'. However, with time the word has developed two additional senses. One sense is closely related to the primary meaning, when the direct object referred to an organization, firm, hotel, store, etc. means 'give one's regular patronage, support; trade with'. In the other sense, when the direct object refers to a person, the word has developed a negative cultural load: 'adopt an air of condescension toward, behave in an offensively condescending manner toward'. This latter sense may have arisen from focusing on the superior position that a patron in the other senses has. This meaning might be a reflection of American way of thinking: Don't patronize me, I know how to do that. You patronize me because you think that I am unable to do (something).

The other side of word meaning in Figure 8.2 is *consense* that should be distinguished from corsense. Coresense is the invariant while consense represents the possible variants. Consense realizes a particular aspect or aspects of the coresense by uniting it with the appropriate word-specific semantic property and/or culture-specific conceptual property when the word is actually uttered in an actual situational context. Consense is a mental representation consisting of a variable set of conceptual features compositionally related to the syntactic structure of the lexical unit. This set may vary with every use of the given expression in actual situational contexts.

Coresense changes diachronically while consense changes synchronically. Systematic, repeated changes in consenses (actual uses) over time will result in changes of coresense. Change in the coresense of the following words over time clearly supports this point: 'mouse', 'gay', 'google'.

Figure 8.2 demonstrates how coresense and consense fit within the dynamic model of meaning. As Figure 8.2 shows, coresense is the interface between the conceptual and lexical level. Word-specific semantic properties are links to the lexical level, while culture-specific conceptual properties are ties to the conceptual level. Consenses are the variations of coresense in context. The actual contextual interpretation of coresense is expressed in a consense connected to consenses of other lexical units to form an utterance.

4 Formulaic language as carrier of culture

4.1 Interplay of prior context and actual situational context

As discussed in the Introduction to this chapter formulaic language demonstrates very well how language, culture, and context are intertwined. Culture is the originator. Both formulaic language and the context that they create or are used in are rooted in culture. However, at the same time they both are 'carriers' of culture and both reflect culture but in a different way. Formulaic language, especially situation-bound utterances are an ideal means to demonstrate the interplay of actual situational context and prior context in meaning construction and comprehension because they are often linguistically transparent and carry a sociocultural load at the same time (Kecskes 2000). Consider the following two conversations:

(7) Sam: Coming for a drink?
Andy: Sorry, I can't. *My doctor* won't let me.
Sam: *What's wrong with you?*

(8) Sam: Coming for a drink?
Andy: Sorry, I can't. *My mother-in-law (my wife)* won't let me.
Sam: *What's wrong with you?*

The situation-bound utterance '*What's wrong with you?*' has two different meanings in (7) and (8) although the only difference between the two conversations is that '*My doctor*' is changed to '*My mother-in-law*'. It is not the actual situational context that creates this difference in meaning. Rather, it is the stigmatic load that is attached to the use of the lexical phrase '*My mother-in-law*', which has a negative connotation in most contexts. If we use a third option '*My wife*', the meaning of '*What's wrong with you?*' will depend on the actual situational context, i.e., on how the hearer processes his friend's expression '*My wife*', based on his knowledge about the relationship between Andy and his wife. In this case, because of the 'weakness' of the conceptual load tied to the expression '*My wife*', dominance of the actual situational context becomes obvious.

In these three situations, dominance seems to be changing and depends on what interpretation the encoded conceptual load of the expression makes possible. If the load is very strong and deeply conventionalized, the actual situational context can hardly cancel it. Some 'interpretation sensitive terms' are interpretation sensitive because of prior context and collective salience of the expression like in the following example.

(9) In one of his films (*The Survivors*) Robin Williams says the following:

— 'I had to sleep with the dogs. Platonically, of course ... '

Why does he feel that he should add 'platonically, of course'? In the context of that movie the utterance 'I had to sleep with the dogs' had no sexual overtone at all. Still the actor added 'platonically, of course' because the sexual connotation of the expression 'sleep with' is so strong that the actual situational context itself can hardly cancel it. This shows that not only conventionalized, prefabricated expressions but also ad hoc created expressions can dominate meaning construction and comprehension if the expression used in the course of conversation refers to some phenomenon or sense of an expression that is strongly carved in the mind of interlocutors for some reason. Interesting, too, that some people more than others fixate on certain meanings, e.g., some people are more attuned to any possible sexual innuendo (what they call 'a dirty mind'). This also supports the argument that although individuals may be the members of a speech community, collective salience is distributed individually.

4.2 Psychological saliency of formulas

The importance of formulaic language was noticed in earlier linguistic research. Hymes (1962) pointed out that an immense portion of verbal behaviour consists of linguistic routines. Bolinger suggested that 'speakers do at least as much remembering as they do putting together' (1976: 2). Fillmore also found that 'an enormously large amount of natural language is formulaic, automatic and rehearsed, rather than propositional, creative or freely generated' (1976: 24). However, with the appearance of huge corpora, understanding formulaic language has become more complicated. Working with large corpora Altenberg (1998) went so far as to claim that almost 80 per cent of our language production can be considered formulaic. Whatever the proportion actually is, one thing is for sure: speakers in conventional speech situations tend to do more remembering than putting together as Bolinger said. Our everyday conversations are often restricted to short routinized interchanges where we do not always mean what we say. So a typical conversation between a customer and a store assistant may look like this:

(10)　Andy: Hi Bob. How are you doing?
　　　Bob: Fine, thank you. How about you?
　　　Andy: I am OK, thanks.

None of the expressions used by the speakers look freely generated. Each of them can be considered a formula that is tied to this particular kind of situation. However, if we consider the following conversation we may see something different.

(11)　Mary and Peter are talking.

　　　M: *If you want* to see me again you will need to do *what I tell you* to.
　　　P: OK, *my love*.

There is no doubt that the expressions in italics consist of words that are frequently used together. But are they formulas here? Do they have some kind of psychological saliency as formulas do for the speakers? We must be careful with the answer because frequency is only one of the criteria based on which we can identify formulaic expressions. The problem is that the role of frequency seems to be overemphasized in present day linguistics, especially in corpus linguistics. Recent research analysing written and spoken discourse has established that highly frequent, recurrent sequences of words, variously called lexical bundles, chunks, and multiword expressions are not only salient but also functionally significant. Cognitive research demonstrated that knowledge of these ready-made expressions is crucial for fluent processing. The recurrent nature of these units is discussed in the relevant literature (McEnery and Wilson 1996; Biber *et al.* 1999). Simpson-Vlach and Ellis (2010) confirmed that large stretches of language are adequately described as collocational streams where patterns flow into each other. Sinclair (1991, 2004) summarized this in his 'idiom principle': 'a language user has available to him or her a large number of semi-preconstructed phrases that constitute single choices, even though they might appear to be analyzable into segments' (1991:110). However, this principle is based not primarily on frequency that results in long lists of recurrent word sequences (e.g. Biber *et al.* 1999, 2004). Those frequency lists can hardly give any chance to distinguish where we have conventionalized formulas or where we have just frequently occurring word chunks that lack psychological saliency. Biber *et al.* (1999: 990), in their study of 'lexical bundles', defined formulaic language as 'sequences of word forms that commonly go together in natural discourse', irrespective of their structural make-up or idiomaticity, and argued that conversation has a larger amount of lexical bundle types than academic prose. However, there seems to be a clear difference from the perspective of psychological saliency between sequences such as 'to tell the truth', 'as a matter of fact' on the one hand, and 'I think you ... ', 'to make it' on the other, although all these expressions are high on any frequency-based list. This is why we need to distinguish between groups of prefabricated expressions that have psychological saliency for speakers of a particular language community and loosely tied, frequently occurring word sequences (usually consisting of common words) such as 'if they want', 'to do with it', 'and of the', 'tell them to', etc. Simpson-Vlach and Ellis (2010) argued that psycholinguistically salient sequences like 'on the other hand', 'suffice it to say' cohere much more than would be expected by chance. They are 'glued together' and thus measures of association, rather than raw frequency, are likely more relevant to these formulaic expressions.

Yes, those expressions are 'glued together' by conventional use that is rooted in culture. They are used in reoccurring scenarios, situational contexts. This is why they become customary in use, which gives them a kind of psychological salience. They are the lexicalization of customs and values in a speech community. This is how culture penetrates language and how language reflects culture. Of course, many of those formulas are frozen metaphors. It would be hard for language users to explain where they come from, why they are the ones that are used in those reoccurring contexts. Expressions such as 'piece of cake', 'kick the bucket', 'it's not my cup of tea', 'stick around', and the like are already functional units where the function they refer to is what really counts not what they actually say. But those formulas represent the heart and soul of a language, which make the use of language idiomatic and hard to learn for people coming with a different language and cultural background. This is how culture basically creates the 'heart and soul' of language, what makes the two inseparable.

5 Future directions

Much has been said about the relationship of language, culture, and context but more is needed.

We are not quite familiar yet with every aspect of this complex relationship. The main direction of future research should focus on investigating the relationship between two sides of context that brings together language and culture.

Let us see how two authoritative sourcebooks define 'context'.

Merriam-Webster's
con·text
noun \' kän-ˌtekst\

- the words that are used with a certain word or phrase and that help to explain its meaning
- the situation in which something happens: the group of conditions that exist where and when something happens

As a reminder let us return to the *Concise Oxford English Dictionary* that also gives a definition in two parts:

- the parts that immediately precede and follow a word or passage and clarify its meaning
- the circumstances that form the setting for an event, statement, or idea

These definitions are exactly the same, only the wording is different. The first part of these definitions refers to a linguistic context, i.e. the parts of language that either precede or follow a word or a passage. The second part of the definitions relates to the wider context, the 'setting'. It is interesting to notice that while the definition points to the effect that the linguistic context has on the meaning of a word or a passage, no reference is made to the influence that the wider context ('setting') may have on the way in which a statement, an event or idea is interpreted.

The main point is that the first part of definitions relates language to context while the second part relates culture to context as if they were separable. No they are not. As I explained above, immediate (actual situational) context can become standard context over time and standard context can create immediate (actual situational) context. For decades linguists and non-linguists worship standard context (what is encoded in the language). Meaning has been attached to the words and sentences of the language rather than to the 'real' world that language is supposed to refer to. After the later Wittgenstein rejected many of the assumptions of the *Tractatus*, arguing that the meaning of words is constituted by the function they perform within any given language game all linguists and non-linguists landed on this side emphasizing the role of 'almighty context' in defining meaning. Future research should focus on the interplay of both sides of context in defining meaning.

Related topics

language, culture, and politeness; culture and language processing; language, culture and interaction; language and cultural scripts; language and culture in intercultural communication

Further reading

Duranti, A. and C. Goodwin (eds). 1992. *Rethinking Context: Language as an interactive phenomenon*. Cambridge: Cambridge University Press. (Language and context are seen as interactively defined phenomena. Rather than functioning solely as a constraint on linguistic performance, context is suggested to be analysed as a product of language use).

Fetzer, A. 2004. *Recontextualizing Context*. Amsterdam: John Benjamins. (This book proposes a model for describing the multifaceted connectedness between language and language use, and between cognitive context, linguistic context, social context and sociocultural context and their underlying principles of well-formedness, grammaticality, acceptability and appropriateness.)

Givón, Talmy. 2005. *Context as Other Minds*. Amsterdam: John Benjamins. (The core chapters of the book outline the reinterpretation of 'communicative context' as the systematic, online construction of mental models of the interlocutor's current, rapidly shifting states of belief and intention.)

Graddol, David, Linda Thompson and Michael Byram (eds). 2007. *Language and Culture*. Clevedon, UK: Multilingual Matters. (A collection of papers discussing the relationship of language and culture from different perspectives.)

Kecskes, Istvan. 2013. *Intercultural Pragmatics*. Oxford: Oxford University Press. (The first book on the subject establishes the foundations of the field, combining the pragmatic view of cooperation with the cognitive view of egocentrism in order to incorporate emerging features of communication.)

Leckie-Tarry, H. 1995. *Language and Context: A functional linguistic theory of register*. London: Pinter. (This book develops a functional theory of language which specifies the notion of 'register', in terms of contextual and linguistic features. Moving beyond the limits of much of today's theory, it develops a theoretical understanding of the relationship between text, context and both the function and form of language.)

References

Altenberg, Bengt. 1998. 'On the phraseology of spoken English: The evidence of recurrent word-combinations'. In *Phraseology: Theory, Analysis, and Applications*, Anthony Paul Cowie (ed.), pp. 101–22. Oxford: Clarendon Press.

Bates, Daniel G. and Plog Fred. 1980. *Cultural Anthropology* (2nd edn). New York: Alfred A. Knopf.

Benedict, Ruth. 1967. *El Hombre y la Culture: Investigación sobre los orígenes de la civilización contemporónea*. Buenos Aires: Editorial Sudamericana.

Biber, Douglas, S. Johansson, G. Leech, S. Conrad, and E. Finegan. 1999. *Longman Grammar of Spoken and Written English*. London: Pearson Education.

Biber, Douglas, S. Conrad, and Viviana Cortes. 2004. 'If you look at … : Lexical bundles in university teaching and textbooks'. *Applied Linguistics* 25(3): 371–405.

Blommaert, Jan. 1991. 'How much culture is there in intercultural communication?'. In *The Pragmatics of Intercultural and International Communication*, Blommaert Jan and Jef Verschueren (eds), pp. 13–31. Amsterdam: John Benjamins.

——1998. 'Different approaches to intercultural communication: A critical survey'. Plenary lecture, Lernen und Arbeiten in einer international vernetzten und multikulturellen Gesellschaft, Expertentagung Universität Bremen, Institut für Projektmanagement und Witschaftsinformatik (IPMI), 27–28 February (retrieved from www.cie.ugent.be/CIE/blommaert1.htm).

Bolinger, Dwight. 1976. 'Meaning and memory'. *Forum Linguisticum* 1: 1–14.

Croft, William and D. Alan Cruse. 2004. *Cognitive Linguistics*. Cambridge: Cambridge University Press.

Croft, William and Esther J. Wood. 2000. 'Construal operations in linguistics and artificial intelligence'. In *Meaning and Cognition: A multidisciplinary approach*, Liliana Albertazzi (ed.), pp. 51–78. Amsterdam: Benjamins.

Cruse, D. Alan. 1992. 'Antonymy revisited: Some thoughts on the relationship between words and concepts'. In *Frames, Fields, and Contrasts: New essays in semantic and lexical organization*, Lehrer Adrienne and Eva Feder Kittay (eds), pp. 289–306. Hillsdale, NJ: Lawrence Erlbaum.

Durkheim, Emile. 1982. *The Rules of Sociological Method*. Halls Wilfred Douglas (trans.). New York: Simon and Schuster.

Elsbach, Kimberly D., Pamela S. Barr, and Andrew B. Hargadon. 2005. 'Identifying situated cognition in organizations'. *Organization Science* 16(4): 422.

Fauconnier, Gilles. 1997. *Mappings in Thought and Language*. Cambridge: Cambridge University Press.

Fillmore, Charles J. 1976. 'The need for a frame semantics within linguistics'. *Statistical Methods in Linguistics* 12: 5–29.

Finkelstein, Sydney, Donald C. Hambrick, and Bert Cannella 2008. *Strategic Leadership: Theory and research on executives, top management teams, and boards*. Oxford: Oxford University Press.

Gumperz, John J. 1982. *Discourse Strategies*. Cambridge: Cambridge University Press.

Gumperz, John J. and Celia Roberts. 1991. 'Understanding in intercultural encounters'. In *The Pragmatics of Intercultural and International Communication*, Blommaert Jan and Jef Verschueren (eds), pp. 51–90. Amsterdam: John Benjamins.

Halliday, Michael A. K. and Ruqaiya Hasan. 1985. *Language, Context and Text: Aspects of language in a social–semiotic perspective*. Victoria: Deakin University.

Hymes, Dell H. 1962. 'The ethnography of speaking'. In *Anthropology and Human Behavior*, Thomas Gladwin and William C. Sturtevant (eds), pp. 13–53. Washington, DC: Anthropology Society of Washington.

Jakobson, Roman. 1959. 'On linguistic aspects of translation'. In *On translation*, A. Brower Reuben (ed.), pp. 232–39. Cambridge, MA: Harvard University Press.

Katz, Albert. 2005. 'Discourse and sociocultural factors in understanding nonliteral language'. In *Figurative Language Comprehension: Social and cultural influences*, Herbert L. Colston and Albert N. Katz (eds), pp. 183–208. Mahwah, NJ: Lawrence Erlbaum.

Kecskes, Istvan. 2000. 'A cognitive–pragmatic approach to situation-bound utterances'. *Journal of Pragmatics* 32(6): 605–25.

——2003. *Situation-Bound Utterances in L1 and L2*. Berlin/New York: Mouton de Gruyter.

——2004. 'Lexical merging, conceptual blending and cultural crossing'. *Intercultural Pragmatics* 1(1): 1–21.

——2007a. 'Formulaic language in English lingua franca'. In *Explorations in Pragmatics: Linguistic, cognitive and intercultural aspects*, István Kecskés and Laurence R. Horn (eds), pp. 191–219. Berlin/New York: Mouton de Gruyter.

——2007b. 'Synergic concepts in the bilingual mind'. In *Cognitive Aspects of Bilingualism*, Kecskés István and Liliana Albertazzi (eds), pp. 29–61. Berlin/New York: Springer.

——2008. 'Dueling contexts: A dynamic model of meaning'. *Journal of Pragmatic* 40(3): 385–406.

——2009. 'Dual and multilanguage systems'. *International Journal of Multilingualism* 1–19.

——2010a. 'The paradox of communication: A socio-cognitive approach'. *Pragmatics and Society* 1(1): 50–73.

——2010b. 'Formulaic language in English lingua franca'. In *Metaphor and Figurative Language: Critical concepts in linguistics*, Patrick Hanks and Rachel Giora (eds). Oxford/New York: Routledge (reprint of 2007 paper).

——2010c. 'Situation-Bound utterances as pragmatic acts'. *Journal of Pragmatics* 42(11): 2889–97.

Knapp, Karlfried and Annelie Knapp-Potthoff. 1987. 'Instead of an introduction: Conceptual issues in analyzing intercultural communication'. In *Analyzing Intercultural Communication*, Knapp Karfried, Enninger Werner, and Annelie Knapp-Potthoff (eds), pp. 1–13. Amsterdam: Mouton de Gruyter.

Levinson, Stephen C. 2003. 'Language and mind: Let's get the issues straight!' In *Language in Mind: Advances in the study of language and cognition*, Gentner Dedre and Susan Goldin-Meadow (eds), pp. 25–46. Cambridge, MA: MIT Press.

McEnery, Tony and Andrew Wilson. 1996. *Corpus Linguistics*. Edinburgh: Edinburgh University Press.

Mandelbaum, David G. (ed.). 1949. *Selected Writings of Edward Sapir*. Berkeley and Los Angeles, CA: University of California Press.

Ocasio, William. 1997. 'Towards an attention-based view of the firm'. *Strategic Management Journal* 18: 187–206.

Rampton, Ben. 1995. *Crossing: Language and ethnicity among adolescents*. New York: Longman.

Rapaport, William J. 2003. 'What did you mean by that? Misunderstanding, negotiation, and syntactic semantics'. *Minds and Machines* 13(3): 397–427.

Scollon, Ron and Suzanne Wong Scollon. 2001. *Intercultural Communication*. Malden, MA: Blackwell.

Simpson-Vlach, Rita and Nick C. Ellis. 2010. 'An academic formulas list: New methods in phraseology research'. *Applied Linguistics* 31(4): 487–512

Sinclair, John. 1991. *Corpus, Concordance, Collocation*. Oxford: Oxford University Press.

——2004. 'New evidence, new priorities, new attitudes'. In *How to Use Corpora in Language Teaching*, John Sinclair (ed.), pp. 271–99. Amsterdam: John Benjamins.

Slobin, Dan Isaac. 1991. 'Learning to think for speaking: Native language, cognition, and rhetorical style'. *Pragmatics* 1(1): 7–25.

——1996. 'From "thought and language" to "thinking for speaking"'. In *Rethinking Linguistic Relativity*, John J. Gumperz and Stephen C. Levinson (eds), pp. 70–96. Cambridge: Cambridge University Press.

Starbuck, W. H. and F. J. Milliken. 1988. 'Executive's perceptual filters: What they notice and how they make sense'. In D. C. Hambrick (ed.), *The Executive Effect: Concepts and Methods for Studying Top Managers*, pp. 35–65. Greenwich, CT: JAI Press.

Wray, Alison. 2002. *Formulaic Language and the Lexicon*. Cambridge: Cambridge University Press.

9

LANGUAGE, CULTURE, AND POLITENESS

Sara Mills

1 Introduction

The terms 'language' and 'culture' are often used in politeness research as if they were synonyms. In this chapter I tease these two terms apart and chart their complex relation with politeness. I firstly discuss traditional models of politeness and impoliteness which analyse politeness in purely formally linguistic terms. I foreground the problems of such an analysis and then I examine the discursive approach to politeness which tries to develop a more context-based approach. This approach is more able to chart the complex relations between the terms language, culture and politeness. I then focus on the way that different cultures have been described in relation to politeness norms, where certain cultures have been labelled as collectivist or individualist cultures, positive or negative politeness cultures, and discernment and volition-based cultures. I question the validity of classifying whole cultures as tending towards certain styles of politeness or impoliteness.

2 Politeness and impoliteness

2.1 Traditional approach to the analysis of politeness

Brown and Levinson's early work on politeness has had a major impact on the research field (1978/1987). They were the first to propose a systematic model of politeness and while there has been much criticism of their work, many theorists still adhere to a great deal of their terminology and concepts, even though some elements of the approach used by Brown and Levinson have since been modified. More specifically, Brown and Levinson proposed that politeness is largely strategic, a calculation that speakers make when interacting with others about the social distance from the other person, the power relation between them and the 'cost' of the imposition on the other (if, say, for example, the speaker is requesting something from the hearer). From this calculation, speakers work out what they need to 'pay' the other person. For Brown and Levinson, individuals need to defend their 'face', that is, the self-image of themselves which they, in interaction with others, agree to maintain. If others maintain your face, you, in turn, will maintain their face. Face threatening acts (FTAs) are classified as any actions which potentially disturb the balance of face maintenance among interactants. For example, requests can be categorized as face threatening as they may put the interlocutor into a difficult position, if they wish to refuse the request. Politeness, for Brown and Levinson, is seen as the mitigation of potential threats to face.[1]

Brown and Levinson characterize politeness as consisting of two elements: negative and positive politeness. Negative politeness is largely concerned with not imposing on the other person, and indicating deference and respect towards them. Thus, apologizing would be categorized as negative politeness, as it is seen to be recognizing the needs and wishes of the other person, putting that other person first and stating that the other person will not be imposed upon. Positive politeness is concerned with stressing the closeness between the speaker and the hearer and indicating that the needs of the hearer and the speaker are very similar. Paying someone a compliment or telling them a joke is characterized as positive politeness, as both of these are seen to be concerned with stressing the closeness of the relationship between interactants.

2.2 Problems with the traditional approach to the analysis of politeness

There are a number of issues which have exercised theorists of politeness since Brown and Levinson's work was first published. These critiques have led theorists to either refine Brown and Levinson's model or attempt to produce new models of analysis. I will deal with several of these criticisms here: universalism; the relation between indirectness and politeness and context

Universalism: Brown and Levinson claimed that their model was a universal description of politeness, that is, that it could describe politeness in all languages. They argued that individual language groups differed in the extent to which they used positive or negative politeness, but that in essence, all languages subscribed to the same system of politeness. In recent years, however, this traditional approach has come under scrutiny, largely because, although this model seems to be adequate to describe English politeness, it certainly is not an effective model for analysing, for example, East Asian languages (Kadar and Mills, 2011; Matsumoto, 1989).[2] In languages such as Japanese or Chinese, the concern with strategy and fulfilling one's own individual needs is not viewed as the primary driver of politeness. Instead, in these cultures, there tends to be a focus on marking one's awareness of one's position in the group and one's position in relation to others. Ide (1989) put forward a distinction between discernment and volition to describe these two opposing concerns. Discernment (*wakimae*) is the concern with marking the awareness of one's social position and one's relationship with the interlocutor. Many East Asian languages seem to exhibit a tendency to mark discernment in politeness usage more frequently than Western European languages, or at least this marking of position seems to be more back-grounded and part of expected or appropriate behaviour, than it is in Western European languages. Volition, on the other hand, is characterized by Ide as the type of politeness where speakers decide on the shape and form of the utterance, and tailor it themselves to what they see as the demands of the context and interlocutor. This is often seen as the type of politeness which characterizes Western European languages largely, being concerned with the individual needs of the speaker – and it is the type of strategic politeness described by Brown and Levinson. Ide (1989) describes these two styles of politeness as being related to Eastern and Western cultures; Mills and Kadar (2011, 2013) have described these two styles as tendencies only, arguing that East Asian languages are not wholly characterized by discernment, nor are Western European languages largely characterized by volition. Instead, these are tendencies which can be found in all languages. Mills and Kadar (2013) have also questioned whether there is such a clear distinction to be made between these two terms, and have argued that in fact discernment can best be opposed to certain types of ritualistic or conventionalized utterances rather than to individualistic volitional statements.

2.2.1 The relation between indirectness and politeness

Brown and Levinson argued that there is a scale of politeness, ranging from indirectness and avoidance of speaking to the directness of bald-on record utterances; indirectness for them is seen to be the most polite form. For them, when someone is indirect, for example when requesting something, the person gives the interlocutor the option of not recognizing or acknowledging the request, and therefore indirect forms allow the hearer some freedom of action. For example, if a speaker says: 'I wonder if you could possibly lend me that book?' using an indirect form rather than the relatively direct form: 'Can I borrow that book?' or the more direct form 'I want to read that book', the hearer is offered more options in terms of being able to refuse the request. In a sense, the indirect form already has the potential of refusal embedded within it. This is a highly elaborated form which signals to the interlocutor that the speaker recognizes that they are making a request which might be refused and signalling also to the hearer that the person has the option to refuse: 'I wonder' – thinking rather than demanding; 'if you' – the use of the conditional rather than a statement; 'could' – use of the past tense rather than the present; 'possibly' – again signalling that there is the option for refusal. All of these elements are highly conventionalized in English and therefore it is difficult to describe the intention or the impact of this type of indirectness in particular interactions. However, overall, using indirectness in English seems to signal an acknowledgement that making such a request involves potentially face threatening behaviour, and because this difficulty has been indicated to the hearer, refusal does not threaten the speaker's or the hearer's face. This type of indirectness is characterized by Brown and Levinson (1978/1987) as universal; others have seen it as stereotypically English (Wierzbicka, 1999). However, others have even argued that this type of indirectness is associated with stereotypically elite forms of politeness in English only (Grainger and Mills, forthcoming).

However, many theorists have drawn attention to the fact that while for elite English, indirectness is seen to be the most polite form, in other languages, indirectness may in fact be considered impolite. Kerkam (forthcoming) has shown that in Arabic, indirectness is rarely used for the purposes of being polite, as directness is the seen as the more expected or appropriate form for requests and excuses. Indirectness used in these contexts would indicate a social or affective distance between the interlocutors, and therefore could give rise to an interpretation of impoliteness. Kerkam also shows that when indirectness is strategically used by interlocutors, it tends to be used for face-threatening acts. She has shown that criticizing and blaming are often achieved through indirect means, where speakers and hearers both recognize that an abstracted, generalized indirect utterance, such as 'British children's clothes are not very nice, are they?' is in fact a particularized criticism of someone's taste in clothes, and perhaps also their orientation to foreign cultures.

Indirectness is not an agreed upon term in all languages; thus, what counts as indirect in English (for example, conventional indirectness, such as 'Could you open the window?') might not be seen as indirect at all in some languages (Wierzbicka, 1999). The supposed widespread use of indirectness for refusals in East Asian languages should be viewed as conventionalized, and is often interpreted by native speakers of these languages as fairly straightforward and not indicating politeness.

Thus, indirectness should be seen to have a complex relationship with politeness, and it is clear that particular languages do not necessarily view or use indirectness in the same way as it is interpreted in English.

2.2.2 Context

Brown and Levinson, while arguing for the importance of context, largely focused on single sentence utterances as indicating politeness or impoliteness. It is quite clear that politeness tends to be an accumulated process, whereby politeness and impoliteness build up over a number of utterances and are contributed to by all participants. Thus we might argue that politeness and impoliteness are co-constructed rather than the product of an individual speaker's intention. Bousfield (2008) has argued that it is important to focus on the way that impoliteness builds up over a long stretch of conversation, rather than assuming that it is somehow 'contained' within one utterance. What is important to analyse is the potentiality of politeness and impoliteness – the way that at certain points in the conversation, an interactant manages to repair potential hints of impoliteness, or manages to steer the conversation away from possible impoliteness (Watts, 2003), as I show in the next section. Mills (2003) has focused on the way that, drawing on a Community of Practice (CoP) approach, within a particular context, groups of people classify certain elements as appropriate or inappropriate (Eckert and McConnell-Ginet, 1998). Within each CoP, there may be slightly different assessments of what counts as polite or impolite. A focus on context leads also to a focus on judgement, because politeness and impoliteness are seen as less inherent in particular speech acts or types of utterance, but more as judgements made by interactants about the appropriateness of utterances, in relation to what they consider to be the CoP norms of behaviour (see also Chapter 25 this volume).

2.3 Discursive approach to the analysis of politeness

The discursive approach to the analysis of politeness developed because of a dissatisfaction with many aspects of Brown and Levinson's theorizing and analysis. Following on from Eelen's (2001) thoroughgoing critique of the work of Brown and Levinson and other politeness theorists, the discursive approach has attempted to develop a form of analysis which either modifies their work or dispenses with their work altogether.

Instead of making universal statements about politeness use, and developing a global model for the analysis of politeness, the discursive approach focuses on the way that context, resources and social forces /ideologies determine the possible meanings and interpretations of politeness. These are the elements which in fact determine whether an utterance is considered to be polite or impolite. Politeness and impoliteness are only that which is judged by interactants to be so, but interactants do not make these judgements in a vacuum. Thus the discursive approach focuses on language use in detail, in much the same way that traditional approaches have, but interpretation, judgement and context are considered crucial (Mills, 2011). For example, a discursive approach to the analysis of politeness would analyse an utterance in a particular context and analyse the way that the utterance seems to be functioning, and seems to be judged by the interactants as polite or impolite. Rather than focusing on second order judgements about the utterance (i.e. the analyst's assessment), discursive approaches tend to focus on first order evaluations (i.e. the judgements that the interactants can be seen to be making) (Watts, 2003; Eelen, 2001).

Locher and Watts (2008) argue that politeness and impoliteness are not inherent in utterances; the analyst can only recognize that politeness is a possible interpretation, and thus they describe politeness as a potential within utterances. It is the hearer who decides whether they will choose to categorize the utterance as polite or impolite (or in fact a different form of relational work).[3] Mills (2003) also shows the way that within family interactions, for example, interactants may decide not to 'take up' potential impoliteness moves; they may decide that in fact they value keeping the peace, rather than recognizing explicitly that someone has been impolite – impoliteness within this type of interaction stays at the 'potential' level. That is not to say, however, that its potential is not recognized by interactants. Parents, for example, have the option of acting as though they did not hear the 'impolite' utterance. Bousfield (2008), in an analysis of impoliteness in a documentary about traffic wardens, examines the way that a traffic warden has the option of classifying an utterance by an irate member of the public as impolite. However, generally the traffic wardens do not classify offensive or aggressive utterances as impolite, despite the fact that they involve swearing and shouting, because their institutional position allows them to accept that the offensive language is directed to the institution rather than to them personally. Culpeper (2011) also considers the question of whether in army training, the language used by sergeants towards their trainees is impolite, since none of the trainees displays in their responses to the sergeants any indication that they consider the language inappropriate or offensive. Thus, discursive approaches to the analysis of politeness and impoliteness focus more on the evaluation of acts as polite within particular contexts, rather than retaining any sense that language items are intrinsically polite or impolite (see Linguistic Politeness Research Group, 2011).

3 Conventional approach to culture and language

Conventional linguistic approaches to politeness and culture have tended to assume that different cultures, for example, Arab cultures or English culture, are fairly homogeneous. Everyone within that community is characterized as agreeing on particular norms and rules of behaviour, values, and beliefs. Hofstede (1984: 8) argues that 'culture is composed of many elements which may be classified into four categories: symbols, heroes, rituals and values'. Damen (1987: 367) argues that culture is 'learned and shared human patterns and models for living, day to day living patterns'. However, I would argue what has been described here as the values and beliefs of a given culture, albeit British or Japanese, tend to be the values and beliefs of the elite which end up being applied to the culture as a whole, when they actually function as stereotypes. This notion that all the individuals who categorize themselves or are characterized as belonging to a particular culture have the same access to that culture's values and beliefs, or would share those beliefs is one that a discursive approach would question.

We often make generalizations about cultures. Cultures are believed to be more or less patriarchal, conservative, upholding or challenging certain ideologies about language, encouraging respect for the elderly, encouraging individual self-fulfilment, and so on. But the important thing to recognize is that these are ideological beliefs about the culture, rather than being statements of facts about a culture.[4] They are generally the values and beliefs of an elite group within the culture, and they are produced and maintained by that elite, and those within society who see it as in their interests to uphold the values of that group.[5] These beliefs about the culture are generally seen/portrayed as enduring values, which have 'always' characterized that particular culture. However, when we examine these ideologies, they may sometimes have developed relatively recently. For example, Inoue (2004) has documented the way that ideologies about 'Japanese women's language' and Japanese standard language developed along with the state's move to present itself as modern in the late nineteenth century.

Instead, I see culture as being a fairly heterogeneous grouping of values, beliefs, and ideologies which are associated with a particular elite group. These values then tend to be identified at a stereotypical level with the culture as a whole and there is stratified access to these particular practices, thus often excluding groups from being recognized as fully belonging to that culture.[6] Politeness is one of the key elements in this view of culture, as politeness is very much about appropriate behaviour, and speech which fits in with social norms of what is expected from an elite group. Within a culture there are also many individuals, who belong to sub-groups, who contest the cultural values of the elite culture, but who would still classify themselves as belonging to that particular culture. For example, British people are generally considered to be self-deprecating and reserved. This is a cultural stereotype, as many British people are not self-deprecating at all. But this ideology of the cool, modest, and reserved male developed particularly within the colonial and imperial period, when this particular set of character traits developed to set British people apart both from the indigenous people and from other colonizing nations. In a sense this set of elite cultural characteristics developed to distinguish British people from other groups of people and to justify them in their imperial role. Cultural stereotypes change slowly and it is interesting that this is one of the stereotypes of British people which both informs other nations' view of British people and also informs some British peoples' notions of themselves and what is appropriate. Thus, I am not arguing that cultures are all the same and that we cannot distinguish between different cultures. Rather what I am arguing is that when we distinguish between cultures we are doing so at a stereotypical, ideological level. These ideological beliefs are not necessarily ones that all of the members of that culture will draw on in their own linguistic repertoire.

It is important to maintain a distinction between these values which form elite culture and the language as a whole. Cultural elites will stress the importance of a concern for individual freedom and rights, or a concern for the social norms as a whole, and these constitute what could be considered a particular culture. These values inevitably influence the form of what is considered linguistically appropriate. But these cultural stereotypes do not constitute the language as a whole. It is possible to use language in ways which deviate from these cultural stereotypes. Working-class British people, for example, may recognize that indirectness is a form which is favoured by middle-class people when making requests, and may even see this concern for the other as characterizing British culture, but they may not in fact use indirectness themselves when requesting, or may even mock using indirectness, seeing it as mannered or over-polite (Mills, 2012).

3.1 Collectivist and individualism

When culture is discussed within conventional linguistic research, especially in relation to politeness, cultures are often split into certain tendencies, such as collectivist and individualist; positive politeness and negative politeness; and discernment and volition cultures. I will discuss each of these in turn.

Collectivist cultures are those where the group is seen to be at the fore and the individual is not seen to be of the greatest value. In collectivist cultures, Triandis *et al.* (1990) argue, the group has primacy and individuals give up their personal autonomy to the group. Individuals are not seen and do not see themselves as isolated but rather solely as part of a social whole. Collectivist cultures emphasize adhering to cultural norms and harmony. One's position within a grouping is at the core of one's value and status. An individual's relationship with their family is seen as central and some cultures which are characterized as collectivist may be seen as relatively conservative in relation to values which are associated with the rights of individuals[7]. In these cultures, often the rights of certain marginalized groups such as gay people and women, are seen to be of less importance than the values of the culture as a whole.

In individualist cultures, the individual is characterized as having a more detached relation to groups such as the family or friendship groups, moving on to other groups relatively easily, if relationships within a group do not work out. Status is derived from one's own strivings and it is one's own individual efforts to achieve status for oneself which is of prime importance. Individualist societies are those where the freedom of the individual from the constraints of the group are paramount, and these cultures may be classified as relatively liberal in relation to the rights of the individual.

While it is possible to recognize broadly speaking tendencies in particular cultures towards collectivism or individualism, what is striking about all cultural groups is that all societies display both collectivism and individualism. Thus, while Arab cultures are often characterized as tending towards collectivist values, individuals nevertheless strive for their individual rights and act as autonomous beings. And while English culture tends to be characterized as concerned with individualist values, individuals nevertheless recognize the importance of their allegiance to social groups such as the family and adjust their behaviour and values to those groups. The values which we are describing when we describe a culture as collectivist or individualist are those of the elite, and while these values may have an influence on individuals within that culture, we need to see that they are only tendencies. Thus, although these terms might be interesting to describe broad brush tendencies in cultures, we cannot assert that cultures are either collectivist or individualist.

3.2 Positive politeness and negative politeness cultures

Brown and Levinson (1978/1987) argued that cultures tend towards either positive politeness cultures (camaraderie) which stresses the social closeness amongst individuals, or negative politeness cultures (deference) which tend to emphasize distance and respect between individuals. They gave as examples Japanese culture which they characterized as a negative politeness culture, whereas American and Australian English are characterized as largely positive politeness cultures. Thus in America, Brown and Levinson argue that one is more likely to use informal language towards strangers; in Mediterranean cultures such as Greece, one is more likely to be concerned to stress one's social closeness to others, rather than one's concern for one's own individual needs and distance from others (Sifianou, 1992). Thus within these positive politeness cultures, it is possible to strike up conversations fairly easily with strangers and even to impose on them for small social favours. In cultures such as Japan or Britain, it is asserted that deference and respect (negative politeness) characterize interaction, so individuals apologize more in negative politeness cultures and do not tend to impose on, or even talk to, strangers. However as Kadar and Mills (2011b) have shown, these are idealized and stereotypical views of cultures and politeness. These may be the ideological visions of cultures which we produce for ourselves, and they may represent tendencies within cultures, but they are not accurate representations of all interactions within that culture. These stereotypical beliefs may have some force in terms of the way that interactants think that they should behave, but we should see them as primarily ideological rather than as accurate representations of culture. As Kadar and Mills (2011b) show, these norms are not ones which are accepted by all people within a cultural group; they are often the norms of the elite, which are contested by subgroups. Mills (2004) has argued that there are differences between working-class and middle-class behaviour and norms within UK society, and these are often at issue and are contested in conversations involving members of different classes.

Furthermore, it is problematic to use these terms, positive and negative politeness, which are difficult enough to use at an individual level, when we are describing cultures (Mills, 2009). Brown and Levinson developed these terms to analyse individual interaction, and theorists have then gone on to use them to describe cultures as a whole. Instead we need to use different terms to describe cultures, for example, we should discuss civility to describe politeness and impoliteness at a cultural level. We should also be aware, as I have remarked, that making generalizations about a culture in relation to politeness will tend to generate stereotypical beliefs about the elite.

3.3 Discernment and volition cultures

As I argued above, Ide developed the notion of discernment and volition to describe tendencies within cultures towards concern for the group as a whole and concern for the individual. For her, certain cultures tend to stress the role of the individual in relation to the group, whereas other cultures tend to stress the role of the individual over the needs of the group. She focused on the use of honorifics in Japanese, arguing that social context and variables such as social distance and power tend to determine that honorifics will be used in an interaction. However, theorists have criticized her work and suggested that the use of Japanese honorifics is not as simple as being determined by an awareness of one's position in the social group (Mills and Kadar, 2013). Instead, as Okamoto and Shibamoto Smith's (2004) collection of essays about Japanese usage illustrates, honorifics are a grammatical resource which individuals draw on in order to negotiate their social role, rather than individuals using honorifics simply to display their acceptance of that role to their interlocutor. Thus, for example, Japanese feminists in the 1970s rejected certain types of honorific use in order to map out for themselves a style of speaking which did not fall into the conventional mode of 'Japanese women's language' (Yukagawa and Saito, 2004). Honorifics can be used to signify a very wide range of different meanings, and not just the desire to indicate one's status in the group and to be polite. Instead they can be used to mark distance, contempt, sarcasm and awareness of aesthetics. By shifting between the plain and the polite style of honorifics, it is possible to indicate to the interlocutor an awareness of a shift in one's role. Thus for example, Cook (2012) has analysed the shift in a teacher's language use from polite honorifics to a plain style, when the teacher moves from trying to get her students to do a particular task, to a plain style when talking in more general terms.

Thus, honorifics, a set of linguistic forms, which are often, but not exclusively, associated with deference and politeness, are here elided with the cultural values of the elite. Honorifics are complex and need to be learned by individuals either explicitly at school or by observing others' usage. The observance of honorifics is viewed to be important, but this linguistic form is not as universally used as it is often characterized – there is some leeway for switching from plain to polite form, without thereby offending others. Furthermore, the use of honorifics does not always indicate a concern for the group values rather than a concern for the individual. Thus Japanese should not necessarily be seen as a culture which stresses the importance of the group, and the Japanese language should also not be seen as a language which only stresses deference and respect in honorifics use.

While it is clear that certain cultures do tend to foreground the individual, or foreground the social group, as I have argued above, all cultures should be characterized as exhibiting both of these tendencies. Cultures are not homogeneous, and languages are much richer and more diverse than many politeness theorists are willing to acknowledge.

3.4 Discursive approach to languages and cultures

Thus, while these oppositions are useful as heuristic devices to describe tendencies which we can observe either at a stereotypical level or at a level where they seem to be informing linguistic choices made in individual interactions, we need to accept that cultures and languages are not homogeneous; cultures are not either positive or negative politeness cultures. There is a tendency for the elite norms of language to be considered to characterize a language and culture as a whole. But individuals within a particular culture, speaking a particular language, manage to negotiate and contest cultural and linguistic norms.

A discursive approach questions the homogeneous nature of languages, and instead focuses on the diversity within any particular language group, which inevitably results in different views of what counts as polite or impolite. Politeness and impoliteness are not simply accepted norms within particular societies but they are ones which are contested. This is illustrated very clearly in Lynn Truss's (2005) popular book about politeness in the UK, where she laments what she perceives to be a move away from negative politeness and traditional respect within British society, towards impoliteness, incivility and perhaps the more positive politeness norms, such as informality and camaraderie associated with American culture. For Truss, the elite politeness norms are being eroded by what she perceives as a lack of civility. Her book shows very clearly how within each society, there are different politeness norms, often in opposition to each other. Truss chooses to align herself with the elite norms of a slightly anachronistic British culture, which she sees as threatened by the influence of more informal behaviour and expression, associated with youth culture and American speech.

A discursive approach to culture does not characterize cultures as simply agglomerations of similar individuals. Perhaps it is more useful to see cultures and the behaviours which are associated with the elite as memes (Blackmore, 2007) which strive to be copied. The elite expend effort to ensure that their behaviours are the ones which others imitate. Blackmore asserts that human societies evolved in the way that they did through a process of memetic copying of behaviour, 'for memetics, language is not an adaptation but a parasite turned symbiotic partner; an evolving system in its own right that fed off the humans who selected, remembered and copied sounds' (2007: 8). This striking view of the way that languages evolved may be adapted to consider the way that we might view languages and cultures in a more heterogeneous way, so that we would be able to describe the different cultural and linguistic norms available within a society. Those elements which are copied are those which serve elite purposes and which maintain the status quo.

The cultural values of the elite groups are embodied in what we consider to be polite behaviour (polished, refined, cultured, civilized). This is the way that the elite groups distinguish themselves from other groups within society. These are the values which are associated with stereotypically polite behaviour. But we should not imagine that these are the only ways that individuals and groups within societies exhibit politeness towards each other. Within Britain, the way that we characterize politeness is largely based on the values associated with middle-class, educated people, and we assume that this negative politeness (deferent, respectful, using indirectness) constitutes the politeness norms of the society as a whole. However, working-class people may well rely on other more positive politeness behaviours (while using negative politeness as well when the context demands).

The elite politeness norms function as a resource which can be drawn on by individuals when they are interacting with others; but in certain contexts other relational norms will override these elite norms, enabling the individual to mock these stereotypical norms or assert other modes of behaviour.

5 Future directions

Because of the difficulties I have mapped out with identifying clearly what 'culture' is and its relation to politeness, it is to be hoped that in future linguists will be much more careful when making generalizations about the politeness norms associated with a particular language group or community. One hopes that linguists will map out the range of possibilities within a particular language group for expressing politeness and impoliteness, rather than assuming that there is only one set of uncontested norms. Furthermore, there will be an understanding of the way that individual speakers and hearers use the resources available within politeness to indicate their own status and to display their awareness of their relationship to interlocutors. Politeness will be seen less as a static, unchanging set of norms but rather as a flexible, ever-changing set of resources which individuals can draw upon.

6 Conclusions

I have argued that traditional politeness theorists have tended to characterize cultures and languages as homogeneous and this results in them assuming that the politeness norms of the elite are taken as the norms of the culture or language as a whole. A discursive approach helps us to question this view of politeness and culture and enables us to strive to describe the variety of politeness norms which exist within each culture. For discursive theorists, it is important to distinguish between culture and language. Language is influenced by the cultural values of the elite group, and this is particularly visible in the case of politeness and impoliteness, which is clearly about appropriate behaviour, but we need to recognize that an individual's linguistic repertoire is infinitely more varied than the elite politeness norms of that language. Politeness theorists need to move away from focusing on the politeness norms of the elite and to analyse the relational work which different classes and groups within a society use.

Related topics

Language and culture in sociolinguistics

Further reading

Kadar, D. and S. Mills (eds) (2011) *East Asian Politeness*, Cambridge: Cambridge University Press. (This collection of essays on East Asian politeness stresses the diversity of politeness repertoires within language communities. There are theoretical chapters on discursive approaches to the analysis of politeness and impoliteness as well as more descriptive chapters on, say, the range of politeness norms available in Vietnam and Korea.)

Linguistic Politeness Research Group (eds) (2011) *Discursive Approaches to Politeness and Impoliteness*, Berlin: Mouton de Gruyter. (This collection of essays engages with the discursive approach to the analysis of politeness and impoliteness, and tries to show through practical analyses, what can be said about politeness from this perspective.)

Okamoto, S. and J. Shibamoto Smith (eds) (2004) *Japanese Language, Gender and Ideology: Cultural Models and Real People*, Oxford: Oxford University Press. (A collection of essays which focuses on a social constructionist approach to the analysis of the relationship between gender, language, and culture in relation to Japanese.)

Scollon, R. and W. Scollon (2001) *Intercultural Communication*, Oxford: Blackwell. (A book which critically examines the role of culture in interaction, and which tries to trace the development of particular styles within language.)

Spencer-Oatey, H. (ed.) (2008) *Culturally Speaking: Culture, Communication and Politeness Theory*, 2nd edn, London: Continuum. (This is a collection of essays which examine the role of culture in the production and reception of politeness. This 2nd edition has a number of new essays which map out the use of the term relational work.)

Notes

1 This is of necessity a very brief discussion of traditional politeness theory; a fuller discussion can be found in Watts (2003); Mills (2003), and Culpeper (2011).

2 Many have also argued that this model is not in fact adequate for the analysis of politeness in English as it assumes that the politeness norms are those of the elite. Other politeness norms are not considered (Mills, 2004).

3 Relational work is the interactional work that individuals do to maintain or damage their relationship discursively. This can consist of politeness and impoliteness, but Locher and Watts set out the way in which relational work consists of far more than simply politeness and impoliteness.

4 I use ideological following the work of Althusser (1984) where he defines ideology as the 'imaginary representation of the real relations of production', that is, those representations of the way things are done, which obscure the exploitative practices within a society.

5 It might be argued that this holds true more for developed societies rather than for largely non-literate and oral societies. Within developed societies there are a range of educational institutional holding elite norms in place.

6 However. It must be noted that for those members of non-elite groups, these values and speech styles are not necessarily valued and they may well be treated with scorn (see Mills, forthcoming).

7 This view of cultures, in classifying collectivist cultures as 'conservative' and individualistic cultures as 'relatively liberal' in relation to the rights of the individual, takes up a position, albeit implicit, that the rights of the individual are paramount. It is quite clear that while gay people and women may well be marginalized in collectivist cultures, they may well also be equally marginalized in those cultures classified as individualist.

References

Althusser, L. (1984) *Essays on Ideology*, London: Verso.

Blackmore, S. (2007) 'Imitation makes us human', in C. Pasternak, ed. *What Makes Us Human?* London: One World.

Bousfield, D. (2008) *Impoliteness in Interaction*, Amsterdam and Philadelphia, PA: John Benjamins.

Brown, P. and S. Levinson (1978/1987) *Politeness: Some Universals in Language Usage*, Cambridge: Cambridge University Press.

Cook, H. (2012) 'A response to "Against the social constructionist account of Japanese politeness"', *Journal of Politeness* Research, 8(2): 269–77.

Culpeper, J. (2011) *Impoliteness: Using Language to Cause Offence*, Cambridge: Cambridge University Press.

Damen, L. (1987) *Culture Learning*, Reading, MA: Addison Wesley.

Eckert, P. and S. McConnell-Ginet (1998) 'Communities of practice: where language gender and power all live', in J. Coates ed., *Language and Gender: A Reader*, Oxford: Blackwell, pp. 484–94.

Eelen, G. (2001) *Critique of Politeness Theories*, Manchester: St Jerome's Press.

Grainger, K. and S. Mills (forthcoming) *Directness and Indirectness*, Basingstoke, Hants.: Palgrave.

Hofstede, G. (1984) *Culture's Consequences: International Differences in Work-Related Values*, London: Sage.

Ide, S. (1989) 'Formal forms and discernment: two neglected aspects of linguistic politeness', *Multilingua*, 8 (2–3): 223–48.

Inoue, M. (2004) 'Gender language and modernity: towards an effective history of "Japanese women's language"', in S. Okamoto and J. Shibamoto Smith, eds, *Japanese Language, Gender and Ideology: Cultural Models and Real People*, Oxford: Oxford University Press, pp. 57–75.

Kadar, D. and S. Mills (eds) (2011a) *East Asian Politeness*, Cambridge: Cambridge University Press.

——(2011b) 'Culture and politeness', in D. Kadar and S. Mills, eds, *East Asian Politeness*, Cambridge: Cambridge University Press, pp. 21–45.

Kerkam, Z. (forthcoming) 'Indirectness and directness in English and Arabic', Ph.D. thesis, Sheffield, Sheffield Hallam University.

Lakoff, R. and S. Ide (eds) (2005) *Broadening the Horizon of Linguistic Politeness*, Amsterdam/Philadelphia, PA: John Benjamins.

Linguistic Politeness Research Group (ed.) (2011) *Discursive Approaches to Politeness and Impoliteness*, Berlin: Mouton de Gruyter.

Locher, M. and R. Watts (2008) 'Relational work and impoliteness', in D. Bousfield and M. Locher, eds, *Impoliteness in Language*, Berlin and New York: Mouton de Gruyter, pp. 77–99.

Matsumoto, Y. (1989) 'Politeness as conversational universals: observations from Japanese', *Multilingua*, 8(2–3): 207–21.

Mills, S. (forthcoming) *Beyond English Politeness*, Cambridge: Cambridge University Press.

——(2012) *Gender Matters*, London: Equinox.

——(2011) *Discursive Approaches to Politeness and Impoliteness*, Linguistic Politeness Research Group, Berlin: Mouton de Gruyter, Berlin, pp. 19–57.

——(2009) 'Impoliteness in a cultural context', *Journal of Pragmatics*, 41(5): 1047–60.

——(2004) 'Class, gender and politeness', *Multilingua*, 23(1–2): 171–91.

——(2003) *Gender and Politeness*, Cambridge: Cambridge University Press.

Mills, S. and D. Kadar (2013) 'Discernment reconsidered', *Journal of Politeness Research*.

Okamoto, S. and Shibamoto Smith (eds) (2004) *Japanese Language, Gender and Ideology: Cultural Models and Real People*, Oxford: Oxford University Press.

Scollon, R and W. Scollon (2001) *Intercultural Communication*, Oxford: Blackwell.

Sifianou, M. (1992) *Politeness Phenomena in England and Greece*, Oxford: Oxford University Press.

Spencer-Oatey, H. (ed.) (2008) *Culturally Speaking: Culture, Communication and Politeness Theory*, 2nd edn, London: Continuum.

Triandis, H., R. Bontempo, M. Villareal, M. Asai, and N. Lucca (1988) 'Individualism and collectivism: cross-cultural perspectives on self-in-group relationships', *Journal of Personality and Social Psychology*, 54(2): 323–38.

Triandis, H., C. McCusker, and H. Hui (1990) 'Multimethod problems of individualism and collectivism', *Journal of Personality and Social Psychology*, 59(5): 1006–1375.

Truss, L. (2005) *Talk to the Hand*, New York: Gotham Books.

Wierzbicka, A. (1999) *Emotions across Languages and Cultures*, Cambridge: Cambridge University Press.

Yukagawa, S. and M. Saito (2004) 'Cultural ideologies in Japanese language and gender studies', in S. Okamoto and Shibamoto Smith, eds, *Japanese Language, Gender and Ideology: Cultural Models and Real People*, Oxford: Oxford University Press, pp. 23–37.

10

LANGUAGE, CULTURE, AND INTERACTION

Peter Eglin[1]

This chapter departs from the conventional handbook format by presenting a more or less continuous argument throughout. Instead of a historical survey of positions, issues, and research contributions, these matters are treated in relation to a single question, namely the proper understanding of language, since this has fundamental consequences for what social inquiry into language, culture, and interaction could possibly be like. The error is to abstract language from its uses as if it was a thing independent of them. Making this mistake confounds the understanding of how words mean. 'Language', 'culture', and 'interaction' are, in the first place, words, expressing concepts. 'Language is an instrument. Its concepts are instruments' (Wittgenstein 1972: 569; see Lee 1991).

Introduction: the problem of language

The fundamental problem, then, is philosophical. It is expressed in the question: how shall language be conceptualized? This is clearly not a question that ordinarily arises when members of society are engaged in the activities of everyday life under the auspices of the natural or practical attitude. Language is not a problem for us in this sense. On the contrary, language is like the air we breathe. It is just there, used but, for the most part, unnoticed. Of course, it can be a problem if you don't speak the language that you need to know in order to understand what others are saying or doing. Neither my wife nor I speak Japanese. It limited our interactional possibilities on a visit to Japan. But we got about Tokyo on that city's wonderful and complex railway system with the aid of maps and diagrams, our existing knowledge of railways from other countries, helpful Japanese who offered their assistance … So language *can* be a problem for the practical actor, though not necessarily an insuperable one. It depends on the circumstances. But then 'language' as the medium of communication and thought, and 'language' as in French, Urdu, or Ojibwa, are not the same thing, though named with the same word. Odd that, if you reflect on it, as philosophers are wont to do, but not odd as you live with it. Quite unremarkable, in fact.

The reflective oddity comes about when one considers that reflecting on multiple meaning (or polysemy) does not generally lead the professional, scientific language inquirer in the direction of noticing further and further variability to the point of losing the determinate object assumed to be named by the word. Instead, professional, scientific inquiry, like the common-sense actor

(Sharrock and Anderson 1991: 56), hangs on to the idea of the determinate object, seeing the variability as just varieties of *it*. *It* remains. But since what is apprehended is the variety, *it* must exist somewhere else than in the realm of apprehension, either the 'reality' beneath the variable 'appearances' or the 'ideal' object realized in the imperfect expressions of it, the abstracted competence generating the degenerate performance.

I speak English, Michel speaks French. One can say this and be understood. It is also true to say, though, that Michel speaks English and I can get by in French. But to say this is to miss the point of saying that I speak English and Michel speaks French (which is true even when neither of us is speaking at all, or speaking 'each other's language'). One can be saying, and be heard to be saying, that my native language is English, Michel's French, that I am an English speaker and that Michel is a French speaker. One may even be (heard to be) saying that I 'am' English and Michel 'is' French. But within France one might say that Michel speaks 'Parisian French' whereas Claude speaks Provençal. But then, again, in the environs of the border between France and Italy one finds people who speak 'varieties of French and Italian' respectively that are mutually intelligible (Hockett 1958: 324). I believe this phenomenon is repeated in the environs of the French and Spanish border, and in many other similar situations. Linguistics tries to capture such variation with the concepts of dialect and, indeed, idiolect, referring to an individual's particular way of speaking. Hockett's classic linguistics textbook does recognize that 'the ease with which people can understand each other, and the degree of resemblance of their speech habits, are both functions of the amount of talking that takes place among them' (1958: 326), but rather than leading the linguist to investigate such talking, including its geographical context for the speakers, mutual intelligibility leads back via 'idiolect differentiation' to the idea of a 'common core' and 'overall pattern' in the structure of the presupposed determinate object, 'language' (1958: 331ff.).

But then what of the 'language' of barter, of auctioneering, of stock market exchange floors, of slam poetry, railway station announcements, nuclear physics, TV weather reports ('up in through'), lecturing, bull sessions, football huddles, and so on endlessly? Where is *it*? There is no core element that is common to all the things that can be called 'games' (Wittgenstein 1972: 66–71). Think, moreover, of what can be a person in law: 'In 1886 the Supreme Court of the United States ruled for the first time, without argument, that business corporations were entitled, as "persons", to protection from the arbitrary authority of the states under the Fourteenth Amendment of the U.S. Constitution, an amendment intended for the protection of freed slaves' (Noble 2005: 117). The abstracted, ideal, named object is just what is *not* real except in the theories of linguistics. If 'language' does not name a determinate object, then what are theories of language? Playful inventions. Like language. Yet this is no problem at all to language speakers or language users, who mostly have no need of theories, and when they do have need of them it's typically to handle some local, situational, contingent matter.

Culture

The same argument may be made about culture. No sooner is an attempt made to establish a formal definition for it (thought of as a determinate thing) – for example, an 'integrated and distinct set of rules which give meaning to activities' (Sharrock and Anderson 1982: 120) or, famously, 'whatever it is one has to know or believe to operate in a manner acceptable to [a society's members], and do so in any role that they accept for any one of themselves' (Goodenough 1957: 167) – than it has to be admitted that in any actual case accommodation will have to be made for subcultures, local cultures, the cultures of particular groups of all sorts and the idea, say, that while some set of cultural practices may be 'shared' by neighbouring societies one of them 'owns' the cultural practices in question and the other has 'copied' them (Sharrock 1974: 49–51). For many of its uses 'culture' may be replaced with 'society', 'values', 'customs', 'mores', 'the way we do things round here' without it ever being possible to pin down once and for all what that 'way' is. Cultures as determinate objects are professional anthropologists' inventions, the product of 'ethnographic work' in the 'organization of fieldwork data' (Anderson and Sharrock 1982). Persons in the conduct of their mundane affairs in the practical attitude of everyday life surely have their uses for the concept of culture (e.g. Katz and Sharrock 1979), but it does not pose the sort of systematic problem for them that it does for professional ethnographers.

To paraphrase further the papers by Anderson and Sharrock just cited, the problem arises for the professional anthropological ethnographer only so long as culture is treated as the presupposition of inquiry rather than its discovered outcome. If, however, the 'native' whose thoughts and actions the professional ethnographer seeks to understand is himself or herself regarded as a (lay) ethnographer of their own culture and society, then how *they* go about finding out 'what gives here' in any actual social situation they encounter can become the subject of analytic inquiry. Rather than supposing that the 'native' is a carrier of the 'native point of view' – with all the problems of accessibility and relativism such a view entails for the professional anthropological (or indeed sociological) ethnographer – treating him or her as themselves an inquirer into the values, mores, habits, rules, and ways of acting appropriate to the event, occasion, situation, setting, and society in which they find themself holds out the promise of discovering the interpretive methods in, through and by which *anyone* navigates their way into and through – and thereby appropriates for themself – their own way of life.

Language and culture: (ethnographic) semantics

Ethnographic semantics, or ethnosemantics (see Chapter 4 this volume), is one field that, straddling the boundary of linguistics and cultural (cognitive) anthropology, has acknowledged the problem of variability in the meaning of words and attempted to deal with it in its own terms. Thus, 'variations are not mere deviations from some assumed basic organization; with their rules of occurrence *they are the organization*' (Tyler 1969: 5). Rules of occurrence can then be adumbrated in terms of 'core' or 'primary' meanings, 'metaphor' or 'extended' meanings, and 'polysemy' and 'homonymy', these last two being used as intermediate disambiguating devices (Scheffler and Lounsbury 1971; Wallace and Atkins 1960). Beyond these devices analysts have invoked a semantic domain's 'fuzzy boundaries', 'probabilistic considerations' and a range of sociolinguistic variables to systematize their accounts of variation. I say 'devices' deliberately in order to draw attention to how 'polysemy', 'homonymy', and the like may be viewed as professional semantic analysts' permissive theoretical methods of making sense, of producing rational results, even where the devices are admittedly problematic (Lyons 1977: 552). This two-sided practice of acknowledging variation while rescuing word meaning by theoretical stipulation is perspicuously evident in John Lyons's magnum opus *Semantics* (1977).

Thus, Lyons is prepared to surmise that it 'may well be that the whole notion of discrete lexical senses is ill-founded' (1977: 554, see also 544), to allow that 'words may be correctly and incorrectly applied to persons and things … for all sorts of reasons, some of which have nothing to do with their denotations' (213), to acknowledge that a 'host of additional complexities' (187) attends indefinite reference, to take half a page to mention family resemblances (212), and to quote Bar-Hillel on the 'essentially pragmatic character' of ordinary language (117). With magnanimity he concedes that 'until we have a satisfactory theory of culture, in the construction of which not only sociology, but also cognitive and social psychology, have played their part, it is idle to speculate further about the possibility of constructing anything more than a rather ad hoc practical account of the denotation of lexemes' (210). Notice the recourse to an as-yet-to-be-invented 'theory of culture' as a solution to the problem of indefinite reference. Culture is the first and last refuge of sense-making, for professional and lay analysts alike (Garfinkel 1967: 71, 76–7), as we shall see again below.

But one feels that these are, in effect, concessionary rejections, ways of dispensing with problems by acknowledging them. For in conjunction with them goes the elaborate work of definition whereby the edifice of linguistics as a discrete, formalistic, natural–scientific enterprise is shored up. This methodological moat-building consists in the liberal use of 'methodological fiat' (742, 566) and in such operations as the following:

(a) preserving 'denotation' to hold 'independently of particular occasions of utterances' (208), and leaving 'reference' as an 'utterance-bound relation' holding of 'expressions in context' (208), then

(b) saving reference by (if we ignore the trick of preferring 'for terminological reasons' to say that *expressions* refer rather than *speakers* (177)) (i) distinguishing between the 'utterance-act' and its product, the 'utterance-signal', and opting for the latter as the analytical object (26), and by (ii) making 'context-of-utterance' a theoretical construct referring only to sources of 'systematic' variation (572; cf. Lyons 1968: 420), while leaving 'random' variation 'to be discounted in terms of

[c] the distinction of competence and performance' (572, 29), that renowned filler of wastebaskets (586), a distinction that itself relies on

(d) the claim that 'idealization is inevitable' (586), 'the very considerable problems involved in [which]' (586) are handled for all practical textbook purposes by defining sub-types, namely 'regularization' (586), 'standardization' (588), and 'decontextualization' (588). Add to these the distinctions between 'productivity' and 'creativity' (549), and 'rules' and 'strategies' (549), and the concept of 'metaphorical transfer' (566).

All this theoretically stipulative, definitional work is directed towards the goal of saving *language* and *linguistics* for each other: 'It is pointless to argue, however, that there is no such thing as a homogeneous language-system underlying the language-behaviour of the whole language-community' (588); the validity of such a concept 'is proved by the practical usefulness of the grammars, phonological descriptions and dictionaries that are produced by descriptive linguistics' (588). The tone here is one of embattled 'constructive analysis' (Garfinkel and Sacks 1970: 340), faintly reminiscent of Phaedrus's impassioned defence of the Church of Reason he has lost his faith in (Pirsig 1976: 146). From within linguistics Roy Harris has most forcefully made the case that 'language' as the determinate object is not to be found since it is a product of human making, as the titles of the two books containing the argument, *The Language Myth* (1981: 9–10 for the 'determinacy fallacy') and the *Language Makers* (1980), indicate: 'Languages do not come ready-made … They are what men make them. As language-makers, men … take part in the many social activities which alone provide the context for a relevant conceptualization of what a language is' (Harris 1980: Preface).

From without linguistics we may turn to Emanuel Schegloff who, through attending rigorously to the data of 'performance' in the form of conversation analysis, came to put the whole question of language as a determinate object in question:

In continually writing of a 'syntax-for-conversation' I mean to treat explicitly as hypothetical what seems to me to be prematurely treated as presupposed fact, and that is the existence of A syntax. That there is a trans-discourse-type syntax may end up to be the case; it should be found, not presupposed. With that, I also mean to make explicitly hypothetical the current sense of 'a language', or 'language'. The notion 'a language' seems to be the product of an assumption about some common, stable, underlying properties of an immense range of human behaviour – from talking to the family to reciting Shakespeare to cadging alms to writing memoranda to lecturing, etc. – each of which is embedded in its own combination of organizational structures, constraints and resources. Much attention has been devoted to these supposedly common features; relatively little to their respective environments of use, which differentiate them.

(1979: 282)

Conversational analysis and a serious treatment of Wittgenstein are conspicuously absent from Lyons's text. As for idealization as an inevitable requirement of scientific methodology – 'Without abstraction and idealization there is no systematization' (Chomsky 1988: 37; Searle 1969: 56) – consider the following on Bar-Hillel's indexical (context-dependent) expressions (which is to say, on all of language):

In a search for rigour the ingenious practice is followed whereby such expressions are first transformed into ideal expressions. Structures are then analyzed as properties of the ideals, and the results are assigned to actual expressions as their properties, though with disclaimers of 'appropriate scientific modesty'.

(Garfinkel and Sacks 1970: 339)

Just as linguistics may be said to have a vested professional interest in preserving the idea of language as a determinate object requiring the expertise of its personnel for its explication, so it may be said that anthropology has such an interest in the determinate existence of culture (and sociology, likewise, in society).

Language, culture, and interaction

Returning to the (ethno-)semantic argument about word meaning, consider the following two data consisting of a sign in a bookstore window advertising a sale, and a two-utterance exchange overheard on a university campus sidewalk as A and B crossed paths.

(1)   Books and paperbacks

(2)   A: Do you want a coffee?
      B: No, I've just eaten

Now while these two cases might at first appear to contradict simple taxonomic relations that one might propose for the domains of 'books' and of 'food' or 'drinks', and thereby cause problems for ethnosemantics, the enterprise can be saved, so it is said, by invoking polysemy. That is, in (1) the contradiction would be resolved in some such fashion as this: allow 'book' to have (at least) two senses, namely that (a) in which it includes hardback and paperback books, and that (b) in which it means hardback books and so contrasts with paperbacks; conclude that thereby the second sense is the one relevant here. In (2) either the dictionary specification for 'a coffee' is allowed to include an additional sense, namely something like 'a snack' (though this seems highly implausible), or the domain of 'food' or 'something to eat' (Frake 1969: 31–2) is so constructed to

145

allow for 'food$_1$' to include both 'food$_2$' and 'drinks'. Here the analyst could appeal to the familiar condition of the head term of a taxonomy also being a category label at a lower level of contrast. Thus Hays (personal communication, 1977) proposed, if informally, that (2) is a case of polysemy, as when someone says 'Let's have a coke', meaning by 'coke' in that context 'any soft drink'. Once again, the dictionary definition of a term, 'coke', will have to be allowed to incorporate the separate sense 'any soft drink'.

The crucial problem with this strategy is, however, '*the fact that distinctions of sense can be multiplied indefinitely*' (Lyons 1977: 554, emphasis added). The prospect is one of an ever-expanding dictionary, its size depending only on the breadth of knowledge, imagination, and endurance of the compiler. This captures neither the point of dictionaries nor, crucially, how members, including professional ethnographers, decide what the terms in (1) and (2) mean and how they mean what they do, 'how' and 'what' being, of course, inseparable. How is it that 'book$_2$', and 'food$_1$' are seen to be the relevant categories in these instances? Appeal to the context, it is always said. Yes, but, allowing for a degree of predictability on syntactic and prosodic grounds (Lyons 1977: 569, 186–7), how is it that one, whether actor or observer, selects just that bit of the indefinite context of these particulars that points to the relevant sense of the terms? Trite though it may seem to say so, we cannot dispense with the notion that members of society rely on each other to *look* and *find* just that relation between context and term that will render the term's use intelligible/sensible/rational/appropriate (Garfinkel 1967; Schegloff 1972: 115). Abstracting from users, Garfinkel and Sacks (1970: 338) put it this way: 'a description, for example, in the ways it may be a constituent part of the circumstances it describes, in endless ways and unavoidably, elaborates those circumstances and is elaborated by them'. Societal members may be said, that is, to orient to one another as practical reasoners in the sense of being inquirers into, ethnographers of, their own social circumstances. No sooner is one, whether as actor or observer, lay or professional analyst of the scene, confronted with the cases at hand than one is elaborating the sense of the items and the occasions in which they (might have) occurred in order to render those uses plausible (Sacks 1976; Wieder 1970: 134). In so doing one draws inevitably and implicitly on presumed, and situationally relevant, common-sense knowledge, yet semantic analysts rarely, if ever, take that knowledge explicitly into account (Hymes 1974: 154).

Thus in (1) one can take it that a person viewing the sign can discover (literally) in the (findable) fact that a book *sale* is being *advertised* by the sign, that whereas some sales are of paperbacks only, and some of hardbacks only, *this* sale is of *both*; moreover, *that* fact is something that a bookshop having a sale might be *interested* in having the people seeing the sign, that is its (now) potential *customers*, be aware of, because as anybody knows who looks in bookshop windows, different if overlapping sets of customers are interested in paperbacks and hardbacks. That interest provides the point of the sign. Recognizing that interest, motivation or intention *in* the sign, or imputing it *to* the sign, provides an intelligible reading *of* the sign and of the terms in it, including that it *is* a sign. There is obviously some connection here with the treatment of intention in speech-act theory (see Wootton 1975: 48), but the general point has been most elegantly formulated, in several places, by Harvey Sacks (1976: G6; 1972a: 57; 1972b: 339).

This analysis is a members' analysis, having recourse to such members' analytical categories as 'interest' (cf. 'intention', 'motive', and so on) and to the related, setting-relevant, membership categorization device 'buyer/seller'. I suggest that professional semantic ethnographers trade on such analyses in order to identify the particular sense in which a term is being employed (Cicourel 1964: 76), but, like members, do not make a topic of that analysis; instead, they theorize it as a case of polysemy, in the name of the definite, if not unitary, sense of lexemes. 'Members' analyses' are the domain of ethnomethodology and conversation analysis (CA). To introduce these sociological approaches to language, culture, and interaction, consider the following, somewhat more elaborated account of the second datum in our corpus. Such an account of (2) might run as follows.

I have said that (ethno)semantics could be expected to resolve the 'contradiction' between 'coffee' and 'eaten' by invoking polysemy whereby 'food$_1$' is the relevant sense on this occasion; and that the question then arose of *how* members, whether actors or observers, decide that 'food$_1$' is the relevant sense on this occasion. To answer this question one needs to see that the *actions* being performed here are an invitation and its declining, and that the two have an adjacency-pair format (Sacks *et al.* 1974: 716ff.; Schegloff 2007: 13–14), whereby the occurrence of the first sets up the relevance of the second occurring next. Moreover, (2) is a case where the invitation is made in the form of a question where that, too, sets up the relevance of a particular action in the following turn, namely an answer, question and answer having an adjacency-pair format also. Indeed one might propose that B's 'No' does provide an adequate answer to A's question, while 'I've just eaten' displays B's hearing of that question as an *invitation*, in that 'I've just eaten' can be heard as a reason for declining an invitation, where a simple 'No', though an adequate answer to a question, might well appear ill-mannered as a declining. In displaying itself as a declining of an invitation B's utterance also points to *what* it is a declining of, namely that sort of small social encounter, say a break or a snack, in which a little eating or drinking or both or none might be done – that is, an occasion in which 'a coffee' and 'eaten' are compatible. It is by virtue of the structure of social occasions (Goffman 1964) and of the sequential properties of speech acts that one can come to see 'food$_1$' as (a rough semantic gloss for) the relevant sense here (see Schegloff 1972: 432 fn. 15).

Let me summarize the argument to this point. I began by saying that the fundamental problem is philosophical, a matter of the nature and use of the concept of language being employed. The same may be said about culture and, indeed, about society. The idea that language, culture, and society are objects the nature of which can be discovered and elucidated by the formal, rational, scientific, analytical, abstracted methods of what Garfinkel (2002: 65–8, 121) called the 'worldwide social science movement' is, in Ryle's terms, a category mistake of the first order (Winch 1970 [1964]: 93). Indeed it is a monumental mistake that continues to mislead the respective disciplines that subscribe to it (Hutchinson, Read, and Sharrock 2008; Winch [1958] 2008). It is a mistake because it mis-takes from the outset the way language – and thereby the concepts that are expressed in it, including 'language', 'culture', and 'society' – operates. It entails a failure to appreciate that the home of language, culture, and society is in social interaction (Watson 1992: 2), in the mutually coordinated actions of human beings going about the business of their everyday affairs (whether commonplace or esoteric), what Schegloff (2007: 264) calls 'the observable, actual conduct in interaction that is the prima facie, bottom-line stuff of social life'; that what a linguistic expression or any other sign or movement signifies is to be found in the situated, occasioned, interactional context that constitutes it as such (Coulter 2009: 391); that therefore what language primarily does is not to describe things, this being the constative or descriptive fallacy (Austin 1965: 3), and certainly not to describe some imagined-to-be-independent realm of reality outside of language, but to be the means and medium for performing actions, including describing and those other actions that incorporate descriptions. 'Stating, describing, &c., are just two names among a very great many others for illocutionary acts; they have no unique position' (Austin 1965: 147–8).

The mistake persists, I argue, despite over one hundred years of subversive efforts to overturn the scientific consensus by Weber, Schutz, Garfinkel, Austin, Wittgenstein above all, Winch, and others of the sociological schools of action theory, symbolic interactionism, phenomenology, and ethnomethodology (Coulter 2009), and despite the partial inroads made by the various schools of analytic practice within and across the disciplines of linguistics, anthropology, sociology, communication studies, psychology, and so on that may be loosely assembled under the banner of language and social interaction, and include ethnography of communication, discourse analysis, pragmatics, interactional sociolinguistics, conversation analysis, language and social psychology and coordinated management of meaning (Leeds-Hurwitz 2010: 6–8). Indeed the mistake persists even within these relatively sophisticated schools of linguistic and cultural analysis. It may take the form of (1) a residual positivism with recourse to causal theorizing, quantitative, distributional analysis of correlations (see Maynard *et al.* 2010: 319–20), 'sound empirical results that can test, inform, and refine abstract theoretical positions' providing 'us with solid general-izations' (Duranti 2009: 22–3) or empiricist appeal to 'proof procedures' and 'evidence' (Coulter 1983; Lynch and Bogen 1994), or, paradoxically, of (2) a version of social constructionism attributing the metaphysical project of reality construction to members' actions (Button and Sharrock 1993; Francis 2005; Hester and Francis 1997), or of (3) a politics (characteristically an identity politics) attributed to members' actions but reflective of the analyst's interests and not demonstrable in the talk-in-interaction under investigation. It is this last form of analytic imposition that I shall endeavour to bring out in the final section of this chapter.

Language, culture, and interaction: describing identity

So I said above (well, actually, 'wrote', but does that mean I didn't 'say' it?) that one can say that they speak English, and be meaning (and be heard) to say they are English. But, switching to the first person, I can also say I am British, from Kitchener, North American, European, from Cherry Park, English Canadian, from Liverpool, Ontarian, from Lancashire, Canadian, from Huyton, from the United Kingdom of Great Britain and Northern Ireland, an easterner, from Central Canada, from Lancashire, from south-western Ontario. Who am I?

The question does not follow, once it is appreciated that each of us may be described in a multitude of ways (Sacks 1972a, 1972b), so that these are all not only correct descriptions of who I am but, more importantly, identifications useable for the interactional context in which they are invoked and which they invoke (Coulter 1991: 41; Schegloff 1972: 81). A characteristic feature of such contexts is the matter of where the party soliciting such an identification says they are from themself. One may describe where one is from in relation to where one's inter-locutor is from, as everybody knows. The point of the identification selection is interactional, that is social in Weber's primordial sense – it takes into account the presence of others. One designs one's utterances, including such descriptions as self-identifications, for their recipients, what CA calls 'recipient design' with a preference for 'recognitionals' (Sacks and Schegloff 1979: 16–17). And this is to speak just of geographical identifications. Adding in all the other possible ways of identifying oneself – an indefinitely large number – is, however, not to conjure up the existential metaphysics of personal identity. Nor does it occasion the maelstrom of unresolvable referential ambiguity (Schegloff 1984: 50–2). Indexicality of reference *as a systematic problem of communication* simply does not arise for interpersonal interaction. Ethnomethodology's take on indexicality is not as a *problem* of language use but as its inexhaustible *resource* (Garfinkel and Sacks 1970; Sacks 1976). Yet if we are to believe much contemporary discourse analysis, including some genres of conversation analysis, talk-in-interaction is never free of the influence of some identities, especially those grounded in the *great extending trilogy* of class, race, and gender, plus sexual orientation, ability (able-ness), and so on.

New directions? The 'new' feminist conversation analysis

Following from its origins in ethnomethodology (Sharrock and Anderson 1986: ch. 5; Schegloff 1992), CA methodology is committed to the principles of 'operational relevance' and 'procedural consequentiality' when ascribing 'social structural identities' to talk's participants (Schegloff 1991: 51). Such identities must be grounded in the observable orientations displayed by conversational participants. The consequentiality of relevant categories for how talk proceeds is to be treated as a members' phenomenon, not an analyst's one.

Motivated by these methodological precepts, in the last fifteen years a 'new' feminist conversation analysis has emerged focused on examining gender as a property of social interaction rather than of individuals (Stokoe 2000: 553), while remaining committed to feminist principles. Rather than assuming a priori gender's omnirelevance, the focus shifts to how members of society employ common-sense gender knowledge ('culture') in their talk. But because feminism is not just an academic perspective that focuses on women but a politics built on a critique of male dominance, it is perhaps not surprising that Stokoe should conclude her 2000 paper by asking: 'What happens when speakers do not explicitly orient to gender, yet the analyst wants to make a claim that the talk is gendered, sexist or heterosexist?' (560), or that in Stokoe (2006: 488) she should endorse the behind-the-scenes concept of culture expressed in the claim, 'the more natural, taken-for-granted and therefore invisible the categorization work, the more powerful it is' (Baker 2000: 111). Here feminist politics contradict CA principles. This is most emphatically demonstrated in the work of a leading exponent of new feminist CA, Celia Kitzinger. Following Wowk's (2007) critique of Kitzinger (2000, 2002), and adapting Francis *et al.* (2010), I want to focus on Kitzinger's (2005) claim that the classical writings and data of CA betray an 'undisclosed heteronormativity'.

> Virtually all the talk on which the classic findings of conversation analysis (CA) are based is produced by heterosexuals, who reproduce in their talk a normative taken-for-granted heterosexual world ... A distinctive feature of these 'displays' of heterosexuality is that they are not usually oriented to as such by either speaker or recipient. Rather, heterosexuality is taken for granted as an unquestioned and unnoticed part of their life worlds.
>
> *(222–3)*

Despite noting that 'there is no sense [in which] references to husbands and wives ... are contrived self-presentations of heterosexuality' (Kitzinger 2005: 238), and, indeed, that 'these invocations of spouses are designed to achieve interactional goals related to the immediate sequential contexts in which they occur' (238), Kitzinger nevertheless characterizes the 'giving off' of identities by the members in the data as '*insistently* heterosexual' (222, 242; emphasis added), or as 'heterosex*ist*' (245; emphasis added) or as 'a mundane instance of heterosexual *privilege*' (255; emphasis added). The 'very inattentiveness to heterosexuality ... reflects and constructs heteronormativity' (223), because 'it is precisely the fact that sexist, heterosexist, and racist assumptions are routinely incorporated in to everyday conversations without anyone noticing or responding to them as such that constitutes a culture' (224; cf. Kitzinger 2000: 171). Notice again the substantive ('knowledge that') and behind-the-scenes characterization of culture here.

How then is Kitzinger 'seeing' or 'hearing' here such that she knows better than the talk's participants what is organizing their talk? Francis (2009: 24) writes, 'It seems to me that Kitzinger's descriptions are, in a relevant sense, a "lesbian activist's descriptions" of the talk'. This is apparent when she writes, 'person reference forms ... also make available – *at least to a recipient for whom such things matter* – the inference of that person's heterosexuality' (Kitzinger 2005: 223–4, emphasis added), and '*for any deviant LGBT participant in (or eavesdropping on) the conversations* in the data corpora from which these fragments have been extracted, a *clamorous* heterosexuality is everywhere apparent' (255–6, emphasis added), and 'the range of interactional activities from which *closeted same-sex couples* are excluded … is vast' (258). In short she is relying on a particular 'gaze', that of the outsider or 'passer', who takes a special, undisclosed interest in how people are talking. In Kitzinger (2000: 171) she writes, 'it would be unbearably limiting to use CA if it meant that I could only describe as "sexist" or "heterosexist" or "racist" those forms of talk to which actors orient as such'. She is treating the talk in the CA data as if it were spoken for an overhearing audience who are then entitled to criticize it (see her 2005: 259), when, in fact, it wasn't (see Schegloff 1984: 50 for the 'overhearer's problem'). Hers is, irremediably, an 'interested' analysis (Turner 1976: 233ff.).

Concluding remarks

Rather than reviewing in turn the various schools of thought that take language, culture (or society), and interaction as their subject I have opted in this chapter to identify and critique the philosophical position on these concepts that, I argue, persists in various guises despite being widely thought to have been abandoned. That position is our old friend the correspondence theory of meaning: language is made of words and structures among words that together provide a picture of the world, the correctness of which is a matter of how well the picture corresponds to said world. Culture is then construed as a substantive body of things ('knowledge that') that, like language (and society), is presupposed to exist independently, behind the scenes, of the inter-action that it shapes and constructs. Since it is professional practitioners of the language, culture and society disciplines that have privileged knowledge of the contents of these domains, it is they who are in a position to stand in judgment of the adequacy of laypersons' practices.

Wittgenstein spent his thinking life first formulating this position, then repudiating it. Of human scientific approaches to inquiry ethnomethodology and ethnomethodologically informed con-versation analysis come closest perhaps to honouring his injunction not to ask for the meaning but to look for the use. That language, culture, and society are collections of conceptual tools for use in interaction is the Wittgensteinian insight the radical implications of which continue to elude many inquirers whose professional status hangs on their subscription to scientific method, mathematical dexterity, cultural insight, and/or political correctness. There is no map of future directions to lay out, only persistent problems to take up again for another first time.[2]

Related topics

ethnosemantics; language, gender, and culture; language, culture, and context; language, culture, and identity; language and culture in cognitive anthropology

Further reading

D'hondt, S., Östman, J.-O. and Verschueren, J. (eds) (2009) *The Pragmatics of Interaction*, Amsterdam: John Benjamins. (A useful collection of summary accounts of Sacks, CA, ethnomethodology, interactional linguistics, Goffman and of various features of the linguistic organization of interaction.)

Francis, D. and Hester, S. (2004) *An Invitation to Ethnomethodology: language, society and interaction*, London: Sage. (This is the most accessible and engaging introduction to ethnomethodology with a first chapter emphasizing social interaction, the contextual availability of meaning, and language-in-use.)

Lee, J.R.E. (1991) Language and culture: the linguistic analysis of culture, in G. Button (ed.) *Ethnomethodology and the Human Sciences*, Cambridge: Cambridge University Press, pp. 196–226. (Lee provides a penetrating ethnomethodological respecification of the range of linguistic efforts – from de Saussure to discourse analysis – to analyse culture based on a faulty concept of language uninformed by Wittgenstein.)

Schegloff, E.A. (1972) Notes on a conversational practice: formulating place, in D. Sudnow (ed.) *Studies in Social Interaction*, New York: Free Press, pp. 75–119, 432–3. (Read this brilliant paper for how

Schegloff develops a richly documented examination of members' common-sense geography in terms of location, membership, and topic or activity analyses so as to illuminate the understanding of insertion sequences.)

Speer, S.A. and Stokoe, E. (eds) (2011) *Conversation and Gender*, Cambridge: Cambridge University Press. (In their Introduction to this collection of studies of membership categorization, repair, recipient design, and action formation, all in relation to gender, including independent contributions by Stokoe and (Land and) Kitzinger, the editors take a much more cautious stance to the question of the relationship between members' practical and situational orientation to the relevance of gender categories and professional analysts' interests deriving from feminist politics.)

Notes

1 I dedicate this chapter to the memory of Stephen Hester, friend, collaborator, and a man of extraordinary sociological talent, who lived his life by ethnomethodology.

2 I am grateful to John Lee for his helpful comments on an earlier draft of this chapter.

References

Anderson, R.J. and Sharrock, W.W. (1982) 'Ethnographic work: some aspects of the organization of fieldwork data', unpublished paper.

Austin, J.L. (1965) *How to Do Things with Words: The William James Lectures Delivered at Harvard University in 1955*, New York: Oxford University Press.

Baker, C.D. (2000) Locating culture in action: membership categorization in texts and talk, in A. Lee and C. Poynton (eds) *Culture and Text: discourse and methodology in social research and cultural studies*, London: Routledge, pp. 99–113.

Button, G. and Sharrock, W. (1993) A disagreement over agreement and consensus in constructionist sociology, *Journal for the Theory of Social Behaviour*, 23(1): 1–25.

Chomsky, N. (1988) *Language and Problems of Knowledge: The Managua lectures*, Cambridge, MA: MIT Press.

Cicourel, A.V. (1964) *Method and Measurement in Sociology*, New York: Free Press of Glencoe.

Coulter, J. (1983) Contingent and a priori structures in sequential analysis, *Human Studies*, 6(4): 361–76.

——(1991) Logic: ethnomethodology and the logic of language, in G. Button (ed.) *Ethnomethodology and the Human Sciences*, Cambridge: Cambridge University Press, pp. 20–50.

——(2009) Rule-following, rule-governance and rule-accord: reflections on rules after Rawls, *Journal of Classical Sociology*, 9(4): 389–403.

Duranti, A. (2009) Linguistic anthropology: history, ideas, and issues, in A. Duranti (ed.) *Linguistic Anthropology: a reader*, 2nd edn, Chichester, UK: Wiley-Blackwell, pp. 1–59.

Eglin, P.A. (1980) *Talk and Taxonomy: a methodological comparison of ethnosemantics and ethnomethodology with reference to terms for Canadian doctors*, Amsterdam: John Benjamins.

Frake, C.O. (1969) The ethnographic study of cognitive systems, in S.A. Tyler (ed.) *Cognitive Anthropology*, New York: Holt, Rinehart and Winston, pp. 28–41; orig. pub. 1962.

Francis, D. (2005) Using Wittgenstein to respecify constructivism, *Human Studies*, 28: 251–90.

——(2009) 'Boating with Owl and Pussycat', paper presented at Manchester Ethnography Group Seminars, Manchester, UK, 9 December.

Francis, D., Hester, S. and Eglin, P. (2010) 'Conversation analysis and gender: a critique of two feminist approaches to studies of gender and discourse', unpublished paper.

Garfinkel, H. (1967) *Studies in Ethnomethodology*. Englewood Cliffs, NJ: Prentice-Hall.

——(2002) *Ethnomethodology's Program: working out Durkheim's aphorism*, ed. and intro. A.W. Rawls, Lanham, MD: Rowman and Littlefield.

Garfinkel, H. and Sacks, H. (1970) 'On formal structures of practical actions', in J.C. McKinney and E.A. Tiryakian (eds) *Theoretical Sociology*, New York: Appleton-Century-Crofts, pp. 337–66.

Goffman, E. (1964) 'The neglected situation', *American Anthropologist*, 66 (6, part 2): 133–6.

Goodenough, W.H. (1957) 'Cultural anthropology and linguistics', in P.L. Garvin (ed.), *Report on the Seventh Annual Round Table Meeting on Linguistics and Language Study*. Monograph Series on Languages and Linguistics 9. Washington, DC: Georgetown University Press, pp. 167–73.

Harris, R. (1980) *The Language-Makers*, Ithaca, NY: Cornell University Press.

——(1981) *The Language Myth*, London: Duckworth.

Hays, T.E. (1977) personal communication.

Hester, S. and Francis, D. (1997) 'Reality analysis in a classroom storytelling', *British Journal of Sociology*, 48(1): 95–112.

Hockett, C.F. (1958) *A Course in Modern Linguistics*, New York: Macmillan.

Hutchinson, P., Read, R. and Sharrock, W. (2008) *There Is No Such Thing as a Social Science: In defence of Peter Winch*, Aldershot, UK: Ashgate.

Hymes, D.H. (1974) *Foundations in Sociolinguistics: An ethnographic approach*, Philadelphia: University of Pennsylvania Press.

Katz, B.A. and Sharrock, W.W. (1979) Eine Darstellung des Kodierens [An account of coding], in E. Weingarten, F. Sack and J. Schenkein (eds) *Ethnomethodologie: Beitrage zu einer Soziologie des Alltagshandlens*, zweite Auflage, Frankfurt: Suhrkamp, pp. 244–71.

Kitzinger, C. (2000) Doing feminist conversation analysis, *Feminism and Psychology*, 10: 163–93.

——(2002) Doing feminist conversation analysis, in P. McIlvenny (ed.) *Talking Gender and Sexuality*, Amsterdam: John Benjamins, pp. 49–77.

——(2005) Speaking as a heterosexual: (how) does sexuality matter for talk-in-interaction? *Research on Language and Social Interaction*, 38: 221–65.

Lee, J.R.E. (1991) Language and culture: the linguistic analysis of culture, in G. Button (ed.) *Ethnomethodology and the Human Sciences*, Cambridge: Cambridge University Press, pp. 196–226.

Leeds-Hurwitz, W. (ed.) (2010) *The Social History of Language and Social Interaction: People, places, ideas*, Cresskill, NJ: Hampton Press.

Lynch, M. and Bogen, D. (1994) Harvey Sacks's primitive natural science, *Theory, Culture and Society*, 11: 65–104.

Lyons, J. (1968) *Introduction to Theoretical Linguistics*, Cambridge: Cambridge University Press.

——(1977) *Semantics*, Cambridge: Cambridge University Press.

Maynard, D.W., Clayman, S.E., Halkowski, T. and Kidwell, M. (2010) Toward an interdisciplinary field: language and social interaction research at the University of California, Santa Barbara, in W. Leeds-Hurwitz (ed.) *The Social History of Language and Social Interaction: people, places, ideas*, Cresskill, NJ: Hampton Press, pp. 313–33.

Noble, D.F. (2005) *Beyond the Promised Land: The movement and the myth*, Toronto: Between the Lines.

Pirsig, R.M. (1976) *Zen and the Art of Motorcycle Maintenance*, London: Corgi.

Sacks, H. (1972a) An initial investigation of the usability of conversational data for doing sociology, in Sudnow, D. (ed.) *Studies in Social Interaction*, New York: Free Press, pp. 31–74.

——(1972b) On the analyzability of stories by children, in J.J. Gumperz and D.H. Hymes (eds) *Directions in Sociolinguistics*, New York: Holt, Rinehart and Winston, pp. 329–45.

——(1976) On formulating context, *Pragmatics Microfiche*, 1(7): F5.

——(1992a) *Lectures on Conversation*, vol. 1, ed. G. Jefferson, intro. E.A. Schegloff, Cambridge, MA: Blackwell.

——(1992b) *Lectures on Conversation*, vol. 2, ed. G. Jefferson, intro. E.A. Schegloff, Cambridge, MA: Blackwell.

Sacks, H. and Schegloff, E.A. (1979) Two preferences in the organization of reference to persons in conversation and their interaction, in G. Psathas (ed.) *Everyday Language: studies in ethnomethodology*, New York: Irvington, pp. 15–21.

Sacks, H., Schegloff, E.A. and Jefferson, G. (1974) A simplest systematics for the organization of turn-taking for conversation, *Language*, 50: 696–735.

Scheffler, H.W. and Lounsbury, F.G. (1971) *A Study in Structural Semantics: The Siriono kinship system*, Englewood Cliffs, NJ: Prentice-Hall.

Schegloff, E.A. (1972) Notes on a conversational practice: formulating place, in D. Sudnow (ed.) *Studies in Social Interaction*, New York: Free Press, pp. 75–119, 432–33.

——(1979) The relevance of repair to syntax-for-conversation, in T. Givon (ed.) *Syntax and Semantics, vol. 12: discourse and syntax*, New York: Academic, pp. 261–86.

——(1984) On some questions and ambiguities in conversation, in J.M. Atkinson and J. Heritage (eds) *Structures of Social Action: Studies in conversation analysis*, Cambridge: Cambridge University Press; Paris: Editions de la Maison des Sciences de l'Homme, pp. 28–52.

——(1991) Reflections on talk and social structure, in D. Boden and D.H. Zimmerman (eds) *Talk and Social Structure: Studies in ethnomethodology and conversation analysis*, Cambridge: Polity Press, pp. 44–70.

——(1992) Introduction, in H. Sacks, *Lectures on Conversation*, vol. 1, ed. G. Jefferson, Oxford: Blackwell, pp. ix–lxii.

——(2007) *Sequence Organization in Interaction: A primer in conversation analysis*, vol. 1, Cambridge: Cambridge University Press.

Searle, J.R. (1969) *Speech Acts: An essay in the philosophy of language*, Cambridge: Cambridge University Press.

Sharrock, W.W. (1974) On owning knowledge, in R. Turner (ed.) *Ethnomethodology: selected readings*, Harmondsworth, UK: Penguin, pp. 45–53.

Sharrock, W.W. and Anderson, R.J. (1982) On the demise of the native: some observations on and a proposal for ethnography, *Human Studies*, 5(1): 119–35.

——(1986) *The Ethnomethodologists*, Chichester and London: Ellis Horwood and Tavistock.

——(1991) Epistemology: professional scepticism, in G. Button (ed.) *Ethnomethodology and the Human Sciences*, Cambridge: Cambridge University Press, pp. 51–76.

Speer, S.A. and Stokoe, E. (2011) An introduction to conversation and gender, in S.A. Speer and E. Stokoe (eds) *Conversation and Gender*, Cambridge: Cambridge University Press, pp. 1-27.

Stokoe, E.H. (2000) Toward a conversation analytic approach to gender and discourse, *Feminism and Psychology*, 10: 552–63.

——(2006) On ethnomethodology, feminism, and the analysis of categorial reference to gender in talk-in-interaction, *Sociological Review*, 54: 467–94.

Turner, R. (1976) Utterance positioning as an interactional resource, *Semiotica*, 17: 233–54.

Tyler, S.A. (1969) Introduction, in S.A. Tyler (ed.) *Cognitive Anthropology*, New York: Holt, Rinehart and Winston, pp. 1-23.

Wallace, A.C. and Atkins, J.R. (1960) The meaning of kinship terms, *American Anthropologist*, 62: 58-90.

Watson, D.R. (1992) The understanding of language use in everyday life, in G. Watson and R.M. Seiler (eds) *Text in Context: contributions to ethnomethodology*, Newbury Park, CA: Sage, pp. 1-19.

Wieder, D.L. (1970) On meaning by rule, in J.D. Douglas (ed.) *Understanding Everyday Life: toward the reconstruction of sociological knowledge*, Chicago: Aldine, pp. 107–35.

Winch, P. (1958, 3rd edn 2008) *The Idea of a Social Science and its Relation to Philosophy*, London and New York: Routledge Classics.

——(1970) Understanding a primitive society, in B.R. Wilson (ed.) *Rationality*, Oxford: Basil Blackwell, pp. 78–111; orig. pub. 1964.

Wittgenstein, L. (1972) *Philosophical Investigations*, 3rd edn, trans. G.E.M. Anscombe, Oxford: Basil Blackwell.

Wootton, A. (1975) *Dilemmas of Discourse: controversies about the sociological interpretation of language*, London: George Allen and Unwin.

Wowk, M.T. (2007) Kitzinger's feminist conversation analysis: critical observations, *Human Studies*, 30: 131–55.

11

CULTURE AND KINSHIP LANGUAGE[1]

David B. Kronenfeld

Introduction

Kinship provides one particularly useful domain for the examination of language and thought relations. There are several advantages it offers, as well as at least one drawback. First, and maybe most importantly, anthropologists and linguists have much clearer analytic control of denotative meaning, connotative associations, and figurative extension than for almost any other domain. This control includes both terminological contrast (i.e. 'an *uncle* as opposed to, for instance, a *father*') and reference (i.e., 'how do you tell if someone actually is an *uncle*'), Second, we have extensive presentations and analyses of the social and cultural structures and forms (including groups, legal rights, behavioural obligations, and so forth) with which different kinds of kinship terminologies are associated. Third, there now exists some collection of systematic data patterns of actual behavior among kinsfolk that can be directly compared with patterns of terminological usage. Fourth, both kinship terminologies and patterned (and socially enjoined) relations among kin are universal and universally important – all cultures have them. Fifth, anthropologists and others have been collecting and publishing systematic data on kinship terminologies, groups, and rights for over 150 years. The one clear drawback is that denotative reference – almost uniquely – is defined by relative products (such as 'uncle' is a 'parent's brother') rather than directly by features (a 'table' is a flat surface on which one places things that typically rests on legs and typically falls within a certain size range, depending on what kind of a table it is) and that, thus, kinterms are binary (one is 'someone's uncle' vs. simply 'an uncle') whereas most other terms are unary (it is simply 'a table'). Connotative associations and figurative extension for kinship terms seem more like what is common for other domains.

This overview will consist of seven sections. The first will lay out the traditional theoretic language and analytic presuppositions. Section II provides a brief overview of the history of kinship studies in anthropology. Section III describes the various ways in which kinship terminological systems have been analysed, with the advantages and disadvantages offered by each. Section IV considers the much thinner history of the formal analysis of behavior between and among kinfolk. A brief section IV (a) uses a comparison of the terminological and behavior analyses to address the relationship between language and thought. Section V treats variability, including within formal denotative systems, between denotative and connotative systems, and in informal figurative usage. Section VI describes the major formal approaches to the analysis of kinship terminologies, including notational systems and their role in analysis. The importance of formal analysis and the assertions that each approach implies regarding language and culture are discussed. Finally, Section VII concludes the chapter with a brief overview and a discussion of potential generalizations from the well- and richly studied world of kinship to other domains.

I Definitions and issues

Kinship in anthropology traditionally includes kinship terminological systems and kin groups – and relations among these. In linguistic anthropology the kinship focus has been on the formal semantic analysis of kinship terminologies, and more recently has a socio-linguistic concern with the conditions of kinterm use. In both cases, there is both a descriptive (ethnographic) concern and a comparative (ethnological) concern with the social or cultural (including economic, historical, and regional) conditions and networks which account for the differences between one system and another. Detailed and careful systematic attention to semantics and usage has forced, in turn, a concern with the cultural pragmatics of kinterms (including cultural presuppositions about attitudes and behavior among kin, about contexts of kinterm use and kin-relevance, and about the relevance of kin groups to kinterm usage). This chapter will address both the sets of kinterms (kinship terminology) that people use to identify classes of kin and the behavior that applies to those kinfolk. The relevance of kin groups and relations among these to kinterms and kin behavior will be included, but kin groups themselves and systematic relations among these will remain outside our purview.[2]

By 'culture' I refer to the collective systems of differentially distributed pragmatic knowledge that underlie and enable collective social life (see Kronenfeld 2011 for a presentation and explanation of this view of culture).

Kinship offers a useful laboratory for studying the relationship between language and culture. Anthropologists have studied kinship terminologies for over 150 years. Kinfolk are important in all cultures, and all languages have kinship terminologies. Kinship terminologies all share significant definitional and structural properties while varying enough from one to another – in rigorously patterned ways – to make interesting their relationship to the wider cultures of their speakers.

Kinterms proper are the set of words for parents, children, and spouses, such as, in English, 'mother', 'father', 'son', 'daughter', 'husband', and 'wife' – and words such as 'sister', 'aunt', 'cousin', etc., defined in terms of them ('aunt' is 'mother's' or 'father's' 'sister', 'cousin' is, *inter alia*, 'aunt's son', etc.) Kinterms are part of the lexicon of a language, and so any general theory of the lexicon must apply to them. At the same time the domain has some special characteristics that make it decidedly atypical – such as its universal parental anchor and its rigorous relative product folk definitions. The relevance and/or status of informal variants – e.g., terms such as 'mama', 'mom', 'mommy', 'ma', etc. – seems to depend on one's descriptive and analytic goals; such variants are often synonyms for less than the whole range of the basic formal terms, and often signal attitudinal colourings.

Conventionally, 'ego' (or, sometimes 'propositus') is used to refer to the person whose relative is being spoken of and 'alter' for that relative. 'Kintype' refers to a particular genealogically defined alter of ego's (such as mother's father's sister's son). The relationship is a binary one (i.e. Joe is someone's 'uncle' vs. 'uncle' simply labelling a referent the way that 'chair' does), which can be seen as a string of (0, 1, or more) linking relatives connecting ego to alter (e.g., Joe is Frank's mother's brother); the single relationship can be examined from either perspective by reversing ego and alter (Frank is Joe's sister's son, and hence 'nephew'), and the terms for alter in the two directions (e.g. 'uncle' and 'nephew') are spoken of as 'reciprocals' or reciprocal terms. One term such as 'uncle' in our English example can have several reciprocals – such as, here, 'niece' and 'nephew'. A collateral consanguineal string runs up from ego to the lowest ancestor shared by ego and alter and then down to alter; the shared ancestor is spoken of as the 'apical ancestor', and the sibling pair immediately below the apical ancestor in the string are spoken of as the 'apical sibling pair'. A lineal string runs directly down from either ego or alter to alter or ego; here, though the expression is not much used in this situation, the apical ancestor would be the senior of the two. Affinal strings go down (from ego or a consanguine of ego) to a marriage link and then up to alter or a consanguine of alter; the minimal case is a direct marriage link between ego and alter.

Early on (see, for example, Morgan) it was noted that kin terminological systems around the world fell into a small number of patterns (or 'types'). Morgan, already in 1871, distinguished 'classificatory' (in which some collateral relatives were classed with lineal ones) from 'descriptive' in which lineals were clearly separated from collaterals.[3] Classificatory systems were further divided by Morgan into categories which, with some renaming and with some subsequent additions, have become today's major types (named, alas, after languages which supposedly exhibited them), which include Hawaiian, Cheyenne, Iroquois, Dravidian, Crow, and Omaha types. Descriptive systems are now referred to as Eskimo type.

In brief, in Hawaiian-type systems relatives are categorized by generation and sex. In the remaining types generation and sex remain basic, but with added distinctions. In Cheyenne-type systems, ascending and descending first generation relatives are further classified as 'parallel' (linked through same-sex sibling ancestors) or 'cross' (linked through opposite-sex sibling ancestors). Iroquois and Dravidian both classify relatives in generations zero and one as cross or parallel, and agree on the classification of ego's closest kin – but they differ significantly in their classification of one's more distant kin. In Dravidian-type systems the parallel vs. cross distinction maps closely onto dichotomous social entities (e.g. own vs. opposed 'moieties'), while Iroquois-type systems do not at all match any social entities. Crow- and Omaha-type systems are like Dravidian type, but with the addition of a rule for overriding generation distinctions for cross relatives in certain contexts. Crow-type wipes out the generational distinction between a woman and her child while Omaha-type wipes out the generational distinction between a man and his child. Crow-type systems thus relate to matrilineal succession while Omaha-type ones related to patrilineal succession. Rights of succession (including inheritance) often structure kin groups, and so unilineal succession often results in corporate descent groups – thus (see Kronenfeld 1991 [2009]: ch. 13]), Crow-type terminologies are often (but not always) associated with matrilineages and Omaha type with patrilineages. See Gould (2000: ch. 9) for full definitions of these types with illustrations.

II History

Morgan's work (discussed above) marked the beginning of systematic theoretical treatment of kinship terminologies in anthropology – though earlier records of terminological systems such as the important one of Dorsey (1884) antedate Morgan's compendium. Morgan defined most of the basic types, and saw an evolutionary progression among them. His particular theory of primitive promiscuity evolving towards Victorian monogamy as parents became aware of their own biological children is naive, does not work, and is best left without further discussion. Kroeber (1909) noted the limited number of features which (across all systems) served to distinguish terminological categories from one another – but without specifying the precise application of these to any specific system. Kroeber emphasized the lexical (as opposed to sociological) nature of kinterms. Subsequent scholars, especially Murdock (1949) further refined the set of types, and explored the correlation of the types with various other social and economic features of the communities using them.

Radcliffe-Brown (1924, 1941), in a more social structural orientation deriving in part from Durkheim, saw kinterms as kinds of role terms which represented particular structural positions and the behavioural concomitants of these. His analytic approach was based on such roles, but, being only semi-formal, allowed him to miss two serious kinds of problems with the role view.

First, the range of denotative reference of the terms is not coterminous with their supposed roles. One of his summary rules for relevant terminologies is 'unity of the [same sex] sibling group'. In a great many unilineal systems to which his rule supposedly applies, (whether patrilineal or matrilineal) any 'father's' 'brother' falls into the 'father' kinterm; close ones will mostly be in father's lineage (and have the relevant rights and privileges), but many more distant ones will not. Similarly he accounts for generational skewing (in Crow- and Omaha-type systems) with a 'unity of the lineage' rule – which effectively for matrilineal systems such as Fanti amounts to delineating 'men of my father's matrilineage'. The problem is that a great many of the generationally skewed male relatives in all Crow-type systems do not fall in father's matrilineage, and Omaha has the same problem with patrilineal systems.

Second, there exist no consistent behavioural correlates of any kinterms in any system – that is, behaviours which apply to all and only members of the given terminological category. The problem occurs as well in work of Tax, Leach, and Schneider (see below).

Tax (1955a, 1955b) developed a more formal and terminologically focused version of Radcliffe-Brown's approach that worked much better at explicating which kind of relative fell in which terminological category. But it was cumbersome and it foundered on problems involving reciprocals of some terms.

Radcliffe-Brown's position was classically opposed to that of Kroeber (1909), who said that kinterms were just words in a language and had no intrinsic sociological importance or relevance. What Kroeber missed was the fact that prototypic (or kernel) members of categories have definite and specific sociological associations – which associations are what enable native speakers to use kinterms to refer to behavioural patterns – as in the Fanti use of their 'father' term (*egya*) to speak of father-like non-relatives in their courtesy pattern of extension. See Kronenfeld 1975 [2009]: ch. 8] for the Kroeber vs. Radcliffe-Brown controversy.

An interesting variant (or application) of Radcliffe-Brown's approach is seen in Leach's early (1945) discussion of Jinghpaw kinship groups, residence, and kinterms. In it he shows how a combination of kin group membership and residence norms can isolate the classes of relatives labelled by the kinterms used by Jinghpaw speakers. The problem is that it only dependably works for a combination of close referents and canonical residence decisions. Still, it is an impressive *tour de force* and it gets at something basic about which categories of relatives come to be terminologically recognized.

In a separate dispute, Schneider in a series of articles (1980, 1984) claimed kinship terms were a cultural phenomenon that had nothing to do with biological reproduction, as opposed to the common view before and since that kinship was particularly where biology and culture came together. He seemed to dismiss apparent genealogical regularities as epiphenomenal by-products of how anthropologists studied kinship. But he never explained how such consistently genealogical patterning which we universally find could be the by-product of something unrelated, and, beyond that, never explained what made kinship systems across all cultures so clearly recognizable and isolatable as a single type of system (which anthropologists typically call a kinship system). Sometimes, and to some degree, he confounded the preceding view with a claim that kinship was not *about* genealogy. This latter version seems more reasonable since for people in many cultures genealogical links merely serve to provide a frame on which important economic, religious, and social relations can to varying degrees be based. The universality of kinship systems seems to come from people everywhere recognizing that children always have a biological mother and father.[4] Since parentage is almost all that is known about a newborn, it seems reasonable that basic social (economic, religious, etc.) ascriptions would be based on that parentage. Genealogies themselves are not directly involved, but are, as an analytic tool, simply the result of combining into a single diagram the concatenations of parent–child relations reaching out from an ego to a surrounding range of kin. These concatenations are the same kinds of chains that we see as defining basic kinterm categories. Members of some cultures do explicitly make use of genealogies, but many do not.

A variant of Schneider's view was independently put forward by Edmund Leach (1958) for Trobriand Islanders, in which he claimed that terms which referred to kin were to be understood by the common elements among all their referents (kin and otherwise) rather than through any sort of privileging of traditional kinterm referents – especially given the loose versions of kinterm semantics then abroad. But Lounsbury in 1965 demonstrated a logically tight and exact, and quite parsimonious, account of Trobriand kinterms based directly on genealogical definitions – much tighter and more parsimonious than Leach's account. Leach's account, in retrospect, seems nicely to summarize the connotations of some key Trobriand kinterms – connotations which are involved in their non-kin extensions – but without offering anything close to clear denotative definitions.

III Terminological analysis

Kinterms in all systems are susceptible to several alternative formal analytic definitional systems. Of the major two, one can be seen as semantic and the other pragmatic.

The first approach, a semantic one, is concerned with the distinctions among terminological categories in the set, such as the difference between a 'table' and a 'chair'. In this approach to kinterm analysis, the contrasts among terms and their referents can be rigorously defined by a combination of paradigmatic contrasts (defined by the intersection of a set of distinctive features) among their focal or prototypic referents and rules for the extension of these terms to ranges of extended referents.

In kinship this distinctive features approach (usually spoken of as 'componential analysis') is based on the features ('components') such as relative generation, sex of relative, relative sex, lineal vs. collateral, mother's vs. father's side, etc. Some of these features such as relative generation are binary (that is, categorize ego relative to alter) while others such as sex of relative are unary (categorizing alter in absolute terms). In this analytic approach kinterm categories are defined by the intersection of distinctive (defining) features.

(1) In one variant the feature definitions are taken as applying to the full range of referents of relevant kinterms; e.g., in English, the 'cousin' category includes a wide range of collateral relatives. At the same time, the responses to requests to 'describe your cousin' or answers to questions such as 'what is a cousin' clearly focus on a 'first cousin' – that is, a parent's sibling's child. One can speak of semantic extension here, but the extension is accomplished directly through the application of the defining features of the category, and distinguishes its prototype from the prototypes of contrasting categories. The classic articles of Goodenough (1956) and Lounsbury (1956, 1964a), as well as the important papers of Wallace and Atkins (1960) and Romney and D'Andrade (1964) employed this form of analysis. The approach was used by Romney and Epling (1958) in an early (and too much ignored) analysis of an Australian system.

However, in some systems such as Fanti, the above approach to semantic extension has problems. In Fanti, ego's father's brother, father's mother's sister's son, and father's sister's son, among many other kinds of kin, fall in the *egya* category which includes ego's actual father. The distinction is emically[5] and ethnographically clear: one's actual father is spoken of by Fanti as the 'real' *egya*, as opposed to those other referents who are described as 'really' *egyas* (even though not one's 'real' *egya*). The problem is that the 'generational skewing' represented by the presence in the category of father's sister's son (ego's 0 generation relative in a basically +1 generation term) cannot be reasonably handled by such a direct application of the category's defining features. And we further note that the preceding genealogically based usage of *egya* is opposed, in turn, to its use for a respected (in some sense father-like) senior friend who can be addressed, or spoken of, as *egya*, but who is 'not really' one – a respect usage not unlike our use in English of 'uncle' for relatively senior family friends. This 'courtesy' usage, similarly, is not amenable to the category's distinguishing features.

Within the preceding distinctive features frame more focused hypotheses based on work in psychology and linguistics have sometimes been explored. For instance, Nerlove and Romney's (1967) sibling typology study was based on Bruner, Goodnow, and Austin's (1956) work on concept formation and Greenberg's (1966 and see 1968) work on marked vs. unmarked categories.[6] It focused on true full siblings, and was followed up on with improvements by Kronenfeld (1974). The study showed that out of 4,140 logical possibilities the 12 types that occurred empirically in a sample of 245 terminologies were all conjunctively defined and 240 fit additional constraints related to marking and other specific measures of cognitive ease.

Per Hage (2001, 1999, 1998, 1997) used marking relations in the context of comparable terms from a set of genetically related languages to reconstruct the historical development of kinship terminological systems in the language families to which the languages belong.

(2) The skewing problem led Lounsbury (1964b – and for the general case, beyond kinship, see Lounsbury 1969) to the other major variant of the distinctive features approach, in which the feature definitions of kinterm categories are taken only as applying to the prototypic referents (often spoken of in the literature as 'kernel' or 'core' referents); other (more distant) referents are linked to the category by some form of equivalence (or extension) rule (such as 'a mother's brother's son is terminologically equivalent to a mother's own son'). These equivalences were created by the analyst in the analyst's analytical language, and were not necessarily directly equivalent to native speaker statements. Their justification was that they worked – and in particular that a very small set of very simple ones worked powerfully across a great many different systems. Lounsbury used three basic rules for consanguines: a 'merging rule' (making same-sex-siblings terminologically equivalent when appearing in a string as linking relatives) of which the immediately preceding example is a partial version, a 'half-sibling rule' (in which half-siblings are made terminologically equivalent to full siblings) and a 'skewing rule' which moves specific relatives up or down a generation. The half-sibling rule seems general in its application; the merging rule applies to the large set of systems defined as 'classificatory'; the skewing rule applies to a subset of those in which some central terminological categories include relatives from several generations. This approach was developed by Lounsbury (1964b, 1965), and further elaborated in various ways by others including Scheffler, Kronenfeld, and Trautmann. In this approach the courtesy usage can be included via extension from the prototype based on features of apparent generation, sex, and a kinship-like attitude towards the courtesy alter.

Within the kin domain, in the context of the above approach, I have looked at the functional and communicative bases and uses of the different kinds of extension (Kronenfeld 1996:172–6, and see 2009:137–40 and in press). For kinship terminologies denotative extension is based on formal extension rules, while connotative extension is based directly on the functional relations implied by the term; figurative extension applies the kin contrasts to another domain. 'Essential properties' seem to apply necessarily only to prototypic referents.

The second approach, a pragmatic one has to do with how the referents of the terms interrelate or interconnect – for example, how are chairs used with tables in which contexts. In the kinterm domain, one basic system of pragmatic relations among terms (related particularly to how native speakers calculate kinterm assignments of relatives) can be formally defined as an algebraic system based on relative products (e.g., in English, 'brother's son' equals 'nephew', but 'son's brother' equals 'son'). Such systems can be ethnographically defined directly on the basis of lexemes in the language or ethnologically (i.e. comparatively) defined in terms of genealogical abstractions from the lexemes' focal definitions. The link to genealogical abstraction stems from the dependence of all kinship terminological systems on the core axiomatic categories (such as father, mother, spouse, and their reciprocals) on which the relative product calculus gets based.

Terms in the parent–children–spouse set are taken as axiomatic in the sense of being defined by events outside the terminology itself – such as birth and marriage – and relative products of these terms are used to define other terms. Sometimes the set of non-axiomatic terms is split into a set of ones (such as 'brother' and 'sister' in English) which can be used in the definition of other terms (as illustrated above) and a set (such as 'grandfather' in English) which are not so used. There exist two major variants of this approach.

(1) One approach, an emic one (for example, see Read 2011, 2001 and Kronenfeld 1980b – reprinted as Kronenfeld 2009: ch. 3), aims at precise ethnographic accuracy. It is focused on the lexical categories of the language system being analysed, and constructs the relative product formalism totally out of those categories – whether literally in the words of that language or in a direct representation of them in some symbolic or graphic meta-language.

(2) The other approach (for example, Gould 2000; Kronenfeld 2001b, 2009: ch. 11, and 2013) is more etic. It aims at precisely representing the structural relations among kinterm categories that define the major ethnological types. This approach represents the categories of the analysed systems (including the distinction between axiomatic and non-axiomatic terminological categories) and tightly models the relations among them with a set of externally defined analytic symbols, but it sometimes leaves out structurally irrelevant labelling anomalies.

In the 1960s there was a big debate about the psychological reality of various componential analyses (modelled on the debate in linguistics concerning the psychological reality of the phoneme). Roger Brown's (1964) statement to the effect that 'you keep asking more and more questions of your analysis until only one is left standing' pointed the way. The additional questions sometimes involved psychological measures of inter-term closeness and the structural models implied by those (Romney and D'Andrade 1964); sometimes they involved native statements about definitions (Keen 1985; Kronenfeld 1980b; Read 2011, 2001, based on earlier work); sometimes they involved psychological/logical measures of simplicity (Wallace and Atkins 1960; Lounsbury 1964a). It eventually became clear, as more analyses and kinds of analysis emerged, that the kinship domain was an overdetermined one – i.e. that the combination of shaping constraints and the regularities that native speakers pulled out of their experience as they learned their terminology allowed of alternative, quite different analytic approaches, as long as each produced more or less the same allocation of referents to terms. And it became clear that sometimes one was asking a comparative analytic question for which any narrow construction of psychological reality was impossible and meaningless (e.g. Gould 2000; Kronenfeld 1992).

The psychological reality debate in kinship studies related closely to another presupposition from linguistics – to the effect that there should exist some one single best analysis that won at the expense of all competitors and that served all relevant analytic purposes. The splintering of the psychological reality argument also ended the kinship version of that presupposition. The game was still – maybe more than ever – an empirical and systematic one, but different kinds of approaches, when successful, were found to serve different analytic ends, and thus potentially to be incommensurable.

Another, third, kind of approach, offered by Wierzbicka (1992: chs 9, 10), uses culture-specific supposedly folk-based definitions of kinterms constructed out of what she sees as universal semantic primes (i.e. universally basic concepts). Her presentation is too brief and minimal for the reader to see how it might apply to the kinds of terminological problems and issues addressed in this chapter; on the face of her presentation of it, there would seem to exist serious logical problems with any such application. See Kronenfeld 1996: 20 and 2000: 211–214 (notes 3 and 4) for discussions of these problems along with some tentative suggestions about how they might be dealt with.

IV Behavior

Pragmatic relations of terms (i.e. categories) to their cultural and communicative uses (including figurative usage) can also be described and analysed. Systematic analytic attention to behavioural implications in the analysis of kinterm systems was proposed by Romney and Epling (1958).

In one study within the Fanti kinship project (Kronenfeld 2009: ch. 4; Kronenfeld 1975 [Kronenfeld 2009: ch. 8]) a set of behaviours was elicited that informants considered relevant to various kinds of kinfolk, or that the ethnographer observed as being relevant. For a sample of informants, each was then asked for each behavior on the list whether or not that behavior could be directed (1) towards each kintype off of a list of kintypes that were relevant to terminological contrasts and (2) towards each of an individually constructed (for each informant) list of individuals who were known to be in relevant terminological categories. The kintype list included 'stranger' and 'friend' as a way of assessing any possible kin-related boundary. The ascribed and remembered data sets were found to be similar to each other in terms of incidence of behavior across kintype categories and across kin-relevant attributes. This behavioural data was compared with kinterm categories and with kin group (i.e., for Fanti, matrilineage) membership, and the ascribed kintype data was directly analysed using a variety of scaling and regression techniques to see what accounted for the incidence of ascribed (to the kintypes) or remembered (for actual specific kin) behavior to kin. In general no necessary or tight relationship was found between ranges of referents of a given kinterm and those behaved towards in the manner associated with the kinterm. Similarly, no necessary or tight relationship was found between behavior patterns and lineage membership – with one exception. Fanti kin groups control inheritance (including succession), and so inheritance itself is limited to lineage members; responses to the 'can inherit from' question did isolate lineage membership. The inheritance finding showed that the methodology was capable of picking up behavioural isolation where it existed, and thus in turn implied that the general lack of fit of behavior with kin categories was not any artefact of that methodology. Instead, the great bulk of behaviours were found to depend directly on a kintype's position on relevant variables – mostly generalized 'seniority' and 'closeness', but sometimes more specific aspects of the relationship.

Informant linking of the behaviours to kinterm categories was not random or casual, however. Where the behavior and the terminology came together was for the category's prototypic (i.e. kernel) referents. In the absence of other, inconsistent, information the term was taken as referring to its prototype and not to its full range.

IV (a) Language and thought, as seen from the kinship laboratory

Since the behavior referred to in the behavioural study was either ascribed or remembered, it was cognitive rather than objectively behavioural, and thus was a part of 'thought', as, of course, is language. This study provides one clear-cut disaffirmation of any Whorfian claim that language dictates thought or provides the categories of thought; lesser biasing effects are not ruled out, and indeed a few are discussed in Kronenfeld (2009: ch. 4, 2000). Instead, language itself can be seen as flexible and subject to creative adaptation by users in its application to the world of users' experience; but such flexibility has to exist within some framework that enables reasonably effective communication. Work on kinship shows the importance of prototype-extension semantics to this flexible functioning – as well as the important role that semantic contrasts among prototypes within a relevant contrast set play in communicatively effective extension.

V Variability and usage

The Fanti kinship terminology (see Kronenfeld 1973 (2009: ch. 1), 1980a (2009: ch. 2), and 1980b (2009: ch. 3)) actually has two alternative patterns of denotative extension via relative products (along with the courtesy pattern's connotative extension). One is the skewed pattern already referred to; the other is an unscrewed (Cheyenne-type) pattern. Both patterns are each internally consistent (i.e. logically rigorous), and everyone in the studied Fanti community was familiar with both alternatives and had been seen to use each, though some used one much more frequently than the other. Both patterns are traditional, and neither shows any of the features that clearly mark English loans in Fanti usage. The three patterns can be seen as forming a 'marking hierarchy' in which – based on the successive addition of definitional elements – the most unmarked is the courtesy pattern, which with the addition of genealogical specification produces the unskewed pattern, which then, with addition of skewing, produces the most marked skewed pattern.

Fanti kinterm usage is quite variable, with first the choice whether or not to use a kinterm (vs. some other title or category term) for someone, and then if, as is common in the village, the choice is to use a kinterm, one has the choice between denotatively correct and connotative usages (easily evaluated by asking the speaker 'why do you call her/him' X?), and within denotative usage between the skewed and unskewed alternatives.

As suggested by Radcliffe-Brown (though seriously mis-defined by him) the skewing rule carries a kind of emphasis on lineage relations; the absence of skewing then suggests more ordinary social interactions. These situational overtones do seem to somewhat bias usage, but with no great consistency. Interactive considerations also significantly affect usage. Fanti culture shows a kind of age-based respect hierarchy which is often expressed in kinterm usage. Kinterm usage is common in the village for both kin and non-kin. Not using a kinterm for an adult non-relative implies some social distance; for relatively close kin, using a courtesy pattern term (that differs from any correct denotatively specified term for that person) similarly connotes distance. In ordinary interactions there is a value on showing respect. The effect of these cultural values on usage was driven home to me when I saw a man address his father's sister's son (a cross-cousin) as *egya* ('father') (using the skewed pattern), to which the other man replied with *nua* ('sibling') (using the unskewed pattern). In the skewed pattern the reciprocal of *egya* is *ba* (child), while in the unskewed pattern the reciprocal of *nua* is *nua* itself. The two men were closely enough related for non-genealogical usage to be disrespectful; given that constraint, for the first man 'father' was more respectful than 'sibling', while for the second man 'sibling' was more respectful than 'child'. Both men knew and used both patterns.

Until recently ethnographers were expected (and pressured) to find the single most traditional (i.e. ethnographically correct) system and so such variability does not much show up in the literature (though there are sometimes hints about it). But it has been suggested that variation such as that exhibited by Fanti is maybe not uncommon – especially among systems described either as Cheyenne-type or as one of the skewed types.

The Fanti system with its alternate patterns of extension is a full-blown version of the more limited variability that we see in English 'cousin' term patterns. In English one pattern is that in which the child of one's first cousin is one's 'second cousin' and the child of that cousin is one's 'third cousin', and in which the children of a pair of first cousins are 'third cousins' to each other. The other English pattern is that in which the child of one's first cousin is a 'first cousin once removed', and the child of that cousin is one's 'first cousin twice removed', and in which the children of a pair of first cousins are 'second cousins'.

VI Formalism and formalization

Formalism – having an explicit set of forms and operations involving these – has been crucial to studies of kinship terminologies. The forms with their attributes have been defined in line with analysts' suppositions about the nature of kinterms, and operations similarly defined in terms of the ways in which analysts considered terms to be combined or to otherwise relate to one another. The application of the formal representation to empirical systems revealed how well the formal definitions matched the range and nature of terms and patterns of terms in the empirical data. It was Lounsbury's formal treatment of Iroquois-type systems which made clear their absolute incompatibility with any kind of moiety system; without that formal mindset Morgan had noted the difference between Iroquois and Dravidian types but had failed to realize the significance of that difference. It was, similarly, an explicit formal treatment that made clear the inadequacy of Radcliffe-Brown's account of terminological regularities in classificatory systems, and a formal representation (even if non-algebraic and with a clumsy set of symbols) was crucial to Lounsbury's improved picture. And it is a formal treatment with formal definitions (as in componential analyses starting with Goodenough 1956 and Lounsbury 1956) that exposes the problem with Kroeber's characterization of the difference between descriptive and classificatory kinship terminologies. And it is Kroeber's lack of any precise application of his collection of distinctive features to any specific system that accounts for why his prescient paper produced no follow-up work, while Goodenough's and Lounsbury's componential analyses set off a flurry of further work. For a fuller discussion of formal work on kinship terminologies see Kronenfeld (2001a). Lehman (2001, 2011) offers rigorous formal treatments of basic issues in the analysis of kinship systems.

A good notational scheme (or symbolic system) for representing items (here, kinterms), their relevant attributes, and relations among them can be a great aid not just to ethnographic completeness and clarity of representation, but also – importantly – to the process of analysis. Different notational schemes lend themselves to different kinds of analyses with their different analytic goals. The primary device for representing a system has of course been mapping kinterms onto an abstracted genealogical tree, but such a tree is hard to work with in many ways – especially in dealing with attributes of individual terms, with considering reciprocals of terms, and with representing some important analytic categories. The traditional scheme in anthropology for representing the kintypes that made up some category was simply abbreviations for the English terms for basic kinds of relative (Mo, Fa, Br, Si, So, Da, Hu, Wi or M, F, B, Z, S, D, H, W – with maybe some other stuff). Besides having no clear boundary between basic kintype representation and kinterm representation this system was awkward to work with (whether finding common features or attributes of kintypes in a kinterm or computing reciprocal expressions, or providing concise summary abstractions).

Two major approaches have been developed providing a more efficient and insightful rigorous formal representation of kintypes and cultural materials based on them.

(1) The older approach, the P/C one, is based on the fact that any kinterm can be seen as a string of parent–child and/or child–parent links connecting ego and alter. Here P represents a

link to a parent and C a link to a child (i.e., P's reciprocal) The problem with this basic form is that sex is not coded. For ego and alter m or f (or equivalents) can be used as an ad hoc modifier, but handling sex of linking relative remains difficult and awkward. One variant aimed at getting around the sex problem was to replace P with M and F (for mother and father, respectively), and C with S and D (for son and daughter, respectively) – sometimes with P and C still available for positions in a string where sex did not matter. In some version B and Z (for brother and sister, respectively) were added. The problem with this early F/M version was that reciprocals were often hard to find and pairs of reciprocals hard to represent in the formalism.

For example, *wofa*, the Fanti maternal uncle term would be MB, while *awofasi*, its reciprocal would be mZC. This asymmetry prevented a clean simple statement of equivalence rules that included reciprocals. And, in a related example, a cross-cousin would include MZC and FBC, with no way to unite the two and no way to show that the one is simply the reciprocal of the other.

A final variant was introduced by Gould (2000) in which the inverse of F is $\bar{F}$ ('fatherling') and of M is $\bar{M}$ ('motherling'), where a fatherling is a man's child of either sex and a motherling a woman's child of either sex. In this variant *wofa*, the Fanti maternal uncle term would be Mm (literally a 'male mother' which, in the formalism, implies mother's brother) and its reciprocal would be m$\bar{M}$ (a male's motherling which, in the formalism, implies a man's sister's child). Similarly a cross-cousin would be M$\bar{F}$ and its reciprocal F$\bar{M}$ – that is, a 'mother's fatherling' (i.e. mother's bother's child) and, reciprocally a 'father's motherling (i.e. father's sister's child). Thus, to get a reciprocal in Gould's variant one need only reverse the order of the symbols and put overbars over non-apical symbols that lacked them while removing overbars from non-apical symbols that had them. In Gould's system, equivalence rules (where ↔ signifies formal equivalence such that the left-side expression can be substituted for the right-side one in any longer expression) such as the Crow Skewing rule F$\bar{M}$ ↔ F automatically imply their reciprocals (M$\bar{F}$ ↔ $\bar{F}$).

(2) The other major approach was Romney's (1965, and Romney and D'Andrade 1964) in which persons were distinguished from relations between persons. Here, m is a male person, f a female person, a and b persons of either sex (where b's come in linked pairs), while + is a child to parent link – parent to child link, and o a sibling link. Additional symbols include ... which signals that some further string must replace the ... (i.e. that the given expression can be embedded in a longer expression), . which signals that nothing further can come where the . is (i.e. that element next to the dot is the beginning or end of the expression), the absence of either ... or . means that that end of the expression can either be final or embedded, and /.../ where what is included within the pair of slashes is self-reciprocal (can be read in either direction, if when changing direction one exchanges pluses for minuses and minuses for pluses). Thus here *wofa*, the Fanti maternal uncle term would be a+fom and its reciprocal mof-a, and the string itself including both directions would be /a+fom/. Kronenfeld (1976 [Kronenfeld 2009: ch. 10]) used Romney's notation scheme with a variation of his extended analytic procedure (Romney 1965: 129) in a computer implementation of Lounsbury's reduction–expansion rules. The program took kintypes with their associated kintypes as input, discovered which (if any) of Lounsbury's rules applied, used the rules to reduce ranges to kernel kintypes, and then used the rules to re-extend the terms to their extended range. The program thus functioned successfully as a kind of limited discovery procedure.

The importance of formal notational schemes is that they make easier and clearer both the statement of the regularities that structure the systems and the analyses that find those regularities. The Romney notational scheme – because of the way in which it enables easy factoring out of item and relational regularities – is particularly well adapted to componential (i.e., distinctive feature) analysis while the Gould one provides a very powerful tool for working out and describing etic relative product analyses.

Emic analyses rely more directly on native-language terms and statements of relations among them. Read (2011, 2001a) embeds those terms and relations in a computer program that provides an explicit and rigorous formalism. Keen (1985) and Kronenfeld (1980b) rely on a systematic working through of native language statements to provide the needed formal rigor, but without any independent formal devices.

VII Conclusion

In sum, who is behaved towards as a 'son' or who is called a 'father' in one or another conversational context, or what attributes (both absolute and relative to some reference person) will be presumed for a 'father' in one or another conversational context depend on the attributes of prototypic referents. The detail of each of these relations varies widely but far from randomly across cultures. Communities with their cultures do not necessarily have even a single kinship terminology, let alone a single kinship system taken more broadly. To describe kinterm systems, with the variation that exists within a culture, and with the regularities that enable effective communication and interaction across that variation, anthropologists have had to develop several formal approaches. The further comparison of these kinterm systems and their variability across different cultures has depended on further formal developments.

Kinship terminologies have proved a useful laboratory for exploring and understanding the semantics and pragmatics of language. Kinterms are, after all, words in a language – and thus subject to any rules or shaping constraints which govern words in general. This special usefulness stems both from their 150-year history of careful description and analysis within anthropology (on top of earlier studies elsewhere), and from special features of the domain – including its biological rootedness, the formal algebraically tight nature of kinterm systems, and the external analytic framework offered by genealogies. At the same time, kinterms are atypical of vocabulary in general in some ways that make generalization from them tricky. Relevant atypical features include their biological roots and derived genealogical framework, their algebraic precision, their binary nature, and the relative product calculus by which native speakers calculate them.

Some areas of potential generalization (or hypotheses) about word meanings from 'kinlab' maybe include

(1)   The usefulness and importance of formal treatments.
(2)   The complexities of what we mean by 'definitions' of terms in a folk system – that is, the distinction between the semantic ways in which we tell terms apart and identify distinctive features and the pragmatic ways in which we assign terms in practice and understand their relevance to the important things in our lives – including the possibility that different uses or different contexts may produce different pragmatic structures within the same domain, and the possibility that different domains may exhibit very different structures.
(3)   The need for a separate (from intra-cultural, intra-language definitions) set of definitions for cross-language and cross-cultural comparison.

Language and culture are both collective social entities, which individuals move in and out of. They both in some sense are shared distillations of the expressed thoughts of the individuals who make up the societies within which they exist. As communal entities they are passively received by individuals, and thus cannot be equivalent to active dynamic individual thought, including the thought that applies them in social interactions.

But language and culture are not – cannot be – equivalent. The one is used to talk about the other, but the contrast between a limited vocabulary and the potential infinity of referents one uses that vocabulary to talk about necessitates that common words be used to refer to a variety of referents – that is, flexibility of usage, but a flexibility based on a clear enough understanding about the conditions of usage to ensure communicative effectiveness.

Language, given the preceding, then cannot provide the underlying medium of thought. But what language does, through the process by which it is learned and relearned, is to provide a compendium of commonly referred to thoughts. This compendium also provides a set of pre-coded thoughts that thus are easy to form and easily used in the assessment of some situation. Language does, thus, certainly bias thought.

Related topics

language, culture, and prototypicality; culture and translation; language and culture in sociocultural anthropology; language and culture in cognitive anthropology; cultural linguistics

Further reading

Gould, Sydney H. (2000) *A New System for the Formal Analysis of Kinship*. Edited, annotated, and with an introduction by David B. Kronenfeld. Lanham, MD: University Press of America. (A mathematician's clear and innovative contribution to the etic algebraic analysis of kinship terminologies is applied wide and full range of examples; this is a major contribution.)

Jones, Doug and Bojka Milicic (eds) (2011) *Kinship, Language, and Prehistory: Per Hage and the Renaissance in Kinship Studies*. Salt Lake City: University of Utah Press. (This historically oriented collection of articles by anthropologists and linguists covers a broader range of approaches and topics than most.)

Kronenfeld, David B. (2009) *Fanti Kinship and the Analysis of Kinship Terminologies*. Urbana and Chicago: University of Illinois Press. (This is a collection of a 35-year range of contributions to the study of kinship terminologies, kinship behavior, kinship groups, and the communicative use of kinship terms re both kin and non-kin.)

Kronenfeld, David B., Giovanni Bennardo, Victor C. de Munck, and Michael Fischer (eds) (2011) *A Companion to Cognitive Anthropology*. Malden, MA: Blackwell. (This is a recent handbook that contains several treatments of kinship in the general context of cognitive anthropology.)

McConvell, Pat, Ian Keen, and Rachel Hendery (eds) (2013) *Kinship Systems: Change and Reconstruction*. Salt Lake City: University of Utah Press. (This is a major collection from a variety of anthropological, linguistic, and historical perspectives.)

Trautmann, Thomas and Peter Whiteley (eds) (2012) *Crow-Omaha: New Light on a Classic Problem of Kinship Analysis*. Tucson: University of Arizona Press. (This is a collection of contributions by major scholars from across the range of theoretical approaches considering examples from around the world.)

Notes

1 Acknowledgements: I am grateful to Nick Allen, E. N. Anderson, Brent Berlin, Roy G. D'Andrade, Marti Doyle, Theodor Gordon, Norman Johnson, Ian Keen, F. K. Lehman, Bojka Milicic, Robert Moore, Martin Orans, Douglas Raybeck, A. K. Romney, Lynn Thomas, and Stephen Tyler for their generous comments, suggestions, or criticism. And, of course, none of them are responsible for what use I have made of their suggestions or criticisms. I also want to thank the Academic Senate of the University of California at Riverside for Intramural Grant support.

2 Kin groups are corporate – at least in the traditional anthropological sense that the group controls some property and can act as a unit without the necessary presence or acquiescence of all of its members. In kinship, corporate groups typically control some property which they (via the decision reached by a designated set of elders) can allocate. By contrast a kinship category references a set of people who share some kinship-relevant property. People bearing the surname 'Smith' (sometimes loosely spoken of as 'the Smith Family') would be one such category. In Fanti, *ebusuas* proper are matrilineal descent groups, but an extended sense of *ebusua* refers to the category of lineages across the Akan region that share the same lineage-clan name (referred to in common anthropological usage as a 'clan').

3 Some scholars, starting with Kroeber (1909), have taken 'descriptive' to refer to systems in which each lexeme referred to only one genealogical position and 'classificatory' to refer to systems in which some lexemes referred a class of genealogical positions. But by this definition there exist no descriptive systems; the example given as descriptive was English, but the English 'cousin' term covers a vast range of genealogical positions.

4 There exist one or two cases in which members of a culture deny the father's role, but these seem on closer examination to be more by way of politics within a matrilineage context than about biology itself. The peoples involved are well involved in animal husbandry, including breeding. And there may exist another one or two that recognize biological fatherhood but deny it any social role or recognition.

5 'Emic' and 'etic' are terms coined by Kenneth Pike in 1954 (see Pike 1967) on the model of 'phonemic' and 'phonetic' in linguistics. As used here they refer, respectively, to analytic categories and operations based directly on native speaker categories and operations vs. categories and operations based on the application of some sort of external machinery to the analysis of native speaker categories and operations.

The distinction is important because any analysis has to be based on some set of categories and operations. The emic set that best captures the detail of some particular system will include at least some parts that are specific to (and, maybe, peculiar to) that system, and thus such a set will prove less felicitous in capturing the regularities of other systems – i.e. less useful for comparative purposes. For comparison one needs some sort of externally derived etic set of categories and operations. Such an external set can be based on one of two approaches. One approach – based on the model of the IPA in phonology – is to draw them from an open set built out of all the categories and operations that have been found in any system, where 'open' means that new items can be added to the set if they show up in new empirical cases. The other approach is to derive the categories and operations from some particular theoretical framework or approach. See Kronenfeld (1992) for a fuller discussion of these issues.

6 The distinction comes from Trubetzkoy's *Principles of Phonology* published in 1939 (see Trubetzkoy 1969), where he distinguished an unmarked base form from a marked form (distinguished by some added phonological attribute or 'mark') derived from it. Greenberg (1966) generalized the opposition to morphology, syntax, and semantics as an unmarked form (representing a conceptual base – or default or generic option) – vs. a conceptually marked derivative specific option. See Kronenfeld (1996: ch. 7) for more on marking and its relationship to semantics.

References

Brown, Roger (1964) Discussion of the conference. In Romney, A. K. and R. G. D'Andrade (eds), *Transcultural Studies in Cognition*, Washington, DC: American Anthropological Association, pp. 243–53.

Bruner, Jerome, J. J. Goodnow, and G. Austin (1956) *A Study of Thinking* (with an appendix on language by Roger W. Brown), New York: John Wiley.

Davis, Kingsley and W. Lloyd Warner (1937) Structural analysis of kinship. *American Anthropologist* 39:291–313.

Dorsey, J. O. (1884) *Omaha Sociology. Third Annual Report of the Bureau of Ethnology to the Secretary of the Smithsonian Institution, 1881–1882.* 3: 205–307.

Goodenough, Ward H. (1956) Componential analysis and the study of meaning. *Language* 32:195–216.

Gould, Sydney H. (2000) *A New System for the Formal Analysis of Kinship*. Edited, annotated, and with an introduction by David B. Kronenfeld. Lanham, MD: University Press of America.

Greenberg, Joseph H. (1949) Logical analysis of kinship. *Philosophy of Science* 16:58–64.

——(1966) *Language Universals with Special Reference to Feature Hierarchies*. The Hague: Mouton (Janua Linguarum No. 59).

——(1968) *Anthropological Linguistics: An Introduction*. New York: Random House.

Hage, Per (1997) Unthinkable Categories and the Fundamental Laws of Kinship. *American Ethnologist* 24:652–67.

——(1998) Proto-Polynesian Kin Terms and Descent Groups. *Oceanic Linguistics* 37:189–192.

——(1999) Marking Universals and the Structure and Evolution of Kinship Terminologies. *Journal of the Royal Anthropological Institute* 5:423–441.

——(2001) Marking theory and kinship analysis: Cross-cultural and historical applications. *Anthropological Theory, 1*, 197–211.

Keen, Ian (1985) Definitions of Kin. *Journal of Anthropological Research* 41:62–90.

Kroeber, A. L. (1909) Classificatory Systems of Relationship. JRAI 39:77–84.

Kronenfeld, David B. (1973) Fanti Kinship: The Structure of Terminology and Behavior. *American Anthropologist* 75:1577–95.

——(1974) Sibling Typology: Beyond Nerlove and Romney. *American Ethnologist* (AE) 1:489–506.

——(1975) Kroeber vs. Radcliffe-Brown on Kinship Behavior: The Fanti Test Case. *Man* 10:257–84.

——(1976) Computer Analysis of Skewed Kinship Terminologies. *Language* 52:891–918.

——(1980a) A Formal Analysis of Fanti Kinship Terminology. *Anthropos*, 75:586–608.

——(1980b) Particularistic or Universalistic Analysis of Fanti Kinterminology: The Alternative Goals of Terminological Analysis. *Man*, 15:1:151–69.

——(1991) Fanti Kinship: Language, Inheritance, and Kingroups. *Anthropos* 86:19–31.

——(1992) Goodenough vs. Fischer on Residence: A Generation Later. *Journal of Quantitative Anthropology* 4:1–21.

——(1996) *Plastic Glasses and Church Fathers*. New York: Oxford University Press.

——(2000) Language and Thought: Collective Tools for Individual Use. In *Explorations in Linguistic Relativity*, edited by Martin Pütz and Marjolijn H. Verspoor, pp. 197–223. Amsterdam and Philadelphia: John Benjamins.

——(2001a) Introduction: The Uses of Formal Analysis re Cognitive and Social Issues. *Anthropological Theory*, 1:147–72.

——(2001b) Using Sydney H. Gould's Formalization of Kin Terminologies: Social Information, Skewing, and Structural Types. *Anthropological Theory*, 1:173–96.

——(2009) *Fanti Kinship and the Analysis of Kinship Terminologies*. Urbana and Chicago: University of Illinois Press.

——(2011) Types of Collective Representations: Cognition, Mental Architecture, and Cultural Knowledge, by Giovanni Bennardo and David B. Kronenfeld. In *A Companion to Cognitive Anthropology*, edited by David B. Kronenfeld *et al.*, pp. 82–101.

——(2013) Kinship Terms: Typology and History. In *Kinship Systems: Change and Reconstruction*, edited by Pat McConvell, Ian Keen, and Rachel Hendery. Salt Lake City: University of Utah Press.

Leach, Edmund (1945) Jinghpaw kinship terminology. JRAI 75:59–72. Reprinted in *Rethinking Anthropology*, pp. 28–53.

——(1958) Concerning Trobriand Class and Kinship Category *Tabu*. In *The Developmental Cycle in Domestic Groups*, edited by Jack Goody, pp. 120–45. Cambridge: Cambridge University Press.

——(1961) *Rethinking Anthropology*. LSE Monographs in Social Anthropology No. 22. London: Athlone.

Lehman, F. K. (2001) Aspects of a Formalist Theory of Kinship: The Functional Basis of Its Genealogical Roots and Some Extensions in Generalized Alliance Theory. *Anthropological Theory*, 1:212–38.

——(2011) Kinship Theory and Cognitive Theory in Anthropology. *A Companion to Cognitive Anthropology*. Edited by David B. Kronenfeld, Giovanni Bennardo, Victor C. de Munck, and Michael Fischer. Malden, MA: Blackwell, pp. 254–69.

Lounsbury, Floyd G. (1956) A Semantic Analysis of the Pawnee Kinship Usage. *Language* 32(1):158–94.

——(1964a) The Structural Analysis of Kinship Semantics. *Proceedings of the Ninth International Congress of Linguists*, The Hague, Mouton. Reprinted in Stephen A. Tyler, ed., *Cognitive Anthropology*. New York: Holt, Rinehart and Winston, pp. 193–212.

——(1964b) A Formal Account of the Crow- and Omaha-Type Kinship Terminologies. In Ward H. Goodenough, ed., *Explorations in Cultural Anthropology*. Reprinted in Stephen A. Tyler, ed., *Cognitive Anthropology*. New York: Holt, Rinehart and Winston, pp. 212–55.

——(1965) Another View of Trobriand Kinship Categories. In *Formal Semantic Analysis* (*American Anthropologist* special publication). E. A. Hammel, ed. pp. 142–85. Washington, DC: American Anthropological Association.

——(1969) Language and Culture. In Sidney Hook, ed., *Language and Philosophy*. New York: New York University Press, pp. 3–29.

Morgan, Lewis Henry (1871) *Systems of Consanguinity and Affinity of the Human Family*. Smithsonian Contributions to Knowledge, No. 218. Washington, DC: Smithsonian Institution.

Murdock, George Peter (1949) *Social Structure*. New York: Free Press.

Nerlove, Sara B. and A. Kimball Romney (1967) Sibling Terminology and Cross-sex Behavior. *American Anthropologist* 69:179–87.

Pike, Kenneth L. (1967) *Language in relation to a unified theory of the structure of human behavior* (2nd edn). The Hague: Mouton.

Radcliffe-Brown, A. R. (1924) The Mother's Brother in South Africa. *South African Journal of Science* 21:542–55. Reprinted in *Structure and Function in Primitive Society*, ed. by A. R. Radcliffe-Brown. pp. 15–31.

——(1941) The Study of Kinship Systems. JRAI. Reprinted in *Structure and Function in Primitive Society*, ed. by A. R. Radcliffe-Brown. pp. 49–89.

——(1952) *Structure and Function in Primitive Society*. Glencoe, IL: Free Press.

Read, Dwight W. (2001a) Formal Analysis of Kinship Terminologies and Its Relationship to What Constitutes Kinship. *Anthropological Theory*, *1*, 239–267.

——(2001b) 'What Is Kinship?' in R. Feinberg and M. Ottenheimer (eds) *The Cultural Analysis of Kinship: The Legacy of David Schneider and Its Implications for Anthropological Relativism*. Urbana, IL: University of Illinois Press.

——(2011) Mathematical Representation of Cultural Constructs. *A Companion to Cognitive Anthropology*. Edited by David B. Kronenfeld, Giovanni Bennardo, Victor C. de Munck, and Michael Fischer. Malden, MA: Blackwell, pp. 229–53.

Romney, A. Kimball (1965) Kalmuk Mongol and the Classification of Lineal Kinship Terminologies. In *Formal Semantic Analysis* (*American Anthropologist* special publication). E. A. Hammel, ed., pp. 146–70. Washington, DC: American Anthropological Association.

Romney, A. Kimball and Roy G. D'Andrade (1964) Cognitive Aspects of English Kinship. In Romney, A. K. and R. G. D'Andrade, eds., *Transcultural Studies in Cognition*. Washington, DC: American Anthropological Association.

Romney, A. Kimball and Philip J. Epling (1958) A Simplified Model of Kariera Kinship. *American Anthropologist* 60:59–74.

Schneider, David (1980) *American Kinship: A Cultural Account*. Englewood Cliffs, NJ: Prentice-Hall.

——(1984). *A Critique of the Study of Kinship*. Ann Arbor, MI: University of Michigan Press.

Tax, Sol (1955a) Some Problems of Social Organization. In: *Social Anthropology of the North American Tribes* (ed.) F. Eggan (enlarged edn). Chicago, IL: University of Chicago Press, pp. 3–34.

——(1955b) The social organization of the Fox Indians. In: *Social Anthropology of the North American Tribes* (ed.) F. Eggan (enlarged edn). Chicago, IL: University of Chicago Press, pp. 243–84.

Trubetzkoy, Nikolai S. (1969) *Principles of Phonology*. Berkeley, CA: University of California Press. Translated from *Grundzüge der Phonologie* (Göttingen: Vandenhoeck & Ruprecht, 1958; 3rd edn, 1962; originally published in Prague, 1939).

Wallace, Anthony F. C. and Atkins, J. (1960) 'The meaning of kinship terms'. *American Anthropologist* 62: 57–80.

Wierzbicka, Anna (1992) *Semantics, Culture, and Cognition: Universal Human Concepts in Culture-Specific Configurations*. Oxford: Oxford University Press.

12

CULTURAL SEMIOTICS

Peeter Torop

Introduction

The concept of 'cultural semiotics' can be interpreted in three ways. First, as referring to a methodological tool which can be recognized simultaneously in various disciplines of contemporary humanities and social sciences. It can also be considered as a concept representing the diversity of methods for analysing various aspects of culture as a research object in semiotic theory and applied semiotics; and finally, as one of the subdisciplines of semiotics and culture studies. In the last case cultural semiotics has a holistic view to culture and features of discipline.

Early development

Cultural semiotics is one of the fields of semiotics still searching for its disciplinary identity, and has been doing so for more than forty years. The Tartu–Moscow School made a programmatic entry into international science in 1973 when Lotman, Ivanov, Toporov, Pjatigorski, and Uspenskij collectively published their *Theses on the Semiotic Study of Cultures*. These theses laid the foundation for the semiotics of culture as a separate discipline, the primary aim of which was 'the study of the functional correlation of different sign systems. From this point of view particular importance is attached to questions of the hierarchical structure of the languages of culture.' Every culture is characterized by a unique relationship between sign systems and therefore in discussing any culture it is important to understand its historical evolution. Lotman has said in his memoirs: 'I personally cannot draw a clear line where a historical description ends and semiotics begins.' Special attention needs the empirically oriented subheading of the 'Theses': 'as applied to Slavic texts'. The publications in English translation followed the same principle: 'The Semiotics of Russian Culture' (Lotman and Uspenskij 1984) and 'The Semiotics of Russian Cultural History' (Lotman, Ginzburg, and Uspenskij 1985).

The study of a unique culture creates the need for new methods of research and thus the study of any new culture also enriches science itself. From here it follows that Russian culture, Estonian culture, or Chinese culture are all equally valuable for science, and each one of them adds something to the understanding of human culture as such. It is from this kind of approach that a general science of culture can evolve. The Tartu–Moscow school is not a representative of a unified system of knowledge in the semiotics of culture. Nevertheless, Juri Lotman was searching for a disciplinary synthesis – a fact that was first noticed by Karl Eimermacher who entitled his introduction to the German collection of Juri Lotman's works as 'Ju. M. Lotman. Bemerkungen zu einer Semiotik als integrativer Kulturwissenschaft' (Eimermacher 1974) ('J. M. Lotman. Notes to a semiotic version of integrative culturology'). 'Integrative' is an appropriate word, taking into account Lotman's special position in the typological studies of culture.

Historically, cultural semiotics grew out of the period of the diffusion of semiotic ideas after Peirce (1914) and de Saussure's (1915) death. The second phase was represented by the creation of general theories of language (Bühler, Hjelmslev, Prague Linguistic Circle, Chomsky), literature (Propp, Tynyanov, Bakhtin), and culture (Malinowski, White, Cassirer, Geertz). The third phase marked the interdisciplinary development of different fields in the humanities (Lévi-Strauss, Barthes, Todorov, Kristeva, Wiener, Eco, Lotman, etc.) and semiotics (Morris, Koch, Winner, Portis Winner). Their aspirations can be summed up as a desire to understand language and culture in as systematic fashion as possible, and fuse together quantitative and qualitative methods in this understanding. The first characteristic feature of semiotics of culture is that in this atmosphere, it attempted to be innovative on both the object level and the metalevel, offer new ways of defining the cultural object of study, and new languages of description (not just one universal language) for carrying out cultural analysis. As a result of all this, the emergence of semiotics of culture also meant the introduction of a new methodology.

Semiotics of culture has been strongly related to the development of general semiotics. One of the examples would be Roman Jakobson's endeavour to create a new science with three distinct disciplinary levels: (1) study in communication of verbal messages = linguistics; (2) study in communication of any message = semiotics (communication of verbal messages implied); (3) study in communication = social anthropology jointly with economics (communication of messages implied) (Jakobson 1971[1967]: 666). Jakobson first demonstrated his model of verbal communication (see Figure 12.1) in 1956 in his article 'Metalanguage as a Linguistic Problem' (1985a [1956]).

On the one hand, the given model ties its components to various functions of language: 'Language must be investigated in all the variety of its functions' (Jakobson 1985a [1956]: 113). On the other hand, along with the various functions of language, it is also important for Jakobson to distinguish two principle levels of language – the level of object language and the level of metalanguage: 'On these two different levels of language the same verbal stock may be used; thus we may speak in English (as metalanguage) about English (as object language) and interpret English words and sentences by means of English synonyms and circumlocutions' (1985a [1956]:117). The actualization of the concept of metalanguage as 'an innermost linguistic

CONTEXT

(REFERENTIAL FUNCTION)

ADRESSER   MESSAGE   ADRESSEE

(EMOTIVE FUNCTION)   (POETIC FUNCTION)   (CONATIVE FUNCTION)

CONTACT

(PHATIC FUNCTION)

CODE

(METALINGUAL FUNCTION)

Figure 12.1 Jakobson's model of communication

problem' (Jakobson 1985a [1956]: 121), which emerges from Jakobson's logic, is important for an understanding of the psychological as well as linguistic and cultural aspects of the functionality of language.

He begins from the metalinguistic aspect of the linguistic development of a child: 'Metalanguage is the vital factor of any verbal development. The interpretation of one linguistic sign through other, in some respects homogeneous signs of the same language, is a metalingual operation which plays an essential role in child language learning' (Jakobson 1985a [1956]: 120). But the development of a child corresponds to the development of an entire culture. For the development of a culture, it is important that the natural language of this culture satisfy all the demands for the description of foreign or of new phenomena and by the same token ensure not only the dialogic capacity but also the creativity and integrity of the culture, its cultural identity: 'A constant recourse to metalanguage is indispensable both for a creative assimilation of the mother tongue and for its final mastery' (Jakobson 1985a [1956]: 121). The very concept of metalanguage turns out to be important both at the level of scientific languages and at the level of everyday communication.

The process of communication is viewed hierarchically by Jakobson, so that a comprehension of his model of communication has to rest not so much on a statistical, theoretical basis as on a dynamic, empirical one. Jakobson in his article calls for a consideration of the specificity of each act of communication and correspondingly sees in the act of communication a hierarchy not only of linguistic but also of semiotic functions: 'The cardinal functions of language – referential, emotive, conative, phatic, poetic, and metalingual – and their different hierarchy in the diverse types of messages have been outlined and repeatedly discussed. This pragmatic approach to language must lead mutatis mutandis to an analogous study of the other semiotic systems: 'with which of these or other functions are they endowed, in what combinations and in what hierarchical order?' (Jakobson 1971d [1968]: 703). The linguistic and semiotic aspects of communication are interrelated and on this basis Jakobson distinguishes two sciences from a semantic point of view – a science of verbal signs or linguistics and a science of all possible signs or semiotics (Jakobson 1985b [1974]: 99).

Some activities in semiotics and semiology are interpretable as parallel to the Jakobsonian movement of thought. For Lévi-Strauss linguistics has a metalingual value for anthropology:

> as a 'semeiological' science, anthropology turns toward linguistics – first, because only linguistic knowledge provides the key to a system of logical categories and of moral values different from the observer's own; second, because linguistics, more than any other science, can teach him how to pass from the consideration of elements in themselves devoid of meaning to consideration of a semantic system and show him how the latter can be built on the basis of the former. This, perhaps, is primarily the problem of language, but, beyond and through it, the problem of culture in general.
>
> *(1963: 368)*

Lévi-Strauss shows an aptitude for finding analogies between language and parts of culture:

> New perspectives then open up. We are no longer dealing with an occasional collaboration where the linguist and the anthropologist, each working by himself, occasionally communicate those findings which each thinks may interest the other. In the study of kinship problems (and, no doubt, the study of other problems as well), the anthropologist finds himself in a situation which formally resembles that of the structural linguist. Like phonemes, kinship terms are elements of meaning; like phonemes, they

acquire meaning only if they are integrated into systems. 'Kinship systems', like 'phonemic systems', are built by the mind on the level of unconscious thought. Finally, the recurrence of kinship patterns, marriage rules, similar prescribed attitudes between certain types of relatives, and so forth, in scattered regions of the globe and in fundamentally different societies, leads us to believe that, in the case of kinship as well as linguistics, the observable phenomena result from the action of laws which are general but implicit. The problem can therefore be formulated as follows: Although they belong to another order of reality, kinship phenomena are of the same type as linguistic phenomena.

(1963: 34)

Barthes, who also dreamed about a new science, differentiated first and second order languages and enlarged the borders of linguistics: 'In fact, we must now face the possibility of inverting Saussure's declaration: linguistics is not a part of the general science of signs, even a privileged part, it is semiology which is a part of linguistics: to be precise, it is that part covering the great signifying unities of discourse. By this inversion we may expect to bring to light the unity of the research at present being done in anthropology, sociology, psycho-analysis and stylistics round the concept of signification' (1967: 11). Language in the context of this logic is both object and metalanguage:

Thus, though working at the outset on non-linguistic substances, is required, sooner or later, to find language (in the ordinary sense of the term) in its path, not only as a model, but also as component, relay or signified. Even so, such language is not quite that of the linguist: it is a second-order language, with its unities no longer monemes or phonemes, but larger fragments of discourse referring to objects or episodes whose meaning underlines language, but can never exist independently of it. Semiology is therefore perhaps destined to be absorbed into a trans-linguistics, the materials of which may be myth, narrative, journalism, or on the other hand objects of our civilization, in so far as they are spoken (through press, prospectus, interview, conversation and perhaps even the inner language, which is ruled by the laws of imagination).

(Barthes 1967: 10–11)

The 1960s was typified by the search for analogies between language and different cultural artefacts for better analysability. Barthes was very influential in this type of methodological thinking: 'We shall therefore postulate that there exists a general category language/speech, which embraces all the systems of signs; since there are no better ones, we shall keep the terms language and speech, even when they are applied to communications whose substance is not verbal' (1967: 25). Also representative of this approach is the book of Metz *Film Language: A Semiotics of the Cinema* (1968) where the author, for example, found analogy between shots and utterances.

Within the same period, Umberto Eco's work *A Theory of Semiotics* was published. In the preface, dated from the years 1967–74, Eco distinguishes between two theories: a theory of codes and a theory of sign production (1977: viii). Eco did not think about disciplinary cultural semiotics but culture was conceptualized as an important semiotic research object:

To look at the whole of culture *sub specie semiotica* is not to say that culture is only communication and signification but that it can be understood more thoroughly if it is seen from the semiotic point of view ... In culture every entity can become a semiotic phenomenon. The laws of signification are the laws of culture. For this reason culture

173

allows a continuous process of communicative exchanges, in so far as it subsists as a system of systems of signification. *Culture can be studied completely under a semiotic view.*

(Eco 1977: 27–8)

It was also the period of time in which there was a movement from typological descriptions of languages to descriptions of the general typology of culture. According to Lotman, the typology of culture should be based on the universals of culture. The most universal feature of human cultures is the need for self-description. Every culture has its own specific means for doing this – its languages of description. The descriptive languages facilitate cultural communication, perpetuate cultural experience, and model cultural memory. The coherence of culture is based on exactly the repetition and interpretation of the same things. The more descriptive languages a culture has, the richer is that culture. Consequently, every culture is describable as a hierarchy of object languages and descriptive languages, where the initial object language is a so-called home language and it is surrounded by semiotic systems related to everyday rituals and bodily techniques. There are certain languages of culture that can serve the function of both, object language and metalanguage from the point of view of everyday cultural experience (depicted in Figure 12.2).

While home language, native language, and everyday rituals as semiotic mediation are object languages, the experience of literature, art, and media can be both object and metalinguistic, depending on their position in and impact on a person's (especially a child's) life. In a common situation it can be claimed that literature, arts, and media channels depict a certain reality; the critic interprets it in a language of a given medium that is easily understandable for the audience; the humanities do it in their metalanguage where strict terms exist alongside metaphors; sciences and natural sciences do it in strict terminological systems (and the process of interpretation takes place) up to formal languages and artistic languages. By means of object languages a human being acknowledges his or her relations to the world and by learning and using metalanguages shapes his or her individual identity. Culture does the same. The more descriptive languages there are in a culture, the more numerous are the possibilities for self-identification and the constitution of cultural identity.

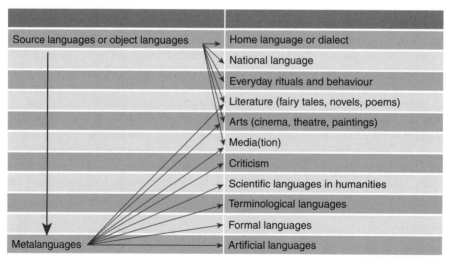

Figure 12.2 Hierarchy of objective and descriptive languages

Cultural semiotics

Cultural semiotics has the means to analyse very different languages of culture not only through the communication processes taking place in a culture but also by seeing these processes as culture's self-communication. In the course of analysing a culture's self-communication we inevitably arrive at the definition of its identity. In today's world, between global and local processes there exists a field of tension in which many ambivalent and hybrid phenomena take place. Because of this, it is especially important to understand that the need of individuals and societies for defining their self, their identity, and the semiotics of culture is becoming increasingly relevant in achieving this understanding. A sign system and language become synonyms in this context, and the notion of language is metaphorized, especially when the notion of a modelling system is added. A field of notions emerges: language – sign system – modelling system, and in addition, object language and metalanguage are differentiated.

The similarity between the notions of (cultural) language and a sign system in the semiotics of culture, gives us the possibility of distinguishing between two typological approaches. The first distinction is based on the juxtaposition of primary and secondary modelling systems.

I   Language as a primary modelling system
II   Secondary modelling systems:

  (1)   language as a higher sign system (myth, literature, poetry),
  (2)   language as a metalanguage or a part of metalanguage (criticism and history of art, music, dance, cinema, etc.), and
  (3)   language as a model or analogue (language of film, dance, music, painting, etc.).

Proceeding from this classification, language as a primary modelling system is the humans' main means of thinking and communicating. As a secondary modelling system, language is the preserver of the culture's collective experience and the reflector of its creativity. As a metalanguage, natural language is the translator and interpreter of all nonverbal systems, and from a methodological perspective, especially during the 1960s and 1970s, language offered cultural analysis the possibility of searching for discrete (linguistic) elements also in such fields of culture where natural language either does not belong to the means of expression, or does so only partially.

The second distinction is based on the possibility of differentiating between the statics and the dynamics of cultural languages.

I   Statics:

  (1)   continual (iconic-spatial, nonverbal) languages, and
  (2)   discrete languages (verbal languages).

II   Dynamics:

  (1)   specialization of cultural languages, and
  (2)   integration of cultural languages:
      (a)   self-descriptions and meta-descriptions,
      (b)   creolization.

While the level of statics is based on the distinction between verbal and nonverbal languages, the level of dynamics is related to the different paces of development of the different parts of culture. This means that during any given period in culture there are certain fields where there is balance between creation and interpretation (criticism, theory, history) and it is possible to speak about specialization and the identity of the field. At the same time, there are fields where, either due to the fast pace of development or for other reasons, a split between creation and interpretation brings about the need to integrate the field into culture. This can be done in two main ways – by using the creators' self-descriptions also for general interpretation, or by borrowing tools of analysis from other fields and, combining them, creating new creolized languages of description.

As a result of descriptive processes, one can talk about cultural self-models. Cultural self-description can be viewed as a process proceeding in three directions. Culture's self-model is the result of the first direction, whose goal is maximum similarity to the actually existing culture. Second, cultural self-models may emerge that differ from ordinary cultural practice and may even have been designed for changing that practice. Third, there are self-models that exist as an ideal cultural self-consciousness, separately from culture and not oriented toward it. By this formulation Lotman does not exclude conflict between culture and its self-models. But the creation of self-models reflects the creativity of culture. In the 1980s Juri Lotman described creativity, calling on the work of Ilya Prigogine. In the article 'Culture as a Subject and Object for Itself', Lotman maintains that: 'The main question of semiotics of culture is the problem of meaning-generation. What we shall call meaning-generation is the ability both of culture as a whole and of its parts to put out, in the "output", nontrivial new texts. New texts are the texts that emerge as results of irreversible processes (in Ilya Prigogine's sense), i.e. texts that are unpredictable to a certain degree' (2000: 640).

Cultural semiotics started from the realization that in a semiotical sense culture is a multi-language system, where, in parallel to natural languages, there exist secondary modelling systems (mythology, ideology, ethics, etc.), which are based on natural languages, or which employ natural languages for their description or explanation (music, ballet) or language analogization (language of theatre, language of movies). The next step is to introduce the concept of text as the principal concept of cultural semiotics. On the one hand, text is the manifestation of language, using it in a certain manner. On the other hand, text is itself a mechanism that creates languages. From the methodological point of view, the concept of text was important for the definition of the subject of analysis, since it denoted both natural textual objects (a book, picture, symphony) and textualizable objects (culture as text, everyday behaviour or biography, an era, an event). Text and textualization symbolize the definition of the object of study; the definition or framework allows in its turn the structuralization of the object either into structural levels or units, and also the construction of a coherent whole or system of those levels and units. The development of the principles of immanent analysis in various cultural domains was one field of activity of cultural semiotics. Yet the analysis of a defined object is static, and the need to also take into account cultural dynamics led Juri Lotman to introduce the notion of semiosphere. Although the attributes of semiosphere resemble those of text (definability, structurality, coherence), it is an important shift from the point of view of culture's analysability. Human culture constitutes the global semiosphere, but that global system consists of intertwined semiospheres of different times (the diachrony of semiosphere) and different levels (the synchrony of semiosphere). Each semiosphere can be analysed as a single whole, yet we need to bear in mind that each analysed whole in culture is a part of a greater whole, which is an important methodological principle. At the same time, every whole consists of parts, which are legitimate wholes on their own, which in turn consist of parts, etc. It is an infinite dialogue of wholes and parts and the dynamics of the whole dimension.

Yet the text will remain the 'middle' concept for cultural semiotics, since as a term it can denote both a discrete artefact and an invisible abstract whole (a mental text in collective consciousness or subconsciousness). The textual aspect of text analysis means the operation with clearly defined sign systems, texts or combinations of texts; the processual aspect of text analysis presupposes definition, construction or reconstruction of a whole. Thus the analysis assembles the concrete and the abstract, the static and the dynamic in one concept – the text (Torop 2009).

The space of communication can thus be further divided into communication and meta-communication. The texts in this space are autonomous and describable through the relations of prototext and metatext, and the possibility of fixing their amount assures the analysability of culture. At this level, culture can be described as a set of texts and we can determine the process of creating new texts from previous texts, which generates coherence in culture. We could say that describing this coherence is a static approach to the space of culture, based on the classification of proto- and metatexts. Another possibility is the dynamic approach, which stems from the intertextual relations between texts. Intertextuality hereby refers to textual relations on different levels: from parts of text (citation, allusion, reminiscence, paraphrase, etc.) to whole texts (parody, plagiarism, travesty, etc.). Intertextual description of culture includes the rules of operating with alien texts. Every text is bounded by many different texts through implicit or explicit references and these texts have overlappings and intertwinings as a result of which the intertextual description of culture is a dynamic network that lacks direct causal relations in contrast to the case of metacommunicational description. Therefore, intertextual space is the space of visible and invisible bonds between texts. In this space, text is a process both from the point of view of its creation (from the first to the final draft) and its reception and interpretation. Thus we have a reason to talk also about intercommunication (see Figure 12.3).

Describing textual relations is fruitful on at least three more levels. First, both meta- and intercommunication are possible not only between verbal texts but between texts fixed in different sign systems. This means that in the space of culture, it is possible to describe any text intersemiotically or that communication always bears an intersemiotic aspect in culture. This is expressed in the mediation of words with images in illustrated books and in ekphrasis as well as in the writing of a ballet based on a literary work or its cinematic adaptations, etc. Second, dis-courses are hierarchized in culture. One and the same message can be translated into different discourses and it is possible to speak of interdiscoursivity or the existence of the message in different modalities and on different levels of culture. Therefore, interdiscoursive space is also multimodal space. Third, in every culture, it is possible to observe the transfers of one message between different media and this means the necessity of using also the notion of intermediality. For instance, the screen adaptation of a novel is on the one hand describable as an intersemiotic translation and the analysis of it presumes the comparison of verbal and audiovisual sign systems. On the other hand, however, literature and cinema are two different media and, complementarily, the influence of medium on the text or the comparison of literariness and cinematicity is important. Therefore, the space of culture is simultaneously the space of different sign systems (intersemiotic),

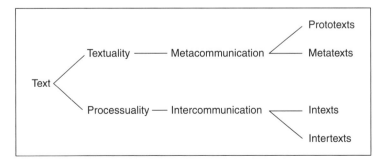

Figure 12.3 Metacommunication and intercommunication

discoursive practices (interdiscoursive) and media (intermedial). These three dimensions of the space of culture allow more versatility in describing the processes of communication. From this perspective, one possibility afforded by this holistic view of culture is to understand culture as a process of total translation (Torop 2008, 2010, 2011).

The original conception of the dynamics of culture came from W. A. Koch, founder of evolutionary cultural semiotics. Koch saw culture as a phenomenon whose true integrative potentialities have not yet been fully discovered or explored. For a semiotics thus conceived, structure and process are not different phases of reality and/or sciences but rather mere faces of a unitary field. His semiotic analysis will be based on premises of macro-integration – or evolution – and of micro-integration – culture (Koch 1989: v). For evolutionary cultural semiotics evolution means the dynamics of the cultural environment as semiosis that evolves from verbal and pictorial media, to start with, towards printed media and then telemedia. Today this process is continuing in the environment of new media. It is a movement from immediate communication towards the diversification of forms of mediated communication and the understanding of communication forms, with the cultural value of technological evolution becoming a part of both the history of science and that of culture.

On one hand, the study of culture would be possible via the semiotization of culture-studying disciplines, which would bring them closer to the essence of culture. The birth of the notion of semiotic anthropology is an example of such a development, which, together with the capability for disciplinary analysis, would increase the level of analysability of culture (see Torop 2006). On the other hand, cultural semiotics offers a systematic approach to culture and creates a complementary methodology, which ensures the mutual understanding of different disciplines studying culture. This is the developmental prospect of cultural semiotics.

The intersection of culture and disciplines studying culture evokes questions raised by Rastier, those about universal trans-semiotics, and differentiates between two poles with respect to the study of culture – there are the sciences of culture (*sciences de la culture*), represented by Ernst Cassirer, and the semiotics of cultures (*sémiotique des cultures*) represented by the Tartu School. Between these two poles lie the questions: one or many sciences? Culture or cultures? (Rastier 2001: 163; see also Posner 2005: 292).

Transdisciplinary effort exists between semiotics and many other disciplines. Semiotic anthro-pology possesses a significant methodological value: 'A further advantage of semiotic anthropology for today's sociocultural anthropologists is that it supports more flexible and expansive approaches to defining where and how we can do our research' (Mertz 2007: 345). In archaeology we can also detect a similar methodological partnership with semiotics – the belief that semiotics offers 'a common language with which we can understand the structure of contrasting interpretative approaches and communicate across these boundaries while at the same time acknowledging the validity of our different theoretical commitments' (Preucel and Bauer 2001: 93). In cultural psychology there exists a strong interest in semiotics: 'The whole semiotic mediation system is viewed as a hierarchical regulatory system of meanings that guarantee the person's psychological distancing from the here-and-now setting' (Valsiner 2005: 203). The purpose is not to show all the contacts between semiotics and other disciplines in cultural research but rather the dialogical value of semiotics.

In both cases of culture as an object of study and culture research sciences as objects of study – it is suitable to recall the picture that emerged from Umberto Eco's reading of Lotman: 'If we put together many branches and great quantity of leaves, we still cannot understand the forest. But if we know how to walk through the forest of culture with our eyes open, confidently following the numerous paths which criss-cross it, not only shall we be able to understand better the vastness and complexity of the forest, but we shall also be able to discover the nature of the leaves and branches of every single tree' (2000: xiii).

Cultural semiotics is disciplinary oriented to the complex analysis of culture, where it is important to balance between the understanding of the part and the whole, statics and dynamics. The specificity of cultural semiotics lies in understanding the complementarity between processes of communication in culture and cultural autocommunication. The historical analysis of culture covers the typological research of cultural self-descriptive languages, the coexistence of these languages and the mutual translatability between them. Contemporary culture is a multilingual dynamic whole where every innovative act from a new novel, through an exhibition or movie to a big social event exists in culture as something unpredictably new. This new will become the part of culture only after being described for culture, when semiotic tools have been found for its research, and when through the adaptations and the transformations of this new component of culture into other cultural forms, a system of metalanguage has been constructed to interpret the new cultural phenomenon. Cultural semiotics serves as a tool for the complex analysis of culture and also for synthesizing the experiences gained from other culture studies disciplines. The disciplinary development of cultural semiotics is at the same time an interdisciplinary development of the dialogue between culture and humanities, on the one hand, and between different culture studies disciplines, on the other.

Related topics

culture and translation; language and culture in intercultural communication; cultural linguistics; language, culture and identity; language and cultural scripts; language, culture and spatial cognition; space, time and space–time: metaphors, maps and fusions; language, gender and context; language and culture in cognitive anthropology; ethnolinguistics

Further reading

Capozzi, Rocco (ed.) 1997. *Reading Eco. An Anthology*. Bloomington, Indianapolis: Indiana University Press. (This collection provides a very good overview of Eco's cultural semiotics and its scientific reception.)

Koch, Walter A. (ed.)1990. *Semiotics in the Individual Sciences*. Vols.1–2. Bochum: Brockmeyer Universitätsverlag. (This volume gives a very good overview of different fields of cultural semiotics: literary studies, linguistics, anthropology, arts, etc.)

Lotman, Yuri M. 2000. *Universe of the Mind. A Semiotic Theory of Culture*. Bloomington, IN: Indiana University Press. (This book is the best source for understanding basic notions of cultural semiotics: text, semiosphere, cultural memory.)

Lotman, Juri 2009. Culture and Explosion. Berlin, New York: Walter de Gruyter. (This is an important book on cultural dynamics, unpredictability in cultural changes and search of new descriptive languages.)

Salupere, Silvi, Torop, Peeter, and Kull, Kalevi (eds) 2013. *Beginnings of the Semiotics of Culture. Tartu Semiotics Library 13*. Tartu: University of Tartu Press. (Overview of history of cultural semiotics and collection of programmatic texts of Tartu–Moscow semiotic school.)

References

Barthes, Roland 1967. *Elements of Semiology*. New York: Hill and Wang.

Eco, Umberto 1977. *A Theory of Semiotics*. London: Macmillan.

——2000. 'Introduction'. In: Lotman, Yuri, *Universe of the Mind: A Semiotic Theory of Culture*. Bloomington, IN: Indiana University Press, vii–xiii.

Eimermacher, Karl 1974. Ju. M. Lotman. 'Bemerkungen zu einer Semiotik als integrativer Kulturwissenschaft'. In: Lotman, Jurij M. *Aufsätze zur Theorie und Methodologie der Literatur und Kultur*. (Eimermacher, Karl, hrsg.) Kronberg Ts.: Scriptor, vii–xxv.

Ivanov, Vyacheslav 1978. 'The Science of Semiotics'. *New Literary History*, 9:2, 199–204.

Jakobson, Roman 1971a [1959]. 'On linguistic aspects of translation'. In: Jakobson, Roman, *Selected Writings. II. Word and Language*. The Hague: Mouton, 260–6.

——1971b [1961]. 'Linguistics and communication theory'. In: Jakobson, Roman, *Selected Writings II: Word and Language*. The Hague: Mouton, 570–9.

——1971c [1967]. 'Linguistics in relation to other sciences'. In: Jakobson, Roman, *Selected Writings. II. Word and Language*. The Hague: Mouton, 655–95.

——1971d [1968]. 'Language in relation to other communication systems'. In: Jakobson, Roman, *Selected Writings. II. Word and Language*. The Hague: Mouton, 697–708.

——1985a [1956]. 'Metalanguage as a linguistic problem'. In: Jakobson, Roman, *Selected Writings. VII. Contributions to Comparative Mythology. Studies in Linguistics and Philology, 1972-1982*. Berlin: Mouton, 113–21.

——1985b [1974]. 'Communication and society'. In: Jakobson, Roman, *Selected Writings. VII. Contributions to Comparative Mythology. Studies in Linguistics and Philology, 1972–1982*. Berlin: Mouton, 98–100.

Koch, A. Walter 1989. 'Bochum publications in evolutionary cultural semiotics: Editorial'. In: Koch, Walter A. (ed.), *Culture and Semiotics*. Bochum: Studienverlag Dr. Norbert Brockmeyer, V.

Lévi -Strauss, Claude 1963. *Structural Anthropology*. New York: Basic Books.

Lotman, Juri 1973 = Лотман, Юрий. Материалы к курсу теории литературы. Выпуск 2: Статьи по типологии културы. Тарту: Тартуский государственный университет.

——2000. *Kul'tura kak subjekt i sama-sebe objekt (Culture as a subject and object for itself)*. J. Lotman. Semiosfera [Semiosphere]. Sankt-Peterburg: Iskusstvo-SPB, 639–47.

Lotman, Juri, Ginzburg, Lidiya, Uspenskij, Boris 1985. *The Semiotics of Russian Cultural History*. Ithaca, NY and London: Cornell University Press, 1985.

Lotman, Juri M. and Uspenski, Boris A. 1984. *The Semiotics of Russian Culture*. (Michigan Slavic Contributions 11.). Ann Arbor, MI: Department of Slavic Languages and Literatures, University of Michigan.

Mertz, Elizabeth 2007. Semiotic anthropology. *Annual Review of Anthropology* 36, 337–53.

Posner, Roland 2005. Basic tasks of cultural semiotics. In: Williamson, Rodney; Sbrocchi, Leonard G.; Deely, John (eds), Semiotics 2003: 'Semiotics and National Identity'. New York, Ottawa, Toronto: Legas, 307–53.

Preucel, Robert W. and Bauer, Alexander A. 2001. Archaeological pragmatics. *Norwegian Archaeological Review* 34:2, 85–96.

Rastier, François 2001. Sémiotique et sciences de la culture. *LINX* 44:1, 149–66.

Torop, Peeter 2006. 'Semiotics, anthropology and the analysability of culture'. *Sign Systems Studies* 34.2, 285–315.

——2010. *La traduzione totale. Tipi di processo traduttivo nella cultura*. Milan: Hoepli.

——2011. *Tõlge ja kultuur (Translation and culture)*. Tartu: Tartu University Press, 2011.

——2009. 'Lotmanian explosion'. In: Juri Lotman. *Culture and Explosion*. Berlin, New York: Walter de Gruyter, xxvii–xxxix.

——2008. 'Translation as communication and auto-communication'. *Sign Systems Studies* 36.2, 375–97.

Valsiner, Jaan 2005. 'Scaffolding within the structure of Dialogical Self: Hierarchical dynamics of semiotic mediation'. *New Ideas in Psychology* 23, 197–206.

13

CULTURE AND TRANSLATION

Nigel Armstrong

Introduction

The term 'culture' splits fairly neatly into two senses: the anthropological, which refers to the totality of practices that distinguish a community, large or small; and the narrower sense of artistic enterprise. Within the former definition, we shall see that culture pervades language in ways that reflect several senses of the term. Within the latter, culture ranges from high to low, from Homer of the *Odyssey* to Homer of *The Simpsons*. Both types of culture offer stiff challenges to the theory and practice of translation, as well as opportunities to theorize and practise the art, or science, in creative ways.

Culture in both senses pervades language down to the deepest structural levels. It is unsurprising that the most superficial linguistic level, vocabulary, should convey cultural reference, given that words, quite obviously, convey meaning, both in denotation and connotation. One form of the Sapir–Whorf hypothesis (Chapter 2 this volume) states that culturally important elements will undergo 'codability', the unintuitive term used to describe compactness of encoding. The phenomenon is easy to understand, but the difficulties it presents to the translator may be considerable; at least, if we accept that expansion of linguistic material from the source to the target language implies translation loss, an issue we consider below. We are not of course referring here to the expansion in the availability of literature that translation provides; this needs no defence.

Sapir-Whorf in the other direction, emphasizing the influence of language on culture, is of most interest where 'grammatical words' like pronouns are concerned. Thus for example, languages having 'T/V' or dual-pronoun systems oblige their speakers to reflect on the relationships they contract in terms of power or solidarity; these are latent in other languages, or appear in different forms, and call for ingenious strategies in their rendering.

Translation problems raised by the first form of Sapir–Whorf referred to above seem however to be more common. In the following section we consider the scope, and to some extent the nature of these issues. In a second section we look at cultural shift or drift as shown in translation. We take examples from English and French in what follows.

Culture with its roots in language

The metaphor is used advisedly; it is possible to uproot a cultural reference and transplant it in another language, although the risk of damage is always present. We said above that culture 'pervades language down to the deepest structural levels'. The three structural levels commonly referred to in linguistics are pronunciation, grammar and vocabulary – in the jargon, phonology, morpho-syntax, and lexis. To illustrate these last two we may proceed by example, using the following extract from an episode of the animated cartoon show *The Simpsons*, which is typical of the cultural richness often found in the show. A transcription must necessarily ignore phonology, but it may be added that the show is exceptionally adept at exploiting social accents and voice quality in the interests of characterization.

The Simpsons: 'Saturdays of Thunder' episode (reference to the stock-car racing movie *Days of Thunder*)

French title: 'Un père dans la course'

Voiceover: Products you could only imagine before:

Voiceover: Des produits que vous n'avez jamais osé imaginer:

– The Foam Dome

– La casquette-buvette

– The Jet Walker

– Le turbo-déambulateur

– Mr. Sugar Cube

– Le sucré-cube

HOMER: That baby changed our lives.

HOMER: Cette p'tite merveille nous change la vie.

TROY: I'm actor Troy McClure. You might remember me from such TV series as 'Buck Henderson, Union Buster' and 'Troy and Company's Summertime Smile Factory'. But I'm here to tell you about 'Spiffy', the twenty-first-century stain remover. Let's meet the inventor, Dr Nick Riviera.

TROY: Je suis l'acteur Troy McClure. Vous vous souvenez certainement de m'avoir vu dans des séries télé comme 'L'homme qui sombre [?] à pic', 'La loi de l'œuf en gelée', ou bien 'Mixion Impossible'. Mais je suis ici pour vous parler de 'Spiffy', le détachant miracle du vingt-et-unième siècle. Mais voici son inventeur, le Dr Nick Riviera.

NICK: Thank you, Troy! Hi, everybody!

NICK: Je vous remercie, Troy. Salut, tout le monde !

ALL: Hi, Dr Nick!

TOUS: Salut, Dr Nick !

NICK: Troy, I brought with me the gravestone of author and troubled soul Edgar Allan Poe!

NICK: Troy, je me suis permis d'apporter la pierre tombale d'un auteur à l'âme tourmentée, Edgar Allan Poe.

TROY: One of our best writers.

TROY: L'un de nos meilleurs écrivains.

NICK: Yes, but unfortunately, a century of neglect has turned this tombstone into a depressing eyesore.

NICK: Oui, mais malheureusement après un siècle de négligence, cette pierre tombale nous offre un spectacle absolument lamentable.

TROY: So what? I guess we're going to have to throw it away.

TROY: Alors j'imagine qu'on va devoir la balancer.

NICK: Not so fast, Troy! With one application of Spiffy, you'll think the body's still warm! [applies some Spiffy, removes all the grime]

NICK: Non, pas si vite, Troy ! Avec une seule application de Spiffy, vous aurez l'impression que le cadavre est encore chaud.

ALL: Ooooooh! Ahhhhhhhh!

TOUS: Aaaaah ! Aaaaah !

TROY: Quoth the raven, 'What a shine!'

TROY: Et comme dit le corbeau, quelle brillance !

HOMER: Ooooh! That's one clean tombstone!

HOMER: Ooooh ! C'est ce qu'on appelle une pierre tombale nickel.

NICK: I'm offering three bottles, enough to clean one thousand tombstones, for only $39.95!

ALL: Booo! [a chair is heaved on stage]

TROY: I'm afraid you're going to have to do better, doctor.

HOMER: Yeah, give us a break, doctor!

NICK: But Troy, how can I make it lower than $39.95?

TROY: Find a way.

NICK: Okay, I'll throw in a fourth bottle, the applicator glove, and a state-of-Kansas jello mould, $29.95! [crowd goes wild]

NICK: Eh bien, je vous offre trois bouteilles, de quoi remettre à neuf un millier de pierres tombales, pour seulement $39.95!

TROY: J'ai l'impression que vous allez devoir faire un petit effort, docteur.

HOMER: Hé, sois pas radin, mon vieux.

NICK: Mais Troy, comment voulez-vous que je descende en dessous de $39.95?

TROY: Alors, débrouillez-vous.

NICK: Très bien, j'ajoute une quatrième bouteille, des gants de protection et un moulin à gâteau rectangulaire Kansas, comme l'état du même nom, pour $29.95!

The extract shown has, as so often in an episode, nothing to do with the main plot. It comes at the beginning of the episode, and it is farce – or satire, should one prefer to see some social purpose beneath the clowning. The first failure in the extract relates to what students of translation have come to call 'encyclopaedic knowledge', or general knowledge outside the jargon. The knowledge in question here is at the same time specialized, since it has to do with characterization achieved through dialogue. Devotees of the show are familiar with the unsuccessful actor Troy McClure and his invariable self-introduction: 'I'm actor Troy McClure. You might remember me from … '. The incongruity resulting from the juxtaposition of 'Buck Henderson, Union Buster' with 'Troy and Company's Summertime Smile Factory', in the present writer's mind at least, reinforces a perception of McClure's lack of success, betrayed by his willing to take on any role whatever; or if this seems too fine-spun, it may be functioning as a comment on the precariousness of the acting profession. The French dialogue replaces this with rather whimsical puns on the titles of some TV action shows, substituting fictional cookery shows instead: 'The Fall Guy' (French title 'L'homme qui tombe à pic'), 'LA Law' ('La loi de Los Angeles') and 'Mission Impossible' (same title). It is perhaps unfair to call these 'failures', but an element of complexity is certainly lost in translation. A straightforward or 'mainstream' cultural reference is apparent in 'Quoth the raven … ', very clearly marked in English by reason of its archaism. That said, one can suggest that the French equivalent, 'Comme dit le corbeau … ', may well convey similar resonance for a French speaker familiar with Poe.

The limits of culture are passed when we consider sequences that can justly be considered as presenting to the translator purely linguistic problems. This is illustrated in the last exchange, where Nick throws in a 'state-of-Kansas jello mould'; five words, or three if we treat 'state-of-Kansas' as one linguistic unit. The obvious point here is that English has the advantage of being able to use compound noun phrases as attributive adjectives, and French can really do nothing with sequences like this, as is shown by the ten words used to render the English. Is this failure? Given the lack of choice open to the translator, it is hardly profitable to discuss the issue in these terms, but expansion from source to target text is generally regarded as unwelcome. From the viewpoint of a near-bilingual student of translation, the blemish is obvious enough, but in specialized discussions like this it is easy to forget that translations are made for monolinguals, who have no basis of comparison, and that the statement made earlier, that 'expansion of linguistic material from the source to the target language implies translation loss', is hard to test. It is quite obvious from an inspection of these two texts that French has more linguistic material, but it is hard to say whether this is an artefact of translation. Shakespeare tells us that brevity is the soul of wit, but it may be that a French speaker would find the jello-mould circumlocution amusing. It is certain that the longer utterances would pass unnoticed.

Culture infused in language

The 'infusion' metaphor, by contrast, implies an indissociable alliance of language and culture. Consider the following limerick:

> Said Watts-Dunton, 'However one searches,
> The Pines remains Putney's best purchase.
> But let's give old Algy a
> Touch of nostalgia
> By changing its name to The Birches.'

The text is a curious blend of high and low culture. Its appreciation depends (at least) on acquaintance with one of the minor by-ways of English literature; the alcoholic Victorian poet Algernon Swinburne ('Algy') spent his later years in the care of his friend Theodore Watts-Dunton, at a house in Putney called The Pines. The last line refers to Swinburne's taste for flagellation. This information is in the province of high culture, but the way in which it is expressed is less easy to define along a simple high–low polarity, and indeed any attempt to define it in this way shows that the polarity metaphor is unsuitable, for culture varies along more than one dimension. Thus limericks often comprise an element of the bawdy, as in this case, although it is obliquely expressed; the best examples also combine wit and fantasy. The combination of 'high' cultural subject matter, irreverent treatment, unserious metre and weak or absurd rhymes are perhaps the chief source of wit, while the fantastical element pervades the whole. From the translator's viewpoint, lexis in this example communicates cultural reference that, when allied with other aspects of culture like literary structure, will seal off a text from the possibility of translation. The limerick is like a jewel, or an egg, sufficient to itself and impossible of access.

At still deeper structural levels of language, we see variation in pronunciation and grammar that has its roots so deep in language as to rule out any but the most desperate attempt at translation, quite irrespective of structural considerations like those relating to the limerick just looked at. Variation of this kind responds to the wider cultural factors that promote 'social identity'. Phenomena like these are perhaps marginal and found mostly in dialogue, but the interest they present to the translation theorist is absorbing.

The deepest or most 'structural' ways in which culture and translation interact are to be seen in pronunciation and grammar. The following examples, taken from Armstrong (2005), show that the linguistic and cultural aspects of translation issues can be fused. Grammatical variation is a salient feature of French, in the sense of being shared by all speakers, to an extent that seems less noticeable in English. So for instance, in informal French a speaker has the option between *quelle* and *quoi* as question words in sequences of the following type. The symbol '~' here means 'varies with'. The second variant is the more informal, and has what some linguists have called a 'QU-final', structure, such that the interrogative word appears phrase-finally.

> tu es de quelle origine? ~ tu es d'origine quoi?

The non-standard alternant of the pair, *tu es d'origine quoi?*, is untranslatable in any literal way into a language that has little social variation in its interrogative system, like English. An attempt to render into English the very informal nature of the second variant would probably have to use resources from a linguistic level other than syntax. The ease with which we can imagine a solution to the translation of a stretch of non-standard language depends on the availability of a feature in the TT that is more or less comparable. For instance, the famous opening passage of *Zazie dans le Métro*, by Raymond Queneau, is presented as straight speech, or more precisely as interior monologue. The first two sentences are as follows:

Doukipudonktan, se demanda Gabriel excédé. Pas possible, ils se nettoient jamais.

Queneau's use of his semi-phonetic system right from the outset, and his tendency to write phrases solid, seem to proclaim his commitment to the celebration of spoken *français populaire* (there are no gaps between words in speech). *Doukipudonktan* seems to mean *D'où qu'il(s) pue(nt) donc tant ?* (Gabriel is standing in an apparently unwashed crowd), translatable as 'Why do they stink so much?' and we can imagine a translation that would replace the non-standard syntax of *d'où que* with English non-standard lexis, perhaps something like either: 'Why do they smell so bloody awful?' or 'Where's that bloody awful hum coming from?', depending on the interpretation of *Doukipudonktan*. Wright's (2000) translation renders these sentences as:

Howcanaystinksotho? Ts incredible, they never clean themselves.

We can see that the translator has resorted to reduction to achieve an approximation to the non-standard effect in the ST: 'they' reduces to 'ay', 'it's to 'ts', and quite ingeniously, 'though' to 'tho', using non-standard spelling to suggest non-standard speech. The rather odd collocation of *nettoyer* with an animate object goes straightforwardly into English using the verb 'clean', which likewise sounds dubious when collocated with people. The non-standard syntax of *d'où que* has no equivalent in English on the grammatical level, and compensation is provided through the means just pointed out.

What is meant by culture in this connection? Clearly, the broad anthropological sense referred to earlier distinguishes the totality of practices that typify a community. These can vary along different sociocultural axes, in this case to do with speakers of different age groups, social classes, and other characteristics, and in situations differentiated by their formality. What is axiomatic in sociolinguistics, but can appear startling on a fresh view, is that speakers 'exploit' linguistic resources in order to express their social identity. The use of quotes is meant to indicate that this exploitation is not conscious. Social identity can be thought of, admittedly in an atomistic way, as being composed of a bundle of cultural attributes like sex, age, class, regional origin, ethnicity, etc. This view can be methodologically convenient, but ignores obviously the fact that social identity is experienced as a complex whole. It remains true however that some linguistic features, known as stereotypes (Chambers and Trudgill 1980: 171–4), convey cultural information in a straightforward and salient fashion. The example these authors cite is the so-called /ʌy/ variable, stereotypical of New York City and giving the effect conveyed in spelling by 'boid' for standard 'bird'. This variable appears now to be recessive, but stereotypes linger on in the cultural consciousness such that they remain available as a way of conveying cultural stereotypes in shorthand, if not always very accurately. A stunning example is found right at the beginning of Dashiell Hammett's first published novel, *Red Harvest*, as follows:

I first heard Personville called Poisonville by a red-haired mucker named Hickey Dewey in the Big Ship in Butte. He also called his shirt a shoit. I didn't think anything of what he had done to the city's name. Later I heard men who could manage their r's give it the same pronunciation. I still didn't see anything in it but the meaningless sort of humor that used to make richardsnary the thieves' word for dictionary. A few years later I went to Personville and learned better.

(first paragraph of Red Harvest, *by Dashiell Hammett (1929))*

A recent translation into French has this attempt:

> J'ai d'abord entendu *Personville* prononcé *Poisonville* au bar du Big Ship à Butte. C'était par un rouquin nommé Hickey Dewey, ouvrier chargé à la mine. Il disait aussi *T-shoit* au lieu de *T-shirt*. Je n'ai rien pensé alors de ce qu'il avait fait subir au nom de la ville. Plus tard, j'ai entendu des hommes qui savaient articuler leurs « r » utiliser la même appellation. Je n'y voyais toujours rien de plus que cet humour dépourvu de sens qui fait dire aux voleurs *Rick Sionaire* à la place de *dictionnaire*. Quelques années plus tard, je suis allé à Personville et j'ai compris.
>
> *(first paragraph of* Moisson Rouge, *translation of* Red Harvest *(2009))*

Hammett's use of the stereotype in this punning sense refers to the plot of the novel, which deals with the narrator's attempts to clean up corruption in the town. The French rendering faithfully follows Hammett's reference to 'men who could manage their r's', which has in fact nothing to do with the stereotype being exploited, since the point at issue is alternation between two vowels, not presence or absence of /r/. The first syllable of 'Poisonville' would in French be pronounced /pwa/ (the New York stereotype is usually transcribed /ɜi/); we must accept, naturally, that the original stereotype is impossible to convey, since it is culturally meaningless in French, and admit the translator's good fortune in having available 'poison' in both languages, since this is the conceptual essence of the word play. Further good fortune is provided by the presence in the French pronunciation of the /r/ consonant in Personville. The translator's heroic attempt to make sense of the 'shirt' ~ 'shoit' alternation involves him in an anachronism, since the first attestation of 'T-shirt' in French occurred some twenty years after the events portrayed in the novel. But 'shirt' in standard French is, to the translator's misfortune, 'chemise'.

The linguistic and cultural interest of the foregoing examples is probably in inverse relation to their representativeness. Cultural reference is no doubt usually a 'bolt-on' that can be conveyed by a circumlocution. Thus the French acronym *ENA*, and its derivatives, notably *énarque* and *énarchie*, refer to an area of cultural practice in the higher-education system that doubtless looms large for a good many French people. If these terms occur in a textbook, where elegance is at a discount, they can be dealt with in footnotes or glossaries.

Is culture translatable?

To try to answer this question we need to distinguish between literary texts and other types. We considered above some extreme examples of cultural untranslatability, caused by literary and linguistic structure, as well as one instance of culture more or less detachable from language, and therefore translatable at the cost of expansion, if indeed we accept expansion as a cost. In looking at the various types of literary production, we need not dive too deep into literary theory to see that the effect of a work of art cannot be thought of in terms of 'communication', at least as that term is ordinarily understood. The difference in this respect between an informative text like a computer manual and a literary narrative is quite patently fundamental.

To adopt for the moment a gloomy (and refutable) view, the principle known as the 'intentional fallacy' states that 'the design or intention of the author is neither available nor desirable as a standard for judging the success of a work of literary art' (Wimsatt, 1954). This implies that even where authors do have a view of their design or intention, and these views are available, they are unreliable and can, indeed must be ignored for the purposes of literary analysis. This is summed up in the tag 'trust the tale, not the teller'. But as the novelist and literary critic David Lodge has pointed out further (1997: 192): 'the fact that the author is absent when his message is received, unavailable for interrogation, lays the message, or text, open to multiple, indeed infinite interpretation. And this in turn undermines the concept of literary texts as communications.' This also undermines the status of the critic as arbiter, implied by Wimsatt; for who is to judge of literary quality when a text is open to infinite, or at least indefinite interpretation? Some readers may be more perceptive than others, or at least more adept at 'interpreting' a text, but for our present purposes the point is simply that different readers respond to texts differently, and the same reader may respond to the same text in different ways on different days, which torpedoes the notion of 'equivalence' in literary translation, if by this is meant the search for an invariant equivalent effect across source and target text. If the author's intention is unreliable and indeed unknowable, and is not in any event concerned with conveying propositional information of the cat-sat-on the-mat kind, and if reactions vary across and within readers, it is possible to wonder what exactly is meant when the notion of a successful translation is evoked. This implies that despite the recent claims of some translators to be artists in their own right, a literary translation is almost always regarded as a secondary text which is not read primarily for its aesthetic quality – which, in this argument, is in any case unknowable. In other words, those who read major authors in translation do so in spite of the translation rather than because of it, and the best that can be hoped for, on the one hand is an avoidance of betrayal by the translator of whatever propositional information is being offered, and on the other of the type of unhandiness in the target text that is sometimes referred to as 'translatorese'. Less bleakly, the literary qualities of interest in translated work are in this view non-linguistic: subtlety of plot and characterization, for instance, and these elements can be thought of as being within the compass of culture, though perhaps not specific to any one culture.

It need hardly be said that the point of view set out above would not find acceptance among theorists or practitioners of translation, and indeed cogent arguments come readily to hand to oppose it. As was pointed out above, translations are neither designed, nor for the most part read, by near-bilingual specialists of translation; the 'translation commentary' of the type that was applied to the extract from *The Simpsons* above is useful for raising awareness among students of translation of certain techniques that for professional translators have become second nature, but can easily inculcate a hypercritical attitude, even extending to the discipline itself. To disprize translation is to forget that a good deal of literature derives from the practice – the Bible is only the most obvious example, but its influence on many literatures has been incalculable. Anyone who has read much imaginative literature will have encountered translations that in their own terms appear successful as works of art. Indeed the rational, or at least sanguine, approach is to distinguish between author's intention and reader's response, recognizing at the same time that one reading of a text is as valid as another, and extending the sense of 'reading' to translation. Wimsatt's claim for the critic's privilege, as was implied above, seems therefore untenable, since no empirical or theoretical argument supports it. In this view, a plurality of viewpoints makes for enrichment rather than chaos. Bassnett and Bush (2007) and Loffredo and Perteghella (2006), among others, have gathered valuable accounts of the creative role of translation.

Cultural shift and translation

We live in the midst of cultural change, and on that account find it difficult to see it whole. It is too large; the elephant in the room of contemporary cliché. It is a widespread belief that recent cultural changes have been more rapid and more momentous than at any previous time, and even if this belief is in part due to the wish to feel that one has lived through a historic epoch, there is solid evidence from sociolinguistics, and no doubt other social sciences, to show that cultural change has been, at least since the 1960s when reliable linguistic data began to become available, on a large scale and in the direction of what one might call informalization. To speak of formality implies relations between people, and indeed it is easier to think in terms of less stiffness in interpersonal contacts, and in culture generally, than to point to the very complex societal mutations underpinning the tendencies. These relate to a process of levelling that has its roots in increased equality and egalitarianism; especially the latter since it works on a largely symbolic level, against a background of increasing general prosperity but continuing sharp inequality.

One consequence of democratization or levelling is an increasing porosity between high and low culture, expressed in the postmodern view that refuses to recognize hierarchies of any kind. We can see this as a return to an earlier state, at least in literature, although of course for different motives; the chasm dividing serious literary forms from the rest is a relatively recent one. In the rest of this chapter we explore the cultural fortunes, as shown in their translation, of an example of the type of literature that straddles high and low: the 'good-bad' book. The example is instructive because it illustrates the cultural shift described above.

Dashiell Hammett

The category of 'good bad books' was defined by Orwell (1968: 19), in an entertaining essay on the subject, as 'the kind of book that has no literary pretensions but which remains readable when more serious productions have perished'. Genre fiction seems to be in the majority in this category. Orwell mentions as an outstanding example the Sherlock Holmes stories, 'which have kept their place when innumerable "problem novels", "human documents" and "terrible indictments" of this or that have fallen into deserved oblivion'. Orwell also cites *Uncle Tom's Cabin* as a book that is hard to take seriously by strictly literary criteria. We might therefore add to the list didactic fiction, and risk the generalization that the category excludes modern mainstream novels, the principal subject of which can perhaps be defined as the complexity of human relationships, dramatized in settings that are not too far removed from the experience of most readers. As mentioned above, this category has emerged fairly recently; since about 1800 in English literature, in contrast to the picaresque that was largely prevalent before then. We consider here as a case study one author, Dashiell Hammett, who made a notable contribution to the good-bad genre that is perhaps most conveniently known as 'crime fiction', a popular-cultural category that includes narratives variously labelled thriller, crime, detective, *noir*, *policier*, etc. We examine this author from the viewpoint of his reception in France, as shown by his treatment in French translators, determined seemingly by a mutation in the French cultural climate over the past fifty years or so. In a comparative optic, we also consider his UK reception.

Dashiell Hammett (1894–1961) is perhaps a borderline candidate for inclusion in the 'good-bad' category, despite having published quite a large quantity of pulp fiction which he himself in later life saw no reason to preserve. Some of his novels are works of art, in passages at least; this is hardly surprising in view of the evident fact that ambitious effects can often be found in the humbler types of fiction, and pedestrian passages in serious texts. Hammett is generally credited with the introduction, or at least the popularization, of the 'hard-boiled' school of detective fiction, characterized by a cynical narrative viewpoint and violence that is sometimes capable of distressing the reader. His fiction marked a sharp departure from the 'body-in-the-library' type, designed largely to provide a puzzle capable of solution through deduction under an agreed set of rules. Hard-boiled fiction as practised by Hammett was more veridical, to the extent that fiction can be; the crimes described in the stories seem at all events to be more likely to occur than the typical country-house murder. He has always been well received in the UK, and aside from his literary merits we can suggest that this is in part because of his cynicism; as Symons points out (1985: 125), in *Red Harvest*, his first novel, 'the police are crooked almost to a man', as indeed they are in most of his fiction, if they are not incompetent. There can be little doubt that the US police were quite largely corrupt during Prohibition, the period when the novels were set, but for the purposes of the present argument it seems legitimate to assume that Symons's very favourable judgement of Hammett's work has a political as much as an aesthetic motive.

In the 1988 *Cambridge Guide to English Literature*, the article on Hammett states that he 'wrote in an unadorned, realistic manner ... that suited his material perfectly'. Statements of this kind are the province of literary theory, and largely beyond our scope here, although it does seem intuitively obvious that the alliance of an unedifying subject matter and a euphuistic style would result in incongruity. Symons (1985: 125) refers to Hammett's 'bareness of ... style in which everything superficial in the way of description has been removed', while acknowledging that he did not write 'realistically in a documentary sense'. The term 'realistic' is of course a difficult one, as is illustrated by the following passage from *The Dain Curse* (1929; 2012: 27–8), Hammett's second novel. A minor character called Rhino Tingley is counting his money, witnessed by the narrator.

> Rhino said: 'Ain't nobody's business where I got my money. I got it. I got' – he put his cigar on the edge of the table, picked up the money, wet a thumb as big as a heel on a tongue like a bath-mat, and counted his roll bill by bill down on the table. 'Twenty – thirty – eighty – hundred – hundred and ten – two hundred and ten – three hundred and ten – three hundred and thirty-five – four hundred and thirty-five – five hundred and thirty-five – five hundred and eighty-five – six hundred and five – six hundred and ten – six hundred and twenty – seven hundred and twenty – eight hundred and twenty – eight hundred and thirty – eight hundred and forty – nine hundred and forty – nine hundred and sixty – nine hundred and seventy – nine hundred and seventy-five – nine hundred and ninety-five – ten hundred and fifteen – ten hundred and twenty – eleven hundred and twenty – eleven hundred and seventy. Anybody want to know what I got, that's what I got – eleven hundred and seventy dollars. Anybody want to know where I get it, maybe I tell them, maybe I don't. Just depend on how I feel about it.'

The first French rendering (1950: 33) shows a compression that is really rather cavalier:

> – Ça regarde personne où je ramasse mon fric, dit Rhino. Je l'ai eu ... J'ai ...
> Il posa son cigare sur le bord de la table, rafla l'argent, humecta un pouce gros comme un poignet avec une langue aussi longue qu'un tapis de bain et compta son magot en empilant les billets un par un sur la table.
> – Vingt, trente, quatre-vingts, cent, cent dix ...
> Il arriva ainsi à onze cent soixante-dix, et reprit :
> – Si quelqu'un veut savoir ce que j'ai, conclut-il, v'là c'que j'ai. Onze cent soixante-dix dollars. Si quelqu'un veut savoir comment j'les ai ramassés, p't'être j'y dis, p't'être j'y dis pas. Ça dépend comment j'suis luné.

The ruthless abbreviation of the 95-word list hardly needs pointing out. We can perhaps count this as writing 'realistically in a documentary sense', to the extent that the most 'realistic' narrative almost always suppresses detail of this kind, and is thus in fact highly conventional. We are brought up short when the convention is flouted, whether our reaction is irritation or admiration.

The 'bareness' referred to above is therefore unevenly distributed, but it remains true that the stories are often characterized by a terseness and lack of sentiment which sit well with the protagonist and anti-hero narrator of many of the stories and two of the novels, the 'Continental Op'. The first sentence of *Fly Paper*, one of the frequently collected stories, is representative: 'It was a wandering daughter job'. The plot is summarized in six words, and the narrator's attitude towards it of weariness and venality established. Examples could be multiplied, but of greater interest here is the serious, perhaps even over-earnest literary intent that informed Hammett's work, evidence of which is to be found even in the early hard-boiled stories. A single example may suffice, taken from *Red Harvest*. Part of the description of Dan Rolff, a minor character, runs as follows: 'His voice was a sick man's and an educated man's.' Stretches of affectation like this are out of tune with the generally demotic nature of the narrative.

The following passage, from *The Dain Curse* (1929; 2012: 35), is especially notable in presenting a display of learning, but in a derisive way that accords with the narrator's cynical and philistine approach. But the general point, that it is 'out of place' in a hard-boiled detective novel, still stands:

> On my way back to the agency I dropped in on Fitzstephan for half an hour. He was writing, he told me, an article for the *Psychopathological Review* – that's probably wrong, but it was something on that order – condemning the hypothesis of an unconscious or sub-conscious mind as a snare and a delusion, a pitfall for the unwary and a set of false whiskers for the charlatan, a gap in psychology's roof that made it impossible, or nearly, for the sound scholar to smoke out such faddists as, for example, the psycho-analyst and the behaviourist, or words to that effect. He went on like that for ten minutes or more, finally coming back to the United States with: 'But how are you getting along with the problem of the elusive diamonds?'

This is 'literary' in the sense that strictly speaking it is redundant in a crime novel of the type that Hammett wrote, since it does nothing to advance the plot, although it may be designed to deflect attention from Fitzstephan as a suspect. It can hardly be described as portentous or overwritten, and the humour, best illustrated by the use of 'or nearly' and the long series of images beginning with 'a snare', is highly developed. Indeed, the passage is fairly complex, in that Hammett contrives to introduce a quite learned flourish and to mock it by presenting it from the narrator's debunking point of view. The first French rendering (1950: 40–1) is as follows:

> Je repris le chemin de l'agence et m'arrêtai chez Fitzstephan pendant une demi-heure. Il était en train d'écrire, me dit-il, un article pour la *Revue Psychopathologique* ou quelque chose de ce genre. Il vaticinait sur son sujet pendant dix minutes, puis revint finalement sur terre en me disant :
>
> – Et ce problème des diamants escamotés, au fait, ça avance?

Here the sixty-odd words in the source text facetiously describing Fitzstephan's article are compressed into the verb 'vaticinait', literally 'prophesied', perhaps suitably translated here as 'pontificated'.

The observations set out above are not new; Robyns (1990) has a detailed account of the quite systematic practice prevalent in French publishing houses during the relevant period of gutting translated detective fiction of much 'extraneous' matter, of the type exemplified above; that is, passages which, irrespective of their literary interest, do little or nothing to further the plot. This appears then to be a very concrete example of the French cultural elitism which prevailed until quite recently. Before examining evidence of Hammett's more recent seeming rehabilitation in France, we examine how the French cultural context has evolved recently. But we provide first of all a brief sketch of the UK situation, which provides highlight by contrast.

The UK and French cultural contexts

It is undeniable that the appreciation of literary value, like any aesthetic value, though real, is entirely subjective. Problems arise when aesthetic judgements are based on sociopolitical criteria, as they so often are in Britain, where a kind of puritan populism is detectable. Judgements based on this viewpoint will in principle see popular-cultural products as good, and refuse to distinguish artefacts which are popular in the sense of being well liked by many from those which, in the pristine French sense of 'populaire', have to do with or promote working-class culture. Wheatcroft suggests (2005: 271): 'Both in academic discourse and in practical politics, class conflict has [in the UK] been superseded by "culture wars"; and the other great truth of the age is that the right has won politically while the left has won culturally'. The obvious socio-historical explanation of the political victory of the right is to be found in the economic history of the past thirty or so years, which saw monetarism mobilized in response to the oil shocks of the 1970s. The doctrine has not been successfully challenged since, and it is a commonplace that politico-economic discourse in the UK and most other comparable countries is now located in the centre-right. That the left has 'won culturally' can perhaps be interpreted simply as the irreversibility of the broadly populist post-war sociocultural developments which have proceeded independently of the rightward economic and political restructuring of recent times. The 'cultural victory of the left', admittedly a vague phrase, seems to refer to a requirement imposed by critics upon writers (indeed all artists) to promote working-class values and attack the 'establishment'.

The view also entails that all art should be didactic or at least 'committed', and explains the contrasting critical fortunes of the spy novelists Ian Fleming and John le Carré. Fleming's fiction is highly implausible, though deftly covered with a veneer of realism. In this sense a parallel with the spy novels of John le Carré is not very close, since the latter author's work seems more 'realistic' (so far as the uninstructed reader can judge) in its portrayal of the less spectacular and more sordid aspects of espionage. As to the viewpoints from which their work is written, the example of le Carré's work shows that spy novels can receive a warm critical reception if they affirm the cultural victory of the left just referred to, in the sense of presenting a 'balanced' picture that eschews any suggestion of the moral superiority of one's own country. The contrast with Fleming's unreflecting patriotism is obvious, and there is a parallel here with Hammett's positive reception in the UK. The French situation does not fit comfortably with the cultural left–right polarity just sketched.

What is especially notable in France is an attitude of social or cultural conservatism in several French commentators whose stance is on the political left. The French situation shows the obvious fact that the political terms 'left' and 'right' are in large measure nation-specific. Almost the entire landscape in France tilts 'left', if by this is meant, in a democratic context, 'characteristic of greater state intervention', in all matters: political, economic, social, cultural. Along with this statism goes an aspiration for cultural uplift. Perhaps the most striking example of a French intellectual who is not notably right-wing but who has attacked cultural democracy is Alain Finkielkraut; the title of his book, *La Défaite de la Pensée* (1987), speaks for itself. He is very vocal in his opposition to cultural levelling of the kind that, for example, refuses to distinguish between the quality of Mozart and rap music (his examples). The prominent left-wing writer Régis Debray (1992: 18) has an analogous approach, as shown by the following quotation:

> La République, c'est la Liberté *plus* la Raison. L'Etat de droit, *plus* la Justice. La Tolérance, *plus* la volonté. La Démocratie, dirons-nous, c'est ce qui reste d'une République quand on éteint les Lumières.[1]

This line of thought shows clearly the element of the republican tradition that lays stress on the republic as a rational enterprise, informed by the Enlightenment ('les Lumières', in the untranslatable pun), and on duties as well as rights, including the citizen's duty of participation in the polity. This in turn depends in education. While other national contexts do not lack discussion of 'dumbing down', notably of institutions like the BBC, which in the Reithian tradition has or has had an educational and even morally improving role, the idea of upward rather than downward levelling, with the aim of full and responsible participation by the citizen in the democratic process, seems more central to the French republican concept.

For the purposes of this discussion, it is significant that French sociocultural élites, including of course publishers and their editors, certainly shared and no doubt to some extent still share the *élitisme républicain* or 'elitism for all' which either disprizes popular culture, or in a seeming paradox seeks to assimilate it to high culture. The paradox is superficial, because in a state where a tradition of official promotion of the arts is firmly entrenched, that promotion will be shaped by the differing views of influential personalities. This tradition is beyond dispute; Looseley (1995: 2), citing the French historian Jean-Pierre Rioux (1991: 10), points out that:

> France has always distinguished itself from other developed nations by 'l'effort séculaire que l'Etat et ses fonctionnaires ont consacré à la transmission, au partage et à l'enrichissement d'une "culture" largement entendue et dont ils ont estimé qu'elle relevait sans conteste du domaine de l'administration générale'.[2]

This is no doubt allied to the sense prevalent in France of the uniqueness of its national culture, expressed in the phrase '*exception culturelle*', in marked contrast to other 'developed' nations, for instance the UK, where arts funding is capable of polarizing the political left and right. Looseley's book traces the influence exercised by the French Culture Minister Jack Lang during the 1981–93 Socialist administration. Lang's promotion of popular culture aroused the fury of high-culture intellectuals like Finkielkraut, in part perhaps because some popular genres like pop music are not native to France. The earlier condescending attitude to Hammett's fiction, as shown by the summary translations accorded to it, may stem partly from the same cause, as well as from the elitism discussed above that sixty years ago saw detective fiction as devoid of literary merit.

Aside from formal initiatives like those described above, pursued in the dirigiste transition, we can point out that popular culture tends very strongly to be assimilated to high culture, just as middle-class language very often adopts, at least in the contemporary period, working-class linguistic forms. For instance, the operettas of Gilbert and Sullivan, despised by many in their day, would now be generally agreed to be highbrow or at least middlebrow culture. While the French Impressionist School was widely regarded at its inception as a bad joke at best, Impressionist paintings now undoubtedly form part of the canon of high culture, to the point of attracting derision from contemporary cultural iconoclasts. Collovald and Neveu (2004: 19), in their study of the contemporary reception of detective fiction (including non-French authors in the genre), have a discussion of those whom they call the 'cultural entrepreneurs' responsible for rehabilitating certain authors. Unsurprisingly, these are publishers, publishers' editors and academics, but also enthusiasts less formally connected with the cultural industry.

The situation is of course complex, and whatever the precise mechanisms responsible for the changing fortunes of some authors, it seems indisputable that Hammett's rehabilitation, or perhaps absorption into respectable culture, is from the French viewpoint well under way, if not complete. This is illustrated by the publication of a 2009 omnibus edition of his five novels translated into French, accompanied by a good deal of biographical and critical information. The translations are moreover highly respectful of the originals. It would be tedious to reproduce the more recent French translation of the scene in *The Dain Curse* where Rhino Tingley counts his money; suffice it to say that the long list is reproduced in full in the recent rendering. The contemporary translation (2009: 307) of the mock-literary intrusion into the same novel, quoted and discussed earlier, is however worth quoting:

> En retournant à l'agence, je fis halte une demi-heure chez Fitzstephan. Il rédigeait, me dit-il, un article pour la *Revue de psychopathologie* (ce titre est probablement erroné, mais c'était quelque chose comme ça) qui condamnait l'hypothèse d'une dimension incon-sciente ou subconsciente de l'esprit, jouant le rôle de leurre et de tromperie, de piège pour l'imprudent et de postiche pour le charlatan, une faille dans la structure de la psychologie qui rend impossible, ou quasiment, pour le spécialiste sain d'esprit de chasser de leurs trous en les enfumant les représentants de professions à la mode tels les psychanalystes et les psychologues comportementalistes, ou je ne sais quelle théorie à l'avenant. Il poursuivit sur sa lancée pendant dix minutes au moins et revint enfin dans le monde réel en disant : « Mais où en est-tu, avec ton problème de diamants envolés ? »

In marked contrast to the 1950 translation, the more recent version is longer than the original – 142 words against 130. The fidelity to the original entails more words, inevitably given that French uses post-modifying constructions where English has the advantage of more compact expression, such that 'faddists' in the original gives 'représentants de professions à la mode', while the phrasal verb 'smoke out' has the unavoidable circumlocution 'chasser [de leurs trous] en les enfumant'. The French tendency to abstraction is illustrated in the rendering of 'a gap in psychology's roof' by 'une faille dans la structure de la psychologie'. The point is worth making because of the high expansion rate usually seen in translation from English to French. The compression in the earlier translation of *The Dain Curse* is therefore radical, and involves considerable cutting throughout.

We referred above to an 'attitude of social or cultural conservatism' noticeable in France. This phrase, like 'the cultural victory of the left', is rather vague but implies an ability to distinguish between politico-sociological and aesthetic judgements. This ability is noticeable in Orwell's writings; he was a man of the left but had strong artistic preferences that were independent of his politics. As we have argued, this approach seems more widespread in France. The aesthetic judgements visited in France upon Hammett, at least by 'cultural entrepreneurs', have mutated in the last fifty or so years, judging by his treatment by French translators. The shift to cultural populism is no doubt common to most comparable nations, but the top-down role played by the French state gives the country a curious uniqueness that does line up quite closely with its self-perception.

Future directions

The highly pervasive influence of culture upon language, and hence translation, hardly needs to be restated here, in view of the space we have devoted to the subject. Cultural shift as shown through translation, as of course through other practices, seems broadly to be proceeding in the same direction across more or less comparable countries, but the subtle inflections that differentiate each case merit further investigation. As was mentioned above, much translation has little to do with culture as discussed here, dealing as it does with purely functional issues, although even computer manuals will be required to conform, for example, to culturally specific politeness norms, and the recent term 'glocalization', adapted to translation, reflects this need. That the market for culture is increasingly global is a commonplace; future directions for the study of cultural factors as they influence translation choices may well be concerned with divergences that are a good deal wider than those discussed here, and with how translators have risen to the challenges they pose.

Related topics

the linguistic relativity hypothesis revisited; language, culture and context; writing across cultures; language, culture and identity; language, literacy and culture; language and culture in sociolinguistics; cultural linguistics; language and culture in intercultural communication

Further reading

The translation literature, like the industry, is enormous. Textbooks tend to concentrate on the linguistic aspects of translation. The small selection below indicates a way into consideration of the wider and narrower senses of culture as treated here. See also the author's own book, referenced below.
Bassnett, S. (2014). *Translation Studies*. London: Routledge. (Probably the most compendious introductory account of the subject.)
Bassnett, S. and A. Lefevere (1998). *Constructing Cultures: Essays on Literary Translation*. Clevedon: Multilingual Matters. (A series of essays covering a broad range of issues, including recent notions like cultural capital.)
Hickey, L. (ed.) (1998) *The Pragmatics of Translation*. Clevedon: Multilingual Matters. (An up-to-date and thorough account of cross-cultural variation in pragmatics, considered in connection with translation.)
Lefevere, A. (1992). *Translation/History/Culture*. London/New York: Routledge. (A panoptic historical account of translation in relation to culture in the narrower literary sense.)
Venuti, L. (1997). *The Translator's Invisibility: A History of Translation*. London/New York: Routledge. (This rather polemical work criticizes 'United Kingdom and United States cultures that are aggressively monolingual', and interprets the translator's status as comparable to that of the original author of the ST.)

Notes

1 The Republic is liberty *plus* reason, the rule of law *plus* justice, tolerance *plus* will. We may say that democracy is what remains of a republic when the lights have been switched off.
2 The constant effort that the State and its servants have devoted to the transmission, sharing and enrichment of a 'culture' understood in a broad sense, and which they have deemed to fall incontestably within the remit of general government.

References

Armstrong, N. (2005). *Translation, Linguistics, Culture*. Clevedon: Multilingual Matters.
Bassnett, S. and Bush, P. (eds) (2007). *The Translator as Writer*. London: Continuum.
Chambers, J. K. and Trudgill, P. (1980). *Dialectology*. Cambridge: Cambridge University Press.
Collovald, A. and Neveu, E. (2004). *Lire le noir: enquête sur les lecteurs de récits policiers*. Paris: Bibliothèque Publique d'information, Centre Pompidou.
Debray, R. (1992). *Contretemps: Eloge des idéaux perdus*. Paris: Gallimard.
Finkielkraut, A. (1987). *La défaite de la pensée*. Paris: Gallimard.

Hammett, D. (1929). *Red Harvest*. New York: Knopf.

——(1950). *Sang Maudit*, French translation by H. Robillot of *The Dain Curse*. Paris: Gallimard.

——(2009). *Moisson Rouge*, French translation by P. Bondil and N. Beunat of *Red Harvest*, in *Dashiell Hammett, Romans*. Paris: Gallimard.

——(2009). *Sang Maudit*, French translation by P. Bondil and N. Beunat of *The Dain Curse*, in *Dashiell Hammett, Romans*. Paris: Gallimard.

——(2012). *The Dain Curse*. London: Orion. First published 1929 by Knopf, New York. Page references are to the 2012 edition.

Lodge, D. (1997). *The Practice of Writing*. Harmondsworth: Penguin.

Loffredo, E. and Perteghella, M. (eds) (2006). *Translation and Creativity: Perspectives on Creative Writing and Translation Studies*. London: Continuum.

Looseley, D. (1995). *The Politics of Fun: Cultural Policy and Debate in Contemporary France*. Oxford: Berg.

Orwell, G. (1968). 'Good bad books', in S. Orwell and I. Angus (eds), *The Collected Essays, Journalism and Letters of George Orwell*, vol. 4. London: Secker & Warburg, pp. 19–22. [First published in *Tribune*, 1945].

Ousby, I. (ed.) (1998). *The Cambridge Guide to English Literature*. Cambridge: Cambridge University Press.

Queneau, R. (1959). *Zazie dans le Métro*. Paris: Gallimard.

——(2000). *Zazie in the Metro*, trans. B. Wright. Harmondsworth: Penguin.

Rioux, J.-P. (1991). L'Evolution des interventions de l'Etat dans le domaine des affaires culturelles. *Administration*, 15.

Robyns, C. (1990). The normative model of twentieth century *belles infidèles*. Detective novels in French translation. *Target* 2:1, 23–42.

Symons, J. (1985). (first edition 1972). *Bloody Murder. From the Detective Story to the Crime Novel: A History*. Harmondsworth: Penguin.

Wheatcroft, G. (2005). *The Strange Death of Tory England*. London: Allen Lane.

Wimsatt, W. K. (1954). *The Verbal Icon: Studies in the Meaning of Poetry*. Lexington, KY: University of Kentucky Press.

14

LANGUAGE, CULTURE, AND IDENTITY

Sandra R. Schecter

Introduction

This chapter focuses on the historical evolution and critical debates associated with research in the area of *language, culture, and identity*, with special attention paid to the different social processes emphasized in representations of the relationships among and between the three concepts. The exposition starts from the premise that although debates about these representations have been at times contentious, the diverse approaches undertaken by researchers over the years reveal underlying preoccupations with different kinds of issues and questions. The larger portion of the chapter is devoted to elucidating these preoccupations and their associated relevancies in diachronic perspective. The final sections of the chapter undertake to problematize the concepts and representations under discussion by elucidating how the relationship between *language, culture, and identity* has been and continues to be used perniciously, to construct vulnerable individuals and groups as 'other'. I also suggest productive avenues for future inquiry, and propose ways in which these constructs may be manipulated, or reconfigured, to empower traditionally marginalized constituencies.

For discussion purposes, I have organized the relevant literature under headings corresponding to three differentiated approaches, representing: a social anthropology perspective, grounded in the study of how boundaries between groups are maintained; a sociocultural perspective, concerned with conditions necessary for individuals and groups to self-sustain and thrive; and a participatory/ relational perspective, interested in culturally situating individuals' authentic selves in what it is that they say and do and with whom. This said, given the breadth of the subject area, we may locate within each of these epistemological traditions additional divergences related to variations in emphases – between 'strong' (identity as structurally determined and durable) and 'weak' (identity as fluid, impermanent, and context-dependent) versions of the concept of *identity* (Grad and Martin Rojo 2008), between 'personal' identity and 'collective' or group identities (Riley 2007), between an individual's sense of a subjective narrative versus the self as a social construction (Edwards 2009; Giddens 1991), between cultural resources seen as sets of collective practices and, alternatively, as capital. It may also be the case (although the incidences were not as frequent as anticipated) that individual researchers have contributed to the development of more than one perspective, as their appreciations of the dynamics involved in these complex, interdependent relationships have evolved, and as the effects of modernization processes have become more evident.

Theorizing the relationship between language, culture, and identity

A social anthropology perspective

Earlier work seeking to theorize the relationship between *language, culture, and identity* emanated from the preoccupations of traditional social anthropologists who were concerned with the boundary work involved in the social construction of differences between groups (Barth 1969). From studies that examined the structuring of social interaction among members of social groups emerged detailed accounts that identified limitations in shared understandings and practices, including criteria for judgement of social value and performance. These limitations were found to correspond to differences in individuals' origins and backgrounds, key features of which were 'native language' and ethnic origin. In this framework, culture is seen as rooted in ethnicity/ nationality and native speaker status as determined through attachments established at birth.

For sociolinguists and anthropologists who take as their primary mission to ensure the survival and well-being of individuals and groups who constitute ethnic minorities within national entities with hegemonic majorities, preservation of linguistic varieties associated with the group's ethno-cultural heritage has been a key concern; for as Joshua Fishman (1995) and others have argued, the loss of a minority language 'forms part of a wider process of social, cultural, and political dislocation' (May 2008: 4). Indeed, there exists within the sociology of language an established corpus of literature that attests to the relationship between minority language maintenance and cultural continuity of endangered groups on the one hand and language loss/shift and ethnocultural attrition on the other (e.g., Edwards 1994; Fishman 1989). Much of this work is housed in edited volumes that issued from conferences devoted to exploring the states of minority languages in national contexts where 'heritage' languages and the cultures with which they were associated were perceived to be threatened with decline or extinction by national or global processes involving rapid modernization and urbanization (e.g., Edwards 1984; Fase *et al.* 1995).

Fishman (1991) further postulated that language and cultural identity were indexically related, that is, that a language (assuming it is intact) that has been most intimately associated with a culture is best equipped to elucidate that culture's values and concerns and to express and contextualize its features and artefacts. From such assertions, the linking of particular languages with corresponding ethnic groups and the assignment of historically associated languages as markers of specific cultural identities were not long to follow (see, for example, Giles *et al.* 1977) – notwithstanding the more nuanced interpretations that were and continue to be available to explain the relationship between language and culture (for example, where maintenance of a linguistic minority variety is evident, language is well positioned to serve as a resource to support ethnic and cultural identification). For Fishman, in particular, cultural and linguistic continuity and change embody an interdependent relationship and, in their interlocked status, may be summoned on a case-by-case basis to characterize specific ethnic or group identities. Based on the premise, then, that language constitutes a 'core cultural value' (Smolicz 1992), studies on the 'ethnolinguistic vitality' of endangered or at-risk minority groups sought to represent the robust-ness of various cultures by assessing dimensions and breadth of language use and usage within different communities (e.g., Allard and Landry 1992; Giles *et al.* 1977). Extensive intragroup use of varieties associated with ethnic categories were affirmed to in themselves constitute 'acts of identity' in that the strengthening of in-group linguistic connections represented a positive step towards cultural maintenance and continuity (Le Page and Tabouret-Keller 1985).

While of a scientific nature, such studies were at the same time unapologetically concerned with the predicament of linguistic-minority families who confronted the unenviable dilemma of whether to remain loyal to their cultural traditions, in so doing, committing to a set of linguistic

197

practices that would ensure the maintenance of the 'heritage' language, or follow an alternative strategy entailing assimilation into the dominant culture, by so doing, improving their children's life opportunities at the perceived cost of cultural maintenance (Fishman 1991). The majority of researchers in the sociology of language endorsed the former orientation, persuaded by the alarming findings of sociolinguistic studies on 'language death' as well as research in language planning that provided evidence of rapid language atrophy and concomitant cultural estrangement in regional contexts, for example, Breton in France (see Ferguson 2006). While state intervention on behalf of endangered varieties was urged, few sociolinguists and applied linguists were convinced that linguistic maintenance could be achieved by means of schooling alone (Edwards 1994). Consequently, prominent linguists and psychologists appealed directly to minority parents, arguing that intergenerational family language transmission was the key to cultural preservation (e.g., Crago et al. 1993; Fishman 1991; Hakuta and Pease-Alvarez 1994).

More recently, claims asserting direct associations between linguistic variety and cultural affiliation have come to be equated with essentialist notions of identity (Norton 2010); and indeed, this critique is not without some merit, as undergirding this ideology rests the premise that one's native language is the 'essence' of one's identity. Pavlenko and Blackledge (2004), among others, have underscored the perils inherent in such an ideology, of which the most insidious, it has been postulated, would be the creation of a hierarchy of authenticity based on a direct correspondence between language and identity and the subsequent dehumanization and even possibly extinction of individuals or groups who are rated low on the hierarchy scale (Myhill 2003).

Nonetheless, a more generous reading of contributions within this tradition would suggest that asserting a causal relationship between language and ethnic identity and/or instantiating theoretical claims concerning authentic group membership based on linguistic affiliation were not the primary concerns propelling the agendas of researchers working within the social anthropology framework. Clearly, colleagues were preoccupied with ensuring the cultural survival of linguistic-minority groups, a goal that they viewed as dependent on securing the 'language rights' of all individuals (Fishman 1991; Secada and Lightfoot 1993). Beyond staving off situations where official policies would predictably lead to ethnolinguistic dislocation and assimilation of minority cultures, many working in the sociology of language and applied linguistics were, doubtlessly, also passionate about the political agenda of creating possibilities for linguistically plural societies (see Edwards 1984).

Other critiques of the social anthropology perspective focus on the ideology's explicit recognition of the 'native speaker' as the normative and appropriate user of language X (Davies 1991). Such critiques additionally question the extent to which features such as a speaker's native language may be relied upon to define or even be determinative of an individual's identity and/or cultural affinities (see Canagarajah 2010). This perspective has ushered in a process of deconstruction of the notion of 'native speaker' through critical discussions that interrogate whether the status is more productively viewed as an empirical fact or a social construct. We will return to this point presently.

A sociocultural perspective

The 1980s through to the first decade of the twenty-first century saw a proliferation of empirical studies that sought to stimulate discussion about the interaction of externally and internally constructed identities (Garza and Herringer 1988) in social acculturation processes through close observation of interactional practices of (mostly socially vulnerable) individuals and groups within their home, school, and peer networks. Much of this research – committed to augmenting the respective sensitivities of researchers, professional educators, and caregivers to the home, school, and infrastructural conditions that foster the cognitive, social, and emotional development of linguistic-minority individuals – incorporated a language socialization approach (Ochs 1988; Schieffelin and Ochs 1986). Researchers working within this orientation considered both the context of interaction and the culturally sanctioned roles of the participants as major determinants of language conventions, genres, and strategies used in given situations and of the norms – including values and skills – with which individuals learn to identify (e.g., Ballenger 1999; Lee 2007). Frequently grounded in inquiry of an ethnographic nature that provided detailed accounts of how language is experienced and used in communities, family groupings, and social networks (e.g., Heath 1983; Michaels 1981), researchers who adopted a sociocultural perspective were motivated to produce integrated, holistic analyses of how 'one's individual and social identities, and their complex interconnections, are inevitably mediated in and through language' (May 2008: 132).

Extending this agenda, scholars working in bilingual and multilingual communities were additionally motivated to consider the patterns of meaning suggested by the use of different language varieties in the speech and literacy performances of individuals as well as well as family, community, and/or societal ideologies concerning the symbolic importance of different varieties (e.g., Guerra 1998; Schecter and Bayley 1997; Zentella 1998). With regard to indigenous multilingual contexts, they also used ethnography to address issues related to how modernity has affected the ways in which children are socialized in and through language and how these changes shape language shift and cultural reproduction, including literacy practices (e.g., Kulick 1992; Patrick 2003).

Much of the method behind this work involved documenting the role of alternate languages and language varieties in the self-definitions of linguistic-minority individuals and groups. Researchers working with groups for whom minority-language transmission was a factor found that in their daily negotiations between dominant and minority groups, and empowered and disenfranchised individuals, subjects confronted questions of discreteness and synthesis of linguistic code at many junctures and levels of self- and other-defining decision making (e.g., Schecter and Bayley 1997; Zentella 1981). Moreover, researchers identified considerable variation in the manner in which individuals who may align to the same census categories engaged these linguistic choices. For example, in their study of Eastside, a Mexicano community located in central California, Vasquez *et al.* (1994) found that bilingual children were able to summon their cultural and linguistic resources to act as translators and cultural brokers between their non-English-speaking parents or elders and institutional representatives such as government agents and medical practitioners. Because communication in both Spanish and English proved a necessity in terms of negotiating the family's needs for children of monolingual Spanish-speaking parents, translation provided children with important opportunities to develop both their languages as well as skills associated with the enhancement of metalinguistic awareness.

Concerned with issues associated with immigration and border crossings of a less formal and often more socially contentious nature, researchers in multilingual settings characterized by transnational migration and flux were confronted with a need to make sense of discontinuities in family and community ideologies concerning the importance of different linguistic varieties in socially embedded contexts. As this corpus expanded, and issues that problematized claims leading to linear representations of the relationship between *language, culture, and identity* presented, increasingly these contributions were embedded in discussions of identity construction that represented the process as complex, multidimensional, and dialogic. For example, in their study of the relationship between home language practices and the development of bilingual and biliterate abilities among Mexican-descent children in California and Texas, Schecter and Bayley (1997) found that subjects with little to no mastery of a language could nevertheless view this same variety as a significant value that is centrally linked to their cultural identity. The same researchers (Schecter and Bayley 2002) also concluded that due to the fluidity of individuals' personal circumstances, subjects evidenced 'shifting locations' with regard to their bilingual persona, suggesting that support for a strategy of maintenance must ensue not from a one-time decision on the part of caregivers but rather from a series of choices that constitute successive affirmations, disavowals, and reaffirmations of a commitment to a bilingual identity.

Influenced by these more nuanced interpretations, an increasing number of researchers underscored the limitations of reductionist constructions of the relationship between *language, culture, and identity* based on linear conceptions by showing that individuals and groups who may be viewed as authentic standard bearers of languages by virtue of primordial attachments (e.g., birthplace, religion) may differ in their views of the salience of specific varieties to their cultural identities and in the extent to which they view language itself as a significant core value linked to cultural identity (e.g., May 2003, 2008; Myhill 2003; Tannenbaum 2005). Indeed, the findings of extensive ethnographic studies have revealed both the mutability of ethnic identity in light of transnational migration and modernization processes and the extent to which language, along with other cultural attributes, vary in their salience to cultural identity (Eastman 1984).

A participatory/relational perspective

Recent scholarship on *language, culture, and identity* has directed attention away from a focus on interactions within primary, secondary, and tertiary networks to interrogate issues of methodology in relation to questions of identity ascription and appropriation. In line with theory that privileges a deterritorialization of notions of social identity, Canagarajah (2014) problematizes the use of the ethnic 'community' as a unit of analysis for language and identity researchers, advocating a shift towards the study of the use of language in places of contact – or 'contact zones' – in which multiple subjects associate and deal with different symbolic and sociocultural systems (Pratt 1987). Working within environments characterized by linguistic and ethnic diversity and fluid communicative contexts, Canagarajah (2007) and colleagues (e.g., Leung 2012) observed the translingual interactions involved in both speakers and listeners negotiating multiple norms of interaction, in situations where interpersonal relationships are reconfigured on an ongoing basis, requiring actors to develop repertoires of mobile semiotic resources that they can use to collaborate with others in social situations. Within this interactional/relational framework, there is an emphasis on procedural (as opposed to propositional) knowledge; hence, as Hall (1996) points out, identities are more dependent on resources that people use than on attributes that people 'have' or 'are'. In the contact zone, then, what matters most in terms of identity in-scription and a-scription is what one can do with one's language. Indeed, following Norton (1997), the question 'Who am I?' can be answered only in reference to the question 'What can I do?'

Contemporary discussions of culture aligning to this recent emphasis on relational and negotiated aspects of interaction have focused on identity as co-emergent with ongoing activity in which individuals participate (see, e.g., Kiely *et al.* 2006). In such a manner, one becomes a Hopi through 'affective acculturation' (Nicholas 2009), or acquisition of an emotional commitment to the ideals of the culture that develops as a result of active participation in contemporary Hopi society and continuous practice of Hopi traditions. Noteworthy within this perspective is that cultural markers of identity may or may not include speaking the indigenous or heritage language (Tannenbaum 2005). As well, within this perspective culture is additionally distinguished from ethnic identity; and while language tends to function as a significant core value in relation to ethnic affiliation (May 2001, 2003; Smolicz *et al.* 2001), subjective interpretations of the relevance of language as a constitutive feature of cultural identity vary widely, inviting a constructivist approach to interpretation of data regarding the salience of language as a cultural marker (Tannenbaum 2009).

Accompanying the focus on the relational dimensions of identity has been a reflective turn towards the study of subjectivity and intersubjectivity as complex and contested constructs. Recent framings of identity have sought to distance themselves from the notion of a unified subjectivity, positioning the construct of 'self' as alternately fluid, multiple, and hybridized – as well as instantiated 'in relation' – rather than as stable and autonomous (Kubota and Lin 2009). A simultaneous focus on intersubjectivity is interested in how individual subjects strive to occupy an intercultural dimension, or 'Third Space', as they navigate multiple worlds. The notion of 'Third Space' was proposed by anticolonial theorist Homi Bhabha (1994) to signal a discursive site or set of conditions where transnational social actors can appropriate, translate, or renegotiate different linguistic resources and social identity repertoires, in so doing, challenging dominant discourses of both their birth and host countries. In this alternative dimension, cultural realities are deconstructed, and reconstructed, through common experience, which privileges representation over a priori defining features (Hall 1996); and language plays an important role in embodying the attitudes and beliefs entailed in these cultural realities (Kramsch 1998), conflictual as they may sometimes appear and, in fact, be. It is therefore not surprising that the carwash attendant that Suresh Canagarajah (2010) identifies in Brampton, Ontario, as Tamil-speaking, on the basis of the first name projected on the chest pallet of his uniform and other signifying features, will have none of his linguistic assailant; for the attendant is determined to elude the reductive identity that he assumes is entailed in the greeting in Tamil that Suresh foists upon him in relieved (at least, initially) anticipation of meeting up with a fellow linguistic traveller in an unfamiliar locale.

To expand on lessons embedded in the preceding example: note how in addition to intercultural ability, within this alternative 'Third Space' (Bhabha 1994), or 'third culture' (Kramsch 2009), if you will, capacity for appropriation is most highly valued. Canagarajah has usurped his subject's autonomy by presuming to ascribe to him a linguistic and cultural identity; and the attendant is quick to assert that this identity can only be instantiated through his own willing and wilful appropriation of it. Similarly, within an interactional/relational perspective a subject's 'community' cannot be established solely by means of analysis of survey data addressing questions related to demographic background, status at birth, and where the subject lives. Rather, an individual 'achieves' community by choosing membership in a certain group – or perhaps even more than one group (Canagarajah 2010) – by participating in activities and acquiring experiences that are associated with membership in this/these group/s (Ivanic 2006), and by using language that is commensurate with this/these respective identity/ies (Ortega 2012; Pennycook 2007). In this manner, researchers interested in characterizing the relationship between *language, culture, and identity* from an interactional/participatory perspective draw on usage-based linguistics methodologies – documenting histories of linguistic practices – where identity is emergent from experience, and experience from participation and practice (Canagarajah 2007; Norton 1997). One notes how within this framework, as concerns the relationship between language and identity, as well as perceptions of proficiency in the dominant variety, experience would appear to displace birthright.

Using this practice-based and adaptive framework to pursue a related interest in local configurations, Pennycook (2007) has situated local cultures at the intersection of how members of a community strategically use language to negotiate meaning, identity, and status and achieve common social goals. As part of a transcultural process, this preoccupation with 'localization' at the same time invites openness to diversity, as individuals who may be considered members of different cultural communities strive to transcend their sociocultural boundaries and to reconfigure as hybridized cultural entities in their immediate locales. Such goals often entail the use and, indeed, command of a lingua franca that serves as a shared vehicle for subjects from diverse linguistic backgrounds and differing life experiences to negotiate norms associated with a common, locally referenced identity. Related discussions here directly reference the large-scale appropriation of English as a vehicle of transnational communication in emergent, global contexts (Canagarajah 2007; House 2003) as well as the 'glocalization' (intersection of the global and local) of Mandarin in societies such as Hong Kong and Singapore in response to the need for individuals to develop multilingual competencies that are compatible with evolution towards a cultural identity that recognizes the dominance of China and the growth of Mandarin as an international language (Tong and Cheung 2011). It is, moreover, clear from these representations that within this perspective subjects cede no authority to the 'native speaker'. Indeed, even the authenticity of the construct *native speaker* has become suspect, as participants who cross national boundaries endeavour to manipulate contextual frames in order to wrest control of influential varieties from those whose appropriation claims, based on innateness, were hitherto uncontested (Kramsch 2009; Nunan and Choi 2010). However, the concept has become suspect for an additional reason, related to inequitable cultural production around the question of who is entitled to have an identity as a native speaker. In the next section I engage these debates.

Pernicious derivations

The preceding arguments against simplistic representations of identity notwithstanding, the research literature abounds with disturbing accounts of how linguistic, cultural, and discursive processes are used and manipulated to fix, or essentialize, marginalized individuals and groups in subject positions that are reductive and often negative, while positive attributes and subject positions are ascribed to society's more privileged individuals (Lin 2008). Ibrahim (2009), for example, describes how a group of immigrant youth from Somalia and Senegal 'became Black' in terms of their ascribed and internalized social identities under the hegemonic gaze of white Canadians in a south-western Ontario town. Similarly, in his investigation of how young immigrants from the Dominican Republic negotiated language and identity in their new habitats in Rhode Island (USA), Bailey (2000) found that the youths' self-identifications as Spanish speakers of Hispanic descent ran counter to the emphasis members of the host society placed on the importance of race in matters of ascribed identity. Based on his findings, Bailey predicted that immigrants of African descent would be largely merged into the African-American population by the second generation, given the manner in which 'constraining, hegemonic forms of inscription – e.g., social classification based on phenotype – are invoked and reconstituted' (2000: 557) within American society.

Within educational settings, we see how linguistic- and especially racial-minority students may be constructed as the other by their mainstream teachers and peers (e.g., essays in Kubota and Lin 2009; Merry 2005), while insidious processes to maintain the teaching profession as white persist and reinforce racial categories (Austin, 2009). Ligget (2009) studied a group of white English language teachers who had difficulty recognizing white as a race and, consequently, themselves as cultural beings who were capable of beliefs, attitudes, and actions resulting in differential exclusion of students based on race. Grant and Lee (2009) focused on the racialized manner in which linguicism operates in the English language teaching profession in South Korea, where a 'globalization policy', adopted in light of perceived economic necessity, ascribes cultural capital to the acquisition of competence in English. Within this commodification context, where power, capital, and knowledge are closely related, only white Americans associated with the standard, mainstream variety of English represent for South Koreans the idealized globalized group; and therefore only whites are recognized as legitimate teachers of English.

Drawing on the work of Foucault (1979) and Bourdieu (1992), researchers (e.g., Skeggs 2004) have brought to light issues related to how technologies for producing a favourable 'self' are not equally available to all and how identity functions as 'a discursive position that privileges those with access to specific cultural resources to both know and produce themselves' (Skeggs 2008: 13). Researchers informed by a discursive (sociolinguistic) perspective have represented identity processes similarly as opportunities to specify particular interests and relationships between groups or communities and to establish dominant practices as the norm (Fairclough 1995; Phillipson 1992). Working in the European context, van Dijk (1993) addressed the discursive reproduction of dominant ideologies and racism through stereotypical representations of minorities as different, backward, lacking modernity and intelligence. Spanish sociolinguists and applied linguists (e.g., Ambadiang and García Parejo 2011; Ambadiang *et al.* 2009; García 2006; see also Schecter, García Parejo, Ambadiang and James 2014), writing on the predicament of Latin American immigrant students in Spain, have described how in Madrid the stigma cast by speakers of the peninsular dialect on the variety of Spanish used by Latin American immigrants results in symbolic construction of bidialectal students and their families as a problematic group. At the same time, the experience of having their language and culture devalued and demeaned by Spanish society provokes in bidialectal Latin American students and their families a sense of alienation and a concomitant desire to abandon any intercultural space with Spaniards. These representations illustrate a dynamic where processes of othering in which elite and minority groups get involved result in spaces that seem to offer potential for being intercultural becoming progressively deserted, with evidence of this dissimulation in the resultant undermining of the role of schooling as a vehicle for social unification.

Future directions

Clearly, the dispiriting results that issue from reductive manipulations of the central concepts stand in stark contrast to the ethos of collaboration revealed in cited recent studies aligning to a relational/participatory perspective. Assuming, as we do, all relevant research to have been carried out in good faith, we are left to account for these radically different interpretations. To this end, the field would stand to benefit from comparative analyses of such divergent contexts and the intersubjectivities that they respectively engender. That is, how is it that under certain conditions sets of relationships get constructed socially, within relations of power, and are sustained through hegemonic discourses that foreclose alternate interpretative frameworks (Ahmed 2004), whereas in other, more fluid ecosystems processes combine with actions to defuse and/or contest identity categories and the conditions under which they may thrive? In this regard, recent inquiry into the co-construction of cosmopolitan spaces that produce a disposition of embodied openness in response to encounters between differences hold promise as a heuristic tool for exploring how identity representations are mediated in moments of intercultural exchange (e.g., Darwhadker 2001; Hull *et al.* 2010; Vasudevan 2010).

As well, sociolinguists are to be encouraged in their attempts to reconcile dialectical tensions between localized, ethnographic accounts of linguistically mediated identity construction with broader, more inclusive approaches that seek to account for how language functions to move individuals out of local cultural identities as they encounter situations that are infused with influences from outside (see Street 2003). Certainly, as evidenced by the research reviewed in this chapter, there is value in both socioculturally 'situated' and more global orientations to the examination of socially constructed epistemological principles about language, identity, and culture. It remains, as colleagues (e.g., Maddox 2001; Street and Leung 2010) have suggested, to link both approaches through a more inclusive theoretical framework that takes account of the role of transcultural processes in identity realignment and shift. By 'more inclusive,' I am referencing as well a shift in tenor from one focused on oppositional, mutually exclusive, interpretations of these processes to one open to a methodological heteroglossia that would view the mobile, nuanced relations we are now documenting as at once localizing and globalizing activities, emergent through practice.

Concluding remarks

I would conclude this discussion with a vision of how the central constructs may be configured, or *re*-configured, to create interpersonal spaces that empower individuals, communities, and groups who have been marginalized by systemic inequalities. First, while there is no question that in order to succeed, minority groups and individuals require access to the social resources and institutionalized standards, including textual practices, of privileged groups within a hierarchical society (see Bourdieu 1977; Bourdieu and Passeron 1990), the research reviewed in this chapter, in combination with successful action-oriented initiatives, suggests a revisiting of dominant interpretations of the notion of 'cultural capital' (see Schecter and Ippolito 2008). Indeed, we have seen evidence of how it is possible for institutions to generate additional sources of cultural capital by acknowledging and valuing the languages, literacies, and diverse experiences of minority groups and individuals as 'community cultural wealth' (Yosso 2005). We have accounts testifying to the development of dynamic subcultures where community resources, including multilingual literacies, are seen as sources of social capital that generate a powerful sense of belonging to the local community and motivation to participate in the society beyond (e.g., Davis *et al.* 2005; Orellana 2001; Schecter and Cummins 2003).

A second, complementary strategy for reconfiguration of the central concepts involves the privileging of a language-as-resource orientation towards processes of self- and other identification (Ruiz 1988). To this end, linguists are well positioned to encourage initiatives on the part of practitioners and policy-makers that foster institutional environments that – more than being respectful of the cultural backgrounds and experiences of linguistic- and ethnic-minority individuals – actively support individuals in sustaining the cultural and linguistic competencies of their communities (Paris 2012). For, in the end, it is strategic to make a collective investment in the formation and maintenance of identity for linguistically and culturally marginalized groups – in the sense that linguistic diversity is a societal resource that may be nurtured for the benefit of all groups (Cummins and Schecter 2003). Research discussed in this chapter has shown how such an investment can be advantageous in modern society for negotiating across domains of interest and power boundaries. It also has shown how such an orientation contributes to a broadening in perceptions of competence, involving a more efficient use of society's human resources and creating opportunities for those who heretofore have been considered peripheral or illegitimate members to have a voice in the collective agenda.

Of course, there is no certainty that such a critical recontextualization can be fully actualized; however, advocacy for these envisioned outcomes promises to contribute to the formation of a political will that will help to secure the status and legitimacy of those whose linguistic claims and public identities remain, for political, historic and economic reasons, tenuous. We all would wish to be ascribed a cultural and linguistic identity that has value and that, moreover, like Suresh's proactive antagonist, we sign on for.

Related topics

linguaculture: the language-culture nexus in transnational perspective; language, literacy and culture; culture and language development; language and culture in sociolinguistics; world Englishes and local cultures

Further reading

Kiely, R., Rea-Dickens, P., Woodfield, H. and Clibbon, G. (eds) (2006) *Language, Culture and Identity in Applied Linguistics*, London: Equinox. (This collection of papers focuses on the relationships individuals forge with communities and institutions, where identities emerge from interaction in work, social, and educational contexts.)

Kramsch, C. (1998) *Language and Culture*, Oxford and New York: Oxford University Press. (Kramsch's classic introductory text contains summary overviews of key topic areas, recommendations for readings in these areas, annotated references, and a glossary of related technical terms.)

Lin, A. (ed.) (2008) *Problematizing Identity: Everyday Struggles in Language, Culture and Education*, Mahwah, NJ: Lawrence Erlbaum Associates. (This important collection of essays address symbolic struggles revolving around linguistic, discursive, and cultural processes of fixing identities and subject positions for subaltern others while creating fluid, favourable identities for selves.)

Riley, P. (2007) *Language, Culture, and Identity*, London: Continuum. (The author presents a model of social epistemology involving relationships among the three constructs from two intellectual traditions – the sociology of knowledge and ethnolinguistics.)

Schecter, S. R. and Bayley, R. (2002) *Language as Cultural Practice: Mexicanos en el Norte*, Mahwah, NJ: Lawrence Erlbaum Associates. (The authors provide an ethnographic account of processes of cultural identification and bilingual development among Mexican-descent children in communities in northern California and south Texas, with implications for a theory of language socialization.)

References

Ahmed, S. (2004) 'Affective economies', *Social Text* 22(279): 117–39. doi:10.1215/01642472-22-2_79-117

Allard, R. and Landry, R. (1992) 'Ethnolinguistic vitality beliefs and language maintenance and loss', in W. Fase, K. Jaspaert and S. Kroon (eds) *Maintenance and Loss of Minority Languages*, Amsterdam: Benjamins.

Ambadiang, T. and García Parejo, I. (2011) 'Identity, power, language and the configuration of the intercultural space: The case of Ecuadorian migrants in Spain', paper presented at the Annual Bloomsbury Round Table, Conference of BAAL Intercultural Communication Special Interest Group, London.

Ambadiang, T., Palacios, A. and García Parejo, I. (2009) 'Diferencias lingüísticas y diferencias simbólicas en el discurso de jóvenes ecuatorianos en Madrid', *Círculo de Lingüística Aplicada a la Comunicación* 40: 3–32. Available HTTP: <http://pendientedemigracion.ucm.es/info/circulo/no40/ambadiang.pdf> (accessed 28 March 2013)

Austin, T. (2009) 'Linguicism and race in the United States: impact on teacher education from past to present', in R. Kubota and A. Lin (eds) *Race, Culture, and Identities in Second Language Education: Exploring Critically Engaged Practice*, New York: Routledge.

Bailey, B. (2000) 'Language and negotiation of ethnic/racial identity among Dominican Americans', *Language in Society* 29: 555–82.

Ballenger, C. (1999) *Teaching Other People's Children: Literacy and Learning in a Bilingual Classroom*, New York: Teachers College Press.

Barth, F. (1969) *Ethnic Groups and Boundaries*, Boston: Little Brown.

Bhabha, H. (1994) *The Location of Culture*, New York and London: Routledge.

Bourdieu, P. (1977) *Towards a Theory of Practice*, Cambridge, England: Cambridge University Press.

——(1992) *Language and Symbolic Power*, Cambridge, England: Polity Press.

Bourdieu, P. and Passeron, J. (1990) *Reproduction in Education, Society, & Culture*, 2nd edn, London: Sage.

Canagarajah, S. (2007) 'Lingua franca English: Multilingual communities and language acquisition', *Modern Language Journal* 91(5): 923–39.

——(2010) 'Achieving community', in D. Nunan and J. Choi (eds) *Language and Culture: Reflective Narratives and the Emergence of Identity*, New York and London: Routledge.

——(2014) 'Theorizing a competence for translingual practice at the contact zone', in S. May (ed.), *The Multilingual Turn: Implications for SLA, TESOL, and Bilingual Education*, New York: Routledge, pp. 78–102.

Crago, M., Annahatak, B. and Ningiuruvik, L. (1993) 'Changing patterns of language socialization in Inuit homes', *Anthropology and Education Quarterly* 24: 205–23.

Cummins, J. and Schecter, S. (2003) 'Introduction: School-based language policy in culturally diverse contexts', in S. Schecter and J. Cummins (eds) *Multilingual Education in Practice: Using Diversity as a Resource*, Portsmouth, NH: Heinemann.

Davies, A. (1991) *The Native Speaker in Applied Linguistics*, Edinburgh: Edinburgh University Press.

Davis, K., Bazzi, S., Cho, H., Ishida, M. and Soria, J. (2005) '"It's our Kuleana": A critical participatory approach to language-minority education', in L. Pease-Alvarez and S. Schecter (eds) *Learning, Teaching, and Community: Contributions of Situated and Participatory Approaches to Educational Research*, Mahwah, NJ: Lawrence Erlbaum Associates.

Dharwadker, V. (ed.) (2001) *Cosmopolitan Geographies: New Locations in Literature and Culture*, New York: Routledge.

Eastman, C. (1984) 'Language, ethnic identity and change', in J. Edwards (ed.) *Linguistic Minorities, Policies and Pluralism*, London: Academic Press.

Edwards, J. (ed.) (1984) *Linguistic Minorities, Policies and Pluralism*, London: Academic Press.

——(1994) *Multilingualism*, London: Routledge.

——(2009) *Language and Identity*, Cambridge, England: Cambridge University Press.

Fairclough, N. (1995) *Critical Discourse Analysis*, New York: Longman.

Fase, W., Jaspaert, K. and Kroon, S. J. (eds) (1995) *The State of Minority Languages: International Perspectives on Survival and Decline*, Lisse, Netherlands: Swets and Zeitlinger.

Ferguson. G. (2006) *Language Planning and Education*, Edinburgh: Edinburgh University Press.

Fishman, J. (1989) *Language and Ethnicity in Minority Sociolinguistic Perspective*, Clevedon, UK: Multilingual Matters (original 1977).

——(1991) *Reversing Language Shift: Theoretical and Empirical Foundations of Assistance to Threatened Languages*, Clevedon, UK: Multilingual Matters.

——(1995) 'Good conferences in a wicked world: On some worrisome problems in the study of language maintenance and language shift', in W. Fase, K. Jaspaert, and S. Kroon (eds) *The State of Minority Languages: International Perspectives on Survival and Decline*, Lisse, Netherlands: Swets and Zeitlinger.

Foucault, M. (1979) *The History of Sexuality:* vol. 1, *An Introduction*, London: Penguin.

García, P. (2006) 'Argentins et Equatoriens à Madrid: deux modes de reconstruction sociale dans un contexte migratoire', *Les Cahiers ALHIM*, 12. Available HTTP: <http://alhim.revues.org/index1452.html> (accessed 4 April 2013).

Garza, R. and Herringer, L. (1988) 'Social identity: A multidimensional approach', *Journal of Social Psychology* 127: 299–308.

Giddens, A. (1991) *Modernity and Self-Identity: Self and Society in the Late Modern Age*, Cambridge, England: Polity Press.

Giles, H., Bourhis, R. Y. and Taylor, T. M. (1977) 'Towards a theory of language in ethnic group relations', in H. Giles (ed.) *Language, Ethnicity, and Intergroup Relations*, New York: Academic Press.

Grad, H. and Martin Rojo, L. (2008) 'Identities in discourse: An integrative view', in R. Dolon and J. Todolf (eds) *Analyzing Identities in Discourse*, Amsterdam: John Benjamins.

Grant, R. and Lee, I. (2009) 'The ideal English speaker: A juxtaposition of globalization and language policy in South Korea and racialized language attitudes in the United States', in R. Kubota and A. Lin (eds) *Race, Culture, and Identities in Second Language Education: Exploring Critically Engaged Practice*, New York: Routledge.

Guerra, J. (1998) *Close to Home: Oral and Literate Practices in a Transnational Mexicano Community*, New York: Teachers College Press.

Hakuta, K. and Pease-Alvarez, L. (1994) 'Proficiency, choice, and attitudes in bilingual Mexican American children', in G. Extra and L. Verhoeven (eds) *The Cross-Linguistic Study of Bilingual Development*, Amsterdam: Netherlands Academy of Arts and Sciences.

Hall, S. (1996) 'Introduction: Who needs identity?' in S. Hall and P. du Gay (eds) *Questions of Cultural Identity*, London: Sage.

Heath, S. B. (1983) *Ways with Words: Language, Life, and Work in Communities and Classrooms*, Cambridge, England: Cambridge University Press.

House, J. (2003) 'English as a lingua franca: A threat to multilingualism?' *Journal of Sociolinguistics* 7: 556–78.

Hull, G., Stornaiuolo, A. and Sahni, U. (2010) 'Cultural citizenship and cosmopolitan practice: global youth communicate online', *English Education* 42(4): 331–67.

Ibrahim, A. (2009) 'Operating under erasure: Race/language/identity', in. R. Kubota and A. Lin (eds) *Race, Culture, and Identities in Second Language Education: Exploring Critically Engaged Practice*, New York: Routledge.

Ivanic, R. (2006) 'Language, learning and identification', in R. Kiely, P. Rea-Dickens, H. Woodfield, and G. Clibbon (eds) *Language, Culture and Identity in Applied Linguistics*, London: Equinox.

Kiely, R., Rea-Dickens, P., Woodfield, H. and Clibbon, G. (eds) (2006) *Language, Culture and Identity in Applied Linguistics*, London: Equinox.

Kramsch, C. (1998) *Language and Culture*, Oxford and New York: Oxford University Press.

——(2009) 'Third culture and language education', in L. Wei and V. Cook (eds) *Contemporary Applied Linguistics*, London and New York: Continuum.

Kubota, R. and Lin, A. (2009) *Race, Culture, and Identities in Second Language Education: Exploring Critically Engaged Practice*, New York: Routledge.

Kulick, D. (1992) *Language Shift and Cultural Reproduction: Socialization, Self and Syncretism in a Papua New Guinean Village*, Cambridge and New York: Cambridge University Press.

Le Page, R. and Tabouret-Keller, A. (1985) *Acts of Identity: Creole-Based Approaches to Language and Ethnicity*, Cambridge, England: Cambridge University Press.

Lee, C. D. (2007) *Culture, Literacy, and Learning: Taking Bloom in the Midst of the Whirlwind*, New York: Teachers College Press.

Leung, C. 'Participatory involvement in linguistically diverse classrooms', paper presented at American Association for Applied Linguistics annual meeting, Boston, 2012.

Liggett, T. (2009) 'Unpacking white racial identity in English language teacher education', in R. Kubota and A. Lin (eds) *Race, Culture, and Identities in Second Language Education: Exploring Critically Engaged Practice*, New York: Routledge.

Lin, A. (ed.) (2008) *Problematizing Identity: Everyday Struggles in Language, Culture and Education*, New York: Lawrence Erlbaum Associates.

Maddox, B. (2001) 'Literacy and the market: The economic uses of literacy among the peasantry in north-west Bangladesh', in B. Street (ed.) *Literacy and Social Development*, London: Routledge.

May, S. (2003) 'Rearticulating the case for minority language rights', *Current Issues in Language Planning* 4(2): 95–125.

——(2008) *Language and Minority Rights: Ethnicity, Nationalism and the Politics of Language*, New York and London: Routledge.

Merry, M. (2005) 'Social exclusion of Muslim youth in Flemish- and French-speaking Belgian schools', *Comparative Education Review* 49(1): 1–22.

Michaels, S. (1981) '"Sharing time": Children's narrative styles and differential access to literacy', *Language in Society* 10: 423–42.

Myhill, J. (2003) 'The native speaker, identity, and the authenticity hierarchy', *Language Sciences* 25: 77–97.

Nicholas, S. (2009) '"I live Hopi, I just don't speak it": The critical intersection of language, culture, and identity in the lives of contemporary Hopi youth', *Journal of Language, Identity, and Education* 8: 321–34.

Norton, B. (1997) 'Language and identity: Special issue', *TESOL Quarterly* 31: 431–50.

——(2010) 'Foreword', in D. Nunan and J. Choi (eds) *Language and Culture: Reflective Narratives and the Emergence of Identity*, New York and London: Routledge.

Nunan, D. and Choi, J. (eds) (2010) *Language and Culture: Reflective Narratives and the Emergence of Identity*, New York and London: Routledge.

Ochs, E. (1988) *Culture and Language Development: Language Acquisition and Language Socialization in a Samoan Village*, Cambridge, England: Cambridge University Press.

Orellana, M. F. (2001) 'The work kids do: Mexican and Central American immigrant children's contribution to households and schools in California', *Harvard Educational Review* 71(3): 366–89.

Ortega, L. (2012) 'Ways forward for a bilingual turn in SLA', paper presented at American Association for Applied Linguistics annual meeting. Boston.

Paris, D. (2012) 'Culturally sustaining pedagogy: A needed change in stance, terminology, and practice', *Educational Researcher* 41(3): 93–7.

Patrick, D. (2003) 'Language socialization and second language acquisition in a multilingual Arctic Quebec community', in R. Bayley and S. Schecter (eds) *Language Socialization in Bilingual and Multilingual Societies*, Clevedon, England: Multilingual Matters.

Pavlenko, A. and Blackledge, A. (2004) 'Introduction: New theoretical approaches to the study of negotiation of identities in multilingual contexts', in *Negotiation of Identities in Multilingual Contexts*, Clevedon, England: Multilingual Matters.

Pennycook, A. (2007) *Global Englishes and Transcultural Flows*, London and New York: Routledge.

Phillipson, R. (1992) *Linguistic Imperialism*, Oxford: Oxford University Press.

Pratt, M. L. (1987) 'Linguistic utopias', in M. Fabb, D. Attridge, A. Durant, and C. MacCabe (eds) *The Linguistics of Writing: Arguments between Language and Literature*, London: Methuen.

Riley, P. (2007) *Language, Culture, and Identity*, London: Continuum.

Ruiz, R. (1988) 'Orientations in language planning', in S. McKay and S. Wong (eds) *Language Diversity: Problem or Resource?*, New York: Newbury House.

Schecter, S. R. and Bayley, R. (1997) 'Language socialization practices and cultural identity: Case studies of Mexican-descent families in California and Texas', *TESOL Quarterly* 31(3): 513–39.

——(2002) *Language as Cultural Practice: Mexicanos en el Norte*, Mahwah, NJ: Lawrence Erlbaum Associates.

——(2004) 'Language socialization in theory and practice', *International Journal of Qualitative Studies in Education* 17(3): 605–25.

Schecter, S. R. and Cummins, J. (2003) *Multilingual Education in Practice: Using Diversity as a Resource*, Portsmouth, NH: Heinemann.

Schecter, S. R., García Parejo, I., Ambadiang, T. and James, C. E. (2014) 'Schooling transnational speakers of the societal language: Language variation policy-making in Madrid and Toronto', *Language Policy* 13(2): 121–44. Doi: 10.1007/s10993-013-9310-y

Schecter, S. R. and Ippolito, J. (2008) 'Parent involvement AS education: Activist research in multilingual and multicultural urban schools', *Journal of Curriculum and Pedagogy* 5(1): 163–83.

Schieffelin, B. B. and Ochs, E. (1986) 'Language socialization', *Annual Review of Anthropology* 15: 163–91.

Secada, W. and Lightfoot, T. (1993) 'Symbols and the political context of bilingual education in the United States', in M. Arias and U. Casanova (eds) *Bilingual Education: Politics, Practice, and Research*, Chicago: University of Chicago Press.

Skeggs, B. (2004) *Class, Self, Culture*, London: Routledge.

——(2008) 'The problem with identity', in A. Lin (ed.) *Problematizing Identity: Everyday Struggles in Language, Culture and Education*, New York: Lawrence Erlbaum Associates.

Smolicz, J. J. (1992) 'Minority languages as core values of ethnic cultures: A study of maintenance and erosion of Polish, Welsh, and Chinese languages in Australia', in W. Fase, K. Jaspaert, and S. Kroon (eds) *Maintenance and Loss of Minority Languages*, Amsterdam: John Benjamins.

Smolicz, J. J., Secombe, M. J. and Hudson, D. M. (2001) 'Family collectivism and minority languages as core values of culture among ethnic groups in Australia', *Journal of Multilingual and Multicultural Development* 22(2): 152–72.

Street, B. (2003) 'What's new in New Literacy Studies? *Current Issues in Comparative Education* 5(2), 77–91.

Street, B. and Leung, C. (2010) 'Sociolinguistics, language teaching and new literacy studies', in N. H. Hornberger and S. L. McKay (Eds.), *Sociolinguistics and Language Education*, Bristol; Tonawanda, NY: Multilingual Matters.

Tannenbaum, M. (2005) 'Viewing family relations through a linguistic lens: Symbolic aspects of language maintenance in immigrant families', *Journal of Family Communication* 5(3): 229–52.

——(2009) 'What's in a language? Language as a core value of minorities in Israel', *Journal of Ethnic and Migration Studies* 35(6): 977–95.

Tong, H. and Cheung, L. (2011) 'Cultural identity and language: A proposed framework for cultural globalisation and glocalisation', *Journal of Multilingual and Multicultural Development* 32(1): 55–69.

van Dijk, T. (1993) *Elite Discourse and Racism*, Newbury Park, CA: Sage.

Vasquez, O., Pease-Alvarez, L. and Shannon, S. (1994) *Pushing Boundaries: Language and Culture in a Mexicano Community*, Cambridge, England: Cambridge University Press.

Vasudevan, L. (2010) 'Literacies in a participatory, multimodal world: The arts and aesthetics of Web 2.0', *Language Arts* 88(1), 43–50.

Yosso, T. (2005) 'Whose culture has capital? A critical race theory discussion of community cultural wealth', *Race, Ethnicity, and Education* 8(1): 69–91.

Zentella, A.C. (1981) '"*Ta bien*, you could answer me *en qualquier idioma*": Puerto Rican code switching in bilingual classrooms', in R. Duran (ed.) *Latino Language and Communicative Behavior*, Norwood, NJ: Ablex.

——(1998) 'Multiple codes, multiple identities: Puerto Rican children in New York City', in S. M. Hoyle and C. T. Adger (eds) *Kids Talk: Strategic Language Use in Later Childhood*, Oxford: Oxford University Press.

15

LANGUAGE AND CULTURE HISTORY: THE CONTRIBUTION OF LINGUISTIC PREHISTORY

Patrick McConvell

Introduction

Historical linguistic evidence is a key element in the reconstruction of prehistoric cultures, the migrations of people bearing cultures, and the diffusion of cultural elements. 'Culture history' in a wider sense, with more of an emphasis on material culture, was widely used as the term for a dominant approach in archaeology in the first half of the twentieth century, but the term went out of favour. The field of linguistic prehistory, however, continues many of the aims and methods of culture history with emphasis on historical linguistic evidence, often combined with the findings of archaeology, and other disciplines such as palaeobiology and biological genetics. The scholar of the Austronesian language family, Robert Blust, a prominent advocate and successful practitioner of opening the 'window' of language on to prehistory, and culture history, reminds us (1996: 28) that humans have been 'inadvertently recording the stuff of social and cultural history in ... daily speech since long before the advent of writing'. This record is largely preserved in the languages spoken in recent times, and can be interpreted by historical linguistics to teach as much as, and in some areas, much more than archaeology can about the prehistoric past.

This chapter examines some important examples of linguistic prehistory such as the detailed work on proto- and early Indo-European culture, on various North American language families, on Africa, Austronesian, and Australian Indigenous languages. The fields of vocabulary highlighted here include material culture and technology, and, in non-material culture, kinship and social organization. Concepts include *linguistic stratigraphy*, in which linguistic changes such as sound changes can show which words are inherited, and which borrowed, and their relative chronology. This method allows alignment of borrowing of cultural words with what is known of cultural contact and diffusion through archaeology and history. Particularly important here are the words for new elements recoverable in the archaeological record, such as material culture and plant remains. These horizons can provide absolute dates, which can then be transferred to the linguistic stratigraphy of other domains such as social organization. Examples of this method are discussed, including in relation to Indigenous Australia.

Boas and Sapir

Franz Boas established a new kind of anthropology in North America at the dawn of the twentieth century, one that encompassed the 'four fields': sociocultural anthropology;

linguistics; archaeology; and physical anthropology. Boasian anthropology kept the fields together usually in single departments, a number of figures practised in more than one field, and cross-fertilization between them occurred, was encouraged (Stocking 1966; Darnell 1998) and often involved diachronic hypotheses. This was in contrast to the varieties of 'British' functionalist social anthropology which emerged soon afterwards, in which these fields were discrete, and dominated by synchronic studies, and in which diachronic hypotheses, especially those dealing with groups without a tradition of literacy, were dismissed as 'conjectural history' (Radcliffe-Brown 1952: 3; Stocking 1983). This attitude on the part of the British school was understandable at the time, in light of the plethora of speculation about the origins and early development of society and culture by late nineteenth century and early twentieth-century scholars, the notorious 'armchair anthropologists'.

The Boasian school also turned away from their speculative forbears, but instead of virtually banning prehistorical reconstruction of society and culture, they tried to establish a more scientific methodology, less in thrall to the evolutionist and diffusionist 'grand schemes' of the day.

In building this kind of new diachronic methodology, Edward Sapir was a key figure. In his pioneering essay 'Time Perspective in American Aboriginal Culture: A Study in Method' (1916) he sets out a manifesto of the new method. Sapir, like Boas, Kroeber, and others of his era, practised both cultural anthropology and linguistics, and was familiar with the rigorous methods of historical comparative linguistics developed in the nineteenth century by European, mainly German, scholars. He brilliantly combined linguistic and other cultural evidence to add the diachronic 'time perspective' to the static picture of Native American societies and cultures, and provided a model of what was later to be called 'linguistic prehistory' – the theme of this chapter.

Indo-European

Attempts to reconstruct a picture of prehistoric cultures from linguistic evidence of course pre-date Boas and Sapir. They formed a part of the body of research on the Indo-European language family dating from the mid-nineteenth century, often referred to by the label *Wörter und Sachen* (German 'words and things'), or *linguistic palaeontology*. By the twentieth century quite detailed and convincing depictions of many aspects of proto-Indo-European culture around 6,000 years ago were being presented, based on linguistic data. The existence of direct evidence from ancient languages up to half this age was helpful, but not indispensable in such a task, as we will see later when we deal with language families which lack this kind of evidence.

One method, used in the Indo-European case and in linguistic prehistory of other language families, was the listing of proto-forms of lexical items for the ancestral language, with meanings covering various cultural domains. The individual reconstructions provided cogent evidence that these items were present in the ancestral language. Further, groups of such proto-forms yield a picture of cultural complexes possessed by the speakers of the proto-language, often going far beyond what archaeology can offer into the realms of ideas, beliefs, and social organization. Proto-Indo-European reconstructed vocabulary now boasts over 1,500 reliable words listed in such publications as the *Encyclopedia of Indo-European culture* (Mallory and Adams 1997).

The enormous boon represented by this kind of work in linguistic prehistory and culture reconstruction is not universally recognized. Some archaeologists, who have most to gain from this research, which fills in huge gaps in their own results, have been sceptical about how reliable the process of reconstruction is, often due to their unfamiliarity with the rigorous methods of comparative historical linguistics. Admittedly there have been, and still are, some scholars practising a kind of linguistic prehistory that lacks rigour, and is highly speculative and unreliable. However, a band of archaeologists have stepped forward to defend linguistic prehistory based on standard historical linguistics. Among these is Colin Renfrew who lent early impetus to this trend with his book *Archaeology and Language* (1987), mainly on Indo–European, and who has nurtured many projects with such interdisciplinary aims. David Anthony's book *The Horse, the Wheel and the Chariot: How Bronze Age Riders from the Eurasian Steppes Shaped the Modern World* (2007) brings together linguistic and archaeological results to present a well-rounded picture of the emergence of early Indo-European language and culture, and their dynamic spread.

The central set of words investigated by Anthony relate to horses, wheels, and vehicles, which together made up a technological complex that transformed the culture of the first proto-Indo-European speakers. 'Wheel' has been reconstructed as $k^wék^wlos$ in proto-Indo-European; we can readily see its relationship to the Greek word which is borrowed into English as *cycle*. Less obvious is that it is a *cognate* of the English word *wheel*: making this connection requires that we know that the changes between these two words, and between all the other words which are cognates of them in Indo-European are the results of *regular sound correspondences* produced by regular sound changes. I will not go into this in detail here, but suffice it to say that one cannot use a method where any word which looks similar can be regarded as a cognate – in fact there are many cases in which being very similar actually rules word pairs out as cognates, because to be cognate (rather than loanwords or accidental resemblances), they should have undergone changes.

There is another aspect of reconstruction which is very important for the task of under-standing the proto-culture – the determination of the meaning of the proto-form. In the case of $k^wék^wlos$ (Anthony 2007: 34) five of the eight branches of Indo-European which have this root, including Germanic, in which English is found, have 'wheel' as a meaning of this word. 'Majority rules' is not a dominant principle in semantic reconstruction, but this kind of pattern does carry some weight. In the other three, the meaning of the cognate of the pIE (proto-Indo-European) root is 'circle', 'wagon', or 'vehicle'. There are a number of examples where 'wheel' comes to mean 'vehicle' (a metonymic change) so that hypothesis about the direction of semantic change is supported, and it is a rule of thumb in semantic change that concrete meanings precede more abstract ones, so this also supports the idea of 'wheel' being the proto-meaning, as opposed to 'circle'. $k^wék^wlos$ is itself derived from a verb $k^wé$ 'to turn' so meant 'thing that turns', reinforcing the fact that 'wheel' is in all probability the earliest meaning.

Other parts of a wagon ('axle' 'hub') also have words in pIE, as well as words implying the use of draft animals ('yoke') and the animals themselves, adding up to a picture of a developed culture using animal-drawn vehicles (Fortson 2004: 36). The combination of this and other reconstructed culture complexes fed into the debate about the location of the pIE homeland, since archaeology can look for places where these features were co-present at one period and in one area. The discoveries and interpretations of the archaeologist Marija Gimbutas about the Kurgan culture (1997) and its emphasis on horses and chariots largely coincided with those of linguistic prehistory and strengthened the case for the Indo-European homeland being located in the Pontic-Caspian Steppe between about 4000 and 3000 BCE.[1]

Linguistic prehistory is not all about material culture and technology, and many other domains have been investigated in depth for proto-Indo-European, such as religious belief systems and practices, and social organization, including kinship, to be discussed later. But material culture is a pivotal area because it connects to archaeology and allows us to develop chronologies, which then can be applied to non-material culture. A method for doing this is discussed in the next section.

Linguistic stratigraphy: chronology from linguistics and archaeology

One of the aims of linguistic prehistory is to provide a chronology of cultural changes, either relative, or where possible, with absolute dates or data ranges. To show how this is done in principle Sapir (1916: 74, fn) takes the example of two lexical roots in Germanic which appear in Anglo-Saxon as *hænap* ('hemp') and *cyrice* ('church'). The first of these shows the effect of the sound change Grimm's law, which occurred at the branching of the Germanic sub-group from the rest of Indo-European. Grimm's law changed *k to x (subsequently h in English). However the second example does not show this change – if it did, our word for 'church' in English today would begin with h. The explanation is that the diffusion of the relevant variety of hemp pre-dated Grimm's law, whereas the diffusion of the institution of churches, together with Christianity and the word for 'church', came after Grimm's law, so the sound change did not apply. Both words came from Greek, *kannabis* and *kyrike* respectively, and spread west.

This example can use written sources to estimate the date of these diffusions of cultural items, although particularly in the case of hemp, archaeological and palaeobotanical findings assist (Barber 1991; McConvell and Smith 2003). Sapir's major interest, though, was in North American indigenous culture history where there are no written sources before the colonial powers entered the picture some 500 years ago, and precious little in many places after that. Sapir, and other linguistic prehistorians of his era, focused on relative chronology, rather than dating, or absolute chronology.

Place names (toponyms) are a useful source of relative chronology, for instance for when a certain group of language speakers entered an area. Among the methods used by Sapir and others is whether a place name is opaque or analysable:[2]

> Mt. Shasta, in northern California, is visible to a considerable number of distinct tribes. The Hupa call it nin-nis-'an lak-gai, a descriptive term meaning 'white mountain'; while the Yana have a distinctive term for it, wa'galu, which does not yield to analysis. We may infer from this that the Hupa, as an Athabaskan-speaking tribe, are newcomers in northern California as compared with the Yana, a conclusion that is certainly corroborated by other evidence.
>
> *(Sapir 1916: 57)*

This descriptive naming on the part of an Athabaskan group may also relate to the resistance of Athabaskan to borrowing loanwords, in contrast to other groups, remarked by writers including Sapir (1921): this tendency may be counted as part of the inherited culture of these language groups. The migration of Athabaskan speakers from southern Canada did not just extend to northern California but also farther into the south-west, to form the large Apachean groups, such as Navajo. Sapir (1936) used meaning change in Athabaskan words as the groups travelled south to chart changes in environment and culture along the migration path. From being hunter-gatherers they adopted agriculture from neighbours when they arrived in the south, and needed words for farming practices. True to their 'purist' bias they did not generally borrow the words but substituted other Athabaskan words and changed their meaning. For instance the term for 'seeds planted in rows' in Apachean languages originally meant 'snowflakes lying in rows' in the Canadian Athabaskan languages, also reflecting the difference in climate and environment of the cold northern homeland and southern areas to which they migrated.

In more recent times, a great deal has been contributed to the picture of Athabaskan migration and cultural change by other disciplines such as human population genetics and archaeology with its ability since the 1960s to date organic material associated with cultural strata.

Another large language family which migrated into the south-west, but in the opposite direction, from Mexico in the south, was Uto-Aztecan, according to the hypothesis of Hill (2010), in which this is a 'farming language dispersal' closely paralleling the spread of maize as a crop.[3] An essential tool in the processing of maize (and other seeds) into flour was the lower grindstone, called in local Spanish and English by its Uto-Aztecan name *metate*. Sapir attempts to apply the 'linguistic stratigraphy' method to the words for this artefact and finds them related, but differing in accordance with known regular sound correspondences. Such a situation makes it difficult to decide whether the words are inherited or early loanwords diffusing before all the relevant sound changes.

> the Uto-Aztekan word for 'metate, grinding stone', metla-(tli) … appears in Nahuatl as metla-tl, in Huichol as mata, in Luiseño as mala-l, in Southern Paiute as mara-tsi-. Linguistically there is nothing to show that these correspondences do not rest on dialectic development from a common Uto-Aztekan source; should this interpretation prove sound, we would be dealing with a very old culture element antedating the tremendous movements of population that have scattered the Uto-Aztekan peoples from Idaho to Central America. If, on the other hand, there should be other than linguistic evidence to show that the metate was gradually diffused from an Aztec centre of distribution to the Sonoran and Shoshonean tribes to the north, the linguistic evidence would still prove a great antiquity for this diffusion, as it must have been consummated before the operation of a number of distinctive phonetic laws of considerable geographical distribution and, therefore, age (assimilation in Sonoran and Shoshonean of e-a to a-a; spirantization of intervocalic -t- to Luiseño -l- and Southern Paiute -r-).
>
> *(Sapir 1916: 75)*

In fact, archaeology, with its dating techniques developed largely since the 1960s, tells us that the artefact known as 'metate' is found sparsely between 9000 and 6000 years ago in the region subsequently occupied by Uto-Aztecan languages, much older than conceivable dates of around 4,000 years old for the spread of the language family or of maize (the metate being used for grinding other plant materials before that, see e.g. Jenkins *et al.* 2004). However, there was an intensification of, and different use of grinding, and different appearance of grindstones, spreading with the spread of maize, and quite possibly with the spread of Uto-Aztecan languages, implying that this was to a great extent an inherited word and new cultural pattern.

In Australia grinding and grindstones are also important markers of cultural and economic change and can be tracked by the form of words for the technology used, in conjunction with archaeology (McConvell and Smith 2003). Again, as in the north-central American case discussed above there are sporadic examples from the late Holocene and early Pleistocene but there was a great efflorescence of what Tindale (1977) called the 'seed grinding economy' using wild grass seeds in central Australia in the mid-Holocene around 3,500 years ago, one of several examples of 'intensification' across the continent involving large-scale harvesting and processing of specific plants.[4]

In the example studied by McConvell and Smith, the focus is not on the bottom grinding stone, but on the top one, or muller. This is known in American archaeology as a *mano*, Spanish for 'hand', and in many of the indigenous languages of north-central America, the word for 'hand', or a derivative of it, is used for muller. Strikingly, the same is true of many Australian indigenous languages. In the languages under examination here, the term for muller is not the plain word for 'hand' but 'hand' with a suffix. The suffixes vary in different languages, but in the specific example considered here, in an earlier stage the form of the word is

mara	– *ngu*	'muller'
hand	belonging	

Mara is a very ancient word for 'hand' in Australia, reconstructable to proto-Pama-Nyungan, and since it appears in a number of non-Pama-Nyungan languages also, perhaps further up the tree towards proto-Australian. *–ngu* is an old suffix too, perhaps dative/genitive in origin but cognates in languages in the region such as Arandic *–nge* have one function which is especially apposite for the 'muller' case, to indicate the part which is used to hold something.

The key point in this connection is that there is a regular sound change in proto-Ngumpin-Yapa from r to rl (a retroflex l) between most vowels including between two a's. This means that the word for 'hand' in Ngumpin-Yapa languages is *marla*, not *mara*. In contrast, the word for 'muller' in Ngumpin-Yapa languages, *marangu*, contains the older form of the word, *mara* before the change r > rl took place. This constitutes evidence that the word for 'muller' is a loanword into Ngumpin-Yapa after the r > rl change stopped operating. This sound change is one of the shared innovations which define the Ngumpin-Yapa subgroup, so the borrowing of the word for 'muller' must come after the stage of the proto-Ngumpin-Yapa language.

Archaeology provides evidence of an increase in mullers used for seed grinding in central Australia around 3,500 to 3,000 years ago. The horizon for such mullers to the north of the centre in the Ngumpin-Yapa group is around 2,500 years ago pointing to a spread of reliance on grass seed as a staple in this area at this time. It is likely that the diffusion of the word *marangu* for this artefact coincides with the spread of this technology and economy. Since this word did not undergo the r > rl change, this diffusion must postdate proto-Ngumpin-Yapa unity, putting the latter at around 3,000 years ago.

We have spent time examining this because it is this kind of inference about material culture items and the words referring to them which can provide a standard of calibration of dates for non-material items. For instance, it can be shown that a word for 'father-in-law' in Ngumpin-Yapa languages *lamparr*, is borrowed from a word *ramparr* for 'mother-in-law', 'avoidance' and 'barrier' in Worrorran (Non-Pama-Nyungan) languages to the north of Ngumpin-Yapa. The change here r > (r) l is the same as the one identified as taking place at the proto-Ngumpin-Yapa stage above. This 'father-in-law' loanword arrived at this stage, around 3,000 years ago – earlier than the 'muller' word around 2,500 years ago, which did not undergo this change. The borrowing of a new word for 'father-in-law' could well have been associated with a change in marriage practices which put more power into the hands of the father-in-law for bestowal of the bride, and this appears to have occurred sometime before the full-scale adoption of the seed-grinding economy in the region (McConvell in press).

Such stratigraphy can be augmented, to provide a more detailed sequence of cultural changes with the possibility of calibrating with absolute dates where archaeological dates can be brought in. Further examples of the linguistic prehistory of non-material culture in kinship and social category terminology are discussed below.

Kinship and social organization

The example discussed above of a kinship term concerned tracing of diffusion of a term. In Australia and elsewhere affinal (spouse and in-law terms) are most commonly diffused, but other consanguineal terms are frequently inherited. In Indo-European (IE) for instance a significant proportion of kinship terms can be traced back to the proto-language, such as 'father', 'mother', 'sister', and 'brother' in English which have cognate forms in nearly all branches of IE. However some consanguineal kin terms are known to have diffused widely between different IE branches in Europe in the early Middle Ages, notably from French – 'cousin', 'aunt', and 'uncle' for instance. This is not just a result of dominance and prestige of the French in culture and politics at that time, or to be explained by these being somewhat peripheral collateral terms which are more easily replaced than 'mother', 'father', etc. (Matras 2009). Arguably the diffusion of the terms is motivated by large-scale cultural changes which were occurring at the time throughout much of Europe, related to the structure of the family, inheritance custom and law. In France between the eleventh and thirteenth centuries the term *oncle*, for instance, lost other meanings and was stabilized around the meaning 'parent's brother' (Maranda 1974).

It is this meaning which is imported into other languages at this time, in the case of English resulting from invasion. In English this meaning of 'uncle' replaced a more complex terminological system in which 'mother's brother' and 'father's brother' were differentiated lexically, and similar changes occurred in the other European languages when the French kinship terms arrived.

Of course, dealing with the medieval period in Europe we are assisted by writings which deal with kinship, such as records of marriages and inheritance, legal cases, and so on. Going back several millennia, proto-Indo-European kinship terminology is no longer documented in written form, but has been investigated using historical linguistics, with a view to drawing conclusions about society and culture at the time. One hypothesis derives inferences about post-marital residence from the presence or absence of in-law terms on the husband's or wife's side in the proto-language in question (Benveniste 1979; Clackson 2007: 201–6). The rationale is that, for instance, if post-marital residence is virilocal or patrilocal (wife living with the husband's family) there is little need for terms for the husband's in-laws since he has little interaction with them, whereas the wife has constant contact with her in-laws – her husband's family.[5] There is a difference along the dimension of sidedness of in-law terms between two sets of Indo-European languages, with a core group, having terms only for the wife's in laws (Greek, Baltic, Slavic, and Armenian) whereas the peripheral groups apply terms to both wife's and husband's kin (Indo-Iranian, Latin, Germanic, Celtic, and Albanian). Using the kind of inferences already mentioned, this has been said to point to different patterns of residence: ancestrally virilocal in the core set, and mainly neolocal (both husband and wife moving to a new location) in the peripheral group. This kind of situation often leads to a stalemate when trying to determine which situation was prior, in the proto-language. Fortunato (2011) uses computational phylogenetics to attempt to assess the probabilities of which of these systems came first – concluding that the earlier and probable proto-IE system was that found mainly in the core: predominantly virilocal with some levels of alternative neolocality. She also cites some genetic evidence which seems to indicate higher levels of non-local females in ancient groups, which would be consistent with the practice of virilocality.

Patterns of kinship terminology also have implications about systems of descent. For instance proto-Indo-European had an Omaha skewing pattern of terminology in which people related in the male line in different generations are referred to by the same term (Friedrich 1966). This kind of patterning (in which for instance 'grandfather' and 'mother's brother'; and 'grandchild' and 'nephew/niece' have the same terms) was transmitted in a number of branches of Indo-European including Latin and early Germanic until the medieval changes referred to above, which overrode this pattern in most languages.[6] This Omaha type of system is strongly associated with descent in the male line across the world, so is one of a number of sources of evidence that proto-Indo-European society was patrilineal. According to Friedrich (1979: 207), the proto-Indo-European (PIE) kinship structure was "patriarchal, patrilocal, and patrilineal," and other features of pIE society 'bride-capture, bride-wealth, polygyny, dominance of the husband, concubinage, and the "appointed daughter status", all articulate functionally with the patrilocal family and patrilineal descent'.

Turning to the other side of the world we will now look at the Austronesian language family, then Australia. Within the broader Austronesian family, which stretches from

Madagascar to Rapanui, there is a very large sub-group, Oceanic, which covers the Pacific Islands. Reconstruction of proto-Oceanic has been the subject of intensive work over a number of years, and has featured in particular lexical reconstruction of cultural and environmental domains. Not unnaturally, seafaring and fishing make up a significant component of the reconstructed vocabulary, but food plants and horticulture are also very significant (Pawley and Ross 1995) and several volumes have been published on different lexical domains, with more to come. The reconstructions are numerous and detailed, affording insight into the culture of the island peoples as they began to colonize the Pacific some 4,000 to 3,000 years ago.

Analysis of kinship and other related terminology in Austronesian languages of Island South-East Asia and the Pacific has been used to come to a different conclusion about the system in proto-Oceanic from that arrived at for Indo-European. It has been argued that linguistic evidence points to the proto-system being matrilineal, and matrilocal (Hage 1998). In this case recent evidence of human genetics has also been claimed to support this hypothesis (Hage and Marck 2003). The genetic make-up of Oceanic peoples includes a strong signal in the mitochondrial DNA (carried in the female line) of an Asian origin (as also backed up by the strong support in linguistics for a Taiwanese origin of Austronesian), but it also has a strong contribution of Melanesian peoples in the y-chromosome (carried in the male line). The argument is that matrilineality and matrilocality are frequently found in situations where people travel away from their home base, as earlier Oceanic colonizers did.

The Austronesian language family has been the site of other important reconstructions of the kinship systems of proto-languages and their associated forms of social organization and culture. One proposal by Robert Blust, the scholar mentioned at the beginning of this chapter, is that marriage in early Austronesian societies was unilateral and specifically matrilateral, with men marrying cross-cousins on the mother's side (e.g. mother's brother's daughter or a classificatory equivalent), rather than bilateral, with cousins on both the father's and mother's side. The linguistic evidence is complex but concerns such polysemies as a reconstructed term *ma(n)tuqa* meaning both 'mother's brother' and 'wife's father' – a straightforward signature of matrilateral marriage. The implications of this difference are profound, since unilateral marriage creates chains of spouses moving in one direction opening up wide alliances whereas bilateral marriage is a system of immediate and local exchange. Lévi-Strauss (1949) sees this as a major divide between types of societies with restricted exchange (with bilateral marriage) and generalized exchange (with unilateral marriage).

In Australia there are also both of these types, found in different regions, and it is possible, by using linguistic evidence combined with anthropological inferences about possible transformations of kinship and marriage systems, to reconstruct the sequence of change. In Australia, systems with bilateral marriage often have a single term for cross-cousins/spouses, mother's brother's child and father's sister's child, and often have typical other equations such as the term for father's father being the same as mother's mother's brother. Such systems are known as 'Kariera' after a group in the Pilbara region of Western Australia which has such an arrangement. 'Kariera' systems are also found in the east of Cape York Peninsula (CYP) in Queensland. In the west of CYP and across the Gulf of Carpentaria among the Yolngu in north-east Arnhem Land there is matrilateral marriage (a man marrying only a maternal cross-cousin). Along with this different system goes a matching kinship terminology, with *different* terms for maternal cross-cousin (marriageable for a man) and paternal cross-cousin (unmarriageable for a man).

Now many of the kinship terms are related in their linguistic form in Cape York Peninsula (the Paman sub-group of the Pama-Nyungan family) and among the Yolngu (another sub-group of Pama-Nyungan). In some cases this is due to their both being Pama-Nyungan languages, but the similarities go further than this. In crucial instances the meaning of terms has changed in significant ways. The term for mother's brother's child or wife('s sibling) among the Yolngu is *dhuway*, which is cognate and closely similar to words for woman's/sister's child on the eastern side of the Gulf; the term for father's sister's child or husband('s sibling) is *galay*, cognate and closely similar to words for 'mother's brother' on the eastern side of the Gulf. This meaning change is a key to deciding which direction the change went in. It is clear that the original meanings were the ones in the eastern languages, and this meaning change provided the necessary terms to distinguish the two kinds of cross-cousins in an asymmetrical marriage system such as that of the Yolngu (McConvell and Keen 2011).

The meaning change was not an arbitrary one just engineered to solve this problem. The changes are exactly those found in the Omaha skewing system in which the term for a maternal uncle is also applied to his son (and 'mother' to his daughter) and the other change from paternal aunt to woman's child is the automatic reciprocal of this. Omaha skewing is widely found with both the senior and junior meanings active under special circumstances in a swathe of languages in Australia as well as elsewhere. This type of skewing seems to accompany expansionary systems and the need for wider alliances, not only in Australia (McConvell 2012).

Hence we can reconstruct a 'Kariera' bilateral system for the immediate forbear of at least the central Paman languages and Yolngu, with the change to a matrilateral system in parts of the western Cape and in Yolngu.[7] This may be an indication that the Kariera system was ancestral in Pama-Nyungan, or more generally in Australia, but we have to be cautious about such claims, bearing in mind that the linguistic prehistory of Australia is as yet in its infancy (McConvell and Bowern 2011).

Another ancient system of social organization in Australia, the section system, seems to fit very well with the Kariera kinship and marriage arrangements, since it assumes or implies bilateral cross-cousin marriage. This is a system of four sociocentric categories which goes beyond language boundaries, actually covering at one time about half of Australia, enabling people to contract pseudo-kinship relations with other people over very long distances. It is possibly unique to Australia.[8] The section terms are not all the same or related. In some areas similar terms are used over very wide regions, but in other part of the continent there are more geographically restricted terminologies. There is another kind of system of eight divisions, subsections, which generally operates in areas with a different kind of marriage, to second cousins (man marries a MMBDD – 'mother's mother's brother's daughter's daughter' – for instance); this is certainly unique to Australia. Subsections have been shown to have arisen from a particular kind of alliance between two section systems in the north of the Northern Territory and diffused from there. Hence subsections are considerably younger than sections, and at least in part replaced earlier sections in the central north. The hypothesis of origin and spread is robust, and is based on solid linguistic evidence about loan morphology and regular sound changes (McConvell 1997).

Perhaps because of their shallower time depth, subsections are more tractable since most of them are related in form across their whole geographical range, whereas sections are related only within ten to a dozen discrete areas. Therefore it is highly unlikely that any one common ancestral section terms will be discovered. It does not necessarily follow though that these groups of sections originated independently in each area: possibly their original common element might have been semantic, for instance names of birds and bees, as are commonly found with moiety (dual division) names.[9]

It should be noted too that these sets of section and subsection terms diffused across their range as *Wanderwörter*, and were not in general inherited from a proto-language. It is not appropriate to assign them to the vocabulary and culture of a particular group of proto-language speakers, as is frequently done in linguistic prehistory. They can be said to belong to a layer or stratum, however, corresponding to the time that they were borrowed into a particular language. As discussed in an earlier section on linguistic stratigraphy, they then can be analysed as arriving before or after or at the same time as other words with cultural meanings. If these words refer to material culture, including diffused words for plants, then the possibility of absolute dating exists through archaeology. There are certainly relative chronological sequences that can be inferred from the differential impacts of sound changes on subsection terms and other cultural words, but when wooden artefacts do not survive long and dating of images from rock art is still problematic, absolute dating of subsection origin and spread remains out of reach, let alone dating of sections, at least for the time being.

Environmental terms and culture

Aside from dating the origin and spread of social categories, there is much that can be learned from words for natural species about their relationship to material culture, and symbolic and spiritual aspects of culture in prehistory. The images of such species, artefacts and related mundane and ceremonial activities in rock art and other graphic representations can assist, as can the archaeology and palaeobotany which can inform research about where the species were located and how they were used. In many cultures there are close connections between natural species and spiritual and mythological identities of individuals and groups, for instance the notion of a 'totem'.

Going back to the south-western United States and Central America, Hill (1992) investigated the 'Flower World' of the early Uto-Aztecan language family – a pervasive set of metaphors which link flowers and colours to gods, spirits, and creative beings. The evidence here is in the links between words themselves and the similarities in poetic language in song, which is still evident today. While it is possible for such schemas to diffuse across cultures, Hill argues that these cultural features were shared at an earlier stage of the language family.

Plant metaphors are deeply embedded in ways of thinking about such issues as social organization in recent Western cultures, a schema which Kövecses (2002: 98) formulates as *complex abstract systems are plants*. This is evident in the very fields examined here: kinship with its 'family trees', 'branches of families', and so on; and in historical linguistics with its use of the same metaphor, and phylogenetics more generally in the sciences.

Similar metaphorical schemas are important in many cultures across the world. For instance in the Austronesian world the growth and propagation of social groups is systematically likened to the structure of plants.

> The idea of 'origin' is commonly designated in a large number of Austronesian languages ... refers to the 'base' or 'trunk' of a tree ... [and] is thus conceived of, in a botanic idiom, as a kind of epistemic development from a 'base' to a 'tip' or more divergently to a myriad of separate 'tips'.
>
> *(Fox 2006: 16)*

> the botanic metaphors of 'trunk' and 'tip' occur not just in rules about the correct 'planting' of house posts, but in ways of talking about kinship, for example women, wife-givers or senior houses are all in particular Indonesian societies contrasted with men, wife-takers or junior houses, as 'trunk' to 'tip'.
>
> *(Waterson 2006: 236)*

Barnes (1979: 29) argues that such systems of 'analogy' are an appropriate target for 'a palaeontology of Austronesian throught'. For instance in Proto-Austronesian *puqu 'trunk of tree' is reflected in some daughter languages as a term of kinship or rank, and may have had such connotations from early times. In Rotinese the sister's son is only referred to by a botanical term *selek* (plant) or *sele-dadik* (planted sprout) – there is no dedicated kinship term (Fox 1971). This indicates the depth of penetration of the plant metaphorical schema into the language itself. When trying to trace if such a schema was similarly active in earlier stages of a language family, good evidence would be the overlap or replacement of kinship or social category terms by terms which can be shown to refer to plants originally. However one should be awake to the possibility that meanings can extend in the opposite direction, from the social to the plant domain as in the case of the proto-Austronesian term *empu* 'affine, ancestor, lord' (Barnes 1979: 21) which turns up in Javanese as empu 'principal node of a tuber' (citing Dempwolff 1938).

While it may be legitimate to reconstruct the plant metaphor schema outlined to an early stage of Austronesian, parallel systems do exist elsewhere without any cultural or linguistic links to Austronesian. Among the Gurindji and neighbouring Eastern Ngumpin speakers of the Northern Territory of Australia, the terms *marnaru* (trunk, base of tree, with an alternative form *marna*) and *jawuku* (tip, end of branch; alternative form *japiyapi*) are used to distinguish relationships between kin and social groups. One function is to distinguish a leading (trunk) from a junior (tip) lineage in a clan. Another is to distinguish two kinds of relations which are referred to by the same kinship term because of Omaha skewing (McConvell 2012), for instance *ngamirni marnaru* (trunk mother's brother) – mother's brother, from *ngamirni jawuku* (tip mother's brother) – mother's brother's son.

In order to establish that a coherent metaphorical cultural schema existed, on linguistic grounds, ideally it is required that the linked elements can all be reconstructed to the same particular proto-language or particular stage or stratum in linguistic prehistory – otherwise the researcher may be mixing elements from different eras and different languages. For instance, in the case of Eastern Ngumpin *marnaru* and *jawuku*, one might try to reconstruct the plant–kinship metaphorical complex to the proto-language of the relevant next highest sub-group, Ngumpin-Yapa (McConvell and Laughren 2004). But while cognates of at least one of the relevant terms are present in Western Ngumpin (e.g., Walmajarri, Richards and Hudson 1990) and Yapa (e.g. Warlpiri, Schwartz 2012), the meaning is related but different and do not point to the same kind of metaphorical schema (as shown in Table 15.1).

The terms *mana* and *marna* in Walmajarri and Warlpiri are doubtful as cognates of Gurindji *marna(ru)* because of difference in sounds and meaning respectively. More likely the original meaning of *marna in Western Pama-Nyungan was 'buttocks' (found in a number of languages) extended to 'base' and 'trunk of tree'. Warlpiri and Walmajarri *japi* are

Table 15.1 The terms *mana*, *marna* and *japi* in Walmajarri and Warlpiri

Language	Word	Gloss
Walmajarri	*japi*	physical features (e.g. rocks or parts of sandhills) near a permanent waterhole, (jila), indicating presence of water snake, (kalpurtu)
Walmajarri	*mana*	tree, stick
Warlpiri	*japi*	end of anything, entrance. As to a humpy, sugar ant';s nest, etc.
Warlpiri	*japujapu alt. japijapi*	coiled, rolled up, folded up, entwined, twisted around.
Warlpiri	*marna*	spinifex, grass in general

cognates related in meaning, since the physical features at a waterhole are signs of an entrance of the snake, or other mythical beings, and the reduplication *japijapi* (cf. Gurindji *japiyapi*) encompasses meanings where the tips or ends of long thin things are brought together. This is related to the Gurindji *japi* 'end or tip' of something (especially a tree, but also head of a river, etc.) in the sense that an entrance is an extremity like a tip. This suggests that the plant metaphor idiom only gained ascendancy at the stage of Eastern Ngumpin, not before that. For further plotting of the prehistory of links between plant metaphor and concepts of social organization in this region, see McConvell (2000), McConvell and Ponsonnet (in press).

Summary and conclusions

This chapter has shown how historical linguistics has made a significant contribution to understanding of culture history and prehistory. The techniques for doing this have been honed for over a hundred and fifty years and received a boost in the early days of American 'four fields' cultural anthropology in the twentieth century. While this kind of endeavour is perhaps not the most active field in either linguistics or anthropology today, there is a great deal of interest on the part of influential archaeologists and the absolute dating techniques coming from archaeology offer great promise for calibrating the linguistic chronologies such as linguistic stratigraphy. Other disciplines are also heavily engaged with linguistic prehistory, such as human population genetics and plant genetics. Linguistic prehistory adds a time dimension to our general appreciation of the links between culture and language by showing how these aspects influence each other over time and the mechanisms which produce change in either or both together.

The range of examples offered here has been necessarily restricted, both thematically and geographically. Thematically, emphasis has been given to the material culture of cultural/economic transitions such as seed-grinding, and to the reconstruction of kinship systems and possible inferences about other aspects of social organization. Geographically, attention has been given to Indo-European, because it is in this field that a lot of early work in linguistic prehistory and 'linguistic palaeontology' was done, but also because of continuing debate about issues in this realm; and to North America because of the pioneering work of Sapir and others, again continuing today with new exciting work. Then the Asia-Pacific claims our attention with work on seed-grinding on Australia particularly on the notion of linguistic stratigraphy, moving on then to the reconstruction of Austronesian kinship and social organization, and topics in the linguistic prehistory of Australian kinship and social categories. The latter has been a field rife with speculation among ethnologists especially at the end of the nineteenth and early twentieth centuries but is benefiting now from a new emphasis on rigorous linguistic work. The final section deals with how two areas of interest in linguistic prehistory, social organization and plants, can be linked in metaphorical schemas and how research can discover the structure of these links in ancient times.

It is unfortunate that so many important areas of progress in linguistic prehistory cannot be covered in this short review. To take one example, linguistic prehistory has made significant contributions to the history of Africa. The work of Christopher Ehret can be highlighted here. He builds on the work of many others in linguistics and archaeology and is a powerful advocate of using linguistic prehistory in a broad kind of history not limited to evidence from written sources. Africa provides striking examples of language spread in the late Holocene, such as Bantu, originating in West Africa north of the Congo and migrating east and south, ultimately entering areas of South Africa occupied by Khoe-San people ('bushmen') in the last few hundred years as European settlers were also making incursions. A number of the African language families are considerably older than Bantu, according to Ehret's calculations stretching back to the late Pleistocene around 15,000 years ago or more.[10]

Ehret uses historical linguistics to plot the history of cultural patterns and changes (see Ehret (2010) for a summary of numerous publications). Many of these are related to changes in economy and mode of subsistence, including major changes from foraging to agriculture and herding, and subsequent additions and modifications to crops, livestock, and technology, which mainly took place in the Holocene (the last 10000 years) and include new crops coming from the Americas in the last few hundred years. Other areas such as ritual, methods of measuring time periods, and kinship are also investigated in detail.

Beyond such regional and thematic studies, there is work on a bigger stage, that of the expansion of humans across the globe and how the spread of languages and cultures relates to that. It is understood by most linguists that there are strict temporal limits to linguistic reconstruction usually estimated at around 10,000 years (although some hold out hope that something can be glimpsed beyond that curtain). Even if this is a barrier though, knowing something about the culture – and aspects of it archaeology might not be able to illuminate – at the beginning of the Holocene gives researchers a better purchase on bridging the gap back to around 100,000 years ago when *Homo sapiens* began to move out of Africa.

Models of why and how people migrate and how languages move with migrating people (as in 'demic diffusion', 'farming language dispersal') or are adopted by language shift is an active field at the theoretical and methodological level. Clear-headed interaction with archaeologists, geneticists, demographers, climate scientists, and others is needed to refine these models, and feed them back into local and thematic studies.

Related topics

ethnosemantics; culture and kinship language; language and culture in sociocultural anthropology

Further reading

Campbell, Lyle. 2004. *Historical Linguistics: an introduction*. Cambridge, MA: MIT Press. Chapter 15 'Linguistic Prehistory' 378–420. (Succinct but thorough chapter on the subdiscipline in a fine textbook.)

Ehret, Christopher. 2010. *History and the Testimony of Language*. Berkeley, CA: University of California Press. (Overview of linguistic prehistory in Africa for the non-specialist, from Ehret's viewpoint.)

Mallory, J. P. and D. Q. Adams. 1997. *Encyclopedia of Indo-European Culture*. London/Chicago: Fitzroy Dearborn. (A rich and enjoyable compendium of discoveries about early Indo-European culture, multidisciplinary but emphasizing linguistic evidence.)

Sapir, Edward. 1916. *Time Perspective in Aboriginal American Culture, a Study in Method*. Geological Survey Memoir 90: No. 13, Anthropological Series. Ottawa: Government Printing Bureau. Reprinted in Sapir, E., ed. D. Mandelbaum 1985. *Selected Writings in Language, Culture and Personality*. 389–402. Berkeley, CA, University of California Press. (An early but magisterial essay setting out methods for linguistic pre-history with examples mainly from North America. Although research has moved on in its discoveries, this work remains surprisingly up to date and relevant.)

Notes

1 Most linguists accept this general line of argument about the age of pIE and the location of the homeland. The archaeologist Renfrew, however, proposed that pIE was located in Anatolia (modern Turkey) and was several thousand years earlier. He also disputed the evidential value of linguistic palaeontology in discovering homelands and dates. His hypothesis fitted with a more general theory that large language families, and Indo-European in particular, spread along with farming dispersal, which is controversial. More recently, techniques of Bayesian inference have been applied to the

problem of Indo-European phylogeny, producing results supporting Renfrew's view, but the jury is still out on this.

2 Similar diagnostic tools can be used for names of groups (ethnonyms). Tindale remarked that opaque 'tribal' names in Australia are ancient (1974); for Australian indigenous ethnonyms and toponyms and their implications for prehistoric culture, see McConvell (2006, 2009).

3 This proposal is overturning earlier hypotheses about the origin of Uto-Aztecan in the south-western USA. However the point being made by Sapir below is independent of the phylogeny and origin point of the family.

4 This is of course a development within the foraging economy, not a 'Neolithic' transition to farming as in the Uto-Aztecan case, but a transformative one nonetheless. The issue of whether a language family or sub-group expansion occurred along with the spread of the seed-grinding economy, as proposed for Uto-Aztecan spread by Hill, needs further research. It seems too late to be linked directly to early spread of the major family Pama-Nyungan across most of the continent, but could be linked to a secondary pulse of this spread into central areas.

5 This is not by itself a particularly strong argument – the wife's in-laws could be key people even if contact is infrequent – and has been challenged for instance by Goody (1969) and Szemerenyi (1977).

6 An alternative view holds that Omaha skewing only developed in some branches of Indo-European and is not necessarily to be reconstructed to pIE. This is the kind of issue encountered already in the discussion of the relation of kinship terminology to residence.

7 Note that a common proto-language is not proposed at this stage for Paman and Yolngu, apart from their common affiliation to the very broad Pama-Nyungan family. This is unlike some of the earlier discussion of Austronesian where validated subgroups proto-languages (such as proto-Oceanic) are said to be the locus of a kinship system or innovation. At this stage we do not have evidence of such a higher-level sub-group as a combination of Yolngu and some eastern sub-group although the kinship terminologies are quite similar.

8 Section systems appear to exist among speakers of Panoan languages in Peru and Bolivia, have been claimed for ancient China, and something similar has existed in parts of Vanuatu.

9 Research is ongoing on such questions through the AustKin2 ARC project.

10 Ehret uses a version of glottochronology to estimate dates along with calibration by archaeology; some of his dates are controversial.

References

Anthony, David. 2007. *The Horse, the Wheel and the Chariot: How Bronze Age Riders from the Eurasian Steppes shaped the Modern World*. Princeton, NJ: Princeton University Press.

Barber, Elizabeth. 1991. *Prehistoric Textiles: The Development of Cloth in the Neolithic and Bronze Ages with Special Reference to the Aegean*. Princeton, NJ: Princeton University Press.

Barnes, Robert. 1979. 'Lord, Ancestor and Affine: An Austronesian relationship name', *Nusa* 7:19–34.

Benveniste, Emile. 1979. *Indo-European Language and Society*. London: Faber and Faber.

Blust, Robert. 1976. 'Austronesian culture history: some linguistic inferences and their relation to the archaeological record', *World Archaeology*. 8.1: 19–43.

——1996. 'Austronesian Culture History: The Window of Language', *Transactions of the American Philosophical Society New Series* 86(5), Prehistoric Settlement of the Pacific, 28–35.

Clackson, John. 2007. *Indo-European Linguistics: An Introduction*. Cambridge: Cambridge University Press.

Darnell, Regna. 1998. *And Along Came Boas: Continuity and Revolution in Americanist Anthropology*. Amsterdam: Benjamins.

Dempwolff, 1938. *Vegleichende Lautlehre des Austronesischen Wortschatzes*. Vol. 3. Beihefte der Zeitschrift der Eingebprenen Sprachen. No. 19 Berlin: Dietrich Reimer.

Ehret, Christopher. 2010. *History and the Testimony of Language*. Berkeley, CA: University of California Press.

Fortson, Benjamin W. 2004. *Indo-European Language and Culture: An Introduction*. Oxford: Blackwell

Fortunato, Laura. 2011. 'Reconstructing the History of Residence Strategies in Indo-European-Speaking Societies: Neo-, Uxori-, and Virilocality'. *Human Biology* 83.1: 107–28

Fox, James. 1971. 'Sister's child as plant: metaphors in an idiom of consanguinity'. In R. Needham ed., *Rethinking Kinship and Marriage*. 219–52. London: Tavistock.

——2006. 'Comparative perspectives on Austronesian houses: An introductory essay'. In Fox ed., 1–30.

——ed. 2006. *Inside Austronesian Houses: Perspectives on Domestic Designs for Living*. Canberra: ANU EPress

Friedrich, Paul. 1966. 'Proto-Indo-European Kinship'. *Ethnology* 5.1: 1–36. Also in booklet, University of Pittsburgh Press.

——1979 *Language, Context and the Imagination*. Stanford, CA: Stanford University Press.

Gimbutas, Marija. 1997. *The Kurgan culture and the Indo-Europeanization of Europe: Selected Articles from 1952–1993*. Eds. Miriam Robbins Dexter and Karlene Jones-Bley. Journal of Indo-European Studies Monograph 18. Washington, DC: Institute for the Study of Man.

Goody, Jack. 1969. *Comparative studies in Kinship*. Taylor and Francis.

Hage, Per. 1998. 'Was Proto-Oceanic society matrilineal?' *Journal of the Polynesian Society*. 107: 365–79.

Hage, Per and Jeff Marck. 2003. 'Matrilineality and the Melanesian Origin of Polynesian Y Chromosomes'. *Current Anthropology*. 45.S5: S121–S127.

Hill, Jane. 1992. 'The Flower World of Old Uto-Aztecan'. *Journal of Anthropological Research* 48.2: 117–44

Hill, Jane. 2010. 'New evidence for a Mesoamerican homeland for Proto-Uto-Aztecan'. *PNAS*, 107.11: E33.

Jenkins, Dennis, Thomas J. Connolly, and C. Melvin Aikens. 2004. 'Early and Middle Holocene Archaeology in the Northern Great Basin: Dynamic Natural and Cultural Ecologies'. In *Early and Middle Holocene Archaeology of the Northern Great Basin* Edited by D. L. Jenkins, T. J. Connolly, and C. M. Aikens. University of Oregon Anthropological Papers 62:1–20

Kövecses, Zoltan. 2002. *Metaphor: A Practical Introduction*. New York: Oxford University Press

Kuper, Adam. 1983. *Anthropology and Anthropologists: The Modern British School*. London: Routledge.

Lévi-Strauss, Claude. 1949 [translation 1969] *The Elementary Structures of Kinship*. Boston, MA: Beacon Press.

McConvell, Patrick. 1997. 'Long-lost relations: Pama-Nyungan and northern kinship'. In Patrick McConvell and Nicholas Evans (eds), *Archaeology and Linguistics Aboriginal Australia in Global Perspective*. 207–36 Melbourne: Oxford University Press.

——2000. '"Born is nothing": Roots, family trees, and other connections to land in the Victoria River District and Kimberleys'. *Aboriginal History* 22: 180–202.

——2006. 'Shibbolethnonyms, Ex-Exonyms and Eco-Ethnonyms in Aboriginal Australia: The pragmatics of Onymization and archaism' *Onoma* 41:185–214

——2009. '"Where the spear sticks up": The variety of locatives in placenames in the Victoria River District, Northern Territory', in Harold Koch and Luise Hercus (ed.), Aboriginal Placenames: Naming and Re-Naming the Australian Landscape. 359–402. Canberra: ANU ePress.

——2012. 'Omaha skewing in Australia: Overlays, dynamism and change'. In Thomas Trautmann and Peter Whiteley (eds), *Crow-Omaha: New Light on a Classic Problem of Kinship Analysis*. 243–60. Tucson: University of Arizona Press.

——[in press]. 'Long-distance diffusion of affinal kinship terms as evidence of late Holocene change in marriage systems in Aboriginal Australia'. In P. Toner, ed. [*title tba*] Canberra: ANU Press.

McConvell, Patrick and Claire Bowern. 2011. 'The Prehistory and Internal Relationships of Australian Languages'. *Language and Linguistics Compass*. 5.1:19–32.

McConvell, Patrick and Ian Keen. 2011. 'The transition from Kariera to an asymmetrical system: Cape York Peninsula to north-east Arnhemland'. In Doug Jones and Bojka Milicic eds, *Kinship, Language and Prehistory: Per Hage and the Renaissance in Kinship Studies*. 99–132. Salt Lake City: University of Utah Press.

McConvell, Patrick and Mary Laughren. 2004. 'Ngumpin-Yapa Languages'. In H. Koch and C. Bowern eds, *Australian Languages: Classification and the Comparative Method* 151–78. Amsterdam: Benjamins.

McConvell, Patrick and Maia Ponsonnet. [in press]. 'Generic terms for subsections ("Skins") in Australia: Sources and semantic networks'. In P. McConvell and P. Kelly (eds) [*title tba*]. ANU Press.

McConvell, Patrick and Mike Smith. 2003. 'Millers and mullers: The archaeolinguistic stratigraphy of seed-grinding in Central Australia'. In H. Andersen (ed.) *Language Contacts in Prehistory: Studies in Stratigraphy*. 177–200. Amsterdam: Benjamins.

Mallory, J. P. and D. Q. Adams. 1997. *Encyclopedia of Indo-European Culture*. London/Chicago: Fitzroy Dearborn.

Maranda, Pierre. 1974. *French Kinship: Structure and history*. Berlin: Mouton.

Matras, Yaron. 2009. *Language Contact*. Cambridge: Cambridge University Press.

Pawley, Andrew and Malcolm Ross. 1995. 'The prehistory of the Oceanic languages: A current view'. In Peter Bellwood, James Fox and Darrell Tryon (eds), *The Austronesians: Historical and Comparative Perspectives*. 39–74. Canberra; Department of Anthropology, Australian National University.

Radcliffe-Brown, A.R. 1952. *Structure and Function in Primitive Society*. Glencoe, IL: Free Press.

Renfrew, A. Colin. 1987. *Archaeology and Language: The Puzzle of Indo-European Origins*. Jonathan Cape.

Richards, Eirlys and Joyce Hudson. 1990. *Walmajarri–English Dictionary*. Darwin: SIL–AAB.

Sapir, Edward. 1916. *Time Perspective in Aboriginal American Culture, a Study in Method*. Geological Survey Memoir 90: No. 13, Anthropological Series. Ottawa: Government Printing Bureau. Reprinted in Sapir, E., ed. D. Mandelbaum 1985. *Selected Writings in Language, Culture and Personality*. 389–402. Berkeley, CA, University of California Press.

——1921. *Language: An Introduction to the Study of Speech*. New York: Harcourt Brace.

——1936. Internal Linguistic Evidence Suggesting the Northern Origin of the Navajo. *American Anthropologist*, 38.2: 225–32.

Schwartz, Stephen. 2012. 'Interactive Warlpiri–English Dictionary: with English–Warlpiri finderlist'. Darwin: AUSIL.

Stocking, George. 1966. 'Franz Boas and the Culture Concept in Historical Perspective' *American Anthropologist* 68:867–82.

——1984. 'Radcliffe-Brown and British Social Anthropology'. In G. W. Stocking, Jr. (ed.), *Functionalism Historicized*, pp. 131–91, Madison: University of Wisconsin Press.

Szemerenyi, Oswald. 1977. *Studies in the Kinship Terminology of the Indo-European Languages*. Leiden: Brill.

Tindale, Norman. 1974. *Aboriginal Tribes of Australia: Their Terrain, Environmental Controls, Distribution, Limits and Proper Names*. Berkeley, CA: University of California Press.

——1977. 'Adaptive significance of the Panara or grass seed culture of Australia'. In R.S.V. Wright (ed.), *Stone Tools as Cultural Markers. Change, Evolution and Complexity*. Prehistory and Material Culture Series No.12. Australian Institute of Aboriginal Studies: Canberra.

Waterson, Roxana. 2006. 'Houses and the built environment in Island South-East Asia: Tracing some shared themes in uses of space'. In Fox ed., 227–42.

PART IV

Language, culture, and cognition

16

EMBODIMENT, CULTURE, AND LANGUAGE

Ning Yu

1 Introduction

This chapter surveys the more recent literature on the embodied grounding of human cognition with a focus on the cognitive linguistic contributions to the study of the embodied cognition hypothesis. In particular, the survey is done from the vantage point of Cultural Linguistics. As a multidisciplinary area of research that explores the relationship between language, culture, and conceptualization and the function of cultural models at the level of cultural cognition, Cultural Linguistics integrates interests and concerns of Cognitive Linguistics with those of linguistic and cognitive anthropology (see Chapter 32 this volume).

The notion of embodiment in the cognitive linguistic paradigm emphasizes the role of the body in grounding and framing cognition within the cultural context. In contrast with the Cartesian mind–body dualism, the embodiment hypothesis claims that the body actually shapes the mind (Gallagher 2005). Such a mind is therefore embodied in that it is crucially shaped by the particular nature of the human body, including our perceptual and motor systems and our interactions with the physical and cultural world. However, the mind is not shaped universally because the body itself may take different 'shapes' in different cultural models in the first place. Cultures may construe the body and bodily experiences differently, attributing different values and significances to various body parts and organs and their functions. Various cultural construals of the body and bodily experiences may motivate different schematizations and conceptualizations, which give rise to varied perspectives in the understanding of the world. To contribute to a better understanding and articulation of the relationship among body, culture, and cognition, this chapter looks in particular at how body and culture interact in the motivation, formation, and operation of human meaning, reasoning, and understanding in abstract domains as manifested in the use of language.

The term *embodiment*, as suggested by the root of the word itself, has to do with the body, but it is really about how the body is related to the mind in the environment, and how this relationship affects human cognition. The basic idea behind embodiment is that the mind emerges and takes shape from the body with which we interact with our environment. Human beings have bodies, and human embodiment shapes both what and how we know, understand, think, and reason. We can know, understand, think, and reason only from and within our bodily experience: 'No body, never mind' (see Pires de Oliveira and Bittencourt 2007). That is, embodiment represents a theoretical approach to the study of mind in cognitive science commonly known as *embodied cognition*. This approach focuses on the co-evolution between minds and bodies, and on the whole behaving organism in its natural context in which individual humans interact in and across groups (Semin and Smith 2008). When cognition is said to be embodied, it offers a radical shift in explanations of the human mind, emphasizing the way cognition is shaped by the body and its sensorimotor interaction with the world (Lindblom and Ziemke 2007). This world, it is worth stressing, is both physical and sociocultural. In the past decades, embodiment has stimulated increasingly growing research in cognitive science as an inter-disciplinary field where a number of disciplines such as anthropology, artificial intelligence, computer science, linguistics, neuroscience, philosophy, psychology converge and overlap for the study of the mind. Scholars have put forward a variety of programmatic theses for the embodiment paradigm, including 'the body in the mind' (Johnson 1987), 'the culture in the mind' (Shore 1996), and 'the culture in the body' (Maalej 2008), which are important theses in the studies of the relationship between body, mind, and culture.

In his book, *Embodiment and Cognitive Science*, Gibbs (2006: 1) states that in cognitive science, embodiment refers to 'understanding the role of an agent's own body in its everyday, situated cognition', namely how our bodies influence the ways we think and speak. He outlines the following as the embodiment premise:

> People's subjective, felt experiences of their bodies in action provide part of the funda-mental grounding for language and thought. Cognition is what occurs when the body engages the physical, cultural world and must be studied in terms of the dynamical interactions between people and the environment. Human language and thought emerge from recurring patterns of embodied activity that constrain ongoing intelligent behaviour. We must not assume cognition to be purely internal, symbolic, computational, and disembodied, but seek out the gross and detailed ways that language and thought are inextricably shaped by embodied action.
>
> *(Gibbs 2006: 9)*

Gibbs suggests that the key feature here for understanding the embodied nature of human cognition is to 'look for possible mind–body and language-body connections' (p. 9) as formed in the interaction between the body and the physical and cultural world.

2 A historical overview

In a general sense, the term *embodiment* collapses the duality of mind and body by infusing body with mind, attributing a more active and constructive role to the body in human cognition. This view is in contrast and reaction to 'disembodied' Cartesian dualism, represented by the French philosopher and scientist René Descartes (1596–1650), which has been the dominant view on the mind–body relations in Western philosophy during the past few hundred years. According to the Cartesian mind–body split, the body, which has material properties and follows the law of physics, works like a machine; in contrast, the mind (or soul), which is a non-material entity that does not follow the law of physics but has the capacity to think, controls the body. Descartes postulated an absolute difference in kind between the mind and the body, the former defining selfhood and personhood and having supremacy over the latter; in his words, 'I think, therefore I am' and 'the mind, by which I am what I am, is entirely distinct from the body' (Synnott 1993: 22). So postulated, Cartesianism tends to deprecate the body in favour of the mind, to privilege the mind over the body, or even to describe the body as an enemy to the mind. The Cartesian mind is disembodied. A problem for Descartes, as for all Cartesianists subsequently, is how to account for the intermingling of mind and body, given their absolute difference and separation even though Descartes gave the mind an ethnolocation and considered the pineal gland in the head as the site for interaction between mind and body. In the modern West, however, the self and the person have been largely conceptualized in terms of oppositions between reason, thought and intellect, on the one hand, and emotion, feeling and desire, on the other, all along the Cartesian dualistic line between mind and body (Strathern 1996; Synnott 1993). The mind–body dualism is also conceptualized metonymically as a dichotomy between head (LOCATION FOR ACTIVITY) and heart (PART FOR WHOLE). The 'abyssal separation between body and mind' is referred to as 'Descartes' error', which treats thinking as an activity quite separate from the body, and celebrates the separation of mind, the 'thinking thing', from the 'nonthinking body' (Damasio 1994: 247–52).

While Cartesianism has dominated Western thought in the past few hundred years, it has faced some challenges. For instance, Neapolitan philosopher and historian Giambattista Vico (1668–1744) responded to Descartes' mechanism with his own humanism, relying on a complex etymology in classical rhetoric and philology. In his *New Science* (1725) he argued for the evolution of human language and cognition as the extension of bodily experiences through human imagination structured by metaphor and metonymy. The magnificent insight is that human language and cognition have evolved with the human mind thinking and knowing on the basis and with the help of the human body (O'Neill 1985). After his *The Origin of Species* (1859) was published, Charles Darwin (1809–82) tried to explain how different species had evolved by assuming a mental linkage between animals and humans. In modern terms, Darwin viewed the mind as embodied and did not believe it to be separate from the body (Lindblom and Ziemke 2007).

In the twentieth century, the Cartesian dualism was seriously challenged by phenomenology represented by French philosopher Maurice Merleau-Ponty (1908–61). Merleau-Ponty's philosophy is an explicit attempt to think beyond the dualism of mind and body. Rather than two separate entities, mind and body are fundamentally interwoven components of an indivisible human whole, a body-subject that is simultaneously physical and mental. He argued that the body is one's general medium for having a world, and that it is through one's body that one understands other people. In Merleau-Ponty's work, the body is described not as a material object of nature agitated by stimuli, but as an organism capable of perceiving and activating itself in organized ways, i.e., the body as a structure of perceptual and behavioural competence. According to him, humans are inserted into the world bodily and human experience of the world comes to human beings through their bodies. That is, the human being is first and foremost a bodily being and human cognition is achieved through its bodily experience. Human thinking is 'a movement of the body', and humans 'are moved into thinking' (Blacking 1977: 20). That is, it is not the brain alone that does the thinking, but the whole body. The body has the necessary knowledge to perform tasks at hand since it knows how to act and how to perceive through the history of its perceptual and sensorimotor interactions with the environment. For him, therefore, the body actually provides meaning or intentionality for the mind, whereas the mind is essentially embodied and interacting with the surrounding world (Lindblom and Ziemke 2007).

The Swiss biologist and psychologist Jean Piaget (1896–1980) also stressed the importance of sensorimotor activity for the emergence of intelligent behaviour. For him, cognition is about the organization of an agent's sensorimotor experiences and interactions with the environment, but his theory, which he claimed as universal, has been criticized as not paying much attention to cultural differences in cognitive development. The role of culture, however, was strongly emphasized by Russian psychologist Lev Vygotsky (1896–1934), who proposed that individual cognitive development requires a sociocultural embedding through certain transformation processes. Thus, the cognitive abilities of an 'enculturated' person are the product of developmental processes, in which primitive and immature humans are transformed into cultural ones through social interactions. Vygotsky's theory is commonly contrasted with Piaget's as having a different focus, although in fact the theories are largely compatible and agree in viewing knowledge as constructed through the interaction of biological and sociocultural factors in the course of cognitive development (Lindblom and Ziemke 2007: 139–41).

In the American context, it is argued, the concept of embodiment in cognition has its philosophical and psychological roots in early American Pragmatism in the works of thinkers such as William James and John Dewey (Johnson and Rohrer 2007). According to the Pragmatist view of cognition as action, cognition emerges from the embodied nature and processes of an organism that is constantly adapting to better utilize relatively stable patterns within a changing environment. This naturalistic approach seeks to explain how meaning, abstract thinking, and formal reasoning could emerge from the basic sensorimotor capacities of organisms as they interact with the environment and one another, with the fundamental assumption that everything we attribute to mind – perceiving, conceptualizing, imagining, reasoning, etc. – has emerged as part of a process in which an organism seeks to survive and grow within different kinds of situations. This evolutionary embeddedness of the organism within its changing environments, and the development of thought in response to such changes, ties mind inextricably to body and environment. On this view, mind is never separate from body, for it is always a series of bodily activities immersed in the ongoing flow of organism–environment interactions that constitutes experience. This rootedness of thinking in bodily experience and its connection with the environment entail that there is no rupture in experience between perceiving, feeling, and thinking (Johnson and Rohrer 2007: 18–23). In short, according to American Pragmatism, human cognition arises from human experience and social interaction, which is an embodied view of mind.

By the mid-twentieth century, the 'cognitive revolution' was underway in reaction to the behaviourism that dominated the first half of the twentieth century. Along with advancements in the field of computer science, this 'cognitive revolution' led to the rise of 'computationalist cognitive science', defined and characterized by the computer metaphor for mind. According to this metaphor, cognition takes place in the head in the form of abstract symbol manipulation, whereas the body only serves as an input and output device, i.e., a physical interface between internal program (cognitive processes) and external world, executing commands generated in the mind through symbol manipulation. In this view, the nature of cognition is such that the minds or brains, which function like computers, accept information, manipulate symbols, store items in memory and retrieve them again, classify inputs, recognize patterns, and so on. The relation between body and mind was considered to be similar to the one between hardware and software in a computer, with the body being viewed as a mere physical implementation of the mind, which however is largely implementation independent. Computationalism in cognitive science became very successful mainly because it seemed to offer an elegant solution to the mind–body problem, bridging the gap between body and biology (hardware) on the one hand and mind and psychology (software) on the other, with the exciting metaphor of mental states and processes acting as the software running on the brain's hardware. It is therefore of no surprise that the computer metaphor became the dominant model of how the mind works (Lindblom and Ziemke 2007: 141–3).

In the late 1970s, however, several criticisms of computationalism emerged, the overall concern being its lack of embodiment and situatedness. As the rational and formalized view was the dominating approach in cognitive science for a long time, the role of the body and the environment, physical as well as sociocultural, was largely ignored. It was pointed out that a computer, as well the computer metaphor for mind, is the product of traditional thinking in Plato's footsteps over 2,500 years. In that sense, the cognitive revolution was nothing but 'old wine in new bottles'. Since the late 1980s, cognitive science has revived theories that acknowledge the embodied, situated, distributed, and sociocultural nature of the human mind. Today, there is a growing interest in embodiment in cognitive science, or rather 'embodied' cognitive science, in contrast with its earlier 'traditional', 'classical' counterpart that is 'computationalist' and 'disembodied' in nature. In short, embodied cognitive science views embodiment as a necessary requirement for intelligence and mind (Lindblom and Ziemke 2007: 143–4).

Today, the centrality of the body and embodiment in human cognition is broadly acknowledged and this has provoked a huge quantity of research throughout a wide range of scientific domains associated with cognitive science. Cognition is seen as depending on the body and its sensorimotor systems in a fundamental way, emerging from our bodily based experience and our sensorimotor interactions with the world that is both physical and sociocultural. This is certainly a more than welcome shift in the traditional Western research paradigm, since this reorientation can help to free it from the old, seemingly unresolvable dualisms between body and mind, between the internal world of immaterial concepts and thoughts and the external world of objectivist reality (Violi 2008).

3 Body as a culturally constructed concept

In the past decades, the meaning of the term *embodiment*, however, 'has been stretched in different directions' as it has become more popular (Strathern 1996: 196). As Violi (2008: 54) points out, 'the present widespread use of the notions of body and embodiment across different fields and with different meanings makes it particularly important to develop a better understanding and clarification of these two notions.'

While embodiment has to do with the physical and biological body, what is embodied, however, is always some set of meanings, values, tendencies, orientations that have derived from the sociocultural realm (Strathern 1996). Embodiment refers to patterns of human behaviour enacted on the body and expressed in the bodily form. In other words, although it is always the same biological and physical body that is said to embody various aspects of human experience, what is embodied is clearly not just the biological and physical but the social and cultural as well. It is socioculturally situated embodiment, as some cognitive linguists and cognitive scientists would call it (see, e.g., Frank *et al.* 2008; Sharifian *et al.* 2008; Ziemke, Zlatev, and Frank 2007).

Gibbs (2006: 36–9) characterizes the relationship between body and culture and the diversity of cultural meanings attached to the body. As he suggests, the body system offers insightful analysis for understanding cultural systems because physical environments in which people and their bodies move are imbued with culture. Anthropologists have demonstrated how many elementary embodied experiences are shaped by local cultural knowledge and practice in a variety of cultural settings. The body is appreciated for its symbolic properties as people instill cultural meanings into bodily processes and activities. Culture does not just inform, but also constitute, embodied experience. Many embodied experiences are rooted in sociocultural contexts. This does not imply that people in various cultures have different physiologies, but only that they weigh their embodied experiences differently in how they interpret their sensorimotor interactions in and with the world around them. It is therefore important to explore the linkages between embodiment and cultural meaning.

In reality, however, 'body' is often taken as a natural, self-evident concept, one that does not need any further elaboration, but it sometimes appears to be, paradoxically, the most misleading (Violi 2008). Metaphorically speaking, the human body is a kaleidoscope capable of producing amazingly diversified and ever-changing colourful patterns of view. As pointed out nicely by Armstrong, 'The body is what it is perceived to be; it could be otherwise if perception were different. The question is not therefore concerned with the nature of the body but with the perceiving process which allows the body's nature to be apprehended' (cited in Yu 2009a: 14). Synnott (1993: 37) summarizes the wide range of meanings, metaphorical and otherwise, which the body carries, as follows:

> In sum, the body has been, and still is, constructed in almost as many ways as there are individuals; it seems to be all things to all people. Thus the body is defined as good or bad; tomb or temple; machine or garden; cloak or prison; sacred or secular; friend or enemy; cosmic or mystical; one with mind and soul or separate; private or public; personal or the property of the state; clock or car; to varying degrees plastic, bionic, communal; selected from a catalogue or engineered; material or spiritual; a corpse of the self.

French author and symbolist poet Paul Valéry once said that the body is commonly used to refer to a wide variety of things. It is the privileged object we possess, although our knowledge of it may be extremely variable and subject to illusions. We speak of it as a thing that belongs to us; but for us it is not entirely a thing; and it belongs to us a little less than we belong to it (Kuriyama 2002). As Kuriyama (2002: 14) suggests, 'The body is unfathomable and breeds astonishingly diverse perspectives precisely because it is a basic and intimate reality. The task of discovering the truth of the body is inseparable from the challenge of discovering the truth about people.' The body is 'never just a purely biological entity but one which has social and cultural dimensions too', being influenced by social and cultural forces which shape or attempt to shape it in their own image (cited in Yu 2009a: 14).

As Violi (2008: 55) has forcefully argued, body is 'a semiotic construal'. The concept of body has resulted from the various discourses that 'construct' it. Even if the phenomenological experience of the body can appear an immediate one, the concept of body certainly does not. Instead, it is taken as 'construals' of it within any disciplinary perspective. 'In other words, the various meanings attributed to the notion of body are the sum of the various effects on its sense of the different disciplines as they investigate and define it.' All different 'bodies' are not reducible to one another. Many of the differences in the use of the very word 'embodiment' depend on the different discourses that construct body in their respective ways as an object of research. Therefore, there is really no such thing as a body 'in itself'. Body cannot be described outside the different practices and discourses that define it, independent of the cultures that shape it. No 'hard' science can escape from this paradox: even the body described by the most sophisticated technologies – radiography, magnetic resonance imaging, spectroscopy, etc. – is but just another way of representing it. Violi, then, further argues, 'Even the body as studied in medicine is a construal, so much so that different medical practices in different cultures construe as many different bodies as there are cultures': the Western body studied in Western medical tradition is not the same as the body mapped by Chinese acupuncture (Violi 2008: 54–5).

Violi's argument echoes Kuriyama's (2002: 8) observation in his *The Expressiveness of the Body and the Divergence of Greek and Chinese Medicine*, which explores the fundamental question of how perceptions of something as basic and intimate as the body can differ so much, as a 'riddle' that 'lies at the heart of the history of medicine': 'The true structure and workings of the human body are, we casually assume, everywhere the same, a universal reality. But then we look into history, and our sense of reality wavers ... accounts of the body in diverse medical traditions frequently appear to describe mutually alien, almost unrelated worlds.' After all, from an anthropological point of view, 'medicine is a culture with its own language, gestures, customs, rituals, spaces, costumes, and practices. Within medical culture, the body becomes the locus that corporealizes culture, enculturates bodiliness' (cited in Yu 2009a: 19).

In short, as Mark Johnson argues, the body does not terminate with the fleshy boundary of the skin, but rather extends out into its environment that is at once physical, social, and cultural, engaging in all sorts of bodily and sociocultural interactions, so that the organism and environment are not independent, but rather interdependent aspects of the basic flow of bodily experience (see Pires de Oliveira and Bittencourt 2007). That is, to fully understand the role of the body in human cognition, we will have to go beyond the body itself (Violi 2008).

4 Embodiment and culture in language

As one approach to the study of language, associated with second-generation, embodied cognitive science, Cognitive Linguistics, especially its conceptual metaphor theory, has for decades seriously challenged the fundamental assumption that most of our thinking about the world is literal, directly corresponding to the external reality, asserting that meaning construction in and through language is not a separate and independent module of the mind, but reflects our overall experience as embodied beings (e.g., Fusaroli and Morgagni 2013; Geeraerts 2006; Gibbs 2006; Lakoff and Johnson 1980, 1999; see Gibbs 2013 for an evaluation of conceptual metaphor theory). There are at least two main aspects to the broad experiential grounding of linguistic meaning in which Cognitive Linguistics is especially interested, as Geeraerts (2006: 5) points out:

> First, we are embodied beings, not pure minds. Our organic nature influences our experience of the world, and this experience is reflected in the language we use … Second … we are not just biological entities: we also have a cultural and social identity, and our language may reveal that identity, i.e. languages may embody the historical and cultural experience of groups of speakers (and individuals).

Indeed, the findings of cognitive linguistic studies have shown that human minds are embodied in the cultural world, and human meaning, feeling, and thinking are largely rooted in bodily and sociocultural experiences. It is argued that 'all cognition is embodied in cultural situations' (Gibbs 1999: 156). While manifesting embodied cognition, language is after all a cultural form and should be studied in its social and cultural context, as conceptualizations underlying language and language use are largely formed and informed by cultural systems (Palmer 1996). These claims by cognitive linguists about human cognition embodied in its sociocultural context, as reflected in language, will be illustrated by some linguistic examples from Chinese in comparison and contrast with English.

(1) a. *zui-ying*   *shou-ruan*
     mouth-tough   hands-soft
     'talk tough but act soft'

   b. *yan-gao*   *shou-di*
     eye-high   hands-low
     'have great ambition but little ability; have sharp eyes in criticizing others but clumsy hands in doing things oneself'

Both of these idiomatic expressions with body-part terms are formed via metaphor and metonymy grounded in our immediate bodily experience, especially with respect to the structure of our body and the functions the parts of our body perform. Thus, in (1a), *zui* 'mouth' stands for talking and *shou* 'hands' for acting, both metonymically. With the two body-part nouns in combination with the two adjectives appealing to the sense of touch, the expression as a whole refers metaphorically to some people's inability or unwillingness to back up in deeds ('hands-soft') their tough talk in words ('mouth-tough'). Example (1b) also contains *shou* 'hands' as well as *yan* 'eyes'. This expression describes, again metaphorically, the inconsistencies of people whose ability does not match their ambition, or who are too critical of others' ability while they themselves are not capable at all. Our eyes set goals, and our hands act to achieve those goals. While we can 'aim high' with our eyes, our aim may be too high for us to 'reach' with our hands. Both examples show how human bodily experience works its way up to shape abstract concepts in human cognition and language (see Yu 2009b).

A contrastive case that exemplifies differences in the shaping of the body by cultural models lies in the fundamental difference between Western and Chinese (along with some other Asian) cultures in the conceptualization of 'person'. This difference can be expressed by two formulas:

(2) a. Western: PERSON = BODY + MIND
     b. Chinese: PERSON = BODY + HEART

These formulas can then be further illustrated as shown in Figure 16.1.

As shown in Figure 16.1, the Western conceptualization of 'person' is dualistic in that a person is 'split' into two distinct and separate parts: the body and the mind. This mind–body dichotomy defines Cartesian dualism, which has been the dominant philosophical view in the West for hundreds of years. According to this dualism, however, the mind does have an interactive site – the pineal gland in the head – where it connects and interacts with the body. In contrast to the Western dualistic view, Chinese takes on a more holistic view that sees the heart as the center of both emotions and thought. In the traditional Chinese conceptualization, therefore, although a person also consists of two parts – the body and the heart (*xin*), these two are however not separate, the latter being an integral part of the former. According to this cultural conceptualization, the heart is regarded as the central faculty of cognition (see Yu 2009a). The contrast outlined above characterizes two cultural traditions that have developed different conceptualizations of person, self, and agent of cognition.

Reflecting Cartesian dualism in the West, as Wierzbicka (1989, 1992) points out, the present-day English word *mind* is basically free of emotions and morally neutral, but instead has the predominantly intellectual and rational orientation, with a modern emphasis on thinking and

Figure 16.1 The difference between Western and Chinese cultures in the conceptualization of 'person'

knowing, not on feeling, wanting, or any other nonbodily processes. Thus, present-day *mind* displays the following characteristics in collocation:

(3) a. ★ *a happy mind* (emotional)
     b. ★ *a fiery mind* (emotional)
     c. ★ *a noble mind* (moral)
     d. ★ *an ignoble mind* (moral)
     e. *an inquisitive mind* (seeking knowledge)
     f. *an inquiring mind* (seeking knowledge)
     g. *a brilliant mind* (good at thinking)
     h. *a keen mind* (active in thinking and seeking to know)
     i. *a good mind* (intellectual)

As is shown, *mind* cannot be in collocation with adjectives of emotion and moral (3a–d). Instead, it can only combine with adjectives related to thought, knowledge, and intellect (3e–i).

In contrast, the Chinese concept of 'heart', because the heart is traditionally conceptualized as the central faculty of cognition, is lexicalized in a great number of compounds and idioms related to all cognitive and affective aspects of a human person, such as mental, intellectual, rational, moral, emotional, dispositional, and so on. The Chinese expressions in the list below (accompanied by literal translations in the parentheses next to them) are just some examples, where their English equivalents are provided in a separate column for comparison and contrast:

(4) **Chinese**   **English**

	Chinese	English
a.	*cheng-xin* (sincere-heart)	*sincerity*
b.	*liang-xin* (good-heart)	*conscience*
c.	*zhi-xin* (knowing-heart)	*intimate; understanding (friend)*
d.	*xin-xiang* (heart-think)	*think to oneself*
e.	*xin-fu* (be heart-convinced)	*be genuinely convinced*
f.	*xin-gan* (be heart-willing)	*be willing*
g.	*hao-xin* (good-heart)	*good intention*
h.	*cheng-xin* (establish-heart)	*on purpose*
i.	*yong-xin* (use-heart)	*with concentrated attention*
j.	*jue-xin* (determined-heart)	*determination; be determined*
k.	*wei-xin* (disobey/violate-heart)	*against one's will*
l.	*heng-xin* (constant-heart)	*perseverance; persistence*
m.	*xiao-xin* (small-heart)	*be careful; be cautious*
n.	*cu-xin* (thick-heart)	*careless; thoughtless*
o.	*jiao-xin* (scorch-heart)	*feel terribly worried*
p.	*kai-xin* (open-heart)	*feel happy*
q.	*xin-zui* (be heart-drunk)	*be charmed; be enchanted*

This list can go on and on. The difference in lexicalization may suggest differing views in the interpretation of the workings of the body and its heart organ in particular and how they are related to the 'mind' in the conceptualization of the person. The Chinese compound words point to an embodied view of 'mind', but this embodiment is situated in the context of Chinese culture that traditionally holds that the heart is the central faculty of cognition (see Yu 2009a).

As a way to help the understanding of the concept of socioculturally situated embodiment, readers are referred to Sharifian *et al.* (2008), which presents an interesting case where different cultures traditionally locate the functions of the human mind in different regions of the human body. That is, the languages studied show abdomen-centring, heart-centring, and/or head-centring conceptualizations of the mind. Thus

> cultural models of the mind and more scientific approaches in philosophy and/or medicine have in various cultures invoked central parts of the human body as the locus of the mind. The major loci have been the abdomen region, the heart region and the head region or, more particularly, the brain region. These three types of conceptualizations can be labelled 'abdominocentrism', 'cardiocentrism', and 'cerebrocentrism' (or 'cephalocentrism'), respectively.
>
> *(Sharifian* et al. *2008: 3–4)*

Specifically, as the studies presented in the chapters of the book show, the 'abdomen-centring' languages include Basque, Indonesian, Kuuk Thaayorre, and Malay; the 'heart-centring' languages include Chinese, Japanese, and Korean; and the dualistic 'heart/head-centring' languages include Dutch, English, Northeastern Neo-Aramaic, Persian, and Tunisian Arabic. The volume makes a collective attempt to explore (a) the ways in which internal body organs have been employed in different languages to conceptualize human experiences such as emotions and/or workings of the mind, and (b) the cultural models that appear to account for the observed similarities as well as differences of the various conceptualizations of internal body organs.

5 Future directions

Based on the preceding sections, this section outlines, from a cognitive linguistic perspective, a couple of directions in which future research on embodiment may be developed. First, there needs to be more studies on the role of culture in the triangular relationship among body, mind, and culture in the embodiment hypothesis which intrigues the second-generation scientists. After decades of effort, there is now much evidence available on the decisive way in which the body shapes the mind, but it is still less known as to how culture mediates this process. Particularly, research that shows more global differences that fundamentally characterize different cultural traditions and civilizations is called for. Studies of this kind (e.g., differences between dualism and holism, among 'abdominocentrism', 'cardiocentrism', and 'cerebrocentrism', touched upon in the preceding section) have the potential of uncovering and unearthing certain deep root causes for intercultural miscommunications, or even ethnical conflicts, among various linguistic groups on a global scale, and of promoting and facilitating harmony and peace among various cultural groups in a global context.

Another related factor that needs further studying is the role of language in the picture of embodiment and culture. As shown in Example (4) in the preceding section, for instance, Chinese has a great number of such idiomatic expressions (compounds, idioms, and proverbs) that manifest a cultural conceptualization of the heart as the central faculty of cognition as well as a particular holistic view of the relationship between mind and body (see Yu 2009b). These linguistic expressions are deeply entrenched, conventionalized over time from the ancient sources of Chinese philosophy and medicine. They are sediments at the bottom of a cultural history, having formed and accumulated through a long cultural tradition of thousands of years. As such, they are by necessity culturally based, and are really inconsistent with, or even contradictory to, modern scientific knowledge. However, because they permeate Chinese discourse about inner lives and mental and emotional experiences, such entrenched expressions may have been acquired unreflectively by Chinese people because of their repeated use on a daily basis. After all, entrenched ways of speaking that are employed unreflectively by far outlives any change in conscious knowledge, and cultural beliefs and scientific knowledge make sense at different levels of human consciousness. It would be interesting to study how human language, with particular linguistic structures and expressions, affect human cognition, along the line of a lighter version of linguistic relativity.

6 Conclusion

From the viewpoint of Cultural Linguistics, this chapter has surveyed some literature on embodied cognition both within the area of Cognitive Linguistics and beyond. In particular, it has focused on the relationship between embodiment and culture and its revelation in language. The central idea is that embodiment is always situated in its sociocultural context. That is, fundamentally, the human body shapes the way humans think and talk because what they perceive and do through the sensorimotor systems of their bodies sets up the contours of what they know and understand. At the same time, however, the way humans think and talk cannot escape the impact of their physical and cultural environment, which constitutes human experience in a fundamental way.

Embodied cognitive science is paying increasing attention to the determining force dynamics of the environment, as well as the body and brain, on the human mind. In his 2010 book *The New Science of the Mind: From Extended Mind to Embodied Phenomenology*, Rowlands elaborates on the *4e* conception of the mind: i.e., the mind is *embodied, embedded, enacted,* and *extended.* According to Rowlands (2010: 3), this new way of thinking about the mind is inspired by, and organized around, not the brain but some combination of the four notions of mental processes. First of all, mental processes are *embodied* in that they are partly constituted by, partly made up of, wider (i.e., extraneural) bodily structures and processes. Second, mental processes are *embedded* in that they have been designed to function only in tandem with a certain environment that lies outside the brain of the subject. In the absence of the right environmental scaffolding, mental processes cannot do what they are supposed to do, or can only do what they are supposed to do less than optimally. Thirdly, mental processes are *enacted* in that they are made up not just of neural processes but also of things that the organism does more generally – that they are constituted in part by the ways in which an organism acts on the world and in which the world also acts back on that organism. Lastly, mental processes are *extended* in that they are not located exclusively inside an organism's head but extend out, in various ways, into the organism's environment. It is claimed that at least some cognitive processes are partly composed of environmental processes.

As can be seen, the essence of this *4e* conception is a path by which the mind has been extended into the body, and then through the body into the environment. That is also the path to follow in the study of the relationship between embodiment and culture.

Related topics

culture and emotional language; language, culture, and prototypicality; language, culture and colour; space, time and space–time: metaphors, maps, and fusions; language, culture, and spatial cognition; cultural linguistics; a future agenda for research on language and culture

Further reading

Frank, R.M., Dirven, R., Ziemke, T., and Bernárdez, E. (eds) (2008) *Body, Language and Mind, Volume 2: Sociocultural Situatedness* (Cognitive Linguistics Research, vol. 35.2), Berlin and New York: Mouton de

Gruyter. (The second volume of a two-volume set introduces and elaborates upon the concept of sociocultural situatedness, understood broadly as the way in which minds and cognitive processes are shaped by their interaction with culturally contextualized structures and practices.)

Gibbs, R.W. (2006) *Embodiment and Cognitive Science*, Cambridge: Cambridge University Press. (This book explores how people's subjective, felt experiences of their bodies in action provide part of the fundamental grounding for human cognition and language.)

Maalej, Z.A. and Yu, N. (eds) (2011) *Embodiment via Body Parts: Studies from Various Languages and Cultures* (Human Cognitive Processing, vol. 31), Amsterdam and Philadelphia: Benjamins. (This volume addresses the question regarding what specific roles individual body parts play in the embodied conceptualizations of emotions, mental faculties, character traits, cultural values, and so on in various cultures, as manifested in their respective languages.)

Sharifian, F., Dirven, R., Yu, N. and Niemeier, S. (eds) (2008) *Culture, Body, and Language: Conceptualizations of Internal Body Organs across Cultures and Languages* (Applications of Cognitive Linguistics, vol. 7), Berlin and New York: Mouton de Gruyter. (The studies in this volume explore how across various cultures internal body organs such as the heart have been used as the locus of conceptualizing mental functions such as feelings, thinking, and knowing.)

Yu, N. (2009) *The Chinese HEART in a Cognitive Perspective: Culture, Body, and Language* (Applications of Cognitive Linguistics, vol. 12). Berlin and New York: Mouton de Gruyter. (This book is a study of Chinese conceptualizations of the heart, traditionally seen as the central faculty of cognition. It shows how the concept of 'heart' lies at the core of Chinese thought and medicine, and its importance to Chinese culture is extensively manifested in the Chinese language.)

Yu, N. (2009) *From Body to Meaning in Culture: Papers on Cognitive Semantic Studies of Chinese*, Amsterdam and Philadelphia: Benjamins. (This collection of essays looks at the relationship between language, body, culture, and cognition. In particular, it looks into the embodied nature of human language and cognition as arising from and situated in the cultural environment.)

Ziemke, T., Zlatev, J, and Frank, R.M (eds) (2007) *Body, Language and Mind, Volume 1: Embodiment* (Cognitive Linguistics Research, vol. 35.1), Berlin and New York: Mouton de Gruyter. (The first volume of a two-volume set focuses on the concept of embodiment, understood in most general terms as the bodily basis of phenomena such as meaning, mind, cognition and language.)

References

Blacking, J. (1977) 'Towards an anthropology of the body', in J. Blacking (ed.) *The Anthropology of the Body*, London: Academic Press, pp. 1–28.

Damasio, A.R. (1994) *Descartes' Error: Emotion, Reason, and the Human Brain*, New York: Grosset & Putnam.

Frank, R.M., Dirven, R., Ziemke, T., and Bernárdez, E. (eds) (2008) *Body, Language and Mind, Volume 2: Sociocultural Situatedness* (Cognitive Linguistics Research, vol. 35.2), Berlin and New York: Mouton de Gruyter.

Fusaroli, R. and Morgagni, S. (eds) (2013) A Special Issue on 'Conceptual Metaphor Theory: Thirty Years After', *Journal of Cognitive Semiotics* 5 (1/2).

Gallagher, S. (2005) *How the Body Shapes the Mind*, Oxford and New York: Oxford University Press.

Geeraerts, D. (2006) 'Introduction: A rough guide to Cognitive Linguistics', in D. Geeraerts (ed.) *Cognitive Linguistics: Basic Readings*, Berlin and New York: Mouton de Gruyter, pp.1–28.

Gibbs, R.W. (1999) 'Taking metaphor out of our heads and putting it into the cultural world', in R.W. Gibbs and G.J. Steen (eds) *Metaphor in Cognitive Linguistics*, Amsterdam and Philadelphia: Benjamins, pp. 145–66.

——(2006) *Embodiment and Cognitive Science*, Cambridge: Cambridge University Press.

——(2013) 'Why do some people dislike conceptual metaphor theory?' *Journal of Cognitive Semiotics* 5 (1/2): 14–36.

Johnson, M. (1987) *The Body in the Mind: The Bodily Basis of Meaning, Imagination, and Reason*, Chicago, IL: University of Chicago Press.

Johnson, M., and Rohrer, T. (2007) 'We are live creatures: Embodiment, American Pragmatism and the cognitive organism', in T. Ziemke, J. Zlatev and R.M. Frank (eds) *Body, Language and Mind, Volume 1: Embodiment*, Berlin and New York: Mouton de Gruyter, pp. 18–54.

Kuriyama, S. (2002) *The Expressiveness of the Body and the Divergence of Greek and Chinese Medicine*, New York: Zone Books.

Lakoff, G. and Johnson, M. (1980) *Metaphors We Live By*, Chicago, IL: University of Chicago Press.

——(1999) *Philosophy in the Flesh: The Embodied Mind and Its Challenge to Western Thought*, New York: Basic Books.

Lindblom, J. and Ziemke, T. (2007) 'Embodiment and social interaction: A cognitive science perspective', in T. Ziemke, J. Zlatev and R.M. Frank (eds) *Body, Language and Mind, Volume 1: Embodiment*, Berlin and New York: Mouton de Gruyter, pp. 129–63.

Maalej, Z. (2008) 'The heart and cultural embodiment in Tunisian Arabic', in F. Sharifian, R. Dirven, N. Yu and S. Niemeier (eds) *Culture, Body, and Language: Conceptualisations of Internal Body Organs across Cultures and Languages*, Berlin and New York: Mouton de Gruyter, pp. 395–428.

Maalej, Z.A. and Yu, N. (eds) (2011) *Embodiment via Body Parts: Studies from Various Languages and Cultures* (Human Cognitive Processing, vol. 31), Amsterdam and Philadelphia: Benjamins.

O'Neill, J. (1985) *Five Bodies: The Human Shape of Modern Society*, Ithaca, NY: Cornell University Press.

Palmer, G.B. (1996) *Toward a Theory of Cultural Linguistics*, Austin, TX: University of Texas Press.

Pires de Oliveira, R. and Bittencourt, R.S. (2007) 'An interview with Mark Johnson and Tim Rohrer: From neurons to sociocultural situatedness', in R.M. Frank, R. Dirven, T. Ziemke and E. Bernárdez (eds) *Body, Language and Mind, Volume 2: Sociocultural Situatedness*, Berlin and New York: Mouton de Gruyter, pp. 21–51.

Rowlands, M. (2010) *The New Science of the Mind: From Extended Mind to Embodied Phenomenology*, Cambridge, MA: MIT Press.

Semin, G.R. and Smith, E.R. (2008) 'Introducing embodied grounding', in G.R. Semin and E.R. Smith (eds) *Embodied Grounding: Social Cognitive, Affective, and Neuroscientific Approaches*, Cambridge: Cambridge University Press, pp. 1–5.

Sharifian, F., Dirven, R., Yu, N. and Niemeier, S. (eds) (2008) *Culture, Body, and Language: Conceptualizations of Internal Body Organs across Cultures and Languages* (Applications of Cognitive Linguistics, vol. 7), Berlin and New York: Mouton de Gruyter.

Shore, B. (1996) *Culture in Mind: Cognition, Culture, and the Problem of Meaning*, New York and Oxford: Oxford University Press.

Strathern, A. (1996) *Body Thoughts*, Ann Arbor, MI: University of Michigan Press.

Synnott, A. (1993) *The Body Social: Symbolism, Self, and Society*, London and New York: Routledge.

Violi, P. (2008) 'Beyond the body: Towards a full embodied semiosis', in R.M. Frank, R. Dirven, T. Ziemke, and E. Bernárdez (eds) *Body, Language and Mind, Volume 2: Sociocultural Situatedness* (Cognitive Linguistics Research, vol. 35.2), Berlin and New York: Mouton de Gruyter, pp. 53–76.

Wierzbicka, A. (1989) 'Soul and mind: Linguistic evidence for ethnopsychology and cultural history', *American Anthropologist*, 91: 1–41.

——(1992) *Semantics, Culture, and Cognition: Human Concepts in Culture-specific Configurations*, New York and Oxford: Oxford University Press.

Yu, N. (2009a) *The Chinese HEART in a Cognitive Perspective: Culture, Body, and Language* (Applications of Cognitive Linguistics, vol. 12). Berlin and New York: Mouton de Gruyter.

——(2009b) *From Body to Meaning in Culture: Papers on Cognitive Semantic Studies of Chinese*, Amsterdam and Philadelphia: Benjamins.

Ziemke, T., Zlatev, J, and Frank, R.M (eds) (2007) *Body, Language and Mind, Volume 1: Embodiment* (Cognitive Linguistics Research, vol. 35.1), Berlin and New York: Mouton de Gruyter.

17

CULTURE AND LANGUAGE PROCESSING

Crystal J. Robinson and Jeanette Altarriba

Introduction

One of the primary means through which we communicate our knowledge, ideas, thoughts, and beliefs is through language. Increasingly, the world has become more and more linguistically diverse, not only in terms of the number of languages that we know of and are aware of, but in terms of the richness of those languages and the degree to which individuals master and use more than one language (Altarriba and Heredia 2008). Yet linguistic knowledge rarely lives devoid of the influence of the cultural context in which it is used. The question that has been at once at the forefront and the backdrop of the study of language and communication has been whether or not language influences thought or, the other way around (see e.g., Carroll 1956). However, it is important to bear in mind that this question assumes that culture is not a moderating variable in that relationship. Culture, for the purpose of this chapter, refers to sociocultural context that may be affecting or affected by language use, form, and function. Yet, the works reviewed in the current chapter underscore the importance of understanding the delicate interplay between language, culture, and cognition, and understanding to what degree the former variables influence the latter and under what conditions.

The following sections begin with an overview of the basic theories related to the interplay between language and thought (e.g., linguistic relativity; thinking for speaking) followed by a discussion of the development of cognitive abilities in bilinguals and monolinguals. Research detailing the influence of these two main variables on creative thinking is reviewed next, followed by a discussion of social behaviour as influenced by cultural scripts, beliefs, and contexts. Emotion and memory also play a role in moderating forms of communication – for example, the use of particular words, reflection on one's past experiences, and consideration of language that is considered 'taboo' within a particular cultural group. A final summary is included in the Appendix at the end of the chapter. The aim of the present work is to underscore the notion that both language *and* culture should be considered in the overall analysis of behaviour, given the ways in which they are intertwined and interlinked in everyday cognitive processing.

Language and thought: the basic theories

Linguistic relativity

It is easy to see why the degree and direction to which language, culture, and thought are related is a question that has, and continues to, plague various disciplines, including Cognitive

Psychology. The linguistic relativity hypothesis (Sapir–Whorf hypothesis) attempts to connect various aspects of language to the way we process information. The principle of linguistic relativity assumes that the structure of language affects the ways in which speakers perceive and conceptualize their world (Carroll 1956; Casasanto 2008; Lucy and Gaskins 2003; see Chapter 2 this volume). The goal of researchers who ascribe to this hypothesis is to determine how we interpret and classify reality depending upon the language(s) we speak. Several scholars have worked on operationalizing the hypothesis, keeping empiricism central to the question. In the strictest sense, this hypothesis suggests that language has a direct influence on thought, but makes very little mention of culture.

In relation to linguistic relativity, various studies have investigated the effect of grammatical number on the categorization of countable objects. A countable object refers to anything that has distinct number quantities (e.g., one book, two books, three books). Grammatical number refers to the way a language differentiates between singular and plural nouns. Languages such as Japanese and Yucatec do not require grammatical markers for the cognitive category of additive plurals. In other words, you cannot always tell whether the noun or object being referred to is singular or plural by the form of the noun (Athanasopoulos and Aveledo 2012). This is particularly clear between speakers of English and Yucatec. John Lucy (1992) found that English speakers could attend to changes in countable objects more readily than could Yucatec speakers in non-verbal picture tasks. Specifically, participants were asked to make similarity judgements on a series of pictures with varying numbers of certain countable objects. Scores were calculated to show each individual's relative sensitivity to the specific number of people and animals, implements, and substances, respectively.

Like object classification, colour categorization is also representative of the way language affects our cognitive processes. A great deal of research on the way we categorize colours in various languages, and as a result, process colour-related stimuli has been conducted in attempts to validate the linguistic relativity hypothesis. The various ways a language partitions the colour space can affect the language user's perceptions and memory for colour-related experiences, and the perceived noticeable difference between colours (Chiu 2011). Kay and Kempton (1984) found that when using colour terms, the subsequent memory is influenced by the specific terms used. A similar pattern of results was found when examining the difference between English and Berinmo, the language of a small tribe of hunter-gatherers that live along the Sepik River in Papua New Guinea. Berinmo, similar to Tarahumara, does not contain specific terms that distinguish between blue and green (Roberson, Davies, and Davidoff 2000). The depth of this colour processing is brought into question when verbal interference is introduced to the experimental design. The results of these verbal interference studies are better accounted for in Slobin's (1996) thinking for speaking hypothesis, which will be discussed in the following section.

Thinking for speaking and conceptual transfer

Slobin (1996) revised the traditional linguistic relativity hypothesis with the thinking for speaking hypothesis. This hypothesis states that speakers are bound by the available expressions within the language in which they are working in when attempting to communicate a concept. Thus, speakers must select language specific ways of conceptualizing reality when in the process of speaking (Athanasopoulos and Aveledo 2012). This hypothesis confines the effects of language to language-specific cognitive processes, and becomes evident when the role of verbal interference on colour categorization and processing is taken into account. It was found that as a result of this interference, the effect of overestimating the perceptual difference between blue and green disappeared in English speakers (Roberson and Davidoff 2000).

These results indicate that cognitive differences only occur when linguistic information is being used directly within the task (see also Regier, Kay, and Khetarpal 2007; Roberson, Pak, and Hanley 2008).

Bylund and Jarvis (2011) further modified the thinking for speaking hypothesis (Slobin 1996) with their conceptual transfer hypothesis, noting that speakers of different languages have different patterns of conceptualization. They also added that these patterns could be transferred from one language to another, drawing specific attention to the possibility of differences between language speakers arising not only as a result of grammar and syntax, but also as a result of sociocultural or biological influences. The formation of this hypothesis was in part due to research concerning the way motion events are processed, depending upon the grammatical characteristics of the language employed during processing. The processing of motion events refers to whether events are typically viewed as oriented towards endpoints, or as ongoing processes. This is generally dependent upon whether the language is considered to be an *aspect* language or not, with an aspect language defined as one which focuses on the continuity of events rather than strict endpoints (Athanasopoulos and Aveledo 2012).

Bylund and Jarvis (2011) found that when Spanish (aspect language) and Swedish (non-aspect language) bilinguals were asked to describe a set of scenes in Spanish, focusing on the movement of the action within the scene, participants with a greater level of Swedish proficiency tended to describe the action within the scene in a way that focused on the end points of the action. However, participants who were less proficient in Swedish tended to continue defocusing the end points of the action, representing motion as continuous within the scene. Perhaps the most interesting aspect of these findings is the degree to which the grammatical conventions in one language affect processing in another language, with opposite conventions (see Schmiedtová, von Stutterheim, and Carroll 2011 for a recent review of similar results). This makes a clear argument for the necessity of studying the bilingual speaker as a unique language user.

Bilingualism and language processing

Athanasopoulos and Aveledo (2012) pointed out that linguistic relativity manifests itself differently in bilinguals than in monolinguals due to the impact of two separate mental lexicons on cognitive functioning. Bilinguals have been identified as unique language users with a complete language system separate from that of language one (L1) and language two (L2), and that the L2 user is an independent communicator as opposed to an imperfect version of the native monolingual ideal (Cook 2003). Most of the research has thus far focused on colour categorization, grammatical number and object, emotion-word processing, and memory. Bilingualism appears to affect these cognitive domains in a varying and disparate manner. The main purpose of the studies within this domain is to question the degree to which bilingual mental representations depend upon the linguistic and cultural context of the speaker, and whether these representations are based upon L1, L2, or a unique synthesis of the two. Green (1998) argued that the process of conceptualization must be language specific, and that bilinguals' conceptualization is dependent upon proficiency in each of the two languages. Green also suggested that bilinguals use languages differentially, depending upon occasion and purpose, placing an emphasis on the cultural impact of the linguistic setting. The majority of the empirical findings up to this point suggest that transfer occurs at the conceptual level. However, this transfer may be due to a result of both linguistic and cultural shift.

When studies regarding grammatical number were extended to Japanese–English bilinguals, the bilinguals were not as efficient at attending to changes in number of countable objects as were English monolinguals, but they also did not perform as poorly as the Japanese monolinguals

(Athanasopoulos 2006). These same results were extended to classifying objects based upon shape and material properties. Imai and Gentner (1997) found that speakers of English were more likely to classify objects based upon common shape rather than common material. Speakers of languages such as Yucatec and Japanese exhibit the reverse pattern of results. This is thought to be due to the lack of grammatical difference between mass (e.g., water) and count nouns (e.g., one tree, two trees, three trees) in these languages. It can also be noted that Japanese–English bilinguals who had lived within an English-speaking country for a longer period of time tended to categorize objects more similarly to English monolinguals. This finding could be due to either increased English proficiency or cultural immersion.

Athanasopoulos (2007) attempted to disambiguate linguistic and cultural effects by extending his original study on Japanese–English bilinguals to account for length of stay in L2 country and proficiency within the two languages. He wanted to determine if Japanese–English bilinguals were working with two separate cognitive representations each being used in accordance with the language of the task, or if the linguistic effects on cognition were deeper, and could withstand task instruction in either language. He found that L2 proficiency was the best predictor regardless of length of stay and regardless of task language. This result seems to suggest that language is playing a predominant role over culture in cognitive processing, and that linguistic category shifts occur at the conceptual level. However, these results do not account for the possibility that culture may be encoded within language.

Research on colour categorization in bilinguals also supports this language-dominant, conceptual transfer view of processing. Athanasopoulos (2009) studied the differences between colour similarity judgements in Greek–English bilinguals and English monolinguals. He was interested in the distinction between light and dark blue, as two distinct terms exist for the two shades in the Greek language. He asked all participants to determine how far apart they thought the two colour spaces were from each other, as well as to make a list of all of the colour terms they could think of. He found that length of stay in an English-speaking country was highly predictive of the amount of space participants perceived between light and dark blue, in such a way that bilinguals would judge less perceptual space between the two shades if they had been living in an English-speaking country for two or more years, approximating the English monolingual response pattern. However, it was also evident that participants' similarity judgements were dependent upon the availability of the two separate colour terms. If participants placed the light/dark blue terms high on the list, they maintained the perceptual space between the two shades.

It is important to mention that findings from Tse and Altarriba (2008) were unable to identify differences between monolinguals and bilinguals in the way they process temporal metaphors, or the way in which they express temporal ordering. Based on the findings from Boroditsky (2001), Tse and Altarriba studied the processing of temporal and spatiotemporal metaphors in Chinese and English. Horizontal spatiotemporal metaphors conceptualize time in a before/after fashion (e.g., June comes before August), while vertical spatiotemporal metaphors conceptualize time in an up–down fashion, where up refers to the earlier event, and down the later. A purely temporal description of time would simply label events as early/late or first, second, third, and so on. This description is void of any particular spatial orientation. It is the case that Chinese speakers tend to label events in both a horizontal and a vertical fashion, with a preference for vertical labels, whereas English speakers prefer horizontal labeling. However, when both Chinese–English bilinguals and English monolinguals were asked to determine whether a temporal or spatiotemporal metaphor was either true or false, Tse and Altarriba found no differences in reaction times between the two language groups. This was regardless of whether the participants had been shown a vertical or horizontal spatial prime prior to reading the metaphors, indicating that neither Chinese–English bilinguals nor English monolinguals process temporal and spatiotemporal metaphors in a linguistically constrained fashion. The similarity between the two groups argues specifically against linguistic relativity in bilinguals, supporting the idea that experience within the two languages, as well as cultural factors, such as the pervasiveness of a vertical calendar system in both Eastern and Western cultures, could be playing a role in cognitive processing.

The bilingual benefit

Another question of concern when examining the effects of bilingualism on processing is whether bilingualism benefits or hinders cognition, and whether this is due to two separate competing lexicons, or cultural interactions. Oller and Eilers (2002) have found vocabulary deficits in fluent bilingual children. It has also been seen that bilinguals tend to produce more tip-of-the-tongue states than do monolinguals. In general, it is thought that bilingualism impairs verbal cognitive tasks, such as picture naming, due to the necessity to search through two separate linguistic codes. However, it has been reported that cognitive tasks that rely on an ability to switch between competing alternatives or selectively attend to a singular stimulus are easier for bilinguals than for monolinguals. This is thought to be due to the fact that bilinguals are accustomed to switching between linguistic frames, and this ability to switch between two frames of thought carries over to other cognitive tasks (Kharkhurin 2010).

Although bilingualism tends to hinder verbal abilities, it may positively influence the speaker's ability to attend to conversational norms, resulting in greater understanding. A recent study on bilingualism and conversational understanding attempted to answer the question of whether bilingual children excel in their sensitivity to conversational rules in comparison to monolinguals (Siegal, Iozzi, and Surian 2009). The study made use of Italian and Slovenian monolinguals, along with Slovenian–Italian bilinguals from the ages of 3 to 6. The main goal of the study was to see if the bilingual children were better able to identify when a conversational maxim, or rule, had been violated. The children were shown a twenty-five-minute video that depicted one character asking two other characters simple questions. Each of the two other characters would give a separate response, and the child was asked to identify which character had said something silly or rude. The violated maxims in the video were based on conversational properties such as efficiency, honesty, relevance, clarity, and politeness. The children were also tested on vocabulary and executive functioning. Vocabulary was determined through a standard picture-naming task in both Slovenian and Italian. Executive functioning was assessed using a card sort and day–night task, which required the shifting of attentional focus. The study demonstrated a bilingual advantage in all areas except in the case of determining the redundancy of a statement. The authors attributed this finding to cultural factors. The study also found no difference in executive functioning between the groups of participants, indicating that the bilingual advantage could not be due to overall higher executive functioning. It could be argued that this advantage is due to cultural factors that produce a bias favoring bilinguals, such as growing up in a household which supports openness to dialogues with others, as is suggested by parents taking the initiative to send their children to bilingual schools. The authors discount this possibility by stating that Slovenians tend to learn Italian in order to advance their social status in society. Although studies such as these produce interesting results, it would be necessary to study this effect in bilinguals who speak two languages that are not as socially intertwined as Italian and Slovenian. It would also be interesting to see if these results persist between two linguistically similar languages such as Spanish and Italian. The following few sections will more closely examine the cultural impact on cognitive processing in relation to language.

The culture–language interaction

Creativity across cultures

Creative abilities tend to differ between bilinguals and monolinguals as a result of the bilingual's ability to switch between two linguistic frames of thought (Kharkhurin 2010). However, culture specific factors may be influencing creative potential as well. Kharkhurin and Samadpour Motalleebi (2008) examined the effect of sociocultural environment on creative potential, noting that people from different cultures maintain different concepts of what constitutes creativity. This study looked at Russian, Iranian, and American monolinguals' scores on the Abbreviated Torrance Test for Adults. This test is comprised of three separate tasks, problem identification, picture completion, and picture construction. The problem identification task asks for an individual to generate as many possible problems that may arise in a given situation. This task relies on verbal creative abilities. The picture completion task gives two incomplete figures and asks for the individual to create as many drawings as possible from the two figures. This task, along with the picture construction task, relies on non-verbal creative abilities. The picture construction task asks the individual to create as many pictures as possible from a 3 x 3 matrix of identical triangles.

Due to the high value that Western cultures place on originality, and the fact that the Torrance Task operationalizes creativity as being, in part, due to originality of responses, it was suspected that American monolinguals would outperform Iranian and Russian monolinguals. The results indicated that Iranians scored lower than Americans and Russians, with Americans out-performing Russians. The Russian results were thought to be due to movement away from traditional collectivist (community-based) ideals, towards more westernized (individual-focused) ideals. These findings show a clear relationship between culture and cognitive processing, making note of how language has been shown to impact culture and cultural processing. As will be seen in the following section, specific grammatical aspects of language may also be affecting this cultural processing.

Social structure and pronouns

Unlike colour categorization and grammatical number, it has been found that the linguistic system of pronouns (e.g., I, you, them, etc.) may encode self-view within a culture. The use of pronouns draws attention to the referent of the particular pronoun, thereby bringing the person out from the backdrop of the conversation and forward as a focal point. Languages like English require the use of first and second person pronouns (e.g., *I* am working), while languages like Spanish allow them to be omitted (e.g., *estoy trabajando* instead of *Yo estoy trabajando*) by making use of verb inflections, or forms of the verb that indicate the subject without needing to make use of the pronoun. Other languages, such as Chinese do not require the use of first and second person pronouns even though the subject cannot be assumed through verb inflection. In languages such as Chinese, the use of a pronoun is determined to be obligatory depending upon whether self and addressee must be made salient within the context of the conversation. This grammatical distinction has been linked to levels of individualism (the tendency for a culture to be more focused on the successes, goals, needs, and desires of the individual) and collectivism (the tendency for a culture to be more focused on the successes, goals, needs, and desires of the community), exhibiting a clear interconnectivity between language and culture (Kashima and Kashima 2003). These findings exemplify one of the ways in which language is reflective of cultural values and behaviours. The manner in which these values are invoked by the linguistic environment will be discussed next.

Shared experiences

Language can be used to encode experiences, particularly shared experiences within a culture, such as a mass exodus or tragic event. Language also carries with it the shared experiences of cultural tales and customs. These shared experiences can be automatically activated when processing information in a particular language. The impact of shared experiences is particularly interesting from the bilingual perspective, as it helps to indicate the degree to which the language specific context evokes cultural ideals (Chiu 2011). It has been found that bilinguals express their attitudes towards a particular ethnic culture differently when being tested in the language of that ethnic culture, than when being tested in their second language. In one set of studies, researchers used the Implicit Association Test (IAT), where participants rapidly categorized words that flash on a computer screen or are played through headphones. The researchers administered the IAT in two different settings: once in Morocco, with bilinguals in Arabic and French, and again in the US with Latinos who speak both English and Spanish. In Morocco, participants who took the IAT in Arabic showed greater preference for other Moroccans. When they took the test in French, that difference disappeared. Similarly, in the US, participants who took the test in Spanish showed a greater preference for other Hispanics. In English, that preference disappeared (Ogunnaike, Dunham, and Banaji 2010). In both of these cases, task language may serve as an implicit prime, activating cultural attitudes.

To further make the case for the impact of culture on processing, Earle (1969) studied the differences in dogmatism, or degree to which long-held beliefs are regarded as true regardless of contrary evidence, between English monolinguals and Chinese–English bilinguals. An increase in the degree to which participants thought their beliefs to be true was found in Chinese–English bilinguals when responding in Chinese as opposed to English. When responding in English, the Chinese–English bilinguals responded that they felt less strongly about long-held beliefs in a fashion that was similar to the degree to which English monolinguals felt their beliefs to be true. Earle assumed these results were due to the highly dogmatized and authoritarian experience of living within Chinese culture. It is interesting to note that these results indicate that the language itself is interacting with culture in a dynamic fashion, such that a cultural shift occurs as a result of a linguistic shift. These implicit attitudes and ideals can be conceptualized as a product of memory for particular events within a cultural context. The impact of these memories on cognitive processing is highly dependent upon the language in which these memories are encoded. The following sections will deal specifically with these issues.

The role of memory in language mediated tasks

Thus far, this chapter has focused primarily on the specific features of a language's grammar and function, particularly in reference to the extent to which they impact various mental processes, and the extent to which culture may be playing a role in informing these observed differences between language speakers. Athanasopoulos and Aveledo (2012) suggest that memory may be playing a key role in many of these processes. They derive this from the 'language as strategy' hypothesis which states that language is employed to facilitate performance in cognitively demanding situations by holding events in working memory while the task at hand is performed and processed. This is made evident through studies that block the participant's ability to use language as a mediator by asking them to repeat non-sense syllables, or processes other task-irrelevant language information. Under these conditions, it is seen that language specific differences diminish or completely disappear. The following sections will focus on the way memory mediates cognitive processes within and between languages, relying a great deal on research from within the field of bilingualism. The role of emotion and emotion-word processing in memory will be considered as a heavily influencing factor.

Autobiographical memory and shared experiences

Memories for personal life events are just as easily influenced by the cultural environment in which they are encoded as the linguistic environment. Wang (2011) points to the constructive nature of memory within culture. Wang and Ross (2005) found that when being primed to focus temporarily on their unique personal self, European and Asian American adults recalled self-focused memories rather than memories dependent upon social interactions. When participants received a relational self prime, the pattern of results reversed. As a follow-up, Wang, Shao, and Li (2010) found that speaking English led to a focus on autonomy when describing the self and personal life events. Participants retrieved memories with detail oriented towards the self. When speaking Chinese, participants focused on relationship networks and social roles during retrieval.

Similar studies involving Polish–Danish bilinguals find culture to be a strongly influencing factor in autobiographical memory. This same effect was found in participants who fled from Poland to Denmark. Ten participants who fled Poland at an average age of 24, and ten participants who fled Poland at an average age of 34 were examined. Among both groups, autobiographical memories from before immigration were more frequently retrieved and reported in Polish, whereas the opposite pattern occurred for memories after immigration. Between the two groups, early migrators reported that more of their current inner speech was in Danish. This is thought to be due to the longer amount of time they had spent in Denmark, as compared to the later migrators (Larsen, Schrauf, Fromholt, and Rubin 2002). Memories which are encoded in a specific language tend to carry with them emotional context. The effect this has on emotion and memory processing across languages and cultures will be discussed in the following sections.

Language, emotion, and memory

Emotion and emotion-word processing are receiving an increasingly large amount of attention within the realm of Cognitive Psychology and language research for various reasons. First, with regards to Cognitive Psychology, it has been seen that emotion words tend to be processed differently from abstract and concrete words (Altarriba, Bauer, and Benvenuto 1999), indicating that they play a specific, and perhaps, independent role in language processing, particularly, memory. Furthermore, differences in emotion-word processing across languages have been examined, leading to insight as to whether cultural factors, linguistic factors, or a dynamic interaction between the two are playing a key role in cognitive processing (Altarriba 2003). Studying emotion processing from the bilingual perspective allows for an examination of both the influence of language in culture by taking into account a language speaker's interaction within each of the linguistic settings and corresponding cultures. It can be the case that meaning representation of a particular word in L1 can completely overlap, partially overlap, or exhibit no similarities with meaning representations of that same word in L2 (de Groot 1992). Emotion processing differences with regards to memory and cognitive processes will be examined in the following sections in reference to the relative impact of cultural and linguistic factors.

Differences between cultures in emotion processing

Differences between language speakers with regards to emotion processing can be seen as a result of cultural regulations and the relationship between a person and others as well as, the way emotions and emotion events are represented in the specific language. Subtle differences in the meanings of emotion words between languages may be a potentially influencing factor on processing. Semin, Gorts, Nandram, and Semin-Goossens (2002) examined how people in various cultures talk about emotions and emotion events, reflecting social differences across cultures. It was noted that individualist cultures tend to use more self-markers when discussing emotions, while collectivist cultures make use of more relationship markers, focusing on the thoughts, feelings, and goals of the group rather than the self. Group goals tend to be denoted by the use of concrete language and interpersonal verbs. Semin *et al.* examined the differences between Hindustani–Surinamese speakers (group focused) and Dutch speakers (individualistic). Participants were asked to generate a list of all emotional terms that came to mind, emotions that occur in critical events, or critical events that may result in the critical emotions, and the relative contribution that others made to the shaping of these life events. Hindustani–Surinamese speakers listed more interpersonal events, and stated that others played a larger role in these events. Dutch speakers used more abstract language and generated a larger list of emotion terms. The resulting pattern revealed a clear interaction between cultural values and usage of the emotion lexicon, despite its relative universality across cultures.

Differences between language speakers could be in part due to differences in emotion knowledge exhibited by members of a specific culture. Emotion knowledge is thought to be culturally construed and formed through participation in everyday sociocultural practices. Individual-focused cultures tend to consider emotion a direct expression of the self. In community cultures there is a premium placed on social harmony and group interests, and emotion is seen as destructive to this harmony in many cases. As a result, when asked to judge the emotional nature of a story or describe situations that likely provoke emotions, members of individual-focused cultures outperformed members of community-focused cultures. Furthermore this increase in emotion knowledge is thought to reflect an increase in access to earlier and more detailed accounts of childhood memories, as these memories are often bound up in their emotional context (Wang 2011).

Applied issues in emotion processing

Bilingualism affects memory in a pervasive fashion, such that memories for events are dependent upon a specific language as a retrieval cue. Specific information may not be available in both languages. Javier, Barroso, and Muñoz (1993) examined memory for person events in Spanish–English bilinguals. Participants were asked to describe an interesting or dramatic event from personal history for five minutes in their native language. They were then asked to retell the event in L2. Javier *et al.* found that the quality of description was richer in L1, and memories encoded in a specific language were better remembered in that same language, regardless of whether it was the native language or not. It is easy to see how this research is applicable to therapeutic settings. Schrauf (2000) found similar results when memories from childhood were examined. He found that memories experienced in the mother tongue were typically richer in terms of emotional significance, particularly when recalled in L1. Benefits of having two languages available for use during therapy are numerous, but include allowing the client to be more expressive, with two languages available. On the other hand, the second language can be used as a distancing function when recalling particularly painful life experiences since most emotion information is encoded in L1. Marcos (1976) defined this effect as the detachment effect, noting the tendency for L2 to be devoid of emotion. This may be due to the cultural or emotional context in which each of the two languages is learned (Altarriba 2003). Typically L2 is learned in a formalized and systematic environment, and speakers rarely have experiences with emotional conflict encoded in this language. This vein of research shows a clear language specific influence over memory retrieval. However, this is not always the case.

Memory for language: culturally dependent?

After reviewing the available body of work that comprises memory and emotion research, it is clear that there exists a great deal of evidence to support the impact of language on memory, particularly with regards to emotion. There is also a clear interaction between culture and language, particularly in the case of autobiographical memories, but culture has yet to be examined independently from language (see Appendix for a summary of relevant findings). It remains difficult to separate out culture from language, as the two, in most cases, develop alongside each other, continuously interacting. The question remains as to whether cultural ideals are imbedded within the language, or rather if language use activates memories for the cultural context. In the body of work examining the effects of categorization, grammar, and linguistic environment on cognitive processing, a clear cultural link exists in many cases, but does not present itself outside of language-constrained situations, supporting the idea that culture does impact cognitive shifts, but is constrained to the language of processing.

Conclusions and future directions

The current chapter suggests that language and culture combine in unique ways to moderate and influence cognitive processing and communication, on various levels. Quantitative and qualitative investigations have provided ample evidence suggesting that behavior that is guided by linguistic processing is in most cases also regulated by the cultural context of the speaker. As explained by Slobin (1996), speakers are often bound, in fact, by the available expressions and terms within a given language, yet it is quite clear that with the introduction of a second and potentially a third language, a speaker's conceptual framework expands rather notably (Altarriba 2003). Moreover, immersion in a given cultural environment tends to moderate the ways in which linguistic terms are used and the ways in which objects and items are categorized indicating that there are important influences of these variables on cognition and cognitive functioning (Imai and Gentner 1997). The importance of these findings cannot be underestimated. For example, it has emerged that recall of information or the recounting of a story or event is heavily influenced by the language that was most dominant at the time the event occurred. Thus, when seeking the recall of events from memory, the strategic use of a given language for a bilingual or multilingual speaker should be emphasized in order to gather the richest set of details from memory (Larsen *et al.* 2002; Wang and Ross 2005). For example, this is of particular importance when considering health and therapeutic settings. Previous research has examined the impact of switching linguistic frames during therapy for the bilingual client (e.g., Altarriba and Santiago-Rivera 1994; Santiago-Rivera *et al.* 2009). Yet there remains room for further exploration on the specific outcomes that can be facilitated for bilingual clients and therapists who engage in language switching during therapeutic sessions. Furthermore, with what we now know concerning the ways in which our linguistic and cultural environment impact the way we process information, there is a need to re-evaluate many of the measurement tools used for the purpose of diagnosis in various health settings. It may be the case that bilinguals, even those who are highly proficient in both languages, may respond differently on such measures when responding in one language versus the other.

Whether in the context of emotional events, creative processes, or recounting a story or an event, both linguistic and cultural factors play a role – sometimes one that is inextricably intertwined – and those factors must be adequately assessed and considered in formulating interpretations or conclusions that bear on a theory or model of human behavior. The current review makes a clear argument for the necessity of considering the bilingual as a unique language user, whose perception and memory are working in conjunction with the specific linguistic and cultural experiences of each individual speaker (e.g., Athanasopoulos and Aveledo 2012; Cook 2003; Green 1998). Thus, when conducting research with bilingual populations, it is crucial to consider both the linguistic and cultural circumstances that encompass that population. For example, a bilingual working with two structurally similar languages may process information in a different fashion than a bilingual working in two languages with disparate grammatical and structural components. The same caution should be taken when considering whether or not the two languages spoken in a given population are culturally intertwined in a way that may uniquely shape a bilingual's perception when switching between languages (Wang and Ross 2005). It is hoped that the current chapter will stimulate greater thinking and further research on the importance of these variables to developing a unified theory of cognition and communication.

Appendix

Table 17.1 Summary of relevant findings

Language dominance	Language–culture interaction	Culture dominance
Grammar: grammatical number differences lead to attenuation to differences in countable objects (Athanasopoulos 2006; Lucy 1992)	*Grammar:* grammatical aspect leads to conceptual transfer (Bylund and Jarvis 2011); Pronoun usage is reflective of individualism/collectivism (Kashima and Kashima 2003)	*Creativity in monolinguals:* higher levels of creativity on Torrance Task are found for members of individualistic cultures (Kharkhurin and Samadpour Motalleebi 2008)
Colour categorization: colour terms lead to differences in perceptual space between colours (Kay and Kempton 1984; Roberson, Davies, and Davidoff 2000)	*Memories and value systems:* Cultural ideals are imbedded within language (Ogunnaike, Dunham, and Banaji 2010). Memory for cultural events is encoded in language (Larsen, Schrauf, Fromholt, and Rubin 2002; Wang and Ross 2005)	*Emotion knowledge:* group-focused cultures tend to exhibit lower levels of emotional knowledge (Semin, Gorts, Nandram, and Semin-Goossens 2002)

Related topics

linguistic relativity hypothesis revisited; culture and emotional language; language, culture and interaction; language, culture and colour

Further reading

Gelfand, M. J., Chiu, C. Y., and Hong, Y. Y. (eds). (2013). *Advances in Culture and Psychology* (vols. 1–4). Oxford, UK: Oxford University Press. (This edited collection provides an overview of multidisciplinary research programs in the fields of Culture and Psychology, examining both similarities as well as differences between the behaviors of various cultures.)

Heredia, R. R. and Altarriba, J. (eds) (in press, 2014). *Foundations of Bilingual Memory*. New York, NY: Springer Science+Business Media, LLC. (This edited collection discusses the latest theories and empirical methods used in the study of bilingual memory, focusing on encoding, storage, and retrieval, as related to bilingual processes.)

Kharkhurin, A. V. (2012). *Multilingualism and Creativity* (vol. 88). Multilingual Matters. (This book provides a thorough discussion of how creativity is measured and how the multilingual environment interacts with these measures of creativity.)

Pavlenko, A. (ed.). (2011). *Thinking and Speaking in Two Languages* (vol. 77). Multilingual matters. (This edited collection explores how the linguistic environment may be interacting with various cognitive processes in the case of bi- and multi-lingual speakers.)

References

Altarriba, J. (2003). Does *cariño* equal 'liking'? A theoretical approach to conceptual nonequivalence between languages. *International Journal of Bilingualism*, 7, 305–22.

Altarriba, J., Bauer, L. M., and Benvenuto, C. (1999). Concreteness, context-availability, and imageability ratings and word associations for abstract, concrete, and emotion words. *Behavior Research Methods, Instruments, and Computers*, 31, 578–602.

Altarriba, J., and Heredia, R. R. (eds) (2008). *An Introduction to Bilingualism: Principles and Processes*. New York: Lawrence Erlbaum Associates.

Altarriba, J., and Santiago-Rivera, A. L. (1994). Current perspectives on using linguistic and cultural factors in counseling the bilingual Spanish-speaking client. *Professional Psychology: Research and Practice*, 25, 388–97.

Athanasopoulos, P. (2006). Effects of the grammatical representation of number on cognition in bilinguals. *Bilingualism: Language and Cognition*, 9, 89–96.

——(2007). Interaction between grammatical categories and cognition in bilinguals: The role of proficiency,cultural immersion, and language of instruction. *Language and Cognitive Processes*, 22, 689–99.

——(2009). Cognitive representation of color in bilinguals: The case of Greek blues. *Bilingualism: Language and Cognition*, 12, 83–95.

Athanasopoulos, P. and Aveledo, F. (2012). Linguistic relativity and bilingualism. In J. Altarriba, and L. Isurin (eds), *Memory, Language, and Bilingualism: Theoretical and Applied Approaches* (pp. 236–55). Cambridge, UK: Cambridge University Press.

Athanasopoulos, P., and Kasai, C. (2008). Language and thought in bilinguals: the case of grammatical number and nonverbal classification preferences. *Applied Psycholinguistics*, 29, 105–21.

Boroditsky, L. (2001). Does language shape thought? Mandarin and English speakers' conceptions of time. *Cognitive Psychology*, 43, 1–22.

Bylund, E., and Jarvis, S. (2011). L2 effects on L1 event conceptualization. *Bilingualism: Language and Cognition*, 14, 47–59.

Carroll, J. B. (ed.) (1956). *Language, Thought, and Reality: Selected Writings of Benjamin Lee Whorf*. Cambridge, MA: MIT Press.

Casasanto, D. (2008). Who's afraid of the Big Bad Whorf? Cross-linguistic differences in temporal language and thought. *Language Learning*, 58, 63–79.

Chiu, C. (2011). Language and culture. *Online Readings in Psychology and Culture*, Unit 4. Retrieved from http://scholarworks.gvsu.edu/orpc/vol4/iss2/2

Cook, V. (2003). The changing L1 in the L2 user's mind. In V. Cook (ed.), *Effects of the Second Language on the First* (pp. 1–18). Clevedon: Multilingual Matters.

de Groot, A. M. B. (1992). Determinants of word translation. *Journal of Experimental Psychology: Learning, Memory and Language*, 18, 1001–18.

Earle, M. (1969). A cross-cultural and cross-language comparison of dogmatism scores. *Journal of Social Psychology*, 79, 19–24.

Green, D. (1998). Bilingualism and thought. *Psychologica Belgica*, 38, 253–78.

Imai, M. and Gentner, D. (1997). A crosslinguistic study of early word meaning: Universal ontology and linguistic influence. *Cognition*, 62, 169–200.

January, D. and Kako, E. (2007). Re-evaluating evidence for linguistic relativity: Reply to Boroditsky (2001). *Cognition*, 104, 417–26.

Javier, R. A., Barroso, F., and Muñoz, M. A. (1993). Autobiographical memory in bilinguals. *Journal of Psycholinguistic Research*, 22, 319–38.

Kashima, Y. and Kashima, E. S. (2003). Individualism, GNP, climate, and pronoun drop: Is individualism determined by affluence and climate, or does language use play a role. *Journal of Cross-Cultural Psychology*, 34, 125–34.

Kay, P. and Kempton, W. (1984). What is the Sapir–Whorf hypothesis? *American Anthropologist*, 86, 65–79.

Kharkhurin, A.V. (2010). Bilingual verbal and nonverbal creative behavior. *International Journal of Bilingualism*, 14, 211–26.

Kharkhurin, A. V., and Samadpour Motalleebi, S. N. (2008). The impact of culture on the creative potential of American, Russian, and Iranian college students. *Creative Research Journal*, 20, 404–11.

Larsen, S. F., Schrauf, R. W., Fromholt, P., and Rubin, D. C. (2002). Inner speech and bilingual autobiographical memory: A Polish–Danish cross-cultural study. *Memory*, 10, 45–54.

Lucy, J. (1992). *Grammatical Categories and Cognition: A Case Study of the Linguistic Relativity Hypothesis*. Cambridge, UK: Cambridge University Press.

Lucy, J. A., and Gaskins, S. (2003). Interaction of language type and referent type in the development of nonverbal classification preferences. In D. Gentner, and S. Goldin-Meadow (ed.), *Language in Mind: Advances in the Study of Language and Thought* (pp. 465–92). Cambridge, MA: MIT Press.

Marcos, L. R. (1976). Linguistic dimensions in the bilingual patient. *American Journal of Psychoanalysis*, 36, 347–54.

Ogunnaike, O., Dunham, Y., and Banaji, M. R. (2010). The language of implicit preferences. *Journal of Experimental Social Psychology*, 46, 999–1003.

Oller, D. K., and Eilers, R. E. (eds), (2002). *Language and Literacy in Bilingual Children*. Clevedon: Multilingual Matters.

Regier, T., Kay, P., and Khetarpal, N. (2007). Color naming reflects optimal partitions of color space. *Proceedings of the National Academy of Sciences of the USA*, 104, 1436–41.

Roberson, D., and Davidoff, J. (2000). The categorical perception of colors and facial expressions: The effect of verbal interference. *Memory and Cognition*, 28, 977–86.

Roberson, D., Davies, I., and Davidoff, J. (2000). Color categories are not universal: Replications and new evidence from a stone-age culture. *Journal of Experimental Psychology: General*, 129, 369–98.

Roberson, D., Pak, H. S. and Hanley, J. R. (2008). Categorical perception of colour in the left and right hemisphere is verbally mediated: Evidence from Korean. *Cognition*, 107, 752–62.

Santiago-Rivera, A., Altarriba, J., Poll, N., González-Miller, N., and Cragun, C. (2009). Therapists' views on working with bilingual Spanish–English speaking clients: A qualitative investigation. *Professional Psychology: Research and Practice*, 40, 436–43.

Schmiedtová, B., von Stutterheim, Ch., and Carroll, M. (2011). Implications of language-specific patterns in event construal of advanced L2 speakers. In A. Pavlenko (ed.), *Thinking and Speaking in Two Languages* (pp. 66–107). Bristol: Multilingual Matters.

Schrauf, R. W. (2000). Bilingual autobiographical memory: Experimental studies and clinical cases. *Culture and Psychology*, 6, 387–417.

Semin, G. R., Gorts, C. A., Nandram, S., and Semin-Goossens, A. (2002). Cultural perspectives on the linguistic representation of emotion and emotion events. *Cognition and Emotion*, 16, 11–28.

Siegal, M., Iozzi, L., and Surian, L. (2009). Bilingualism and conversational understanding in young children. *Cognition*, 110, 115–22.

Slobin, D. I. (1996). From 'thought and language' to 'thinking for speaking'. In J. J. Gumperz, and S. C. Levinson (eds), *Rethinking Linguistic Relativity* (pp. 70–96). Cambridge University Press.

Tse, C. S., and Altarriba, J. (2008). Evidence against linguistic relativity in Chinese and English: A case study of spatial and temporal metaphors. *Journal of Cognition and Culture*, 8, 335–57.

Wang, Q. (2011). Autobiographical memory and culture. *Online readings in psychology and culture*, Unit 5. Retrieved from http://scholarworks.gvsu.edu/orpc/vol5/iss2/2

Wang, Q., and Ross, M. (2005). What we remember and what we tell: The effects of culture and self-priming on memory representations and narratives. *Memory*, 13, 594–606.

Wang, Q., Shao, Y., and Li, Y. J. (2010). 'Do you like pizza or shao-mai?' The bilingual and bicultural self in Hong Kong Chinese children and adolescents. *Child Development*, 81, 555–67.

18

LANGUAGE, CULTURE, AND PROTOTYPICALITY

Frank Polzenhagen and Xiaoyan Xia

1 Introduction

Prototype theory is closely linked to the work of the American cognitive psychologist Eleanor Rosch and her colleagues. This work has profoundly changed the mainstream model of human categorization, far beyond its original home territory in psychology. Although several elements of what was to become 'prototype theory' had been established and worked out by earlier researchers, it is the studies of Rosch and her colleagues (see below for references and the overview in Rosch 1978) that have convinced researchers across the various disciplines that it is not necessary to describe their data in terms of the classical model of categories. The significant impact of these studies is reflected by the term 'Roschian revolution', which is commonly used for the perspective shifts they initiated in the 1970s.

The survey given in our chapter will be primarily concerned with the specific repercussions of prototype theory in linguistics. In line with the general focus of the present handbook, the main part of our account is devoted to research that highlights cultural dimensions of prototypicality and their linguistic manifestations. The rationale underlying our discussion is straightforward: prototypicality is context sensitive and context dependent, and sociocultural patterns are a crucial contextual factor in this respect. Specifically, we will explore some of the ways in which the sociocultural context influences and establishes prototypicality.

Our chapter is structured as follows: in section 2, we will briefly review the original framework of the theory, its basic concepts, and some of the elaborations it has received within Cognitive Linguistics (CL). We will also point to some critical and controversial issues linked to prototype theory. In sections 3 and 4, we will provide an overview of studies and approaches that analyse prototypicality from a cultural perspective. Most of our examples come from varieties of English. While this choice admittedly corresponds to our own research focus, it is also, and perhaps first and foremost, motivated by the fact that English is firmly rooted in numerous and often quite different cultural contexts across the globe (see Chapter 31 this volume, for discussion). Hence it is an excellent case in point to show that the specific form of a language spoken by a particular group readily reflects the group's specific cultural conceptualizations. Furthermore, this scope is justified by the fact that a great deal of intercultural communication takes place in English (see Chapter 30 this volume, for discussion), which makes this particular language the preferred object of investigation for our present concern.

In section 3, we will review representative empirical studies that apply the methods of Rosch's classic goodness-of-example and attribute-listing tests with an explicitly cross-cultural scope. Our reference point is the notion of 'culturally blended concepts' (Schmid *et al.* 2008). We will discuss cultural differences in prototypicality that can be observed between corresponding concepts in native English and second-language (L2) varieties, and we will point to some factors that determine or influence the degree of conceptual blending from two cultures in the minds of non-native speakers of English. We will then sketch the interpretation of such data against the background of the notion of 'cultural models' (Holland and Quinn 1987; see Chapter 32 this volume, for discussion).

In section 4, we will place the notion of 'prototype' in the context of cognitive sociolinguistics. Our starting points are Geeraerts's (2008: 27) observation that 'stereotypes are prototypes seen from a social angle' and the old insight that specific linguistic features are both perceived of and used as markers of sociocultural background and identity (on the issue of language, culture, and identity, see Chapter 14 this volume, for discussion). We will then link these obviously related points and review recent work on the sociocultural meaning of allophones, showing that prototypical lectal renderings of phonemes serve as reference points in social cognition and categorization, which, in turn, influences the development of the centre–periphery structure of the linguistic category itself. We will also include the historical perspective on linguistic stereotypes and their modelling in terms of shifting prototypes. In section 5, we will summarize the main points of our chapter.

2 Theoretical issues

Prototype theory was proposed in the early 1970s as an alternative to the so-called 'Classical' or 'Aristotelian' view of categories that had been prevalent by then. The 'Classical' model may be characterized, to borrow from MacLaury (1991: 55), by the CONTAINER metaphor: categories, under this view, are BOXES that contain a discrete set of elements. Individual members have an equal status within the category. Category membership is established when a specific set of necessary and sufficient features is met. This view was endorsed in structuralist semantics, most prominently, by Katz and Fodor (1963), and was aptly described by Fillmore (1975) as 'checklist semantics'.

The persistent dominance of the classical model over the centuries is due to the fact that reflections on the notions of 'categories' and 'categorization' were almost exclusively confined to philosophical discourse. This changed when these notions entered the research agenda of other disciplines, notably cultural anthropology and cognitive psychology. When research interest in these fields turned to actual patterns of human categorization and their expression in natural languages, the classical model proved to be untenable. Hallmark studies on colour categorization across languages (e.g. Berlin and Kay 1969; Heider 1971; see Chapter 19 this volume, for discussion), followed by further empirical studies on a range of other categories (e.g. Rosch 1975a; Erreich and Valian 1979), led to a rapid paradigm shift in the view of human categorization. Among the alternative models proposed in the 1970s and 1980s in order to account for the empirical data, the most notable ones are prototype theory (Rosch 1973, 1975b) and, closely related, exemplar-based models (e.g. Medin and Schaffer 1978; for a comparative survey of these two approaches see, e.g., Murphy 2002).

What these two alternative models share is, first of all, the insight that category members do not have equal status, a phenomenon commonly referred to as *graded membership* or *gradience*. Categories, to borrow the metaphor used by Hampton (2006: 89), are SPACES with a central region (or several sub-centres) and a periphery. Individual members are located within this centre–periphery structure. Textbook examples are the studies by Rosch (e.g. 1975a) on categories like BIRD, FURNITURE, and FRUIT, which showed that some category members are indeed better examples of the category than others. The asymmetry between central and peripheral instances was found to be present not only in goodness-of-example rating tests but also in various other experiments, e.g. on similarity rating, order and probability of item output and true–false verification speed. A second crucial insight which these studies yielded in the nature of categories concerns their boundaries. Some categories, e.g. BIRD, do have clear-cut edges. Others, e.g. FURNITURE and FRUIT, however, are less clearly delineated, as suggested by the hesitation shown by informants when confronted with 'controversial' items such as *carpets* and *tomatoes*. The recognition that the boundaries of some categories are fuzzy and overlapping with the terrain of neighbouring categories is, again, in stark contrast to the classical view, which, to put it in terms of the CONTAINER metaphor again, regards categories as clearly delineated, discrete BOXES.

What distinguishes prototype theory from the alternative but otherwise related exemplar-based models is the assumption that categorization involves considerable abstraction from actual category members (see e.g. Voorspoels, Storms and Vanpaemel 2011). In prototype theory, the category is thought of as being represented by an 'abstract summary' of what its specific instances are generally like, as a schematic representation of the most salient or central characteristics associated with members of the category. Prototypicality effects are accounted for by the similarity between individual members and the abstract prototype. In exemplar-based model, by contrast, the category is solely represented by its previously encountered members, i.e. it is made up of stored exemplars alone. Under this view, prototypicality effects arise from a high similarity with one or more of the stored instances, especially with those which are more central. In fact, the latter view was implied in some of Rosch's (e.g. Rosch and Mervis 1975; Rosch 1977) early writings, which characterize prototypes as being concrete, such as the best example, the clearest case, a typical member of a category or the member with highest 'cue validity'. The adoption of such a concrete notion of prototype can also be found in later research (e.g. Brown 1990; Tversky 1990).

Although the debate between prototype and exemplar-based models is far from being settled (e.g. Medin and Schwanenflugel 1981; Medin and Smith 1984; Minda and Smith 2011; Nosofsky and Zaki 2002; Smith and Minda 1998), a shift can be detected in this heated argument. While much of the earlier research was devoted to deciding which of the two models is correct, recent studies seem to be more interested in the question of whether a single formal model of representation can account for human categorization. One proposal is that we might have multiple systems of categorization based on both prototype abstractions and exemplar memorization, rather than a unitary one (e.g. Medin and Smith 2001; Smith and Minda 2000). Voorspoel, Storm, and Vanpaemel (2011) have provided more empirical support for this multiple-system view. They argue that different factors such as the complexity of the hierarchical structure of a given category, its size and its internal coherence, seem to favour different modes of representation. For instance, exemplar-based models were often observed to make better predictions for lower-level categories with few members, whereas the abstract-prototype view performed better in the case of higher-level categories with many members.

Not surprisingly, the 'Roschian revolution' in psychology had an immediate and enthusiastic reception among the first generation of cognitive linguists and was readily made part of their endeavour to initiate a paradigm shift in their own discipline. Whereas exemplar-based models came to be more popular, if not dominant, among psychologists in the subsequent decades, CL drew almost exclusively from Roschian prototype theory. This is certainly due to the fact that the assumption of an abstracted prototype was more attractive to CL than the exemplar view, given the programmatic commitment of CL to 'generalization' and its objective to extract higher-level schematic representations. Thus Taylor (2003: 64), for instance, defines a prototype as 'a fairly abstract representation, which abstracts away from the properties of individual instances and individual subcategories'.

Further ingredients of the specific Roschian theory were appealing to the CL approach, too. The notion of 'family resemblance', for instance, which Rosch and Mervis (1975) took from Wittgenstein, provided a welcome handle to model chaining relationships among category members in semantics and elsewhere, and it later found its way into the CL concept of 'radial categories', developed, most notably, by Lakoff (1987). Likewise, Rosch and cognitive semanticists shared the recourse to principles of *gestalt* psychology; *gestalt* features and notions like 'good shape' are central to the prototype view. Almost naturally, then, Roschian prototype theory has become a corner stone of CL. However, exemplar models have also come to be a part of CL approaches, e.g. in CL phonology.

Like any other theory, prototype theory has not gone without some criticism. On-principle objections against prototype theory are raised by advocates of strongly compositional models of meaning (e.g. Fodor and Lepore 1996; Connolly *et al.* 2007). Their central argument is that the prototype view fails to provide an adequate account of composite concepts; see e.g. Fodor and Lepore's (1996) discussion of the item *pet fish*. A number of critical issues have also been voiced by CL scholars, who are, however, favourable to prototype theory in general. An overview of potential shortcomings of prototype theory is given, for instance, in Croft and Cruse (2004: 87–91), definitional problems are addressed in Geeraerts (2006: 146–58), and Wierzbicka (1990) is an early warning against the overuse of the notion of 'prototype' in linguistics. Such criticism certainly calls for further refinement of prototype theory and points to its potential limits.

However, prototype theory has clearly proved to be descriptively and theoretically fruitful in many respects. In particular, it can account for the learning of many visual categories (i.e. dot patterns) and categories with a strong family-resemblance structure (see Minda and Smith 2011). Likewise, it is undeniable that it is successful at explaining phenomena like polysemy, vagueness, typicality, genericity, and opacity (see Hampton 2006; Lewandowska-Tomaszczyk 2007). Prototype theory has also found its way into practical lexicography (see Geeraerts 2007 for an overview). Furthermore, the overwhelming evidence for widespread prototypicality effects in semantic categories has inspired a wide and productive application of the prototype model of categorization to various linguistic domains such as grammar, phonology, and pragmatics.

Already among the early proponents of prototype theory there was a strong and programmatic awareness of the culture-specific nature of prototypes and, more broadly speaking, the impact of context on categorization. This does not come as a surprise, since many of them had a background in cultural anthropology and were generally committed to cross-linguistic research. With the wide adoption of prototype theory in various disciplines, more and more studies have surfaced that explore the cultural and contextual dimensions of prototypicality. A well-known example showing the crucial role of context in prototype and category formation is presented in Barsalou's (1983) research on goal-derived categories such as WHAT TO TAKE FROM ONE'S HOME DURING A FIRE. Ad hoc categories of the kind described by Barsalou do not exist until the context (or goal) is released to the participants (Barsalou 1983, experiment 4). A further often-cited early study is Labov's (1973) experiment on the boundaries of the category CUP, in which he showed that categorization judgements on the same object vary with changing situational and functional contexts. Likewise, the crucial role of culture in prototype formation has long been reported in empirical studies. Both prototypical exemplars and typicality gradients were found to differ across cultures (e.g. Kempton 1981; Schwanenflugel and Rey 1986).

A development within CL that was crucial to the study of the culture-specific nature of prototypes was the analysis of prototypicality against the background of the more encompassing notion of 'cultural models' (for overviews, see Ungerer and Schmid 2006; Lewandowska-Tomaszczyk 2007). This approach is already implied in Fillmore's (1975) well-known critical reanalysis of BACHELOR and was shaped by Lakoff's (1987) notion of 'Idealised Cognitive Models' (ICM) and his standard example of the ICM of MOTHER. Lakoff showed that kinship terms like *mother* can be and are used against the background of several cognitive models (see Lakoff 1987: 74–6), e.g.:

the genetic model: the biological mother
the nurture-and-care model: the woman who nurtures and raises the child
the marital model: the father's wife

This list is not exhaustive, and several other notions can come into play. Further important studies include Quinn's (1987) account of the cultural model of MARRIAGE and Sweetser's (1987) reinterpretation of the earlier prototype analysis of LIE by Coleman and Kay (1981). In the second part of the next section we will return to Lakoff's account of the ICM of MOTHER and reconsider it from a cross-cultural perspective. We will also link the study of prototypicality to a further relevant theoretical CL notion, i.e. 'culturally blended concepts'.

3 Culture-specific prototypes, blended concepts, and cultural models in L2 contexts

Conceptual categories are regarded in CL as being shaped by the human interaction with and perception of the objective world, by the physical and psychological peculiarities of the human being and by the cultural environment (e.g. Lakoff 1987: 304–37; Gyori 1996: 161). On the one hand, the shared nature of our body assures that both the basic principles we abide by in categorizing the world and the fundamental structure of our conceptual categories are universal. On the other hand, the cultural experience and knowledge we gain from our situatedness in a particular culture inevitably shapes our thoughts, making the conceptual categories not only embodied but also 'encultured' (see Chapter 16 this volume, for discussion). Under a cross-cultural perspective, prototype theory predicts not only that translation-equivalent categories from two cultures exhibit a centre–periphery structure, but also that the prototype and proto-typicality gradation among the category members are culturally situated. This hypothesis has been consistently verified in the relevant literature (e.g. Schwanenflugel and Rey 1986; Kövecses 2000; Malt, Sloman and Gennari 2003; Athanasopoulos 2009). The resulting differences at the conceptual level reflect specific physical environments and varied cultural beliefs and values. The variation in cultural experiences determines the extent to which conceptual categories are universal, widespread, or culture specific.

Language, from a CL point of view, is 'a collection of form-meaning pairs, where the meanings are concepts in the conceptual system' (Lakoff 1987: 539). This characterization of language implies that learning a language other than one's mother tongue is not only a matter of familiarizing oneself with another set of linguistic forms but also an issue of adopting new ways of perceiving and conceptualizing the world, a stance that was already famously expressed by Humboldt against the background of his notion of 'world-view':

Thus, learning a foreign language ought to be the attainment of a new standpoint in the previously held world view. And, in fact, this is the case to a certain extent, since every language contains the entire fabric of concepts and the way of conceptualising of a part of the human kind. Yet as one always carries over, to a greater or lesser degree, one's own world view and even one's personal linguistic habits, this attainment will not be felt to be complete and pure.

(Hamboldt 1992 [1830–5]: 53f.; our translation)

One key issue of modern L2 research is, accordingly, whether there is a unitary conceptual system that maps onto the different languages commanded by a speaker, or whether the learning of an L2 involves the construction of a separate conceptual system. A CL notion that addresses this issue is that of 'culturally blended concepts' (Schmid *et al.* 2008). This notion is inspired by Blending Theory (e.g. Fauconnier and Turner 2002) and provides an analytical tool to model the effects that language-contact and culture-contact situations may have at the conceptual level. One has to bear in mind, however, that 'blend', in the sense of Fauconnier's model, refers to an ad hoc concept made up in online cognition. The target of Schmid *et al.* (2008), however, is blended concepts that have stabilized through repeated usage in an L2, and it is in this sense that we will employ this term. We will now turn to two respective studies with a specific background in prototype theory that investigate blended concepts in two different cultural settings.

Schmid *et al.* (2008) give substance to their notion of 'culturally blended concepts' through a small-scale empirical study which brings us to the West African context. Their object of investigation is one of the so-called 'New Englishes' spoken there, namely Nigerian English. The authors begin with the observation that the New Englishes are subject to influences from native English and the related culture, on the one hand, and from local languages and cultures, on the other. Following the well-attested view that the New Englishes have adapted to their respective cultural and linguistic setting, a process referred to in the literature as 'contextualisation' or 'indigenisation', Schmid *et al.* (2008) addressed the following questions: (1) do culturally blended concepts vary in their degree of 'blendedness'?; (2) what are the moderating factors that influence the degree of 'blendedness'? and (3) which methodological problems exist for the study of conceptual blending concepts?

In their study, they chose three groups of informants: native speakers of Hausa (group 1; n = 45), speakers of Nigerian (Hausa) English, i.e. L2 speakers of English (group 2; n = 39, all of them also in group 1) and a reference group of native speakers of American English (group 3; n = 47). Groups 2 and 3 were confronted with everyday English lexical items like *cap, airplane, wheelchair* and Group 1 with the respective Hausa translation equivalents. Adopting the 'attribute-listing task' used by Rosch in her studies, Schmid *et al.* asked their informants to list the attributes that the designated objects possess. Frequency statistics were established in order to determine the degree of prototypicality of the collected attributes, i.e. whether an attribute is a significant element of the conceptual structure of a given word. Based on a comparison of the collected prototypical attributes provided by the three groups of informants, Schmid *et al.* (2008) found that the Nigerian English concepts displayed different degrees of mixture of conceptual components from the two cultures involved.

In order to measure the degree of blending in individual concepts, the authors put forward a three-parameter tool inspired by Ogden and Richards' semiotic triangle and distinguish between referent-related, concept-related, and form-related parameters. Consider the results obtained for *cap*: the Nigerian informants listed attributes like 'round', 'hand-made', and 'worn (mostly) by men', both for the English word *cap* and its Hausa equivalent (*hula*). For them, the typical cap is the Hausa *hula*. For the American informants, by contrast, it is the baseball cap, i.e. a quite different referent. While the concept associated with *cap* in Nigerian English clearly reflects the Hausa concept and is hence strongly 'contextualized', the comparison with the list obtained for *hula* also reveals that the latter concept is richer than the former. It contains, for instance, attributes like 'ornamental' and 'part of garment', which reflect the role of the *hula* in Hausa culture and which are missing on the list for *cap* in Nigerian English.

Other items tested by Schmid *et al.* show a different profile. *Wheelchair*, for instance, has a referent-related constellation that is similar to the one with *cap* above: the typical Nigerian wheelchair differs from the American one in that it is hand-driven via pedals and a chain. This is reflected in the Hausa term *keken guragu*, which literally means 'bicycle for cripples', and the list obtained from the Hausa group indeed contains attributes like 'chain' and 'pedal'. The list for the Nigerian English group, however, suggests that the concept associated with the English item *wheelchair* is much closer to the American one. Interestingly, at the form-related level, this list reflects the Hausa term in that it contains the attribute 'bicycle', but at the same time it also reflects the English term in that it contains the attribute 'chair', the latter being absent from the Hausa list. This leads Schmid *et al.* (2008: 112) to calling Nigerian English WHEELCHAIR a 'true blend' of notions from both cultures. By means of the three-parameter analytical tool, Schmid *et al.* hence demonstrate the complexity of culturally blended concepts that arises from the interplay between moderating factors such as linguistic forms, extra-linguistic referents, mental concepts, and tacit cultural knowledge.

Culture-specific prototypicality effects in another setting, namely among Chinese L2 learners of English, are explored by Xia and Leung (2014). Their study focused on the question of whether prototypicality effects were L1 based or L2 based in an L2 context. The objects under investigation were polysemous words. The reason for looking into polysemous words was twofold: first, words have long been identified as a fertile object of study in order to investigate the associations between language, cognition, and culture (e.g. de Groot 1993; Singleton 1995). From a diachronic point of view, words in a language are a miniature of a particular people's categorization of the world. From a cross-cultural point of view, words in a language draw 'a map of the preoccupation of a culture' (Hatch and Brown 1995: 119). Second, polysemous words are particularly suited for this type of research because, from a CL point of view, their senses constitute a complex category (Lakoff 1987: 18; Rice 2003: 246). Hence, as far as cultural differences in people's categorization and conceptual blending are concerned, culture-loaded polysemous words are ideal objects of investigation from a prototype-theory perspective.

The examples under investigation in Xia and Leung (*fc.*) include the conceptual categories linked to the polysemous items *red* and 红 (*hong*, translation equivalent in Chinese). The *senses of red* category consists of such members as *vicious, hot, angry, bloody, aggressive, passionate*, etc., while the *senses of* 红 (*hong*) category has *prosperous, festive, fortunate, passionate, bloody, hot*, etc. as its members. A combination of qualitative and quantitative approaches was adopted to address the above question. The qualitative data, obtained from a free sense-listing task and a prototypicality-rating task completed by both native Chinese (n = 50) and native American English speakers (n = 40), were used to locate cultural variations in the prototypicality of the collected senses of 17 polysemous words. In the next step, quantitative data were obtained by a no-cue English-word-learning and immediate-cued-recall task. Here, the Chinese participants had to learn English words for instances that differed in terms of their prototypicality within the respective English and Chinese category. The hypothesis examined was that they would recall English words for category instances that are prototypical in Chinese but not in English (henceforth *Cp–Enp* instances) better and faster than those that are prototypical in English but not in Chinese (henceforth *Ep–Cnp* instances).

In the word-learning section, Chinese participants were instructed to learn by themselves pairs of English words for either *Cp–Enp* instances (e.g. *prosperous* from *senses of* 红) or *Ep–Cnp* instances (e.g. *vicious* from *senses of red*). No cues were given while they were completing the learning task. In the cued–recall section, the participants were told to recall the previously learned word senses (e.g. *prosperous, vicious*) according to the given cues (e.g. *red* or 红). Related-sample T tests, frequency statistics and Chi-Square tests were used to assess the obtained quantitative data. The results consistently confirm the existence of Chinese-based prototypicality effects in English vocabulary learning. English labels designating the Chinese-based psychologically salient category members are more easily learned and more quickly retrieved by Chinese learners. This finding indicates that L2 learners indeed follow the L1 pattern of categorization in their L2, especially at the initial stage of L2 learning.

However, Xia and Leung (2014) also found evidence of 'culturally blended concepts' in their data. In the recall task for *senses of dragon* and 龙 (*long*, translation equivalent in Chinese), Chinese participants performed equally well with the English words for the *Cp–Enp* instances and with those for the *Ep–Cnp* instances in their responses to the given cues of *dragon* and 龙 (*long*). Chinese-based prototypicality effects (in the form of *Cp–Enp* instances being both better and more quickly retrieved than *Ep–Cnp* instances) were not obtained for the *dragon* and 龙 (*long*) categories.

Taking a closer look at the data, Xia and Leung (2014) noticed, however, that their participants did show a preference for the prototypical instances, namely those of the *Cp–Enp* and *Ep–Cnp* types, as opposed to the non-prototypical instances. This observation indicates that both the *Cp–Enp* and the *Ep–Cnp* instances were psychologically salient in Chinese learners' minds. It suggests that the DRAGON concept of the Chinese participants is a blend of elements from Chinese culture and American English culture, which reflects the increasing interaction between these two cultures. Based on such findings, Xia and Leung (2014) proposed the following assumptions about the formation of 'culturally blended concepts' in L2 learners' minds: L2 learners integrate the L2-specific conceptual elements into the existing, L1-based conceptual representation and this cross-cultural conceptual integration is a dynamic process rather than a static result, being influenced by such factors as L2-proficiency level, formal instruction and exposure to L2 culture. The ideal stage of this conceptual integration is that L2-based prototypical instances also gain a psychologically salient status in the minds of L2 learners.

Another domain to which prototype theory has been fruitfully applied is the realm of kinship terms. Since kinship systems are addressed in detail in a separate chapter of the present volume (Chapter 11 this volume, and, for key texts on this issue in anthropology, the reader by Parkin and Stone 2003), we will confine our discussion to the immediate L2-English context. An early explicitly prototype-oriented study of kinship terms is Alo (1989), which brings us back to the Nigerian setting. His empirical basis is questionnaire data obtained among Yoruba speakers of English (n = 304) on their use of five English kinship terms (*father, mother, brother, sister, uncle*). Alo analysed the semantic properties of these items in Yoruba English along with their range of application. The findings clearly show that the use of these terms in Yoruba English follows, by and large, the pattern of the Yoruba kinship terms and hence differs significantly from the pattern in British English. Within the realm of biological kinship, the British pattern has an almost exclusive focus on the 'nuclear family', while the reference point of the Yoruba system is the so-called 'extended family'. Furthermore, the English kinship terms were applied by the Yoruba informants to express a broad range of bonds beyond biological kinship, in particular those relating to notions like 'respect', 'solidarity', and 'age'. They hence express a wide spectrum of what is referred to in cultural anthropology as 'genealogical relations', i.e. the entire set of 'socially recognised' bonds (see e.g. Goodenough 2001).

Findings as those by Alo readily lend themselves to a more encompassing analysis against the background of the notion of 'cultural models'. At this point, we can return to the list of cognitive models underlying the use of kinship terms proposed by Lakoff (see section 2). In the light of cross-cultural data, this list needs to be extended to include further potential models, e.g.

the respect model: e.g. PERSONS OF RESPECT ARE FATHERS/MOTHERS
the in-group/community model: GROUP/COMMUNITY MEMBERS ARE KIN

the age model: e.g. OLDER PERSONS (IN A GROUP) ARE FATHERS/MOTHERS
the leadership model: e.g. LEADERS ARE FATHERS

Cultures differ with respect to the specific *salience* or *gradience hierarchy* in which they apply these models; hence, in a given cultural group, these models are not equally prominent, rather, they are arranged in a specific centre–periphery structure. In modern Anglo-Saxon culture, for instance, the prototypical reference points are the biological and the marital model of kinship with a focus on the 'nuclear family' (on the historical development of this focus, see e.g. Goody 2000; Sabean, Teuscher and Mathieu 2007). Appeal to the other models is relatively rare and limited to specific contexts. In the West African setting, in turn, we meet a fully-fledged kinship-based community model in which the conceptualizations listed above figure prominently. A comprehensive analysis of this model is given in Wolf and Polzenhagen (2009). The cultural-model approach they take allows them to address a broad range of aspects of this model, e.g. its spiritual dimension and its repercussions in African politics, along with its various linguistic manifestations beyond the use of kinship terms. Congenial work on kinship models in some other varieties of English is also on its way. The best-researched variety is Australian Aboriginal English (see Sharifian 2011 for an overview). Hui (2004, 2005) has analysed the FAMILY schema in Chinese Australian English. Some initial findings on Hong Kong English are presented in Polzenhagen and Wolf (2010). The body of literature along these lines is, however, still small, and research is invited to investigate further varieties from this perspective.

4 And who /r/ you? Allophones, stereotypes, and social cognition

Advocates of both exemplar-based models and abstract-prototype models agree that (proto-) typical elements serve and facilitate categorization by providing relevant cognitive reference points. The aim of the present section is to show that prototypes can function as reference points in yet another respect, namely in social cognition. We will use the example of allophone variation to illustrate this insight; however, a parallel account could be given with respect to variation in other realms, e.g. syntax or lexis. With this scope, our discussion is located at the intersection between (cognitive) phonology, social psychology and variationist sociolinguistics (on the notion of culture in sociolinguistics, see Chapter 25 this volume).

It is an old observation that particular linguistic features are 'socially diagnostic' in that they betray the regional and/or sociocultural origin of a speaker. Such features, or linguistic stereotypes, have come to be referred to as *shibboleths*. This term is derived from the following passage in the Hebrew Bible, which recounts how the pronunciation of the word *shibboleth* was used by the Gileadites to identify Ephraimites (the dialect of the latter lacked the phoneme /ʃ/):

> Gilead then cut Ephraim off from the fords of the Jordan, and whenever Ephraimite fugitives said, 'Let me cross', the men of Gilead would ask, 'Are you an Ephraimite?' If he said, 'No', they then said, 'Very well, say *Shibboleth*'. If anyone said, 'Sibboleth', because he could not pronounce it, then they would seize him and kill him by the fords of the Jordan. Forty-two thousand Ephraimites fell on this occasion.
>
> (New Jerusalem Bible*, p. 247 [Judges 12:5–6])*

The list of historical and modern shibboleths is long. In the field of variationist sociolinguistics, it was William Labov who first made the social meaning of allophones a genuine object of linguistic investigation. In his seminal studies on the distribution of rhotic and non-rhotic speech in New York City department stores and on vowel renderings in Martha's Vineyard, Labov showed that the choice of a particular realization correlates with and is indicative of sociocultural parameters (Labov 1966, 1972). Meanwhile, there is also a rich body of literature dealing with evaluative reactions to accents, ranging from early work such as Lambert *et al.* (1960) and Giles (1970) to current accounts like Coupland and Bishop (2007). These and related subjects have also come to be a central concern of sociolinguistic approaches under labels like 'perceptual dialectology' and 'folk linguistics', which are most prominently represented by the work of Dennis Preston (e.g. Preston 1999; Niedzielski and Preston 2003).

Recently, Preston (2010a, 2010b) has elaborated on this approach with a strong attention to the cognitive foundations of his notion of 'language regard'. In Preston (2010a: 500–1), he uses a hallmark feature of Southern speakers in the US, namely the monophthongisation of the PRICE vowel to [a:] (the shibboleth phrase is *nice white rice*), in order to illustrate how regard responses come about based on the association between particular language features and stereotypes about speakers and groups. In the first step (noticing), the hearer recognizes the monophthongal realization of the PRICE vowel. In the second step (classification), he classifies this realization as 'American Southern'. In the third step (imbuing), stereotypes about 'Southern Americans' are activated by the hearer and he imbues the noticed monophthongal realization with them. These stereotypes evidently depend on the background of the hearer: Among Northerners in the US, for instance, stereotypes about Southerners have been shown to include characteristics like 'prejudiced', 'poorly educated', and 'violent', on the one hand, and 'friendly', 'genuine / down to earth', and 'sympathetic', on the other (see Preston 2010a, 2010b). Step four is the hearer's regard response, i.e. a deliberate reaction to the speaker's language. In this model, the link between the relevant language feature and the cultural stereotypes is established via the retrieval of conceptions of the respective group, i.e. indirectly. Preston (2010a: 501), however, suggests that this link can also be a direct one, without passing through appeal to the group, when it is entrenched through frequent previous instances of imbuing.

Preston's model is close in spirit to recent explicitly cognitive–linguistic approaches to language variation and social cognition, represented most prominently by Kristiansen (2003, 2006, 2008, 2010). In the remaining part of the present section, we will sketch out some aspects of such a cognitive–linguistic account. The example we have chosen for the sake of illustration is the various realizations of the phoneme /r/ across varieties of English along with their associated sociocultural meaning. Our discussion starts from the observation that the association of linguistic features with specific cultural stereotypes described above is, essentially, an entrenched metonymic link between prototypes. At the one end of this link, we are dealing with proto-typical allophones in a given accent. We will address this point against the background of the view of phonemes as radial categories held in cognitive phonology (e.g. Taylor 2003; Nathan 2007). At the other end, we are dealing with social categories that are organized in terms of centre–periphery structures, too.

From the perspective of phonological theory, the phoneme /r/ is certainly among the most challenging families of sounds. There is no common set of features shared across its various allophones that would motivate their membership in this category in a straightforward and distinctive way, neither in terms of articulation nor of acoustic properties. Not surprisingly, prototype-oriented descriptions of /r/ were proposed relatively early (most prominently in Lindau 1985). They model this phoneme in terms of a centre–periphery structure whose members are linked via chained family-resemblance relations, i.e. in terms of a radial category.

In varieties of English, /r/ comes in a broad range of allophones. Which one is 'chosen' depends on the respective phonetic environment, on the regional and social background of the speaker, on the respective speech style (e.g. formal or casual speech), and some renderings are idiosyncrasies of individual speakers. The various realizations are amply documented in the rich sociolinguistic literature on varieties of English (e.g. Wells 1982; Schneider *et al.* 2004). For our present concern, we will only pay attention to some of the allophones that can be said to be 'diagnostic' in social cognition. The specific issue of rhotic vs. non-rhotic accents will be addressed below from the same perspective. Well-known examples of socially and regionally diagnostic allophones of /r/ include (based on Trudgill 2004: 71):

A retroflex approximant [ɹ]. This is a hallmark, first of all, of General American and Canadian English. In England, it is stereotypically associated with the South-West counties. It is also referred to as *pirate r*; many of the pirates in the heydays of piracy were indeed of SW origin and, more importantly, the SW accent, and the [ɹ] in particular, has been the model of pirate speech since the early days of pirate movies ('Arr, matey!').

A voiced uvular fricative [ʁ]. In England, this rendering is linked to traditional North-East dialects and, then, referred to as *Northumbrian Burr*. A range of variants exists, e.g. a voiced velar fricative and uvular taps and trills (see Påhlsson 1972 for details). The *Northumbrian Burr* is, however, becoming rare, and it is more and more confined to rural areas.

An alveolar trill [r]. 'Rolling your r's' is first and foremost associated with Scotland and constitutes one of the main linguistic stereotypes about Scottish English. It has, however, lost ground in Scottish English, with approximant and other realizations getting more and more frequent among younger speakers (see e.g. Stuart-Smith 2003 for details).

An alveolar tap [ɾ]. This rendering is indicative of, for instance, Scottish English and Afrikaans English. Older RP speakers, too, use tapped realizations.

A labiodental approximant [ʋ]. This feature is associated with infant speech and, if an adult shows it, it is often regarded as a speech defect. However, over the last decades labialized renderings have spread in South-East England, especially in urban speech and among younger speakers (see Foulkes and Docherty 2000). In fact, labialized renderings have a long history; as early as 1866, Smith (1866: 29) complains that it has come to be 'fashionable' to turn the 'fine, manly sound' of r 'into that of *W*, and he bans this rendering as 'ridiculous', 'more worthy a monkey than a man' and an indicator of 'foppish manner'.

This list is, of course, far from exhaustive, but it should suffice for our present concern. Two points are particularly relevant from a cognitive perspective (also see Kristiansen 2006): (1) speakers have detailed (receptive) knowledge of various allophones that are not part of their own active inventory of renderings and recognize them as realizations of /r/. Furthermore and crucially, they are aware of prototypical realizations in other accents. Hence, these allophones must be mentally represented as parts of the category /r/ for these speakers. How detailed this knowledge is varies from speaker to speaker. However, knowledge of linguistic stereotypes is certainly transmitted during socialization. (2) The internal structure of the category /r/ differs considerably from accent to accent, in particular with respect to what constitutes the centre; from the perspective of RP, for instance, the alveolar approximant without retroflexion is central, while from the angle of General American English, it is the retroflex rendering.

   From the perspective of social cognition, linguistic stereotypes such as the allophones of /r/ and of other phonemes are not only crucial for their socially and regionally diagnostic character but also in that they function as in-group and identity markers. This point is illustrated by the following early description of one of the /r/-renderings mentioned above, namely the *Northumbrian Burr*; this account comes from Daniel Defoe and attests to the long history of this feature:

   I must not quit Northumberland without taking notice, that the Natives of this Country, of the antient original Race or Families, are distinguished by a *Shibboleth* upon their Tongues, namely, a difficulty in pronouncing the Letter R, which they cannot deliver from their Tongues without a hollow Jarring in the Throat, by which they are plainly known, as a Foreigner is, in pronouncing the Th: This they call the *Northumbrian* R, and *the Natives value themselves upon that Imperfection, because, forsooth, it shews the Antiquity of their Blood.*

(Defoe 1727: 196; emphasis added)

The role of allophones as in-group and identity markers has been analysed, for instance, by Altendorf (2004) for the case of another shibboleth, namely t-glottalling in Britain. Her study shows that the value attached to this highly stigmatized feature differs markedly among her subjects, who are London schoolgirls from different social backgrounds. For the working-class girls, the glottal realization of /t/ was the only or dominant realization of /t/ across the various styles and phonetic contexts. Upper-middle-class girls used glottal stops, but fully avoided them in the most stigmatized phonetic contexts, i.e. intervocalically (as in *butter*) and in pre-lateral position (as in *bottle*). As regards the latter context, middle-class girls patterned with the working-class girls in informal speech and joined the upper-middle-class speakers in formal style. For them, t-glottalling is a means of presenting themselves as 'modern' and 'daring' in the former style. In formal contexts, however, they apparently wish to avoid being regarded as 'common' and 'uneducated' (see Altendorf 2004 for a detailed discussion).

Studies like that by Altendorf document change in progress: specific features are 'copied' and spread from one social or regional group to others. In terms of the radial-category view sketched above, we are dealing with shifting prototypes, i.e. particular realizations move from the periphery to the centre and oust earlier prototypes. Such studies suggest that sociocultural notions attached to specific features are certainly among the driving forces behind this development. Again, /r/-renderings are an excellent case in point to show this dynamic process, and we will now pick up, for the sake of illustration, the issue of rhotic versus non-rhotic accents of English postponed above.

The varieties of English are well known to fall within two global groups as regards rhoticity. The so-called 'r-full' (rhotic) accents have one or the other sound from the family of rhotics in all positions of the syllable, be it onset or coda. In the so-called 'r-less' (non-rhotic) accents, this is only true for syllable onsets. In syllable codas, historical /r/'s in these accents have, somewhat informally speaking, 'weakened' and merged in various ways with the nucleus vowel; effects on the nucleus vowel include lengthening and qualitative changes like the formation of centring diphthongs (gliding towards schwa, obtained from r-vocalization). The shift towards non-rhoticity had its historical origin in urban South-East England speech and, in social terms, it was a 'shift from below'. It spread socially and regionally during the eighteenth century and achieved a stable basis in the South-East during the nineteenth century. However, what was to become a hallmark and a prestige feature of the emerging RP was still looked down on and banned by some nineteenth-century advocates of 'proper English'.

An in-depth analysis of the historical discourse on this and other sound changes is given by Mugglestone (1995), in her seminal book on the rise of accents as social symbols. In this discourse, the 'dropping of *r*' was made by some an explicit sociocultural shibboleth: it was associated with the speech of the Cockney 'vulgar', the 'illiterate', and 'careless', and condemned accordingly. The retention of *r*, in turn, was promoted as 'educated' and 'elegant' speech (see Mugglestone 1995: 99–103). People who reacted to this discourse with a hypercorrect exaggeration of r-fulness were, on the other hand, the target of ridiculing in other 'proper English' manuals; Mugglestone cites the following passage from one of these manuals, which draws from yet another linguistic stereotype: 'Some of our public speakers, who push accuracy of utterance beyond a wholesome limit, get the habit of trilling the *r* so much that one would think they wished to be thought unlettered Scotch or Irish peasants' (*Hard Words Made Easy*, 1855; cited in Mugglestone 1995: 103). The general trend towards non-rhoticity in the South-East, however, continued almost unaffected by this correctness debate, and made its way into the RP standard.

5 Conclusions

Prototype theory and exemplar-based accounts are well established and will continue to be productive models. From the discussion given in the present chapter, we see three challenges to future cultural–linguistic research in this field. The first one is to stay in touch with developments from neighbouring disciplines, as regards both theoretical issues and applications. The example we highlighted (section 2) is the ongoing testing of prototype or alternative models as to their explanatory power and psychological reality. Further issues include the question of whether the knowledge stored in categories is rather general or fairly detailed (see Kristiansen 2006 for discussion). The second challenge is to provide broader interpretational frameworks for findings on prototypicality effects. We focused on two notions that are promising in this respect, namely 'culturally blended concepts' and 'cultural model'. The former sheds light on the dynamics of concept formation in language-contact and culture-contact situations and can be fruitfully applied, *inter alia*, in the context of L2 teaching. The integration into cultural-model research, in turn, allows for the systematic and substantial cultural interpretation of otherwise isolated data on prototypicality. The third challenge we see is closely related and it is in line with current trends in CL: greater attention needs to be paid to culture-related variation in varieties of one and the same language, in addition to the traditional focus on cross-linguistic variation.

Generally, the further exploration of the intimate relationship between linguistic and social categories is a highly fertile research path. As we hope to have shown, linguistic prototypes play a key role in this liaison in that they serve as anchor points for social (re)cognition. This observation is in line with what Eckert (2003: 115) has called the 'semiotic potential of variation', and we agree with Eckert's position that the full acknowledgement of this potential 'leads to the abandonment of the view of variation as simply reflecting social categories in favor of a view of variation as being part of what constructs these categories'. Under this view, it is predictable and not surprising that social categories may induce or block developments within linguistic categories, as illustrated in section 4 with the example of shifting prototypes of phoneme realizations.

Since its early days, prototype theory has been acutely aware of the cultural dimension of human categorization and has produced valuable insights into the cultural situatedness of concepts. Furthermore, due to its wide acceptance, it is part of the common ground between a broad range of sciences. This makes it per se a highly beneficial element of cultural linguistics with its programmatic commitment to the interdisciplinary study of the interaction of language, cognition, and culture.

Related topics

cultural linguistics; language, culture and context; linguistic relativity; language and culture in cognitive anthropology; culture and kinship language; language, culture and identity; language and culture in sociolinguistics; world Englishes and local cultures; language and culture in second language learning; language and culture in intercultural communication

Further reading

Geeraerts, D. (1997) *Diachronic prototype semantics: A contribution to historical lexicology.* Oxford: Clarendon Press. (This book provides a general discussion of prototype theory and develops a framework for its application in a cognitive-linguistic modelling of language change.)

Geeraerts, D. (2006) *Words and their wonders. Papers on lexical and semantic topics.* [Cognitive Linguistics Research 33]. Berlin/New York: Mouton de Gruyter. (This volume is a collection of Geeraerts's contributions to the cognitive–linguistic approach to lexical semantics. Section 1 provides a discussion of prototypicality and salience, section 2 is devoted to the issue of polysemy and section 5 explores consequences and applications of prototype theory in lexicography.)

Kleiber, G. (1990) *La sémantique du prototype.* Paris: PUF. (This early, theoretically oriented, introduction to prototype theory is an adequate representation of the state of the art at its time of publication, i.e. at the prime time of prototype theory.)

Lakoff, G. (1987) *Women, fire and dangerous things: What categories reveal about the mind.* Chicago, IL: University of Chicago Press. (This key text of cognitive linguistics includes an overview of major studies on prototypes in various disciplines. Furthermore, it elaborates the universality of prototypicality in linguistic categories and phenomena and addresses its embeddedness in cultural–cognitive models.)

Murphy, G.L. (2002) *The big book of concepts.* Massachusetts: MIT Press. (This book provides a balanced account of prototype theory and its alternatives, e.g. exemplar-based models, and a very comprehensive and fair review of the relevant literature and empirical studies.)

Taylor, J.R. (2003 [1989]) *Linguistic categorization. Prototypes in linguistic theory* (3rd edn). Oxford: Clarendon Press. (This highly readable book is still the standard reference of the conception of prototype theory in cognitive linguistics and its position in the overall framework of this paradigm. It covers several areas of application including semantics, (morpho-)syntax and phonology.)

Tsohatzidis, S.L. (ed.) (1990) *Meanings and prototypes: Studies on linguistic categorization.* Oxford: Routledge. (This collective volume comprises both case studies and theoretical discussions on prototype theory, including early influential criticism of this model.)

References

Alo, M.A. (1989) 'A prototype approach to the analysis of meanings of kinship terms in non-native English', *Language Science, 11*(2): 159–76.

Altendorf, U. (2004) 'Language change and changing ideologies in and around RP', in M. Pütz, J. Neff-van Aertselaer and T.A. van Dijk (eds) *Communicating ideologies: Multidisciplinary perspectives on language, discourse, and social practice* (pp. 203–24). Frankfurt (Main): Peter Lang.

Athanasopoulos, P. (2009) 'Cognitive representation of color in bilinguals: The case of Greek blues', *Bilingualism: Language and Cognition, 12*(1): 83–95.

Barsalou, L.W. (1983) 'Ad hoc categories', *Memory and Cognition, 11*(2): 211–27.

Berlin, B. and Kay, P. (1969) *Basic color terms: Their universality and evolution.* Berkeley: University of California Press.

Brown, C.H. (1990) 'A survey of category types in natural language', in S.L. Tsohatzidis (ed.) *Meanings and prototypes: Studies on linguistic categorization* (pp. 17–47). London: Routledge.

Coleman, L. and Kay, P. (1981) 'Prototype semantics: The English verb LIE', *Language, 57*(1): 26–44.

Connolly, A.C., Fodor, J.A., Gleitman, L.R. and Gleitman, H. (2007) 'Why stereotypes don't even make good defaults', *Cognition, 103*(1): 1–22.

Coupland, N. and Bishop, H. (2007) 'Ideologised values for British accents', *Journal of Sociolinguistics, 11*: 74–93.

Croft, W. and Cruse, D.A. (2004) *Cognitive linguistics.* Cambridge: Cambridge University Press.

de Groot, A.M.B. (1993) 'Word-type effects in bilingual processing tasks: Support for a mixed-representational system', in R. Schreuder and B. Weltens (eds) *The bilingual lexicon* (pp. 27–52). Amsterdam: Benjamins.

Defoe, D. (1727 [1724–7]) *A Tour Thro' the Whole Island of Great Britain. Divided into Circuits or Journies. Giving a Particular and Diverting Account of Whatever is Curious, and worth Observation.* Vol. III. London: G. Strahan.

Eckert, P. (2003) 'Social variation in America', in D.R. Preston (ed.) *Needed research in American dialects* (pp. 99–121). Durham, NC: Duke University Press.

Erreich, A. and Valian, V. (1979) 'Children's internal organization of locative categories', *Child Development, 50*(4): 1071–7.

Fauconnier, G. and Turner, M. (2002) *The way we think: Conceptual blending and the mind's hidden complexities.* New York: Basic Books.

Fillmore, C.A. (1975) 'An alternative to checklist theories of meaning', *Proceedings of the First Annual Meeting of the Berkeley Linguistics Society*: 123–31.

Fodor, J.A. and Lepore, E. (1996) 'The red herring and the pet fish: why concepts still can't be prototypes', *Cognition, 58*(2): 253–70.

Foulkes, P. and Docherty, G.J. (2000) 'Another chapter in the story of /r/: 'labiodentals' variants in British English', *Journal of Sociolinguistics, 4*: 30–59.

Geeraerts, D. (2006) 'Prototype theory', in D. Geeraerts (ed.) *Cognitive linguistics: Basic readings* (pp. 141–65). Berlin/New York: Mouton de Gruyter.

——(2007) 'Lexicography', in D. Geeraerts and H. Cuyckens (eds) *The Oxford handbook of cognitive linguistics* (pp. 1160–74). Oxford: Oxford University Press.

——(2008) 'Prototypes, stereotypes, and semantic norms', in G. Kristiansen and R. Dirven (eds) *Cognitive sociolinguistics: Language variation, cultural models, social systems* (pp. 21–44). Berlin/New York: Mouton de Gruyter.

Giles, H. (1970) 'Evaluative reactions to accents', *Educational Review, 22*: 211–27.

Goodenough, W. (2001) 'Conclusion: Muddles in Schneider's model', in R. Feinberg and M. Ottenheimer (eds) *The cultural analysis of kinship. The legacy of David Schneider* (pp. 205–18). Urbana: University of Illinois Press.

Goody, J. (2000) *The European family. An historico-anthropological essay.* London: Blackwell.

Gyori, G. (1996) 'Historical aspects of categorization', in E.H. Casad (ed.) *Cognitive linguistics in the Redwoods: The expansion of a new paradigm in linguistics* (pp. 175–206). Berlin/New York: Mouton de Gruyter.

Hampton, J.A. (2006) 'Concepts as prototypes', *Psychology of Learning and Motivation, 46*: 79–113.

Hatch, E. and Brown, C. (1995) *Vocabulary, semantics, and language education.* Cambridge: Cambridge University Press.

Heider, E.R. (1971) '"Focal" color areas and the development of color terms', *Developmental Psychology, 4*(3): 447–455.

Holland, D. and Quinn, N. (eds) (1987) *Cultural models in language and thought.* Cambridge: Cambridge University Press.

Hui, L. (2004) 'Cultural knowledge and foreign language teaching and learning: A study of Chinese family schemas in language, culture and intercultural communication', *Hong Kong Journal of Applied Linguistics, 9*(2): 17–37.

——(2005) 'Chinese cultural schema of education: Implications for communication between Chinese students and Australian educators', *Issues in Educational Research, 15*(1): 17–35.

Humboldt, W. v. (1992 [1830-35]) *Schriften zur Sprache.* Ed. by M. Böhler. Stuttgart: Reclam.

Katz, J.J. and Fodor, J.A. (1963) 'The structure of a semantic theory', *Language, 39*(1): 170–210.

Kempton, W. (1981) *The folk classification of ceramics: A study of cognitive prototypes.* New York: Academic Press.

Kövecses, Z. (2000) 'The concept of anger: Universal or culture specific?', *Psychopathology, 33*(4): 159–70.

Kristiansen, G. (2003) 'How to do things with allophones', in R. Dirven, R. Frank and M. Pütz (eds) *Cognitive models in language and thought: Ideologies, metaphors, and meanings* (pp. 69–120). Berlin/New York: Mouton de Gruyter.

——(2006) 'Towards a usage-based cognitive phonology', *International Journal of English Studies, 6*(2): 107–40.

——(2008) 'Style-shifting and shifting styles: A socio-cognitive approach to lectal variation', in G. Kristiansen and R. Dirven (eds) *Cognitive sociolinguistics: Language variation, cultural models, social systems* (pp. 45–88). Berlin/New York: Mouton de Gruyter.

——(2010) 'Lectal acquisition and linguistic stereotype formation', in D. Geeraerts, G. Kristiansen and Y. Peirsman (eds) *Advances in cognitive sociolinguistics* (pp. 225–63). Berlin/New York: Mouton de Gruyter.

Labov, W. (1966) *The social stratification of English in New York City.* Washington, DC: Center for Applied Linguistics.

——(1972) *Sociolinguistic patterns.* Philadelphia: University of Pennsylvania Press.

——(1973) 'The boundaries of words and their meanings', in C.J.N. Bailey and R.W. Shuy (eds) *New ways of analyzing variation in English* (pp. 340–73). Washington, DC: Georgetown University Press.

Lakoff, G. (1987) *Women, fire, and dangerous things: What categories reveal about the mind.* Chicago: University of Chicago Press.

Lewandowska-Tomaszczyk, B. (2007) 'Polysemy, prototypes, and radial categories', in D. Geeraerts and H. Cuyckens (eds) *The Oxford handbook of cognitive linguistics* (pp. 139–69). Oxford: Oxford University Press.

Lindau, M. (1985) 'The story of /r/', in A. Fromkin (ed.) *Phonetic linguistics: Essays in honor of Peter Ladefoged* (pp. 157–68). New York: Academic Press.

MacLaury, R. (1991) 'Prototypes revisited', *Annual Review of Anthropology*, *20*: 55–74.

Malt, B.C., Sloman, S.A. and Gennari, S.P. (2003) 'Universality and language specificity in object naming', *Journal of Memory and Language*, *49*(1), 20–42.

Medin, D.L. and Schaffer, M.M. (1978). 'Context theory of classification learning', *Psychological Review of Psychology*, *85*: 207–38.

Medin, D.L. and Schwanenflugel, P.J. (1981) 'Linear separability in classification learning', *Journal of Experimental Psychology: Human Learning and Memory*, 7: 355–68.

Medin, D.L. and Smith, E.E. (1984) 'Concepts and concept-formation', *Annual Review of Psychology*, *35*(1): 113–38.

Minda, J.P. and Smith, J.D. (2001) 'Prototypes in category learning: The effects of category size, category structure, and stimulus complexity', *Journal of Experimental Psychology: Learning Memory, and Cognition*, 27: 775–99.

——(2011) 'Prototype models of categorization: Basic formulation, predictions, and limitations', in E.M. Pothos and A.J. Wills (eds) *Formal approaches in categorization* (pp. 1–20). Cambridge: Cambridge University Press.

Mugglestone, L. (1995) *Talking proper: The rise of accent as social symbol*. Oxford: Clarendon Press.

Murphy, G.L. (2002) *The big book of concepts*. Massachusetts: MIT Press.

Nathan, G.S. (2007) 'Phonology', in D. Geeraerts and H. Cuyckens (eds) *Handbook of cognitive linguistics* (pp. 611–31). Oxford: Oxford University Press.

New Jerusalem Bible (1999) Complete Text of the Ancient Canon of the Scriptures. Standard edition. 1999. Edited by H. Wansbrough. New York: Doubleday (Random House).

Niedzielski, N. and Preston, D.R. (2003) *Folk linguistics*. (Revised edition). Berlin/New York: Mouton de Gruyter.

Nosofsky, R.M. and Zaki, S.R. (2002) 'Exemplar and prototype models revisited: Response strategies, selective attention, and stimulus generalization', *Journal of Experimental Psychology: Learning, Memory and Cognition*, 28: 924–40.

Påhlsson, C. (1972) *The Northumbrian Burr: A sociolinguistic study*. Lund: CWK Gleerup.

Parkin, R. and Stone, L. (eds) (2003) *Kinship and family: An anthropological reader*. Oxford: Blackwell.

Polzenhagen, F. and Wolf, H.-G. (2010) 'Investigating culture from a linguistic perspective: An exemplification with Hong Kong English', *(ZAA) Zeitschrift für Anglistik und Amerikanistik*, 58(3) [Special issue: Linguistics and Cultural Studies, ed. by Chr. Mair and B. Korte]: 281–03.

Preston, D.R. (2010a) 'The cognitive foundation of language regard', in *Cognitive sociolinguistics: Language variation in its structural, conceptual and cultural dimensions* (pp. 494–522). Papers of the 34th International LAUD Symposium. Essen: LAUD.

——(2010b) 'Variation in language regard', in E. Zeigler, P. Gilles and J. Scharloth (eds) *Variatio delectate: Empirische Evidenzen und theoretische Passungen sprachlicher Variation* (pp. 7–27). Frankfurt (Main): Peter Lang.

Preston, D.R. (ed.) (1999) *Handbook of perceptual dialectology*. Amsterdam: Benjamins.

Quinn, N. (1987) 'Convergent evidence for a cultural model of American marriage', in D. Holland and N. Quinn (eds) *Cultural models in language and thought* (pp. 173–92). Cambridge: Cambridge University Press.

Rice, S. (2003) 'Growth of a lexical network: Nine English prepositions in acquisition', in H. Cuyckens, R. Dirven and J.R. Taylor (eds) *Cognitive approaches to lexical semantics* (pp. 243–260). Berlin/New York: Mouton de Gruyter.

Rosch, E.H. (1973) 'On the internal structure of perceptual and semantic categories', in T.E. Moore (ed.) *Cognitive development and the acquisition of language* (pp. 111–44). New York: Academic Press.

——(1975a) 'Cognitive representations of semantic categories', *Journal of Experimental Psychology: General*, *104*: 192–233.

——(1975b) 'Universals and cultural specifics in human categorization', in R.W. Brislin, S. Bochner and W.J. Lonner (eds) *Cross-cultural perspectives on learning* (pp. 177–206). New York: Sage Publications.

——(1977) 'Human categorization', in N. Warren (ed.) *Studies in cross-cultural psychology. Vol. 1* (pp. 1–49). London/New York/San Francisco: Academic Press.

——(1978) 'Principles of categorization', in E.H. Rosch and B.B. Lloyd (eds) *Cognition and categorization* (pp. 27–48). Hillsdale, NJ: Erlbaum.

Rosch, E.H. and Mervis, C.B. (1975) 'Family resemblances: Studies in the internal structure of categories', *Cognitive Psychology*, 7(4): 573–605.

Sabean, D.W., Teuscher, S. and Mathieu, J. (eds) (2007) *Kinship in Europe. Approaches to long-term development (1300–1900)*. Oxford/New York: Berghahn Books.

Schmid, H.-G., Ibriszimow, D., Kopatsch, K. and Gottschligg, P. (2008) 'Conceptual blending in language, cognition, and culture. Towards a methodology for the linguistic study of syncretic concepts', in A. Adogame, M. Echtler and U. Vierke (eds) *Unpacking the new: Critical perspectives on cultural syncretization in Africa and beyond* (pp. 93–124). Zurich/Berlin: LIT Verlag.

Schneider, E.W., Burridge, K., Kortmann, B., Mesthrie, R. and Upton C. (eds) (2004) *A handbook of varieties of English. Vol. 1: Phonology*. Berlin/New York: Mouton de Gruyter.

Schwanenflugel, P.J. and Rey, M. (1986) 'The relationship between category typicality and concept familiarity: Evidence from Spanish- and English-speaking monolinguals', *Memory and Cognition*, *14*(2): 150–63.

Sharifian, F. (2011) *Cultural conceptualisations and language. Theoretical framework and applications*. Amsterdam/Philadelphia: Benjamins.

Singleton, D. (1995) 'Review of *The bilingual lexicon* (ed. by R. Schreuder and B. Weltens)', *Applied Linguistics*, *16*(1): 125–7.

Smith, C.W. (1866) *Mind Your H's and Take Care of Your R's. Exercises for Acquiring the Use & Correcting the Abuse of the Letter H. With Observations and Additional Exercises on the Letter R*. London: Lockwood & Co.

Smith, J.D. and Minda, J.P. (1998) 'Prototypes in the mist: The early epochs of category learning', *Journal of Experimental Psychology: Learning, Memory and Cognition*, *24*: 1411–36.

——(2000) 'Thirty categorization results in search of a model', *Journal of Experimental Psychology: Learning, Memory and Cognition*, *26*: 3–27.

Stuart-Smith, J. (2003) 'The phonology of modern urban Scots', in J. Corbett, J.D. McClure and J. Stuart-Smith (eds) *The Edinburgh companion to Scots* (pp. 110–37). Edinburgh: Edinburgh University Press.

Sweetser, E. (1987) 'The definition of "lie". An examination of the folk models underlying a semantic prototype', in D. Holland and N. Quinn (eds) *Cultural models in language and thought* (pp. 43–66). Cambridge: Cambridge University Press.

Taylor, J.R. (2003 [1989]) *Linguistic categorization. Prototypes in linguistic theory* (3rd edn). Oxford: Clarendon Press.

Trudgill, P. (2004) *New dialect formation. The inevitability of colonial Englishes*. Edinburgh: Edinburgh University Press.

Tversky, B. (1990) 'Where partonomies and taxonomies meet', in S.L. Tsohatzidis (ed.) *Meanings and prototypes: Studies on linguistic categorization* (pp. 334–44). Oxford: Routledge.

Ungerer, F. and Schmid, H.-J. (2006) *An introduction to cognitive linguistics*. 2nd edn. Harlow: Pearson Education Limited.

Voorspoels, W., Storms, G. and Vanpaemel, W. (2011) 'Representation at different levels in a conceptual hierarchy', *Acta Psychologica*, *138*: 11–18.

Wells, J.C. (1982) *Accents of English* (3 vols). Cambridge: Cambridge University Press.

Wierzbicka, A. (1990) '"Prototypes save": On the uses and abuses of the notion of "prototype" in linguistics and related fields', in S.L. Tsohatzidis (ed.) *Meanings and prototypes: Studies on linguistic categorization* (pp. 347–67). Oxford: Routledge.

Wolf, H.-G. and Polzenhagen, F. (2009) *World Englishes: A cognitive sociolinguistic approach*. Berlin/New York: Mouton de Gruyter.

Xia, X.Y. and Leung, J. [2014] 'L1-based prototypicality effects in L2 vocabulary learning', in L. Filipović and M. Pütz (eds) *Multilingual cognition and language use: Processing and typological perspectives* (pp. 207–308). Amsterdam/Philadelphia: Benjamins.

19

COLOUR LANGUAGE, THOUGHT, AND CULTURE

Don Dedrick

Introduction

Do the ways that we talk about colour play a role in the ways that we can think about colour? If two languages have different colour words, does that mean that speakers of those languages think about colour in different ways? Are some colour words or colour concepts more significant, more 'basic' than others? And if so why and in what way does that matter, if at all? These questions, and there are others, related, are the basis for an extended research tradition more than forty years old. In this chapter, I aim to describe the parts of this research tradition relevant to understanding the ways that colour language might be thought to influence colour cognition. It is, however, impossible to address this general question without acknowledging the size and scope of the relevant research. It ranges from ethnography and descriptive linguistics to cognitive psychology and neuroscience. Virtually every element of this research tradition is contested.[1] The seemingly innocuous questions with which this chapter begins have been the ground for high controversy: 'the battlefield of colour' (Regier *et al.* 2010). In this chapter, I will address those parts/aspects of the tradition as well as those elements of the controversy that are relevant to understanding colour language, specifically, in relation to thought and culture.

In the late 1960s and early 1970s the linguist Paul Kay, the anthropologist Brent Berlin, and the psychologist Eleanor Rosch launched a critique of linguistic cultural relativism as it had been thought to obtain for the case of colour language and color concepts. As Kay has said, linguistic relativism made its strongest case in the domain of colour language and colour concepts, and for this reason it was a significant target.[2] *Basic Color Terms: Their Universality and Evolution* by Berlin and Kay was published in 1969, followed by supportive work on colour prototypicality by Eleanor Rosch and colleagues in the 1970s. This work on colour language and colour concepts (called 'categories' by psychologists) has set the agenda for an extensive research tradition that remains active and vital. Today, each month of the year, one can find a number of new publications that address the issues engendered by Berlin and Kay, and Rosch's original work. In this sense, colour is an important and contested site in the larger discussion of the relations between language, mind, biology, and culture. Perhaps no other topics, save IQ, gender, and race have generated the same degree of linguistic-cognitive-biological-and-anthropological *Sturm und Drang*.

Prior to the publication of *Basic Color Terms* in 1969, colour language and colour concepts were viewed as a best-case argument for linguistic cultural relativity. Color terms differ across languages, and the differences were viewed through the lens of culture. As the anthropologist V. Ray wrote, in 1953, 'each culture has taken the spectral continuum and divided it on a basis which is quite arbitrary except for pragmatic considerations' (1953: 102). Berlin and Kay acknowledged that there was a great deal of variation in color nomenclature across cultures but they argued that if you place a filter on that variable set you will find that some color terms are more 'basic' than others. The basic terms, according to Berlin and Kay's set of linguistic and psychological criteria number eleven ('black', 'white', 'grey', 'red', 'yellow', 'green', 'blue', 'orange', 'purple', 'pink', and 'brown') and they claimed that every language contains at most eleven and at least two basic color terms. When there are fewer than eleven terms in a language, as with the Himba of Namibia the claim, by Berlin and Kay, is that the Himba's five colour terms map the entire colour space,[3] but do it with fewer terms. Himba, for instance, does not distinguish green and blue lexically as does English. We shall have more to say about these differences later. Berlin and Kay also argued that there is an 'evolutionary sequence' through which the development of basic color terminology passes. If a language adds more basic terms to its lexical stock, the additions will follow a predictable path of development. These are very general and very strong claims: (1) that there is a 'universal' set of basic colour terms from which any language 'chooses' a subset; (2) that the subsets chosen are ordered in an 'evolutionary' sequence reconstructed from the examination of extant colour vocabularies.

There is nothing empirical in *Basic Color Terms* that bears directly on the relation between language and thought for it merely reports some hitherto unexpected results as to the patterning of colour language cross-culturally. Eleanor Rosch's work (Rosch 1972; Rosch and Olivier 1972, 1974) connects these linguistic regularities to psychological regularities, arguing that there are non-linguistic cognitive 'prototypes' which are the non-linguistic cognitive anchors for the basic colour terms, and help explain their universality.

Talk of 'universality' and 'evolution' suggest the bad old days of imperialist anthropology (e.g. Tylor 1871; Morgan 1877) and it is thus not surprising that Berlin and Kay's work came under fire from anthropologists almost immediately. While numerous problems have been identified with Berlin and Kay's original research,[4] and there have been some emendations to the very general claims it expresses,[5] Berlin and Kay's work has provided the basis for remarkably fecund if contested research tradition. It is that tradition that is the primary focus of this chapter.[6] There is a great deal of ground to cover. Section 1 provides an overview that covers the 'classical' period of research: early language-cognition work, followed by its critical evaluation in the work of Berlin and Kay, and Rosch. Section 2 focuses on central areas of contemporary controversy, for this topic not only began in controversy, but remains in such. The conclusion, section 3, comments on the ways in which this debate matters in its own terms as well as in relation to the larger question about the relationships between mind and language and culture. Much of the literature relevant to understanding colour language and colour concepts is not discussed here, not because it is irrelevant or uninteresting, but because it is not directly related to questions about the effects of language on mind. As we shall see, though, it can be hard to draw a line between what is relevant and what is not.

1 The 'classical' period of colour language research

Brain, mind, language, culture, and colour: historical stage setting[7]

If the *locus classicus* for the contemporary debate about colour language, culture, and cognition is to be found in Berlin and Kay (1969), the interest in colour language dates to earlier times. In the third volume of his *Homer and the Homeric age* William Gladstone (1809–98), classicist and Prime

Minister of Great Britain, argued that the colour words one found in Homer were applied in ways foreign to his contemporary English (Gladstone 1858). How could one square the application of a single colour term to 'iron, copper, horses, lions, bulls, eagles, wine, swarthy men and smoke?' (quoted in Biggam 2012: 11). Gladstone's ultimate conclusion was that they could not be squared and, crucially, it would have to be physiology that explained the Homeric deviation from contemporary colour names: 'I conclude, then, that the organ of colour and its impressions were but partially developed among the Greeks of the heroic age' (ibid.). The ancient Greeks spoke about colour differently because they saw colours differently. As Biggam writes, and as it seems to be universally agreed, 'Gladstone drew the wrong conclusion' (ibid.: 12).

There are numerous ways in which it is wrong. Let us consider the way Gladstone has conceptualized the matter as a guide to his mistakes. In the first place, he has pointed to two different things: (a) one's linguistic practice in applying colour words to things and (b) 'the organ of colour and its impressions'. Note that (b) conflates two things: a person's *seeing* (their 'impressions') and their *physiology* (their 'organ of colour'). While one cannot doubt that what one can see constrains what one can name, seeing and its perceptual content is distinct from the physiological systems that generate, cause, or realize that content. There are the events in one's brain, and then there are the perceptual states such events engender.[8] There is, in other words, a distinction in Gladstone between psychological states and biological states that needs to be articulated more clearly. Something else, prima facie, is absent in the sketch of Gladstone's views provided here. There is no mention of context or culture. To be fair to Gladstone he considered both of these notions to be of interest, and even imagined that a culture distinct from his own might deploy colour terms differently (ibid.: 11–12). And yet, in the end, Gladstone settled on the physiological/perceptual account: if the Greeks do not have names for colours (that Gladstone's contemporaries have), that is because they cannot see them; if the Greeks *do* have names for different colours than Gladstone's contemporaries (defined in terms of their referents as determined through textual analysis), that is because the Greeks see colours differently, and in accord with those names. Why Gladstone adopted this reductive position is unclear but, with only some anachronism in order to make things explicit, Gladstone introduces us to the major players in the classical and contemporary debates:

biological states, the 'organ of colour', *the brain*

psychological states, chromatic perceptual content, *the mind*

linguistic behaviour, colour words, *language*

socially transmitted information, context, *culture*

All four of these dimensions are active in accounts of colour naming, whether they are explicitly recognized or not. Gladstone, for instance, takes it that differences in the 'organ of colour' fixes differences in linguistic behaviour. Mind and/or culture, though they are present, have subsidiary roles in explaining Greek colour words (or Victorian English colour words, for that matter). That is one way to interpret the relations among these four dimensions, but there are others. One might, for example, think that culture and language are inseparable, and that language reflects culturally transmitted, group specific information, with the brain and the mind as conduits. This would account for the differences in colour nomenclature one sees across cultures, and it is the sort of idea that Steven Pinker (2002) criticizes as involving a 'blank slate' view of the mind. Or: one could imagine a more subtle version of Gladstone's view that exploits the distinction between mind and brain: perhaps the brain is responsible for generating perceptual states which differ in psychological salience, where psychological differences between more and less salient perceived colours bias humans towards the adoption of certain colour words (e.g., Kay and Maffi 1999). This view downplays the role of culture, and its main proponents are discussed later in this chapter (e.g. Berlin and Kay 1969; Rosch 1972) Such a view could even be 'fine-tuned' to include culture: perhaps socially transmitted information can 'bias the bias', so to speak, causing some differences in colour language to express themselves relative to particular cultural/linguistic groups (Reiger, Kay, and Cook 2005). The point is that, depending on emphasis, these four basic dimensions or parameters can generate a range of different accounts as to the nature of colour language and its relationships to mind, brain, and culture. One aim in this chapter is to direct the reader's attention to these differing emphases.

Gladstone was not the only writer of his generation, and generations prior to the mid-twentieth century, to concern himself with colour and colour language. Hugo Freidrich Magnus (1842–1907), a German ophthalmologist, developed Gladstone's views into a diachronic model of colour language development constructed from the evidence of synchronic colour term application. As with Berlin and Kay, Magnus detected the refinement of colour term reference in a variety of distinct synchronic sources and proposed a diachronic developmental sequence to explain such refinement. Gladstone accepted Magnus's idea and regarded it as 'an evolutionary process which all races experience' (Biggam 2012: 13).

Even so, talk of the 'evolution' of colour vision (the evidence for which, for Gladstone and Magnus, was differences in colour language) drew criticism from the nascent science of evolution: Darwinism. In his *The Colour Sense* (1879) Grant Allen (1848–99), a Darwinian, pointed out that colour vision was both acute and an adaptation in both contemporary humans and in closely related animals. Thus it made sense to think that, phylogenetically, colour vision is inherited, much as it presently functions, from a common ancestor. In this sense its 'evolution' pre-dated differences observed in literate human cultures. Allen also argued, on the basis of an intensive consideration of literary texts, including those of Homer, that the best explanation for differences in colour language resided not in differences in physiology but in differences in context: that colour language develops in relation to the needs of speakers but not in relation to a vision system that is more or less uniform across not only humans but related animals, a view we now know to be correct (e.g. Surridge, Osorio, and Mundy 2003). Allen, in other words, rejected the simple relationship Gladstone and Magnus proposed between physiology and language, and offered up a view similar to that proposed by anthropologists in the first half of the twentieth century, a century that witnessed the development and spread of a modern cultural relativism, proposed in American circles by, most famously, the linguists Edward Sapir, Benjamin Lee Whorf, and the anthropologist Franz Boas. Sapir and Whorf are famous for the hypothesis that bears their name, 'the Sapir–Whorf hypothesis' which asserts that, as Whorf has famously put it:

> We dissect nature along lines laid down by our native languages. The categories and types that we isolate from the world of phenomena we do not find there because they stare every observer in the face; on the contrary, the world is presented as a kaleido-scopic flux of impressions which has to be organized by our minds – and this means largely by the linguistic system in our minds.
>
> *(Whorf 1956: 213)*

For Whorf, language was essentially an expression of culture such that language encodes culturally specific content that affects the way people think. Speakers of different languages may think and behave differently depending on the language that they use. Before discussing this hypothesis in more detail, it is worth noting how nicely it seems to apply to the case of colour and colour concepts. The visible spectrum is a continuum, distinct types of colours – I shall now refer to them as 'colour categories' (a rubric consistent both with Whorf and much of the research to be discussed) – do not, it seems, 'stare us in the face' but have to be isolated from their natural source. The process of isolation is accomplished by linguistic categorization, the linguistic system in our minds, which is shaped by the particulars of culture. This view is well summarized in the quotation from Ray we saw earlier: 'each culture has taken the spectral continuum and divided it on a basis which is quite arbitrary except for pragmatic considerations' (1953: 102). This, indeed, describes 'Whorfianism' in the context of colour categorization and it is a view significantly different from Gladstone's. Recall the four dimensions that can figure in explanations of colour categorization

biological states, the 'organ of colour', *the brain*

psychological states, chromatic perceptual content, *the mind*

linguistic behaviour, colour words, *language*

socially transmitted information, context, *culture*

Gladstone linked biological states directly to linguistic behaviour, downplaying the role of mind and culture. Mind – the relevant perceptual states – are themselves fused to the organ of colour for Gladstone; culture is not discussed in Gladstone's account of ancient Greek colour names. The Whorfian view described here sees culture as the driving force: it is expressed in language and via language shapes the way that encultured individuals think about the world. The biology of colour vision is the odd man out in this account, but that is not because the Whorfian has nothing to say about the biology of colour but because she has an entirely clear position on it. Of course it matters that perception is structured the way that it is. One can only see what one can see. That said, it is of the essence of Whorfianism that the perceptual states delivered by the brain are not bundled discretely into categories such as red, yellow, green, and blue. (The unbroken colour continuum provides prima facie evidence for this.) Colour categorization is, thus, a culturally driven linguistic operation in the mind, operating on perceptual material that is category free.[9] This is the nature of the contemporary debate: is the origin of colour categories – colour concepts in the mind – more like the way Gladstone sees it or more like the way the Whorfian sees it? With this stage setting complete let us move to a discussion of what I shall call 'experimental Whorfianism (I)'.

Experimental Whorfianism (I): colour language and colour cognition

It is widely agreed that there are two versions of the Sapir–Whorf hypothesis (what I will sometimes call 'Whorfianism' to accord with contemporary literature on colour language). The first is a *strong version* and claims that language determines or constrains mental operations. The second, *weak version* claims that language influences mental operations. It is also widely agreed that the strong version is problematic (see Chapter 2 this volume, for a history of linguistic relativity). That language should *influence* thought – that version of the thesis is considered viable and is, indeed, the motivating idea for this volume. None of this is news to those familiar with Whorfianism. What may be news (though it is old news) is that this weak–strong distinction, as well as a general interest in the relationships between language, mind, and culture were topics of considerable interest to the first generation of cognitive psychologists, mainly in the USA, and mainly at Harvard.

In 1954 two of the most influential psychologists from the first self-identifying generation of cognitive psychologists published 'A Study in Language and Cognition' (Brown and Lenneberg 1954). Roger Brown and Eric Lenneberg wanted to see if one could show effects of language on cognition, and they aimed to do so by examining the relationship between colour language and colour cognition. Were they probing the strong or the weak version of the hypothesis? The Harvard psychologist Jerome Bruner, in his intellectual autobiography, reports it was the latter, claiming that Brown did not view the strong version as 'empirical' (1983: 158).

While there seems to be no evidence of this claim in Brown's corpus (Bruner is reporting the gist of a talk at Harvard in 1956) it is not difficult to see why one might view the strong version of the hypothesis as non-empirical. Suppose it is true that language and mind are related such that language *determines* mental operations. If this were so, language and mind could not come apart (much as Gladstone seemed to think that colour language and the impressions of the colour organ could not come apart). If language and mind cannot come apart, it will not be possible to manipulate one or the other in order to show an effect of one upon the other, to specify, as psychologists would say, dependent and independent variables. If Brown was not convinced that the strong version of Whorf's hypothesis was empirically tractable, 'A Study in Language and Cognition' is clearly an attempt to test the weak version, and experimental Whorfianism in cognitive psychology was born.

Brown and Lenneberg were interested in the relationship between language and cognition. In order to examine this relationship they developed a measure they called 'codability' defined in both linguistic and psychological terms.[10] The core idea, following on the heels of Whorf's hypothesis, was that colour terms that were more codable would be more memorable. Codability was intended as a measure of cultural significance (thus connecting language and culture) and, if Whorfian ideas were correct, manipulations of codability should show an effect in memory recognition. And this is what Brown and Lenneberg's study demonstrated. If a colour term was more codable, it was more likely to be successfully recalled on a memory task. If less codable, then less likely to be successfully recalled. It is true that this result is far from Whorf's occasionally expressed idea of speakers of different languages living in different worlds. Nonetheless, it appears to show that the way one thinks about colours is affected by the way one can talk about them.

Whorf's hypothesis applies to singular cultures and across cultures. One way to think of it: when we see differences in languages, between cultural groups, we can interpret those differences as, potentially, culturally driven differences in cognition. What then are we to make of 'A Study in Language and Cognition', a study restricted to the psychologist's typical experimental subjects (in this case Brown's Harvard undergraduates)? The inference (prediction) is clear: were the study to be conducted cross-culturally we would/should find the same pattern: more culturally significant = more codable = more memorable. Brown and Lenneberg did not conduct cross-cultural experiments, but others did. Lenneberg and Roberts published a field study of Zuni Indians that demonstrated similar results (Lenneberg and Roberts 1953) and Lantz and Stefflre (1964), in an explicitly cross-cultural study, demonstrated that a variable associated with codability – they called it 'communication accuracy' – was positively correlated with codability such that subjects, given a colour name, were better at picking an appropriate colour from a display of colour samples if that colour was more codable. All in all, this adds up to a significant push to empirically support Whorf's hypothesis for the case of colour language and cognition. In 1968 (one year before the publication of Berlin and Kay's *Basic Color Terms*), the psychologist Robert Krauss described Brown and Lenneberg's study as 'one of the most elegant and interesting experiments relating language to cognitive processes' (1968: 269). Times were about to change.

Berlin and Kay's basic colour terms

I have already stated the main claims of Berlin and Kay's *Basic Color Terms* (1969). These claims were: (1) there is a 'universal' set of basic colour terms ('black', 'white', 'grey', 'red', 'yellow', 'green', 'blue', 'orange', 'purple', 'pink', and 'brown') from which any language 'chooses' a subset; (2) the subsets chosen are ordered in an 'evolutionary' sequence reconstructed from the examination of extant colour vocabularies. In this chapter the focus is on (1), since it is not entirely clear that the claims about colour term 'evolution' are indicative of language influencing thought.[11]

Since the legitimacy and significance of Berlin and Kay's work depends upon the concept of a basic colour term, it is worth commenting on how the authors arrived at it. Much as with Brown and Lenneberg, Berlin and Kay utilized a mixture of linguistic and psychological criteria intended to identify culturally salient colour terms. The four primary criteria for a colour word being basic were

(i) It is monolexic: that is, the meaning is not predictable from the meaning of its parts.
(ii) Its signification is not included in that of any other colour term.
(iii) Its application must not be restricted to a narrow class of objects.
(iv) It must be psychologically salient for all informants. Indices of psychological salience include, among others, (1) a tendency to occur at the beginning of elicited lists of color terms, (2) stability of reference across informants, (3) occurrence in the idiolects of all informants.

(Berlin and Kay 1969: 6)

These criteria are not intended to be definitional and there are four supplemental criteria for cases where it is difficult to apply the four primary criteria. One should also note that, for different reasons, various scholars have refined and added to the list: *nineteen* criteria are now available.[12] It would be an understatement to say that these criteria have been controversial. Yet the idea that some colour language is 'basic' in the sense of referring essentially to the domain of colour, not being tied to the colour of specific objects, and having a greater degree of cultural salience has proved attractive and useful to many colour language researchers, and pre-dates *Basic Color Terms*.[13] The main scientific critics of the universalist claims accept basicness as legitimate in their own research (e.g. Roberson, Davies, and Davidoff 2000) and it is not my point to question the concept here.

The research reported in *Basic Colour Terms* proceeded as follows. Having identified the basic colour terms for a language, Berlin and Kay asked their informants to specify, on a colour chart,[14] the boundaries of their colour categories. This task involves indicating all the samples in the array that the informant is willing to identify as, say, 'red'. Boundary placements were idiosyncratic across informants, and even speakers of a given language did not agree as to the boundaries. Informants were also asked to specify the best examples of their basic colour terms, and the results of this task were quite different. Informants picked colour chips from a restricted cluster of samples, and this result not only obtained across the speakers of a given language, but was robust across different languages (twenty different languages in total were spoken by the informants). Berlin and Kay called the best examples 'focal points' or 'focal colors' and claimed that they were universal. Previous research claiming significant cultural/linguistic variation in colour categories concentrated upon boundary placement rather than the best example, focal colours they had identified. Musing on the biological basis they believed their results to have indicated Berlin and Kay wrote

Chomsky and Lenneberg have argued that the complexities of language structure, together with some known limitations of human neurophysiology, imply that human language cannot be considered simply as a manifestation of human intelligence. Rather it must be recognized as a species-specific ability, ultimately based on species-specific bio-morphological structures.

And more specific to the topic at hand, colour language:

The study of the biological foundations of the most peculiarly and exclusively set of human behavioral abilities – language – is just beginning, but sufficient evidence has accumulated to show that such connections must exist for the linguistic realms of syntax and phonology. The findings reported here concerning the universality and evolution of basic color lexicon suggest that such connections are also to be found in the realm of semantics.

(Berlin and Kay 1969, p. 109–10)

The reference to Chomsky reflects something of the Zeitgeist in linguistics circa 1970. Even so, generative grammar provides, prima facie, a model for thinking about the supposed universality of basic colour terms and focal colours. In *Aspects of the Theory of Syntax* (1965) Chomsky introduced a distinction between linguistic competence and linguistic performance. The former, competence, is concerned with the (unconscious; tacit) knowledge that a speaker has and which is the basis for his linguistic ability. Linguistic performance, on the other hand concerns everything that is involved with the production of linguistic behaviour. For Chomsky, performance issues concern the realm of human linguistic behaviour, complete with false starts, memory limitations, distractions, errors, individual physiological differences, and so forth. Performance is not the proper object of study for linguistic *theory*, according to Chomsky. It is competence, defined in terms of the specification of a rule based grammar that, when one idealizes and abstracts from all the vagaries of performance – and of surface linguistic features that are contingent properties of natural languages – explains the ability of humans and only humans to learn language.

Chomsky's views are controversial (more so recently than in 1970),[15] but they provide one way to think about basic colour terms. Perhaps Berlin and Kay had discovered a universal colour semantics (or constraints upon such), innate and biologically based, which is obscured by superficial differences, and masked, perhaps by cultural specifics. A historical or anthropological linguist might look to the languages of the world and see linguistic differences that appear profound. And yet for those convinced of 'universal grammar' there is something that is not different but is shared and that all humans have in common: the ability to learn a language (grounded in their innate competence), as opposed to the language that they learn, which is contingent. So too, one might say, for superficial differences in colour language among different linguistic and cultural groups. As with language writ large, the differences may seem over-whelming, but the range of variation is radically reduced by the application of criteria designed to identify commonalties: the basic colour terms and more significantly, the focal colours. While Berlin and Kay do not explicitly connect the competence–performance distinction to their colour semantics, that distinction is far from inconsistent with their theoretical discussion in *Basic Color Terms*.

No matter how one feels about a Chomskian interpretation of Berlin and Kay's work, one of the most significant results that has come out of that work is the concept of the 'focal colour' or 'focal point'. If boundaries are not reliable for speakers and if focal colours are, what might the explanation be for that? Two crucial sets of experiments by the psychologist Eleanor Rosch addressed this issue and set the stage for contemporary discussions of the relationship between language, thought, biology, and culture.

Experimental Whorfianism (II): Rosch, focality, and prototypicality

Eleanor Rosch was familiar with Brown and Lenneberg's codability claims, which appeared to support a weak version of Whorf's hypothesis (Rosch was Brown's doctoral student at Harvard). In an article published in 1972, Rosch and her colleague Donald Olivier tested 'a different kind of operational claim derived from the Whorfian position, a claim that verbal color coding acts on memory imagery such that the structure of colors in memory comes to resemble the structure of color names in a given language' (Heider Rosch, and Olivier 1972: 338). The idea is this: if informants name colours differently will they, on a cognitive measure (recognition or memory, say), perform differently? If I have only two colour words – basic terms – in my vocabulary, will I tend to confuse distinct shades within the boundaries of those two named colour categories or, to put the question comparatively, will I do worse than a speaker whose language has more than two basic terms? Suppose my language has only two basic colour terms: one for 'warm-lightish' colours (red and yellow plus white) and one for 'cool-darkish' colours (blue and green plus black). Suppose another language, such as English, has terms for red, yellow, green, and blue. Will the speaker without terms to differentiate red and yellow (or green and blue) confuse the same-named reds and yellows (or greens and blues) in memory? Rosch's study was explicitly cross-cultural. Her subjects were USA English speakers, and the Durgum Dani of Irian Jaya in Indonesian New Guinea, an aboriginal people that had been described as possessing warm-lightish and cool-darkish terms such as those described above. The results were not as the Whorfian hypothesis of Rosch and Olivier would predict (i.e. that naming structure would influence memory structure). Instead, Rosch discovered that naming structures, which were clearly different for the two sets of informants did not carry over to the memory structures which, at least superficially, appeared similar[16] (Rosch and Olivier 1972: 350).

What is the difference between experimental Whorfianism (I) and experimental Whorfianism (II)? The research focusing on codability had claimed to demonstrate an effect of language on memory: more codable colours were more memorable. Further, codability was explained in cultural terms: culturally important colours were more codable and hence more memorable, thus an effect of language on thought. Note, however, that the direction of causality, from

cultural significance -> codability -> memorability

is determined by the initial assumptions of Whorfianism (this is not strictly a failing, for that is the hypothesis being tested). Is it possible these assumptions are mistaken? Perhaps it is memorability that determines codability and that what is assumed to be 'culturally significant' is more of an *outcome* of this biologically grounded psychological salience. Berlin and Kay had set the table for such an account, by arguing for the universal salience of their focal colours, and Rosch was to supply a key premise to that argument.

In an extremely influential study published in 1972, conducted again with the Dani and others, Rosch was interested in the following question: 'Could it be that these examples of color names, these focal colors, designated areas of the color space that were perceptually (and thus universally) salient, and that it was this perceptual salience that determined both which colors were more memorable and which colors were more codable?' (reported in Rosch 1988: 377). Her results supported a positive answer to these questions. A series of experiments, with the Dani as well as speakers of the major linguistic groups, discovered that focal colours were more codable than non-focal colours. Focal colours were also better remembered than non focal colours. Since the Dani did not have many basic terms, Rosch constructed a task that involved invented names for focal and other colours, and the result was that categories that involved focal colours were more easily learned and remembered in long-term memory than invented names for categories that did not involve focal colours.

The experiments reported in 'Universals in Colour Naming and Memory' explicitly connect Rosch's work to that of Berlin and Kay. As she wrote in the final paragraph of that article:

> Given the attributes of focal colors – their occurrence as exemplars of basic color names, their linguistic codability across languages, and their superior retention in short- and long-term memory – it would seem most economical to suppose that these attributes are derived from the same underlying factors, most likely having to do with the physiology of primate color vision. In short, far from being a domain well suited to the study of the effects of language on thought, the color space would seem to be a prime example of the influence of underlying perceptual cognitive factors on the formation and reference of linguistic categories.
>
> *(Heider 1972: 20)*

Returning to the different dimensions relevant to explanations of colour naming

biological states, the 'organ of colour', *the brain*

psychological states, chromatic perceptual content, *the mind*

linguistic behaviour, colour words, *language*

socially transmitted information, context, *culture*

we find the first three are covered: physiologically based factors of primate colour vision account for the perceptual cognitive factors ('attributes') that play a formative role in the development of linguistic categories. Culture is nowhere to be found, though presumably it has a role in explaining surface variability of colour language.

Reference to physiological factors (the brain), and perceptual cognitive factors (the mind) amount to more than wishful thinking on Rosch's part. With respect to the latter, Rosch developed the concept for which she is most famous as a psychologist, that of a 'prototype'. This notion, which was to have a profound effect on psychological theories of concepts and categories was developed in the context of Rosch's work on colour (Rosch 1974, 1975). It, or something like it, was necessary to mark the distinction between the linguistic and psychological dimensions relative to colour naming. Consider Berlin and Kay's notion of a 'focal color'. One arrives at a focal color for an individual by asking him to identify his best example of a basic color term. A focal color, then, is a linguistic and behavioural concept. Like Brown and Lenneberg, Rosch demonstrated that colour language and colour memory could 'come apart'. Unlike Brown and Lenneberg, who were guided by a Whorfian hypothesis and thus discovered seeming Whorfian effects of language on cognition, Rosch claimed to uncover a different type of psychological salience: a salience that transcends language. The Dani had two focal colours because they only had two basic colour terms and focality is partly defined in terms of basicness. And yet the Dani performance on a variety of experimental tasks indicated certain regions of the colour space were psychologically salient for them. These colours, which corresponded to Berlin and Kay's focal colours, were salient for informants, whether or not they had a full complement of basic terms; these colours were deemed to be 'natural prototypes ... for the development and learning of color names' (Rosch 1974: 114).

As for the claim that physiological factors were responsible for the psychological salience of the colour prototypes, a connection has been made. As Berlin and Kay's own research and the research tradition in general became more sophisticated, in light of various criticisms as well as exposure to much larger data sets than those described in *Basic Color Terms*, the authors and colleagues modified their ideas, coming to hold that the 'Hering primaries' of opponent colour theory (red, yellow, green, blue, white, black) were the basis for the salience of primary colour prototypes and, as well, helped explain synchronic and especially diachronic data that Berlin and Kay described as an 'evolution'. There is, in other words, much more than a promissory note on behalf of biology's role in the explanation of colour naming, however problematical its precise articulation has turned out to be.[17]

Rosch's work stood the earlier language and cognition studies on their heads. Differences in language did not predict differences in thought. One could derive nothing but surface linguistic variation from Rosch's work. But this is not where the story ends.

2 Experimental Whorfianism (III): Rosch revisited

Rosch Heider's (1972) results have been widely accepted as proving the case for universal basic color categories, but some potentially serious flaws have been pointed out in both the design and interpretation of her studies.

(Roberson, Davies, and Davidoff 2000: 370)

The effect of Rosch's experimental work on colour was profound in psychology. Not only did her notion of a prototype revolutionize thought about concepts and concept formation in general but, coupled with Berlin and Kay's ideas about basic colour terms, they formed an influential view about how to understand colour categorization, and, indeed, how to understand Whorf's hypothesis. Colour language could no longer be thought of as the paradigm case of language influencing thought. As Roberson, Davies, and Davidoff (ibid.: 371) note, this is a strong conclusion to draw from a few experiments that, as they say, have some 'potentially serious flaws'. Before we discuss those flaws, it is worth considering the relationship between prototypes and colour categories.

Recall that Berlin and Kay found the boundaries of the colour categories named by a basic term to be unreliable. Focal colours were not as unreliable and Rosch's contribution was to show that one could separate focality from prototypicality (linguistic salience from psychological salience) such that the later, non-linguistic property of the mind, perhaps fixed by biological factors (as both Berlin and Kay and Rosch had suggested) explained the linguistic saliences. The natural salience of the colour prototyes could thus be viewed as playing a role in colour category formation: categories, with their uncertain boundaries, form in relation to prototypes that are psychologically salient cognitive anchors. Indeed, the experiments discussed above demonstrated that informants found it easier to learn artificial colour categories structured 'prototypically', harder to learn categories lacking in such structure. On this view, prototypes are *cognitively* basic and boundaries are defined in relation, somehow,[18] to prototypes. Both of these claims, that cognitive prototypes are cognitively basic to categorization, and that boundaries could only be defined in relation to cognitively basic prototypes were challenged by Roberson and colleagues, beginning with a landmark article appearing almost two decades after Rosch's influential work: 'Color Categories Are Not Universal: New Evidence from a Stone-Age Culture' (Roberson, Davies, and Davidoff 2000). In the introduction to their article Roberson *et al.*, make a number of interesting observations, including: (1) the influence that Rosch's experiments had on the way people have come to think about language–thought research; (2) the fact that it seemed overreaching to tar non-colour language–thought research with the brush of colour proto-typicality; (3) it was not entirely clear that Rosch's data could support her conclusions to say nothing of their far-ranging implications, that is, (1) and (2). The 'potentially serious problems', as Roberson *et al.* put it, concern the interpretation of Rosch's data (there were scaling and statistical issues) and the generally poor performance of the Dani (their performance on the memory tasks was statistically significant given the task design, yet remarkably bad in general).[19] Given these issues – and given the significance attached to Rosch's work, Roberson *et al.* set out to replicate the three most important of Rosch's experiments – just those discussed section 1 of this chapter: (1) colour memory is independent of colour naming (2) focal colours are better remembered than non-focals, regardless of language differences (3) focal colours positively influenced the learning and memory of artificial colour categories taught to informants.

The work by Rosch that we have discussed was explicitly cross-cultural. She compared USA English speakers with the Durgum Dani of Irian Jaya in Indonesian New Guinea (a people described as 'stone-age' by Rosch, a description repeated in Roberson *et al.*'s title). For political reasons, it was not possible to visit the Dani. The comparison population, also from New Guinea, were native speakers of Berinmo, a language identified as possessing five basic colour terms. This would seem to be a significant difference from the Rosch studies, yet as Roberson *et al.* point out, there was some uncertainty as to whether the Dani possess two or more than two terms (ethnographically, other two-term systems have not been discovered), an uncertainty shared by Rosch herself (1972a). Thus, despite the more 'advanced' state of the Berinmo basic colour language, Roberson *et al.* were of the opinion that Berinmo was both 'sufficiently limited and that color as an attribute of objects in their [Berinmo speakers] natural world was of suffi-ciently limited salience to make them a suitable target population on which to attempt a long overdue replication of Rosch Heider's most important original studies' (Roberson, Davies, and Davidoff 2000: 370).

Roberson *et al.* found that (with some caveats),[20] for each of the three main types of study executed by Rosch and discussed above, Rosch's results were *not* replicated. Specifically: (1) colour memory was not independent of colour naming: there was 'a greater intralanguage similarity between naming and memory than interlanguage similarity of memory patterns' (ibid.: 386); (2) there was no advantage for Berlin–Kay focal colours over non-focals for either Berinmo or English speakers (ibid.); (3) focality did not predict superior learning of artificial categories – on a task that could not be completed by Berinmo informants (ibid.) and had to be modified. Similar results for another five-term language, Himba, which is spoken in Northern Namibia, yielded similar results (Roberson, Davidoff, Davies, Shapiro 2005).

As we have seen, prototypicality, which underwrites focality in the Berlin–Kay–Rosch research, is the non-linguistic basis for Rosch's theory of categorization. Categories form in relation to the psychological salience of a prototype. If Berinmo and Himba have colour categories, and if focal colours/prototypes are not salient for those categories, what explains categorization? Is there some process, non-prototypical in nature, accounting for the existence of colour categories? Roberson *et al.*, having failed to replicate Rosch's work, look in that direction.

'Categorical perception' occurs when the categories possessed by an individual effect their perception of stimuli at the boundaries between their categories (Harnad 1987). So, for a domain of stimuli that is continuous, such as the colour continuum, possession of the categories green and blue would, if there is categorical perception, make it easier to distinguish colour samples that are green on the one hand, blue on the other (i.e. between category discrimina-tion) from colour samples that are both blue or both green (i.e. within category discrimination).

Categorical perception has been demonstrated for speech, colour, and for other domains (Goldstone 2010) and it can be exploited to detect effects of language on thought. Suppose that language A has five basic chromatic colour categories (so specified in terms of the criteria for basicness). Language B has eight basic chromatic colour terms (so specified in terms of the criteria for basicness). Such languages differ in both the number of terms, and the placement of boundaries for the categories named by their terms since, let us say, language A does not have distinct terms for what are called 'green' and 'blue' in Language B. Given categorical perception for colour, and given distinct names, categories, and boundaries, will categorical perception be *different* for the two languages and in accord with the linguistic differences? If the answer is yes, that is evidence that linguistic colour categories have affected perception – thought – in a manner dependent on language. And this is what Roberson *et al.* demonstrated to be the case with Berinmo (Roberson *et al.* 2000) and later Himba (Roberson, Davidoff, Davies, and Shapiro 2005). As Roberson and Hanley (2010: 187) summarize this research 'The results indicated that all three groups of participants [English, Berinmo, Himba] showed CP [categorical perception], but only at color boundaries that were explicitly marked in their own language. Crucially, there was no effect of the proposed universal boundary between green and blue for speakers of Himba and Berinmo whose languages do not make this distinction.'

So: experimental Whorfianism III challenged both Rosch's claims about the psychological salience of colour prototypes, and, in doing so, their role in the cognitive construction of colour categories (if there are no prototypes, they cannot be the cognitive anchors of colour categories). Prototypes dispatched, the authors, in a series of articles, turned to the much maligned boundaries of colour categories arguing that these were linguistic constructs responsible for linguistically driven categorical perception. As with Rosch before them, Roberson *et al.* derived very general conclusions from their studies. Thus the authors propose that 'color categorization is largely culturally and linguistically relative' (Roberson, *et al.* 2000: 394).

There is much that has been elided in this account of Roberson's relativist position, including important and interesting questions concerning how boundaries are constructed without prototypes and what explains the cross-linguistic patterning described by Berlin and Kay (but see Roberson and Hanley, 2010). As important as those matters may be, the claims that there is categorical perception at the boundaries of colour terms, and those effects are due to local differences in languages have been accepted by those critical of the relativist position, Paul Kay (and colleagues) in particular. Kay and Reiger write that

> there is ample evidence that differences in color category boundaries between languages may influence color memory, learning or discrimination ... These results have for the most part been established by comparing a behavioral color response between speakers of English and one of a handful of languages, all differing from English in the placement of some lexical color category boundary.
>
> *(2007: 294)*

And on another occasion:

> Roberson *et al.* ... have presented considerable evidence that the cross-linguistically varying boundaries of linguistic color categories can affect nonlinguistic color cognition.
>
> *(Reiger, Kay, and Cook 2005a: 8391)*

One would think that this is good news for relativist Whorfians such as Roberson and Davidoff and, of course, it is. Davidoff, for instance, writes 'we are pleased that it is now generally acknowledged that language plays a substantial role in the establishment of even basic level color categorical perception' (Davidoff *et al.* 2009). Yet significant disagreement remains. In the previous quotation, Davidoff is referring to an article by Reiger *et al.* Here is how *they* summarize their view in that article:

> at least in the color domain, there are clear universals governing the semantic distinctions that languages make – but there may also be some limited element of arbitrariness in exactly where category boundaries are drawn. This is an ultimately universalist finding, but with a relativist twist.
>
> *(Reiger, Kay, Gilbert, and Ivey 2010: 180)[21]*

This makes for a remarkably weak concession[22] to the relativist view (how much of a Martini is the twist?) and seems to be a long way from the claim that 'color categorization is largely culturally and linguistically relative' (Roberson *et al.* 2000). How is it that Kay and colleagues reject the relativist account of categorization, yet accept that categorical perception is largely a function of linguistically specified categorical boundaries?

Where do colour categories come from (I)?

1. Are semantic distinctions in languages determined by largely arbitrary linguistic convention?
2. Do semantic differences cause corresponding cognitive or perceptual differences in speakers of different languages?

(Reiger and Kay 2009)

In the article these questions are taken from, Reiger and Kay argue that the questions must be viewed as distinct. One can agree that semantic differences in the reference of terms cause the sort of Whorfian effects described by Roberson and colleagues, while holding that there are significant cross-cultural regularities as to boundaries for colour categories that cannot be accounted for on the view, (1), that all semantic distinctions are 'arbitrary'. Is this a straw person? In other words, are the relativists we have discussed committed to the view that colour categorization is 'arbitrary'? The answer to this question, in large part, is yes. As we have seen, Roberson *et al.* view colour categorization as 'largely culturally and linguistically relative' (2000: 394). They think, in other words, that once one has dispensed with prototypes, and given the variability of boundaries, *and* given language specific effects that are culturally relative, categories are essentially linguistic/cultural constructs.[23] This is not to say that Roberson, Davidoff, and colleagues believe categorization is *strictly* arbitrary. It observes a *similarity constraint*, which serves as a grouping principle (colour presentations are not randomly assorted into categories but grouped on the basis of their similarity to one another) and it observes what might be called a *linearity constraint* (colour categories appear as ordered sets cut out from the colour continuum such that a category red/yellow is possible (and actual) but a category blue/yellow is not – blue and yellow are not contiguous – see Dedrick (1998) for a detailed discussion of these and related issues). Systems of colour categorization in distinct languages might also come to resemble one another due to various forms of linguistic and political imperialism – in part explaining cross-cultural regularities. All this said, the authors do not believe there are universal constraints beyond the weak ones identified here. Categories are, as Davidoff would have it, nurture not nature (Davidoff, Goldstein, and Roberson 2009). To put things as simply as possible: Davidoff, Roberson, and colleagues argue that categories come from language and culture, they are not there prior.

One might be surprised to find that Kay and colleagues do not claim to know where universal colour categories (or constraints on such categories) come from, offering a number of possible explanations (e.g., Reiger, Kay, and Cook 2005). Instead they offer arguments *against* arbitrariness (including the weak constraints mentioned above). For example, they compute both category foci ('centeroids') and category boundaries across a large data set, including the languages of western and non-western peoples, and conclude the probability of the similarities that appear across these different languages makes it extremely likely that there are universal constraints.[24] They also argue that even the boundaries of Berinmo and Himba – Roberson's counter-examples to universality – are not *radically* different from other five-term systems they have data for (Kay and Reiger 2007). Thus, though they know not where the categories come from, they are confident they are not arbitrary.

Returning to the different explanatory dimensions discussed throughout this chapter

biological states, the 'organ of colour', *the brain*

psychological states, chromatic perceptual content, *the mind*

linguistic behaviour, colour words, *language*

socially transmitted information, context, *culture*

For the relativists we have discussed, cultural information encoded in language transforms thought in ways amenable to Whorf – and to Brown and Lenneberg, for that matter (Agrillo and Roberson 2009). While the brain cannot be irrelevant to colour naming and cognition we might want to think of it as plastic in relation to colour name learning (more on this later), always an encultured process. For Kay and colleagues, the view would seem to be one where linguistic regularities, with the exceptions of marginal cultural modification to some boundaries, stand on their own. Since the universalist has no confident account of where colour categories come from, the position merely (but not insignificantly for the relativist) is that they do not come from culture, by and large. Yet there is a confident account of where colour categories come from, one that has generated a great deal of current and unresolved controversy. Like all the threads of discussion in this chapter, it has a significant connection to research that goes back decades, research that claims at least some psychological colour categories to be innate.

Where do colour categories come from (II)?[25]

In an article published in 1976 the psychologist Marc Bornstein claimed that non-linguistic 4-month-old infants exhibited categorical perception of colour, and that the colors so categorized corresponded to some of the colour categories denominated as basic colour terms – colours that were also the 'Hering primaries' of opponent colour theory (Bornstein, Kessen, and Weiskopf, 1976). The evidence, roughly, was that non-linguistic infants group perceptually non-identical stimuli into hue categories; that they pay less attention to within-category perceptual differences than to between-category perceptual differences; that the categories which are not linguistically specified (how could they be, the infants have no language?) correspond to the colour categories that are grounded in the nature of the vision system: the Hering primaries. Bornstein's work is important to a biological argument for the salience of basic colour terms. Linguistic (basic) colour terms have, as their referents, a variety of colour samples that are not identical and the fact that such categories are, putatively, innate suggests that these colour categories, which are just the sort of things that are named ('red', 'yellow', and so forth) precede language development.

Bornstein's initial experiments claiming categorical perception of colour in infants utilized a habituation task. This task, common in studies of infant perception and cognition, assumes that babies will look longer at novel stimuli and will pay less attention to familiar stimuli. Bornstein claimed that infants perceive colour categorically (group non-identical stimuli together) because the infants are more interested in a newly presented stimulus that belongs to a distinct colour category than a newly presented within-category stimulus. Here is how the experiment works: the infant is shown stimulus *a* and it is, say, red. The infant habituates – loses interest – in that stimulus. Then the infant is presented with stimulus *b*. If stimulus *b* is within-category – another sample of red not identical to stimulus a – the infant will habituate more quickly than if stimulus *b* belongs to a different category, is, say, yellow. These pairs of stimuli are, as we have called them, within-category and between-category, respectively. Bornstein *et al.* (1976) drew the conclusion that infants recognize categorical boundaries, do group similar but non-identical within-category stimuli into hue based-classes; do have colour categories that precede the acquisition of colour language by years.

Critics have noted there are methodological issues that potentially defeat Bornstein's results (Franklin and Davies 2006). One concern was with luminance: did the stimuli match in terms of their brightness, were they 'isoluminant'? There is some reason to think not, and thus, perhaps, it was differences in terms of brightness that were driving the results. Another concern was with the perceptual distance between the paired stimuli. Bornstein used wavelength to specify his stimuli, but arithmetical differences in wavelength do not correspond to perceptual differences across the spectrum. Thus, perhaps, the infants are responding to asymmetries in the stimulus pairs, attending longer to stimuli that are perceptually 'farther away' regardless of categorical differences. Finally, there were concerns with saturation: the stimuli were highly saturated monochromatic lights. Given such stimuli are unfamiliar to infants, perhaps their response was influenced by the high saturation of the light.

In a series of publications beginning in 2004, Anna Franklin and colleagues concluded that 'even when the stimulus separations were equated with a perceptually uniform metric, even when stimuli are at natural saturation levels and are reflective not radiant, and even when the three dimensions of colour are controlled, four-month-old infants still respond categorically to colour' (Franklin and Davies 2006: 108). Bornstein's ideas are vindicated, as far as Franklin and Davies are concerned, and colour categories are pre-linguistic, a fact that is problematical for a relativistic, linguistic theory that claims culture and language to provide the explanation for colour categories. But how much of a problem, actually, is it?

In defending Bornstein's view that there are pre-linguistic colour categories, Franklin might seem to strike a final blow to a strong relativist view. Not only are there universal tendencies in colour naming (as Kay, Reiger, etc. argue), but colour categories themselves precede language and thus, it would seem, it cannot be language and culture that are responsible for colour categorization. As compelling as this critique may seem, things are not so straightforward.

In 1985, writing about his own research on pre-linguistic categories, Bornstein proposed

> An otherwise reasonable surmise from the fact that hue characterization precedes color naming developmentally would be that, in this one realm at least, linguistic identification simply overlays perceptual cognitive organization and thereby facilitates semantic development. Paradoxically, it does not.
>
> *(1985: 74)*

Suppose that there is an innate predisposition to the categorical perception of colour categories: a disposition to group non-perceptually matching colour samples into colour categories such as red, yellow, green, and blue. Now suppose that your language expresses those colour categories linguistically. Is it reasonable to think that your perceptual cognitive organization facilitates linguistic development? Bornstein proposes that the answer is 'yes' and 'Bornstein's paradox', as Dedrick (2002) has called it, arises from the fact that such facilitation seems *not* to occur. Children have a difficult time learning their colour names, even in languages that possess basic color terms (e.g., Bornstein 1985; Backscheider and Shatz 1993; Sandhofer and Smith 1999; Dedrick 2002; Pitchford and Mullen 2003; Roberson, Davidoff, Davies and Shapiro 2004; O'Hanlon and Roberson 2006; Franklin 2006; Kowalski and Zimiles 2006) Bornstein's paradox turns up, on numerous occasions, in the literature critical of universal colour categories. Jules Davidoff writes that:

> One argument against an innate basis is that it would mean a considerable amount of unlearning for speakers of most of the world's languages where categories (e.g., blue, green) do not exist in the adult's language.
>
> *(2006: 337)*

And:

> Bornstein (1985) recognized that some difficulties arise from the proposal of innate color categories. The first is explaining the well-known difficulty children have in learning color names. If the physiological apparatus is already in place at 4 months, it seems odd that it takes another 18 months to learn the first color word during the time the child shows a spurt of word learning.
>
> *(Davidoff and Fagot 2010: 105)*

In the first quotation Davidoff suggests that the presence of pre-linguistic categories should confuse individuals who have to learn different, non-English (and more generally non-western) colour names: 'unlearning' is required. And yet these subjects have no more and no less trouble learning their colour names. In the second quotation, Davidoff *et al.* echo Bornstein's paradox more directly: why does it take so long to learn the names of colour categories that are already there, innate in the mind? (See Roberson and Hanley 2010 for similar remarks describing Bornstein's paradox.) Even Franklin poses this discontinuity as a problem

> The finding that perceptual colour categorization is shown before the acquisition of colour terms, in some ways, raises more questions than it answers. For example, if there is an innate set of perceptual colour categories, why do different languages segment the colour space differently from each other? Why does language not follow on from perception?
>
> *(Franklin and Davies 2006: 115)*

Is the paradox really paradoxical? The authors cited never give a rationale for paradoxicality that goes beyond its obviousness, and there are models for other cognitive domains that suggest learning very much like this is discontinuous (e.g. Carey 2009). The more interesting point, relative to the research at hand, is that colour name learning by children really does not show any advantage to children that have to learn Berlin and Kay basic terms, as opposed to some other non-standard set (say that of Berinmo). Indeed, learning colour words, to adult competence for the full set of basic terms in a language, any language, takes a while (Wagner, Dobkins and Barner 2013).

The debate as to whether there are or are not pre-linguistic categories is mired in very detailed controversy.[26] If that much is clear, what is not clear is that it matters as much as the protagonists believe. It is true that the existence of pre-linguistic categories seems inconsistent with the relativist view. But if the existence of such categories does not matter to the colour categories learned – if it's not easier to learn these colour categories, as the evidence suggests, then we seem to be in a position where one's cultural colour categorical learning may 'override' their universal grounding in perception and biology. On the other hand, as Kay and colleagues have argued, one's learned colour categories, however difficult they are to learn, end up looking like they obey universal constraints. Puzzles remain, but perhaps the greatest reconciliation of the two views lies, surprisingly, in biology, in the brain.

Where do colour categories come from (III)?

So far, talk of the brain in this chapter has been intended as a placeholder for unknown processes that, for instance, generate psychological salience, or soft-wire linguistically driven categorical perception. The hypotheses to be considered here look to brain-based research on colour categorization. The left hemisphere of the brain is dominant for language. The visual fields of the right and left eyes project contralaterally. Might it be the case that the vision of our right eye, or right visual field, is influenced by language, while vision in the left visual field is unsullied (or less influenced) by language? This idea was first tested by Aubrey Gilbert *et al.* in a study that proposed three hypotheses:

> *First*, discrimination between colors from different lexical categories (i.e., that have different names) should be faster when stimuli are displayed in the RVF than when they are displayed in the LVF because the lexical distinction will enhance the perceptual difference. *Second*, discrimination between colors from the same lexical category should be slower in the RVF than in the LVF, because the assignment of the same name to two colors will diminish the perceptual difference. *Third*, these laterality effects should be disrupted when language resources are taxed by the demands of an interference task.
>
> *(Gilbert* et al. *2006; italics are mine)*

The tasks designed to test these hypotheses exploit categorical perception to show (or not) an effect of language on perception. The idea is this: in the right visual field that projects to the language dominant left hemisphere we expect results like those we have already seen in cases of categorical perception. The left visual field, which projects to the right hemisphere that is not dominant for language, should not exhibit such an effect, should be language neutral, with no or little linguistic effect on discrimination. This is exactly what Gilbert *et al.* found. To describe one of the experiments briefly: subjects were asked to discriminate a target from a set of distractors, where the distractors were all the same colour (a shade of blue, say). The target was either within-category (a shade of blue perceptually distinct from the distractors) or between-category (a shade of green, say). Language effects on perception were discovered in the right visual field but not in the left, leading Reiger and Kay (2009) to subtitle an article 'Whorf Was Half Right'.

How does Franklin's work claiming categorical perception in infants (and thus innate pre-linguistic categories) connect to the 'Lateralized Whorf'? (Kay *et al.* 2009). It would seem to fit uneasily. Language comes very late in the evolutionary history of *homo sapiens*. If the hemisphere that is language free does not show categorical perception in adult subjects, how could there be pre-linguistic colour categories in infants (for they are, by definition, language free)? This issue is obviously of concern to Franklin, and she has addressed it in a set of experiments. Without explaining her results in detail, its upshot is this:

there is a form of CP [categorical perception] that is nonlinguistic and RH [right hemisphere] based (found in infancy) and a form of CP that is lexically influenced and biased to the LH [left hemisphere] (found in adulthood). Color CP is found for both infants and adults, but the contribution of the LH and RH to color CP appears to change across the life span.

(Franklin et al. 2008 : 3224)

This is quite remarkable for it seems that, for reasons unknown, categorical perception switches from the right hemisphere to the left hemisphere, sometime in the transition from infancy to adulthood.

These results, though they are not well understood, have implications for Bornstein's paradox discussed in the last section. The air of paradox derived from the fact that, according to Bornstein's research (and later Franklin's), infants appear to possess pre-linguistic categories. And yet the possession of such categories did not seem to assist in or to predict the speed of colour name learning. If infants start out with categorical perception in their right hemisphere and end up without it as adults, possessing linguistically mediated categorical perception in their left hemisphere – that might suggest that instead of building on infant categorical perception, as Bornstein and others thought *ought* to be the case, the development of lexical categories in the brain overwrites infant, non-linguistic categorical perception in the right hemisphere. How this might occur, is mysterious, yet it gives some credence to the idea that linguistic categories really do 'overwrite' one's innate categorical predispositions, and really do play a significant role in the psychology of colour categorization.[27]

3 Concluding remarks and future directions for research

It is difficult to draw general conclusions about this literature. Much is still contested. What we can say is that both the universalists and the relativists about colour categorization agree that there are some aspects of colour categorization that show an effect of language on thought and others that seem resistant to such effects. In fact, that is not quite right. Roberson, Davidoff, and colleagues hold a strong Whorfian view, a 'simple contrast' between nature and nurture on which they side with nurture. Kay and colleagues accept there is categorical perception at the boundaries of colour terms, but even those boundaries, on their view, are fairly uniform across languages. Their view, as we have seen, is that culture can generate categorical perception in the margins of universal categories.

There is much that is not understood. The literature concerning hemispherical specialization is especially perplexing. How does categorical perception switch from the right hemisphere to the left? Are there implications for cognition in general? At another level one might say 'is that all there is?' After forty years of addressing the issue of language–thought relations for colour and colour categorization, does it come down to marginal effects on thought, such as categorical perception, with even that debated as to its origins? It would be exciting to find that colour categorization is mainly a function of language and culture. But such a claim, though Roberson and Davidoff subscribe to it, is contested by the universalist arguments discussed here.

As for the impact of colour categorization research on broader questions concerning the effect of language on thought: the days when this was the exemplar for Whorfian language–thought relations – those days are gone. While work on colour language and thought is of remarkable interest and detail, it is not a good model for the relationship between language and thought in general, and that may well be because there is no interesting general model of the relationship between language and thought.

One thing that is remarkable about the colour-cognition literature is its depth and inter-disciplinarity. Virtually all of the sciences, natural and social, have been involved at one point or another. This makes it a model for the practice of the cognitive sciences, if nothing else. In terms of future directions it would seem that there is a great deal of interest in the hemispherical results discussed above. They are unusual, and for reasons that will ensure further investigation. One would also expect that an interest in children's learning and mastery of adult colour language will persist (there is still much controversy in that domain (see, e.g., Davidoff, Goldstein, and Roberson 2009; Franklin, Wright, and Davies 2009; Wagner, Dobkins, and Barner 2013) as well as much left to understand about the relationship between infant colour perception and categories, and adult categorication and naming. One can, less specifically, be sure that this literature will expand further, continuing its forty-year trajectory well into the foreseeable future.

Related topics

linguistic relativity: precursors and transformations; the linguistic relativity hypothesis revisited; ethnosemantics; language, culture, and prototypicality; language and culture in cognitive anthropology; a future agenda for research on language and culture.

Notes

1 See Saunders and van Brakel (1997) and the attached commentary to get some idea as to how lively the debate can get.
2 Personal communication.
3 Some languages, it seems, do not map the full colour space, leaving some colour unnamed. See for example, Levinson (2000).
4 For detailed accounts of the criticism of the original research and responses to that criticism, see Dedrick (1998a); Kay (2006); Biggam (2102).
5 Berlin, Kay, and colleagues' views about basic colour terms and the evolutionary sequence circa 1969 have been modified over the years. The so-called 'Hering primaries' of contemporary opponent colour theory (black, white, red, yellow, green, blue) have come to play a major role in their thought, to the point where there is much less discussion of non-Hering colours (brown, purple, pink, grey, orange). See, for example Kay and McDaniel (1978); Reiger, Kay, and Cook (2005).
6 I define the 'research tradition' ecumenically: it includes not just those in agreement with Berlin and Kay's universalist project, but those critical of it as well.
7 For more detailed discussion of this history see Dedrick (1998: ch. 1) and especially the more recent Biggam (2012: ch. 3).
8 There are philosophical debates about the relationship between brain states and perceptual content and it is not my intention to take a position in those debates. I rest my claim here on the more prosaic fact that perceptual content requires concepts such as (but not restricted to) hue, saturation, and brightness for its description, while brain states do not.
9 This is what Saunders and van Brakel (1997) have in mind when they claim there are 'no-non trivial constraints' on colour naming: that is the point of their controversial article.
10 One might say that the use of linguistic and psychological criteria begs the question in that it builds cognitive effect into a linguistic measure. This is not as bad as it sounds: the psychological criteria involve things like speed of production of a name when presented with a colour sample. Brown and Lenneberg, as with Berlin and Kay to follow, made reasonable psychological inferences on the basis of third-person behaviour (e.g. a name that is very quickly produced has greater psychological salience for a speaker than a name produced less quickly).
11 The relationship between the evolutionary claim and the universality claim is uncertain. Basic colour terms could be universal without it being the case that there is an evolutionary sequence. "Evolu-tionary" in this context is not a biological notion of evolution, in so far as biologists do not believe that evolution by natural selection has a direction. Current ideas about the change of basic terminology essentially reject the idea of directed change replacing it with the idea that the number of terms present

in a language tends to satisfy an optimality constraint so that, if you have, say, four or five basic terms, those terms tend to partition colour space in an optimal fashion, relative to the number of terms (e.g. Regier, Kay, and Khetarpal 2007).

12 Biggam (2012: ch. 3) is the definitive source for discussion of the criteria for basicness.

13 Kay noted that relativists writing prior to the publication of *Basic Color Terms* assumed it made sense to talk about different colour terms and to compare them cross-culturally, as do Berlin and Kay (Kay 2006).

14 The 'colour chart' was based on a restricted set of highly saturated samples drawn from the larger Munsell colour space. For a discussion of this stimulus set, issues with it, and modifications to it as well as to the experimental procedure used by other researchers, see MacLaury (1997); Kay (2006).

15 For an example of how contemporary non-Chomskians understand syntax, see Perfors, Tenenbaum, and Regier (2011).

16 The reliability of Rosch's statistical claims is discussed later in this chapter, in the context of Roberson, Davies, and Davidoff (2000).

17 See, in particular, Kay and McDaniel (1978); Bornstein (1985). Hardin and Maffi (1997) is an excellent source for interdisciplinary discussion of the relations among biology, psychology, and colour naming. For a more programmatic argument as to the relationship between biology, psychology, and naming, see Hardin (1988: 155–68). Reviews are to be found in Dedrick (1998); Biggam (2012).

18 The relationship between boundaries and focal colours has always been in tension. Berlin and Kay formulated their idea of universality in relation to focal colours, and yet one cannot make sense of colour categories without saying something about boundaries: does one, for instance, want to say that two colour categories are 'the same' just because they have the same focus? If so, then a red category for English would be 'the same' as the putative Dani-named category that was focused in red but included other 'warm colours' such as yellow and orange and white? This is a general problem for understanding different categories in different languages as 'the same' (see Dedrick 1998: ch. 5, for discussion). Since Kay and McDaniel (1978), the interest in mapping boundaries has increased (see, in particular, Reiger, Kay, and Cook (2005)).

19 See Roberson, Davies, and Davidoff (2000: 370–1) for an explanation of these issues.

20 Roberson *et al.* made an effort to be faithful to Rosch's methods. That said, they used a lightbox that controlled for illumination differences. They also found, and this reflected a longstanding criticism of Rosch's work (e.g. Collier (1973); Lucy and Shweder (1979)) that focal colour salience appeared to be a function of a non-randomized display. In other words, if subject were shown a full display of colour chips, they tended to choose Berlin and Kay focal colours. Not so with a randomized display. Roberson *et al.*'s failure to replicate Rosch's results involve randomized displays, unlike the original research. So far as this author can tell, this has not been treated as a confounding factor by anyone.

21 Kay's sympathy to the marginal Whorfian position is not surprising. Kay and Kempton (1984) make a case for marginal (as they see it) Whorfian effects that are a function of culture.

22 It should be said that Kay and Kempton argued *for* Whorfian effects in Kay and Kempton (1984). Kay has, since then at least, viewed some Whorfian effects as compatible with his universalist views.

23 Thus Roberson *et al.* (2000: 395) comment that *mehi*, the Berinmo word for red could be grounded in a universal prototype, but it is also the name for a fruit the cultural salience of which, rather than prototypicality, could explain its linguistic salience.

24 There are a number of articles making some form of a 'large data' argument: Reiger, Kay, and Cook (2005); Kay and Reiger (2007). It is worth pointing out that the authors, though they often use interesting data-modelling techniques by and large determine boundaries and focal colours by simply averaging individual choices. Many individual differences – and language specific differences disappear – when this simple method is applied. For instance: if a subject picks a colour sample that is in the extension of English 'green' as focal for her basic term yellow, and that choice is averaged towards English focal green, in what sense is focal yellow (being green for this subject) psychologically salient for this subject? There is a remarkable range of individual differences in focal choice, even for speakers of western languages (MacLaury (1997); Kuehni (2001).

25 This section is based on but not identical with (Dedrick 2014).

26 The reader is directed to compare Franklin, Wright, and Davies (2009), and Davidoff, Goldstein, and Roberson (2009) as a case in point.

27 The literature on hemispheric categorical perception is growing, and branching out into both evoked potential (ERP) methodology, as well as fMRI studies (e.g. Tan (2008)). See Kay, Regier, Gilbert, and Ivry (2009) for a discussion of techniques and results.

Further reading

Berlin, B. and Kay, P. (1969). *Basic color terms: Their universality and evolution*. University of California Press. (2nd edn, 1991). (With all its warts, still the foundational work for the research described here.)

Biggam, C. (2012) *The semantics of colour*. Cambridge: Cambridge University Press. (This book provides detailed advice to those wishing to engage in historical colour semantics, but it is also an excellent guide to many of the topics discussed in this chapter.)

Lucy, J. (1997). The linguistics of 'color', C. L. Hardin and L. Maffi (eds), *Color categories in thought and language*. Cambridge: Cambridge University Press. (John Lucy has long been a critic of basic colour terms, and the Berlin–Kay model, but see the comments on Lucy's work, same volume).

Roberson, D. and Hanley, J. R. (2010) Relatively speaking; An account of the relationship between language and thought in the color domain. B. Malt and P. Wolff (eds), *Words and the world: How words capture human experience*. Oxford University Press. (A contemporary summary of the relativist position on colour categorization.)

Webster, M. A. and Kay, P. (2012) Color categories and color appearance. *Cognition*. 122, 375–92. Recent empirical research about language, thought, categorical perception, and individual differences in colour categorization.

References

Agrillo, C. and Roberson, D. (2009) Colour language and colour cognition: Brown and Lenneberg revisited. *Visual Cognition*, 17, 412–30

Allen, C. G. B. (1879). *The colour sense: Its origin and development: An essay in comparative psychology*. English and Foreign Philosophical Library 10. London: Trubner.

Backscheider, A. G. and Shatz, M. (1993). Children's acquisition of the lexical domain of color. In K. Beals *et al.* (eds), *What we think, what we mean, and how we say it*. CLS 29 (vol. 2). Chicago, IL: Chicago Linguistic Society.

Berlin, B., and Kay, P. (1969). *Basic color terms: Their universality and evolution*. Berkeley, CA: University of California Press.

Biggam, C. P. (2012). *The semantics of colour*. Cambridge University Press.

Bornstein, M. (1985). Human infant color vision and color perception. *Infant Behavior and Development*, 8, 109–13.

Bornstein, M., Kessen, W., and Weiskopf, S. (1976). Color vision and hue categorization in young human infants. *Journal of Experimental Psychology: Human Perception and Performance*, 2, 115–129.

Brown, R. W. and Lenneberg, E. H. (1954) A study of language and cognition. *Journal of Abnormal and Social Psychology*, 49: 454–62.

Bruner, J. (1983). *In search of mind*. London: HarperCollins.

Carey, S. (2009) *The origin of concepts*. Oxford: Oxford University Press.

Chomsky, N. (1965) *Aspects of the theory of syntax*. Cambridge MA: MIT Press.

Collier, G. A. (1973). Review of basic color terms. *Language*, 49(1): 245–48.

Davidoff, J. B. (2006). Color terms and color concepts. *Journal of Experimental Child Psychology*, 94: 334–8.

Davidoff, J., and Fagot, J. (2010). Cross-species assessment of the linguistic origins of color categories. *Comparative Cognition and Behavior Reviews*, 4, 66–85.

Davidoff, J. B., Goldstein, J., and Roberson, D. (2009). Nature versus nurture: The simple contrast. *Journal of Experimental Child Psychology*, 102(2): 246–50.

Dedrick, D. (1998). *Naming the rainbow: Colour language, colour science, and culture*. Dordrecht: Kluwer.

——(1998a) The Foundations of the universalist tradition in color-Naming Research (and their supposed refutation). *Philosophy of the Social Sciences*, 28(2).

——(2002). The roots/routes of colour term reference. B. Saunders and J. van Brakel (eds), *Theories, technologies, instrumentalities of color: Anthropological and historical perspectives*. Lanham, MD: University Press of America.

Franklin, A. (2006). Constraints on children's color term acquisition. *Journal of Experimental Child Psychology*, 94, 322–27.

Franklin, A., and Davies, I. R. L. (2006). Converging evidence for pre-linguistic colour categorisation. In C. P. Biggam and N. Pitchford (eds), *Progress in Colour Studies: Psychological Aspects* (pp. 101–20). Amsterdam: Benjamins.

Franklin, A., Drivonikou, G. V., Bevis, L., Davies, I. R. L., Kay, P. and Regier, T. (2008). Categorical perception of color is lateralized to the right hemisphere in infants, but to the left hemisphere in adults. *PNAS*, 105, 3221–5.

Franklin, A., Wright, O., and Davies, I. R. L. (2009). 'What can we learn from toddlers about categorical perception of color? Comments on Goldstein, Davidoff, and Roberson'. *Journal of Experimental Child Psychology*, 102, 239–45.

Gilbert, A., Regier, T., Kay, P., and Ivry, R. (2006). Whorf hypothesis is supported in the right visual field but not the left. *PNAS*, 103, 489–94.

Gladstone, W. E. (1858). *Studies on Homer and the Homeric Age III*. Oxford: Oxford University Press.

Goldstone R. L. and Hendrickson, A. T. (2010). Categorical perception. *Wiley Interdisciplinary Reviews: Cognitive Science*, 1(1): 69–78

Hardin, C. L. (1988). *Color for philosophers: Unweaving the rainbow*. Indianapolis, IN: Hackett.

Harnad, S. (1986). *Categorical perception: The groundwork of cognition*. Cambridge: Cambridge University Press.

Kay, P. (1975) Synchronic variability and diachronic change in basic color terms. *Language in Society*, 4, 257–70.

——(2006) Methodological issues in cross-language color naming. In *Language, Culture and Society*. Christine Jourdan and Kevin Tuite (eds). Cambridge University Press, pp. 115–34.

Kay, P. and Kempton, W. (1984) What is the Sapir–Whorf hypothesis? *American Anthropologist*, 86, 65–79.

Kay, P. and McDaniel C. K. (1978) The linguistic significance of the meanings of basic color terms. *Language*, 54, 610–46.

Kay, P. and Maffi, L. (1999). Color appearance and the emergence and evolution of basic color lexicons. *American Anthropologist*, 101, 743–60.

Kay, P. and Reiger, T. (2007). Color naming universals: The case of Berinmo. *Cognition*, 102, 289–98.

Kay, P., Regier, T., Gilbert, A.L., and Ivry, R. (2009) Lateralized Whorf: Language influences perceptual decision in the right visual field. In: Minett, James W. and Wang, William S.-Y. (eds), *Language, Evolution, and the Brain*. Hong Kong : City University of Hong Kong Press, pp. 261–84.

Kowalski and Zimiles (2006). The relation between children's conceptual functioning with color and color term acquisition. *Journal of Experimental Child Psychology*, 94, 301–21.

Kraus. R. (1968). 'Language as a symbolic process in communication: A psychological perspective'. *American Scientist*, 56: 265–78.

Kuehni, R. (2001) Focal colors and unique hues. *Color Research and Application*, 26(2): 171–72.

Lantz, D. and Stefflre, V. (1964) Language and cognition revisited. *Journal of Abnormal and Social Psychology*, 69, 472–81.

Lenneberg, E., Roberts, J. (1953). The denotata of language terms. Paper presented at the Linguistic Society of America, Bloomington, Indiana.

Levinson, S. C. (2000) Yélî Dnye and the theory of basic color terms. *Journal of Linguistic Anthropology*,10: 3–55.

Lucy, J. (1997). The linguistics of 'color'. C. L. Hardin and L. Maffi (eds), *Color categories in thought and language*. Cambridge: Cambridge University Press.

Lucy, J. and Shweder, R. A. (1979) Whorf and his critics: Linguistic influences on color memory. *American Anthropologist*, 81, 581–607.

MacLaury, R. (1997) *Color and cognition in Mesoamerica*. University of Texas Press.

Morgan, Lewis H. [1877] (1982). *Ancient society*. University of Arizona Press.

O'Hanlon, C., and Roberson, D. (2006). Learning in context: Linguistic and attentional constraints on children's color term learning. *Journal of Experimental Child Psychology*, 94, 275–300.

Perfors, A., Tenenbaum J., and Regier T. (2011). The learnability of abstract syntactic principles. *Cognition*, 118, 306–38.

Pitchford, N. and Mullen, K. (2003). The development of conceptual colour categories in pre-school children: Influence of perception on categorization. *Visual Cognition*, 10, 51–77.

Pinker, S. (2002). *The blank slate*. New York: Penguin.

Ray, V. (1953). Human color perception and behavioral response'. *Transactions of the New York Academy of Sciences*, 2(16): 98–105.

Regier, T. and Kay, P. (2009). Language, thought, and color: Whorf was half right. *Trends in Cognitive Sciences*, 13, 439–46.

Regier, T., Kay, P., and Cook, R. S. (2005). Focal colors are universal after all. Terry Regier, Paul Kay and Richard S. Cook. PNAS, 102: 8386–91.

Regier, T., Kay, P., Gilbert, A., and Ivry, R. (2010). Language and thought: Which side are you on, anyway? In B. Malt and P. Wolff (eds.), *Words and the mind: How words capture human experience*, pp. 165–82. New York: Oxford University Press.

Regier, T., Kay, P., and Khetarpal, N. (2007). Color naming reflects optimal partitions of color space. *PNAS*, 104, 1436–41.

Roberson, D., Davies, I., and Davidoff, J. (2000) Color categories are not universal: Replications and new evidence from a Stone-age culture. *Journal of Experimental Psychology: General*, 129, 369–98.

Roberson, D., Davidoff, J., Davies, I. R. L. and Shapiro, L. R. (2004). The development of color categories in two languages: a longitudinal study. *Journal of Experimental Psychology: General*, 133, 554–71.

——(2005) Colour categories in Himba: Evidence for the cultural relativity hypothesis. *Cognitive Psychology*, 50, 378–411.

Roberson, D., and Hanley, J.R. (2010). Relatively speaking: An account of the relationship between language and thought in the color domain. In B.C. Malt and P. Wolff (eds.), *Words and the mind: How words capture human experience* (pp. 183–98). New York: Oxford University Press.

Rosch, E. (1974). Linguistic relativity. In A. Silverstein (ed.), *Human communication: Theoretical perspectives*. New York: Halstead.

——(1975). Cognitive representations of semantic categories. *Journal of Experimental Psychology: General*, 104, 192–233.

Rosch Heider, E. (1972). The structure of the color space in naming and memory for two languages. *Cognitive Psychology*, 3(2): 337–54

——(1972a). Probabilities, sampling, and the ethnographic method. *Man*, 7(3): 448–66.

Rosch Heider, E. and Olivier, D. (1972) Universals in color naming and memory. *Journal of Experimental Psychology*, 93, 10–20.

Sandhofer, C., and Smith, L. (1999). Learning color words involves learning a system of mappings. *Developmental Psychology*, 35, 668–79.

Saunders, B. A. C. and van Brakel, J. (1997) Are there non-trivial constraints on color categorization? *Behavioral and Brain Sciences*, 20, 167–78.

Surridge, A. K., Osorio, D. and N. I. Mundy. (2003) Evolution and selection of trichromatic vision in primates. *Trends in Ecology and Evolution*, 18, 198–205.

Tan, L. H., Chan, A. H. D., Kay, P., Khong, P.-L., Yip, L. K. C. and Luke, K.-K. (2008) Language affects patterns of brain activation associated with perceptual decision. *Proceedings of the National Academy of Sciences*, 105, 4004–9.

Tylor, E. *Primitive culture* (1). 1871. J. Murray.

Vejdemo-Johansson, M., Vejdemo, S., Ek, C. (2014) 'Comparing distributions of color words: Pitfalls and metric choices mail, Susanne, Carl-Henrik Ek'. *PLOS one*. DOI: 10.1371/journal.pone.0089184

Wagner, K., Dobkins, K., and Barner, D. (2013). Slow mapping: Color word learning as a gradual inductive process. *Cognition*, 127, 307–17.

Whorf, B.L. (1956). *Language, Thought, and Reality: Selected Writings of Benjamin Lee Whorf*. Cambridge, MA: Technology Press of Massachusetts Institute of Technology.

20

LANGUAGE, CULTURE, AND SPATIAL COGNITION

Penelope Brown

Introduction

Space is a fundamental attribute of the world all mobile foraging creatures live and operate in, and all display biological adaptations for representing – in some sense – locations, directions and movements in space. Conceptualizing where things are, and where things are going, and acting on these conceptualizations, is central to human cognition, and provides the framework for concrete thinking about objects and events. Since Kant (1768 [1991]), space has been taken to provide the basis for organizing a major component of human cognition, and underlies more abstract conceptualizations of, for example, time, kinship, and social relations.

Humans also *talk* about space – they tell each other where things are, plan where they will go, report where events occurred. And since languages vary widely in the linguistic resources and strategies for talking about space, this raises the Whorfian question of whether the language of space influences how people think about spatial relations even when they are not talking. Over the past two decades spatial language and cognition has played a central role in the revival of Neo-Whorfianism, modern approaches to the idea of 'linguistic relativity' attributed to Sapir and Whorf (see Chapters 2 and 30 this volume). Neo-Whorfian explorations of how language-specific categories affect human thinking include, among others, Bender, Bennardo, and Beller (2009); Boroditsky (2012); Bowerman and Levinson (2001); Gentner and Goldin-Meadow (2003); Gumperz and Levinson (1996); Levinson (1996, 2003a, 2003b); Lucy (1992a, 1992b).

A foil to this work has been research in the cognitive sciences, where over the past twenty-five years space has become a core research topic across several disciplines, especially among those in cognitive psychology, linguistics, anthropology, and child language development centrally concerned with the relations between language and thought. Reflecting the prevailing climate of universalism in the cognitive sciences, strong claims have been made about the universality of how humans conceptualize space based on the left–right asymmetry of their bodies – for example by Clark (1973); Miller and Johnson-Laird (1976); Talmy (1983, 2000). Yet in much of this work there is a complete lack of awareness of the ways in which people of different languages and cultures talk and think about space.

In largely independent lines of work in linguistics and anthropology, detailed descriptions of spatial words and constructions in particular languages have accumulated evidence for major cross-linguistic variability in the semantics of, for example, spatial adpositions like *in*, *on*, *under* (Levinson and Meira 2003), of verbs of motion like *go*, *come*, *enter*, *exit* (Wilkins and Hill 1995, Kita 2008) and of caused motion or placement verbs like *put*, *take* (Kopecka and Narasimhan 2011; Slobin *et al.* 2011). Cross-linguistic variability is also evident in where in the clause spatial meanings are expressed – this may be not only in the familiar European adpositions but in verbs, nouns, cases, and adverbs, and often in several of these at once (Sinha and Kuteva 1995). Even closely related languages can vary in where it is in the clause that essential spatial information is encoded, for example in adpositions vs. verbs in two Mayan languages (Bohnemeyer and Brown 2007; Brown 1994). Where the verbal component of locative statements is semantically specific, it can impose a spatial categorization on objects in the world (e.g., vertically.upright vs. horizontally extended vs. in.concave. container) that is depicted in gestures used when talking of putting and taking things, providing a window on the possible cognitive consequences of these categorizations (Ameka and Levinson 2007).

Some grounding in conceptual distinctions will set the stage for our discussion of the language of spatial relations. Despite the omnipresence of 'where' questions across languages, suggesting some common conceptualization of space as the answer to 'where' things are, languages do not treat space as a unitary semantic domain. Rather there are distinct sub-domains that may be handled quite differently both within a language and across languages. Location of a figure object (the object to be located, F) is generally specified by relating it to another object, the ground (G), or to a named place; distinct linguistic systems are involved when the figure is static as opposed to in motion, and, if static, when the figure is in contact with the ground or separated from it. On the vertical dimension, gravity provides a universally salient asymmetry motivating an axis used to distinguish 'up/down' relations. On the horizontal dimension, however, there is no such naturally given axis, so that some form of coordinate system is required to provide a search space for locating a figure in relation to a ground.

There are three basic types of coordinate system that languages can draw on: an 'absolute' or geocentric system that uses fixed axes external to the spatial scene (e.g., 'north of the house'), a 'relative' or viewpoint-dependent system that uses facets of the viewer's body to project axes (e.g., 'left of the house'), and an 'intrinsic' system that uses parts of the ground object to locate the Figure (e.g., at the back of the house') (see Levinson 2003a for explication). In order to describe spatial relations on the horizontal plane it is necessary to take a perspective on the scene, regardless of whether the figure is in motion or static, or whether a direction or location is being specified. Perspectival representations like those underlying these three types of linguistically coded frames of reference are probably unique to humans; they are among the features language provides us that have enormous significance for our capabilities (Warneken and Tomasello 2009).

Languages vary radically in their lexical resources for spatial description and in their spatial semantics; they also vary in their preferred choice of coordinate systems. This chapter focuses on spatial language and its relation to frames of reference, where the bulk of research on variation in the language–cognition interface has concentrated. I will present evidence for language variation in frame of reference usage, its correlation with conceptualization of spatial relations in non-linguistic thinking, and evidence from adult and child language and co-speech gesture for the influence of language on habitual patterns of thought. I will end with a discussion of the nature of the relations between language, interactional practices, and cultural scaffolding, which places the locus of the language–thought interface in culturally shaped situated interactional practices.

Spatial language and cognition across cultures

Frames of reference in language and cognition

Beginning in the 1990s, the Language and Cognition group at the Max Planck Institute for Psycholinguistics in the Netherlands developed a comparative approach to exploring variation in spatial language and its cognitive correlates; this was applied over more than ten years with more than forty researchers in over forty languages (Levinson and Wilkins 2006). Their method for eliciting comparable spatial language across diverse linguistic and cultural settings involved designing interactive 'space games', adapted from the referential communication task introduced by Clark and Wilkes-Gibbs (1986), where a native-speaker 'director' communicates to a 'matcher' about the spatial array in front of the matcher; they sit facing in the same direction but visually screened from each other. The matcher's task is to select the matching photo or to recreate the spatial array with an equivalent set of objects, relying solely on the director's verbal description and coordinating solely through speech exchanges. The spatial arrays used in these tasks were standardized, designed to elicit descriptions that differentiate minimal differences – e.g., between a man facing forwards or backwards and standing left or right of a tree. To encourage widespread collection of comparable data in different cultural contexts, the spatial stimuli and task instructions were produced in Field Manuals.[1] The 'Nijmegen Method' of using tasks consisting of sets of controlled stimuli with identical procedures in different field sites by researchers fluent in the local language and culture has revolutionized the study of linguistic relativity in the spatial domain.

It soon became apparent that the linguistic resources speakers utilized in these 'space games' varied systematically: in some languages speakers relied predominantly on relative (left/right/front/back) descriptions (e.g., 'The man is standing left of the house'), in others the main strategy was absolute (e.g., 'The man is north of the house'), and in others an intrinsic strategy was preferred ('The man is at the corner of the house'). The discovery of linguistic and cultural settings characterized by dominant use of an absolute strategy relying on fixed directions for describing spatial relations even on small-scale ('table-top') space was startling, and suggested the possibility that speakers of such languages – which require permanent and automatized awareness of the absolute directions – might actually think somewhat differently about space than speakers of the familiar European languages, who rely on a relative 'left/right/front/back' system. To take a specific example, in the Tzeltal Mayan community of Tenejapa in the mountains of southern Mexico, speakers have no productive use of relative 'left/right/front/back' terms. Instead, they use an absolute system with three terms ('uphill', 'downhill', 'across') in a frame of reference abstracted from the overall lay of the land downhillwards towards the north. Tzeltal speakers describe tabletop arrays in terms like 'The bottle is uphillwards (i.e., southwards) of the bowl', and even on flat areas they routinely express object locations in absolute terms ('The machete is downhillwards of the doorway'), and motion in absolute directions ('He is going downhillwards' (i.e., north). Absolute directions permeate the lexicon of Tzeltal, appearing in spatial nouns ('uphill', 'downhill', 'across'), in motion verbs ('ascend', 'descend', 'go across'), in directional adverbs ('upwards', 'downwards', 'acrossways'), and in positional verbs ('be positioned above', 'be positioned across'). In order to talk, speakers of this language must be constantly subliminally aware of where the abstract directions are, including indoors, at night, and in unfamiliar territory (Brown 2006; Brown and Levinson 1993b; Levinson 2003a; Levinson and Brown 1994).

To test for cognitive effects of the habitual use of such a system, a range of informal non-linguistic experiments based on a rotation paradigm were developed. The basic idea is this: if you view an array of toy animals where a pig, a cow, and a sheep are positioned orthogonally to your line of sight, and are asked to memorize 'how they are', a relative thinker will remember the array retaining the relationship relative to his body (as e.g., pig to the left, cow in the middle, sheep to the right). An absolute thinker, however, will remember the array keeping the animals' relationship to, say, 'north' or 'uphill' constant (e.g., pig uphillwards, cow in middle, sheep downhillwards). How can we know what people are thinking? If the participant is then rotated 180 degrees, asked to walk to another table and recreate the array 'just the same', a relative thinker will rotate the array (keeping the pig still to his left, consonant with his egocentric perspective) but an absolute thinker will not, and will recreate the array with the pig still uphillwards – i.e., on the right after rotation. A range of memory and reasoning tasks exploiting this design were carried out in a variety of different cultural settings, and sure enough, in absolute-dominant languages and cultures subjects performed differently on these tasks (keeping the absolute direction of the array after rotation) from those in relative-dominant cultures. (For Tzeltal, see Brown and Levinson 1993a, Levinson 2003a; for the Australian aboriginal language Guugu Yimidhirr, see Levinson 1997. For a comparative study of ten languages see Pederson *et al.* 1998.) This, then, is clear evidence for what have been called 'Whorfian effects': the language you speak affects the way you habitually think about spatial relations even when not talking.

Another study (Haun *et al.* 2011) found similar effects in Namibia. They compared performance on spatial reconstruction tasks by Dutch and Hai//kom-speaking Namibian school children; these two communities differ in the way they predominantly express spatial relations in language, with Hai//kom favoring an absolute frame of reference and Dutch favouring relative. Cognitive strategy preferences were investigated across different levels of task complexity and instruction, and, as in the Guuyu Yimidhirr and Tzeltal Mayan studies, a clear correlation between the dominant linguistic frames of reference and performance patterns in non-linguistic spatial memory tasks was found. The correlation was stable even when the complexity of the spatial array was increased, and participants were not easily able to switch strategies to their non-preferred frame of reference. These results, the authors argue, indicate a difference not only in preference but also in competence, and contribute to the accumulating evidence that across different human groups, spatial language and non-linguistic preferences and competences in spatial cognition are systematically aligned.

This conclusion is strengthened by studies of gestural accompaniments to spatial language in communities where absolute spatial systems are dominant. Briefly, speakers of absolute languages gesture absolutely, that is, veridically, to the actual place in the world being referred to. A phenomenon first noted in the gestures of speakers of Guugu Yimidhirr in Australia (Haviland 1993, 1998; Levinson 1997), it is also apparent in various Mayan groups. Haviland, Levinson, and Le Guen have described in detail the semiotic complexity of the precisely oriented pointing gestures of different Mayan groups, often with characteristics of the terrain and the relative location of objects – even when distant and out of sight – gesturally indicated (Haviland 1996, 2003, 2005; Kita, Danziger, and Stolz 2001; Levinson 2003; Le Guen 2009, 2011a, 2011b). These studies on gesture use in cultures where absolute systems dominate have shown that gesture is deeply integrated into the system of directional reference, providing an important source of insight into the cognitive background to absolute systems. They make it clear that these are not simply linguistic systems but broader communicative ones, and have contributed significantly to our understanding of how spatial frames of reference are invoked, communicated, and switched in conversational interaction (Brown 2014).

Spatial frames of reference in child language and thought

Parallel work has shown comparable linguistic relativity effects in other cultural groups, focusing on children. In an innovative study in Namibia, where Hai//kom speakers also rely on an absolute system, Haun and Rapold (2009) found that children aged 4–12, when asked to recreate a simple dance movement after rotation, recreated it absolutely (arms up on north side, requiring a switch of arm direction, from a body perspective), whereas German children, unsurprisingly, used their relative system and raised the arms leftwards again.

This prompts the question: how do children acquire such a habitual frame of reference? Is there a 'natural' frame of reference – a 'cognitive wild type' – that they start out with, and then adapt to the frame of reference preferences of the culture and language they are embedded in? These questions have only recently been addressed. Haun (2007; Haun *et al.* 2006) carried out experiments comparing the spatial memory of non-human great apes and German children to test for a cognitive 'wild type' for spatial cognition. The task involved remembering where a target was hidden, using cues of place (the target is in the same place but under a different container) vs. 'feature' (the target is under the container with a certain feature). Both apes and pre-linguistic 1-year-old children showed a preference for place over feature, but a third group of children age 3 switched the preference to feature. The implication is that by age 3, language and culture mask the native tendencies inherited from our primate ancestors.

The literature on children's acquisition of spatial language begins with Piaget (Piaget and Inhelder (1956 [1948])), who argued that infant's sensory-motor experience laid the groundwork for their spatial understanding, and that topological concepts were conceptually simpler than the geometry underlying frames of reference. This is consistent with the evidence from child language studies of children in western industrialized societies where relative systems dominate: children learn topological terms (*in*, *on*) from around age 2, then intrinsic uses (e.g., intrinsic 'front/back'), and around the age of 4 get some relative uses ('front/back' projected from ego's point of view). Projective use of 'left/right' terms is very late, in line with Piagetian theory.

This might suggest a handicap for children learning languages with dominant absolute systems, which have the geometrical properties Piagetians predict would be difficult. Yet children in these societies – in so far as the limited evidence so far suggests – do not seem to start their spatial language learning with a universal notional core – e.g. egocentric – and only later learn the absolute system. Rather, they adapt to the local category system from very early. In a study of children's acquisition of an absolute frame of reference anchored in an 'uphill/downhill' distinction, De León (1994) found that Tzotzil Maya children moved from a concrete landmark interpretation of the 'up/down' terms around age 4 to a later acquisition of the absolute meanings (up = eastwards). Brown's research on the closely related Tzeltal 'uphill/downhill' system found that Tzeltal children use intrinsic terms along with absolute terms from age about 4, and show evidence of an abstract absolute up/down axis in novel tasks from about 5 and a half; there is no evidence of starting with presumably easier landmark meanings or vertical meanings for these terms (Brown 2001; Brown and Levinson 2000, 2009; de León 1997, 2001).

Finally, Cablitz, (2002) studied children's acquisition of the Marquesan absolute 'inland/seaward/across' system, and discovered three factors that play a role in the child's acquisition of the system: perceptual clues from the environment such as the local inclination of the land, the familiarity of surroundings (at home vs. an unknown place), and the child's difficulty of localizing his/her own current position. These factors interact; as a result Marquesan children do not master the comprehension of their system until the age of 7 or later, in contrast to the earlier age of acquisition of the Tzeltal and Tzotzil systems. In all three languages, however, children master the absolute system well before western children master projective left–right.

An independent line of evidence comes from a major comparative set of studies of children's use of frames of reference in four cultural settings: Bali, India, Nepal, and Switzerland (Dasen and Mishra 2010; Wassman and Dasen 1998). They found moderate linguistic relativity effects, with children in rural Bali and in Katmandu using their absolute systems from age 4; more complex mixed usage patterns appear in the communities with both absolute and relative systems available. Dasen and Mishra prefer an 'ecological' explanation for choice of frames of reference to a (strong) linguistic relativity one, emphasizing the tendency for absolute dominance to characterize rural communities while left/right systems are preferred in urban ones.

In short, all of these studies found that children master the basics of their absolute system relatively early, compared with the acquisition of projective left/right in European children. This conclusion is consonant with the results obtained in much other work on child spatial language showing that children display very early sensitivity to language-specific semantic differences, adapting to the local system of categories from the beginning (e.g., Bowerman 1996; Bowerman and Choi 2001; Choi and Bowerman 1991). This suggests that in this domain the child must *construct* the relevant categories; these are not given by innate endowment as developmentalists have often assumed (Levinson 1998).

Correlation vs. causality, flexibility, and the role of ego in frames of reference usage

The claim that language can influence non-linguistic cognition has not gone down well in some cognitive psychological circles; it is anathema to those who believe firmly that spatial cognition is primary and universal. Controversy centres on two sources of discrepant interpretations.

First, what do we mean by 'thought' and 'cognition'? This has been a major sticking point for acceptance of Whorfian effects – just how strong an effect do we have in mind? Many cognitive psychologists can accept that language influences thinking when we are preparing to speak (Slobin's (1996) 'thinking for speaking'), but resist the idea that the effects of language on thought could be more pervasive than that. The disagreement about the nature of cognitive effects of linguistic usage is framed by Papafragou (2007) as *the salience hypothesis* vs. *the streamlining hypothesis*. She argues that the former is true – language can indeed make certain concepts more salient, drawn into attention – but the latter is not – language does not streamline or constrain the process of thinking itself.

Yet it seems undeniable that reliance on an absolute frame of reference requires attunedness to abstract absolute directions and refined forms of tracking of them as one moves through space. In any communication that relies on an absolute system for routine spatial description, speakers' mental computations must be adapted to enable this and various cultural practices will support it (e.g., gestures, attention to movements of the sun, etc.). As Levinson (1997: 100–1) expresses it:

> it is necessary to carry out a specialized kind of background computation of orientation and direction. Further, these computations must be carried out well in advance of (indeed independently of) speaking, and the results must be memorized, be available for inference and other psychological process, and in general pervade many aspects of cognition. Thus the fact that absolute directional information is a fundamental prerequisite for speaking … must have pervasive psychological implications.

A second source of controversy stems from the cross-talk due to conflicting understandings of spatial concepts. There is still considerable disagreement and confusion about the conceptual parameters necessary for specifying spatial relations. For example, the misinterpretation of the Levinson group's results as a claim that an absolute language prevents it speakers from thinking egocentrically has motivated some direct attacks on the Levinson programme. Li and Gleitman (2002) carried out a simplified version of the MPI 'Animals in a Row' task with American students as subjects, and argued that they could induce either absolute or relative coding by changing the conditions of the task. They found students coded relatively when indoors, but produced a mixed relative/absolute result outdoors, and when a salient 'landmark' (duck on pond) was placed at alternate ends of the stimulus and response tables, subjects responded in line with the landmark. Li and Gleitman conclude that all humans think in both relative and absolute terms, and can be induced to do so by manipulating the task conditions. Their study, however, displays a misunderstanding of the nature of the frames of reference involved in the task: using a salient landmark on the end of the table induced an intrinsic response, as Levinson *et al.* (2002) showed with a new experiment where subjects were rotated 90 degrees instead of 180. Dutch-speaking subjects placed the animals heading left (relative) or towards the pond (intrinsic), *not* south (absolute). When the memory load was increased by adding to the number of animals to be placed, the subjects reverted to a relative solution.

A direct challenge to the claims of Brown and Levinson for the cognitive effects of the Tzeltal Mayan absolute linguistic system was launched by Li and Gleitman through their student Linda Abarbanell, who conducted a series of experiments with Tenejapa Tzeltal speakers intended to debunk the Brown–Levinson claims (Li *et al.* 2011). They showed that Tenejapan subjects, despite the dominance of their absolute linguistic frame of reference, can be trained to use an egocentric frame of reference in rotation tasks, and under certain task conditions find an egocentric frame actually easier. Unfortunately, again their task designs reflect a confusion between egocentric and intrinsic results. Their findings do not adequately address the Brown–Levinson claims, which were never that Tenejapans cannot use an egocentric frame of reference but rather that they habitually, unreflectively, prefer an absolute frame even when not speaking.

In the work of Li and their colleagues, the collapse of the relative/absolute/intrinsic distinctions made by languages to the two-way 'egocentric' vs. 'allocentric' distinction more familiar to psychologists is a major source of crosstalk. Undoubtedly all humans can take both kinds of perspectives – an egocentric perspective is necessary in perception for vision, etc.; it is also necessary in language for what are likely to be universally available deictic semantic distinctions (e.g., near/far from ego, coming towards/going away from ego). An allocentric perspective is universally available for way-finding over long distances; an axis based on concrete landmarks is allocentric (though not absolute) and ad hoc landmarks are probably usable in all languages ('it's near the doorway, the bed, the telephone pole', etc.). Both perspectives, and an intrinsic one as well, are used by children by age 5 (Nardini *et al.* 2006). It is not surprising, then, that speakers of an absolute-dominant language can be trained or influenced by task design to adopt an egocentric perspective in certain tasks.

Other work more sympathetic with the idea of Whorfian effects of language on thought makes it clear that task design can indeed influence the choice of frame of reference in these kinds of experiments. This is shown in the results of a major comparative project on Mesoamerican space headed by a former MPI colleague Bohnemeyer, where new referential communication tasks were employed in a range of different Mexican cultural settings. An important finding of the MesoSpace project was the flexibility of frame of reference usage in communities that have access to more than one. The use of a frame of reference in non-linguistic tasks is sensitive to the nature of the task – exactly what contrasts are presented and the precise instructions can shift usage to a different frame. This task specificity was found for Tzeltal (Polian and Bohnemeyer (2011), and for Yucatec Maya (Bohnemeyer (2011), suggesting that the Brown and Levinson findings need to be relativized to task. (See the special issue of *Language Studies* that reports results of this project, O'Meara and Pérez Báez 2011.)

In short, there is robust evidence for several unrelated languages and cultures (from Mexico to Australia to Africa to Nepal and Bali) that people's frame of reference usage in non-linguistic cognition matches that of their language use (Levinson 2003b). Together, this work demonstrates that there is in effect a 'cognitive style' associated with habitual use of an absolute frame of reference, supported by many attributes of cultural environment and practices. It is not a straitjacket – even if their language lacks terms for relative 'left' 'right' 'front' and 'back', speakers can certainly switch to an egocentric frame of reference to use deictic terms, or to an intrinsic frame of reference for spatially contiguous objects, both of which are available in all languages. But reliance on an absolute frame of reference is a habit of thought and speech that comes to be associated with other habits (of gesture, of route-finding, of navigation), and imposes some conceptual coherence across different domains of activity. This habit can permeate language use in other lexical domains – e.g., use of Tzeltal landscape terms (Brown 2008b); it may even extend to time. Bender, Bennardo, and Beller (2005), for example, show that 'the rare type of spatial frame of reference used in Tongan is indeed reflected in the temporal domain', suggesting 'a homology between the two domains'. (For other evidence of linguistic relativity in time expressions, see Boroditsky 2000; Casasanto and Boroditsky 2008; Lai and Boroditsky 2013; see also Chapter 21 this volume.)

The cognitive style associated with absolute frame of reference usage is most readily demonstrable in language communities – like that of the Australian aboriginal Guugu Yimdhirr group – that are heavily reliant on one system, while others are simply not available for small-scale spatial descriptions. Complications – and a much less clear picture – arise in bilingual communities and for bilingual speakers (e.g. the younger generation) where the two languages provide alternative systems.

The interpenetration of language, cognition, and culture

Much of what has been reviewed here might seem rather remote from the concerns of anthropologists. Indeed, it has to a large extent been addressed to the cognitive science audience, and the embedding of the linguistic practices associated with spatial frames of reference in social interaction and ethnography – with the notable exception of gesture studies – has been relatively neglected. Of course anthropologists have long been interested in documenting cultural conceptualizations of space–time in calendrical systems, navigation systems, geographical awareness, kinship and social relations (see e.g. Feld and Basso 1996; Hirsely and O'Hanlon 1995; Hugh-Jones 1980; Low and Lawrence-Zuniga 2003; Villa Rojas 1973).

But much more limited attention has been focused on the variety of practices dealing with space and associated linguistic systems. A major exception is Hanks's (1990) meticulous study of spatial deixis usage in Yucatec Maya daily life. Another is Widlok's (1996, 1997) study of way-finding among the Hai//Kom, a group of Namibian hunter-gatherers, as an example of socially shared cognition that emerges through social interaction. A third is Bennardo's (2009) analysis of Tongan radial representations of spatial relationships that extend into other knowledge domains (possession, navigation, religion, kinship). More ethnography of cultural construals of social spaces and detailed examination of the use of spatial language in situated interactions would clarify the connection between tests of thinking and how this thinking could arise in a cultural context.

It would also help to defuse the aura of controversy that has surrounded evidence of Whorfian effects, by showing how language is part of, and not separable from culture. Nor are the language effects always distinguishable from cultural effects (Jensen de López, Hayashi, and Sinha 2005; Sinha and Jensen de López 2000). How we talk about space is related to interactional and cultural practices and structures, and a geocentric or 'absolute' cognitive style is reflected in many aspects of the built and lived-in environment. Cognition in this domain, as in many others, is distributed across interacting participants, it does not just reside in individual minds. Hence the answer to the puzzle of how a child learns it: 'A thousand little details of the built environment and, more importantly, the conduct of interaction … will inform the discerning toddler again and again … Because we think in line with how we speak, so clues are not all in the language but in the environment and distributed throughout the context of language learning' (Levinson 2003b; see also Boroditsky 2012). An integrated approach to the language–cognition–interaction interface (as in e.g., Enfield and Levinson 2006) would greatly improve the discourse.

Conclusion and future directions for research

Linguistic variation is a unique resource for understanding what is distinctive about humans as a species – humans are designed for variation both in habitat and in communication system (Levinson 2006). Although the extent and significance of linguistic variation is still hotly debated (see, e.g., Evans and Levinson 2009; Levinson and Evans 2010), there is accumulating evidence for cognitive consequences of language variability. The interpretation of these effects remains controversial in cognitive psychology circles, as we have seen, at least among those who want to defend to the death the dogma of the primacy of cognition over language.

Research on the language of space over the past twenty-five years has made a big splash in linguistic circles, resulting in the systematization of language typology in the spatial domain and a new field of semantic typology which carefully examines the semantic distinctions languages make in a particular domain, asking what is universal about these and what is language specific (e.g., Levinson and Wilkins 2006), i.e., what are the limits to variation. This pursuit has been extended to looking at how language-specific categories appear across word classes in a particular language, leading to the proposal (Levinson and Burenhult 2009) of 'semplates', semantic templates (e.g. an absolute frame of reference) for a set of distinctions that crop up in the semantics of a variety of word classes and constructions, and stamp the language with a particular flavour.

We now have access to a great deal more information about spatial semantics in different languages than was available thirty years ago, including not only detailed descriptions of the language of space in particular languages: as collected in special issues and edited volumes (e.g., de León and Levinson 1992; Danziger 1998; Dirven and Pütz 1996; Levinson and Wilkins 2006), in Ph.D. dissertations (e.g., Cablitz 2001; Hellwig 2003; Seifart 2005), but also areal surveys of spatial language (e.g., Levinson and Haviland 1994 for Mayan languages; Senft 1997 for Oceanic languages, and O'Meara and Pérez Báez 2011 for Mesoamerican languages. There are also cross-linguistic comparisons of spatial language in particular semantic domains, for example, landscape (Levinson and Burenhalt 2008), body parts (Majid, Enfield, and van Staden 2006), locative verbs (Ameka and Levinson 2009), placement verbs (Kopeka and Narasimhan 2011), and space–time metaphors (e.g. Majid, Boroditsky, and Gaby 2012). There is therefore much more visibility for the range of cross-linguistic variation that exists in the spatial domain and in its extensions to more abstract domains.

What does the future hold? It can be expected that there will be further demonstrations of the ways in which spatial language influences cognition in a cultural context and vice versa (the 'inter-penetration' of language, culture, and thought), moving beyond frames of reference to explore other spatial domains – topological relations, deixis, and motion. Intense debate will doubtless go on concerning the nature of this interpenetration, its extent, and its flexibility. Increased acceptance of the extent of linguistic and cultural variation will, it is hoped, lead to more detailed studies of linguistic systems – this is urgent, given the alarming rate of language death around the world. This will feed into and improve the semantic typology for the language of space.

An important task will be tightening up the conceptual distinctions needed for analysis of frames of reference, topology, and motion expressions. There are still multiple systems in use in different disciplines (e.g., for spatial and temporal frames of reference), radically limiting inter-disciplinary understanding and cross-fertilization. It is especially important to clarify the problem of deictic origos, to distinguish the frames of reference qua coordinate systems from the various origins (deictic and non-deictic) that these systems can have (Levinson 2003a); in any frame of reference ego can be used as origo (e.g., 'North of me' is absolute, utilizing an abstract axis extrinsic to the spatial scene, 'To the left of me/at my left hand' is intrinsic, with the axis pro-jected from my body parts, and 'Left of X from my point of view' is relative). Reformulations have been proposed of some of the conceptual distinctions in frames of reference made by the Levinson team (Levinson 2003a; Levinson and Wilkins 2006), especially concerning the need to distinguish different subtypes of absolute and intrinsic systems which have different properties: true (abstract) absolute vs. locally fixed absolute (anchored to landscape features like mountain/sea) vs. ad hoc landmarks, and the role of ego in all three (Bohnemeyer 2011; Danziger 2010; Haviland 1998; Pederson 2003). But there is still no consensus.

Similarly, the experimental tools for examining the relationship between language and cognition will undoubtedly be refined, going beyond similarity judgments and rotation tasks testing memory and reasoning to exploit new tools, for example, eye-tracking capabilities. The neuro-cognitive correlates of linguistic variability in the spatial domain is another topic currently being pursued, producing for example evidence about how frames of reference are instantiated in the brain (Janzen, Haun, and Levinson 2012).

Closer to the concerns of anthropologists, the ethnography of spatial concepts and detailed examination of the use of spatial language in situated interactions is urgently needed (Sidnell and Enfield 2012; Brown and Levinson (in press) will address this need for the Tzeltal Maya case). Further developments in the anthropology of space can be expected, studying for example spatial concepts for construing social relationships (as in Bennardo 2009; Keating 1998,), the uses and technologies of navigation and way-finding, and the sociocultural significance of physical layouts. And we can expect that research into linguistic relativity effects will move beyond the domains of space and time where they have so far been largely focused, to provide a deeper understanding of the cognitive effects of language structure and use in other domains, for example causality, number concepts, emotions, kinship, and social relations.

Space has proved to be a very fertile domain for exploring the interrelationships between language, culture, and cognition, and for prompting interdisciplinary collaboration – and controversy – via the answers that have so far emerged.

Related topics

the linguistic relativity hypothesis revisited; space, time and space-time: metaphors, maps and fusions; culture and language development

Further reading

Bennardo, G. (2009) *Language, Space and Social Relationships: A Foundational Cultural Model in Polynesia*, Cambridge: Cambridge University Press. (This book analyses spatial language and the mental organization of spatial knowledge in the Polynesian kingdom of Tonga, and proposes a cultural model, 'radiality', to explain how space, time and social relationships are expressed both linguistically and cognitively in this community.)

Hanks, W. (1990) *Referential Practice: Language and Lived Space in a Maya Community*, Chicago: University of Chicago Press. (This classic book on deictic language as actually used in everyday life in a Yucatec

Mayan community examines the routine conversational practices in which Maya speakers refer to themselves and to each other, to their immediate contexts, and to their physical and social world.)

Levinson, S. C. (2003a) *Space in Language and Cognition: Explorations in Cognitive Diversity*, Cambridge: Cambridge University Press. (This book draws on collaborative, interdisciplinary research conducted in many languages and cultures around the world to outline a typology of spatial coordinate systems in language and cognition and provide evidence that non-linguistic cognition mirrors the systems available in the local language.)

Levinson, S. C. and Wilkins, D. P. (eds) (2006a) *Grammars of Space: Explorations in Cognitive Diversity*, Cambridge: Cambridge University Press. (In this edited volume, scholars review the spatial domain across a variety of languages and show that there is wide variation in the way space is conceptually structured across languages.)

Majid, A., Bowerman, M., Kita, S., Haun, D., and Levinson, S.C. (2004) 'Can language restructure cognition? The case for space', *Trends in Cognitive Sciences* 8(3): 108–14. (This article presents a concise overview of the evidence that the use of frames of reference in language, cognition and gesture varies cross-culturally, and that children can acquire different systems with comparable ease, showing that language can play a significant role in structuring a fundamental cognitive domain.)

Note

1 These are available on the MPI website, www.mpi.nl

References

Ameka, F. K. and Levinson, S. C. (eds) (2007) *The Typology and Semantics of Locative Predication: Posturals, Positionals and Other Beasts* [special issue], *Linguistics*, 45(5).

Bender, A., Bennardo, G. and Beller, S. (2005). 'Spatial frames of reference for temporal relations: a conceptual analysis in English, German, and Tongan', in B. G. Bara, L. Barsalou, and M. Bucciarelli (eds) *Proceedings of the Twenty-Seventh Annual Conference of the Cognitive Science Society*, 220–5, Mahwah, NJ: Lawrence Erlbaum.

Bennardo, G. (2009) *Language, Space and Social Relationships: A Foundational Cultural Model in Polynesia*, Cambridge: Cambridge University Press.

Bohnemeyer, J. (2011) 'Spatial frames of reference in Yucatec: referential promiscuity and task-specificity', *Language Sciences* 33(6): 892–914. [special issue]

Bohnemeyer, J. and Brown, P. (2007) Standing divided: dispositional predicates and locative predications in two Mayan languages. *Linguistics* 45(5–6): 1105–1151.

Boroditsky, L. (2000) 'Metaphoric structuring: understanding time through spatial metaphors', *Cognition* 75(1): 1–28.

——(2012) 'How the languages we speak shape the ways we think: the FAQs', in M. J. Spivey, K. McRae, and M. F. Joanisse (eds), *Cambridge Handbook of Psycholinguistics*, 615–32. Cambridge: Cambridge University Press.

Bowerman, M. (1996) 'The origin of children's spatial semantic categories: cognitive vs. linguistic determinants', in J. J. Gumperz and S. C. Levinson (eds), *Rethinking Linguistic Relativity*. Cambridge: Cambridge University Press.

Bowerman, M. and Choi, S. (2001) 'Shaping meanings for language: universal and language-specific in the acquisition of spatial semantic categories', in M. Bowerman and S. C. Levinson (eds) *Language Acquisition and Conceptual Development*, 475–511, Cambridge: Cambridge University Press.

Bowerman, M. and Levinson, S.C. (eds) (2001) *Language Acquisition and Conceptual Development*, Cambridge: Cambridge University Press.

Brown, P. (1994) 'The INs and ONs of Tzeltal locative expressions: the semantics of static descriptions of location'. *Linguistics*, 32, 743–90.

——(2001) 'Learning to talk about motion UP and DOWN in Tzeltal: is there a language-specific bias for verb learning?' In M. Bowerman and S. C. Levinson (eds) *Language Acquisition and Conceptual Development*, 512–43, Cambridge: Cambridge University Press.

——(2006) 'A sketch of the grammar of space in Tzeltal', in S. C. Levinson and D. Wilkins (eds) *Grammars of Space*, 230–72, Cambridge: Cambridge University Press.

——(2014) 'Gestures in native Mexico and Central America: Tzeltal, Tzotzil, Yucatec Maya', in C. Müller, E. Fricke, S. Ladewig, A. Cienki, D. McNeill, and S. Teßendorf (eds), *Handbook Body – Language – Communication*. Volume 2. Berlin: Mouton de Gruyter.

Brown, P. and Levinson, S. C. (1993a) 'Linguistic and nonlinguistic coding of spatial arrays: explorations in Mayan cognition', Working Paper 24, Nijmegen, Netherlands: Cognitive Anthropology Research Group, Max Planck Institute for Psycholinguistics.

——(1993b) '"Uphill" and "downhill" in Tzeltal', *Journal of Linguistic Anthropology* 3(1): 46–74.

——(2000) 'Frames of spatial reference and their acquisition in Tenejapan Tzeltal', in L. Nucci, G. Saxe, and E. Turiel (eds) *Culture, Thought, and Development*, 167–97, Mahwah, NJ: Erlbaum.

——(2009) 'Language as mind tools: learning how to think through speaking', in J. Guo, E. V. Lieven, N. Budwig, S. Ervin-Tripp, K. Nakamura, and S. Ozcaliskan (eds) *Crosslinguistic Approaches to the Psychology of Language: Research in the Tradition of Dan Slobin*, 451–64, New York: Psychology Press.

——(in prep.) *The Language and Cognition of Space in a Mayan Community*. Cambridge: Cambridge University Press.

Cablitz, G. H. (2001) 'Marquesan: A grammar of space', Ph.D. dissertation, Kiel: Christian-Albrechts-Universität.

——(2002) 'The acquisition of an absolute system: learning to talk about space in Marquesan (Oceanic, French Polynesia)', in E. V. Clark (ed.) *Papers of the 2002 Stanford Child Language Research Forum*, 40–9, Stanford, CA: CLSI.

Casasanto, D. and Boroditsky, L. (2008) 'Time in the mind: using space to think about time', *Cognition* 106, 579–93.

Choi, S. and M. Bowerman (1991) 'Learning to express motion events in English and Korean: the influence of language-specific lexicalization patterns', *Cognition*, 41, 83–121.

Clark, H. H. (1973) 'Space, time, semantics, and the child', in T. E. Moore (ed.) *Cognitive Development and the Acquisition of Language*, 28–64, New York: Academic Press.

Clark, H. H. and D. Wilkes-Gibbs (1986) 'Referring as a collaborative process', *Cognition*, 22:1–39.

Danziger, E. (ed.) (1998) *Language, Space, and Culture*, special issue of *Ethos* 26(1).

——(2010) 'Deixis, gesture and cognition in spatial Frame of Reference typology', *Studies in Language* 34(1): 167–85.

Dasen, P. R. and Mishra, R. C. (2010) *Development of Geocentric Spatial Language and Cognition: An Eco-Cultural Perspective*, Cambridge: Cambridge University Press.

de León, L. (1994) 'Exploration in the acquisition of geocentric location by Tzotzil children', in J. Haviland and S. C. Levinson (eds) *Spatial Conceptualization in Mayan Languages*, special issue, *Linguistics* 32(4/5): 857–84.

——(1997) 'Vertical path in Tzotzil (Mayan) acquisition: cognitive vs. linguistic determinants', in E. V. Clark, (ed.) *Proceedings of the 28th Child Language Research Forum*, 183–97, Stanford: Center for the Study of Language and Information.

——(2001) 'Finding the richest path: the acquisition of verticality in Tzotzil (Mayan)', in M. Bowerman and S. C. Levinson (eds) *Cognitive Development and Language Acquisition*, 544–65, Cambridge, Cambridge University Press.

de León, L. and Levinson, S. C. (eds) (1992) Spatial Description in Mesoamerican Languages. Special edition of *Zeitschrift für Phonetik, Sprachwissenschaft und Kommunikationsforschung* 45(6).

Dirven, R. and Pütz, M. (eds) (1996) *The Construal of Space in Language and Thought*. Berlin: de Gruyter

Enfield, N. and Levinson, S.C. (2006) *Roots of Human Sociality: Culture, Cognition and Interaction*. Oxford: Berg.

Feld, S. and Basso, K. (eds) (1996) *Senses of Place*. Santa Fe: School of American Research Press.

Gentner, D. and Goldin-Meadow, S. (eds) (2003) *Language in Mind: Advances in the Study of Language and Cognition*, Cambridge, MA: MIT Press.

Gumperz, J. J. and Levinson, S. C. (eds) (2001) *Rethinking Linguistic Relativity*, Cambridge: Cambridge University Press.

Haun, D. (2007) 'Cognitive cladistics and the relativity of spatial cognition', Ph.D. dissertation, Radboud University Nijmegen.

Haun, D. B. M., Call, J., Janzen, G., and Levinson, S. C. (2006) 'Evolutionary psychology of spatial representations in the Hominidae', *Current Biology* 16: 1736–40.

Haun, D. B. M. and Rapold, C. J. (2009) 'Variation in memory for body movements across cultures'. *Current Biology*, 19(23), R1068–R1069.

Haun, D. B. M., Rapold, C. J., Call, J., Janzen, G., and Levinson, S. C. (2006) 'Cognitive cladistics and cultural override in Hominid spatial cognition', *PNAS*, 103(46): 17568–73.

Haun, D. B. M., Rapold, C. J., Janzen, G., and Levinson, S. C. (2011) 'Plasticity of human spatial memory: spatial language and cognition covary across cultures', *Cognition* 119: 70–80.

Haviland, J. B. (1993) 'Anchoring, iconicity and orientation in Guugu Yimithirr pointing gestures', *Journal of Linguistic Anthropology* 3(1): 3–45.

——(1996) 'Projections, transpositions, and relativity', in J. J. Gumperz and S. C. Levinson (eds) *Rethinking Linguistic Relativity*, 269–323, Cambridge: Cambridge University Press.

——(1998) 'Guugu Yimithirr cardinal directions', *Ethos* 26(1): 25–47.

——(2003) 'How to point in Zinacantán', in S. Kita (ed.) *Pointing: Where Language, Culture, and Cognition Meet*, 139–70, Mahwah, NJ/ London: Lawrence Erlbaum Associates.

——(2005) 'Directional precision in Zinacantec deictic gestures: (cognitive?) preconditions of talk about space', *Intellectica* 2–3(41–2): 25–54.

Hellwig, B. (2003) 'The grammatical coding of postural semantics in Goemai (A West Chadic language of Nigeria)', Ph.D. dissertation, Catholic University Nijmegen.

Hirsely, E. and O'Hanlon, M. (eds) (1995) *The Anthropology of Landscape: Perspectives on Place*. Oxford: Clarendon.

Hugh-Jones, C. (1980) *From the Milk River: Spatial and Temporal Processes in Northwest Amazonia*. Cambridge: Cambridge University Press.

Janzen, G., Haun, D. B. M., and Levinson, S. C. (2012) 'Tracking down abstract linguistic meaning: neural correlates of spatial frame of reference ambiguities in language', *PLoS One* 7(2): e30657.

Jensen de Lopez, K., Hayashi, M., and Sinha, C. (2005) 'Early shaping of spatial meaning in three languages and cultures: linguistic or cultural relativity?', in A. Makkai, W. J. Sullivan, and A. R. Lommel (eds), *LACUS Forum XXXI: Interconnections*, Houston, TX: LACUS.

Kant, E. (1768 [1991]) 'Von dem ersten Grunde des Unterschiedes der Gegenden im Raume' [Translated as: 'On the first ground of the distinction of regions in space'], in J. van Cleve and R. E. Frederick (eds) 1991, *The Philosophy of Right and Left: Incongruent Counterparts and the Nature of Space*, 27–34, Dordrecht: Kluwer.

Keating, E. (1998) *Power Sharing: Language, Rank, Gender and Social Space in Pohnpei, Micronesia*, Oxford: Oxford University Press.

Kita, S. (ed.) (2003) *Pointing: Where Language, Culture and Cognition Meet*, Mahwah, NJ: Erlbaum.

——(2008) 'Figure–ground indeterminacy in descriptions of spatial relations: a construction grammar account', in M. Bowerman and P. Brown (eds), *Crosslinguistic Perspectives on Argument Structure: Implications for Learnability*, 89–110. New York: Taylor and Francis.

Kita, S., Danziger, E. and Stolz, C. (2001) 'Cultural specificity of spatial schemas, as manifested in spontaneous gestures', in M. Gattis (ed.) *Spatial Schemas and Abstract Thought*, 115–46, Cambridge, MA: MIT Press.

Kopecka, A. and Narasimhan, B. (eds) (2011) *Events of Putting and Taking: A Crosslinguistic Perspective*, Amsterdam: Benjamins.

Lai, V. T. and Boroditsky, L. (2013) 'The immediate and chronic influence of spatio-temporal metaphors on the mental representations of time in English, Mandarin, and Mandarin–English speakers', *Frontiers in Psychology* 4:142.

Le Guen, O. (2009) 'Geocentric gestural deixis among Yucatec Maya (Quintana Roo, Mexico)', in *18th IACCP Book of Selected Congress Papers*, 123–36, Athens, Greece: Pedio Books Publishing.

——(2011a) 'Speech and gesture in spatial language and cognition among the Yucatec Mayas', *Cognitive Science* 35(5): 905–38.

——(2011b) 'Modes of pointing to existing spaces and the use of frames of reference', *Gesture* 11(3): 271–307.

Levinson, S. C. (1996) 'Frames of reference and Molyneux's question: cross-linguistic evidence', in P. Bloom, M. Peterson, L. Nadel and M. Garrett (eds) *Language and Space*, 109–69, Cambridge MA: MIT Press.

——(1997) 'Language and cognition: the cognitive consequences of spatial description in Guugu Yimithirr', *Journal of Linguistic Anthropology* 7(1): 98–131.

——(1998) 'Studying spatial conceptualization across cultures: anthropology and cognitive science', *Ethos* 26(1): 7–24.

——(2003a) *Space in Language and Cognition: Explorations in Cognitive Diversity*, Cambridge: Cambridge University Press.

——(2003b) 'Language and mind: Let's get the issues straight!', in D. Gentner and S. Goldin-Meadow (eds), *Language in Mind: Advances in the Study of Language and Cognition*, 25–46. Cambridge, MA: MIT Press.

——(2006). 'Introduction: The evolution of culture in a microcosm', in S. C. Levinson, and P. Jaisson (eds), *Evolution and Culture: A Fyssen Foundation Symposium*, 1–41. Cambridge: MIT Press.

Levinson, S. C. and Brown, P. (1994) 'Immanual Kant among the Tenejapans: anthropology as empirical philosophy', *Ethos* 22(1): 3–41.

Levinson, S. C. and Burenhult, N. (2009) 'Semplates: a new concept in lexical semantics?' *Language* 85: 153–74.

Levinson, S. C., and Evans, N. (2010) 'Time for a sea-change in linguistics: response to comments on "The myth of language universals"', *Lingua*, 120, 2733–58.

Levinson, S. C. and Haviland, J. B. (eds) (1994) 'Space in Mayan languages' [special issue]. *Linguistics*, 32(4/5).

Levinson, S. C., Kita, S., Haun, D., and Rasch, B. (2002) 'Returning the tables: language affects spatial reasoning', *Cognition* 84: 155–88.

Levinson, S. C. and Meira, S. (2003) '"Natural concepts" in the spatial topological domain – adpositional meanings in crosslinguistic perspective: an exercise in semantic typology', *Language* 79(3): 485–516.

Levinson, S. C. and Wilkins, D. P. (eds) (2006) *Grammars of Space: Explorations in Cognitive Diversity*, Cambridge: Cambridge University Press.

Li, P., Abarbanell, L., Gleitman, L., and Papafragou, A. (2011) 'Spatial reasoning in Tenejapan Mayans', cognition 120: 33–53.

Li, P. and Gleitman, L. (2002) 'Turning the tables: language and spatial reasoning', *Cognition* 83(3): 265–94.

Low, S. M., Lawrence-Zuniga, D. (eds) (2003) *The Anthropology of Space and Place: Locating Culture*. New York: Wiley.

Lucy, J. A. (1992a) *Language Diversity and Thought: A Reformulation of the Linguistic Relativity Hypothesis*, Cambridge: Cambridge University Press.

——(1992b) *Grammatical Categories and Cognition: A Case Study of the Linguistic Relativity Hypothesis*, Cambridge: Cambridge University Press.

Majid, A., Boroditsky, L., and Gaby, A. (eds) (2012) Time in terms of space [Research topic] [Special Issue]. *Frontiers in cultural psychology.* www.frontiersin.org/cultural_psychology/researchtopics/Time_in_terms_of_space/755

Majid, A., Bowerman, M., Kita, S., Haun, D., and Levinson, S. C. (2004) 'Can language restructure cognition? the case for space', *Trends in Cognitive Sciences* 8(3): 108–14.

Miller, G. and Johnson-Laird, P. (1976) *Language and Perception*, Cambridge, MA: Harvard University Press.

Nardini, M., Burgess, N., Breckenridge, K., Atkinson, J. (2006) 'Differential developmental trajectories for egocentric, environmental and intrinsic frames of reference in spatial memory', *Cognition* 101(1):153–72.

O'Meara, C. and Pérez Báez, G. (2011) 'Spatial frames of reference in Mesoamerican languages', *Language Sciences* 33(6): 837–52.

Papafragou, A. (2007) 'Space and the language–cognition interface', in P. Carruthers, S. Laurence, and S. Stich (eds) *The Innate Mind: Foundations and the Future*, 272–89, Oxford: Oxford University Press.

Pederson, E. (2003) 'How many reference frames?', in Freksa, C., Brauer, W., Habel, C., Wender, K. F. (eds) *Spatial Cognition III: Routes and Navigation, Human Memory and Learning, Spatial Representation and Spatial Learning*, 287–304, Berlin: Springer.

Pederson, E., Danziger, E., Wilkins, D., Levinson, S., Kita, S. and Senft, G. (1998) 'Semantic typology and spatial conceptualization', *Language* 74: 557–89.

Piaget, J. and Inhelder, B. (1956 [1948]), *The Child's Conception of Space*, London: Routledge and Kegan Paul.

Polian, G. and Bohnemeyer, J. (2011) 'Uniformity and variation in Tseltal reference frame use', *Language Sciences* 33(6): 868–91.

Seifart, F. (2005) 'The structure and use of shape-based noun classes in Mirana (northwest Amazon)', Ph.D. dissertation, Catholic University Nijmegen.

Senft, G. (ed.) (1997) *Referring to Space: Studies in Austronesian and Papuan Languages*, Oxford: Clarendon Press.

Sidnell, J. and Enfield, N. J. (2012) 'Language diversity and social action: a third locus of linguistic relativity', *Current Anthropology* 53(3): 302–33.

Sinha, C. and Jensen de López, K. (2000) 'Language, culture and the embodiment of spatial cognition', *Cognitive Linguistics* 11: 17–41.

Sinha, C. and Kuteva, T. (1995) 'Distributed spatial semantics', *Nordic Journal of Linguistics* 18, 167–99.

Slobin, D. I. (1996) 'From "thought and language" to "thinking for speaking"', in J. Gumperz and S. Levinson (eds) *Rethinking Linguistic Relativity*, 70–96, Cambridge: Cambridge University Press.

Slobin, D. I., Bowerman, M., Brown, P., Eisenbeiss, S., and Narasimhan, B. (2011) 'Putting things in places: developmental consequences of linguistic typology', in J. Bohnemeyer and E. Pederson (eds) *Event Representation in Language and Cognition*, 134–65, New York: Cambridge University Press.

Talmy, L. (1983) 'How language structures space', in H. Pick and L. Acredolo (eds) *Spatial Orientation: Theory, Research and Application*, 225–82, New York: Plenum Press.

——(2000) *Toward a Cognitive Semantics*, vols 1 and 2, Cambridge, MA: MIT Press.

Villa Rojas, A. (1973) 'The concepts of space and time among the contemporary Maya', in M. León-Portilla (ed.) *Time and Reality in the Thought of the Maya*, 121–67, Boston, MA: Beacon Press.

Warneken, F. and Tomasello, M. (2009) 'Cognition for culture', in P. Robbins and M. Aydede (eds) *The Cambridge Handbook of Situated Cognition*, 467–79. Cambridge: Cambridge University Press.

Wassman, J. and Dasen, P.R. (1998) 'Balinese spatial orientation: some empirical evidence for moderate linguistic relativity', *Journal of the Royal Anthropological Institute* 4(4): 689–711.

Whorf, B. L. (2011 [1956]) *Language, Thought and Reality*, 2nd edn, Cambridge, MA: MIT Press.

Widlok, T. (1997) 'Orientation in the wild: The shared cognition of Hai//kom Bushpeople', *Journal of the Royal Anthropological Institute* 3: 317–32.

——(2006) 'Landscape unbounded: space, place and orientation in ≠Akhoe Hai//kom and beyond', *Language Sciences* 30: 362–80.

21

SPACE, TIME, AND SPACE–TIME

Metaphors, maps, and fusions

Chris Sinha and Enrique Bernárdez

Introduction and overview

Space and time are frequently considered to be universal, transcultural domains of human language and thought, and the language of space, time, and motion has been intensively researched in recent decades. Space is widely viewed as the principal source domain for the linguistic and conceptual structuring, through metaphoric mapping, of time. At lexical and constructional levels, the spatial and temporal domains are closely related. In many languages, temporal meanings have been shown to be expressed by words and construction types whose primary meanings are analysed as being spatial. Typological studies have shown that lexical space–time mapping is indeed wide-spread (Haspelmath 1997), and constructional space–time mapping been analysed in languages as typologically and geographically disparate as English (Clark 1973; Lakoff and Johnson 1999), Aymara (South America: Núñez and Sweetser 2006), Chinese (Yu 1998, 2012), and Wolof (West Africa: Moore 2006).

Recent studies have also, however, revealed wide, sometimes dramatic, cross-linguistic variation in the language of space and time, and both domains (as well as their metaphoric inter-domain relations) have been prominent testing grounds for neo-Whorfian research (Levinson 2003; Boroditsky 2001). Much of the evidence adduced in support of Whorfian effects in spatial language involves cross-linguistic variation in the dominant spatial frame of reference (FoR) (Levinson 2003; Chapter 20 this volume). In analogous fashion, it has been suggested that the principal cross-linguistic differences in temporal language (sometimes leading to non-linguistic cognitive differences between speakers) consist not in the existence of space–time metaphor per se, but in the orientational frames of reference within which space–time metaphors are schematically constructed and construed (Radden, 2011).

The analysis of space–time metaphoric mapping in terms of conceptual metaphor theory and the theory of embodied cognition (Lakoff and Johnson 1980, 1999) has been particularly influential in proposals that *linguistic* space–time mapping, being based upon universal *non-linguistic* cognitive processes (Boroditsky 2000; Casasanto and Boroditsky 2008), can be considered as universal (Fauconnier and Turner 2008; Núñez and Cooperrider 2013). Bernárdez (2013) has criticized, however, the tendency in conceptual metaphor research either to neglect entirely the cultural dimension of metaphor, viewing it exclusively through the lens of cognitive universalism; or, when cultural issues are addressed, to conflate cultural variation with linguistic variation – a conflation that, according to Reynoso (2013), coexisted with a conflation of culture and psychology in the writings of Sapir and Whorf.

A number of recent studies, however, challenge the universality of space–time linguistic mapping (Levinson and Majid 2013; Sinha *et al.* 2011) and/or contextualize linguistic space–time mapping by situating it in wider patterns of cultural knowledge and world view (e.g. Hurtado de Mendoza 2002; Núñez and Cornejo 2012). We describe these and other recent studies in some detail below, since they point the way to a richer, more encompassing and more genuinely *cultural* understanding of the sources of both linguistic and cognitive variation.

What is at stake, methodologically, in a thoroughgoing cultural contextualization of the language of space and time? In the disciplines of anthropology and archaeology, language has traditionally been classified, along with belief systems, ritual and other linguistic–behavioural practices, as the foundation of *symbolic* culture; in contrast to *material* culture, the physically constructed human world. From this perspective, space and time, as dimensions of symbolic culture, are articulated not just in grammar and lexicon, but also in cosmologies and world views. In prehistoric, historical, and contemporary societies, questions of cultural identity ('Who are we?') are framed by the answers to 'Where and When' questions such as 'Where do we come from, where are we going, when did the world begin, and when will it end?'

However, the distinction between material culture and symbolic culture has been under increasing challenge in contemporary anthropology (Boivin 2008). Space and time are not only universal domains of language and thought; they are the fundamental situating dimensions of human socio-cultural and cognitive ecology, of what Bourdieu (1977: 86) has called *habitus*. Habitus spans, and unifies, material and symbolic culture in ways that are specific to particular cultures and societies. Social structure is not only *embedded*, conceptually and materially, in space and time, it is also *realized* through material spatial and temporal structures (Hornborg 2005; Hornborg and Hill 2011).

The sociocultural structuring of space and time is achieved by practices involving the construction and use of artefacts and artefact systems that blend the material and the symbolic at different scales. These include familiar, and historically evolved, artefacts such as compasses, clocks, calendars, and other time interval systems based on language (Birth 2012; Sinha *et al.* 2011). Material symbolic artefacts also include, however, the built environment (such as architecture, village and city layout); and the natural and humanly shaped landscape (including megaliths, geomorphic earthworks, and monuments). The meanings of these material symbolic artefact systems range from the expression of social differentiation (gender, rank, clan, etc.) in spatial and temporal dimensions; through architectural renderings of cosmological and religious beliefs; to the spatio-temporal ordering of normatively organized activities by means of time reckoning artefacts.

The materiality of meaning, and meaningfulness of materiality, is not only a key theme in contemporary anthropology. It is also central to recent approaches in cognitive science that emphasize the importance of objects in extended cognitive embodiment (Sinha and Jensen de López 2000); and in which cognition and communication are distributed over material–symbolic cognitive niches (Clark 2006; Hutchins 1995; Magnani 2009; Sinha 2006, 2009, 2013). The sociocultural contextualization of language and cognitive diversity in recent work, together with a general theoretical perspective of extended material–symbolic cultural embodiment, suggests a new, post-Whorfian perspective on the interrelations between language, cognition and culture, and their co-variation.

Historical and contextual perspectives

It is, at least for English speakers, difficult to think of and talk about time without employing metaphors, and many of these have as their source domain space and spatial motion. Take for example Sir Isaac Newton's exposition, in his *Philosophiae Naturalis Principia Mathematica* of 1686, of his theoretical understanding of time. Newton believed time, like space, to be absolute and infinite: 'Absolute, true, and mathematical time, in and of itself and of its own nature, without reference to anything external, flows uniformly and by another name is called duration. Relative, apparent, and common time is any sensible and external measure (precise or imprecise) of duration by means of motion; such a measure – for example, an hour, a day, a month, a year – is commonly used instead of true time.' Paradoxically perhaps, in asserting the metaphysical reality of time as a dimension independent of space, Newton availed himself of a '"passage" metaphor, of the "flow" (or passage) of the "River of Time"' (Smart 1949).

Newton's separation of time from space was challenged in the early twentieth century by the Special Theory of Relativity (Einstein 1920). As Einstein's contemporary, the mathematician Minkowski (1964: 927) put it, 'henceforth space by itself, and time by itself, are doomed to fade away into mere shadows, and only a kind of union of the two will preserve an independent reality'. The ontological status of time remains undecided in physics and the philosophy of science; but whatever its status in the physical universe, there is no denying that time is a fundamental aspect of the experiential, phenomenal life-world. It is important, however, to try to distinguish this temporal aspect of experience, which we can reasonably assume to be transcultural, from the highly culturally variable conceptualizations of time that we shall explore below.

In particular, in describing temporality in experience, we should avoid as far as possible (or at least be cautious about) the tempting but culture-specific use of metaphors, not just of 'flow' and 'passage' (which imply motion 'in time' analogously with motion in space); but also of stative 'location in time'. This is because, even if the experiential grounding of time is transcultural, *concepts* of time vary considerably, and it is not necessarily the case that time is transculturally conceptualized using spatial conceptual resources. Drawing an explicit parallel with Einstein's theory, Benjamin Lee Whorf formulated what he called 'The Principle of Linguistic Relativity' on the basis of his analysis of concepts of time and temporality in the Native American Hopi language (Chapter 2, this volume). Hopi time, he claimed, is 'non-Newtonian': that is, the Hopi speaker 'has no general notion or intuition of time as a smooth flowing continuum in which everything in the universe proceeds at an equal rate, out of a future, through a present, into a past; or, in which, to reverse the picture, the observer is being carried in the stream of duration continuously away from a past and into a future' (Whorf 1950: 27).

Whorf did not report how, or even whether, he directly investigated the existence of passage metaphors in Hopi. His conclusions were challenged by Malotki (1983), who provides a number of examples of what appear (if we accept his glosses) to be passage metaphors involving verbs of motion such as 'come' and 'arrive'. Malotki's critique of Whorf has itself been criticized (Leavitt 2010; Lee 1996), on, among other grounds, his alleged tendency (like Whorf himself, but in mirror-image) to over-interpret his data (which, it must be said, are far more comprehensive than those published by Whorf).

Regardless of the specifics of his analysis of Hopi time, Whorf's contention that 'Newtonian time' is not a universal cultural model has received support from later research, some of which is reviewed below. Can we, nonetheless, postulate some generally valid analytic categories that can serve as the basis for a comparative analysis of time across languages and cultures? Time as experienced is made up of the properties of events, which have two basic, perceptible aspects: duration and succession (or sequential order). We can take as our starting point, then, the plausible-seeming hypothesis that in all cultures people experience, and are able to talk about, events and inter-event relationships in terms of duration and succession; but that the particular words and concepts denoting temporal duration and temporal landmarks, although they may be based in universal human experiences such as awareness of the diurnal cycle, are based in specific cultural and civilizational traditions, and to that extent are language and culture specific. We explore later what the consequences of this variability might be for the presence or absence of linguistic space–time metaphorical mapping.

Duration: cultural time interval concepts

The cultural conceptualization and linguistic expression of *time intervals* (that is, lexicalized concepts of intervals of temporal duration) is known to be widely culturally variable. Much anthropological linguistic research has addressed variability in calendric (or quasi-calendric) systems, and in the social practices of 'time reckoning' (Evans-Pritchard 1939, 1940) that they permit. True calendric systems are *quantificational*, in the sense of being based upon a measurement system, and therefore can be considered as *time based*, segmenting and measuring temporal duration in the abstract and reified 'Newtonian fourth dimension' that Sinha *et al.* (2011) label 'Time as Such'. Time-based time intervals, such as 'hour' and 'week', make up what are often referred to as 'Clock Time' and 'Calendar Time' (Levine 1997; Postill 2002).

Time-based time intervals can be distinguished from event-based time intervals. Time-based time intervals are *chronological* (ancient Greek *chronos* = time), metric and referenced to an objective measure of 'elapsed time', whereas event-based time intervals are *kairotic* (ancient Greek *kairós* = [the right] moment; Birth 2012), qualitative and normative in nature, non-metric, and referenced to 'happenings' (including activities). Event-based time intervals are intervals whose boundaries are constituted by the event itself. In this sense, there is no cognitive differentiation between the time interval and the duration of the event or activity which defines it, and from which in general the lexicalization of the time interval derives. The reference event is often natural (such as 'spring', e.g. 'let's take a holiday in the spring'), but sometimes conventional (such as 'coffee break', e.g. 'let's discuss this during coffee break'). The event-based time interval may be characterized as a change of state (e.g. 'sunrise'), as a stative event attribute (to use an example from the Amondawa language of Amazonia, discussed below, the word *ara* means 'daylight'); or as an activity whose lexicalization may be metonymic, as in Amondawa *pojiwete*, 'when we start work'.

In some cases, event-based time interval terms derive from terms that refer both to activity and to place (or change of place). For example, modern English 'while', a term coordinating the duration of events, derives from the Old Germanic term meaning 'rest', and is related to modern Icelandic *hvíla*, which means both 'rest' and 'bed' (place of rest); while the old Norse cognate of 'rest', *rǫst*, meant 'the length of a journey between two stops', and later acquired a more precise spatial meaning as a distance of 12 km. The polysemy of temporal and spatial meaning in this and other such examples is better thought of as involving a metonymic fusion than a metaphoric mapping, an issue to which we return below.

Although time-based time intervals are based upon natural (astronomical) cycles of events, their divisions are conventional, and measurement of temporal duration is arrived at by counting in a number system. The terminology of *reckoning* or *telling* time has its etymological roots in Germanic words for *counting* (and *recounting* or telling) (e.g. modern Dutch *rekenen*, 'to count'). It is noteworthy that the Indo-European root *reg-* which is the origin of *reckon*, *rekenen*, etc. meant 'to move in a straight line' (a cognate is English *row*), an etymology that itself attests to the significance of path and motion in the conceptualization of number and the number line (Lakoff and Núñez 2000).

Calendric systems usually possess a recursive structure such that different time intervals are embedded within each other, and/or a structure of metrically overlapping intervals. These intervals are typically cyclical in nature, with both embedded and overlapping cycles. The most familiar to us is the now internationally adopted lunar and solar (more strictly, monthly and annual) Gregorian calendar. A dramatic example of the complexity that numerically based calendric systems can attain is provided by the classical Mayan civilization of Central America, which used three different calendar systems. The Long Count could be used to specify any day in Maya history, and could generate time references in an (in principle) infinite scale, a fact which both structured Mayan cosmology and was the main motivation and function for Mayan mathematical knowledge; this worked with place value and the number zero, both unknown to Mediterranean classical antiquity. The *Tzolkin* (counting days or Sacred Year) calendar was a ceremonial calendar, with 20 periods of 13 days, thus completing a ritual cycle every 260 days. The *Haab* was a civil calendar based on a year of 360 days consisting of 18 periods of 20 days. Five days were added at the end of the Haab year to approximately synchronize it with the solar year (Edmonson 1976; Wright 1991). The 260-day ritual cycle was not unique to the Maya, and possibly did not originate with them: the slightly earlier classical Zapotec state of Central America also employed this time interval (Flannery and Marcus 2012: 371).

Calendric systems are not merely 'timekeepers', they are expressive of cultural beliefs and values. The Gregorian calendric system, for example, conceptually superimposes on its cyclic structure a linear model of time (Bernárdez, 2003), as involving motion from an origin (the birth of Christ) to a notional endpoint (the End of Days). This dualistic cyclical–linear conceptualization (with varying relations of dominance between cyclicity and linearity) is characteristic also of other calendric systems, such as the Mayan, the Islamic, and the Vedic (Keyes 1975). Schieffelin (2002) documents the linguistic changes occurring in Bosavi Kaluli (Papua New Guinea), involving both erasure and innovation in lexicon, grammar and speech genres, consequent on the introduction by missionaries of Christian time concepts and by government agencies of the Gregorian calendar.

The classic early study of non-quantificational, but systematic event-based time intervals was by Evans-Pritchard (1939, 1940), who described what he termed the Nuer 'cattle clock' or 'occupational time'. Time in Nuer society, he proposed, was based on environmental changes and associated social activities. The concept of time in Nuer society was thus a product of the interplay between 'ecological time' and 'social structure time'. Although it had names for (roughly) lunar months, Nuer society as described by Evans-Pritchard did not count or measure Time as Such; the language had no word either for the abstract notion of time, or for units of abstract time, and temporal reference points were provided by social activities. 'Nuer have no abstract numerical system of time-reckoning based on astronomical observations but only descriptive divisions of cycles of human activities ... since the months are anchored to oecological [*sic*] and social process the calendar is a conceptual schema which enables Nuer to view the year as an ordered succession of changes and to calculate to some extent the relation between one event and another in abstract numerical symbols' (Evans-Pritchard 1939: 197, 200). Nuer months were not strictly lunar, nor based upon any other fixed number of days. Rather, they were conventionally, if indeterminately, based on both lunar and ecological cycles, and the associated rhythm of social activities. In summary, time for the Nuer consisted in a schematized relation between socially and environmentally defined events, and Nuer time reckoning was not a strict calculation of, or in, Time as Such, but a rough estimate, only infrequently numerically expressed, based on social-structural relationships and activities.

Nuer time is not the only system of time intervals reported in the anthropological literature that employs approximately specified lunar months in a non-quantified system. The time interval system of the Ainu culture of Southern Sakhalin, which in other respects (economy, social structure, and cosmological time) is quite different from the Nuer system, includes lunar months which regulate ritual as well as trapping and fishing activity. However, 'the Ainu are quite oblivious to names of the months as well as the number of months in the year' (Ohnuki-Tierney 1973: 289), and the Ainu, whose basic number system (non-derived numbers) extends to five, rarely or never reckon time intervals numerically, using the opposition between two or three and the derived number six to contrast short with long durations.

While the Nuer event-based time interval system can be thought of as quasi-calendric, permitting rough time-reckoning practices, the unnamed Ainu lunar months do not participate in anything resembling a yearly calendar. Ohnuki-Tierney concludes that 'the Ainu concept of time is basically qualitative; quantitative measurement of time is little developed. Therefore, no temporal divisions represent measurable units; they are distinguished from other units in the same time scale by the special meaning which the Ainu attach to them' (ibid.: 292).

A different conjunction of a small number system (four numbers) and a non-quantificational time interval system is found in the Tupí-Guarani language Amondawa of Western Amazonia (Sinha *et al.* 2011; Silva Sinha *et al.* 2012). The Amondawa time interval system is non-calendric, in the sense that it lacks names for month, week and year; larger time intervals are based upon seasons and their subdivisions (eight terms in all), and smaller ones upon segments of the day.

Amondawa is not a unique case. Preliminary analysis of data collected by Sampaio and Silva Sinha (2012) suggests that other, genetically related and unrelated, Amazonian languages have a similar profile. Moreover, the entirely unrelated, isolate language Yélî Dnye, spoken on Rossel Island, 450 km off Papua New Guinea, also has no calendric terms, although (like in Ainu) the term for 'moon' can designate an approximate lunar month. Yélî Dnye also has four seasonal terms, and contrasting terms for day and night. Levinson and Majid (2013: 3) report that 'this seems to exhaust the indigenous time units'. Intriguingly, both Amondawa and Yélî Dnye appear to employ no constructional space–time metaphors, although both display limited lexical space–time mappings or fusions. We return below to this conjunction of findings.

Temporal relational schemas and spatial metaphors

Duration is temporal *extension*. Succession is temporal *position*. In stating this, we are, indeed, immediately inviting an analogy between duration and spatial extension, and succession and spatial position (in front–behind, before–after). Events are in some respects like objects; but they are also different. Objects are located in space, and endure, however fleetingly, in time. They have properties like mass and energy. Events are 'located' in time, as well as in the space occupied by the objects involved in the event, having properties of duration and succession. Furthermore, we employ temporal (event) landmarks to orient ourselves in time, just as we employ spatial (object) landmarks to orient ourselves in space. Temporal duration words include adjectives such as 'long' and 'short', but also measured time intervals such as 'ten seconds' and 'four months'. Temporal landmarks include adverbials such as 'today', 'yesterday', and 'tomorrow', named times of day (midnight, 3.30), dates (1 May), and other calendrically structured events (Easter, my birthday, graduation day).

While spatial landmarks are employed in the service of literal navigation in space, involving physical motion, we cannot physically travel in time, other than by being 'carried onwards by the flow of time'. Our temporal navigation is therefore entirely conducted in the mind and in linguistic discourse, through remembering, imagining and what we call the 'forward planning' of actions, events and the locations of actions and events.

The analogy between temporal succession and spatial order was the basis for a distinction first made by the philosopher John McTaggart (1908) between what we would nowadays call two different schematic *frames of reference*. McTaggart's 'A-series' can be thought of as events seen from the standpoint of the present moment. Since the present moment is ever-changing, events 'pass' from future to past, hence its designation by some philosophers as 'passage' time. Núñez and Cooperrider (2013) refer to A-series time as *D-time* (for deictic time; see also Evans 2013; Le Guen and Pool Balam 2012). D-time is the schematic basis of grammatical tense, in languages which have tenses, and it is also the time of adverbial deictics like 'tomorrow' or 'yesterday', and of temporal landmarks such as 'next Christmas'.

McTaggart's 'B-series', in contrast, is tenseless, in that it represents events solely in terms of their ordering in a sequence of events, each of which can be marked as 'earlier' or 'later' than other events, and in which no event constitutes a privileged deictic centre. Sinha *et al.* (2011) refer to this 'B-series' as positional time, and Moore (2011) refers to it as the 'field-based' frame of reference (in contrast to the 'A-series', which he designates the 'ego-perspective' frame of reference). For consistency, we shall use Núñez and Cooperrider's abbreviation of *S-time* (for sequence time). S-time is the time in which relations are specified by 'before' and 'after', as well as 'earlier' and 'later', 'first', and 'last'.

Both D-time and S-time can be schematically depicted as linear time lines, and S-time as a recurrent cycle; but as we shall see such attributions should be treated with caution, as not necessarily possessing psychological reality for a given speaker. Calendric time is, by definition, S-time representation, but this does not mean (contra Gell 1992) that S-time events are intrinsically 'dated' with reference to a calendar; they are, rather, intrinsically *ordered*.

Although in a given language particular lexical resources (e.g. words corresponding to 'before' and 'after', as in Yucatec Maya: Bohnemeyer 2002) or grammatical resources (e.g. verbal tense, as in Chinese) may be absent, there are no reported 'timeless' languages, lacking either or both S-time and D-time expressions. We may reasonably assume, then, that not only do all normally developed human beings experience duration and succession, but also that all languages have resources for communicating the time of a referred-to event, relative either to another referred-to event (S-time); or to the time of utterance (D-time). This leaves open, however, the question of whether all languages linguistically encode *both* D-time and S-time relations, and if this is the case, whether languages vary in the degree to which these two fundamental temporal relational schemas are elaborated.

As McTaggart himself noted, it seems natural to construe D-time metaphorically, in terms of passage, or motion, in which either 'we say that events come out of the future [or] we ourselves move towards the future' (McTaggart 1908: 470, n. 1). These two metaphoric schemas, involving either the motion of an event in relation to the 'now' of an experiencer or the motion of an experiencer in relation to a temporal landmark, were labeled by Clark (1973) the 'moving time' (*MT*) metaphor and the 'moving ego' (*ME*) metaphor. They are exemplified by expressions such as 'the vacation is coming up' (MT), 'she is coming up to her exams' (ME), 'the deadline has passed' (MT).

MT and ME constructions are both particular cases of a more general class of D-time metaphors of 'passage', whose source domain is spatial motion. Passage metaphors may, but need not, involve explicit use of verbs of motion such as *come*, *go*, *pass*, *arrive*, and so on; they may rely instead on the metaphoric interpretation of adverbial phrases such as 'the year ahead', and can be stative and orientational as well as dynamic, sometimes involving fictive motion (Talmy 1999): e.g. 'my childhood is behind me', 'he faces a severe jail sentence'. Well-known conceptual metaphors such as 'life is a journey' (Lakoff and Johnson 1980) could be considered as generalized schemas derived from similarly structured passage metaphors, an interpretation that differs from viewing specific passage constructions as instantiations of pre-existent, transcultural conceptual metaphors.

S-time, as well as D-time, can be metaphorically conceptualized in terms of spatial relations, with the difference that the relations are between events, rather than between an experiencer and an event, even though the same spatial terms may be employed that can also be used in passage metaphors. So we can say that 'check-in is ahead of boarding', or 'beyond the first rite of passage lie many more tests'. S-time is always *positional* in meaning, that is, the inter-event relations of temporal antecedence and succession are invariant, whereas the relations of past and future are relative to an ever-changing present moment. We propose then to call spatial metaphors for S-time positional metaphors.

S-time is often said to be conceptualized from an external perspective, but this is not necessarily the case, as can be seen from some of the examples just provided, which are anchored to the point of view of a speaker or experiencer from a position within a time line. S-time is also often thought of as stative, with events sequenced like beads on a string; but verbs of motion may also be employed in positional metaphors, for example 'the cocktail comes ahead of the buffet' or 'questions will follow the lecture'.

As these examples suggest, whereas non-metaphoric S-time expressions (such as 'check in at least 40 minutes earlier than boarding') do not imply a speaker perspective, positional metaphors such as 'check-in at least 40 minutes ahead of boarding', like spatial expressions involving, for example, deictic front–back relations, do imply such a perspective. The existence of perspective, then, is common to both passage and positional space–time metaphors, even though only passage metaphors express deictic (D-time) temporal relations. Furthermore, some positional metaphors that depend on fictive motion, such as 'check-in ahead of boarding', seem themselves to be schematically derived from an ME passage metaphor. The difference between passage and positional metaphors is the semantic contrast between the underlying relativity (D-time) vs. invariance (S-time) of the conceptualized temporal relation.

The asymmetry of D-time and S-time in cross-linguistic perspective

To our knowledge, there are no reports that any language lacks lexical resources for D-time marking, although its grammaticalization is not universal. There are tenseless languages, and there are languages in which D-time is marked on the noun (Nordlinger and Sadler 2004) rather than through verbal tense; but all languages seem to have at the very least a repertoire of deictic adverbials indicating gradations of pastness and futurity of events with respect to the time of utterance. Lexical D-time systems can be of considerable complexity: Yéli Dnye, for example, has very specific monolexemic ordinal terms for days from 'the day before yesterday' to 'the 10th day in the future', and a productive system specifying days further into the future; and its tense system also references the specific day of the referred-to event (Levinson and Majid 2013: 2). The Yéli Dnye ordinal day-count system is particularly interesting because, although the language entirely lacks a calendar, the day-count system is positional, and thus could be said to share or blend properties of S-time with those of D-time.

We are not aware of any languages in which S-time inter-event relations are grammaticalized separately from the tense system, which, although it is deictically anchored to the time of utterance, can also specify sequence, e.g. 'she had left when he arrived'; sometimes in concert with before/after terms, e.g. 'he arrived after she had left.'

S-time is more cross-linguistically variable in its lexical expression and conceptualization than D-time. Consequently, it is more difficult to establish whether its lexicalization is common to all languages. As noted above, despite claims for the universality of the lexical concepts 'before' and 'after' (Goddard 2010), not all languages have these terms (Bohnemeyer 2002). Although we know of no languages that have been reported to lack lexemes that can be glossed as 'early' and 'late', in many cases these are deictic adverbs and it is not clear whether the S-time meanings 'earlier [than Event]' and 'later [than Event]' are analytically or discursively distinguishable from the D-time meanings 'earlier' and 'later' [than now]. For example, the Papuan language Mian has a term *sino*, derived from *sin* 'old', that is glossed as 'formerly, before, earlier' (Fedden and Boroditsky 2012: 5). More generally, we can say that in both non-metaphorical and metaphorical expressions, the same words and constructions may be used to express both D-time and S-time relationships.

Even if a language lacks both tense and before/after lexical equivalents, speakers are able to employ other grammatical resources to express S-time inter-event temporal relations. For example, speakers of Yucatec Maya employ completive and other aspectual markers to convey temporal sequence, in conjunction with the iconic mirroring in the order of mention of events of the order of their occurrence (Bohnemeyer, 2009; Le Guen and Pool Balam, 2012). Thus, what might be regarded as 'gaps' in grammar and lexicon constrain, but do not preclude the conceptualization and expression of S-time. This point is further reinforced when we consider the universality across cultures of narrative (which by definition involves the representation of event sequences) as a linguistic artefact, often also represented by other, for example pictorial, means. In fact, linguistic, pictorial and material–symbolic artefacts can be considered to be important, in some cases the primary, means for enabling the expression of culturally significant S-time concepts.

Although pictorial or other material–symbolic representations of S-time may be absent (as in Amondawa and Yélî Dnye), it may still be represented by linguistically transmitted symbolic systems. Not only calendric systems, but non-calendric seasonal and diurnal time interval systems may be regarded as culture-specific S-time artefacts. Kinship systems, genealogical memory and some naming systems also clearly involve temporal sequence. A striking example of the latter is the Amondawa onomastic system, in which individuals change their names at transition points in their 'passage' through different life stages, drawing from an inventory structured by gender and moiety as well as the named life stages (Silva Sinha *et al.* 2012).

We conclude from this brief survey that although both D-time and S-time schemas are almost certainly transculturally present, there is considerable variation in the specific ways in which these are organized and expressed in different languages. There has been much more linguistic research on D-time, because it is fundamental to tense systems, than on S-time, which is not conventionally grammaticalized separately from D-time, and which is expressed both lexically and in constituents of symbolic culture at a level higher than individual words or sentences (narratives, time interval and kinship systems); often involving other semiotic resources (e.g. pictorial) than language. Investigations of these artefactual systems has been the preserve more of cultural anthropology and psychology than linguistics. S-time representation, we suggest, is more culturally variable than D-time. Furthermore, we shall argue, it is the specific means of mediation and representation of S-time that seems to be correlated with, and possibly causally linked to, the existence of passage and positional space–time metaphors.

Spatializing time around the world

As noted above, several recent studies have investigated whether cross-linguistic differences in space–time mapping patterns involve correlations between spatial and temporal frames of reference. As well as linguistic analyses, two methodologies that have been frequently employed in these and other studies are the recording of situated co-speech gesture, and the elicited positioning by speakers of pictures or other material symbols representing temporally ordered events. At the time of writing, no cross-culturally consistent picture has emerged from these studies. Some investigations have found systematic isomorphisms between spatial and temporal frames of reference, linguistically and non-linguistically (Gaby 2012; Núñez *et al.* 2012). Others have found no such relationship, and/or have found response patterns suggestive that native speakers do not constitute a uniform sample: language contact and educational experience being independent mediating variables (Brown 2012; Le Guen and Balam 2012; Levinson and Majid 2013).

On the basis of their investigations in, respectively, Tzeltal and Yélî Dnye, Brown (2012: 10) concludes that 'there is no automatic transfer of spatial frames of reference to those for time'; and Levinson and Majid (2013: 10) that their study 'casts doubt upon a strong universal tendency for systematic space–time mapping'. Le Guen and Balam (2012: 14) investigated, in a multi-methodological study, both D-time and S-time in Yucatec Maya, finding that neither of them is mapped to a metaphoric time line. S-time, they report, is conceptualized as 'a succession of completed events not spatially organized', in which 'cyclicity' is attributed to both single events and event sequences. They conclude that 'the use of a geocentric [spatial] FoR instead of providing a way of mapping time to space, prevents it, and only allows a space-to-time mapping that opposes current and remote (past and future) time'.

It is important to note, nonetheless, that in no cultural context so far investigated have participants failed to understand, in at least one task, the task demand of representing temporal sequence by producing a spatially ordered positional layout, even in cases where systematic linguistic, gestural or artefactual space–time mapping has been found to be absent (Figure 21.1). This supports the hypothesis that the prerequisite cognitive capacity or tendency for space–time mapping is a transcultural human universal. It should equally be noted, however, that it is by no means the case that all such spatial representations of S-time are rectilinear; they are often curved lines, and the same holds for D-time spatial representations, which may not be organized with linear asymmetry at all (Le Guen and Balam 2012). In other words, even if space–time mapping rests on universal cognitive foundations, there is nothing universal about the notion of

Figure 21.1 An Amondawa speaker spatially maps the seasonal time intervals

a 'time line'. In all likelihood, the linear time-line concept has historically developed in synergy with the concept of a number line, which has also been shown not to be a transcultural universal (Dehaene *et al.* 2008).

In evaluating the claim that spatialization of time is universal, we need to distinguish (1) occasional, non-systematic space–time mappings, correspondences, and fusions from (2) systematic mappings involving the transposition of a spatial FoR to D-time and or S-time; and/or the widespread recruitment of spatial motion and location constructions in passage or positional metaphors. It seems likely that many, perhaps all languages manifest instances of (1) without (2) being necessarily implied (this is the case, for example, for both Amondawa and Yélî Dnye, both of which lack systematic space–time metaphor).

Non-systematic mappings may be metaphoric, metonymic, or fusional. An example of metonymic mapping is the Amondawa inflected word meaning 'along the path of the sun', provided by a speaker in translation of 'today' (Sampaio and Silva Sinha 2012). It should be noted that we do not yet know whether this is an entrenched usage, or relatively recent coinage; but it serves to demonstrate that the absence of systematic space–time mapping does not imply the complete absence of productive space–time mapping, especially at the lexical level. In other cases, such as the use of the same lexemes (e.g. 'long') for spatial and temporal extension, or old Norse *rǫst*, discussed above, which has both a duration and a distance meaning, the 'mapping' is arguably a polysemous fusion. The same fusional character can be seen in the use in many languages of the same term or gesture to signify both spatial and temporal here and now; that is, a unified spatio-temporal deictic centre. None of these non-systematic space–time metonymic mappings and/or fusions are, in our view, *contra* Núñez and Cooperrider (2013), readily classifiable as 'spatial construals of time'.

The notion of 'fusion' returns us to a consideration of the opposition between the Newtonian vision of space and time as distinct domains, and the singular domain of space–time introduced to Western thought by Einstein, and attributed by Whorf to Hopi language and thought. There is extensive documentation of the lexicalization of a unified, or fused, space–time concept in at least two languages, Aymara and Quechua. Aymara and Quechua are phylogenetically unrelated Andean languages (Adelaar 2004) that share cultural conceptualizations and practices, and vocabulary, especially in the domain of space–time. Space–time is called in both languages *pacha*, from which are derived the Aymara terms *pachamama* (Mother Earth), *akapacha* (this time and epoch) (Núñez and Cornejo 2012), and many other compounds.

The Aymara terms *nayra*, 'front' and *qhipa*, 'back', correspond, respectively, to the Quechua cognates *ñawpaq* and *qhipa*. Núñez and Sweetser (2006) showed that Aymara speakers employ a deictically anchored D-time line in which the future is conceptualized as being in front of the speaker/experiencer, and the past behind them. This 'reversal' of the directionality of the Western schema, in which the future is thought of as in front, and the past behind, is manifested not only in Aymara speech but also in co-speech gesture. Quechua employs what appears to be an identical D-time line to Aymara (Hurtado de Mendoza 2002); although Faller and Cuéllar (2003) dispute this, arguing that Quechua *ñawpaq* and *qhipa* do not in fact correspond to 'past' and 'future', but are rather S-time expressions corresponding to 'earlier than' and 'later than'. This indeed appropriately characterizes their use in the seventeenth-century Huarochirí manuscript (Arguedas 2011), analysed by Bernárdez (2013); but we may note that temporal relational terms can be used with both D-time and S-time meanings in many languages; the equivalent Aymara terms appear to be so used.

An in-depth analysis of Aymara spatial usage of *nayra* and *qhipa* by Núñez and Cornejo (2012) revealed that, intriguingly, the use of terms is situated in an absolute frame of reference (Chapter 20, this volume), in which *nayra* corresponds to East and *qhipa* corresponds to West. This schematization is transferred by Aymara people to the Andean variety of Spanish, and can

Table 21.1 Space–time correspondences in the genetically unrelated Andean languages Aymara (Nuñez and Cornejo 2012) and Quechua (e.g. Hurtado de Mendoza 2002; Bernárdez, 2014)

Language	Lexical term	Glosses	Spatial relational meaning	Associated cardinal direction	Associated S-time meaning	Associated D-time meaning	Visibility
Aymara	*nayra*	face front eye	in front of	East	earlier [before]	Past	Visible
	qhipa	back	behind	West	later [after]	Future	Invisible
Quechua	*ñawpaq*	front	in front of		earlier [before]	Past (?)	Visible
	qhipa	back	behind		later [after] [following]	Future (?)	Invisible

lead to situations such as that in which a speaker can say that he is *qhipa* (Aymara) or *atrás de* (Spanish 'in back of') someone sitting directly facing them (Núñez and Cornejo 2012: 972). Núñez and Cornejo also analyse how these correspondences, which implicate visibility as well as cardinal direction, are expressed or materialized in the built environment. We do not have space here to go into the details of this and other studies, but a summary of the complex of correspondences that characterize *pacha*, Andean space–time, is provided in Table 21.1.

In contrast with the non-systematic metaphoric–metonymic mappings and fusions discussed above, Andean space–time correspondences are highly systematic and informed by a cultural world-view. Should we regard this structured ensemble of mappings and correspondences as *metaphoric*? Or should we rather follow the indigenous languages and their shared cultural model in regarding the correspondences as existing within a *single conceptual domain* of space–time? We regard the latter as preferable for several reasons. First, the testimony of speakers, pointing out that movement in space *is* simultaneously movement in time, and denying that *ñawpaq* and *qhipa* are just equivalents of 'front' and 'back' should be taken seriously (see for example Hurtado de Mendoza 2002: 71).

Second, upon closer investigation, the Aymara–Quechua *nayra/ñawpaq–qhipa* axis is *not* simply the Western past–future time line, reversed and with additional correspondences. The word for 'ancestor' in Quechua is *ñawpaqkuna*, meaning the ones in front, who are guides to right conduct (Calvo Pérez 1995: 21). This centrality of the ancestors in a space–time that is also a moral universe is shared by other Amerindian cultures too. For example, Basso (1988: 112) highlights the role of Apache place names: 'in positioning people's minds to look "forward" (*bidááh*) into space, a place name also positions their minds to look "backward" (*t'qqzhi'*) into time. For as persons imagine themselves standing in front of a named site, they may imagine that they are standing in their ancestors' tracks (*nohwizá'yé biké'é*).' The ancestors are also key to Navajo time and life, which follows a curved return line in which 'the gradual completion of one's life is seen as a continuous process of growth right back into ancestry; while growing older one continuously changes, gradually to become an ancestor (which, in the West, we would situate "in the past")' (Pinxten 1995: 240) (see Yu 2012, for a discussion of ancestor schematizations in Chinese and other cultures).

Third, while the experience of time is transcultural, the concept of autonomous and reified Time as Such is, as argued by Sinha *et al.* (2011), a historical and cultural invention, not a universal cognitive domain. It is only when this domain is constructed, through the numerical–calendric organization of S-time, that systematic space–time metaphorical mapping emerges. *Pacha*, we would argue, is also a historical and cultural construction, the result of a different and divergent process. Although metaphoric reasoning would have been central to this construction process, to view Andean space–time as a 'spatial construal of time' imposes a Eurocentric distortion on indigenous culture and languages.

Summary and future directions

On the basis of the research reviewed, we conclude that:

Space–time linguistic metaphor and/or space–time fusion are widespread in the world's languages and are likely motivated by universal cognitive processes.

However, there is mounting evidence that *systematic* space–time metaphorical mapping is *not* universal in language.

The motivation of linguistic structure by cognitive process (even given that the latter is putatively universal) is *never* direct, but *always* mediated by material and symbolic cultural patterns and processes.

Language variation in space and time is *culturally situated* in systematic multilevel sociocultural variation, expressed in practices and artefacts as well as belief systems.

The conceptualization of space and time in languages is determined as much or more by shared worldviews in broad cultural–geographical areas as by phylogenetic relations, yielding cross-linguistic patterns such as Andean *pacha*.

Space is not the only source domain for the linguistic and cultural conceptualization of time, which draws also on cosmological and kinship systems.

Research in this field will continue to employ qualitative and quantitative multi-methodological designs, and we suggest it will increasingly add archaeology to the list of represented disciplines. Research should record number systems, cosmology, and relevant material culture and associated practices, as well as the linguistic and gestural conceptualization of space and time. The main challenge in coming years will be to go beyond the documentation and classification of variation to develop an encompassing theoretical account of both the causes of and constraints on variation.

Related topics

language, culture, and spatial cognition; research on language and culture: a historical account; the linguistic relativity hypothesis revisited

Further reading

Bernárdez, E. (2013) On the cultural character of metaphor. Some reflections on universality and culture specificity in the language and cognition of time, especially in Amerindian languages. *Review of Cognitive Linguistics* 11: 1–35. (Critiques the presumed universality of space–time metaphor and provides a detailed description of Amerindian space–time in different languages.)

Birth, K. 2012. *Objects of Time: How things shape temporality*. New York: Palgrave Macmillan. (Focuses on the role of cognitive artefacts in the historical construction of time concepts, and examines multiple temporalities in different cultures.)

Nuñez, R. and Cooperrider, K. (2013) The tangle of space and time in human cognition. *Trends in Cognitive Science* 17: 220–9. (Reviews both non-linguistic and linguistic evidence for spatial construals of time and their cross-linguistic variation, from a universalist perspective.)

Sinha, C., Silva Sinha, V. da, Zinken, J. and Sampaio, W. (2011) When time is not space: The social and linguistic construction of time intervals and temporal event relations in an Amazonian culture. *Language and Cognition* 3–1 (2011), 137–69. (Documents a language lacking space–time metaphor and proposes the socioculturally based mediated mapping hypothesis.)

Special thematic issues of journals can be consulted on the following relevant topics: *Current Anthropology* (2002 vol. 43, no. S4) on repertoires of timekeeping in anthropology; *Frontiers in Cultural Psychology* (2012–13 doi: 10.3389/fpsyg.2013.00554), on time in terms of space; *Journal of Pragmatics* (2011 vol. 43, issue 3, pp. 691–922) on the language of space and time.

Chris Sinha and Enrique Bernárdez

References

Adelaar, W. with P. Muysken (2004) *The Languages of the Andes*. Cambridge: Cambridge University Press.

Arguedas, J. M. (2011) *El manuscrito de Huarochirí*. Bilingual version by José María Arguedas. Ed. J. I. Úzquiza González. Madrid: Biblioteca Nueva.

Basso, K. H. (1988) 'Speaking with names': language and landscape among the Western Apache. *Cultural Anthropology* 3(2): 99–130.

Bernárdez, E. (2003) Toward a common history of the Germanic and European languages in the Middle Ages. *SELIM [Journal of the Spanish Society for Mediaeval English Language and Literature]* 12: 5–32.

——(2013) On the cultural character of metaphor. Some reflections on universality and culture specificity in the language and cognition of time, especially in Amerindian languages. *Review of Cognitive Linguistics* 11: 1–35.

Birth, K. (2012) *Objects of Time: How things shape temporality*. New York: Palgrave Macmillan.

Bohnemeyer, J. (2002) *The Grammar of Time Reference in Yukatek Maya*. Munich: LINCOM.

——(2009) Temporal anaphora in a tenseless language. In W. Klein and L. Ping (eds.) *Expression of Time*. Berlin: Mouton de Gruyter, pp. 83–128.

Boivin, N. (2008) *Material Cultures, Material Minds: The role of things in human thought, society and evolution*. Cambridge: Cambridge University Press.

Boroditsky, L. (2000) Metaphoric structuring: understanding time through spatial metaphors. *Cognition* 43: 1–22.

——(2001) Does language shape thought? Mandarin and English speakers' conceptions of time. *Cognitive Psychology* 43: 1–22.

Bourdieu, P. (1977) *Outline of a Theory of Practice*. Trans. R. Nice. Cambridge: Cambridge University Press.

Brown, P. (2012) Time and space in Tzeltal: is the future uphill? *Frontiers in Psychology* 3 doi: 10.3389/fpsyg.2012.00212.

Calvo Pérez, J. (1995) *Introducción a la lengua y cultura quechuas*. Valencia: Universitat de València.

Casasanto, D. and Boroditsky, L. (2008) Time in the mind: using space to think about time. *Cognition*, 1062, 579–93.

Clark, A. (2006) Language, embodiment and the cognitive niche. *Trends in Cognitive Science* 10: 370–4.

Clark, H. H. (1973) Space, time, semantics and the child. In Moore, T. E. (ed.) *Cognitive Development and the Acquisition of Language*. New York: Academic Press, pp. 27–63.

Dehaene, S., Izard, V., Spelke, E. and Pica, P. (2008) Log or linear? Distinct intuitions of the number scale in Western and Amazonian indigene cultures. *Science* 320: 1217–20.

Edmonson, M. (1976) The Mayan Reform of 11.16.0.0.0. *Current Anthropology* 17(4):713–17.

Einstein, A. (1920) *Relativity: The Special and the General Theory*. London: Methuen.

Evans, V. (2013) *Language and Time*. Cambridge: Cambridge University Press.

Evans-Pritchard, E. E. (1939) Nuer time-reckoning. *Africa: Journal of the International African Institute* 12 (2):189–216.

——(1940) *Nuer*. Oxford: Oxford University Press.

Faller, M. and M. Cuéllar (2003) *Metáforas del tiempo en el quechua*. (CD-ROM publication).

Fauconnier, G. and Turner, M. (2008) Rethinking metaphor. In Gibbs, R. (ed.) *The Cambridge Handbook of Metaphor and Thought*. Cambridge: Cambridge University Press, pp. 53–66.

Fedden, S. and Boroditsky, L. (2012) Spatialization of time in Mian. *Frontiers in Psychology* 3 doi: 10.3389/fpsyg.2012.00485.

Flannery, K. and J. Marcus (2012) *The Creation of Inequality: How our prehistoric ancestors set the stage for monarchy, slavery and empire*. Cambridge, MA: Harvard University Press.

Gaby, A. (2012) The Thaayore think of time like they talk of space. *Frontiers in Psychology* 3 doi: 10.3389/fpsyg.2012.00300.

Gell, A. (1992) *The Anthropology of Time: Cultural constructions of temporal maps and images*. Oxford: Berg.

Goddard, C. (2010) The natural semantic metalanguage approach. *The Oxford Handbook of Linguistic Analysis*. Oxford: Oxford University Press, pp. 459–484.

Haspelmath, M. (1997) *From Space to Time: Temporal adverbials in the world's languages*. Munich and Newcastle: Lincom.

Hornborg, A. (2005) Ethnogenesis, regional integration, and ecology in prehistoric Amazonia: Toward a system perspective. *Current Anthropology* 46(4):589–620.

Hornborg, A. and Hill, J. (eds.) (2011) *Ethnicity in Ancient Amazonia: Reconstructing Past Identities from Archaeology, Linguistics, and Ethnohistory*. Boulder, CO: University of Colorado Press.

Hurtado de Mendoza, S. W. (2002) *Pragmática de la Cultura y la Lengua Quechua*. Quito: Abya Yala.

Hutchins, E. (1995) *Cognition in the Wild*. Cambridge, MA: Bradford Books.

Keyes, Charles F. (1975) Buddhist pilgrimage centers and the twelve-year cycle: Northern Thai moral orders in space and time. *History of Religions* 15: 71–89.

Lakoff, G. and Johnson, M. (1980) *Metaphors We Live By*. Chicago: University of Chicago Press.

——(1999) *Philosophy in the Flesh: The embodied mind and its challenge to Western thought*. New York: Basic Books.

Lakoff, G. and Núñez, R. E. (2000) *Where Mathematics Comes from: How the embodied mind brings mathematics into being*. New York: Basic Books.

Leavitt, J. (2010) *Linguistic Relativities: Language diversity and modern thought*. Cambridge: Cambridge University Press.

Lee, P. (1996) *The Whorf Theory Complex: A critical reconstruction*. Amsterdam: John Benjamins.

Le Guen, O. and Pool Balam, L.I. (2012) No metaphorical timeline in gesture and cognition among Yucatec Mayas. *Frontiers in Psychology* 3 doi: 10.3389/fpsyg.2012.00271.

Levine, R. (1997) *A Geography of Time. The temporal misadventures of a social psychologist, or: How every culture keeps time just a little bit differently*. New York: Basic Books.

Levinson, S. (2003) *Space in Language and Cognition: Explorations in cognitive diversity*. Cambridge: Cambridge University Press.

Levinson, S. and Majid, A. (2013) The island of time: Yélî Dnye, the language of Rossell Island. *Frontiers in Psychology* 4 doi: 10.3389/fpsyg.2013.00061.

McTaggart, J. (1908) The unreality of time. *Mind: A Quarterly Review of Psychology and Philosophy*. 17, 456–73.

Magnani, L. (2009) *Abductive Cognition: The epistemological and eco-cognitive dimensions of hypothetical reasoning*. Cognitive Systems Monographs 3. Berlin: Springer.

Malotki, E. (1983) *Hopi time: A linguistic analysis of the temporal concepts in the Hopi Language*. Berlin: Walter de Gruyter.

Minkovsky, H. (1964) Space and time. In Smart, J. J.C. (ed.), *Problems of Space and Time* London: Macmillan, p. 927.

Moore, K. E. (2006) Space-to-time mappings and temporal concepts. *Cognitive Linguistics* 17: 199–244.

——(2011) 'Ego-perspective and field-based frames of reference: temporal meanings of FRONT in Japanese, Wolof, and Aymara'. *Journal of Pragmatics* 43: 759–76.

Newton, I. S. (1686) *Philosophiæ Naturalis Principia Mathematica*. London: Royal Society.

Nordlinger, R. and L. Sadler (2004) Nominal tense in crosslinguistic perspective. *Language* 80(4):776–806.

Núñez, R. and Cooperrider, K. (2013) The tangle of space and time in human cognition. *Trends in Cognitive Sciences* 17: 220–9.

Núñez, R., Cooperrider, K., Doan, D., and Wassmann, J. (2012) Contours of time: topographic construals of past, present, and future in the Yupno valley of Papua New Guinea. *Cognition* 124: 25–35.

Núñez, R., and Cornejo, C. (2012) Facing the sunrise: cultural worldview underlying intrinsic-based encoding of absolute frames of reference in Aymara. *Cognitive Science*, 36(6), 965–91.

Núñez, R. and Sweetser, E. (2006) With the future behind them: convergent evidence from Aymara language and gesture in the crosslinguistic comparison of spatial construals of time. *Cognitive Science* 30: 1–49.

Ohnuki-Tierney, Emiko (1973) Sakhalin Ainu Time Reckoning. *Man*. New Series 8(2): 285–99.

Pinxten, R. (1995) Comparing time and temporality in cultures. *Cultural Dynamics* 7: 233–252.

Postill, J. (2002) Clock and calendar time: a missing anthropological problem. *Time and Society* 11(2/3): 251–70.

Radden, G. (2011) Spatial time in the West and the East. In M. Brdar, M. Omazic, V. Pavicic Takac, T. Gradecak-Erdeljic, and G. Buljan (eds.) *Space and Time in Language*. Frankfurt: Peter Lang, pp. 1– 40.

Reynoso, C. (2013) *Lenguaje y pensamiento: Tácticas y estrategias del relativismo lingüístico* unpublished manuscript, Universidad de Buenos Aires. Versión 13.04.04 Downloaded 07/05/2013 from *http://carlosreynoso.com.ar*.

Sampaio, W. and Silva Sinha, V. (2012) *Dados Espaço-Tempo (Projeto Açaí) 2012*. Unpublished data archive.

Schieffelin, B. (2002). Marking time: The dichotomizing discourse of multiple temporalities. *Current Anthropology* 43, S4: S5–S17.

Silva Sinha, V. da and Sampaio, W. (2012) Unpublished data corpus of space–time mappings in Amazonian languages.

Silva Sinha, V. da, Sinha, C., Sampaio, W. and Zinken, J. (2012) Event- based time intervals in an Amazonian culture. In Filipovič, L. and Kasia M. Jaszczolt (eds), *Space and Time across Languages and Cultures Vol. II Language, Culture and Cognition*. Amsterdam: John Benjamins, pp. 15–35.

Sinha, C. (2006) Epigenetics, semiotics and the mysteries of the organism. *Biological Theory* 1(2) 1–4.

——(2009) Language as a biocultural niche and social institution. In Evans, V. and S. Pourcel (eds.) *New Directions in Cognitive Linguistics*. Amsterdam: John Benjamins, pp. 289–310.

——(2013) Niche construction, too, unifies praxis and symbolization. *Language and Cognition* 5: 261–71.

Sinha, C. and Jensen de López, K. (2000) Language, culture and the embodiment of spatial cognition. *Cognitive Linguistics* 11, 17–41.

Sinha, C., Silva Sinha, V. da, Zinken, J. and Sampaio, W. (2011) When time is not space: The social and linguistic construction of time intervals and temporal event relations in an Amazonian culture. *Language and Cognition*, 3: 137–69.

Smart, J. J. C. (1949) The River of Time. *Mind*. New Series, 58(232):483–94.

Talmy, L. (1999) Fictive motion in language and 'ception'. In P. Bloom, M. Peterson, L. Nadel, and M. Garrett (eds), *Language and Space*, 211–76. Cambridge, MA: MIT Press.

Whorf, B. L. (1950) An American Indian model of the universe. *International Journal of American Linguistics* 16, 67–72.

Yu, N. (1998) *The Contemporary Theory of Metaphor: A Perspective from Chinese*. Amsterdam: John Benjamins.

——(2012) The metaphorical orientation of time in Chinese. *Journal of Pragmatics* 44: 1335–54.

22

CULTURE AND LANGUAGE DEVELOPMENT

Laura Sterponi and Paul F. Lai

1 Introduction

In *The Language Instinct*, Steven Pinker celebrates the acquisition of language as 'one of the wonders of the natural world', the mundane yet remarkable ability of human beings to 'shape events in each other's brains' with words (1994: 15–16). By the utterance of a sequence of sounds, for instance, a 1-year-old child manipulates the mental awareness of a caretaker to an undetected soiled diaper or a preference for warm or cold milk. Yet Pinker argues, along the lines of various innatist or linguistic nativist perspectives, this ability is 'not a cultural artifact ... but a distinct piece of the biological makeup of our brains' (ibid.: 18). Chomsky (1965) famously postulated a theory of Universal Grammar which sought to explain how young children could so readily adopt most of the complex deep structures embedded in any language, not to mention creatively generate acceptable sentences of incredible variety. Chomsky (ibid.) argued this feat could only be accomplished by means of a genetically inherited Language Acquisition Device, a hypothesized cognitive structure of pre-programmed constraints and possibilities, which exists *a priori* in children as a set of 'switches' (for instance, between a Subject–Verb–Object or a Subject–Object–Verb pattern) that are then calibrated to the specific primary language a child is reared in.

Nativist perspectives dismiss culture as a relevant variable to include in their developmental model, allowing only for a secondary influence of the environment, conceptualized exclusively as linguistic input (e.g. Regier and Gahl 2004). A different treatment of culture is found in critiques to the Chomskian theoretical lineage.

However, what is meant by the term 'culture' in these alternative perspectives is not homogeneous. A central distinction points back to Herder's *Reflections on the Philosophy of the History of Mankind* ([1784] 1968), where the German philosopher marked out the difference between *Kultur* and *Cultur*. The German *Kultur* shared semantic territory with the idea of 'civilization', that which distinguishes humanity from animals and facilitates our development. But Herder advocated the other usage, the German *Cultur*, which emphasized cultures (plural) in their diversity and their particularity, as opposed to the notion of a single, universal trajectory of social development.

These two conceptions of culture, one as a singular system acting as a developmental mechanism in humans, the other as an ongoing proliferation of specific and irreducible social contexts, have bearing on the question of how culture functions in language acquisition. Put simply, culture can be said to be the resource that underpins people's universal proficiency with language (in contrast to, say, a language gene). Or, culture can be said to be the distinctive social situation in which each child is apprenticed into local systems of meaning. *Culture* structures *Language*, or *cultures* structure *languages*. But are those conceptions mutually exclusive?

In a thought-provoking, in her own words 'heretical', paper published in 1990, prominent scholar in linguistic anthropology and founder of the language socialization research paradigm Elinor Ochs has contended that culture is both 'a universal property of the human condition' and 'local, particular, unique' (1990a: 1). In effect, culturally embedded uses of language must be a species-wide resource for the development of linguistic structures as well as a local and unique context within which meaning is found. In this chapter we embrace such tensions and consider ways in which both *universally* and *specifically* culture structures language development.

To this aim we engage two research paradigms, which have different disciplinary roots: the usage-based approach, from developmental psychology, and the language socialization approach, from linguistic anthropology. We argue that these two research traditions offer insights on the relationship between culture and language development that are not only *compatible* with each other but also and most importantly *complementary* to each other. In this chapter we thus outline the main distinctive contributions of each research paradigm and the ways one supplements the other. Our aim is to offer a comprehensive account of current understanding of the cultural universals and the cultural specifics of language development.

2 Culture and cultures

In their attempt to provide an alternative approach of language development to the Generative Grammar model, both the usage-based and the language socialization paradigms have granted culture the central stage. As we shall outline in this section, however, the treatment of culture related to each paradigm is profoundly different.

Culture is what Michael Tomasello (2000a, 2009b), the leading figure of the usage-based approach, posits to be the key distinctive feature between humans and non-human species (including those exhibiting complex forms of social organization and advanced cognitive capacities, notably chimpanzees). In Tomasello's perspective what is distinctive is not only the impressive variety of artefacts – material, such as tools, and symbolic, such as languages – that culture produces over historical time but also the coevolved uniquely human capacity to acquire them at ontogenetic scale. Human beings can engage in forms of learning that cannot be found consistently in non-human animals. These forms of learning underpin the transmission of culture and have coevolved precisely to enable such transmission. Because of this mutually implicative relationship, these specific forms of learning are referred to as *cultural learning* (Tomasello *et al.* 1993).

The most basic and consequential form of cultural learning is *imitative learning* (ibid.), which occurs when the child reproduces 'the adult's actual behavioral strategies in their appropriate functional contexts, which implies an understanding of the intentional states underlying the behavior' (ibid.: 497). In human ontogeny, imitative learning is followed by instructed learning and collaborative learning. Without going into detail to depict these two other forms of learning, it suffices to say that each entails a more sophisticated type of perspective-taking. Indeed, underpinning all forms of cultural learning is a social cognition milestone: the perspective-taking ability, or, put slightly differently, the capacity to perceive other persons as intentional agents (Carpenter *et al.* 1998). This distinctive capacity emerges within the first year of human life and comprises the ability to coordinate attention with an interactional partner towards an object (*joint attention*) and the ability to recognize the adult as intentional agent with specific goals (*intention reading*) (Tomasello and Farrar 1986; Tomasello 2001). We thus have a set of mechanisms specific to the human species whereby individual beings appropriate the community cultural inheritance. Cultural learning enables a child to acquire language (see section 3).

Culture does not only underpin language development but also situates it within a historically contingent social matrix whose impact on language learning is no less significant. In this situated sense, culture is plural, particular, and ideological. In a brief commentary to the seminal article on *Cultural Learning* by Tomasello *et al.* (1993), Jerome Bruner points to this situated conceptualization of culture, inviting the reader to think about it as a way to 'buttress' Tomasello *et al.*'s key contribution. In Bruner's own words:

> Far more needs to be said about how collectivities of people operate to empower, sustain, pattern, and enforce these acquisitions. An example: Tomasello *et al.* acknowledge that human mothers become enormously diligent and skillful in 'teaching the culture', as illustrated in their management of imitative, instructed, and collaborative activity in their children's language acquisition (e.g., Ninio and Bruner 1978). But Tomasello *et al.* tend to ignore the fact that mothers also impose strong normative expectations on their children in the process. What 'should' be done or said becomes as important in the child's conception of agency as the act itself. Felicity conditions are usually imposed more rigorously than syntactical rectitude. The representation of the intentions and beliefs of others is as deontic as it is epistemic: full of oughts, musts, and notions like 'good manners' ... So, although Tomasello *et al.* are compelling as far as they go, I sorely miss a discussion of the normative, deontic side of participating in a human culture.
>
> *(1993: 516)*

The language socialization theory has engaged the deontic and normative dimensions of human culture by delineating the *cultural ecologies* of language acquisition (Ochs and Schieffelin 1995), that is by attending to the systems of beliefs, norms, preferences, and social orders that profoundly affect the processes of teaching and learning to talk (Schieffelin and Ochs 1986a). The scope of language socialization inquiry is not simply to document the variety of learning contexts and social activities that are associated to acquiring the mother tongue across different speech communities. Language socialization posits that such diversity is to be illuminated by an analysis of the indexical order of speech community's communicative practices. As we shall see in section 4, such an analysis layers the deontic and ideological onto the epistemic and cognitive dimensions of language development.

Culture is both related to the psychological make-up of the individual and to the socio-historical contexts in which s/he is born and develops. Children acquire culture and learn culturally. Culture permeates the subjective and the intersubjective. The usage-based and the language socialization approaches provide a set of conceptual and methodological tools to illuminate the many facets of the intersection between language development and culture.

3 Cultural learning and the usage-based theory of language acquisition

The usage-based approach to language acquisition has countered generativist claims of the necessity of *a priori* mental structures for language learning, building upon an empirical foundation to demonstrate that children's language develops through *cultural learning* and exploiting the cognitive skills of intention-reading and pattern-finding (Tomasello 2003, 2009a). Rather than speculating about the miraculous mechanics of a 'distinct piece of the biological makeup of our brains' (Pinker 1994: 18) specifically devoted to language acquisition, Usage-Based Language

Acquisition posits that children's general cognitive capabilities provide the means to learn, if not the deep structures proposed in a hypothesized Universal Grammar, then a range of linguistic constructions relative to surrounding inputs and communicative occasions. If language structures are not inherent in the mind but induced from the surrounding context, how cultural learning results in language development requires a research-grounded account.

As previously mentioned, the usage-based approach identifies the foundation of language acquisition in the infant capacity to attain joint attention. Joint attention is not solely a cognitive phenomenon but also an interactional process as it entails the engagement of an interactant, with whom the child co-orients attention (Bakeman and Adamson 1984). The engagement in repetitive, hence predictable interactive episodes scaffolds the child's detection and tracking of the adult's attentional focus and his/her intended linguistic (or gestural) referents (Bruner 1981; Tomasello and Farrar 1986).

Starting from roughly their first birthdays, children build from joint attention to the social cognitive skills of *imitative learning*, utilizing tools, artefacts, and symbols according to the models of adults around them. When infants begin to reproduce those sounds they see and hear adults around them using as conventionalized linguistic symbols, they engage in the imitative process of cultural learning. While imitative learning might bring to mind the image of an adult picking up an object, naming it, and asking the child to repeat the name of the object, in reality such a process accounts for a very limited portion of language, of caregiver behaviours, and of cultural practices in the world. Instead, children read the intentional goals of adults as those adults interact in habitual ways with objects, artefacts, and symbols, and they imitate the use of the same tools for the same intentional means, not only learning about things in the world *from* adults, but learning about things in the world *through* adults and what they do (Tomasello 1999: 514–15).

This is why, among the available theories for the beginnings of children's language learning (notably Bloom 2000; Golinkoff *et al.* 1994; Smith 2000), Usage Based Language Acquisition subscribes to a social-pragmatic theory (Nelson 2007; Tomasello 2003), which analyses as its fundamental unit the *utterance* (Croft 2009). The utterance as a basic unit emphasizes the fact that meaningful language units are used in particular contexts with specific communicative intents behind their usage. Social-pragmatic theories of early word-learning suggest that rather than the accessibility of concepts, the ease of association between words and things, or the pre-existence of mental categories, what makes words and phrases meaningful to young children is the salience of the social situation, undergirded by children reading the communicative intent of people in their surrounding context. Rather than hearing words and simply fast-mapping them to an array of concepts (Bloom 2000), the earliest sequences of sounds that children learn, whether words or phrases, are ones that they encounter 'in situations in which it is easiest to read the adult's communicative intentions' (Tomasello 2003: 49). These early utterances include the more easily individuated concrete nouns predominant in nascent lexicons (*chair, milk*), but also less tangible nominals (*dinner*) and other types of words (*sit, thank you, warm*) that have interpersonal and social relevance in children's worlds. These phrases and words – utterances – can be easily imagined surrounding the children in joint attentional interactions with caregivers and siblings, attached to others' intentions in meaningful usages of linguistic tools. Meanings are made in this interpersonal, cultural territory.

Thus, when children begin to produce their own utterances, they do so as imitative cultural learning, attempting to reproduce not only the sounds of individual words, but entire 'goal-directed act[s]' (Tomasello 2000b: 65). Instead of children speaking their first words, Usage-Based Language Acquisition suggests that children imitate in *holophrases*, single-word or single-phrase stand-ins for larger whole utterances, such as 'doll' for 'Where's the doll?' (Barrett 1982; Dore 1975). Those utterances are not limited to words and their denotations, but larger schema that might include certain occasions, participants, and other contextual aspects of an utterance's use. In fact, some usage-based proponents would contend that the idea that words map onto privately held, firm denotative concepts is misguided. In keeping with the later Wittgenstein, Nelson for instance argues that there is no such thing as a 'private language', the meaning of particular symbols not dependent on the conceptualizations of individuals but on a community's norms and rules of usage for those symbols (Nelson 2009). In other words, children begin not with concepts and their labels, but with culturally grounded meanings and rules for communicative utterances.

Similarly, when children begin to utilize syntactic units, the so called 'pivot schemas' that characterize early acquisition across languages, such as 'Where's the X?' or 'Put X here', these utterances should not be analysed according to adult-like categories of syntax that linguists attribute to them (Tomasello 2009a). Added to the joint attention and intention-reading that supports imitative learning, Usage-Based Language Acquisition also rests upon the empirically established *pattern-finding* cognitive abilities of young children (Goldberg 1995, 2006; Tomasello 2009a). These pattern-finding capabilities include children's competence with schematization, exemplar-based categorization, distributional analysis, and analogy recognition (Gentner and Markman 1997; Tomasello 2003). Usage-Based Language Acquisition argues that these domain-general, rather than language-specific, cognitive competencies lead the way to constructing the grammar of language users.

Here, Usage-Based Language Acquisition reveals its theoretical origins in Cognitive Linguistics, an alternative to the dominant generative traditions of North American linguistics. Classically, the problem of how children go from simple word-learning to more complex syntactic constructions is the challenge for generative grammar: it both necessitates and yet still confounds the Chomskian invocation of a Language Acquisition Device. When researchers begin with the varieties and constraints of the syntactic structures of a generativist account of grammar, and then proceed to study what children can understand and produce, the leaps appear to be unaccountable. But Tomasello observes in empirical research on children more support for the description of grammar of cognitive linguists, who, rather than abstracting syntax from the context of meaning and use, recontextualize grammar in human experiences, conceptualizations, and meanings. In particular, Goldberg (2006) delineates a fundamental unit of *constructions* that, as opposed to words, phrases, clauses, or sentences, mirrors the units of language which any caregiver can testify that children acquire – whatever chunk they have associated with some level of meaning. Children learn idiosyncratic and idiomatic sentences, collocations, interjections, and streams of discourse in haphazard but culturally based ways, developing inventories of particular constructions from repeated and situated occasions of adult and peer usage. This approach to language learning is known as Construction Grammar (Goldberg 1995, 2006; Tomasello and Brooks, 1999).

For a usage-based approach, Construction Grammar can explain the acquisition of language by providing a model of language where particular items or tokens can be schematized into the grammar that language users master. In Construction Grammar, a particular token instance of language serves multiple functions, functions at the level of a whole construction and sub-functions for component parts. Take for example an older sister's request, 'Can I have some *more*?' to a parent in front of her 1-year-old brother during a meal. First, there is a communicative function of the construction as a whole, a petition for more that leads to another helping served. Then there is the meaningful sub-construction of a question-inflected utterance of *more*, which perhaps the 1-year-old also recognizes and even uses in other such request situations. And then again, the older child's question provides another token instance of a question construction modal auxiliaries or that, at this point, the 1-year-old will not analyse or appropriate, but will serve as an exemplar, a case of use, that will accumulate to a later schematization of question constructions for the younger language learner. And, thus, constructions exist at nested levels with varying complexity. The important point is that each instance of use is both a concrete utterance token and an exemplary type. Meanwhile, the language learner moves from part to whole and from whole to part, recognizing patterns, appropriating, and gradually schematizing from specific phrases to more abstract constructions (Dabrowska and Lieven 2005). As language develops, construction chunks are blended in various ways to generate the creative array of utterances displayed in language in use (Kemmer and Barlow 2000).

4 Situating language acquisition in cultural contexts: language socialization

Language development cannot be characterized simply in terms of lexical wealth, semantic complexity, and syntactic virtuosity. When, how, and why young children apprehend grammatical forms is not solely informed by a uniquely human psychological endowment. It is also 'culturally reflexive' (Ochs and Schieffelin 1995: 74), that is, shaped by local dispositions, beliefs, and norms that structure communicative practices and the child's participation therein.

The study of language acquisition as sociocultural process has emerged in the early 1980s, within linguistic anthropology. The methodology is not only longitudinal but also ethnographic; and the scope of the inquiry includes an examination of the speech community's social organization, world-view, and communicative habitus. Such an approach to the study of language acquisition is known as *language socialization* (Ochs and Schieffelin 1984; Schieffelin and Ochs 1986a). Developing their programme at a time when the nativist perspective prevailed within language acquisition research, language socialization scholars set out to discern the impact of culture on the acquisition of language, thereby beginning to debunk claims of universal developmental patterns as well as homogeneity in learning conditions and outcomes across societies (Heath 1983; Schieffelin and Ochs 1986b).

Drawing on Hymes's theorization (1967, 1971), language socialization research developed as a multidimensional enterprise: it examined child directed communication and the child's language development as influenced not solely by cognitive and psychological factors but also by a number of culture-specific elements, notably (a) the community's communicative repertoire, with special attention towards communicative behaviours directed to infants and young children; (b) the role of speaking in native conceptions of cultural transmission and modes of teaching; (c) conceptions of children's communicative intentions and capacities; (d) the speech community's attitudes towards linguistic codes in relation to valued social roles and subject positions. Hymes conveyed the broader scope of his research programme through the idea that infants and young children begin by acquiring not simply a system for creating an infinite number of grammatically correct sentences (which Hymes referred to as *linguistic competence*), but rather a tool for carrying out culturally appropriate communicative actions. In Hymes's words: 'We have then to account for the fact that a normal child acquires knowledge of sentences, not only as grammatical, but also as appropriate. He or she acquires competence as to when to speak, when not, as to what to talk about with whom, when, where, in what manner' (1972: 278). The focus is thus on *communicative competence* (ibid.) in which linguistic ability is qualified by appropriateness norms, related to social roles and cultural expectations.

To illuminate the relation of language to sociocultural constructs and processes, and thereby discern the intricacies of acquiring communicative competence, language socialization scholars have engaged the semiotic notion of indexicality. Drawing from Charles S. Peirce's (1974) account of the ways in which meaning can be conveyed through signs, linguistic anthropologists have brought to light how members of each speech community associate particular linguistic features – as elementary as morphemes and particles, and more complex grammatical forms or registers – to specific types of speakers or contexts (Agha 2007; Hanks 1990; Ochs 1990b; Silverstein 1976). Thus linguistic forms do not solely convey symbolic content but also bear indexical meaning, which is based on connections with the social context. In turn, the inherent indexical value of linguistic forms is such that every instance of use contributes to reconstituting the relevant sociocultural context.

A broad spectrum of sociocultural information can be indexed through linguistic forms, notably gender, social status, affective and epistemological stances, ethnicity, and identity. Indexical relationships, however, are more complex than one-to-one direct associations (Ochs 1990b; Silverstein 2003). On the one hand, a single linguistic feature may index a wide range of possible social contexts. The use of the pronoun *vous* as second-person singular address form in French is a case in point: it can index a power asymmetry between the speaker and the person being addressed, but it can also index the encounter between individuals with no prior relation or one that is unknown to the individuals; or it can index the encounter as formal (Morford 1997). On the other hand, linguistic forms also occur in clusters, which as a whole index some contextual meaning. Register is a good example of this kind of indexical complexity, being constituted by clustered and patterned linguistic, paralinguistic, and discursive features that as a whole signal and enact certain ethnic identities, social roles, or subject positions (Agha 2004). A well-known example of register is baby talk (see section 5). Further, indexical meanings may be conveyed through direct relations between one or a cluster of linguistic forms and some dimensions of context. Alternatively, certain sociocultural information is conveyed indirectly, via the mediation of another indexical relation. Evidential markers (e.g. the modals *may* and *might*, the clause *I think*, the adverbs *surely* and *maybe*), for instance, may index the speaker's epistemic stance, and via a claim of knowledge (or lack thereof), they may index authority and power asymmetry (Ochs 1996).

When children acquire language they thus experience, apprehend and deploy the indexical scope of grammatical structures (Ochs 1990a, 1990b). In acquiring language children are socialized into certain subject positions, social relationships, ways of knowing, relating, and acting (Ochs and Schieffelin 1995; Kulick and Schieffelin 2004).

By taking into account the indexical scope of linguistic structures, certain documented patterns of language development that would be conundrums if evaluated only according to linguistic complexity and frequency in the input can be better understood. In traditional Western Samoan communities, for instance, young children have been documented to master the deictic verb *aumai* ('to bring/give') before the deictic verb *sau* ('to come') (Ochs 1988; Platt 1986). Both verbs are used in imperative constructions, to summon others (*sau*) and to demand or request goods (*aumai*), and they are widely used in the social environment in which young children are immersed. If the order of acquisition of these deictic verbs were to be predicated on their relative frequency of usage in the children's communicative environment, or on their semantic structure and on the cognitive load that structure demands for comprehension and production, one would expect *sau* to be mastered before *aumai*. *Sau* is semantically simpler than *aumai*: unlike the former, *aumai* is a causative verb and its informational content is wider than *sau*'s (Platt 1986). But in Samoan society, the documented order of acquisition can be explained by the hierarchical organization of the community, in which physical movement is associated with relatively lower-status individuals. Higher-status persons tend to minimize movements and delegate to lower-status community members actions that require a change of physical location. The deictic verb *sau* is chiefly used to orchestrate those actions and movements. Young children are usually the lowest-ranking people in the household, so while they are frequently summoned with *sau* imperatives, there are few opportunities for them to use the verb appropriately. In contrast, *aumai* is the verb conventionally employed to carry out the act of begging, which is considered an appropriate and indeed expected action for young children to perform (in so far as it implies that the beggar is in a submissive position). We thus need to take the sociocultural context into account in order to explain the acquisition pattern of the two deictics in Samoan.

This example clearly illustrates the tight and complex relationship between language and social practices: grammatical forms are used to carry out social acts. These in turn are connected to social identities and cultural activities, whose meanings reflect and instantiate a community's beliefs and world-view. Language acquisition is a situated process, deeply connected to the life worlds of the community of speakers.

5 Rethinking input in language development

The treatment of input in first language acquisition is traditionally highly debated (Ellis 2002; Zyzik 2009). While nativist theories contend that input under-determines linguistic competence (primarily on the basis of the poverty of stimulus argument: e.g. Crain 1991; Hornstein and Lightfoot 1981), the usage-based approach puts a premium on it, considering input a key determinant of language acquisition (Lieven 2010). Naturalistic as well as laboratory studies have recorded frequency effects for morphological, lexical, and syntactic phenomena (e.g. Huttenlocher *et al.* 2002; Lieven 2008; Reali and Christiansen 2005). At the same time, a number of factors interacting with frequency have been identified, notably form-function mapping (Cameron-Faulkner *et al.* 2007), neighbourhood relations (Dabrowska and Szczerbinski 2006), and multiple cues (Dittmar *et al.* 2008).

Usage-based studies have thus offered nuanced analyses of input as linguistic phenomenon. Language socialization research offers a complementary and equally important treatment of input as a sociocultural phenomenon. The speech to which young children are exposed is characterized in terms of social actions embedded in social activities constitutive of the community's repertoire of cultural practices (Ochs 1990a, 1990b). The child vocalizations as well are examined in relation to the course of action in which they are produced and to the interpretation that they receive by the interlocutors.

This approach has unveiled that variability in the input extends well beyond linguistic terms and is indexical of culturally specific dispositions and world-views (Kulick 1992; Ochs and Schieffelin 1984). We can take the key topic of *baby talk* as a case in point. Baby talk, a simplified register used to address young children, has traditionally been considered a universal phenomenon, in fact the indispensable input for children's language acquisition. In the early 1980s, language socialization pioneers Elinor Ochs and Bambi Schieffelin (1984) put forward a groundbreaking reconceptualization of baby talk based on their fieldwork in Western Samoa and Papua New Guinea respectively. Ochs and Schieffelin revealed that child-directed speech does not exhibit the same characteristics across cultures; notably, simplification is not universally as pervasive as in Euro-American child-directed communication. In addition, they demonstrated that dyadic exchanges are not always the primary communicative set-up in which the child is exposed to and apprehends her mother tongue (see also Akhtar 2005; Blum-Kulka and Snow 2002; de Léon 1998).

Ochs and Schieffelin's contribution did not stop at documenting the cultural variability in child-directed speech. Most significantly, they offered an analytic framework that allows us to understand that such variability reflects (that is, is indexical of) distinct systems of beliefs, epistemological orientations, and social orders. For instance, among the Kaluli in Papua New Guinea, infants are considered unable to understand or communicate (Schieffelin 1985, 1990). Mothers do not engage them in dyadic (proto)conversation or take infant vocalizations as precursors of speech endowed with communicative intention. The exposure to language is nevertheless rich, as Kaluli infants are always carried on their mother's body and held facing outward; hence, they are continuously immersed in activities and conversations among adults and older children. In addition, Kaluli mothers often initiate triadic exchanges in which they ventriloquate for their babies using a high-pitched, nasalized voice to engage an older child or adult in conversation. In voicing for their infants, Kaluli mothers use well-formed and unsimplified language.

The Kaluli child is treated as an interlocutor only once she or he begins uttering the words *no* and *bo*, 'mother' and 'breast' respectively (Schieffelin 1990). At that point, the child becomes the target of explicit language instruction. The most frequent language instructional practice is a prompting routine that consists of offering a model for what the child should say followed by the imperative *a:la:ma* ('Say it like that'). No simplification or prosodic alteration is featured in this instructional practice. Indeed, Kaluli caregivers believe that simplification is counterproductive to language acquisition. Learning to talk is a hardening process whose goal implies both mastering 'hard words' and overcoming the vulnerability of infancy.

In other cultural groups – such as American and European middle-class communities – newborns are considered intentional communicators, and infants and young children are expected to take on the demanding communicative roles of addressees and speakers. Infants' vocalizations are treated as speech acts (e.g., requests, assessments, complaints) and are often taken up and ratified through repetition or expansion. Indeed, caregivers as well as occasional interlocutors extensively simplify their own linguistic production when talking to children (Ochs and Schieffelin 1984).

The treatment of input as sociocultural phenomenon across cultures compels researchers in language development to extend the examination beyond child-directed communication to include an analysis of how the child is positioned, spatially and semiotically, within communicative interaction (Ochs *et al.* 2005). The presupposition of many language acquisition studies that infants receive linguistic input directly through dyadic verbal interaction does not withstand the evidence of cross-cultural studies. In many cultures, a child's first display of communicative competence is that of attuned listener (e.g., de León 1998, on the Zinacantec Mayans; Gaskins 1996, on the Yucatec Mayans; Toren 1990, on the Fijians). Infants are not recruited as interlocutors, either as speakers or addressees, but are nevertheless engaged in the flow of communication and activities in ways that require them to be attentive – that is, active peripheral participants (Rogoff *et al.* 2003).

As previously mentioned, among the Kaluli, preverbal children are not treated as communicative partners (Schieffelin 1985). However, as early as the first six months of life, infants are often involved in triadic interactions with an adult caregiver and an older sibling. An older sibling may be prompted to address rhetorical questions or imperatives to younger brothers or sisters in order to get them to change their course of action. Infants are not expected to respond verbally; in fact, they are not assumed to understand the propositional content of what they are told. The goal of the activity is a behavioural adjustment by the infant, which is usually effectively accomplished.

Among Zinacantec Mayans, infants' vocalizations, gestures, and eye gaze are interpreted as conveying communicative intention, which adults respond to in two ways: either by producing a verbal gloss or by quoting the baby (employing a reported speech frame) (de León 1998). Both speech acts are addressed to other co-present family or community members. Infants are thus considered proto-speakers long before they begin to talk, but they are not recruited as addressees and speakers in dyadic exchanges. A triadic participation format is more common with children who have begun babbling or uttering words. In elicitation routines, the child is addressed and at the same time invited to speak to a co-present third party.

In summary, both usage-based and language socialization approaches assign an essential role to input in language development and have contributed to deepening our understanding of it.

Usage-based studies have shown that input cannot be considered solely in terms of frequency effects, bringing to light complex relationships between concurrent language phenomena. Language socialization studies have revealed that children's language learning does not depend on the child being addressed (in simplified or other form) by adults and other competent speakers, or on being treated as an intentional communicator beginning in infancy. Different participant structures recruit children to language socialization practices. These forms of participation and the children's allocations therein vary developmentally and cross-culturally. On the one hand, they are associated with stages of expertise and maturation; on the other, they are related to local theories of socialization and childhood. In this sense, acquiring communicative competence encompasses taking on culturally appropriate subject positions.

6 Conclusion

This chapter has examined the relationship between culture and language development through the lens of two developmental models that feature culture centrally. The usage-based approach posits that underpinning language acquisition is a uniquely human form of learning, which has coevolved with cultural practices.

The language socialization paradigm argues that language development is intertwined with, as well as constitutive of the process of becoming a competent member of the social group. The two perspectives are *compatible* because the conceptions of culture that each adheres to stand in a reconcilable tension: culture is a species-wide resource of ontogenetic development, but cultures are dynamic and differentiated systems particular to times and places. The two perspectives are *complementary* because while the usage-based approach explains how the rules of language use are gained from context, language socialization examines the ways that the context of language use structures those rules.

Both the usage-based and the language socialization paradigms have solid empirical foundations (a basis that the nativist model to which they reacted does not hold). The usage-based approach focuses 'on the specific communicative events in which people learn and use language' (Tomasello 2000b: 61). The language socialization scholar examines 'socializing routines – recurrent, situated activities that provide structured opportunities for children to engage with caregivers and other community members' (Garrett and Baquedano-López 2002: 343). The dimensions of context that these two paradigms examine are however different: the usage-based model considers the specific interactional event as an activity format, which constitutes the functional grounding for the child's and her interlocutor's linguistic acts (Nelson 2009). The language socialization scholar examines the social structuring of the communicative event in which the child is engaged, and illuminates the ideological substratum that informs how she is positioned therein, what stances and actions she is exposed to and is prompted to perform.

We have argued in this chapter that the dimensions of context brought to bear in usage-based and language socialization research are non-equivalent and interdependent. The way these dimensions of context are laminated onto each other and interact is yet to be examined. We thus propose a research agenda that ambitiously aims to illuminate the intersection of activity and practice in language development. We posit that such research enterprise entails some arbitration of different theoretical pronouncements as well as a methodological synthesis; indeed a much needed deepening of collaborations across disciplines.

Despite their strong emphasis on the role of context in language development, neither the usage-based model nor the language socialization approach is deterministic or unidirectional, and both position the child as agent, creatively engaged in her learning experience (Carpenter *et al.* 1998; Ochs and Schieffelin 2012; Tomasello 2000b). In usage-based research we see the child appropriate and deploy linguistic construction in the expression of her own intentions. She also displays remarkable audacity in blending constructions and creating novel utterances. In language socialization studies we see that as children take up – through language and with language – expected social roles and subject positions, they also creatively negotiate and manipulate – through language and with language – their social and existential spaces (Goodwin and Kyratzis 2012; Paugh 2005; Pontecorvo *et al.* 2001). Language as both a system and a social practice is continually object and instrument of improvisation and change.

Related topics

ethnopragmatics; linguaculture: the language–culture nexus in transnational perspective; culture and language processing; language, culture and interaction

Further reading

Bavin, E. (ed.) (2009) *The Cambridge Handbook of Child Language*. Cambridge: Cambridge University Press. A comprehensive survey of language acquisition and development research. Organized by topic, the handbook traces the development of language from pre-linguistic infancy on. The volume also includes chapters on bilingualism, sign languages, and language impairments.

Duranti, A., E. Ochs, and B. B. Schieffelin (eds.) (2012) *The Handbook of Language Socialization*. Malden: Wiley-Blackwell. This edited collection provides an invaluable introduction to language socialization research. The field's theoretical underpinnings and methodological commitments are discussed before considering studies spanning across the life span, a multitude of cultures and institutional settings.

Kramsch, C. (ed.) (2002) *Language Acquisition and Language Socialization: Ecological Perspectives*. London: Continuum. A remarkable interdisciplinary collection which offers insights into the social, cognitive, and semiotic processes that shape both the acquisition of language and the formation of the subject and the social.

Rogoff, B. (2003) *The Cultural Nature of Human Development*. Oxford: Oxford University Press. Winner of the William James Book Award and translated into several languages, this book present a compelling argument for appreciating human development as a cultural process, not simply a biological or psychological one.

Wootton, A. (1997) *Interaction and the Development of Mind*. Cambridge: Cambridge University Press. An illuminating longitudinal case study that focuses on key developmental issues through the study of spontaneous interaction. A sophisticated social constructionist approach to children's language and cognitive development.

References

Agha, A. (2004) 'Registers of language', in A. Duranti (ed.) *A Companion to Linguistic Anthropology*. Oxford: Blackwell, pp. 23–45.

——(2007) *Language and Social Relations*. Cambridge: Cambridge University Press.

Akhtar, N. (2005) 'The robustness of learning through overhearing', *Developmental Science*, 8(2): 199–209.

Bakeman, R. and L. Adamson (1984) 'Coordinating attention to people and objects in mother–infant and peer–infant interaction', *Child Development*, 55: 1278–89.

Barrett, M. J. (1982) 'The holophrastic hypothesis: Conceptual and empirical issues', *Cognition*, 11(1): 47–76.

Bloom, P. (2000) *How Children Learn the Meanings of Words*. Cambridge, MA: MIT Press.

Blum-Kulka, S. and C. E. Snow (eds.) (2002) *Talking to Adults: The Contribution of Multiparty Discourse to Language Acquisition*. Mahwah, NJ: Lawrence Erlbaum.

Bruner, J. (1981) 'The pragmatics of acquisition', in W. Deutsch (ed.), *The Child's Construction of Language*. New York: Academic Press, pp. 35–56.

Cameron-Faulkner, T. *et al.* (2007) 'What part of no do children not understand? A usage-based account of multiword negation', *Journal of Child Language*, 34: 251–82.

Carpenter, M., N. Akhtar and M. Tomasello (1998) '14- through 18-month-old infants dfferentially imitate intentional and accidental actions', *Infant Behavior and Development*, 21: 315–30.

Chomsky, N. (1965) *Aspects of the Theory of Syntax*. Cambridge, MA: MIT Press.

Crain, S. (1991) 'Language acquisition in the absence of experience', *Behavioral and Brain Sciences*, 14: 597–650.

Croft, W. (2009) 'Toward a social cognitive linguistics', *New Directions in Cognitive Linguistics*, 1: 395–420.

Dabrowska, E. and E. Lieven (2005) 'Towards a lexically specific grammar of children's question constructions', *Cognitive linguistics*, 16(3): 437–74.

Dabrowska, E. and M. Szczerbinski (2006) 'Polish Children's productivity with case-marking: The role of regularity, type frequency and phonological diversity', *Journal of Child Language*, 33: 559–97.

De Léon, L. (1998) 'The emergent participant: interactive patterns in the socialization of Tzotzil (Mayan) infants', *Journal of Linguistic Anthropology*, 8(2): 131–61.

Dittmar, M. *et al.* (2008) 'German children's comprehension of word order and case marking in causative sentences', *Child Development*, 79: 1152–67.

Dore, J. (1975) 'Holophrases, speech acts and language universals', *Journal of Child Language*, 2(01): 21–40.

Ellis, N. C. (2002) 'Frequency effects in language processing', *Studies in Second Language Acquisition*, 24: 143–88.

Garrett, P. and P. Baquedano-Lopez (2002) 'Language socialization: Reproduction and continuity, transformation and change', *Annual Review of Anthropology*, 31: 339–61.

Gaskins, S. (1996) 'How Mayan parental theories come into play', in S. Harkness and C. M. Super (eds.), *Parents' Cultural Belief Systems: Their Origins, Expressions, and Consequences*. New York: Guilford, pp. 345–63.

Gentner, D. and A. B. Markman (1997) 'Structure mapping in analogy and similarity', *American Psychologist*, 52(1): 45.

Goldberg, A. (1995) *Constructions: A Construction Grammar Approach to Argument Structure*. Chicago, IL.: University of Chicago Press.

——(2006) *Constructions at Work: The Nature of Generalization in Language*. Oxford: Oxford University Press.

Golinkoff, R. M., C. B. Mervis and K. Hirsh-Pasek (1994) 'Early object labels: The case for a developmental lexical principles framework', *Journal of Child Language*, 21: 125–55.

Goodwin, M. H. and A. Kyratzis (2012) 'Peer language socialization', in A. Duranti *et al.* (eds.), *The Handbook of Language Socialization*. Malden: Wiley-Blackwell, pp. 365–90.

Hanks, W. (1990) *Referential Practice: Language and Lived Space among the Maya*. Chicago, IL: University of Chicago Press.

Heath, S. B. (1983) *Ways with Words*. Cambridge: Cambridge University Press.

Herder, J. G. ([1784] 1968). *Reflections on the Philosophy of the History of Mankind*. Trans. T. O. Churchill. Chicago, IL: University of Chicago Press.

Hornstein, N. and D. Lightfoot (1981) *Explanation in Linguistics: The Logical Problem of Language Acquisition*. London: Longman.

Huttenlocher, J. *et al.* (2002) 'Language input and child syntax', *Cognitive Psychology*, 45(3): 337–74.

Hymes, D. H. (1967) 'Models of the interaction of language and social settings', *Journal of Social Issues*, 23: 8–28

——(1971) 'On linguistic theory, communicative competence, and the education of disadvantaged children', in M. Wax *et al.* (eds.), *Anthropological Perspectives on Education*. New York: Basic Books, pp. 51–66.

——(1972) 'On communicative competence', in J. B. Pride and J. Holmes (eds.), *Sociolinguistics*. Harmondsworth: Penguin, pp. 269–93.

Kemmer, S. and M. Barlow (2000) 'Introduction: A usage-based conception of language', in S. Kemmer (ed.), *Usage-Based Models of Language*, Stanford, CA: CSLI Publications, pp. 7–28.

Kulick, D. (1992) *Language Shift and Cultural Reproduction: Socialization, Self, and Syncretism in a Papua New Guinean village*. Cambridge: Cambridge University Press.

Kulick, D. and B. Schieffelin (2004) 'Language socialization', in A. Duranti (ed.), *A Companion to Linguistic Anthropology*. Oxford: Blackwell, pp. 349–68.

Lieven, E. (2008) 'Learning the English auxiliary: A usage-based approach', in H. Behrens (ed.), *Corpora in Language Acquisition Research: Finding Structure in Data*. Amsterdam: Benjamins, pp. 60–98.

——(2010) 'Input and first language acquisition: Evaluating the role of frequency', *Lingua*, 120: 2546–56.

Morford, J. (1997) 'Social indexicality in French pronominal address', *Journal of Linguistic Anthropology*, 7(1): 3–37.

Nelson, K. (2007) *Young Minds in Social Worlds: Experience, Meaning, and Memory*. Cambridge, MA: Harvard University Press.

——(2009) 'Wittgenstein and contemporary theories of word learning', *New Ideas in Psychology*, 27(2): 275–87.

Ochs, E. (1988) *Culture and Language Development*. Cambridge: Cambridge University Press.

——(1990a) 'Cultural universals in language acquisition', *Papers and Reports on Child Language Development*, 29: 1–19.

——(1990b) 'Indexicality and socialization', in J. Stiegler *et al.* (eds.), *Cultural Psychology: Essays on Comparative Human Development*. Cambridge: Cambridge University Press, pp. 287–308.

——(1996) 'Linguistic resources for socializing humanity', in J. Gumperz and S. Levinson (eds.), *Rethinking Linguistic Relativity*. Cambridge: Cambridge University Press, pp. 407–37.

Ochs E. and B. Schieffelin (1984) 'Language acquisition and socialization: three developmental stories and their implications', in R. Shweder *et al.* (eds.), *Culture Theory: Essays on Mind, Self, and Emotion*. New York: Cambridge University Press, pp. 276–320.

——(1995) 'The impact of Language Socialization on grammatical development', in P. Fletcher and B. MacWhinney (eds.), *The Handbook of Child Language*. Oxford: Blackwell, pp. 73–94.

——(2012) 'The theory of language socialization', in A. Duranti *et al.* (eds.), *The Handbook of Language Socialization*. Malden: Wiley-Blackwell, pp. 1–21.

Ochs, E., O. Solomon and L. Sterponi (2005) 'Limitations and transformations of habitus in child-directed communication', *Discourse Studies*, 7(4–5): 547–83.

Paugh, A. (2005) 'Multilingual play: Children's code-switching, role play, and agency in Dominica, West Indies', *Language in Society*, 34: 63–86.

Peirce, C.S. (1974) *Collected Papers*. Cambridge, MA: Harvard University Press.

Pinker, S. (1994) *The Language Instinct*. New York: Harper Perennial Modern Classics.

Platt, M. (1986) 'Social norms and lexical acquisition: A study of deictic verbs in Samoan child language', in B. Schieffelin and E. Ochs (eds.), *Language Socialization across Cultures*. New York: Cambridge University Press, pp. 127–52.

Pontecorvo, C., A. Fasulo and L. Sterponi (2001) 'Mutual apprentices: The making of parenthood and childhood in family dinner conversations', *Human Development*, 44: 340–61.

Reali, F. and M. Christiansen (2005) 'Uncovering the richness of stimulus: Structure dependence and indirect statistical evidence', *Cognitive Science*, 29: 1007–28.

Regier, T. and S. Gahl (2004) 'Learning the unlearnable: The role of missing evidence', *Cognition*, 93: 147–55.

Rogoff, B., R. Paradise, R. M. Arauz, M. Correa-Chávez and C. Angelillo (2003) 'Firsthand learning through intent participation', *Annual Review of Psychology*, 54(1): 175–203.

Schieffelin, B. (1985) 'The acquisition of Kaluli', in D. Slobin (ed.), *The Cross-linguistic Study of Language Acquisition. Vol. 1: The Data*. Hillsdale, NJ: Erlbaum, pp. 525–93.

——(1990) *The Give and Take of Everyday Life*. New York: Cambridge University Press.

Schieffelin, B. and E. Ochs (1986a) 'Language socialization', *Annual Review of Anthropology*, 15: 163–91.

Schieffelin, B. and E. Ochs (eds.) (1986b) *Language Socialization across Cultures*. New York: Cambridge University Press.

Silverstein, M. (1976) 'Shifters, linguistic categories, and cultural description', in K. Basso and H. A. Selby (eds.), *Meaning in Anthropology*. Albuquerque, NM: University of New Mexico Press, pp. 11–56.

——(2003) 'Indexical order and the dialectics of sociolinguistic life', *Language and Communication*, 23: 193–229.

Smith, L. B. (2000) 'Learning how to learn words: An associative crane', in R. M. Golinkoff and K. Hirsh-Pasek (eds.), *Becoming a Word Learner*. Oxford: Oxford University Press, pp. 51–80.

Tomasello, M. (1999) 'The human adaptation for culture', *Annual Review of Anthropology*, 509–29.

——(2000a) 'Culture and cognitive development', *Current Direction in Psychological Science*, 9(2): 37–40.

——(2000b) 'First steps toward a usage-based theory of language acquisition', *Cognitive Linguistics*, 11(1/2): 61–82.

——(2001) 'Perceiving intentions and learning words in the second year of life', in M. Bowerman and S. Levinson (eds.), *Language Acquisition and Conceptual Development*. Cambridge: Cambridge University Press, pp. 132–58.

——(2003) *Constructing a Language: A Usage-Based Theory of Language Acquisition*. Cambridge, MA: Harvard University Press.

——(2009a) 'The usage based theory of language acquisition', in E. L. Bavin (ed.), *The Cambridge Handbook of Child Language*. Cambridge: Cambridge University Press, pp. 69–87.

——(2009b) *The Cultural Origins of Human Cognition*. Cambridge, MA: Harvard University Press.

Tomasello, M. and P. J. Brooks (1999) 'Early syntactic development: A Construction Grammar approach', in M. Barrett (ed.), *The Development of Language: Studies in Developmental Psychology*. New York: Psychology Press, pp. 161–90.

Tomasello, M. and M. J. Farrar (1986) 'Joint attention and early language', *Child Development*, 57(6): 1454–63.

Tomasello, M., A. Kruger and H. Ratner (1993) 'Cultural learning', *Behavioral and Brain Sciences*, 16: 495–552.

Toren, C. (1990) *Making Sense of Hierarchy: Cognition as Social Process in Fiji*. Atlantic Highlands, NJ: Athlone.

Zyzic, E. (2009) 'The role of input revisited: Nativist versus usage-based models', *L2 Journal*, 1(1): 42–61.

23

LANGUAGE AND CULTURAL SCRIPTS

Anna Wierzbicka

Introduction

Cultural scripts are representations of cultural norms which are widely held in a given society and are reflected in language. To be faithful to the 'insider perspective' and at the same time intelligible to the outsider, these representations are formulated in simple words and phrases which are cross-translatable between English (the main lingua franca of the globalizing world) and any other natural language. Such a mode of representation depends on the outcomes of the decade-long cross-linguistic semantic research conducted within the Natural Semantic Metalanguage programme (see Chapter 5 this volume). As discussed in Chapter 5, the Natural Semantic Metalanguage (NSM) is believed to correspond to the 'intersection of all languages'. As illustrated in the present chapter, cultural scripts articulate cultural norms, values, and practices using this metalanguage as a medium of description and interpretation. For a selection of NSM-based publications on cultural scripts, see, for example, Ameka (2006), Gladkova (2014a), Goddard (2010), Hasada (2006), Nicholls (2014), Peeters (2013), Priestley (2014), Travis (2006), Wong (2006), Ye (2006) and Yoon (2004). See also Goddard (2006), Wierzbicka (2006), Goddard and Wierzbicka (2004), and Levisen (2012). (For a broader perspective on the theme of this chapter, including a discussion of the historical perspectives, critical issues, and future directions, see Chapter 5 this volume.)

Cultural scripts and bilingual experience

The eminent Oxford historian of ideas Isaiah Berlin was an Englishman, a Russian, and a Jew. He was born in pre-revolutionary Riga (1909), moved with his family to Petrograd (St. Petersburg) in 1916, and thence to London in 1921. For most of his life, Oxford was his geographical and intellectual home, but culturally and emotionally he lived in three worlds – and in two languages. He was a close friend of the Russian-born Jewish scientist and Zionist Chaim Weizmann (who became in 1949 the first President of the State of Israel), and of Weizmann's Russian-born wife Vera. For many years Berlin kept up an intimate epistolary correspondence with the Weizmanns. As a recent book about Berlin (Dubnov 2012) puts it, in these conversations 'Russian proved to be a powerful interpersonal glue'. Here is an extract from Berlin's own testimony:

> [It] is our Russian conversations which I adore & look forward to & think about and remember the longest ... I can never talk so ... to anybody in England ... Russian to

me is more imaginative, intimate and poetical than any other [language] – & I feel a curious transformation of personality when I speak it – as if everything becomes easier to express, & the world brighter and more charming in every way.

(quoted in Kelly 2013: 51)

Testimonies of this kind are quite common among people living, like Isaiah Berlin, with two languages and cultures (see e.g. Besemeres 2002; Besemeres and Wierzbicka 2007; Hoffman 1989; Kellman 2003; Pavlenko 2006). Until recently, however, linguistics as a discipline did not try to account for those aspects of bilingual and bicultural people's language and cultures which underpin such experience.

Why should anyone feel a transformation of personality when switching from English to Russian, the way Berlin did? And how could scholars pin down the objective realities underlying such subjective feelings?

No doubt many different approaches can be taken here, including a systematic analysis of bilingual memoirs, testimonies, and interviews. When conducted sensitively and imaginatively, such analyses can offer the reader a great deal of insight into bilingual lives and bilingual minds. At some point, however, it is good if the art of interpretation can be combined with a 'science of interpretation' equipped with a methodology that can be explicitly stated, shared and taught.

This is where the theory of cultural scripts comes in.

The 'cultural scripts' approach to bilingual and cross-cultural experience demonstrates that many aspects of it can be explained if we identify certain tacit – or semi-tacit – cultural norms which speakers of different languages share and which are embedded in their vocabulary, grammar, and speech routines.

The way many people talk in a particular language promotes certain models of verbal (as well as non-verbal) interaction. Other people adopt and imitate these models more or less sub-consciously, and take the assumptions which underpin them for granted. In principle, however, these assumptions can be brought to the surface of people's consciousness and sometimes one can see them articulated, in some form, in ordinary discourse.

Anticipating more precise discussion of such tacit but verbalizable cultural scripts, I will start by trying to identify, in an informal way, two broad themes which inform many Russian cultural scripts and which contrast with some of the central cultural themes and assumptions of Anglo culture embedded in English. These themes can be hinted at with terms such as 'self-expression' and 'communion', but they can be made much more intelligible if we try to articulate them in simpler and more self-explanatory words and phrases, along the following lines (see also scripts from [G] to [N] in the second half of this chapter):

[A] **A Russian cultural script**

    at many times, it is good if someone wants to say to someone else:

        'I think like this now, I feel something because of this'

Perhaps one reason why Berlin felt that, in Russian, 'everything becomes easier to express' was that when he was writing to Chaim and Vera Weizmann in Russian some basic Russian cultural scripts allowed him, indeed encouraged him, to reveal thoughts and feelings which in English he would have been inclined to censor and shape, in advance, into carefully chosen forms.

In the cultural universe of Russian interpersonal interaction, two key concepts are 'duša' (roughly, 'soul/heart') and 'obščenie' (roughly 'communion', from *obščij* 'common, shared'). (For detailed discussion see, e.g., Gladkova 2009, 2014b; Wierzbicka 2002). There is a strong cultural discourse on these two leading Russian themes (see e.g. Pesmen 2002), and an extended literature devoted to it. The cultural script approach offers certain linguistic tools for identifying these themes, and the communicative norms related to them, in a precise as well as illuminating fashion.

Getting inside other people's minds

To formulate a plausible hypothesis about other people's tacit assumptions we have to be acutely aware that their assumptions are likely to be different from our own. In the case of our own speech community, the meaning of words can provide us with an intuitive guide to many assumptions that are widely shared. Outside our own speech community, however, we don't have such an intuitive guide, and we are almost certain to attribute some of the tacit assumptions embedded in our own languages to the speakers of other languages – and thus to get a distorted picture of how those other people think, and what their tacit assumptions are.

For example, the English word *generous* carries with it a certain cognitive scenario, and a positive evaluation. This identifies for speakers of English a cultural norm which at a certain level can be spelled out like this: 'it is good if someone is generous'. For people learning English, and especially for immigrants to English-speaking countries, it is important to find out what exactly the word *generous* means: by learning the meaning of this word they can learn a certain cultural value shared by many speakers of English, and a widely shared cultural norm.

But not all languages have a word matching the English word *generous* in meaning, although many languages have words overlapping in meaning with it. For example, for Russian, the *Oxford English–Russian Dictionary* (1984) assigns two different glosses to *generous*, namely, *velikodušnyj* and *ščedryj*, each of which partly overlaps with it in meaning – but only partly. Thus, we have lexical evidence for existence of the cultural norms in Russian culture: 'it is good if someone is *velikodušnyj*', 'it is good if someone is *ščedryj*'. We can't, however, 'read' this evidence unless we have a methodology which would enable us to pinpoint the meanings of the words *velikodušnyj* and *ščedryj* without distorting them through the English word *generous*.

What applies to Russian, applies even more so to Australian Aboriginal languages, where 'generosity' is said to be a key cultural value. For example, anthropologist Les Hiatt has written: 'Probably everywhere in Aboriginal Australian the highest secular value is generosity' (Hiatt 1982: 14–15, quoted in Peterson 1993).

Another anthropologist, Nicolas Peterson, endorses Hiatt's statement in a widely quoted paper in which the word *generosity* appears in the title: 'Demand Sharing: Reciprocity and the Pressure for Generosity among Foragers' (1993). But 'generosity' in what sense? Peterson emphasizes that in Aboriginal Australia we find 'a different construction of the ethic of generosity' (ibid.: 870) than that found in Western culture. As he puts it, Westerners associate 'unsolicited giving with generosity' and see it as something positive, whereas in Aboriginal culture 'moral obligation and commitment to others is construed not in terms of giving freely, but in terms of responding positively to their demands' (ibid.).

However, if the cultural ideal of 'generosity' is associated with 'unsolicited giving' and the Aboriginal ideal usually described in English with the word *generosity* is not, then it is not clear why this Aboriginal ideal should be described in terms of the Anglo/English concept of 'generosity'. Surely, it is not a 'different ethic of generosity' but simply a different ethic, which it would be good to try to understand from the insider's point of view and to describe in words cross-translatable into Aboriginal languages, rather than in terms of any culturally shaped Anglo ideals. At least such is the view underlying the NSM approach to comparative semantics and pragmatics and the theory of cultural scripts. Using the Natural Semantic Metalanguage (NSM) we can compare different cultural norms associated with different languages without an Anglo/English bias which is inherent in the use of English conceptual vocabulary for describing meanings and ideas embedded in languages other than English (Wierzbicka 2014).

Scripts of 'avoidance' in Australian languages

To start with a simple example, I will first look at the issue of 'avoidance' between certain categories of relatives, which is one of the hallmarks of social cognition in Aboriginal Australia. Hiatt (2007: 11) introduces this topic as follows:

> **Affinal reserve**. Propriety requires reserved behaviour between men and their affines. The requirements (entailing physical and social distance) and associated sentiments (embarrassment, shame) are conspicuous if not exaggerated in the case of the mother-in-law.

As evidence of the cognitive reality of the need for such 'affinal reserve' Hiatt cites, *inter alia*, the Warlpiri word *minyirri*, with his own definition of it and the consultants' comments aimed at explaining and illustrating its meaning:

> *minyirri*: respectful behaviour to in-laws, appropriate behaviour to in-laws, avoidance, shame, circumspection, inhibited, embarrassed.
> Definition: behaviour appropriate to interaction with one's spouse and one's spouse's close kin.
> *Kajikanparla makurntanyanuku – wajamirnirlanguku – miniyirri-jarrimi.*
> 'You would be circumspect and respectful with regard to your wife's mother or uncle.'

But Warlpiri doesn't have words with meanings like 'physical', 'social', and 'distance', used in Hiatt's preliminary explanation of 'affinal reserve'. Furthermore, most of the words and phrases used in the English gloss of *minyirri* also come from the English conceptual vocabulary ('appropriate behaviour', 'avoidance', 'circumspection', 'interaction', etc.), so to try to formulate a hypothesis about the content of the norm in question as construed from an indigenous point of view, we need to go beyond such phrases and to posit a cultural script couched in words cross-translatable into Warlpiri itself.

Before proposing such a script for Warlpiri, I will refer to a particularly well-known example of what Hiatt calls 'affinal reserve': the special 'mother-in-law language' described in R. M. W. Dixon's book on another Australian language, Dyirbal. Thus, Dixon (1972: 32) writes:

> Each speaker [of Dyirbal] has at his disposal two separate languages: a Dyalŋuy, or 'mother-in-law language', which was used in the presence of certain 'taboo' relatives; and a Guwal, or everyday language, which was used in all other circumstances. Each dialect had a Guwal and a Dyalŋuy. The 'everyday language' is called *guwal* in the Dyiral and Giramay dialects, and *ŋirma* in the Mamu dialect.
>
> No man or woman would closely approach or look at a taboo relative, still less speak directly to them. The avoidance language, Dyalŋuy, had to be used whenever a taboo relative was within earshot. The taboo was symmetrical – if X was taboo to Y so was Y to X. Taboo relatives were:

[1]   a parent-in-law of the opposite sex; and, by the symmetry rule, a child-in-law of
      the opposite sex.
[2]   a cross-cousin of the opposite sex – that is, father's sister's or mother's brother's child.

Category [2] covers just those relatives who are of the section from which ego must
draw a spouse, but who must be avoided on the grounds that they are too close kin.
Thus, the rules for using Dyalŋuy, together with the section system, precisely indicate
who is sexually available for any person.

On the basis of Dixon's account, I would propose the following cultural script for Dyribal:

[B]   The 'mother-in-law script' in Dyirbal

> if a woman is the mother of a man's wife, it is like this:
>   he can't say things to her,
>   he can't look at her,
>   he can't be very near her,
>   if he wants to say something to someone else when she can hear it,
>   he can't say it like he can say it at other times

As the quote from Dixon's book makes clear, the category of 'taboo relatives' extends far beyond
the focal category of 'mother-in-law', so clearly, several other cultural scripts will be needed to
account for this aspect of Dyirbal speech practices. Rather than attempting such further Dyirbal
scripts here, I will now sketch a 'mother-in-law script' for Warlpiri, drawing in particular on
anthropologist M. J. Meggitt's classic 1962 book *Desert People*. The comments quoted below
focus on the potential, rather than actual, 'mothers-in-law':

> The ban on intercourse with mothers-in-law is one of the strongest taboos operating
> in Walbiri society, and I have never seen any of the accompanying rules broken … The
> Walbiri continue to avoid mothers-in-law despite countervailing European pressures that
> often force 'm.m.b.d.' [mother's mother's brother's daughter] and 'm.b.d.s.' [mother's
> brother's daughter's son] into close contact. If both are riding in a motor-truck, the
> men stand facing the front and the women sit facing the back. A man who has to
> enter a building where women are working will not do so without first announcing
> his identity and then waiting for the 'm.m.b.d.' to leave.
>
> *(p. 153)*

This suggests the following cultural script:

[C]   The 'potential mother-in-law script' in Warlpiri

> if a woman can be the mother of a man's wife, it is like this:
>   he can't say things to her,
>   he can't look at her,
>   he can't be very near her

To provide one more example of a 'script of avoidance' in an Australian language, I will draw on
Cliff Goddard's work on yet another Australian language, Pitjatjantjara/Yankunytjatjara. Thus, in
the entry on the word *umari*, Goddard (1996: 198) writes:

umari *noun*

person with whom you have an 'avoidance relationship', due to ceremonial and/or marital arrangements. You are not allowed to speak with, sit with, pass things to, or look closely at such a person. The strongest avoidance relationship is between a man and his potential or actual wife's parents. Avoidance works both ways, so that, for instance, a woman's *umari* are her daughter's husband and potential husbands.

To translate this information, and the lexical evidence contained it is, into a cultural script, I would tentatively propose the following formula:

[D] **The '*umari* script' in Pitjatjantjara/Yankunytjatjara**
people can't not think like this about many other people at many times:

'I can't say things to this someone
I can't look at this someone
I can't be very near this someone'

a man can't not think like this about a woman if she is the mother of his wife,
this woman can't not think like this about this man
a man can't not think like this about another man if this other man is the father
of his wife
if someone can't not think like this about someone else,
this other someone can't not think in the same way about this someone

As the information provided in the dictionary entry indicates, while the word *umari* refers to some specific categories as prototypes, it focuses, more generally, on a *kind* of relationship that requires, roughly speaking, mutual avoidance.

It is worth noting that cultural scripts such as those presented in this section transcend the distinction between 'law' and 'morality', which, as Hiatt notes, is not made in Australian languages. Hiatt cites in this context the following example from the Warlpiri dictionary: 'That old woman said about herself, "I did the wrong [*maju*, 'bad'] thing. I did. 'Did your son-in-law meet up with you?' 'Yes, that's it" (Hiatt 2007: 7).

The psychological reality of cultural scripts of the kind presented here is supported by comments such as those made by the 'insider' Margaret Kemarre Turner in her book *Iwenhe Tyerrtye – What It Means to Be an Aboriginal Person* (2010: 86–90):

Ikirrentye is a word meaning respect … *Ikirrentye* covers all ways people behave to each other. What you *can* do as well as what you can't do. Because of *ikirrentye*, you can't say the wrong things to your *nyurrpe* ['opposite-side'] side. You must know what you can do and what you can't do … That is the way of Aboriginal people … You can [i.e. must] act in one way for your *mwere*, your son-in-law, and in a different way towards your father.

(ibid.: 86)

The sacredness of *ikirrentye* comes from the Land. Because of that it's a really strict relationship – son-in-law and mother-in-law can't sit next to, or do anything with each other.

(ibid.: 90)

Both the 'mother-in-law scripts' and the '*umari* script' formulated here are very tentative, and their optimal phrasing is a matter for further research. What matters in the present context is the methodological principle: in order to constitute plausible hypotheses about indigenous cultural norms, cultural scripts need to be formulated in words and sentences cross-translatable into the indigenous languages themselves, and not in terms dependent on the conceptual vocabulary of English.

The scripts of 'doing good things for others' in Australian languages

There are many words in Australian languages whose meanings can give us helpful clues for identifying the indigenous cultural norms in question in an authentic way, not through the prism of Anglo cultural norms and values. Hiatt's (2007) study 'The moral lexicon of the Warlpiri people of Central Australia' offers much valuable material towards such a project, including material bearing on the norms for 'doing good things for others'. I will cite two relevant examples, drawn by Hiatt from the *Warlpiri Dictionary* (Laughren *et al.* 2006), both including the word 'generous' in the explanations. (I am omitting here the Warlpiri sentences offered by the consultant and present only the English glosses):

[1] *jama* generous, giving, kind
     Jama is *good* person who gives freely. He can give you bread or meat or money even. That is what *jama* is.

[2] *yulkinji* unselfish, generous
     Definition: person who is not interested in having a lot of food for self or things for self.
     Yulkinji is like a *generous person* who gives away anything and who promises things to other people, or who sees food or meat and doesn't take it for himself but who leaves it for other people or just gives away food, meat, anything.

Hiatt (2007: 6) rightly expresses his concern that in describing the Warlpiri normal lexicon 'the English gloss is not [i.e. should not be] importing moral judgement into a Warlpiri text that doesn't contain them'. Arguably, however, the problem goes deeper than Hiatt was ready to acknowledge: *any* English word used in the English gloss is likely to import Anglo-English ways on thinking, unless it is a word which has an exact semantic equivalent in the indigenous language itself. For example, if the Warlpiri word *jama* is glossed as 'generous, kind', then the English words *generous* and *kind* import Anglo/English cognitive scenarios which are not contained in any Warlpiri words or texts. Even the innocent-looking translation of the Warlpiri folk definition which says '*Jama* is a good person who gives freely' also imports some English ways of thinking embedded in the word *freely* and in the English phrase 'to give freely'. In fact, this phrase can have two different interpretations in English. The *Collins Cobuild English Dictionary* formulates these two interpretations as follows: '[1] *Freely* means in large quantities or often, especially without restraint. [2] Something that is given or done *freely* is given or done willingly.' So the gloss 'a good person is someone who gives freely' is unhelpful as it does not make clear what exactly is valued in a person when they are called 'jama' ('giving a lot', or 'giving willingly').

Examining the material reviewed in Peterson's and Hiatt's articles I would suggest that there are probably many different cultural norms reflected in it, including some focused specifically on one's 'relations'. Thus, in a section headed 'Helping relatives' Hiatt (2007: 17) includes the following extracts from the *Warlpiri Dictionary* (again, I am omitting here the Warlpiri sentences, presenting only the English glosses):

> Helping relatives
> **kunka-jinta** mutual support, on same side, back each other
> You don't have to ask me to fight. I'll just back you anyway. We should stick together because we have the same father and the same mother and so we should stick up for each other.
> **wardu-pi-nyi Sense 1:** depend on, trust, give confidence to, have confidence in, support, count on ...
> With food or with meat, two people trust and help each other – or in a fight. 'You don't ask me to fight, I just support you so that we should always back each other, like in a fight.

These examples offered by the consultant (and both including the key word *kunka-jinta*) suggest the following cultural script:

[E]   **The kunka-jinta script in Warlpiri**
      people can't not think like this about many other people:

> 'I don't want something bad to happen to this someone
> I want to do something good for this someone'

someone can't not think like this about someone else
      if they can say about the same woman: 'this is my mother'
someone can't not think like this about someone else
      if they can say about the same man: 'this is my father'

if someone can't not think like this about someone else,
      this other someone can't not think in the same way about this someone

Turning now to one of the norms which are not focused specifically on relatives, here is what Hiatt cites from the Warlpiri dictionary entry on the word *ngampa-ngampa* (again, I'm only including the English translation of the consultant's comments):

> *ngampa-ngampa* responsible, helpful, active, willing to work, feel sorry for, kindly disposed towards, sympathetic, kind, concerned for
> *Ngampangampa* is when a person is very sorry for someone. And he just gives away food to people who are hungry like when other people, who are not related to him, ask him. Like when people ask him for anything he simply gives something to them as he feels sorry for them and is kindly disposed towards them.

This suggests the following cultural script, applying to anyone to whom 'something very bad is happening' (for example, hunger):

[F]   **The ngampa-ngampa script in Warlpiri**
      if is good if someone is like this:

> when something very bad happens to someone else,
>   this someone feels something bad because of this
> because of this, this someone wants to do something good for this other someone

Revealing one's current thoughts to others

As we have seen, cultures can differ a great deal in their norms about revealing to other people what one is currently thinking. In some cultures, for example, in Aboriginal Australia, speakers appear to feel free to reveal their thoughts and wants to some categories of people, but not to others. In others, for example, in Malay culture (Goddard 2000), there is a broad cultural norm 'Think first' (i.e. don't say spontaneously what you are thinking, without any 'premeditation'). In Anglo culture, too, there are some scripts encouraging caution and care, though quite different from the Malay ones. By contrast, Russian culture is, roughly speaking, disapproving of 'guardedness' in ordinary interpersonal relations, especially among friends; and cultural scripts valuing, roughly speaking, unguardedness and communicative spontaneity are a salient part of Russian cultural tradition (as evidenced by the Russian key word *iskrennost* – see Wierzbicka 2002).

One example of such 'unguardedness' *à la russe* is the readiness to tell people whom one has not seen for some time what one notices about their changed appearance, for example, that they have aged or evidently put on weight. For example, in Chekhov's *Three Sisters* Maša tells Veršinin, when she meets him after many years (English glosses from Karl Kramer's translation, Chekhov 1997): 'Oh, how you've aged! (Through tears): How you've aged!' Similarly, in *The Cherry Orchard* (Michael Frayn's translation), the middle-aged Ljubov' Andreevna tells the student Trofimov after a few years' absence: 'What's this, Petya? Why have you lost your looks? Why have you aged so?' And then she continues: 'You were still only a boy before, just a nice young student. You're surely not still a student?' After that, she turns to her brother Leonid, kisses him, and tells him: 'You've aged, too, Leonid.' Ljubov' Andreevna's gentle, kind-hearted grown-up daughter Varya makes similar remarks to Trofimov – without any malice but simply in recognition of the truth: 'oh, but Petya, you've grown so ugly, you've aged so!'.

Arguably, what happens in such speech situations is that the speaker says to the addressee: 'I think like this now', without censoring his or her thoughts in any way. Evidence suggests that such lack of censorship is not only allowed but even valued in Russian culture, especially if the speaker's good feelings towards the addressee can be taken for granted. This can be portrayed in the following cultural scripts:

[G] **A Russian cultural script**
  at many times, it is good if someone wants to say to someone else:
    'I think like this now'

[H] **A Russian cultural script**
  sometimes it is good if someone wants to say to someone else:
    'I think something bad about you now'

From an English speaker's point of view, such comments may seem to reflect a strange indifference to the addressee's feelings, or even a perverse willingness to 'hurt someone's feelings'. As I discussed in my earlier contrastive work on cultural scripts (e.g. Wierzbicka 2001, 2002, 2008; see also Hoffman 1989), however, the focus on 'not hurting someone else's feelings' is part of Anglo culture, not a universal human priority. In Russian, as in Polish and Ukrainian, it is far more important to show good feelings towards the addressee than to protect the addressee from feeling something bad. It is also more important to reveal one's current thoughts and feelings to the addressee, spontaneously and truthfully, than to avoid causing offence or displeasure: it is the current feeling which justifies the negative comment about the addressee and makes it acceptable.

The culturally licensed willingness to express one's current thoughts is not by any means restricted to situations where the speaker is on especially friendly terms with the addressee. I will illustrate this here with one extended example: a collection of recent Facebook posts on the divorce of the Russian President Vladimir Putin and his wife. From a contrastive English–Russian point of view, one of the most striking features of this discussion is the prevalence of sentences including the untranslatable Russian particle *vot*. The *Oxford Russian–English Dictionary* assigns to this particle the primary meaning 'here (is), there is, this is', illustrating it with the sentence 'vot moj dom', glossed as 'here is my house'.

But in the collection of Facebook posts on the divorce only the compiler's introductory sentence with *vot* could be translated with the word 'here' ('Here are some commentaries on the Putins' divorce posted by journalists, political scientists, public figures'). In all the other sentences, *vot* points to a spot in the speaker's mental space: the here and now of what the speaker is thinking. Sometimes this reference to the speaker's current thinking is quite explicit:

A ja vot vse dumaju, v Amerike kak-to po-drugomu k ètomu otnosjatsja.
'And I *vot* keep thinking, in America people have a different attitude to such things.'
A ja vot tože dumaju, novogo sroka-to, poxože, ne budet.
'And I *vot* also think: there will be no new term [for the President].'

In other sentences, 'thinking' it not explicitly mentioned, but the reference to the speaker's current thinking seems clear. For example:

Vot by on ešče so stranoj, civilizovanno razvelsja'.
'*Vot* if only he'd get a civilised divorce from the country as well.'
Vot pišut, čto i Petr razvodilsja, i Ivan Vasil'evič.
'*Vot* they write that the [tsar] Petr also got a divorce, and [tsar] Ivan Vasil'evič, too.'

As one would expect, such non-spatial uses of the particle *vot* have been noted in large monolingual Russian dictionaries, but their connection with the basic sense 'here' has usually been left unexplained, the usual gloss for the non-spatial meaning being something like 'emphatic' or 'intensifying'. But there are many other common particles in Russian which are used in discourse in very different ways and which are also glossed as 'emphatic' (see for example my analysis of the particles *da* and *nu* in Wierzbicka 2011.) By linking the use of non-spatial *vot* with the current thought we can explain why *vot*, rather than, for example, *da* or *nu*, is appropriate in sentences like *A ja vot dumaju* ('And I am *vot* thinking'), and why a deictic particle, used 'in pointing to something that is before one's eyes' (Ožegov 1978: 283) is commonly used in expressing an abstract thought. At the same time, the common use of this deictic particle in relation to one's current thought highlights the Russian cultural norm encouraging speakers to 'show' their current thoughts to their interlocutors, in accordance with script [G].

I would add that the gloss 'here is, there is, this is' does not adequately capture the primary meaning of the particle *vot*, thus obscuring the 'immediacy' implied by it in both spatial and non-spatial uses. Monolingual Russian dictionaries are usually more helpful in this respect, as they link this particle with the phrase 'neposredstvenno pered glazami', 'directly before one's eyes' (see e.g. Ožegov 1978). In my opinion, however, this phrase is not quite sufficient either, because it fails to specify that *vot* refers to an event occurring at the moment of speech. For example, the sentence 'vot moj dom', glossed by the *Oxford Russian Dictionary* as 'here is my house', implies, in addition: 'I see it right now' and 'you can see it right now'. Thus, *vot* is an interactive particle referring to the moment of speech – and this applies to the non-spatial use of *vot* as much as to the spatial one.

As discussed by the American correspondent in the *Moscow Times* Michele Berdy (*Moscow Times*, 15 August 2013), *vot* enters into innumerable set phrases in colloquial Russian. Berdy appears to suggest that in each such phrase *vot* has a different meaning. In fact, however, the contribution of *vot* to the meaning of most, if not all, of these phrases can be explained in terms of the one invariant meaning posited here.

The prominent use of the particle *vot* in Russian is in striking contrast with the prominent use of the particle *well …* in English. Roughly speaking, *well …* indicates that the speaker does not want to reveal his or her current thoughts and wants to gain some time before deciding what to say to the addressee and how to put it. This is particularly clear in interviews with politicians, whose replies to questions from journalists often start with 'well' (for example, 'Well, yes. But … ', 'Well, no. But … '). This is not an exact opposite of the Russian *vot* by any means, but the overall orientation is clearly different: Russian offers the speaker a convenient ready-made tool for 'showing' the addressee one's current thought just as it is in the speaker's mind (*vot*); whereas English provides its speakers with a tool for delaying the expressing of one's thoughts and for shaping one's forthcoming verbal response before it is put on record (see Goddard 2011: 171–5; Wierzbicka 2011).

[I] **An Anglo cultural script**
at many times, when someone wants to say something to someone else about
something it is good if this someone thinks like this:

'I want to say it well

because of this, I want to think about it for some time before I say it'

Many scripts of this kind appear to have developed in Anglo culture relatively recently, as part of the new Anglo discourse generated by the anti-rhetoric campaign of seventeenth-century England and of the trend towards epistemic and linguistic caution prompted in large part by John Locke's *Essay on Human Understanding* (1690), as I discussed in more detail in (Wierzbicka 2012).

Richard Bauman and Charles Briggs (2003) tell the story of this massive campaign to 'remake language' (i.e. to remake English), which took place in seventeenth-century England. The main goal of that campaign, aimed at 'making language safe for science and society', was fighting 'rhetoric' and thus, in Locke's words, 'removing some of the rubbish that lies in the way to knowledge' ([1690] 1959: 14).

As discussed by Bauman and Briggs (2003: 20), Francis Bacon saw language as 'the greatest obstacle to modernity and progress'. This was taken up by the scholars associated with the Royal Society, who denounced words as intrinsically unreliable instruments in scientific thinking, rejected rhetoric and promoted a new type of discourse characterized by understatement and moderation (rather than exaggeration), epistemological and verbal caution (rather than a tone of certainty), conciseness (rather than rhetorical amplification), dispassion (rather than passion), and rationality (rather than emotionality and flights of imagination).

It is interesting to note that although these new cultural norms did not take hold of English before the end of the seventeenth century, already in Shakespeare's *Hamlet* one can find the advice (from father to son): 'Give thy thoughts no tongue', which prefigures some of the modern Anglo cultural scripts that are strikingly at odds with some of the central scripts of Russian culture. These Anglo cultural scripts are very much in evidence in Sir Isaiah Berlin's fine English prose in his books and essays, and arguably the contrast between them and the

Russian scripts explains a good deal about Berlin's personal testimony quoted at the outset of this chapter.

If one were to triangulate between Anglo, Russian, and Australian Aboriginal cultures one might say that, from a Russian point of view, English speakers tend to treat all other people as if they were 'taboo relatives', that is, with what Hiatt calls 'affinal reserve', entailing physical, social, and psychological distance.

Arguing in Russian

The desire to reveal to another person what one is currently thinking does not exclude 'bad thoughts' that one may be currently having about the addressee. On the contrary: revealing such thoughts to the addressee seems to be almost particularly valued, especially in relation to one's friends. Many different cultural scripts may be simultaneously at play here. Some of them have to do with arguing, which in the Russian context is often combined with an intense desire to change the addressee's way of thinking by vigorously attacking his or her current view. A good example of such a robust argument between friends is provided by an extended verbal exchange between two close friends, Nerzhin and Rubin, in Alexander Solzhenitsyn's novel *The First Circle* (see Wierzbicka 2011).

Looked at from an Anglo point of view, the conversations between Solzhenitsyn's protagonists seem full of abusive terms of address and comments about the addressee. What is even more strange (from an Anglo point of view) is that phrases which seem to imply a very negative judgment about the addressee alternate with affectionate, even tender forms of address. Here are some examples, with Willetts's English translations (R stands here for Russian and E, for English):

R. Žalkaja ličnost'! Eto-iz lučšix knig dvadcatogo veka!

(p. 34)

E. You pathetic person! It's one of the best books of the twentieth century!

(p. 27)

R. Merzavec. No esli xočeš', v ètom est'-taki racional'noe zerno …

(p. 41)

E. Swine. But if you like, there is a rational kernel in all that.

(p. 35)

R. Man'jak! – Ot durandaja slyšu!

(p. 44)

E. Madman! (p. 37) – It's an idiot who says so!

(p. 37)

R. Kamennyj lob!

(p. 48)

E. Of all the pigheadedness!

(p. 41)

R.   Da ne vera – naučnoe znanie, obaldon!

E.   It isn't a matter of belief, you dunderhead, but of scientific knowledge!

(*p. 41*)

R.   Potomu čto u tebja uma nc xvatalo, dura!

(*p. 48*)

E.   Because you weren't clever enough, fathead.

(*p. 42*)

R.   Da durak ty nabityj!

(*p. 49*)

E.   Fathead, idiot!

(*p. 42*)

R.   Duren'! Ty beznadežno otravlen isparenijami tjuremnoj paraši!

(*p. 343*)

E.   Idiot! The fumes from the night bucket have gone to your head!

(*p. 338*)

R.   Sobaka! Sterva! … Golosa klassificirovat' vmeste … čtož mne teper' – odnomu rabotat'?

(*p. 344*)

E.   You dog! You scoundrel! We learned how to classify voices together. What am I supposed to do now? Work by myself?

(*p. 341*)

Most of these verbal attacks on the addressee (some of which have been softened in the English translations) denounce the addressee's stupidity, allegedly shown in the preceding utterance. Thus, words like *dura*, *duren'*, *durandaj*, *durak* (all, essentially, 'fool') and expressions like *kamennyj lob* (lit. stone forehead) are particularly prominent in the discussions between Rubin and Nerzhin. They do not indicate, needless to say, that the friends regard one another as stupid, nor that they want to insult one another. Rather, every time when one of these words is used, it indicates that the speaker regards the interlocutor's preceding utterance as stupid and that he feels strongly about that. In Anglo speech culture, speakers would normally not feel free to express such a reaction to the interlocutor's utterance for fear of offending him or her; and there are strong cultural scripts operating in this area. Among friends, it may be okay to say 'rubbish' or 'nonsense', but not to call the addressee 'fathead' or 'idiot', and especially not in an intellectual discussion, where dispassion is seen as a condition of rationality.

Not so in Russian. Here, feeling strongly about the matter, and expressing one's feelings, is a necessary part of a good *spor* (argument), and one culturally sanctioned way of expressing one's current feelings in an argument is to say some 'strong' negative words about the addressee.

There are many reasons why seemingly aggressive terms of address don't have to be deeply offensive in Russian. One is that it is understood – by virtue of Russian cultural scripts – that they express only momentary 'bad thoughts' and bad feelings. For example, by calling the addressee 'dura' (fool, a feminine form, and so particularly offensive when addressed to a man), the speaker does not express an *opinion* about the addressee but a contemporaneous thought about what the addressee is now saying. This can be a fleeting thought, and the bad feeling which accompanies it can be a fleeting one, too. The momentary, transient character of bad feelings towards the addressee expressed again and again in the conversations between Nerzhin and Rubin is made abundantly clear by the frequent expression of good feelings in the same conversations.

Many Russian cultural scripts are reflected in arguments such as the one between Nerzhin and Rubin. I will only mention these four:

[J] **A Russian cultural script**
at many times, it is good if someone wants to say to someone else:
'I think like this now'

[K] **A Russian cultural script**
at many times, it is good if someone can say to someone else:
'I think like this now'

[L] **A Russian cultural script**
sometimes it is good if someone can say to someone else:
'I think something bad about you now'

[M] **A Russian cultural script**
at many times, when someone feels something very bad
because this someone thinks something about something
it is good if this someone wants to say to someone else:
'I think like this about it'

Revealing one's feeling as one speaks

In their book *Key Ideas of the Russian Linguistic Picture of the World* the founders of the Moscow school of cultural semantics Anna Zalizniak, Irina Levontina, and Aleksej Šmelev (2005: 11) list eight ideas which they see as central to Russian culture. One of them is this: 'It is good when other people know what a person feels'. As key items of linguistic evidence for this key idea the authors mention the adjective *iskrennij* ('totally sincere and spontaneous'), *xoxotat'* (roughly, to laugh with a loud and totally uncontrolled laughter, often described as *zdorovyj*, 'healthy'), and the phrase *duša naraspašku* ('the soul/heart wide open, like an unbuttoned shirt'), which implies high praise.

To understand the value placed on a 'wide-open soul' and related ideas linked with the concept of 'soul', one needs to bear in mind that the Russian word *duša*, normally glossed as 'soul', doesn't really mean the same as the English *soul*, and that it is often seen by Russian speakers as, above all, the organ of emotions. For example, in their account of the 'naive picture of the world' embedded in the Russian language, linguists Jurij and Valentina Apresjan explicitly link thinking with 'the intellect', and emotions with *duša*, which the English translation of their essay renders as 'soul' (Apresjan 2000: 208).

The contrast between Anglo and Russian cultural scripts relating to the expression of emotions is an enduring source of puzzlement and bemused commentary on the part of Russian émigrés in England and other English-speaking countries. Discussing such Russian perceptions, Russian linguist Tatjana Larina (2009: 103) quotes *The Xenophobe's Guide to the English* by Antony Miall and David Milstead (2001: 21), according to whom, 'English children are taught, literally from birth, not to show their real feelings, in other words, to be hypocritical, to suppress any spontaneity, lest by some chance they may accidentally offend someone'. In the same context, Larina (2009: 104) adduces a quote from the Russian writer Ovchinninkov (1986: 347):

> My Russian heart likes to pour itself out in lively, intimate conversations, it loves volatile eye contact, rapid changes in facial expressions, expressive movements of the hands. The Englishman says little, appears to be indifferent and speaks as if he were reading, without ever revealing the inner impulses of the soul [*duša*].

As Larina's discussion illustrates, from a Russian cultural point of view, English speakers tend to worry too much about 'not hurting other people's feelings' (an expression which doesn't have an equivalent in Russian), and not enough about connecting with other people, on a deeper level, by revealing to them what is happening in the speaker's 'heart' and 'soul' (*duša*).

The Russian word *duša* plays an extremely important role in Russian speech, quite unlike the English *soul*. Suffice it to say that the frequency of occurrences of *duša* in the Russian National Corpus is more than ten times higher than that of *soul* in the Collins Wordbanks. (The Russian counterpart of *heart*, *serdce*, is also used a lot – in fact, twice as often as the English *heart*; Gladkova 2009.)

As the quotes adduced by Larina illustrate, from a Russian speaker's point of view it is good to let one's emotions speak (through one's words, voice, eyes, facial expressions, and so on). From a Russian listener's point of view, on the other hand, it is good to know what the speaker feels. Both these perspectives can be captured at the same time in the following cultural script:

[N]   **A Russian cultural script**
>   if someone feels some things when this someone is saying something to
>   someone else
>   it is good if this other someone can know it

Concluding remarks

The theory of cultural scripts and the analytical practice based on it have been evolving over the last 20 or 25 years and they continue to do so. The optimal formulation of a given cultural script can only be found by trial and error in a process of consultation with other scholars and with native speakers. The general format for different types of cultural scripts can also be determined only by trial and error, through wide-ranging practice of writing, and rewriting, specific scripts for many languages and cultures.

The work of the last two decades suggests that most scripts can be framed either in terms of evaluative phrases such as 'it is good if … ', 'it is not good if … ', 'it is bad if … ', or in terms of 'proscriptive' terms such as 'I can (so, say, etc.) … ', 'a man can't … ', 'people can't … '. The scripts presented in the present chapter have all gone through many versions and may go, with time, through some further reformulations. It is a process of gradual improvement and increased accuracy.

The key point is that the tacit cultural norms reflected in different languages should be formulated in a stable and standardized metalanguage, in non-technical words and phrases cross-translatable into the conceptual language of the speakers whose social cognition they are trying to model. The reasons why this cross-translatability is crucial have been clearly summed up by Goddard (2007: 537):

> First, it means that they are accessible to the people whose speech practices are being described. Native speaker consultants can discuss, assess, and comment on them. This makes for increased verifiability and opens up new avenues for evidence. Second, translatability is crucial to the practical value of cultural scripts in intercultural education and communication, i.e., in real-world situations of trying to bridge some kind of cultural gap, with immigrants, language-learners, in international negotiation etc. (cf. Goddard & Wierzbicka 2004, 2007). Third, the fact that cultural scripts are expressible in the native language of speakers gives them a *prima facie* better claim to cognitive reality than technical formalisms which are altogether unrecognizable to native speakers.

Related topics

ethnosyntax; ethnopragmatics; language, culture and context; language, culture, and interaction; culture and kinship language

Further readings

Besemeres, Mary. 2002. *Translating One's Self: Language and Selfhood in Cross-Cultural Autobiography*. Oxford: Peter Lang. (This book, which explores the work of seven major contemporary bilingual writers, is the first in-depth study of lived cross-cultural experience. It shows the reality of 'cultural scripts' in people's lives, as seen from the insider's perspective.)
Besemeres, Mary and Anna Wierzbicka (eds.). 2007. *Translating Lives: Living with Two Languages and Cultures*. St Lucia: University of Queensland Press. (This book is a collection of moving personal stories tracing the experiences of twelve people living in Australia who speak – and 'live in' – more than one language. Through their eyes, the readers can see how language, culture, and identity are intrinsically connected.)
Goddard, Cliff (ed.). 2006. *Ethnopragmatics: Understanding Discourse in Cultural Context*. Berlin: Mouton de Gruyter. (This edited collection shows how speech practices can be understood in terms of values, norms, and beliefs of speakers themselves. Using cultural scripts, the studies in this book cover a gamut of culturally shaped ways of specking from settings around the world.)
Goddard, Cliff and Anna Wierzbicka (eds.). 2004. *Intercultural Pragmatics* 1(2). Special issue on cultural scripts. (The studies presented in this volume show in detail how the cultural scripts model makes it possible to describe cultural norms and practices in a way which combines an insider perspective and intelligibility to outsiders, is free from Anglocentrism, and lends itself to direct practical applications in intercultural communication and education.)
Levisen, Carsten. 2012. *Cultural Semantics and Social Cognition: A Case Study of the Danish Universe of Meaning*. Berlin: Mouton de Gruyter. (This book is an insightful and engaging investigation of Danish cultural keywords and cultural scripts, and a model for exploring languages and cultures in an integrated and coherent framework, with special attention to a society's values and cultural scripts.)

References

Ameka, Felix. 2006. '"When I die, don't cry"': the ethnopragmatics of "gratitude" in West African languages'. In Cliff Goddard (ed.) Ethnopragmatics: Understanding Discourse in Cultural Context. Berlin: Mouton de Gruyter, 231–66.
Apresjan, Juri D. 2000. *Systematic Lexicography*. Translated by Kevin Windle. Oxford: Oxford University Press.
Bauman, Richard and Charles L. Briggs. 2003. *Voices of Modernity: Language Ideologies and the Politics of Inequality*. Cambridge: Cambridge University Press.

Besemeres, Mary. 2002. *Translating One's Self: Language and Selfhood in Cross-Cultural Autobiography*. Oxford: Peter Lang.

Besemeres, Mary and Anna Wierzbicka (eds). 2007. *Translating Lives: Living with Two Languages and Cultures*. St Lucia: University of Queensland Press.

Chekhov, Anton. 1997. *Chekhov's Major Plays: Ivanov, The Seagull, Uncle Vanya, The Three Sisters*. Karl Kramer, trans; *The Cherry Orchard*. Lanham, MD: University Press of America.

Collins Wordbanks Online. www.collinslanguage.com/content-solutions/wordbanks

Collins Cobuild English Language Dictionary. 1991. London: HarperCollins.

D'Andrade, Roy. 1995. *The Development of Cognitive Anthropology*. Cambridge: Cambridge University Press.

Dixon, Robert M. W. 1972. *The Dyirbal Language of North Queensland*. Cambridge: Cambridge University Press.

Dubnov, Arie M. 2012. *Isaiah Berlin: The Journey of a Jewish Liberal*. New York: Palgrave Macmillan.

Gladkova, Anna. 2009. 'The discourse of *duša* in Russian language and culture'. Paper presented at conference Cross-culturally Speaking, Speaking Cross-culturally, Macquarie University, Sydney, 6–8 August.

——2014a. '"Is he one of ours?" The cultural semantics and ethnopragmatics of social categories in Russian'. *Journal of Pragmatics*.

——2014b. '"Intimate"' talk in Russian: Human relationships and folk psychotherapy'. In Goddard, Cliff (ed.) special issue 'Semantics and/in social cognition' *Australian Journal of Linguistics*.

Goddard, Cliff. (ed.) 1996. *Pitjantjatjara/Yankunytjatjara to English Dictionary*. Alice Spring: IAD Press.

——2000. '"Cultural scripts" and communicative style in Malay (*Bahasa Melayu*)'. *Anthropological Linguistics* 42(1): 81–106.

——(ed.) 2006. *Ethnopragmatics: Understanding Discourse in Cultural Context*. Berlin: Mouton de Gruyter.

——2007. 'A response to N. J. Enfield's review of *Ethnopragmatics* (Goddard, ed. 2006)'. *Intercultural Pragmatics* 4(4): 531–38.

——2010. 'Cultural scripts: applications to language teaching and intercultural communication'. *Studies in Pragmatics* (Journal of the China Pragmatics Association) 3: 105–19.

——2011. *Semantic Analysis*, 2nd edn. Oxford: Oxford University Press.

Goddard, Cliff and Anna Wierzbicka. 2004. 'Cultural Scripts: What are they and what are they for?' *Intercultural Pragmatics* 1(2): 153–66.

——(eds). 2004. *Intercultural Pragmatics* 1(2). Special issue on cultural scripts.

——2007. 'Semantic primes and cultural scripts in language teaching and intercultural communication'. In Farzad Sharifian and Gary Palmer (eds), *Applied Cultural Linguistics: Implications for second language learning and intercultural communication*. Amsterdam: John Benjamins, 105–24.

Goddard, Cliff, Anna Wierzbicka and Rie Hasada. 2006. 'Cultural scripts: Glimpses into the Japanese emotion world'. In Cliff Goddard (ed.), *Ethnopragmatics: Understanding Discourse in Cultural Context*. Berlin: Mouton de Gruyter, 171–98.

Hiatt, L. R. 1982. 'Traditional attitudes of land resource'. In R. M. Berndt (ed.), *Aboriginal Sites, Rites and Resource Development*. Perth: University of Western Australia Press, 13–26.

——2007. 'The moral lexicon of the Warlpiri people of Central Australia.' *Australian Aboriginal Studies* 1: 4–30.

Hoffman, Eva. 1989. *Lost in Translation: A life in a new language*. New York: Dutton.

Hymes, Dell. 1968. 'The ethnography of speaking'. In J. Fishman (ed.). *Readings of the Sociology of Language*. The Hague: Mouton, pp. 99–138.

Kelly, Aileen. 2013. '*Isaiah Berlin: The Journey of a Jewish Liberal*'. *New York Review of Books* LX.11.

Kellman, Steven G. (ed.) 2003. *Switching Languages: Translingual writers reflect on their craft*. University of Nebraska Press.

Larina, Tatjana. 2009. *The Category of Politeness and the Style of Communication: A comparison of the English and Russian linguo-cultural traditions* [In Russian]. Moskva: Jazyki Slavjanskix Kul'tur.

Laughren, Mary, Kenneth Hale and Warlpiri Lexicography Group. 2006. *Warlpiri–English Encyclopaedic Dictionary*. *Electronic files*. St Lucia: University of Queensland.

Lee, P. (1996) *The Whorf Theory Complex: A critical reconstruction*. Amsterdam: John Benjamins.

Levisen, Carsten. 2012. *Cultural Semantics and Social Cognition. A case study of the Danish universe of meaning*. Berlin: Mouton de Gruyter.

Locke, John. 1959 [1690]. *An Essay Concerning Human Understanding*. Oxford: Clarendon Press.

Meggitt, M. J. 1962. *Desert People*. Sydney: Angus & Robertson.

Miall, Antony and David Milstead. 2001. *The Xenophobe's Guide to the English*. London: Oval Books.

Nicholls, Sophie. 2014. 'Cultural Scripts in Roper Kriol'. In Goddard, Cliff (ed.) special issue 'Semantics and/in social cognition' *Australian Journal of Linguistics*.

Ovchinninkov, Vsevolod. 1986. *Sakura i dub* [In Russian]. Kiev.

Oxford English–Russian Dictionary. 1984. Oxford: Oxford University Press.

Ožegov, S. I. 1978. *Slovar' russkogo jazyka,* 9th edn. Moscow: Sovetskaja Enciklopedija.

Pavlenko, Aneta. 2006. 'Bilingual Selves'. In Aneta Pavlenko (ed.) *Bilingual Minds: Emotional Experience, Expression, and Representation.* Tonawanda, NY: Multilingual Matters, 1–33.

Peeters, Bert. 2013. 'Râler, râleur, râlite: discours, langue et valeurs culturelles'. In C. Claudel, P. von Münchow, M. Pordeus, F. Pugnière-Saavedra and G. Tréguer-Felten (eds) *Cultures, discours, langues: nouveaux abordages.* Limoges: Lambert-Lucas, 117–41.

Pesmen, Dale. 2000. *Russia and Soul: An Exploration.* Ithaca, NY: Cornell University Press.

Peterson, Nicolas. 1993. 'Demand sharing: reciprocity and the pressure for generosity among foragers'. *American Anthropologist* 95(4): 860–74.

Priestley, Carol. 2014. 'Social categories based on shared experience, examples from Koromu (PNG)'. In Goddard, Cliff (ed.) special issue 'Semantics and/in social cognition' *Australian Journal of Linguistics.*

Quinn, Naomi. 2005. Universals of child rearing. *Anthropological Theory.* 5(4): 475–514.

——2006. The self. *Anthropological Theory.* 6(3): 365–87.

Russian National Corpus www.ruscorpora.ru

Shweder, Richard. 1991. *Thinking through Cultures: Expeditions in Cultural Psychology.* Cambridge, MA: Harvard University Press.

Solzhenitsyn, Aleksandr. 1991. *V kruge pervom.* Moscow: INKOM NV.

——2009. *In the First Circle.* Translated by Harry T. Willets. New York: Harper Perennial.

Travis, Catherine. 2006. 'The communicative realization of confianza and calor humano in Colombian Spanish'. In Cliff Goddard (ed.) *Ethnopragmatics: Understanding Discourse in Cultural Context.* Berlin: Mouton de Gruyter, 199–230.

Turner, Margaret Kemarre. 2010. *Iwenhe Tyerrtye – What It Means to Be an Aboriginal Person.* Alice Springs: IAD Press.

Wierzbicka, Anna. 1994. '"Cultural scripts": A semantic approach to cultural analysis and cross-cultural communications'. In L. Bouton and Y. Kachru (eds), *Pragmatics and Language Learning.* Urbana-Champaign, IL: University of Illinois, pp. 1–24.

——2001. 'A culturally salient Polish emotion: *Przykro* (pron. *pshick*ro)'. In Jean Harkins and Anna Wierzbicka (eds) *Emotions in Crosslinguistic Perspective.* Berlin: Mouton de Gruyter, 337-357

——2002. 'Russian cultural scripts: The theory of cultural scripts and its applications'. *Ethos* 30(4): 401–32.

——2006. 'Anglo scripts against "putting pressure" on other people and their linguistic manifestations. In Cliff Goddard, ed. *Ethnopragmatics: Understanding Discourse in Cultural Context.* Berlin: Mouton de Gruyter, 31–63.

——2008. 'A conceptual basis for intercultural pragmatics and world-wide understanding'. In Martin Pütz and JoAnne Neff-van Aertselaer, eds. *Developing Contrastive Pragmatics: Interlanguage and Cross-cultural Perspectives.* Berlin: Mouton de Gruyter, 3–45.

——2011. 'Arguing in Russian: Why Solzhenitsyn's fictional arguments defy translation'. *Russian Journal of Communication.* 4(1/2): 8–37.

——2012. 'The history of English seen as the history of ideas: Cultural change reflected in different translations of the New Testament'. In Terttu Nevalainen and Elizabeth Closs Traugott (eds). *The Oxford Handbook of the History of English* Oxford: Oxford University Press, 434–45.

——2014. *Imprisoned in English: The Hazards of English as a Default Language.* New York: Oxford University Press.

Wong, Jock. 2006. 'Social hierarchy in the "speech culture" of Singapore'. In Cliff Goddard (ed.), *Ethnopragmatics: Understanding Discourse in Cultural Context.* Berlin: Mouton de Gruyter, 99–125.

Ye, Zhengdao. 2006. 'Why the "inscrutable" Chinese face? Emotionality and facial expression in Chinese'. In Cliff Goddard (ed.) *Ethnopragmatics: Understanding Discourse in Cultural Context.* Berlin: Mouton de Gruyter, 127–69.

Yoon, Kyung-Joo. 2004. 'Not just words: Korean social models and the use of honorifics'. In: Cliff Goddard and Anna Wierzbicka. *Intercultural Pragmatics* 1(2) (special issue on Cultural Scripts) 189–210.

Zalizniak, Anna, Irina Levontina and Aleksej Šmelev. 2005. *Ključevye idei russkoj jazykovoj kartiny mira.* [Key ideas of the Russian linguistic picture of the world]. Moscow: Jazyki Slovjanskix Kul'tur.

24
CULTURE AND EMOTIONAL LANGUAGE

Jean-Marc Dewaele

Introduction

In answer to the question 'In which language does the phrase "I love you' feel stronger?", Rie, a native speaker of Japanese with English as a second language (L2), points out that the Japanese avoid expressing their emotion overtly: 'silence is beautiful in Japanese society. We try to read an atmosphere' (Dewaele 2008: 1768). Veronica Zhengdao Ye, a Chinese scholar who immigrated to Australia, had made a similar point about the expression of emotion in China compared to how it is done in the West: 'We do not place so much emphasis on verbal expression of love and affection, because they can evaporate quickly' (2004: 140). She explains that she prefers the Chinese way of expressing emotions: 'subtle, implicit and without words' (ibid.: 139–40). She describes her first parting from her parents, just before boarding the plane that would take her to Australia: 'we fought back our tears and urged each other repeatedly to take care; we wore the biggest smiles to wave good-bye to each other, to soothe each others' worries. Just like any other Chinese parting between those who love each other – there were no hugs and no "I love you". Yet I have never doubted my parents' profound love for me' (ibid.: 141). Ye explains that at the beginning of her stay in Australia, when she was clearly expected to verbalize her feelings, it made her feel 'stripped and vulnerable' (ibid.: 140). She was struck by the ease with which Australians use 'honeyed words'. She gradually understood that these expressions are pleasantries for social purposes (ibid.). She needed some time before she was able to recognize the emotions displayed in the Australian context accurately and deal with them appropriately. Interestingly, two years later, at the end of a visit home, Ye decides to give her parents 'a long and tight embrace' at the same airport gate (ibid.: 142).

These two observations highlight the basic fact that the expression of emotions varies across cultures. That is, there are cultural differences in the prevalent, modal, and normative emotional responses (Mesquita, Frijda, and Scherer 1997). Ye's story also illustrates my belief that 'emotions are first and foremost a type of connection with our social worlds' (Mesquita 2010: 83). In this view 'emotions themselves are social phenomena that in the moment constitute a relationship and are constituted by it' (ibid.: 84).

Ye also offers a glimpse of the fascinating cultural differences in the communication and perception of emotion in East and West. Moreover, her exposure to Australian culture seems to affect the way she interacts with her parents on a return visit to China. It seems a good illustration of emotional acculturation of immigrants, namely the fact that individuals' emotional patterns shift in response to changes in their sociocultural context (De Leersnyder, Mesquita, and Kim 2011). In other words, emotions are 'ongoing, dynamic, and interactive processes that are socially constructed' (Boiger and Mesquita 2012: 221). Multilingual and multicultural individuals are an ideal group to investigate the relationship between culture and emotional language as they have developed a unique capacity to navigate between the different norms of their different languages (Dewaele 2010a).

The present chapter will present an overview of the empirical work carried out by cultural psychologists, cognitive psychologists and applied linguists on the relationship between culture and emotion in bilinguals and multilinguals. The work reviewed will come from both sides of the epistemological and methodological divides, starting with the etic – quantitative approach which characterizes much of the psychological work, and the emic – qualitative approach which is more frequent in multilingualism research. Researchers who adopt an etic approach use carefully defined and relatively stable concepts from the analytic language of the social sciences (Pike 1954). This makes them useful for comparative research across languages, situations, and cultures, and they are ideally suited to look into automatic processes. Researchers who prefer an emic approach, on the other hand, incorporate the participants' perspectives and interpretations of behaviour, events, and situations using the descriptive language of participants (Pike 1954). This approach is particularly useful for volitional acts (freely chosen) such as language choices, sense of self. Both approaches have strengths, the etic – quantitative approach allows to establish the existence of general patterns in data collected from large samples, while the emic – qualitative approach allows researchers to explore what a small group of individuals say about their behaviour and the reasons underlying that behaviour. We feel that in research on multilingualism/multiculturalism and emotion both approaches are needed to shed light on the complexity of the phenomena under investigation (Dewaele 2010a).

Cultural–psychological perspectives

Markus and Kitayama (1991) attribute the differences in the display of emotion between Easterners and Westerners to different views of the self: 'While in the West the self is viewed as independent, self-contained, and autonomous, it is considered interdependent in Asian, African, Latin-American and many southern European cultures' (225).

For those with independent selves own goals and desires are the priority. These individualists will resist interference from the outside in what they consider to be their own interests. As a consequence, they express their emotions freely and frequently. Indeed, an individual has a sacred right in individualist cultures to be self-sufficient, autonomous and to strive for personal goals, which implies the freedom to express both negative and positive emotions to members of the in-group and strangers alike. For those with interdependent selves, however, emotional restraint is the norm (ibid.: 236). Individuals in collectivist cultures learn that they have a duty to the in-group and that they have to strive for group harmony in order to maintain social cohesion. Emotional restraint is seen as a sign of maturity, and is particularly important in dealing with superiors: 'in Japanese society, the overt expression of anger and verbal attack is interpreted as evidence of immaturity and childishness' (ibid.: 281).

Emotions thus seem to have more or less intrapersonal meaning depending on the culture. Personal feelings, and their free expression, reaffirm the importance of the individual compared to social relationships (Suh *et al.* 1998). These cultural differences between East and West in the display of emotions are also linked to life satisfaction. While individuals in individualist cultures set up their own expectations, those in collectivist cultures internalize the expectations of family, friends, and teachers. Suh *et al.* (ibid.) looked at the effect of internal versus external standards in life satisfaction judgements among over 60,000 participants of 61 countries. They found that in collectivist countries those who were living close to external standards felt happier while those from individualist countries were happier when they were able to live a life congruent with their internal standards.

In Japanese culture socially engaging emotions such as friendly feelings or shame (both signal the acknowledgment of social rules) are more frequent than socially disengaging emotions such as pride and anger, which are more prevalent in the American independent cultural context. Indeed, 'Socially disengaging emotions tend to signal and contribute to the boundedness and independence of an individual, and thus fit the goals in independent contexts' (Mesquita 2010: 96).

A comparison of a European–American sample and a Japanese sample revealed that disengaged emotions were more frequent in the former, while engaged emotions were more frequent in the latter (Kitayama *et al.* 2006). Interestingly, the disengaged emotions were the best predictors of happiness in the American sample while the engaged emotions were the best predictors of happiness among the Japanese participants.

Mesquita (2010: 98) reports that emotions themselves 'may differ in the ways that fit the cultural models'. A study on experiences of offense among Japanese and American participants showed that offense triggered anger in both groups but that the prevalent action was very different: only 30 per cent of Japanese reported being aggressive in response to the offense compared to 70 per cent of Americans. A majority of Japanese reported doing nothing, which is consistent with the Japanese preoccupation to preserve relationship harmony (ibid.).

Differences between Japanese and Westerners also exist in how they establish the emotional state of their interlocutor. Tanaka *et al.* (2010) argue that individuals rely on a combination of multiple emotional cues including the voice and the face of interlocutors in their perception of emotion. The authors found that participants' cultural background modulates the multisensory integration of affective information. Japanese participants were more attuned to vocal processing in the multisensory perception of emotion while Dutch participants focused more on facial expression (ibid.: 1259).

Cultural differences have also been linked to memory for emotional experiences (Oishi *et al.* 2007). A comparison of European Americans and Asian Americans in their retrospective frequency judgements of emotions revealed that emotional events congruent with personal values remain in memory longer and influence retrospective frequency judgements of emotion more than do incongruent events. How well emotional experiences are remembered is not just a matter of congruence but also whether the recall happens in the language in which the event happened. Immigrants recalling L1 memories from childhood in an L2 typically lose some emotional intensity. Moreover, immigrants' memories that were experienced in the L1 were generally richer in terms of emotional significance when recalled in that L1 (Schrauf and Durazo-Arvizu 2006).

Cognitive psychological and applied linguistic perspectives

Bilinguals' processing of emotion words

Cognitive psychologists have examined lower-level and automatic processes in bilinguals' handling of emotion words. This included reaction times (RTs) experiments with affective priming and measurement of skin conductance response (SCRs), which reflect the level of arousal. Altarriba and Canary (2004) found that bilinguals who had learned their English as an L2 in a school context had reduced affective priming effects, possibly because the words had fewer emotional connotations. Harris, Ayçiçegi, and Gleason (2003) looked at SCRs of Turkish–English university students to emotion words in both languages. They had learned English later in life and were enrolled in an American university. The researchers found that reactions to taboo words and reprimands in the L1 resulted in significantly higher SCRs compared to equivalent words and expressions in the L2. Caldwell-Harris and Ayçiçeği-Dinn (2009) confirmed these findings with Turkish–English bilinguals living in Istanbul who displayed higher SCRs to emotional phrases presented in an L1 compared to emotional phrases in English L2.

Eilola and Havelka (2011) combined SCRs of native and non-native English speakers during emotional and taboo word Stroop tasks. Significantly slower RTs were found for negative and taboo words when compared to neutral words in both groups of participants (Eilola and Havelka 2011). SCRs were different in both groups: native English speakers responded with significantly higher SCRs to negative and taboo words when compared with neutral and positive words. No such difference was observed in non-native speakers. Aycicegi-Dinn and Caldwell-Harris (2009) also found emotion memory effects among the bilingual participants, i.e. emotion words were more frequently recalled than neutral words. Overall emotion-memory effects were similar in the two languages, with reprimands having the highest recall, followed by taboo words, and non-emotional words. This phenomenon has been linked to the 'emotional contexts of learning hypothesis', arguing that language emotionality is independent of age of onset of acquisition, but linked to the emotional context in which the language was acquired and used (Harris *et al.* 2006: 276–7). Pavlenko (2012) reviewed this literature and argued that affective processing in the L1 is more automatic than in the L2, hence fewer interference effects and less electrodermal reactivity to taboo emotional stimuli in the L2. She also suggests that for some late bilinguals, their languages may be differentially embodied, with languages learned later in life processed semantically but not affectively.

Caldwell-Harris *et al.* (2011) interviewed Chinese–English bilinguals residing in the US about their experience of using emotional expressions. Participants reported L1-Mandarin expressions as feeling stronger than L2-English expressions. They did prefer to express their emotions in English, citing more relaxed social constraints in English-speaking environments. Electrodermal monitoring on a similar sample of Chinese–English bilinguals showed that participants with both good Mandarin and good English proficiency had similar magnitude SCRs in English and Mandarin emotional expressions. The only exception was the category of endearments (e.g., 'Thank you', 'I miss you', 'I love you'), where larger SCRs occurred for English expressions. The authors speculate that English-speaking societies encourage more open expression of positive emotion than do Chinese cultures, which means that the frequent exposure to English endearments 'may have led to easy retrieval of personal situations with strong emotional resonances; these memories then resulted in increased affect and increased SCRs' (ibid.: 329). Surprisingly, ratings of the emotional intensity of endearments were similar in Chinese and English, in contrast with the SCRs findings. Finally, 'English childhood reprimands were rated as less intense than L1-Mandarin reprimands, consistent with other studies showing that childhood reprimands are felt to be more intense in the native language' (ibid.).

A surprising finding of automatic processing of emotion words by bilinguals emerged from a study by Wu and Thierry (2012). Participants were native speakers of Chinese with advanced knowledge of English. They were asked to indicate whether or not pairs of English words were related in meaning while monitoring their brain electrical activity (ERP) and skin conductance. Unbeknownst to the participants, some of the word pairs hid a sound repetition if translated into Chinese. The authors observed the expected sound repetition priming effect for positive and neutral words, but English words with a negative valence such as 'failure' did not automatically activate their Chinese translation. It thus seems 'that emotion conveyed by words determines language activation in bilinguals, where potentially disturbing stimuli trigger inhibitory mechanisms that block access to the native language' (ibid.: 6485). The authors point out that the explanation advanced in the work of Caldwell Harris and Dewaele about differences in emotional resonance of L1 and L2 cannot account for their findings. It is unlikely that late L2 learners would acquire negative and positive words in systematically different contexts, in different periods of life, or master them at relatively different levels (ibid.: 6488). The valence-specific effects can therefore not be attributed to differences in the emotional resonance between languages (ibid.). The authors suggest that a cognitive suppression mechanism may involve interactions between the limbic system and the caudate nucleus which plays a role in inhibitory control during code-switching (ibid.: 6489). The authors conclude that 'emotional processing unconsciously interacts with cognitive mechanisms underlying language comprehension' (ibid.).

Perception of emotion in a foreign culture

The story of Veronica Zhengdao Ye in the introduction was a good illustration of the difficulty facing an individual suddenly transplanted in an environment with a different set of emotional norms. Recognising the emotion of interlocutors and judging its intensity is the first difficult step before the immigrant can hope to react to these emotions appropriately in interactions.

A pioneering study in this area is Rintell (1984) who asked foreign students of Spanish, Arabic and Chinese origin, enrolled in an American Intensive English Program, to identify which emotion – pleasure, anger, depression, anxiety, guilt, or disgust – best characterized each tape-recorded conversations played to them. Participants were also asked to rate the intensity of each emotion. Their responses were compared to those of a control group of native English speakers, among whom there was a high level of agreement. Cultural background and language proficiency played a significant role in the students' performance. Language proficiency had the strongest effect, with intermediate and advanced students scoring significantly higher than beginners. However, even the most advanced students in the sample, who identified the emotions conveyed in the conversations only about two thirds of the time, had significantly lower scores than the control group. In addition, when learners of the three groups at comparable levels of proficiency were compared to each other, it was found that Chinese students had most difficulty with the task, followed by the Arab students and finally the Spanish students.

Graham, Hamblin, and Feldstein (2001) found similar patterns for the identification of emotion in English voices by native speakers of Japanese and native speakers of Spanish in an EFL programme. The control group of native English speakers obtained the highest rate of correct identification across all conditions, followed by the Spanish and the Japanese students. An analysis of the misjudgements revealed a mostly systematic pattern across related pairs of emotions (anger confused with hate and vice versa) for the English and Spanish students. The Japanese students manifested more non-systematic confusions than the Spanish students.

Emotion concepts in bilinguals

Pavlenko (2008: 147) demonstrated that 'emotion concepts vary across languages and that bilinguals' concepts may, in some cases, be distinct from those of monolingual speakers'. She defines emotion concepts as 'prototypical scripts that are formed as a result of repeated experiences and involve causal antecedents, appraisals, physiological reactions, consequences, and means of regulation and display' (ibid.: 150). She distinguishes three possible relationships between emotion concepts encoded in two different languages: complete overlap, partial overlap or no overlap at all. This sets the stage for seven conceptual processes in the bilingual lexicon: '(1) co-existence;

(2) L1 transfer; (3) internalization of new concepts; (4) restructuring; (5) convergence; (6) shift; and (7) attrition' (ibid.: 153).

The first case is illustrated in the work of Stepanova Sachs and Coley (2006) on Russian–English bilinguals and two monolingual control groups. The authors focused on differences in the mapping of envy and jealousy in both languages. In Russian 'revnuet' is used to refer to the emotion of jealousy while 'zaviduet' is used to refer to the emotion of envy. In English, on the other hand, the word jealous is applied to both jealousy and envy. Participants had to select a word to describe a jealousy or an envy story they had heard. Russian monolinguals chose the most appropriate term while the English monolinguals considered the words envious and jealous as being equally appropriate for describing the emotions of characters in envy stories. For bilinguals, testing language determined responses. They behaved like Russian monolinguals in Russian, and when they were tested in English, they responded like English monolinguals.

In a second experiment, involving a free sorting task, English monolinguals and bilinguals were more likely to group envy and jealousy situations together than were Russian monolinguals (2008: 225). It thus seems that bilinguals' familiarity with the emotion terms in both languages alters their conceptual representation of these emotions.

Pavlenko and Driagina (2007) offered evidence for L1 transfer in the domain of emotion concepts with advanced American learners of Russian. The learners used the copula verbs and emotion adjectives in contexts where Russian monolinguals use emotion verbs. This is evidence that 'that in discussing emotions in Russian the learners draw on the dominant L1 concept of emotions as states and have not yet internalized the representation of emotions as processes' (Pavlenko 2008: 153–4). Pavlenko and Driagina (2007) found that internalization does not always accompany L2 learning. Although the American learners of Russian were aware of the meaning of the Russian emotion verb 'perezhivat' (to experience things keenly) they did not use this verb in narrative tasks where Russian monolinguals did.

Evidence of conceptual restructuring was found in Stepanova Sachs and Coley (2006). The Russian–English bilinguals grouped situations eliciting jealousy and situations eliciting envy together in the sorting task, while Russian monolinguals separated the two situations.

Panayiotou (2006) also found evidence of conceptual restructuring among her Greek–English bilinguals for the concepts of guilt ('enohi') and shame ('ntropi') in Greek Cypriot culture. Although the terms have linguistic equivalents in Greek and English, 'the meanings of these translations differ in the cultures examined' (2006: 203). Interestingly, some participants realized that their use of the English 'guilt' had affected the narrower conceptual category of 'enohi' and had led them to produce inappropriate statements in Greek such as 'I feel guilty for eating too much cake', which caused surprised stares from their interlocutors (ibid.: 196). The participants acknowledged that they borrowed emotion terms from two emotional universes but insisted that these universes 'are interconnected and guided by one unified 'experiencer' of the terms' (ibid.: 204).

Pavlenko (2008: 154) reports to have found no examples of conceptual convergence in emotion concepts of bicultural bilinguals. However, she did find ample evidence of conceptual shift, which 'takes place in the lexicons of L2 users residing in the L2 context, whose representations of partially overlapping concepts have shifted in the direction of L2-based concepts' (ibid.). She observed this shift in her own work on Russian–English bilinguals 'who in their Russian narratives appealed to combinations of change-of-state verbs and adjectives to describe emotions as states, rather than as processes, thus displaying L2 influence on their L1 performance' (ibid.).

De Leersnyder, Mesquita, and Kim (2011) looked at conceptual shift among immigrants, labelling it 'emotional acculturation'. The authors point out that the emotional experiences of people who live together (dyads, groups, cultures) tend to be similar and that immigrants' emotions probably approximate host culture patterns of emotional experience. They carried out a study on Korean immigrants in the United States and on Turkish immigrants in Belgium using an Emotional Patterns Questionnaire that allowed them to collect data on emotional experiences of immigrants and host group members. The degree of immigrants' emotional similarity to the host group was reflected in a correlation value of their individual emotional patterns with that of the average pattern of the host group. Immigrants' exposure to and engagement in the host culture predicted emotional acculturation (ibid.: 460). In other words, immigrants who had spent a larger proportion of their life in the host country were more likely to have emotionally acculturated as a result of intercultural interactions and relationships (ibid.: 461). The authors raise the question about the changes that underlie the shifts in emotional patterns: 'Emotional patterns may change either because immigrants who are introduced in the new culture will experience different situations or because immigrants start appraising the same situations differently' (ibid.). The authors argue that this combination of external and internal components of acculturation is not mutually exclusive.

The final process described by Pavlenko (2008: 155) is conceptual attrition, where, due to prolonged contact with the L2, bilinguals cease to rely on a L1 conceptual category to interpret their experiences. Evidence of such attrition was found in Pavlenko (2002) where monolinguals and bilinguals retold the same short film, portraying an emotional situation. While the Russian monolinguals mentioned two central emotion concepts, 'rasstraivat'sia' (to be getting upset) and 'perezhivat', the Russian–English bilinguals, however, only used the first notion 'that has a lexical and conceptual counterpart in English but did not invoke the language- and culture-specific notion of "perezhivat"' (Pavlenko 2008: 155).

Language preferences of multilingual and multicultural individuals

A number of significant patterns emerged concerning language choices of multilingual and multicultural individuals in the data collected through the Bilingualism and Emotions Questionnaire (BEQ) (Dewaele and Pavlenko 2001–3) from more than 1500 multilinguals (Dewaele 2010a). Emotional speech acts happened most frequently in the multilinguals' dominant language, which was generally the L1 in the BEQ.

Ryoko (Japanese L1, English L2), for example, observes that her languages are used in particular domains. She uses English – which she teaches – for her academic writing, while Japanese seems to emerge spontaneously when she writes about her feelings:

> Ryoko: I chose the language I feel like using for that day or even on the same day I switch languages following my urge … I feel that whenever I write in English, my thoughts become clearer than in Japanese. This is why I prefer writing papers (academic) in English. On the other hand, I tend to enjoy the vagueness and the poetic/artistic way Japanese comes out when you make sentences … If I write about my emotions, Japanese sounds much more suitable to my feelings than English.
>
> *(2010a: 89)*

However, some participants reported occasionally using their other languages to express emotion depending on their communicative intentions. Participants who had learned a foreign language through classroom instruction but had also used that language in authentic interactions outside the classroom tended to use that language more frequently for swearing than participants who had purely formal instruction. A similar pattern emerged for age of onset of acquisition: participants who had an early start in the acquisition of the foreign language used swearwords in that language more frequently than later starters. General frequency of use of a language showed a highly significant positive relationship with language choice for swearing in all languages. An analysis of individual variation in perceived emotional force of swearwords in the multilinguals' different languages revealed similar patterns (Dewaele 2004b). L1 swearwords were rated highest in emotional force and swearwords in languages learned later in life had gradually lower emotional force. Participants who had learned a language only through classroom instruction gave lower ratings on emotional force of swearwords in that language than participants who learned their language(s) in a naturalistic – or mixed – context. High levels of proficiency in a language and frequent use of that language was linked with more emotional force of swearwords.

Similar patterns were uncovered in Dewaele's (2008) study on the perceived emotional weight of the phrase 'I love you'. The phrase 'I love you' was felt to be strongest in multilinguals' L1. It appeared to be linked with self-perceived language dominance, context of acquisition of the L2, age of onset of learning the L2, degree of socialization in the L2, nature of the network of interlocutors in the L2, and self-perceived oral proficiency in the L2. Japanese participants made some interesting comments about the expression of love.

One Japanese participant who wished to remain anonymous, YT, a female (Japanese L1, English L2), argues that the phrase 'I love you' has no proper equivalent in Japanese:

> YT (Japanese L1, English L2): 'I love you' does not exist in Japanese. Even though we can translate it to 'Aishiteimasu' 'Aishiteiru' 'Aishiteru'. This word is translation from English word. The feeling is there. Why should we have to say that? It seems that you have a doubt in love. Even if I heard that in English the word does not move me. Sounds sweet but this is just a word.
>
> *(2008: 1768)*

Dewaele (2011) selected of subsample of 386 multilinguals from the BEQ who reported to be equally proficient in their L1 and L2, and used both languages constantly. The analysis revealed that despite their maximal proficiency in the L1 and L2, participants preferred the L1 for communicating feelings or anger, swearing, addressing their children, performing mental calculations, and using inner speech. The L1 was also perceived to be emotionally stronger than the L2 and participants reported lower levels of communicative anxiety in their L1. The qualitative analysis of the Multilingual Lives corpus, where participants were interviewed on the topics covered by the BEQ, confirmed the finding that the L1 is usually felt to be more powerful than the L2, but that this did not automatically indicate a preference for the L1. Longer immersion in the L2 culture was linked to a gradual shift in linguistic practices and perceptions where the L2 started to match the L1 in their hearts and minds.

Dewaele (2010b) focused on language choice for swearing in the same sample of multilinguals from the BEQ and found that despite equal levels of proficiency and use, the L1 was used significantly more for swearing and L1 swearwords were reported to have a much stronger emotional resonance than L2 swearwords. Interview data confirmed that L1 swearwords are perceived to be stronger. However, the L1 was not always the preferred language for swearing. Participants who had socialized into their L2 culture reported picking up local linguistic practices (including swearing). L2 swearwords evolved from being 'funny' words without any emotional connotation or social stigma, to proper swearwords, ready to be used, but not necessarily matching the emotional force of L1 swearwords.

AH points out that swearwords in her L2 lack power:

> AH (German L1, Italian L2, English L3): I rarely use them (swearwords) in my L2. Also I find saying such things sounds really really funny.

Mustafa (Kurdish and Turkish L1, German L2, French L3, Arabic L4 and English L5) had lived in the UK for 12 years and reported feeling dominant in Turkish and English. He explained that swearing in English and Turkish allowed him to escape the social constraint that weighs on him in Kurdish.

> Mu: I feel really swearing is always kind of in these two languages Turkish and English.
> Interviewer (B): OK.
> Mu: But not Kurdish.
> B: Not Kurdish, why?
> Mu: Because there aren't many swearwords in Kurdish, and there are extremely rude and undignified kind of expressions, it's kind of cultural, so even in Kurdish there aren't many swearwords that I can use, they are usually Turkish.
>
> *(Dewaele, 2010b: 608)*

Michelle (Taiwanese L1, Mandarin L2, English L3) had lived in the UK for 17 years and feels very fluent in English which she uses all the time. She reported that despite the fact that Chinese sociocultural norms forbid her from swearing, she did use mild English swearwords with her Chinese friends in London:

> Mi: It's funny, you do get by isn't it without swearing, you still get by, but I just think that even now I swear, I swear when I'm with my friends, Chinese friends, you have to say 'oh shoot' or 'sugar' or whatever, and you know and then you say that in English, so …
> B: While you speak in Chinese?
> Mi: Yeah.
>
> *(Dewaele 2010a: 208)*

The effect of strong socialization in English has an effect on linguistic choices to express angry emotions among Japanese who returned to Japan:

> Ryoko (Japanese L1, English L2): I tend to use English when I am angry, Japanese when I'm hurt or sad, both when I am happy or excited … My other bilingual friends who are all returnees like me said the same thing about using English when they're angry. I guess I like the sound of the swearing words since I heard it so many times during my stay in the US. This swearing doesn't happen so often in Japan. It's a cultural difference.
>
> *(ibid.: 120)*

Another Asian participant, Miho (Japanese L1, English L2, Thai L3, German L4, dominant in L1 and L2) explains that she prefers English to express strong emotions but that she uses either English or Japanese with a monolingual interlocutor. She is a bit surprised when asked what she would say in Japanese to express anger, and explains that she would communicate her feelings non-verbally:

> B: You're angry at a Japanese friend who doesn't understand English, which language do you use?
> M: Um, Japanese.

B: Ah-ah.
M: but I don't know how to say.
B: So what do you say?
M: I just show angry face?
B: Ah ah.
M: Yeah.

(ibid.: 209)

Quipinia (Cantonese L1, English L2) reported that her family suppressed the expression of emotion at home, 'therefore I feel a lot easier to use another language to express the feelings and the different personality inside me' (ibid.: 120). She recalls an incident in which she burst out in English at her parents who know English but with whom she usually speaks Cantonese:

Quipinia: But I remember one time when they were arguing with me and I was soooooooooo angry that I shouted out 'IT'S UNFAIR!!!!' I guess it's regarded quite impolite if I shouted at my parents (you know Chinese Traditional family) but at that point I feel that I had to express my anger and let myself just do it in another language; perhaps I feel I'm another person if I say that in English.

(ibid.: 120)

Bilingual selves

Quipinia's observation about being a different person in English shows that the systematic choice of a particular language in a particular emotional context can lead to a perception of different selves in different languages. A pioneer is this domain is Koven (1998, 2001, 2006) who elicited stories of different kinds of personal experience of two French–Portuguese bilinguals telling a story to a social peer. They were then asked to tell the same story in the other language and subsequently interviewed about the experience of telling the story. Koven looked at how the women presented themselves and also analysed their own impressions of their 'verbally produced selves' which she combined with the listeners' impressions. Koven found that both participants:

perform(ed), enact(ed), or inhabit(ed) the role of their characters in the stories
    quite differently ... Isabel sounds like an angry, hip suburbanite in French, whereas in Portuguese, she seems a frustrated, but patient, well-mannered bank customer who does not want to draw attention to the fact that she is an émigré.

(1998: 435)

Koven noted that the evaluators tended to report that the women seemed to let themselves be pushed around more when they spoke Portuguese and stood up for themselves more when they spoke French (Koven 1998). Koven suggested that using different languages allowed speakers to 'perform a variety of cultural selves' (2001: 513). Koven focused specifically on the performance of affect by Linda, who was asked to tell twelve stories about a bad experience twice each, once in Portuguese and once in French, to a Portuguese–French bilingual of her own age (Koven 2006). Her accounts were recorded and formally analysed in terms of interlocutory devices and different styles. Five bilingual listeners gave commentaries on the recordings of each story. The findings showed that she was 'angrier, more forceful and more aggressive in French' (ibid.: 107), despite recounting the stories in similar ways in both languages. Koven reports that Linda is aware that she 'contains' herself in Portuguese and does not have access to profane or vulgar vocabulary in that language. Koven notes that 'Linda may not be free to perform an aggressive persona in Portuguese' (ibid.: 108).

Panayiotou (2004a) investigated Greek–English and English–Greek bilinguals' reactions to the same story read to them in both languages. It concerned a young professional – Andy or Andreas as appropriate – who neglected his girlfriend and his care for his elderly mother because of work pressure. When asked what advice they would give to Andy/Andreas, participants were found to be much more tolerant of Andy's behaviour compared to Andreas's behaviour. Panayiotou suggests that participants' judgements differed according to the linguistic repertoires and cultural frames they were drawing from (Cultural Frame Switching).

Pavlenko (2006) used the feedback from 1,039 participants of the BEQ (Dewaele and Pavlenko 2001–3) to the question whether participants feel that they become different people when they change languages. She found that almost two-thirds of participants offered an affirmative response to the question, a quarter of participants gave a negative response, with the remaining 10 per cent of participants giving an ambiguous response (Pavlenko 2006: 10). Many participants answered that they felt more 'real' and 'natural' in their L1, and more 'fake', 'artificial' in later learned languages (ibid.: 18). The perception of different selves was not restricted to late or immigrant bilinguals, 'but is a more general part of bi- and multilingual experience' (ibid.: 27).

This finding was confirmed in a smaller-scale study (Dewaele and Nakano 2012), where 106 multilinguals reported feeling gradually less logical, less serious, less emotional and increasingly fake when using the L2, L3 and L4 compared to their L1.

Conclusion and future directions

This overview has shown that research on culture and emotion happens with different approaches and methods across a wide range of disciplines. The study of differences between emotions in Eastern and Western cultures has spawned a considerable body of work. It shows that culture permeates the experience and communication of emotion. Psychologists have become more interested in the emotional change that immigrants experience as they settle in a new culture. Applied linguists and psychologists have also delved into the unique emotional behaviour of multilinguals, their emotion concepts and their selves in their various languages. Most research has been cross-sectional, i.e. focused on variation between individuals at the moment of data collection. Much less research has focused on diachronic variation among the same individuals, i.e. in change over time as a result of acculturation and socialization into a new culture. This is not surprising given the fact that change can occur gradually over a period of several years and that few researchers can wait that long. Testimonies by multilinguals do allow researchers to obtain a glimpse of the process of change in progress. As these are typically case studies, it is hard to generalize the findings. One research question that deserves future attention in the etic and emic paradigms is why some multicultural individuals shift further and faster than others? To what extent is the speed and extent of change linked to sociocultural or psychological variables? Do age and gender mediate these changes? It would be particularly interesting to see to what extent variance in lower-level and automatic processes can be explained by stable sociobiographical and psychological variables, and whether volition can explain any variance. In other words, will the multilingual who is particularly motivated to master a particular language or culture display different lower-level and automatic processes compared to those who might be slightly less motivated? Further research is also warranted on various emotional variables, to establish the effect of new and additional languages and cultures on existing emotion concepts and automatic processes.

Related topics

culture and language processing; language, culture and context; language, culture, and politeness; language and cultural scripts; language and culture in intercultural communication

Further reading

Berry, J.W., Poortinga, Y.P., Breugelmans, S.M., Chasiotis, A. and Sam, D.L. (2011) *Cross-Cultural Psychology: Research and Applications*. Cambridge, MA: Cambridge University Press. (The authors discuss all domains of behaviour (including emotion and perception), and present the cultural, culture-comparative and indigenous traditions in cross-cultural psychology. They also discuss acculturation and intercultural relations.)

Kitayama, S. and Markus, H.R. (1997) *Emotion and Culture: Empirical Studies of Mutual Influence*. Washington, DC: American Psychological Association. (The authors argue that emotions are not 'hardwired' biological events, but are influenced and shaped through social, cultural, and linguistic processes. Culture is shown to penetrate into every component process of emotion: cognitive, linguistic, physiological and neurochemical elements.)

Kövecses, Z. (2003) *Metaphor and Emotion: Language, Culture, and Body in Human Feeling*. Cambridge: Cambridge University Press. (The author addresses the question of whether human emotions are best characterized as biological, psychological or cultural entities. He shows how cultural aspects, metaphorical language and human physiology are part of a complex integrated system.)

Pavlenko, A. (2005) *Emotions and Multilingualism*. Cambridge, MA: Cambridge University Press. (This is the first book to consider the relationship between language and emotions in bi- and multilinguals, condemning the monolingual bias in much psychological research and delving into autobiographical literature and empirical research.)

Wierzbicka, A. (1999) *Emotions across Languages and Cultures: Diversity and Universals*. Cambridge, MA: Cambridge University Press. (The author combines psychological, anthropological and linguistic theories to understand how emotions are expressed and experienced in different cultures, languages and social relations.)

Zhu Hua (2013) *Exploring Intercultural Communication: Language in Action*. Abingdon, Oxon.: Routledge. (This book shows how intercultural communication (a process of negotiating meaning, cultural identities between people from various cultural and linguistic backgrounds) permeates everyday life. It investigates what is needed to achieve effective and appropriate intercultural communication, and then considers the link between language, culture and identity.)

References

Altarriba, J. and Canary, T. M. (2004) 'Affective priming: The automatic activation of arousal', *Journal of Multilingual and Multicultural Development*, 25, 248–65.

Aycicegi-Dinn, A. and Caldwell-Harris, C.L. (2009) 'Emotion memory effects in bilingual speakers: A levels-of-processing approach', *Bilingualism: Language and Cognition*, 12, 291–303.

Ayçiçeği -Dinn, A. and Caldwell-Harris, C.L. (2009) 'Emotion memory effects in bilingual speakers: A levels-of-processing approach', *Bilingualism: Language and Cognition*, 12, 291–303.

Boiger, M. and Mesquita, B. (2012) 'The construction of emotion in interactions, relationships, and cultures', *Emotion Review*, 4, 221– 9.

Caldwell-Harris, C.L. and Ayçiçeği -Dinn, A. (2009) 'Emotion and lying in a non-native language', *International Journal of Psychophysiology*, 71, 193–204.

Caldwell-Harris, C.L., Tong, J., Lung, W. and Poo, S. (2011) 'Physiological reactivity to emotional phrases in Mandarin–English bilinguals', *International Journal of Bilingualism*, 15, 329–52.

De Leersnyder, J., Mesquita, B. and Kim, H. (2011) 'Where do my emotions belong? A study on immigrants' emotional acculturation', *Personality & Social Psychology Bulletin*, 37, 451–63.

Dewaele, J.-M. (2004a) 'Blistering barnacles! What language do multilinguals swear in?!', *Estudios de Sociolinguistica*, 5, 83–106.

——(2004b) 'The emotional force of swearwords and taboo words in the speech of multilinguals', *Journal of Multilingual and Multicultural Development*, 25, 204–23.

——(2006) 'Expressing anger in multiple languages', in A. Pavlenko (ed.) *Bilingual Minds: Emotional Experience, Expression and Representation*, pp. 118–51. Clevedon: Multilingual Matters.

——(2008) 'The emotional weight of 'I love you' in multilinguals' languages', *Journal of Pragmatics*, 40, 1753–80.

——(2010a) *Emotions in Multiple Languages*. Basingstoke: Palgrave Macmillan.

——(2010b) '"Christ fucking shit merde!" Language preferences for swearing among maximally proficient multilinguals', *Sociolinguistic Studies*, 4, 595–614.

——(2011) 'The differences in self-reported use and perception of the L1 and L2 of maximally proficient bi- and multilinguals: A quantitative and qualitative investigation', *International Journal of the Sociology of Language*, 208, 25–51.

Dewaele, J.-M. and Nakano, S. (2012) 'Multilinguals' perceptions of feeling different when switching languages', *Journal of Multilingual and Multicultural Development* 34, 107–20.

Dewaele, J.-M. and Pavlenko, A. (2001–3) *Web questionnaire Bilingualism and Emotions*. University of London.

Eilola, T. and Havelka, J. (2011) 'Behavioural and physiological responses to the emotional and taboo Stroop tasks in native and non-native speakers of English', *International Journal of Bilingualism*, 15, 353–69.

Harris, C.L., Aycicegi, A. and Berko Gleason, J. (2003) 'Taboo words and reprimands elicit greater autonomic reactivity in a first than in a second language', *Applied Psycholinguistics*, 24, 561–78.

Harris, C.L., Gleason, J.B. and Aycicegi, A. (2006) 'When is a first language more emotional? Psycho-physiological evidence from bilingual speakers', in A. Pavlenko (ed.) *Bilingual Minds: Emotional Experience, Expression and Representation*, Clevedon: Multilingual Matters.

Koven, M. (1998) 'Two languages in the Self/The Self in two languages: French–Portuguese verbal enactments and experiences of self in narrative discourse', *Ethos*, 26, 410–455.

——(2001) 'Comparing bilinguals' quoted performance of self and others in telling the same experiences in two languages', *Language in Society*, 30, 513–58.

——(2006) 'Feeling in two languages: A comparative analysis of a bilingual's affective displays in French and Portuguese', in A. Pavlenko (ed.) *Bilingual Minds: Emotional Experience, Expression and Representation*, pp. 84–117. Clevedon: Multilingual Matters.

Markus, H.R. and Kitayama, S. (1991) 'Culture and self: Implications for cognition, emotion, and motivation', *Psychological Review*, 98, 224–53.

Mesquita, B. (2010) 'Emoting. A contextualized process', in B. Mesquita, L. F. Barrett and E. Smith (eds), *The mind in context*. New York: Guilford, pp. 83–104.

Mesquita, B., Barrett, L.F. and Smith, E. (2010) *The Mind in Context*, New York: Guilford.

Mesquita, B., Frijda, N.H. and Scherer, K.R. (1997) 'Culture and emotion', in P. Dasen and T.S. Saraswathi (eds), *Handbook of Cross-Cultural Psychology. Basic Processes and Human Development* (vol. 2, pp. 255–97). Boston, MA: Allyn and Bacon.

Oishi, S., Schimmack, U., Diener, E., Kim-Prieto, C., Scollon, C.N., Choi, D.W. (2007) 'The value–congruence model of memory for emotional experiences: An Explanation for cultural differences in emotional self-reports', *Journal of Personality and Social Psychology*, 93, 897–905.

Panayiotou, A. (2004a) 'Switching codes, switching code: Bilinguals' emotional responses in English and Greek', *Journal of Multilingual and Multicultural Development*, 25: 124–39.

——(2004b) 'Bilingual emotions: The untranslatable self', *Estudios de Sociolingüística*, 5, 1–19.

——(2006) 'Translating guilt: An endeavour of shame in the Mediterranean?', in A. Pavlenko (ed.) *Bilingual Minds: Emotional experience, expression, and representation*, pp. 183–208, Clevedon: Multilingual Matters.

Pavlenko, A. (2002) 'Bilingualism and emotions', *Multilingua*, 21, 45–78.

——(2006) 'Bilingual selves', in A. Pavlenko (ed.) *Bilingual minds: Emotional experience, expression, and representation*, pp. 1–33, Clevedon: Multilingual Matters.

——(2008) 'Emotion and emotion-laden words in the bilingual lexicon', *Bilingualism: Language and Cognition*, 11, 147–64.

——(2012) 'Affective processing in bilingual speakers: Disembodied cognition?' *International Journal of Psychology*, 47, 405–28.

Pavlenko, A. and Driagina, V. (2007) 'Russian emotion vocabulary in American learners' narratives', *Modern Language Journal*, 91, 213–34.

Pike, K. L. (1954) *Language in Relation to a Unified Theory of the Structure of Human Behaviour*, The Hague: Mouton.

Rintell, E. (1984) 'But how did you feel about that? The learner's perception of emotion in speech', *Applied Linguistics*, 5, 255–64.

Schrauf, R. W. and Durazo-Arvizu, R. (2006) 'Bilingual autobiographical memory and emotion: Theory and methods', in A. Pavlenko (ed.), *Bilingual minds: Emotional experience, expression, and representation*, pp. 284–311, Clevedon: Multilingual Matters.

Stepanova Sachs, O. and Coley, J.D. (2006) 'Envy and jealousy in Russian and English: Labelling and conceptualization of emotions by monolinguals and bilinguals', in A. Pavlenko (ed.) *Bilingual Minds: Emotional Experience, Expression and Representation*, pp. 209–31, Clevedon: Multilingual Matters.

Suh, E., Diener, E., Oishi, S. and Triandis, H. C. (1998) 'The shifting basis of life satisfaction judgments across cultures: Emotions versus norms', *Journal of Personality and Social Psychology*, 74, 482–93.

Tanaka A., Koizumi A., Imai H., Hiramatsu S., Hiramoto E., and de Gelder B. (2010) 'I feel your voice. Cultural differences in the multisensory perception of emotion', *Psychological Sciences*, 21, 1259–62.

Ye, Veronica Zhengdao (2004) 'La Double Vie de Veronica: reflections on my life as a Chinese migrant in Australia', *Life Writing*, 1, 133–46.

PART V

Research on language and culture in related disciplines/sub-disciplines

25

LANGUAGE AND CULTURE IN SOCIOLINGUISTICS

Meredith Marra

Introduction

Within the wider field of linguistics, sociolinguistics is distinguished by the emphasis placed on social context as a central and contributing factor for understanding language use. We argue that language conveys social meaning within the contextual bounds in which it occurs; for sociolinguists, context both shapes and supports our interpretation of language. Amongst the complex array of components that comprise context, 'culture', especially in the form of cultural background and culturally based practices, offers potential explanations for many linguistic choices.

As a macro-level social category (like age, gender, status and ethnicity), culture influences interaction via distinctive values and norms for communicating. We might argue that a particular cultural group typically prioritizes directness and explicitness (as scholars such as Juliane House (2005) and Suzanne Günthner (2008) have argued about speakers from Germany) or that another community has a distinctive register with stable and describable features for talking to important leaders (chiefly Samoan as described by Peggy Fairbairn-Dunlop (1984), for example). These are often broad-brush claims which suggest some form of consistency in communicative behaviour within a culture. The goal of such approaches is to demonstrate wider group patterns, especially where this serves as an explanation for cultural differences.

At a more micro-level of linguistic detail, sociolinguists also consider the ways in which individual speakers signal their membership of a cultural group. In my own home country of New Zealand, a speaker who uses a higher frequency of Māori lexical items in their English, especially using pronunciation approximating Māori language norms, is typically interpreted as being part of the Māori community (the indigenous people of New Zealand). So, for example, someone who identifies as Māori might use commonly understood vocabulary items, such as *hui* ('gathering, meeting') or *kai* ('food, meal'), as a component of their cultural identity.

In both these examples, there is an assumption that linguistic choices, whether macro or micro, can be mapped to the relevant cultural group. This represents one dominant understanding within the field, exemplified by Interactional Sociolinguistics (see Gumperz 1982a; Gordon 2011). There is a competing approach which places greater emphasis on the role of negotiation between participants as a central element in our understandings of the contextual environment, illustrated in this chapter by social constructionism (see Holmes 2003). In this second approach, the focus is more likely to be on the way in which cultural identity emerges through interaction, the way this identity is dynamically negotiated, and the role of the interactional collaboration between interlocutors. Thus Māori lexical items as described above signal ('index') many different meanings depending on the speakers, the topic, the setting, and other contextual features. These meanings could include a particular cultural identity (either New Zealander or Māori, or both), but might also suggest an educated identity, or an urban identity or even a younger identity, each depending on the specific discourse environment.

When applying either of the two major approaches, the social context in which participants are operating is a key consideration for interpreting interaction. The dominance of one approach over the other has changed throughout the years in which sociolinguists have been investigating culture, although both are still in use. In this chapter, I track sociolinguistic research from earlier pattern-based approaches to more recent dynamic, negotiated approaches to culture, incorporating the major theoretical stances which dominate these investigations, namely Interactional Sociolinguistics and Social constructionism.

Interactional Sociolinguistics: the importance of 'gravy'

Increasing interest in the role of culture in sociolinguistics in the 1970s and 1980s was facilitated by a coinciding turn towards discursive approaches to analysis (for a discussion, see Harré 1995; also see discussion of discursive approaches in Chapter 9 this volume). This contrasted with the more traditional regional and social dialectology research which had previously represented the core of the field. Thus, rather than counting isolated linguistic phenomena as indicators or markers of a particular social group (such as age, status or ethnicity), interactional scholars embraced a more qualitative approach in their empirical research. While large-scale quantitative investigations, such as those of William Labov in his Lower East Side Study (1966), had involved extensive data collection and recording of a wide range of people, qualitative sociolinguists adopted data collection procedures which necessitated gathering in-depth information about a particular speech community using ethnographic techniques. Here there was a strong influence from anthropology, especially via the Hymesian framework known as the Ethnography of Speaking (Hymes 1974). The methodological practices incorporate participant observation to help establish norms for interpretation and rules of interaction. The rich descriptions of communication norms which resulted from the approach offered new and exciting insights with enormous relevance for scholars interested in culture.

In the discursive approach of Interactional Sociolinguistics, for example, culture is considered foundational; miscommunication based on cultural differences is a central motivation in its application. Interactional Sociolinguistics views language, culture and society as situated processes and aims to make explicit the knowledge that we use in our everyday interaction. This approach blends the traditions of two scholars in particular, sociologist Erving Goffman (1963, 1974) and linguistic anthropologist John Gumperz (1982a, 1982b). In Interactional Sociolinguistics we view language as social interaction, taking a speaker-oriented perspective (following Goffman), and we identify 'contextualization cues' which allow participants to offer situated signals for how to interpret utterances (following Gumperz). With these goals, the analyst uses quality recordings of naturalistic social interactions (which are typically transcribed) to facilitate repeated revisiting of subtle features. The analytic practice focuses on what participants do in interaction, including how other interactants respond to the contributions to ascertain how an utterance is interpreted.

In a particularly useful description outlining the important contribution made by Gumperz, Cynthia Gordon (2011) describes the approach as offering both theories and methods for exploring the social processes inherent in interaction. During research in which he had applied the Ethnography of Speaking noted above, Gumperz witnessed countless examples of diversity based on linguistic and cultural presuppositions. This led to his interest in intercultural communication. As an approach, interactional sociolinguistics helps us access 'signalling mechanisms' – linguistic/discursive, prosodic and paralinguistic – which speakers use in the process of conversational inferencing in order to interpret interaction in its culturally shaped context (2011: 67). Because of our previous communicative experiences within cultural groups, we learn how to both understand and make use of these contextualization cues. Groups recognize different features as counting as a cue and can have different understandings for how a particular cue typically operates. Within the interactional sociolinguistic understanding of language use, these differences are seen as having the potential to lead to communication breakdown. To explore this potential, proponents make use of the discourse-based approach which is well suited to investigating communication that occurs between those from different cultural backgrounds, and which makes use of attention to close linguistic detail in the analysis of naturally occurring talk.

At the core of Interactional Sociolinguistics, therefore, culture is conceptualized as a source of potential miscommunication and a top-down category for explaining differences. This provided a starting point for important research in the area of workplace interaction in particular (my own interest, and a focus which therefore impacts upon my descriptions of culture throughout this chapter). In a groundbreaking piece of research, now known by the shorthand 'gravy' within sociolinguistic and sociopragmatic circles, Gumperz (1982a) used Interactional Sociolinguistics to explicate a cause of miscommunication among staff at a busy UK airport. There were rising concerns and complaints in the workers' canteen by both the Indian and Pakistani food service workers and the British baggage-handling staff. Gumperz identified one small interactional feature as offering a key element in his analysis of the interactions: the intonation pattern on the word *gravy*. The women who worked in the canteen thought they were offering gravy to the staff; the British staff thought the falling inflection used by the servers (rather than the rising inflection normally associated with offers) was an unhelpful, and consequently impolite, statement, perhaps even suggesting that they must have gravy with their meal. People are quick to use culture as a scapegoat or blanket excuse for miscommunication and there were claims that there was significant and irreparable communication breakdown between the two groups. The British workers thought the women were rude, and the women felt they were the target of discrimination. Gumperz pointed out the difference and was able to show the damning effect of small interactional differences when they are not recognized.

Adopting the techniques established by Gumperz, Celia Roberts and her colleagues used interactional sociolinguistics to investigate misunderstanding in multi-ethnic workplaces, this time with an explicit focus on language and discrimination. Within a larger research project involving the UK Industrial Language Training Service, they also investigated the vital gate-keeping role served by job interviews (Roberts, Davies and Jupp 1992). The original aims were to research the English language needs of ethnic-minority workers, but analysis showed the importance of communication factors which went well beyond linguistic competence. In this context, even minor differences like the intonation patterns described by Gumperz can result in serious and tangible consequences for those who are not from the majority group. Subtle differences based on diverse interactional norms can be interpreted by the gatekeeper as evidence that you are not fit for the job. The analysis by Roberts and her team explicated the 'hidden agenda' in such encounters. By recording and analysing data from this discourse context, they were able to establish schemas and frames which characterized the interaction. This analysis also identified the contextualization cues used by majority group speakers to understand what is 'required' from the interviewee.

As their data indicated, as majority group speakers the illocutionary meaning behind a question is typically part of the shared knowledge that community members have. For example, in Western work environments when asked why we want the job for which we have applied, we tend not to give factually accurate answers like 'because I need a job' or 'because I want more money'. Instead we know to provide an answer which demonstrates a good match with the requirements of the organization, even if this seems to show incoherence with the question if taken at face value.

Embracing a goal of empowering the minority group members with whom they worked, and simultaneously educating the majority group members, the team analysed the structure of the interview and gave a gloss for the typical action that occurred in each phase: greeting, discussion of previous employment, nature of work, level of skills etc. This was based on recordings of both British and non-British workers. By focusing on where patterns were successfully followed and where interviewees deviated from the patterns, Interactional Sociolinguistics enabled the researchers to provide evidence of a cultural norm.

An excellent illustrative example is provided by the two contrasting jobcentre interviews presented below (from Roberts *et al.* 1992: 137–41). These examples represent the 'nature of work' category in the schema. In both cases the employment advisor who acts as interviewer is Mrs E, a 'white woman'. In example 1, the client is Mr M, a 'white main in his fifties', and thus also a majority group member. In example 2, the client is Mr A who is of a similar age to Mr M, but who comes from Bangladesh.

Example 1
E: Can you tell me a little bit about
     the job, you know, what you
     actually did?
M: Well in respect of L _____ it was
     maintaining and looking after the
     machinery so that, so that if any
     faults cropped up ...

(Roberts et al. *1992: 138)*

In the first example, Mr M understands that he is not just providing information about his day to day activities or *what he actually did*. Instead he gives an overview which defines a particular, transferable skill set, and one which we could expect to match the potential requirements of a future job. To see how the participants understand (or do not understand) the hidden agenda represented by the question and answer pair, the authors encourage readers to compare this interview with the interview below. In each case I have extracted the same phase from the longer interview for easy comparison.

Example 2
E: and what was your job there?
A: Spinning job
E: You were a spinner, yeah
A: Yes, spinner
E: Yeah right. Can you tell me a little bit about the job, what you actually did? ...
     you know, as a spinner, what
     were you doing?
A: Well ... er spinning job ... machinery job ... so I controlled
     my machine

(Roberts et al. *1992: 140)*

Mrs E attempts to elicit the information using slightly differently wording (*what was your job there* vs. *what did you actually do*) but in both cases she is requesting information about the nature of the interviewee's previous employment. In contrast with Mr M's full, seemingly rehearsed and positively packaged answer, Mr A provides a short but nevertheless factual response. Evidence that this answer is problematic can be seen in the reformulation of the question by Mrs E. First she rephrases his answer as suggesting an occupation (*spinner*) and asks for confirmation. When this does not signal to Mr A that he should provide an answer in the vein of Mr M's response, she explicitly asks for more information, interestingly choosing the expression she used successfully in the first interview (*can you tell me ... what you actually did?*). While Mr M understands the contextualization cue represented by her question, the intention is clearly opaque to Mr A. When prompted for more information he gives an answer which is relevant (*I controlled my machine*), but not with the elaboration or detail expected. His hesitation could also be explained by his probable knowledge that the person with whom he is talking, an experienced advisor working in the 'heart of the declining Lancashire cotton industry' (1992: 141), knows exactly what spinning involves. The long, negotiated response to provide an answer which is 'bureaucratically processable' (Campbell and Roberts 2007), and therefore culturally appropriate, clearly puts him at a disadvantage.

The interactional sociolinguistic approach which this research represents with its corresponding focus on cultural differences was adopted into other areas within sociolinguistics. For example, in research which captured significant media and lay attention, Deborah Tannen used an interactional sociolinguistic approach to explore gender in discourse (see Tannen 1990). She argued that gender differences could be likened to cultural differences, providing evidence of contrasting cultural patterns for interaction. The equal-but-different approach that she promoted for understanding communication breakdown in everyday conversation among men and women was also later applied to the business environment (Tannen 1994) to explain differences in interactions in the workplace context. Thus 'culture' began to enjoy a wider definition beyond the ethnicity or regional-based understanding which had permeated much of the research to that point.

One of the disadvantages of the interactional sociolinguistic approach, however, is the foundational assumption that cultural differences should be equated with potential miscommunication. Similarly there seems to be an underlying assumption that there is an identifiable 'culture' within a speech community. This suggests at least some degree of homogeneity within a group and tends towards culture being conceptualized as a largely fixed social category (albeit with a degree of flexibility as recognized through the discursive approach).

Social constructionism: a dynamic view of culture

The turn to social constructionism within sociolinguistics in the early 1990s offered a less rigid and more fluid perspective through which to consider culture. In a move which actively challenged the more essentialist understanding of categories (like biological sex or ethnicity based on blood lines), the central argument in the social constructionist paradigm is the notion that social identities are brought into being through interaction, in other words they are discursively constructed in negotiation with others. These social identities therefore do not exist outside of interaction. While in interactional sociolinguistics the focus is cultural presuppositions, in a social constructionist approach the analyst examines how people use language to construct, maintain, and modify particular social identities. Thus social categories are subject to constant change.

Social constructionists argue that our knowledge of the world is constrained not by empirical observation but by the categories (linguistic and conceptual) we use to define it (Holmes 2003;

see also Burr 2003). Talk itself actively creates different styles and constructs different social contexts and social identities as it unfolds. Within this philosophical stance, we are encouraged to question the ideas of social categories as 'given' and instead focus on the dynamic process of creating meaning and social order. Our identity, or rather identities, are not static – we place emphasis, consciously or inadvertently, on aspects of our 'selves' as we interact with others to create social meaning. For example, at various points in the same conversation we may highlight our identity as female, a boss, a friend, an expert, a New Zealander, etc. Different aspects emerge as more or less relevant depending on the interaction. So, rather than culture being considered a top down category as in interactional sociolinguistics, within social constructionism, culture must emerge and *become* relevant.

In terms of the application of this theoretical perspective within sociolinguistics, the traditions of interactional sociolinguistics are extremely influential. Social constructionists in the field use ethnographic information to gain knowledge of community norms and to 'warrant' interpretations (Swann 2002; Cameron 2009); the data is typically naturally occurring audio and video recordings, transcribed to capture linguistic and paralinguistic detail to aid analysis; the negotiated and emergent nature of identity construction is evidenced through a focus on interaction. It is clear that interactional sociolinguistics typically underpins and guides much of the analytic practice. The distinctive theoretical stance, however, which claims no *a priori* categories, is absolutely crucial to the approach. As described by Corder and Meyerhoff (2007: 452), for social constructionists no identity is 'pre cultural', but rather it comes into being through interaction with others.

To give some illustration of this rather different theoretical perspective, I provide an example captured in an interaction between a skilled migrant (Henry) and his local mentor in a New Zealand workplace.

Example 3[1]
1 Henry: also when I worked in China we I I think maybe
2   it's a culture difference because you stator [status]
3   is higher than me because you are my mentor also …
4   so usually the Chinese with a lower stator will
5   speak like … not very loud
6   because you are not the have the right
7   have the authority to speak as loud as you might

At one level, culture is made visible in this interaction because cultural difference is signalled as the topic of conversation by Henry. In this extract he draws on a Chinese identity by giving a meta description of Chinese interactional norms, namely that junior staff members speak more quietly (line 5) because of their reduced status (line 2) and reduced authority (line 7). At another level his cultural identity is foregrounded in the pronunciation which is recognizable as a 'Chinese' non-native speaker to New Zealand ears. Although the transcript (a written representation of the spoken interaction) does not give much evidence of accent, there are still indicators of his non-native use of English, such as *stator* for *status* and *you are not have the right* rather than *you do not have the right*. It is important to also recognize the discourse context of the turn. It is a response to a suggestion from his mentor that Henry should speak up after feedback from other colleagues that he speaks very quietly. This is not an unsolicited suggestion, but rather the duty of the mentor who is tasked with the job of helping Henry integrate into the New Zealand workplace as part of a supported internship.

For the purposes of illustration I have provided an analysis which is somewhat simplified. My intention was to show a range of features which might be taken into account in a social constructionist paradigm, including content, pronunciation and grammatical features, but importantly those which have meaning for the participants. I also wanted to highlight the role of the other participants. A key consideration, and one that makes a vital contribution to our understanding in this case, is a particular discourse choice made by Henry. The content seems to suggest that he is actively following norms for constructing a Chinese identity in this interaction, especially by his attention to providing evidence of legitimate business experience in China (line 1) and by his explanation of the cultural norm he was following to justify his behaviour. A subtle but important element is the way in which this is delivered, namely in a loud, confident voice. This helps create elements of his professional identity too; while he might be constructing an identity of 'Chinese-origin employee' he is also showing that he is willing to enact the advice of his mentor.

In analysis, one of the things we can focus on is how the speakers 'index' their cultural group membership by making use of particular linguistic and discursive tools which have relevance for the interlocutors (see, for example, Bucholtz and Hall (2005): indexicality is one of five principles outlined in their description of current sociolinguistic research on identity). In example 3, indexing relevant discursive and pragmatic choices help construct a complex identity, including Henry's explicit mention of China, his accent, his reference to previous employment, etc. Henry's choice to speak in a loud voice and the juxtaposition between the content and the delivery of his utterances also allows him to signal a challenge to the identity ascription his mentor is making.

Thus far, the discussion has surrounded the identity of an individual which in some ways seems to stand in contrast with the heavy emphasis placed by social constructionism on negotiation. The recognition of the role of the group in social constructionism is most usefully seen in the notion of a Community of Practice, which has provided a valuable analytic tool for sociolinguists (Eckert and McConnell-Ginet 1992, 2003; Holmes and Meyerhoff 1999). This concept draws and builds on constructionist views by exploring the role of group norms in interaction. Within this frame, and as described below, culture can be regarded as a set of negotiated group practices which dynamically contribute to normative constraints on talk.

A Community of Practice framework

The Community of Practice (CoP) framework was initially proposed within the context of situated learning (Lave and Wenger 1991; Wenger 1998). Through participation we can begin as peripheral members of a group and through shared practices built up over time in the form of an apprenticeship we can progress to core members of a community. A CoP is thus particularly relevant for demonstrating the focus on process and interaction: negotiating your membership of a group is bound up in your interaction with the group and signalling your membership is achieved by indexing shared norms. This means the focus is neither completely on the individual, nor solely on the group. Instead it recognizes the interplay and interdependence of the two levels alongside elements of the discourse context. Through interaction members are actively in the process of (re)constructing what it means to be a member of the group. This complex circularity allows us to recognize that the shared linguistic repertoire is constantly available for negotiation. As succinctly described by Penny Eckert (2000) the individual, group, activity and meaning are 'mutually constitutive'.

The concept of a CoP permeated the field more widely after it first appeared in work within language and gender at a time where gender as a fixed category was being challenged and questioned. In a highly influential paper, Eckert and her colleague Sally McConnell-Ginet (1992: 464) defined a CoP as:

> An aggregate of people who come together around mutual engagement in an endeavor. Ways of doing things, ways of talking, beliefs, values, power relations – in short, practices – emerge in the course of this mutual endeavor. As a social construct, a CofP (community of practice) is different from the traditional community, primarily because it is defined simultaneously by its membership and by the practice in which that membership engages.

The three definitional characteristics in this description (joint enterprise, mutual engagement and a shared repertoire of linguistic resources built up over time) are used in considering whether a group constitutes a CoP. This focus on practices is a significant defining characteristic and provides an important contrast with the more static concept of *speech community* which is used as the bounded group in the Hymesian approach. As the CoP label suggests, practice is crucial to membership. In order to learn how to become a member of a CoP you have to learn how to interact or construct your identity as a community member. The approach bridges the micro (in the form of linguistic processes) with more macro patterns, either in the form of enacting them, or challenging them.

Making use of the CoP concept allows the focus on culture to spread to a wider range of groups than is the case with the more targeted notion of culture as used in Interactional Sociolinguistics. Individuals can belong to more than one CoP and these CoPs may intersect or overlap. Because the focus is shared norms which are built up over time, a CoP could refer to a sports group, or a book club, or a professional group provided there is a shared goal, regular interaction between members and a repertoire of linguistic practices. (See discussion of CoPs in Chapter 5 this volume.)

This wider understanding of culture is evident in the following example. The extract is taken from a project which focuses on the language used on building sites in New Zealand. In the example Max, an apprentice, has been given a drill by the site manager and sees this as an indication of his increasing status (in theoretical terms, evidence of his progress along the trajectory from legitimate peripheral membership towards core membership). He is talking to his foreman, Tom, and a group of tradesmen (TM1-3) who regularly work with the team as technical specialists.

There are many elements of the interaction that are relevant to an analysis which focuses on the CoP and its interactional/cultural norms. While Max and Tom belong to the same team, namely the team we were following in the recording process, they are also part of a wider group working together and committed to successfully finishing the build of this house (representing their joint enterprise). They have mutual engagement through their interactions on site, and there is evidence of shared linguistic resources which they have built up over time.

Example 4
1 Max: this is going to be fun + same same as yours
2 Tom: did he give you one
3 Max: yeah
4 Tom: sweet
5 Max: yeah sweet as + we have to label them I guess ++
6   mine will be the cleanest
7 Tom: I'll fix that [dabs paint on drill] [...]

8 TM 1:   you know you're a tradesman now mate
9   yeah you're a proper tradesman mate
10 Max: one day
11   I've had it for three hours
12 TM 2:   you throw it on the ground like that
13 TM 3:   [laughs] + I'll fix that mate
          [Tradesman 3 puts more paint on drill]
14 Max: [laughs]: what oh [name] oh: +
15   I'm gonna get your van eh [general laughter]

Max has been given the drill by the boss who is implicitly referred to as *him*, a reference which is understood by the others. The new drill appears to be an artefact and marker of core rather than peripheral status. We see evidence of a shared understanding of what it means to be a member of the team on this building site because Max is now a *proper tradesman*. We also see evidence of discourse norms in this interaction. The core members of the group (who are also older) tease Max that the drill is new and unadorned with the normal paint splatters etc which are typical of a drill which has seen action on site. Several of the men contribute to this teasing (line 7, line 12, line 13). Max demonstrates his membership in the way that he accepts the good-humoured ribbing (suggested by the shared laughter in lines 13, 14 and 15). An additional indication of his membership is his response to paint being dripped on his drill when he teases TM3 that he will reciprocate by *getting* his van. Based on this and other extracts, we could claim that the CoP norm is that teasing is encouraged, and that core members should be able to give as well as take this teasing.

There are also other relevant factors which contribute to the way in which these CoP members interact which index other aspects of identity. There is overlap with gendered patterns of behaviour which suggest masculine norms (such as the competitive teasing, also discussed in Holmes and Marra 2002). The use of *sweet/sweet as* (lines 4–5) to mean 'good' and *eh* as a invariant tag question are also well recognized features of New Zealand English, typically (although not exclusively) associated with, and therefore indexing, younger and male speakers (Marsden 2013).

The lens I have offered for understanding this extract is the work team as a CoP, together with the fact that the 'culture' of the team, based on their shared repertoire, orients towards normative associations of masculinity and toughness. In investigations of other workplace teams, my colleagues and I have labelled CoPs as 'gendered' where feminine or masculine norms dominate the repertoire (Holmes and Stubbe 2003) and 'ethnicized' where the core business of the team (the joint enterprise) is aligned with an ethnicity, and shared norms actively draw on practices which index ethnically marked discourse practices (Schnurr, Marra and Holmes 2007). It should be clear that this approach has much to offer sociolinguists because of the wider understanding of culture and how this influences and shapes the way we interact. In each case, however, the major focus is the way that these 'cultures' emerge in the identity construction of individuals within the context of their community.

Because of the central role of the ongoing (re)construction of the linguistic repertoire of the community, most investigations which make use of a CoP model are necessarily a 'snapshot' of the norms of a particular group at, or over, a particular period of time. It is rare for researchers to track the development of a community's norms, the changes in the shared repertoire and the disestablishment of the community. This would require longitudinal ethnographic field work which is often beyond the scope of the kinds of projects current researchers can undertake (see Wilson 2011 and King 2014, as exceptions). This limitation on constructionist views of culture is important, but recognized.

Future directions

The two approaches described above are still strongly represented in current research in socio-linguistics. When Gumperz passed away in 2013, the impact of his work with Heathrow staff in the 1960s and the value of his use of micro-level detail and naturally occurring recordings was brought back into the public arena. His findings on the misunderstanding caused by a subtle difference in intonation patterns demonstrate the explanatory power of the approach which continues to be used today. Similarly, the dynamic, emergent approach offered by social constructionism for investigating negotiated group norms is still highly relevant for those taking a qualitative, discursive approach. The subtle, nuanced interpretations afforded by the CoP framework are recognized as offering many advantages for empirical research into the influence of group differences on interaction.

However, it should also be acknowledged that the term 'culture' is regarded with a certain amount of unease in sociolinguistics: it is considered slippery and ephemeral. As Scollon *et al.* (2012: 3) argue when describing their discourse approach to intercultural communication, '[t]he biggest problem with the word culture is that nobody seems to know exactly what it means, or rather, that it means very different things to different people'. They argue that we should think of culture as a verb, that is something that we 'do', a heuristic describing a 'tool for thinking', and a way of dividing people up. These three options still suggest an extremely broad definition.

Exactly what does and does not count is still hard to pinpoint and it seems that attempts at descriptions are never, and can never, be complete. Some might even go so far as to argue that we should avoid the term altogether. However appealing that might sound as a solution to the unease we face as analysts, there is still widespread use of culture as a 'floating signifier' for participants (Glynos and Angouri 2009). Participants happily blame miscommunication on what they willingly label as cultural differences, and when constructing and ascribing identity we see speakers orienting to and indexing supposed cultural traits. In this same vein, intercultural communication is well established as a field of enquiry and important empirical research offers information about the role of group difference on interaction. We clearly have mental models for what culture entails and it is something that we orient to as a macro category in our everyday interactions. It seems that culture is highly relevant to speakers and naturalized as a social category, whatever we may want to argue as analysts.

A more tempered approach is offered by a 'realist' stance (see Coupland 2001 and the discussion in Holmes *et al.* 2011). At the most basic level, this view means that we recognize that 'real world material conditions and social relations ... constrain and shape the discursive construction of organisational reality in any particular socio-historical situation' (Reed 2005: 1629). So, the way we interact is influenced (or constrained) by broad societal norms and structures such as beliefs about how we should behave and who counts as important, etc. These structures provide us with frames for understanding what is meant.

Realism as a theoretical perspective combines the dynamic, negotiated focus of social con-structionism with the notion of norms as constraints on interaction. It allows us to make use of a shifting concept of culture as well as highlight the role of interaction and practices on our understandings of what should be included under the heading.

Following these lines, it would seem that the field is likely to place significant emphasis on practices and the influence of group ideologies and norms on these practices in future investigations of culture. More fully deconstructing what counts as culture is the inevitable next step for the field, much in same way that we have deconstructed gender to go beyond a oversimplified binary biological category, or how we problematize ethnicity as encapsulating more than race. An approach which (a) recognizes 'culture' as a normative constraint and which (b) highlights the emergent and negotiated nature of 'culture' in interaction affords movement towards a more nuanced approach for the field. We have swung from static and fixed understandings of cultural difference in the more essentialist models where culture is a 'category', to the other extreme where cultural identity is created only in interaction. The obvious way forward in our sociolinguistic understandings of culture is a middle ground of some kind that embraces the best of the two approaches described in the chapter.

Related topics

language, culture and interaction; language and culture in intercultural communication; language, culture and politeness; language, culture and context; language, gender and culure

Further reading

Eckert, P. and McConnell-Ginet, S. 1992. 'Communities of practice: Where language, gender and power all live'. In: Hall, K., Bucholtz, M., and Moonwomon, B. eds. *Locating Power: Proceedings of the Second Berkeley Women and Language Conference*, Berkeley: Berkeley Women and Language Group, University of California, pp. 89–99. (In this article, the authors describe Wenger's community of practice framework and the relevance of a group's shared linguistic resources built up over time. The article encouraged sociolinguists to adopt the framework into their research, first within the area of language and gender, and then more widely.)

Gumperz, J.J. 1982. *Discourse strategies*. Cambridge: Cambridge University Press. (The now famous 'gravy' example is described in this seminal book on discourse approaches to intercultural interaction.)

Hymes, D. 1974. *Foundations in sociolinguistics: An ethnographic approach*. Philadelphia: University of Pennsylvania Press. (In this book, Dell Hymes outlines an ethnography of speaking approach and the SPEAKING grid for describing the various components of a communicative event. Culture is described most obviously under the category of 'Norms of interpretation'.)

Sarangi, S. 1994. 'Intercultural or not? Beyond celebration of cultural differences in miscommunication analysis'. *Pragmatics* 4(3): 409–27. (Sarangi challenges an essentialist, fixed understanding of culture which had previously permeated studies of intercultural interaction.)

Notes

I thank my colleague, Prof Janet Holmes, who read and commented on a draft of this chapter. I also acknowledge the research collaboration of the Language in the Workplace team which has contributed to my understandings.

1 Examples 3 and 4 have been selected from the corpus of naturally occurring interactions collected by the Wellington Language in the Workplace project. They were recorded by volunteers as they went about their everyday business. The selection of these examples represents both my own research interests in workplace discourse and the continuation of the workplace theme provided by the work of both Gumperz and Roberts, Davies and Jupp.

The examples have been edited for ease of reading. The following transcription conventions have been applied:

+   Untimed pause of up to 1 second
[   ]::   Paralinguistic and other editorial comments in square brackets.
           Colons indicate start and end
...   Material omitted

(My thanks go to the participants who willingly donated their interactions to our data set.)

References

Bucholtz, M. and Hall, K. 2005. 'Identity and interaction: A sociocultural linguistic approach'. *Discourse Studies* 7(4–5): 585–614.

Burr, V. 2003. *Social constructionism* (2nd edn). London and New York: Routledge.

Cameron, D. 2009. 'Theoretical issues for the study of gender and spoken interaction'. In: Pichler, P. and Eppler, E.M. eds. *Gender and spoken interaction*. London: Palgrave Macmillan, pp. 1–17.

Campbell, S. and Roberts, C. 2007. 'Migration, ethnicity and competing discourses in the job interview: Synthesizing the institutional and personal'. *Discourse & Society* 18(3): 243–71.

Corder, S. and Meyerhoff, M. 2007. 'Communities of practice in the analysis of intercultural communication'. In: Kotthoff, H. and Spencer-Oatey, H., eds. *Handbook of applied linguistics 7: Intercultural communication*. Berlin: Mouton de Gruyter, pp. 441–61.

Coupland, N. 2001. 'Introduction: Sociolinguistic theory and social theory'. In: Coupland, N., Sarangi, S. and Candlin, C. eds. *Sociolinguistics and social theory*, London: Longman, pp. 1–26.

Eckert, P. and McConnell-Ginet, S. 1992. 'Communities of practice: Where language, gender and power all live'. In: Hall, K., Bucholtz, M. and Moonwomon, B. eds. *Locating power: Proceedings of the second Berkeley women and language conference*, Berkeley: Berkeley Women and Language Group, University of California, pp. 89–99.

——2003. *Language and gender*. Cambridge: Cambridge University Press.

Fairbairn-Dunlop, P. 1984. 'Factors associated with language maintenance: The Samoans in New Zealand'. *New Zealand Journal of Educational Studies* 19(2):99–113.

Glynos, J. and Angouri, J. 2009. 'Managing cultural difference and struggle in the context of the multi-national corporate workplace: Solution or symptom?' *Working Paper in Ideology and Discourse* 26, www.essex.ac.uk/idaworld/paper261209.pdf

Goffman, E. 1963. *Behaviour in public places*. New York: Free Press.

——1974. *Frame analysis*. New York: Harper and Row.

Gordon, C. 2011. Gumperz and interactional sociolinguistics. In: Wodak, R., Johnstone, B. and Kerswill, P. eds. *The Sage handbook of sociolinguistics*. London: Sage, pp. 67–84.

Gumperz, J.J. 1982a. *Discourse strategies*. Cambridge: Cambridge University Press.

——ed. 1982b. *Language and social identity*. Cambridge: Cambridge University Press.

Günthner, S. 2008. 'Negotiating rapport in German–Chinese conversation'. In: Spencer-Oatey, H., ed. *Culturally speaking* (2nd ed). London: Continuum, pp. 207–26.

Harré, R. 1995. 'The discursive turn in social psychology'. In: Schiffrin, D., Tannen, D. and Hamilton, H.E. eds. *The handbook of discourse analysis*. London: Blackwell, pp. 688–706.

Holmes, J. 2003. Social constructionism. In: Frawley, W.J., ed. *International encyclopedia of linguistics* (2nd edn) vol. 4, pp. 88–92.

Holmes, J. and Marra, M. 2002. 'Having a laugh at work: How humour contributes to workplace culture.' *Journal of Pragmatics* 34: 1683–1710.

Holmes, J., Marra, M. and Vine, B. 2011. *Leadership, discourse, and ethnicity*. Oxford: Oxford University Press.

Holmes, J. and Meyerhoff, M. 1999. 'The community of practice: theories and methodologies in language and gender research'. *Language and Society* 23(2): 173–83.

Holmes, J. and Stubbe, M. 2003. '"Feminine" workplaces: stereotype and reality'. In: Holmes, J. and Meyerhoff, M. eds. *The handbook of language and gender*. Oxford: Blackwell, pp. 573–99.

House, J. 2005. 'Politeness in Germany: Politeness in Germany?' In: Hickey, L. and Stewart, M., eds. *Politeness in Europe*. Clevedon: Multilingual Matters, pp.13–28.

Hymes, D. 1974. *Foundations in sociolinguistics: An ethnographic approach*. Philadelphia: University of Pennsylvania Press.

King, B. 2014. 'Tracing the emergence of a community of practice: Beyond presupposition in sociolinguistic research'. *Language in Society* 43(1): 61–81.

Labov, W. 1966. *The social stratification of English in New York City*. Washington, DC: Center for Applied Linguistics.

Lave, J. and Wenger, E. 1991. *Situated learning: Legitimate peripheral participation*. Cambridge: Cambridge University Press.

Marsden, S. 2013. 'Phonological variation and the construction of regional identities in New Zealand English', Ph.D. thesis. Wellington: Victoria University of Wellington.

Reed, M. 2005. 'Reflections on the "realist turn" in organisation and management studies'. *Journal of Management Studies* 42(8): 1621–44.

Roberts, C., Davies, E. and Jupp, T. 1992. *Language and discrimination: A study of communication in multi-ethnic workplaces*. London: Longman.

Schnurr, S., Marra, M. and Holmes, J. 2007. 'Being (im)polite in New Zealand workplaces: Māori and Pākehā leaders'. *Journal of Pragmatics* 39: 712–29.

Scollon, R., Wong-Scollon, S. and Jones, R. 2012. *Intercultural communication: A discourse approach* (3rd edn). Malden, MA: Wiley-Blackwell.

Swann, J. 2002. 'Yes, but is it gender?' In: Litosseliti, L. and Sunderland, J. eds. *Gender identity and discourse analysis*. Amsterdam: John Benjamins, pp. 43–67.

Tannen, D. 1990. *You just don't understand. Women and men in conversation*. New York: Ballantine.

——1994. *Talking 9 to 5. Women and men at work*. New York: William Morrow.

Wenger, E. 1998. *Communities of practice: Learning, meaning and identity*. Cambridge: Cambridge University Press.

Wilson, N. 2011. 'Leadership as communicative practice: The discursive construction of leadership and team identity in a New Zealand rugby team', Ph.D. thesis. Wellington: Victoria University of Wellington.

26

LANGUAGE AND CULTURE IN COGNITIVE ANTHROPOLOGY[1]

Claudia Strauss

Introduction

Cognitive anthropology has been defined as 'the study of the relation between human society and human thought' (D'Andrade 1995: 1). Human thought has two aspects: it is both a process (thinking) and a product (thoughts). Cognitive anthropologists tend to divide between those who focus on the process of thinking (e.g., cognition in practice, distributed cognition studies) and those who study the content, form, organization, and distribution of cultural understandings (e.g., cultural models, cultural consensus, and cultural domain studies). Both of these approaches and various schools within them will be described in this chapter, as well as some that bridge the thinking–thoughts divide.

Culture is analysed differently in these two main approaches. For cognitive anthropologists who study thinking processes, the immediate social and material context is more important than shared cultural understandings. By contrast, culture is central to the work of cognitive anthropologists who study thoughts. In the latter approach culture includes a significant ideational component that differs between human groups and portraying those ideas is their primary concern.

Language plays different roles in these two paradigms as well. In the study of thinking as a process language is considered to be one tool or resource among many, whereas in the study of cultural beliefs, lexicons or discourse are the primary data that researchers mine for category systems, explicit beliefs, and implicit understandings.

Both approaches in cognitive anthropology have important applications to the study of language and culture. Cognition-in-practice researchers created the concept of communities of practice, a currently influential way to theorize communicative practices. Cultural models researchers and others who focus on cultural understandings have methods and theories that have been applied to the study of communicative competence and that are relevant to indexical associations and language ideologies, as I explain below.

The study of cultural understandings has defined the mainstream of cognitive anthropology. As a result, some anthropologists who study cognitive processes do not identify with that label. Nonetheless, not only do researchers from both perspectives share an interest in cognition, but also both schools share certain key theoretical and methodological assumptions that set them apart from many other anthropologists. Neither accepts the Durkheimian dictum that collective representations should be considered apart from individuals (Lave 1988; Strauss and Quinn 1997). Cognitive anthropologists dispute that the cultural meanings lie in collective representations themselves; instead, meanings arise when people create, learn, interpret, and use these collective representations. Methodologically, cognitive anthropologists' conclusions do not rest on decentred discourses, texts, or symbols, but on observations of what specific people say and do. For example, consider the value of success in the United States. Cognitive anthropologists do not deduce cultural meanings of success from movies, self-help books, and the like. A cognitive anthropologist concerned with cultural understandings might talk to Americans to find out how they interpret such sources and what success means to them. A cognitive anthropologist concerned with thinking processes might look at how people use characters from movies or slogans from self-help books as motivational tools or at the specific social contexts in which people learn a group's success-striving practices.

These two major paradigms do not exhaust research in past and present cognitive anthropology. This subfield has included studies of perception, rationality, decision making, mathematical thought, cognitive modularity, evolved cognitive tendencies, and cognitive development among other topics, but there is insufficient space to discuss these in this chapter. Cognitive anthropologists have contributed to studies of linguistic relativity (whether and how thought is shaped by language), but that topic is thoroughly reviewed by Wolf (Chapter 30 this volume), so will not be covered here.

Since the two main approaches to cognitive anthropology have different genealogies, I will describe each approach separately, starting with cognitive anthropological studies of cultural understandings. My focus will be on differences among cognitive anthropologists in their theories of culture.

Cognition as thoughts: the study of cultural understandings

The study of socially varying belief systems has been a central focus of cultural anthropology since its inception. Early in the twentieth century Franz Boas divided anthropology into just two subfields, one devoted to biology and the other (what would now be called sociocultural and linguistic anthropology) to 'the influence of the society' on 'the habits of action and thought of the individual' (quoted in Stocking 1992: 318–19). That statement of the goals of sociocultural anthropology is close to D'Andrade's (1995) definition of cognitive anthropology. How did cognitive anthropologists come to pursue a way of studying cultural beliefs that was different from what most cultural anthropologists did?

Part of the answer lies in cultural theories that motivated some anthropologists to move away from Boas's emphasis on the individual. That part cannot be pursued here. Another part of the answer lies in the influence of interdisciplinary cognitive studies on the anthropologists who initiated cognitive anthropology. Psychology, artificial intelligence, and linguistics all had an impact, with the greatest influence coming from linguistics. The cultural anthropologists who started the subfield later known as cognitive anthropology were inspired both by rigorous descriptions of linguistic knowledge and by various theories of how linguistic knowledge is mentally represented.

Ward Goodenough is widely credited with setting an agenda for contemporary cognitive anthropology. Later in this review I describe some problematic aspects of Goodenough's agenda, but it is important to recognize the impact of his famous definition of culture:

> A society's culture consists of whatever it is one has to know or believe in order to operate in a manner acceptable to its members, and to do so in any role that they

387

accept for any one of themselves. Culture, being what people have to learn as distinct from their biological heritage, must consist of the end product of learning: knowledge, in a most general, if relative, sense of the term. By this definition, we should note that culture is not a material phenomenon; it does not consist of things, people, behavior, or emotions. It is rather the organization of these things. It is the forms of things that people have in mind, their models for perceiving, relating, and otherwise interpreting them.

(1957: 167)

In other words, Goodenough defined culture as ideational rather than material and located those ideas in people's minds rather than in public symbols and events.[2] Cognitive anthropologists do not have to subscribe to Goodenough's narrow definition of culture as only mental representations (see D'Andrade 1995; Keesing 1972; and Strauss and Quinn 1997 for criticisms of that part); it is enough to appreciate his point that such knowledge is a significant part of culture, it is structured, and it directs the way people interpret what is going on and act (see also Hallowell 1955).

At this stage one of the key roles of linguistics was to provide the analogy of grammatical descriptions. Goodenough's doctoral dissertation was entitled 'A grammar of social interaction'. Another early practitioner, Charles Frake, stated that the goal was 'productive descriptions ... which, like the linguist's grammar, succinctly state what one must know in order to generate culturally acceptable acts and utterances appropriate to a given socio-ecological context' (Frake 1962, quoted in Keesing 1972: 302).

As Keesing (1972) notes, figuring out context-specific models of performance was more ambitious than what linguists were attempting in the late 1950s and 1960s, but for these anthropologists the analogy was close enough. Their research into local notions of appropriateness helped stimulate ethnographies of communication that described norms of communicative competence, including the cultural understandings of settings, social roles, event sequences, goals, and dangers that guide participants' interactions in communicative events (Hymes 1974; Tyler 1978).

However, the analogy of cultural knowledge with linguistic knowledge also raises some red flags. Is cultural knowledge as systematic as grammatical knowledge has been portrayed as being? Probably not.

Nonetheless, systematic formal analyses have been an ideal to which some cognitive anthropologists aspired, following the example of linguists' grammars. In a less-quoted part of Goodenough's influential article he says that a second feature of a good description of culture is its 'elegance' (Goodenough 1957: 168). One elegant model in the late 1950s was structural linguistics, which described the features whose presence or absence differentiated linguistic elements such as phonemes for speakers of a particular language. Early cognitive anthropologists took that basic approach and applied it to an aspect of cultural knowledge that showed promise of systematicity: the category systems that underlie terminology in a cultural domain (e.g., kinship categories, diseases, plants, or colours). While cognitive anthropologists in the late 1950s and 1960s were also concerned with rules for social behaviour, much of their attention during this period turned to sets of words and their meanings. Such studies were known for a while as *ethnoscience* because many of the domains studied were aspects of the natural world. The broader term *ethnosemantics* is more common today.

Yet while the early generation of cognitive anthropologists appreciated formal descriptions, most also wanted models that had *psychological reality*, as Wallace and Atkins (1960) put it. This put a salutary check on their model building. To have psychological reality, it was necessary to understand 'the world as [a member of the society] perceives and knows it, in his own terms' (Wallace and Atkins 1960: 75). In Goodenough's definition of culture, the psychological validity of a model was not a concern: a cultural description was adequate if following it would produce behaviour that was judged normal in a society. However, from the early 1960s on, many cognitive anthropologists went further, devising additional procedures to see, for example, if the implicit semantic dimensions that the analyst thought were important in fact seemed to guide similarity judgements made by members of the society (D'Andrade 1995: 50ff.). As I describe below, there have been significant shifts in the methods and theories of cognitive anthropologists who study cultural understandings since the late 1950s, but a consistent emphasis that has differentiated the cognitive approach from run-of-the-mill anthropological studies of cultural knowledge has been a commitment to ferreting out what particular members of a society think.

Cultural knowledge as meanings of words in contrast sets

Because ethnosemantics is the sole focus of Leavitt's chapter of this volume, and because there are excellent histories of cognitive anthropology that cover this phase of the subfield (D'Andrade 1995; see also Blount 2011), I will touch on it only briefly here.

You can appreciate the underlying intuition that motivated cognitive anthropologists' attention to the lexicon in a domain if you agree with Whorf that 'the world is presented in a kaleidoscopic flux of impressions which has to be organized by our minds – and this means largely by the linguistic systems in our minds' (1956: 213). Whorf, like his teacher Sapir, was more interested in grammatical systems than lexical ones, but his observation is commonly tied to lexicons. (Think of the Eskimo-words-for-snow urban legend.) The assumption is that if a group has a word for something, it must have some cultural significance and if it uses different names in the same domain, they encode culturally relevant distinctions. The focus of this approach is dimensions of meaning that apply to all the words in a lexical contrast set, which is a set of names for things that are part of the same larger category, such as words for different emotions. The focus of ethnosemanticists on lexical contrast sets was influenced by structural linguists' assumption that meanings are not attached to individual signs but derive from a whole local system for differentiating among possible alternatives.

Ethnosemanticists devised a variety of procedures for determining local category systems. Their *emic* descriptions could be very insightful and some of the ingenious methods they devised are still used in cultural domain analysis, described below. A particularly important development was to move beyond word denotations, that is, the local criteria that define what makes something an x rather than a y (as Goodenough 1956 preferred), to the culturally juicier realm of word connotations. Researchers began paying attention to connotations when they listened to what was important in local discourse (see review in Boster 2011 and D'Andrade 1995: 76–7). For example, the defining features of a lexicon for alcoholic beverages might be the main ingredient (barley, rye, grapes, etc.) and whether the drink is distilled. Depending on what group you listened to however, the kinds of connotations that might be salient would have to do with whether the drink is sophisticated, how quickly it gets you drunk, whether it is appropriate to serve at certain kinds of social gatherings, and so on. Researchers interested in such connotative features could then create an elicitation frame to systematically inquire for each item in the lexicon whether it has that feature (e.g., 'Can drinking one cup of ___ make you drunk?').

Studying word connotations based on locally salient features was an important step towards greater psychological reality and broader cultural understandings. Yet that too was limited. For some topics there is not a large vocabulary labelling different types of objects. My current research concerns the way unemployed Americans interpret their situation. There is no lexicon

I could analyse that would begin to reveal the moral, religious, social, economic, and political interpretive frameworks they draw upon. Even in domains where there is a large lexicon, the study of words in a contrast set does not take us very far towards uncovering cultural knowledge, as some commentators began observing by the 1970s (e.g., Colby 1975; Frake 1977; Kay 1978; Keesing 1972). If you want to know what members of a group think about drinking alcohol, is analysing their lexicon for alcoholic beverages really the best approach? The way they categorize wine, beer, and whisky gives only a small glimpse of their cultural understandings of drinking.[3]

There was also a growing realization that testing for psychological validity is not the same as modelling members' mental organization of their cultural knowledge. Is it a set of propositions? Concepts and their logical relations? Abstract rules (D'Andrade 1995; Quinn 2011b)?

Dissatisfaction with analysis of lexical contrast sets led to a variety of other approaches, described next.

Domain analysis and consensus analysis

Although ethnosemantics turned out not to be the key to cultural understanding, its practitioners were clever in devising a variety of methods for eliciting and analysing members' cultural knowledge. Some of these methods yielded quantitative and qualitative findings that could be analysed by following replicable procedures. Some cognitive anthropologists have continued to apply these techniques and have added new ones, even as their focus has broadened beyond word meanings.

Free listing is a simple method that can be used to elicit cultural knowledge. It is often the first step in a study of lexical contrast sets ('list all the kinds of x you can think of'), but it can also be used not just to generate lists of terms but also to find conceptual associations. For the latter purpose the method consists of asking participants to list everything that comes to mind in connection with something. The analyst then considers what is listed most often, what is mentioned near the top of people's lists, and whether certain items tend to cluster near each other. For example deMunck *et al.* (2011) asked informants in Russia, Lithuania, and the US to list all the things they associate with romantic love. While there was some cross-society overlap, there were also national differences. For example, words like 'friendship', 'comfortable', and 'secure' were among the top ten most commonly named associations by the US sample but were almost completely absent in the Russians' and Lithuanians' free lists.

Consensus analysis was developed by Romney, Weller, and Batchelder (1986) to study what beliefs are shared and by whom. This view draws upon a definition of culture as a 'socially transmitted information pool' (D'Andrade 1981: 180). The basic assumption of consensus analysis is that in many cultural domains there are some agreed-upon propositions among expert members of a group – but not everyone is an expert. If the researcher observes a response pattern in which there is convergence among some participants on a set of answers and no competing agreed-upon answers (and they are not discussing the topic with each other while answering the questions), the consensual answers are considered cultural knowledge and those who gave the culturally correct responses are considered to have greater competence in that domain. Consensus analysis is generally conducted with true–false or multiple-choice questions.

Consensus analysis is useful for studying the distribution of beliefs, including patterns of subgroup variation. This method can also be used to uncover competing understandings of the correct answer and can suggest underlying social flows of information (Boster 1986). One of its weaknesses is that its standardized elicitation procedures limit participants' opportunity to reveal their thinking beyond the questions asked. It is common for cultural consensus modellers to begin with open-ended interviews to derive their closed-choice questions. Others (e.g., Kempton, Boster, and Hartley 1995) also use cultural models research, described next, to present a fuller description of members' beliefs.

Cultural models

As the above review of work on ethnosemantics explains, by the 1970s cognitive anthropologists had several concerns about that approach. Chief among them were the realizations that studying the meaning of words in a contrast set left out considerable cultural knowledge and that this whole approach was long on methods but short on theoretical models of the mental organization of cultural knowledge. Schema theory in the cognitive sciences provided a more satisfying way of understanding what cultural knowledge consists of, and inspired new methods for studying it. The result was the body of work that became known as *cultural schemas* or *cultural models* research.

As elaborated in psychology, linguistics (especially frame semantics, e.g., Fillmore 1975), and artificial intelligence starting in the 1970s, schemas (also called 'frames', 'scripts', 'scenes', and other terms) are mental structures representing the relations among the typical elements of any type of concrete or abstract thing. We have schemas for everything we encounter or learn about, from the mundane and concrete (how to recognize and use everyday objects) to the lofty and abstract (what is a desirable life course, whether there is a higher power, folk psychology, folk economics, and so on). Cultural schemas are derived from learned, shared experiences, either ones personally experienced by multiple members of a group or ones communicated among them. Cultural schemas are local models of how the humanly created, natural, supernatural, interpersonal, and wider sociopolitical worlds work.

Since a schema is an interrelated whole, anything that evokes part of the schema will bring the rest to mind, consciously or unconsciously. Thus, we can leave a lot unsaid because a hint or indirect reference will evoke the rest of the schema in the hearer's mind. Schemas have been posited to enter into all phases of cognition, explaining how we interpret perceptions and emotions, how we reconstruct memories, and how we plan future actions, in addition to producing and interpreting ongoing verbal and nonverbal behaviour. Schemas are simplified, generic concepts like stereotypes, but without the connotation of prejudicial beliefs necessarily, although they can include prejudicial stereotypes because schemas encode our assumptions regarding what is typically associated with what.

Another important characteristic of cultural models is that they are connected to feelings and motivations (D'Andrade 1981; D'Andrade and Strauss 1992). In D'Andrade's (1984) words, cultural schemas have 'directive force', that is, they are not neutral explanations but also include evaluations and goals that motivate action, or at least create discomfort if they are not enacted.

While cognitive anthropologists who study cultural schemas agree on the above, there are some subtle differences in how they conceptualize such schemas. For example, D'Andrade draws upon Mandler's definition of a schema as a 'bounded, distinct, and unitary representation' (Mandler 1984 cited in D'Andrade 1995: 122). For D'Andrade it is not a schema unless it comes to mind as a unit, and if it comes to mind as a unit, it is restricted in size and complexity by the number of chunks that can be held in working memory,[4] hence the terminological distinction he draws between simpler *cultural schemas* and more complex *cultural models*, which has led to a current preference on the part of some researchers for the former term over the more familiar latter one (see Quinn 2011b: 36).[5]

In Quinn and Holland's introduction to *Cultural Models in Language and Thought* (1987), by contrast, the definition of schemas as bite-sized enough to arise in working memory is not mentioned. They chose to narrow the idea of cultural models as follows: 'Cultural models are presupposed, taken-for-granted models of the world that are widely shared (although not necessarily to the exclusion of other, alternative models)' (Quinn and Holland 1987: 4). That puts the focus of cultural research on beliefs that have become so naturalized that they are not even seen as beliefs, the aspect of culture that Pierre Bourdieu (1977: 164) termed *doxa* rather than *dogma*. It is common in cultural studies to focus on explicitly propounded dogmas; in the cultural models approach, by contrast, the focus is turned to understandings that are so generally accepted that they form the shared presuppositions underlying different opinions about a topic. That approach is consistent with the way many anthropologists have thought about culture (as the water in which a fish swims, as what we 'see with' but do not see), but it limits the researcher's focus to the most consensual type of cultural understanding. In practice, cultural models researchers have also studied the way debated cultural understandings interact with more taken-for-granted ones (e.g., Fong 2007; Holland *et al.* 1998; Quinn 1996; Strauss 2007, 2012), so cultural models research as it has developed is broader than is implied by that early definition.

The difference between taken-for-granted and debated ideas is relevant to linguistic anthropologists studying *language ideologies* (also called *linguistic ideologies*). As Woolard (1998) explains, one definition of language ideologies is 'shared bodies of commonsense notions about the nature of language in the world' (Rumsey 1990: 346, quoted in Woolard 1998: 4).[6] Rumsey gives the example of a common-sense Western distinction between 'mere talk' and action, an excellent example of a cultural schema in Quinn and Holland's (1987) sense. By contrast, Michael Silverstein's definition of linguistic ideologies is 'sets of beliefs about language articulated by users as a rationalization or justification of perceived language structure and use' (Silverstein 1979: 193, quoted in Woolard 1998: 4). An example would be the idea held by many Americans that nonstandard English dialects are 'sloppy'. That, too, is a widely held cultural schema, but it is more controversial than the assumed separation of talk and action.

While the focus on consensus is somewhat out of fashion (however important it remains), there is a respect in which cultural models analysts have taken a leading role in rethinking conceptions of culture. Notice that D'Andrade (1995) emphasizes that schemas are bounded and distinct, but not that cultures are bounded and distinct. A cultural schema is by definition shared, but groups do not share all of their schemas. Centring research on schemas and the experiences that might give rise to them usefully problematizes, rather than assumes, the extent to which members of a locality, ethnic group, or nation state share the same cultural models. Some schemas may be limited to a family or a circle of friends; others may be shared among those who follow the same pop culture globally. D'Andrade rejects the idea that culture is 'a thing' (1995: 250). In criticizing Geertz's metaphor of culture as being like an octopus, he responds, 'culture looks more like the collected denizens of a tide pool than a single octopus … Each cultural model is "thing-like", but all the models together do not form any kind of thing' (1995: 249). His tide pool analogy could be taken to imply some degree of integration (we would expect organisms in an ecosystem to affect each other), but he does not pursue the partially integrative tendencies his metaphor suggests.

In *A Cognitive Theory of Cultural Meaning* (1997), Naomi Quinn and I consider the issue of cultural integration. We start with a dynamic understanding of schemas as consisting of elements that come to be strongly interconnected through repeated association or vivid encounters in the learner's experience. Schemas are built up through interactions between people and the worlds they construct, and culture 'consists of regular occurrences in the humanly created world, in the schemas people share as a result of these, and in the interactions between these schemas and this world' (Strauss and Quinn 1997: 7). Thus, we see culture as both intrapersonal and extrapersonal, both shared schemas and the experiences that create and are created by them. We then consider what social and psychological factors lead to schemas being shared in a group or more divergent; motivating or given lip service only; durable or more fleeting; and integrated thematically versus at odds.

The connectionist model of cognition[7] we draw upon also yields a distinctive way of thinking about cultural meanings. Cultural meanings are not the same as cultural schemas. Instead, meanings or interpretations are 'the thoughts, feelings, and less conscious associations evoked when people's schemas meet the world at a given moment' (Strauss and Quinn 1997: 54). The meaning a person will give to a particular experience depends on what combination of elements of different schemas will be activated by the particular features of an event. It can be a novel blend.

If cultural schemas are usually left unsaid, how do cognitive anthropologists study them? In ordinary conversation, speakers and hearers rely on their schemas to fill in what is left unsaid. Cultural schema researchers, similarly, look at extended discourse to see what is presupposed by what is said. As D'Andrade puts it, 'I have found it is better not to ask informants directly about their models, but rather to ask something that will bring the model into play; that is, something that will make the person *use* the model' (D'Andrade 2005: 90). A typical cultural models study will draw upon lengthy semi-structured interviews because the topic in question comes up at unpredictable times in daily life, making extended talk about it difficult to capture with participant observation (Quinn 2005b). Other kinds of discourse, such as proverbs, stories, and online communications (Mathews 1992; Price 1987; Strauss 2007; White 1987) can be collected, as well as observations of the models in action (e.g., Kusserow 2004).

There are different ways of analysing the large corpus of discourse collected by cultural models researchers. Quinn (2005a) states, 'My assumption is that the shared understandings I seek lie behind what people said – not, as our folk "Whorfian" theory of language makes us prone to assume, that these are meanings embedded in the words themselves' (ibid.: 45). For example, Quinn (1991) has examined the metaphors her interviewees use for talking about marriage. Her assumption is not that thinking about marriage is essentially metaphorical, but rather that people use metaphors to articulate their cultural understandings of the properties of typical and ideal marriages. Those views are elaborated in her critique of Lakoff and Johnson's (1980) metaphor theory (Quinn 1997).

While cultural models research requires a verbatim record of people's words, much linguistic detail is not relevant if the goal is to figure out tacit cultural understandings. In the last section I consider other approaches that attend to discourse features that reflect the form as well as the content of cultural understandings.

Cognition as thinking

An alternative major approach within cognitive anthropology is to focus on cognition as an activity (thinking) rather than on shared mental representations. Anthropologists who study thinking as a process do not start with Goodenough's definition of culture as what members know and believe. For example, Edwin Hutchins (1995) rejects Goodenough's definition and criticizes D'Andrade's (1981) division of labour in which psychologists study cognitive processes and anthropologists study cognitive contents. Instead, for Hutchins, 'Culture is a human cognitive process ... and the "things" that appear on list-like definitions of culture are residua of the process.[8] Culture is an adaptive process that accumulates partial solutions to frequently encountered problems' (1995: 354; see also Bender *et al.* 2010).

The study of thinking in particular social and cultural contexts can be found in classic anthropological accounts such as Evans-Pritchard's careful description of the way Azande draw inferences regarding past events or future activities from the reactions of chickens to small doses of poison (1976 [1937]). Some of the more recent work on cognition as a contextually embedded practice has been influenced by the theories of Lev Vygotsky (e.g., Vygotsky 1962, 1978) and other Soviet-era Russian psychologists. Vygotsky took Marx's interest in the way humans transform nature with tools and extended it to the intellectual tools that humans create to mediate the effect of material conditions on their thoughts. Vygotsky was interested in the process by which socially created tools become internalized mental tools. Intellectual tools or *mediating devices* include whole sign systems (e.g., language, writing) as well as particular artefacts (e.g., calculating devices) or actions (e.g. gestures, Hutchins 2006) that aid and shape memory, problem solving, decision making, communication, and so on. Alexei Leontiev took the Soviet cultural–historical school of psychology approach in another direction by focusing on goal-directed human activities as the unit of analysis (Cole and Scribner 1978; Holland and Valsiner 1988).

As Nardi (1996) explains, some anthropologists who study processes of thinking are influenced more by the activity theory of Leontiev, which means they are concerned with the goals that actors have in mind (e.g., Holland and Reeves 1994), while others focus instead on the affordances of the immediate situation (e.g., Lave 1988) or the way information processing is distributed among humans and material artefacts (e.g., Hutchins 1995). These theoretical differences among different approaches to the study of cognition as a process have methodological implications. Nardi points out that close analysis of videotaped interactions are useful for *distributed cognition* or *cognition in practice* or *situated action* studies of interactions in the immediate situation, but long-term observation and interviews with participants are more appropriate for activity theorists concerned with participants' goals in a continuing activity (Nardi 1996).

Researchers who focus on the immediate context of thinking have tended to polemically reject the importance of mental representations or have downplayed their importance as a reaction to mainstream cognitive anthropology (e.g., Lave 1988). More recent writings by at least some researchers acknowledge that some earlier work went too far in that direction. These researchers now more fully integrate mental representations into thinking in context (e.g., Hazlehurst 2011; Holland and Cole 1995; Hutchins 2005).

Cognition-in-practice researchers have made an important contribution to linguistic anthropology with the concept of communities of practice. The term 'community of practice' was proposed by Jean Lave and Etienne Wenger (1991). Lave and Wenger looked at the way learning of any sort (formal or informal) takes place in communities. They emphasized that by community, '[W]e do not imply some primordial culture-sharing entity. We assume that members have different interests, make diverse contributions to activity, and hold varied viewpoints. In our view, participation at multiple levels is entailed in membership in a *community of practice*' (Lave and Wenger 1991: 98). Although members of a community of practice may have diverse cultural backgrounds, what they share is an orientation towards a common activity. Lave and Wenger downplay the role of talk in such communities as a way of passing on knowledge. Instead, they focus on talk as a facilitator of social participation (ibid.: 109). An application of this approach is to look at beliefs as contextually and socially negotiated.

Future directions

What the reader probably expects at this point are directions for the future that unite studies of cognition as thoughts and cognition as thinking in a happy synthesis. However, I think it is fair to say that the most interesting cutting-edge work in cognitive anthropology is not oriented towards a synthesis for its own sake but instead pushes the boundaries of the paradigm in which it arose by asking new questions or using new methods. More ecumenical approaches are often a result.

One new direction in cognitive anthropology is a focus on narrative. As Mattingly and Garro (2000: 17) note, stories are 'ways of thinking through the past, ways of making sense of ongoing situations and guides for future actions'. A good story fits cultural schemas (e.g., about how you are supposed to portray your choice of a career, Linde 1993, or finding a life partner, McCollum 2002, or events in your marriage, Quinn 2011a, or your life as an alcoholic, Cain 1991), and examining life stories can reveal these cultural schemas. However, stories describe particular events that may deviate from the generic patterns represented in cultural models (Price 1987), and they can reveal the personal associations that a speaker makes between shared cultural models and their own life events (Strauss 1992, 2005). Narratives can also be seen as Vygotskian mediating devices (Holland and Valsiner 1988: 263). Stories are good to 'think with' because they memorably combine information with implications for action (e.g., when my friend cheated the consequences were terrible, so I shouldn't do that) (Mathews 1992; Price 1987). As Garro (2001) has noted, ordering experience in narratives, like using a schema to judge that a current situation is an example of something you have encountered before, is an example of the 'effort after meaning' that the mid-twentieth-century psychologist Frederick Bartlett said was part of all human cognition (Garro 2001: 110).

Another new body of work is in cultural epidemiology. Cultural epidemiologists study the distribution of ideas and practices and what explains that distribution to understand why some catch on more than others (Sperber 1985). For example, Atran *et al.* (2005) consider a variety of definitions of culture, rejecting some on the mentalistic side as assuming consensus and stability within identity groups and some on the practice side as paying insufficient attention to mental content and processes. They use cultural consensus analysis to study the ecological beliefs of three ethnic groups in Guatemala, then considered factors that affected the distribution of knowledge within and between the groups, such as the late arrival of one of the Mayan groups to this lowland area and the reliance of the Ladino group on experts from the better established of the two Mayan groups. Thus, they combine some of the contextual factors that are important in studies of cognition in practice with methods for studying cultural content.

Wide distribution of ideas is also facilitated when generic schemas are frequently repeated in a formulaic way. In Strauss (2012) I argue that most people's opinions about topics such as immigration reform and national health insurance in the United States are drawn from hetero-geneous conventional discourses. A conventional discourse is a schema, but unlike cultural schemas that are presupposed, conventional discourses represent schemas that are debated or repeated because they are seen as in need of defence. For example, one conventional discourse about immigration in the United States is Foreigners Taking Our Jobs, which expresses the schema that immigrants as well as workers in foreign countries are taking jobs away from native-born Americans or depressing their wages. Its common rebuttal is the Jobs Americans Don't Want discourse, which expresses the schema that immigrants are only taking jobs that people born here do not want to do. Conventional discourses have characteristic rhetorical markers, whether they are keywords and phrases (such as *jobs that Americans can't /won't do*), tone (e.g., resentful, proud, or matter of fact), mode of argumentation, and speaker's projected social location (e.g., that of the working-class native-born for Foreigners Taking Our Jobs).

I also argue that cultural models in the early Quinn and Holland (1987) sense of 'presupposed, taken-for-granted models of the world that are widely shared' represent just one point on a cultural standing continuum that ranges from controversial opinions, to debatable opinions (speakers recognize there is more than one widely held view on the subject in their opinion community), to common opinions (widely shared in an opinion community but threatened by outsiders, backsliders, or radicals), to understandings that are presupposed to the point that locals rarely recognize them as beliefs that could be questioned (Strauss 2004, drawing on Bourdieu 1977). I would broaden culture to encompass beliefs and practices that are widely held (whether presupposed or articulated) or well respected (even if they are not widespread) or that are *perceived* to be widely held or well respected (Strauss 2012: 32). Speakers are expected to mark the cultural standing of their ideas when they speak (e.g., by hedging or not hedging) and such expected markers, as well as paralinguistic features of delivery such as hesitation or disfluency, can be analysed for evidence of the speaker's perception of the cultural standing of their ideas (Strauss 2004). This expands the aspects of discourse that are examined from underlying content to manner of expression.

It also shifts the notion of culture from propositions all propagated and held in the same way to cultural beliefs as publicly and mentally represented in different ways. Views that have to be defended from challenges within or outside the opinion community are more likely to be made explicit in public forums and represented propositionally in members' minds. By contrast, assumptions about what goes with what, such as indexical associations of clothing, manner of speaking, and so on with types of people or communicative contexts, may never be explicitly propounded and need not be internalized as propositions. Instead, they might be learned simply as strong connections in a neural network such that someone's dress, appearance, and ways of communicating will bring a flood of associations to the minds of those interacting with him or her, whether or not they are conscious of them (Strauss and Quinn 1997). While analysts must use language to describe what people believe, the cognitive content of cultural knowledge is not necessarily discursive and thinking processes include both verbal and nonverbal elements (see also Tyler 1978).

In a commentary about cultural models research Roger Keesing (1987: 388) complained, 'cognitive anthropology remains, I think, curiously innocent of social theory' that examines 'the production, control, distribution, and ideological force of cultural knowledge'. Although that was never uniformly true of cognitive anthropology (see, e.g., Holland and Eisenhart 1990; Kay 1978; Lave 1988; Quinn 1992), it is less true today than ever. As I hope this review has shown, recent work in cognitive anthropology is highly relevant to questions about the relation of social forces to the formation, expression, enactment, and distribution of products and processes of human thought.

Related topics

the linguistic relativity hypothesis revisited; language, culture and prototypicality; ethnosemantics; language, culture and colour, culture and kinship language, language and cultural scripts, cultural linguistics

Further reading

Bender, Andrea, Edwin Hutchins, and Douglas Medin. 2010. 'Anthropology in Cognitive Science', *Topics in Cognitive Science* 2 (2010) 374–85. (This article explains the bumpy history of cognitive anthropology's place in the cognitive sciences and cites much research not covered here.)

Bennardo, Giovanni and Victor de Munck. (in press) *Cultural Models: Genesis, Methods, and Experiences.* New York: Oxford University Press. (This book reviews methods and findings of cultural models research broadly construed to include both qualitative and quantitative research.)

D'Andrade, Roy. 1995. *The Development of Cognitive Anthropology.* Cambridge: Cambridge University Press. (This is still the best one-volume introduction to the history of cognitive anthropology, especially the mainstream traditions that focus on cultural understandings.)

Kronenfeld, David B., Giovanni Bennardo, Victor C. de Munck, and Michael D. Fischer, eds. 2011. *A Companion to Cognitive Anthropology.* Malden, MA: Wiley-Blackwell. (The 29 chapters by different contributors provide an up-to-date comprehensive overview of theories, methods, and applications from different approaches in cognitive anthropology.)

Quinn, Naomi, ed. 2005. *Finding Culture in Talk: A Collection of Methods.* New York: Palgrave Macmillan. (The contributors provide theoretical background and concrete examples of anthropological approaches to discourse analysis, with an emphasis on the cultural models approach.)

Notes

1 Acknowledgements: I am grateful for comments on an earlier draft from Naomi Quinn.
2 Goodenough's definition of culture is thus like Chomsky's I-language, i.e., native speakers' mental representations of linguistic knowledge (Chomsky 1986).
3 See Quinn 2011b and D'Andrade 1995:126ff. on his discovery that his studies of Americans' lexicon of illnesses did not reveal their ideas about germs.
4 The idea that some mental representations are easily brought to mind while others are more complex and less readily graspable was helpful to me in distinguishing between the simple mental representations I call *conventional discourses* and discourses in Foucault's sense (Strauss 2012: 18).
5 Casson (1981, 1983) used *cultural schemata*. Subsequently *cultural models* was popularized by the influential volume *Cultural Models in Language and Thought* (Holland and Quinn 1987; see also D'Andrade and Strauss 1992).
6 Some anthropologists instead would contrast culture (taken-for-granted) with ideology (contested).
7 Connectionism (also *parallel distributed processing* or *neural network models*) is a way of modelling cognition that is inspired by the simultaneous information processing of neurons in the brain rather than the sequential symbolic processing of most computers. For an accessible introduction see Garson (2010) or Strauss and Quinn (1997).
8 By 'list-like definitions' Hutchins has in mind, for example, Tylor's famous definition of culture as 'that complex whole which includes knowledge, belief, art, morals, law, custom, and any other capabilities and habits acquired by man as a member of society' (Tylor 1871, quoted in Hutchins 1995: 353).

References

Atran, S., Medin, D.L. and Ross, N.O., 2005, 'The cultural mind: Environmental decision making and cultural modelling within and across populations', *Psychological Review*, 112(4), 744–76.
Bender, A., Hutchins, E. and Medin, D., 2010, 'Anthropology in Cognitive Science', *Topics in Cognitive Science* 2, 374–85.
Blount, B. G., 2011, 'A history of cognitive anthropology', in D. B. Kronenfeld, G. Bennardo, V. C. de Munck and M. D. Fischer (eds), *A Companion to Cognitive Anthropology*, Wiley-Blackwell, Malden, MA, pp. 11–29.
Boster, James S. 1986, 'Exchange of varieties and information between Aguaruna manioc cultivators', *American Anthropologist* 88, 429–36.
——2011, 'Data, method, and interpretation in cognitive anthropology', in D.B. Kronenfeld, G. Bennardo, V.C. de Munck and M.D. Fischer (eds), *A Companion to Cognitive Anthropology*, Wiley-Blackwell, Malden, MA, pp. 131–52.
Bourdieu, P., 1977, *Outline of a Theory of Practice*, R. Nice, trans., Cambridge University Press, New York.
Cain, C., 1991, 'Personal stories: Identity acquisition and self-understanding in Alcoholics Anonymous', *Ethos* 19 (2), 210–53.
Casson, R.W., 1981, 'Language, culture, and cognition', in R. W. Casson (ed.), *Language, Culture, and Cognition: Anthropological Perspectives*, Macmillan, New York.
——1983, 'Schemata in cognitive anthropology', *Annual Review of Anthropology* 12: 429–62.
Chomsky, N., 1986, *Knowledge of Language*. New York: Praeger.
Colby, B.N., 1975, 'Cultural grammars', *Science* 187, 913–19.
Cole, M. and Scribner, S., 1978, 'Introduction', in M. Cole, V. John-Steiner, S. Scribner and E. Souberman (eds), *Mind in Society: The Development of Higher Psychological Processes*, Harvard University Press, Cambridge, MA, pp. 1–14.
D'Andrade, R.G., 1981, 'The cultural part of cognition', *Cognitive Science* 5,179–95.
——1984, 'Cultural meaning systems', in R.A. Shweder and R.A. LeVine (eds), *Culture Theory: Essays on Mind, Self, and Emotion*, Cambridge University Press, Cambridge, UK, pp. 88–119.
——1995, *The Development of Cognitive Anthropology*, Cambridge University Press, Cambridge, UK.
——2005, 'Some methods for studying cultural cognitive structures', in N. Quinn (ed.), *Finding Culture in Talk: A Collection of Methods*, Palgrave Macmillan, New York, pp. 83–104.
D'Andrade, R.G. and Strauss, C. (eds), 1992, *Human Motives and Cultural Models*, Cambridge University Press, Cambridge, UK.
de Munck, V.C., Korotayev, A., de Munck, J. and Khaltourina, D., 2011, 'Cross-cultural analysis of models of romantic love among U.S. residents, Russians, and Lithuanians', *Cross-Cultural Research* 45(2), 128–54.

Evans-Pritchard, E.E., 1976 [1937], *Witchcraft, Oracles, and Magic among the Azande*, abridged edn, Oxford University Press, Oxford.

Fillmore, C., 1975, 'An alternative to checklist theories of meaning', in C. Cogen, H. Thompson, G. Thurgood, K. Whistler and J. Wright (eds), *Proceedings of the First Annual Meeting of the Berkeley Linguistics Society*, University of California Press, Berkeley, CA, pp. 123–31.

Fong, V., 2007, 'Parent–child communication problems and the perceived inadequacies of Chinese only children', *Ethos* 35, 85–127.

Frake, C.O., 1962, 'The ethnographic study of cognitive systems', in T. Gladwin and W. Sturtevant (eds), *Anthropology and Human Behavior*, Washington, DC: Anthropological Society of Washington pp. 72–85.

——1964, 'Notes on queries in ethnography', *American Anthropologist*, 66 (3), 132–45.

——1981 [1977], 'Plying frames can be dangerous: Some reflections on methodology in cognitive anthropology', in R. W. Casson (ed.), *Language, Culture, and Cognition: Anthropological Perspectives*, Macmillan, New York, pp. 366–77.

Garro, L., 2001, 'The remembered past in a culturally meaningful life: Remembering as cultural, social and cognitive process', in C.C. Moore and H.F. Mathews (eds), *The Psychology of Cultural Experience*, Cambridge University Press, Cambridge, UK, pp. 105–47.

Garson, J., 2010, 'Connectionism', *Stanford Encyclopedia of Philosophy*, http://plato.stanford.edu/entries/connectionism/#StrWeaNeuNetMod, accessed 24/07/13.

Goodenough, W., 1956, 'Componential analysis and the study of meaning', *Language*, 32 (1), pp. 195–216.

——1957, 'Cultural anthropology and linguistics', in P. Garvin (ed.), *Report of the Seventh Annual Round Table Meeting in Linguistics and Language Study, Monograph Series on Language and Linguistics*, no. 9, Georgetown University, Washington, DC, pp. 167–73.

Hallowell, A.I., 1955, *Culture and Experience*, University of Pennsylvania Press, Philadelphia.

Hazlehurst, B., 2011, 'The distributed cognition model of mind', in D.B. Kronenfeld, G. Bennardo, V. C. de Munck and M.D. Fischer (eds), *A Companion to Cognitive Anthropology*. Wiley-Blackwell, Malden, MA, pp. 471–88.

Holland, D. and Cole, M., 1995, 'Between discourse and schema: Reformulating a cultural–historical approach to culture and mind', *Anthropology and Education Quarterly* 26 (4), 475–90.

Holland, D. and Eisenhart, M., 1990, *Educated in Romance : Women, Achievement, and College Culture*, University of Chicago Press, Chicago.

Holland, D. and Quinn, N. (eds), 1987, *Cultural Models in Language and Thought*, Cambridge University Press, Cambridge, UK.

Holland, D. and Reeves, J.R., 1994, 'Activity theory and the view from somewhere: Team perspectives on the intellectual work of programming, *Mind, Culture, and Activity* 1 (1–2), 8–24.

Holland, D., Skinner, D., Lachicotte, W. and Cain, C., 1998, *Identity and Agency in Cultural Worlds*, Harvard University Press, Cambridge, MA.

Holland, D. and Valsiner, J., 1988, 'Cognition, symbols, and Vygotsky's developmental psychology', *Ethos*, 16 (3), pp. 247–72.

Hutchins, E., 1995, *Cognition in the Wild*, MIT Press, Cambridge, MA.

——2005, 'Material anchors for conceptual blends', *Journal of Pragmatics* 37, 1555–77.

——2006. 'Imagining the cognitive life of things', in workshop, The cognitive life of things: recasting the boundaries of the mind, McDonald Institute for Archaeological Research, Cambridge. Online at: http://liris.cnrs.fr/enaction/docs/documents2006/ImaginingCogLifeThings.pdf

Hymes, D., 1974, *Foundations in Sociolinguistics: An Ethnographic Approach*, University of Pennsylvania Press, Philadelphia.

Kay, P., 1978, 'Tahitian words for race and class', *Publications de la Société des Océanistes* 39, 81–93.

Keesing, R.M., 1972, 'Paradigms lost: The new ethnography and the new linguistics', *Southwestern Journal of Anthropology*, 28 (4), 299–32.

——1987, 'Models, "folk" and "cultural": Paradigms regained?' in D. Holland and N. Quinn (eds), *Cultural Models in Language and Thought*. Cambridge University Press, Cambridge, UK, pp. 369–93.

Kempton, W., Boster, J.S. and Hartley, J.A., 1995, *Environmental Values in American Culture*, MIT Press, Cambridge, MA.

Kusserow, A., 2004, *American Individualisms: Child Rearing and Social Class in Three Neighborhoods*, Palgrave Macmillan, New York.

Lakoff, G. and Johnson, M., 1980, *Metaphors We Live By*, University of Chicago Press, Chicago.

Lave, J., 1988, *Cognition in Practice: Mind, Mathematics and Culture in Everyday Life*, Cambridge University Press, Cambridge, UK.

Lave, J. and Wenger, E., 1991, *Situated Learning: Legitimate Peripheral Participation*, Cambridge University Press, Cambridge, UK.

Linde, C., 1993, *Life Stories: The Creation of Coherence*, Oxford University Press, New York.

McCollum, C., 2002, 'Relatedness and self-definition: Two dominant themes in middle-class Americans' life stories', *Ethos* 30 (1–2), 113–39.

Mandler, G., 1984, *Mind and Body: The Psychology of Emotion and Stress*, Norton, New York.

Mathews, H.F., 1992, 'The directive force of morality tales in a Mexican community', in R.G. D'Andrade and C. Strauss (eds), *Human Motives and Cultural Models*, Cambridge University Press, Cambridge, UK, pp. 127–62.

Mattingly, C. and Garro, L., 2000, *Narrative and the Cultural Construction of Illness and Healing*, University of California Press, Berkeley.

Nardi, B.A., 1996, 'Studying context: A comparison of activity theory, situated action models, and distributed cognition', in B. Nardi (ed.), *Context and Consciousness: Activity Theory and Human-Computer Interaction*, MIT Press, Cambridge, MA, pp. 69–102.

Price, L., 1987, 'Ecuadorian illness stories: Cultural knowledge in natural discourse', in D.C. Holland and N. Quinn (eds), *Cultural Models in Language and Thought*, Cambridge University Press, Cambridge, UK, pp. 313–42.

Quinn, N., 1991, 'The cultural basis of metaphor', in J. Fernandez (ed.), *Beyond Metaphor: Trope Theory in Anthropology*, Stanford University Press, Stanford, CA, pp. 56–93.

——1992, 'The motivational force of self-understanding: Evidence from wives' inner conflicts', in R.G. D'Andrade and C. Strauss (eds), *Human Motives and Cultural Models*, Cambridge University Press, Cambridge, UK, pp. 90–126.

——1996, 'Culture and contradiction: The case of Americans reasoning about marriage', *Ethos* 24, 391–425.

——1997, 'Research on shared task solutions', in C. Strauss and N. Quinn, *A Cognitive Theory of Cultural Meaning*, Cambridge University Press, Cambridge, UK, pp. 137–88.

——2005a, 'How to reconstruct schemas people share, from what they say', in N. Quinn (ed.), *Finding Culture in Talk: A Collection of Methods*, Palgrave Macmillan, New York, pp. 35–81.

——2005b, 'Introduction', in N. Quinn (Ed.), *Finding Culture in Talk: A Collection of Methods*, Palgrave Macmillan, New York, pp. 1–34.

——2011a, 'Event Sequencing as an Organizing Cultural Principle', *Ethos* 39 (3): 249–278.

——2011b, 'The history of the cultural models school reconsidered: A paradigm shift in cognitive anthropology', in D.B. Kronenfeld, G. Bennardo, V.C. de Munck and M.D. Fischer (eds), *A Companion to Cognitive Anthropology*, Wiley-Blackwell, Malden, MA, pp. 30–46.

Quinn, N. and D. Holland, 1987, 'Culture and cognition', in D.C. Holland and N. Quinn (eds), *Cultural Models in Language and Thought*, Cambridge University Press, Cambridge, UK, pp. 3–40.

Romney, A.K., Weller, S.C., Batchelder, W.H., 1986, 'Culture as Consensus: A Theory of Culture and Informant Accuracy', *American Anthropologist* 88, 313–38.

Rumsey, A., 1990, 'Wording, meaning, and linguistic ideology', *American Anthropologist*, 92(2), 346–61.

Silverstein, M., 1979, 'Language structure and linguistic ideology', in P.R. Clyne *et al.* (eds), *The Elements: A Parasession on Linguistic Units and Levels*, Chicago Linguistic Society, Chicago, pp. 193–247.

Sperber, D., 1985, 'Anthropology and psychology: Towards an epidemiology of representations', *Man* 20, 73–89.

Stocking, G., 1992, 'Polarity and plurality: Franz Boas as psychological anthropologist', in T. Schwartz, G.M. White, C.A. Lutz (eds), *New Directions in Psychological Anthropology*, Cambridge University Press, Cambridge, UK, pp. 311–23.

Strauss, C., 1992, 'What makes Tony run? Schemas as motives reconsidered', in R.G. D'Andrade and C. Strauss (eds), *Human Motives and Cultural Models*, Cambridge University Press, Cambridge, UK, pp. 197–224.

——2004, 'Cultural standing in expression of opinion', *Language in Society* 33(2), 161–94.

——2005, 'Analyzing discourse for cultural complexity', in N. Quinn (ed.), *Finding Culture in Talk: A Collection of Methods*, Palgrave Macmillan, NY, pp. 203–42.

——2007, 'Blaming for Columbine: Conceptions of agency in the contemporary United States', *Current Anthropology* 48(6), 807–22.

——2012, *Making Sense of Public Opinion: American Discourses about Immigration and Social Programs*, Cambridge University Press, New York.

Strauss, C. and Quinn, N., 1997, *A Cognitive Theory of Cultural Meaning*, Cambridge University Press, Cambridge, UK.

Tyler, S.A., 1978, *The Said and the Unsaid: Mind, Meaning, and Culture*, Academic Press, New York.

Tylor, E.B., 1871, *Primitive Culture: Researches into the Development of Mythology, Philosophy, Religion, Langue, Art, and Custom*, John Morrow, London.

Vygotsky, L.S., 1962, *Thought and Language*, E. Hanfmann and G. Vakar (eds), MIT Press, Cambridge, MA.

——1978, *Mind in Society: The Development of Higher Psychological Processes*, M. Cole, V. John-Steiner, S. Scribner and E. Souberman (eds), Harvard University Press, Cambridge, MA.

Wallace, A.F.C. and Atkins, J., 1960, 'The meaning of kinship terms', *American Anthropologist* 62, 58–80.

White, G.M., 1987, 'Proverbs and cultural models: An American psychology of problem solving', in D.C. Holland and N. Quinn (eds), *Cultural Models in Language and Thought*, Cambridge University Press, Cambridge, UK, pp. 151–72.

Whorf, B.L., 1956 (1940), 'Science and linguistics', in J.B. Carroll (ed.), *Language, Thought, and Reality: Selected Writings of Benjamin Lee Whorf*, MIT Press, Cambridge, MA.

Woolard, K.A., 1998, 'Introduction: Language ideology as a field of inquiry', in B.B. Schieffelin, K.A. Woolard and P.V. Kroskrity (eds), *Language Ideologies: Practice and Theory*, Oxford University Press, Oxford.

PART VI

Language and culture in applied domains

PART VI

Language and culture as applied domains

27

LANGUAGE AND CULTURE IN SECOND LANGUAGE LEARNING

Claire Kramsch

The teaching of culture in foreign language (FL) learning is facing new challenges associated with the globalization of linguistic and cultural exchanges across the world. The proliferation of global media and electronic social networks, the fragmentation within national boundaries of majority and minority languages, foreign, second and heritage language learners, and, beyond national boundaries, the deterritorialization of national languages and their cultural characteristics due to increased migration and the formation of diaspora communities – all these developments have transformed the nature and the role of culture in FL learning. What used to be the cultural and historical context in which languages were taught and used has now become truncated memories and projected stereotypes, constructed in and through discourses whose authenticity is uncertain as they are both local and global, real and imagined. I first pass in review the changes that have occurred in the last thirty years, I then examine the paradoxes and the challenges of the language–culture duo in FL learning today. Finally I explore some of the suggestions that have been made for redefining the relationship of language and culture in FL education.

1 Language and culture: the uncontested duo

In the twentieth century, language in FL learning was seen as indissociable from culture. Based on the eighteenth-century view that 'every nation speaks … according to the way it thinks and thinks according to the way it speaks' (Herder cited in Kramsch, 2004), it was taken for granted that speech communities, whether they be nationally, regionally, or ethnically defined, were held together not only by a common language but also by common ways of thinking, behaving and otherwise making sense of the world – in other words their 'culture'. If speech communities differed, it was not only because of their different linguistic systems but also because of the different speech habits of their native speakers/writers and their way of life. The speech habits of native speakers in formal, written, or academic situations were captured by the big C culture of literature and the arts, the speech habits of native speakers in informal conversations were captured by the little c culture of everyday life (Kramsch, 1993, 1998).

Until the 1960s, the focus in FL learning was placed on big C culture. The traditional *raison d'être* of learning foreign languages was to be able to one day read the foreign literature in the original, become a cultured, educated person, and be able to hold sophisticated conversations with educated native speakers. After the communicative revolution of the 1960s, little c culture came into focus as did the need to be communicatively competent when interacting with native and other non-native speakers in everyday life. Little c culture took the form of pragma-linguistic and sociopragmatic competence and the ability to use language in culturally appropriate ways. In communicative language teaching, the link between culture and discourse was made explicit (Scollon, Scollon, and Jones, 2012), so that intercultural competence came to be equated with interdiscursive competence (Young, 2009). Some scholars have distinguished between foreign language study that includes both big c and little c culture, and second language learning that deals with the little c culture of homes and workplaces (Gass and Selinker, 2008). But the distinction is not clear cut in the context of general education and is, rather, symptomatic of a growing trend to de-school language learning and replace it with apprenticeship in an authentic immersion context or community of practice.

Note that, whether culture was seen as mostly literate (as in 'literature and the arts') or mostly oral (as in 'way of life'), it was always considered to be the shared characteristic of a homogeneous speech community, whose members had a common way of remembering the past, defining the present and imagining the future. That speech community occupied an identifiable place on the map, which was outside the learner's national borders in the case of foreign languages, or inside these borders but in minority enclaves in the case of heritage languages. Even for an international language like English, English was taught around the world as the language of native speakers living in Kachru's first circle countries (Kachru, 1990) – the UK, the USA, or Australia, and their respective national cultures.

The cultural component of FL learning was, in the twentieth century, relatively easy to identify. Applied linguistic research focused on operationalizing various kinds of cultural competence in a foreign language. Cross-cultural pragmatics explored the dimensions of pragmatic appropriateness across cultures or culturally different ways of realizing speech acts (see, e.g., Blum-Kulka *et al.*, 1989), while research on the intercultural (Byram, 1997; Kramsch, 2012b; Risager, 2007) and the transcultural (Kramsch, 2010; MLA, 2007) focused on the exchange of linguistic, ideational, and economic resources in a world of increased international relations.

The conception of culture discussed above is a modernist conception (see Kramsch 2009a, 2012a) that is still with us today. Even though 'culture' remains for many language teachers difficult to define and to operationalize in the classroom, it is still talked about as 'membership in a discourse community that shares a common social space and history, and common imaginings. Even when they have left that community, its members may retain, wherever they are, a common system of standards for perceiving, believing, evaluating, and acting. These standards are what is generally called their 'culture' (Kramsch 1998: 10). Language learners are well aware that the linguistic structures they are learning have a different meaning for native speakers than they have for them, who come from a different discourse community with different cultural standards. The pleasure – and the difficulties – of learning another language come not from differences in structure but from differences in the semiotic value attached to these structures.

The National Standards promoted by the American Council for the Teaching of Foreign Languages (ACTFL) represented a modernist view when they proposed their five C goals of foreign language learning in the US:

> *Communication*: communicate, i.e., provide and obtain information, express feelings and emotions, and exchange opinions, in languages other than English.
> *Cultures*: gain knowledge of and understand the relationship between the practices and perspectives of the cultures studied.

Connections: connect with other disciplines and acquire information through the foreign language.

Comparisons: develop insight into the nature of language and culture through comparison with your own.

Communities: participate in multilingual communities at home and around the world, both within and beyond the school setting.

(ACTFL, 1996)

These standards, that are still applied today in teacher training and textbook writing, make three assumptions about language and culture, learners of language and culture, and language and culture education. The first assumption is that language is a direct gateway to and expression of culture ('The study of another language enables students to understand a different culture *on its own terms*' (ibid.: 43)). Culture is 'generally understood to include the philosophical perspectives, the behavioral practices, and the products – both tangible and intangible – of a society' (ibid.: 43). Perspectives (meanings, attitudes, values, ideas), practices (patterns of social interactions), and products (books, tools, foods, laws, music, games) constitute 'the true content of the foreign language course, i.e., the cultures expressed through that language' (ibid.). According to this definition, mastery of a foreign grammar and lexicon will give the learner access to, connection with and even participation in 'the global community and marketplace' (ibid.: 7). The second assumption is that 'all students can be successful language and culture learners' and that 'all can benefit from the development and maintenance of proficiency in more than one language' (ibid.). This assumption reaffirms the multicultural nature of American society and includes heritage language learners in the efforts to contribute to the global linguistic and cultural diversity. The third assumption is that language and culture education contributes to the enhancement of the two main tenets of American public school education: 'basic communication skills and higher order thinking skills' (ibid.: 7).

In sum: a twentieth-century view of FL learning has been called 'modernist' in that it assumes a positivistic, objective link between one language and one culture. It is predicated on the following tenets:

- Language is a tool to express pre-existing thoughts, a neutral conduit for the transmission of ideas and intentions.
- The meaning of words is enclosed in grammars and dictionaries and can find its rough equivalents in the dictionaries of another language.
- Communication is mostly about the accurate, concise, and effective exchange of information.
- Cultures are clearly bounded by territorial, ethnic or ideological boundaries.
- Cultures can be compared by comparing, for example, verbal and non-verbal behaviours in one's own and in the target culture.
- Communities have their rules of behaviours that need to be observed if communication is to proceed smoothly.

2 The new global age

Since the late 1980s, which scholars agree is the time when economic globalization took off (Cameron, 2006), the deregulation of business and commerce has accelerated the mobility of people and capital around the globe (for a discussion of the sociolinguistics of globalization, see Blommaert, 2010). It has been facilitated in part by the new global information technologies, global media, and a neo-liberal ideology of a free market entrepreneurial culture that has taken over all sectors of public life, including education, in this era of late capitalism (Block *et al.*, 2012; Heller, 2003; Ward, 2011). As Heller and Duchêne (2012) describe it, globalization has weakened the traditional role of the nation state's schools as monolingual gatekeepers of the citizens' grammatical accuracy and pragmatic appropriateness and as the exclusive warrant of legitimate literacy practices. Corporate interests have far outpaced national interests in promoting a different kind of literacy and communicative competence – one based less on cultural pride and more on commercial profit.

In a perspective based on cultural pride, learning another language is getting access to a wealth of historical knowledge, a culture shaped by centuries of language use by members of the same national, regional or ethnic community, who take pride in their membership in that community. Words have a cultural meaning that is shared by the members of the community, they refer to and evoke a way of categorizing reality, of conceptualizing experience, of mediating thoughts, emotions, memories, and fantasies (Kramsch, 2009b) that is common to all speakers within the well-bounded 'imagined communities' (Anderson, 1983) evoked by maps and other territorial materialities.

By contrast, in a perspective based on individual profit, learning another language is acquiring a skill that will enable learners to gain access to resources that give them more social power, and more freedom to play with the constraints imposed by the social and cultural structures of society. Language is seen less for its use value than for its exchange value (Heller, 2003), i.e., it gives its users a profit of distinction on the market of symbolic exchanges. While learners may learn a language less to read its literature in the original than to gain an edge on the job market or in the competition to enter graduate school, pride and profit need not be exclusive from one another. Pride in one's knowledge of the literate culture may be turned into a profit for foreign language learners seeking employment and commercial profit can boost the ethnic pride of heritage language learners (Heller, 2003).

In the new global economy, becoming bi- or multilingual increases one's semiotic potential and one's ability to carve out for oneself a hybrid identity that is at once multiple, changing, and conflictual (Norton, 2000). This new subjective and highly symbolic way of making meaning does not do away with the historical and material realities of what constituted communication, language, and culture in local contexts. It has only resignified them within another, more global culture of linguistic and cultural participation, social profit and economic power. Within educational institutions this global culture is restructuring the very knowledge we research and teach (Ward, 2011). The new meaning of communication, language, and culture has to be apprehended within a postmodernist framework that is used below.

Communication

In communicative language teaching in the eighties, communication was understood as the 'interpretation, expression, and negotiation' of intended meanings and language learning was seen as 'learning how to communicate as a member of a particular socio-cultural group' (Breen and Candlin, 1980: 90). Communication was seen as not only following the social conventions of the group but 'also of negotiating through and about the conventions themselves' (ibid.). It thus included a strong element of reflexivity in an attempt to interpret and negotiate cross-cultural differences, a two-way exchange of views on how to proceed. Under the influence of global media, neo-liberal ideology, and the proliferation of electronic social networks, communication across cultures has come to mean less an arduous effort at interpretation and negotiation of intended meanings than social contact and the sharing of what Castells calls 'the value of communication' itself (2009). Human contact, that has become less dependent on face-to-face interaction and happens increasingly on line, is now sought for its own sake, not for the sharing of cultural values or a deep engagement with difference, but for phatic communion, displays of knowledge or affection, impression management, and group affiliation or identification (see Magnan *et al.*, 2014). Communication in this new age has become mostly: presentation of self, participation, playfulness, and an increased tendency to use multiple codes and modalities to bring one's message across.

But there is a concern that FL learning is becoming impoverished in the process. The growing commodification of English as a global skill risks spreading to other languages that might also be learned not as cultural but as instrumental languages, unless they are heritage languages. In answer to the question: 'Is English as a lingua franca a threat to national languages and to multilingualism?', some scholars, like Juliane House, see a welcome division of labour between 'languages for communication' and 'languages for identification' (2003: 556). According to her, English as a lingua franca (ELF) is linked not so much to a speech community as to a 'community of practice', characterized by 'mutual engagement, joint negotiated enterprise and a shared repertoire of negotiable resources' (ibid.: 572). As such, ELF 'can be seen as strengthening the complementary need for native local languages that are rooted in their speakers' shared history, cultural tradition, practices, conventions, and values as identificatory potential' (ibid.: 562). The risk, however, is that it might devalue native local languages precisely by confining them to the local while confirming the pre-eminence of English on the global stage.

Communication in a global age is thus both transmission of facts and participation, both sharing of content and self-positioning. It is as much about acquiring a voice and making yourself heard, as it is about negotiating differences in intended meaning (Hull *et al.*, in press). For L2 learners, it is about the construction and re-construction of selves in dialogue with others (Pavlenko and Lantolf, 2000). The emancipatory potential of such a concept of communication and its potential for greater power and control is what distinguishes it from its modernist counterpart that saw in communication mainly an exchange of factual information.

Language

Second language acquisition research has been predicated on the notion that the target language is a coherent, intricate linguistic system that is to be acquired incrementally over several years following natural sequences of acquisition in interaction with speakers of the language. A learner's interlanguage has been viewed as approximating ever more closely the language of the native speaker (NS). To the development of grammatical competence communicative language teaching added a sociolinguistic, pragmatic, discourse, and strategic competence that understands language as language-in-use. Besides grammatical and lexical structures, language came to include also speech functions, politeness strategies, discourse skills such as cohesion, genre, and register manipulation, schemas of interaction and interpretation, learning and communication strategies, and literacy practices of various kinds.

While modernist conceptions of language learning still consider the monolingual NS as the model language user and the target of instruction, late modernist views have problematized the monolingual speaker as an appropriate model for a learner who, by definition, is striving to become bilingual, not doubly monolingual. In a global world of multilingual encounters, is it even desirable to teach the totality of one linguistic system? SLA researchers like Lourdes Ortega have reconceptualized SLA research as an apprenticeship in bilingualism (2012) and most foreign language educators today would agree that learning another language is learning to make meaning in multiple ways, not just in a different code (English, French, German) but also in different modes (spoken, written, virtual) and modalities (verbal, visual, musical) (see Kress, 2010). Some researchers argue that what L2 learners need in a global world is not knowledge of whole linguistic systems, but a variety of linguistic repertoires (Cenoz and Gorter, 2011), also called by Blommaert 'truncated repertoires' (Blommaert, 2010: 23) or disposable linguistic resources that can be activated according to the needs of the moment.

Where does all this leave the language learner in the twenty-first century? The growing diversification of learners' needs, interests and opportunities around the world have made it difficult to use the same definition of language in all FL learning contexts. For some, language will be seen as a skill to establish contact, make friends, and participate in global exchanges using a variety of verbal and non-verbal resources. For others, language will be the entrance to another cultural community in a specific local context. For yet others, it will be seen as giving access to the high culture of literature and the arts. These different conceptions of what language is do not easily map out on different levels of instruction, as the differential reception of the ACTFL National Standards (1996) and the MLA Report (2007) in the US seem to suggest, e.g., language as skill for elementary and secondary education, and language as cultural study for post-secondary education. For example, some schools are primarily interested in providing skills for the immediate job market while others are more interested in giving their students an all-purpose general education. Each educational context requires a different pedagogic approach and different criteria of success. Hence the need to localize methods and materials and train teachers to deal with a variety of contexts of language use.

Culture

Before the 1980s, as mentioned above, getting to know a foreign culture was the uncontested rationale for learning a foreign language. Culture was seen as composed of: material artefacts, customs of everyday life, often called 'food, fairs and folklore' and was therefore seen as rather separate from language. Because of the increased pressure to produce learners with a usable language proficiency or communicative competence, language teachers increasingly complained of a lack of time to teach culture. Communicative activities in the classroom took up so much of lesson time! Many students themselves resented having culture forced upon them (Chavez, 2002; Byram and Kramsch, 2008) when all they wanted was the ability to communicate and interact with young people from around the world. Thus, despite decades of research on the nature and the role of culture in FL learning, there is still a great deal of ambiguity regarding the obligation to teach culture in foreign language classrooms.

However, advances in cognitive science, sociolinguistics, and linguistic anthropology in the last twenty years have brought the teaching of language and the teaching of culture closer together. It is now a widely recognized fact that language and thought are closely related to one another in the brain and that we apprehend reality through conceptual metaphors expressed in verbal terms (Lakoff, 1987). The words we use to characterize people, things, and events are in fact categories of the mind that reveal a great deal about a speaker's way of cutting up and thus of making sense of social reality. Culture is no longer just the objective way of life of a certain speech community but the subjective way in which the members of that community give meaning to events. It's the meaning that constitutes the culture, not the artefacts themselves. That meaning is sometimes conventionalized through schooling, the media and commercial stereotypes, but most of the time it is idiosyncratic, emerging from dialogic interaction among people in conversation. It is therefore variable and up for interpretation.

The current perplexity of language teachers regarding the teaching of culture is a sign of how hybrid national cultures have become, how fluid the boundaries are now between lived culture and the culture represented on the screen, between the real and the virtual. What Thurlow and Jaworski call 'tourism discourse' (2010) has permeated the textbooks and the websites of the internet. As a metaphor for a neo-liberal mindset, tourism discourse denotes less actual tourists' ways of talking than a way of interacting with places and people based on playful, fleeting encounters without any desire to negotiate, let alone resolve, differences in meaning. It encourages a tourist gaze that 'seeks *encounters* not relationships, *contact* not engagement, *service* not commitment' (ibid.: 235). This sobering view of culture is countered by language educators who applaud the greater accessibility of foreign cultures provided by computer environments and their promise of 'authentic' human contact. But beyond contact, engaging with and understanding other world-views has become a much more complex endeavour given the growing diversity and semiotic uncertainty both within nations and among different communities, groups, and generations.

In sum: the twenty-first-century view of FL learning captured in this section has been called 'postmodernist' in that it assumes a relational, subjective link between language and culture. It is predicated on the following tenets:

– Language is a social semiotic that both expresses and constructs emergent thoughts, a process in which identities are constructed through repeated subject positionings according to the demands of the situation.
– The meaning of words depends on who speaks to whom about what under which circumstances.
– Communication is an attempt to shape a context in which words will help categorize social reality and evoke meanings that will, it is hoped, be shared among the participants.
– Cultures are portable schemas of interpretation of actions and events that people have acquired through primary socialization and which change over time as people migrate or enter into contact with people who have been socialized differently.
– Cultures can be compared only if the totality of their contexts of use is taken into account.
– Communities in an era of globalization have become too hybrid and too complex to have well-defined rules of behaviours that need to be observed if communication is to proceed smoothly. Pragmatic appropriateness must now be negotiated on a case by case basis.

Postmodernist views have not replaced modernist views on language and culture. Even though modernist views might not correspond to the current global reality, they still survive and get resignified in the memories of teachers, textbooks, movies and novels; they are reproduced in marketing stereotypes and brand logos.(1)

3 New ways of conceiving of the relation of language and culture in FL learning

The challenge

FL learning today is caught between the need to acquire 'usable skills' in predictable cultural contexts and the fundamental unpredictability of global contexts. Foreign language teaching is caught between the need to teach an academic literacy that learners can share with educated native speakers in Paris and Berlin and the realization that most of those educated native speakers now all speak English. Much of the little c culture of everyday life has been infiltrated by a global culture of consumerism that is no longer specific to any particular country. It has become difficult to reconcile the local and the global, the traditionally monolingual mandate of FL education ('you study French in order to get to know the French') and the multilingual realities of our age ('you study French in order to be able to speak with Koreans, Africans, or Tunisians, to code-switch between French, English, Korean, Swahili or Arabic'). Today, FL study is torn between its national premise and its transnational/global entailments. In the words of a teacher of Russian at an American university:

> My problem is that I am not sure *what* we should be teaching in college language classes – mostly because we do not have a specific task anymore such as getting the students ready to read Russian literature or do Russian linguistics. It is not clear that we are getting them ready to go to Russia or talk to Russians either. I feel like I am trying to do everything to try to make it the richest experience I can in as many ways as possible, but with not enough time.

Hence the major paradox with which the teaching and learning of foreign languages at secondary and post-secondary institutions around the world is confronted. On the one hand, mindful of their mission to teach the national language, literature, and culture of a given national speech community, teachers strive to impart a mastery of the standard language that will enable learners to become educated users of the language, to communicate with native speakers and to read the literature written by and for native speakers. On the other hand, as global communications have become more and more multimodal and multilingual and potential interlocutors are not necessarily monolingual native nationals but other multilingual non-native speakers, foreign language learners have to learn, as the 2007 MLA Report advocates, how to 'operate between languages' (ibid.: 35), i.e., how to develop a linguistic and cultural competence across multilingual contexts. While this multilingual imperative has been the theme of a special issue of the *Modern Language Journal* on multilingualism (Cenoz and Gorter, 2011), and while applied linguists have put forth a range of suggestions for embracing multilingualism, it has not yet been taken seriously by FL teachers in departments of foreign languages and literatures at educational institutions. How can FL teachers take into account the changing contexts of language use for which they are preparing their students, without losing the historical and cultural awareness that comes from studying one national language, literature and culture?

Solutions proposed

Several suggestions have been made to render the teaching of foreign languages more 'translingual and transcultural' (MLA 2007: 237). Some are a response to the ACTFL National Standards (Magnan *et al.*, 2014) and to the MLA Report (Phipps and Levine, 2010), others elaborate on the Common European Framework of Reference (Byram, 1997; Council of Europe, 2000), yet others come from scholars in literacy education interested in exploring the use of computer technology to teach language in new and more inclusive ways (Hull *et al.*, in press; Kern, 2012). I take each one in turn.

Revisiting ACTFL's National Standards (1996)

The National Standards for the teaching of foreign languages first published in 1996 by the American Council for the Teaching of Foreign Languages are now being revisited in light of globalization. If FL learning is claimed to give access to the five C's, then teachers should be aware that these five C's themselves may have acquired different meanings from when they were first used fifteen years ago. Each of the C's presents difficult challenges.

Communication, as mentioned above, used to mean the expression, interpretation, and negotiation of intended meaning. Now new information technologies and social networks have more often than not transformed information into info bites, feelings and emotions into emoticons, and the exchange of opinions into chat over likes and dislikes.

Cultures in FL education used to mean mostly national cultures; today the link between one national language and one national culture has been significantly weakened as people belong to different cultures and change cultures many times over the course of their lifetime. National cultures themselves have become hybrid and fragmented.

Connections with other disciplines, that led to the foreign-languages-across-the-curriculum (FLAC) efforts, are not as easy now that scholars are realizing how much their discipline is mediated by the language in which it is framed, and how different countries construct knowledge differently within different intellectual traditions. For example, Chinese history taught in Mandarin Chinese might be very different from the same history taught in English.

Comparisons of foreign cultures with American learners' own culture have become inordinately more difficult now that American society is more and more divided economically, socially and politically. What does it even mean for Americans to compare the foreign culture 'with their own'?

Communities are no longer bound by their national languages; speech communities have for the most part become deterritorialized, portable communities, real and imagined, that people carry in their heads. And, given the growth of anti-Americanism around the world, 'participating in communities around the world' has become a more complex and challenging enterprise.

While many of the changes brought about by globalization were slow in the making, we recognize them and they don't seem that unfamiliar. But the increase in the speed and scope of the change make visible some contradictions that would have been overlooked ten years ago, for example, *communication* now includes both eagerness for contact and fear of engagement and possible rejection; *cultures* indexes both embrace of diversity and fear of the foreign; *connections* entails both a call for more connections and the fear of losing control; *comparisons* means being able to see ourselves through the eyes of others and yet continue to believe in American exceptionalism; *communities* brings to the fore the paradox of both an eagerness to seize job opportunities on the global scene and the fear of having to compete with multilingual global actors.

Recently, Sally Magnan and her colleagues reported on a survey that revisits the ACTFL Standards (Magnan *et al.*, 2014) and the *Modern Language Journal* published a special issue to address the challenges and opportunities posed by globalization to FL education in the US (Kramsch, 2014).

Operationalizing the MLA Report and its recommendations (2007)

In the 2007 report of the Ad Hoc Committee on Foreign Languages of the American Modern Language Association, the goals of foreign language education at the college level are redefined in accordance with the increasingly interconnected world which we are preparing our students to enter.

> The language major should be structured to produce a specific outcome: educated speakers who have deep translingual and transcultural competence. Advanced language training often seeks to replicate the competence of an educated native speaker, a goal

that post-adolescent learners rarely reach. The idea of translingual and transcultural competence, in contrast, places value on the ability to operate between languages.

(MLA, 2007: 237)

This kind of foreign language education systematically teaches differences in meaning, mentality, and worldview as expressed in American English and in the target language. Literature, film, and other media are used to challenge students' imagination and to help them consider alternative ways of seeing, feeling, and understanding things. In the course of acquiring functional language abilities students are taught critical language awareness, interpretation and translation, historical and political consciousness, social sensibility, and aesthetic perception

(ibid.: 238).

It has only been five years since the publication of the MLA Report and already notions such as 'translingual and transcultural competence' and 'operating between languages' are in need of recontextualizing in the face of globalization. While the phrase 'translingual and transcultural competence' drew on Marie Louise Pratt's work in post-colonial studies and acknowledged the power and status differential between speakers of majority and minority languages, the spread of electronic social networks has levelled the communicative playing field and transformed the nature of communication across time and space. The use of computer-mediated communication to teach foreign languages has grown tremendously in the last five years; it is affecting students' social habitus and their conversational practices. Some educators (see Cenoz and Gorter, 2011) equate 'operating between languages' with code-switching and the situational use of various linguistic resources according to need, but more often than not it has to do with the much more complex task of managing various identities and group memberships that are sometimes incompatible.

The Report focuses on the dichotomous relation between an L1 and an L2 and seems to assume that there is a homogeneous C1 culture and an equally homogeneous C2 culture, and that each of them expresses itself through its respective national language. Today this view can seem too simplistic; however, it does put the emphasis not on the transmission of information or the solving of communicative tasks, but rather on understanding 'differences in meaning, mentality, and worldview', in part through a process of interpretation and translation.

Some FL scholars (e.g., Kern, 2000; Kramsch and Huffmaster, in press; Malinowski and Kramsch, 2014) have built on the MLA Report to propose a multilingual approach to the teaching of foreign languages that includes under multilingualism also: heteroglossia (or the ability to use multiple voices, registers, and styles), multiliteracy (or the ability to use various genres and create new ones), and multimodality (or the ability to make meaning not just through language but also through visuals, music, gestures, film, and video). If we extend the notion of translation to a pedagogic principle that leads to translingual and transcultural competence, then 'trans-lation' would become central to the multilingual mindset that teachers need to develop. It would mean systematically designing exercises in translation, transcription, transposition – exercises that would systematically practice the transfer of meaning across linguistic codes, discourse frames, media, and modalities.

Common European Framework of Reference (Council of Europe, 2000) and Byram's Five Savoirs (1997)

Globalization is also affecting the way the Common European Framework of Reference (CEFR) is interpreted, specifically the five *savoirs* identified by Byram (1997) as essential for the development of intercultural competence: *savoir, savoir comprendre/faire, savoir apprendre, savoir être,* and *savoir s'engager*. *Savoir être* involves 'attitudes of curiosity and openness, readiness to suspend disbelief about other cultures and beliefs about one's own'. *Savoir s'engager* as critical cultural awareness is 'the ability to evaluate, critically and on the basis of explicit criteria, perspectives, practices and products in one's own and other cultures and countries' (Byram, 2012). These last two *savoirs* imply an ethical and political vision of tomorrow's global citizen. In their recent work Byram (2012), Risager (2007), and Byram and Risager (1999) call for an 'engagement' that is at once knowledge and practice. *Savoir s'engager*, in particular, is a decentring process in which learners are to assess others' ways of living, to reflect on the criteria they are using and why they have chosen those criteria and not others, and to critique their own social group's ways of living. Learning is designed so as to put learners in contact with L2 speakers in real-world situations, much like service learning is meant to get college age students to use their L2 skills to help others in the community.

These goals of the CEFR apply mainly to adolescent FL learners at secondary institutions who are in the process of developing their own sense of identity and are thereby challenged to broaden their horizon through the acquisition of a systematically inculcated intercultural competence that will serve them well as citizens of a multilingual and multicultural Europe.

Revisiting L2 literacy practices and the use of language learning technologies

Globalization has not only changed our ways of speaking. Combined with global information technologies, it has also transformed the way we produce and use texts. Since FL learning is for a large part dependent on literacy practices of writing, reading, and exchanging texts of various kinds, research on L2 literacy is of crucial importance. As computer technology magnifies the parameters of social reality by compressing time and space and presenting us with a hyperreality that imitates the real, it both enhances and distorts communication. By eschewing the social pressure of face-to-face exchanges and by favouring anonymity, informal chat and free access to distant others, the computer with its email, blogs, and tweets has democratized the written word. By changing the temporal and spatial scale of human exchanges, and by making language endlessly retrievable, it has subtly transformed texts into hyper-'texts', book pages into web-'pages', real friends into Facebook-'friends'. Language has been complicit in this transformation as the same lexical categories are used for the real and the virtual, thus giving the virtual an appearance of authenticity that has been the object of controversy.

Language educators have quickly understood the immense benefit that electronic communication can bring to the teaching of literacy among underprivileged youth (Hull *et al.*, 2014) and to the teaching of L2 literacy and culture (Kern, 2014), but some concerns have been voiced that FL education might thereby lose the sense of the 'foreign' on which it has always been predicated (Malinowski and Kramsch, 2014).

Conclusion

Over the last thirty years globalization has changed the way we think and talk about language and culture in FL learning. With the mobility of goods and people across the globe, the immediate and constantly available connection with distant cultures, the global media, and the spread of electronic social networks, the triad: communication, language, and culture has changed meaning. This change is at once exciting and worrisome. On the one hand, globalization brings with it the prospect of increased participation, sense of community, plurality of voices, and human agency. It makes space for people to be heard and to change the culture of their everyday lives. It can potentially change the balance of power between the haves and the have-nots. On the other hand, globalization also ushers in the instrumentalization of language, a consumerist, touristic mindset, that goes hand in hand with greater competitiveness, and, ultimately, greater and more invisible power and control.

If culture is redefined as a meaning-making process, then it has to be seen as constructed by the speech acts and discursive practices of individual speakers and writers as they use the language and other symbolic systems for communicative purposes. Language teachers, who have to teach both the standard language and its variations in discourse cannot help but teach culture, even in its stereotypical forms. The challenge is how to seize the moment to move the students from the security of the stereotype to its exhilarating but risky variations, and how to engage them with the differences in world-views indexed by these variations.

Related topics

language and culture in intercultural communication; culture and language development; language, culture, and interaction; language, culture, and identity; the linguistic relativity hypothesis revisited; language, literacy and culture

Further reading

Blackledge, A. and Creese, A. (eds) (2014) *Heteroglossia as Practice and Pedagogy*. Berlin: Springer. (This edited collection provides an excellent overview of current thinking on multilingualism as not only diversity of codes, but complexity of various ways of making meaning).

Heller, M. (ed.) (2007). *Bilingualism: A social approach*. Basingstoke, UK: Palgrave Macmillan. (This volume provides a critical examination of the notion of bilingualism, moving it away from the coexistence of two linguistic systems to a set of socially and politically embedded language practices.)

Kramsch, C. (2009) 'Third culture and language education'. In V. Cook and L. Wei (eds) *Contemporary Applied Linguistics. Vol. 1 Language Teaching and Learning* (pp. 233–54) London: Continuum. (A literature review of the notion of 'third place' in FL learning and language education in general.)

Kramsch, C. and Whiteside, A. (2008) 'Language ecology in multilingual settings: Towards a theory of symbolic competence.' *Applied Linguistics* 29(4): 645–71. (A study of the multilingual practices of Yucatec Maya immigrants to San Francisco leads to a theory of symbolic competence, to supplement that of communicative competence in the multilingual and multicultural environments of today's globalized world.)

Weber, J.J. and Horner, K. (2012). *Introducing Multilingualism: A social approach*. London: Routledge. (An eminently accessible introduction to multilingualism from a sociolinguistic perspective, with abundant suggestions for discussion topics and fieldwork activities. Ideal for both undergraduate and graduate students.)

Note

1 The distinction made in this chapter between modernist and postmodernist views on language and culture are related to but slightly different from the one made by Wolf in this volume (see Chapter 30). Indeed, large-scale migrations and global modes of communication have produced language users whose cultural habitus is much more hybrid than it used to be, and whose behaviours and world-views must be understood not through reference to the culture of any particular social group but to memories, identifications, affiliations, and imagined identities that may be explored through critical discourse analysis (e.g., Blommaert, 2005) or cognitive linguistics (Fauconnier and Turner, 2002). Such a postmodernist stance, however, does not, as Wolf suggests, have a 'functionalist leaning' in the sense he gives to the term, i.e., an exclusive focus on communicative effectiveness. On the contrary, applied linguists who advocate a postmodernist approach to studying language in cultural contexts of use (e.g., Blommaert, 2005; Cameron, 2005; Kramsch, 2009c; McNamara, 2012; Pennycook, 2001) argue that the discourses and ideologies that give meaning to social reality are to be found simultaneously on

multiple timescales of experience that are sometimes in conflict with one another. A postmodernist pedagogy strives less for greater communicative effectiveness than for a greater awareness of the symbolic power of discourse to give meaning to our lives.

References

American Council for the Teaching of Foreign Languages (ACTFL) (1996) *Standards for Foreign Language Learning. Preparing for the 21st Century*. Yonkers, NY: ACTFL.

Anderson, B. (1983) *Imagined Communities. Reflections on the origin and spread of nationalism*. New York: Verso.

Block, D., Gray, J., and Holborow, M. (2012) *Neoliberalism and Applied Linguistics*. Abingdon, Oxon.: Routledge.

Blommaert, J. (2005). *Discourse*. Cambridge: Cambridge University Press.

——(2010) *The Sociolinguistics of Globalization*. Cambridge: Cambridge University Press.

Blum-Kulka, S., House, J. and Kasper, G. (eds) (1989) *Cross-Cultural Pragmatics: Requests and Apologies*. Vol. XXXI in the series of Advances in Discourse Processes, Roy O. Freedle (ed.). Norwood, NJ: Ablex.

Breen, M. and Candlin, C. (1980) 'The essentials of a communicative curriculum', *Applied Linguistics* 1(1): 97–112.

Byram, M. (1997) *Teaching and Assessing Intercultural Communicative Competence*. Clevedon, UK: Multilingual Matters.

——(2012) 'Reflecting on teaching "culture" in foreign language education', in D. Newby (ed.) *Insights into the European Portfolio for Student Teachers of Languages (EPOSTL)*. Newcastle: Cambridge Scholars Publishing.

Byram, K. and Kramsch, C. (2008) 'Why is it so difficult to teach language as culture?', *German Quarterly* 91(1): 21–35.

Byram, M. and Risager, K. (1999). *Language Teachers, Politics and Cultures*. Clevedon, UK: Multilingual Matters.

Cameron, D. (2005) 'Language, gender, and sexuality: Current issues and new directions', *Applied Linguistics* 26(4): 482–503.

——(2006) 'Styling the worker: Gender and the commodification of language in the globalized service economy', *Journal of Sociolinguistics* 4(3): 323–47.

Castells, M. (2009) *Communication Power*. Oxford: Oxford University Press.

Cenoz, J. and Gorter, D. (eds) (2011) 'Toward a multilingual approach in the study of multilingualism in school contexts', *Modern Language Journal*, special issue, 95(3): 339–43.

Chavez, M. (2002) 'We say "culture" and students ask "what?". University students' definition of foreign language culture', *Unterrichtspraxis* 35(2): 129–40.

Council of Europe (2000). *Common European Framework for Language Learning, Teaching and Evaluation*. Strasbourg: Council of Europe.

Fauconnier, G. and Turner, M. (2002) *The Way We Think. Conceptual blending and the mind's hidden complexities*. New York: Basic Books.

Gass, S. and Selinker, L. (2008) *Second Language Acquisition. An introductory course*. 3d edn. London: Routledge.

Heller, M. (2003) 'Globalization, the new economy, and the commodification of language and identity', *Journal of Sociolinguistics* 7(4):473–92.

Heller, M. and Duchêne, A. (2012) 'Pride and profit: Changing discourses of language, capital and nation-state', in Duchêne, A. and Heller, M. (eds) *Language in Late Capitalism. Pride and profit* (pp. 1–21). Abingdon, Oxon.: Routledge.

House, J. (2003) 'English as a lingua franca: A threat to multilingualism?' *Journal of Sociolinguistics* 7(4): 556–78.

Hull, G., Stornaiuolo, A., and Sterponi, L. (2014) 'Imagined readers and hospitable texts: Global youths connect online', in D. Alvermann, N. Unrau, and R. Ruddell (eds) *Theoretical Models and Processes of Reading* (6th edn). Newark, DE: International Reading Association.

Kachru, B. (1990) *The Alchemy of English: The spread, functions, and models of non-native Englishes*, Chicago, IL: University of Illinois Press.

Kern, R. (2000). *Literacy and Language Teaching*. Oxford: Oxford University Press.

——(2012) 'Teaching communication in a global age: new goals for language/culture teacher education', in H.W. Allen and H. Maxim (eds), *Educating the Future FL Professoriate for the 21st Century* (pp. 1–16). Boston, MA: Heinle.

——(2014) 'Technology as *pharmakon:* The promise and perils of the Internet for foreign language education', *Modern Language Journal*, special issue, 98(1).

Kramsch, C. (1993). *Culture and Context in Language Teaching*. Oxford: Oxford University Press.

——(1998) *Language and Culture*. Oxford: Oxford University Press.

——(2004) 'Language, thought, and culture', in A. Davies and C. Elder (eds) *The Handbook of Applied Linguistics* (pp. 235–61). Oxford: Blackwell.

——(2009a) 'Cultural perspectives on language learning and teaching', in W. Knapp and B. Seidlhofer (eds) *Handbook of Applied Linguistics* (pp. 219–46). Berlin: Mouton de Gruyter.

——(2009b). *The Multilingual Subject*. Oxford: Oxford University Press.

——(2009c) 'Discourse, the symbolic dimension of intercultural competence', in A. Hu and M. Byram (eds) *Intercultural competence and foreign language learning. Models, empirical studies, assessment* (pp. 107–22). Tübingen: Gunter Narr.

——(2010) 'Theorizing translingual/transcultural competence', in Phipps, A. and Levine, G. (eds), pp. 15–31.

——(2012a) 'Language, culture and context', in C. Chapelle (ed.) *Encyclopedia of Applied Linguistics. Vol. Language and Culture*, Karen Risager (ed.).

——(2012b) 'Teaching culture and intercultural competence', in C. Chapelle (ed.) *Encyclopedia of Applied Linguistics Vol. Language Learning and Teaching,* Lourdes Ortega (ed.).

——(2014) 'Teaching foreign languages in an era of globalization: Introduction', special issue, *Modern Language Journal* 98(1): 296–311.

Kramsch, C. and Huffmaster, M. (2014) 'Multilingual practices for the monolingual classroom', in Cenoz, J. and Gorter, D. (eds.) *Multilingual Education. Navigating between language learning and translanguaging.* Cambridge: Cambridge University Press.

Kress, G. (2010) *Multimodality. A social semiotic approach to contemporary communication.* London: Routledge.

Lakoff, G. (1987) *Women, Fire, and Dangerous Things.* Chicago, IL: University of Chicago Press.

McNamara, T. (2012) 'Poststructuralism and its challenges for applied linguistics', *Applied Linguistics* 33(5):473–82.

Magnan, S., Murphy D., and Sahakyan, N. (2014) *Goals of Collegiate Learners and the Standards for Foreign Language Learning. Modern Language Journal.* Vol. 98 Supplement.

Malinowski, D. and Kramsch, C. (2014) 'The ambiguous world of heteroglossic computer-mediated language learning', in Blackledge, A. and Creese, A. (eds) *Heteroglossia as Practice and Pedagogy* (pp. 155–178). Berlin: Springer.

MLA Ad Hoc Committee on Foreign Languages (2007) 'Foreign Languages and Higher Education: New Structures for a Changed World', *Profession 2007,* pp. 234–45.

Norton, B. (2000) *Identity and Language Learning.* London: Longman

Ortega, L. (2012) 'Ways forward for a bi/multilingual turn in SLA', in S. May (ed.) *The Multilingual Turn. Implications for SLA, TESOL and bilingual education* (pp. 32–53). Abingdon, Oxon.: Routledge.

Pavlenko, A. and Lantolf, J. (2000) ' Second language learning as participation and the (re)construction of selves', in Lantolf, J. (ed.) *Sociocultural Theory and Second Language Learning* (pp. 155–78). Oxford: Oxford University Press.

Pennycook, A. (2001) *Critical Applied Linguistics. A critical introduction.* Mahwah, NJ: Lawrence Erlbaum.

Phipps, A. and Levine, G. (eds) (2010) *Critical and Intercultural Theory and Language Pedagogy.* Boston, MA: Heinle.

Risager, K. (2007) *Language and Culture Pedagogy. From a national to a transnational paradigm.* Clevedon, UK: Multilingual Matters.

Scollon, R., Scollon, S.W. and Jones R.H. (2012) *Intercultural Communication. A discourse approach.* 3rd edn. Oxford: Wiley-Blackwell.

Thurlow, C. and Jaworski, A. (2010) *Tourism Discourse. Language and global mobility.* London: Palgrave Macmillan.

Ward, S. (2011) *Neoliberalism and the Global Restructuring of Knowledge and Education.* London: Routledge.

Young, R. (2009). *Discursive Practices in Language Learning and Teaching.* Malden, MA: Wiley Blackwell.

28

WRITING ACROSS CULTURES
'Culture' in second language writing studies

Dwight Atkinson

1 Introduction

For the past 50 years, culture has been one of the most contested concepts in Western academia. This is due in part to: (1) the notorious difficulty of defining the term (Williams 1983); and (2) its use as a causal explanation of individual behaviour. But certainly the biggest source of 'culture trouble' over the past half-century has been the development of anti-foundationalist, neo-Marxist, and postcolonial 'critical' philosophies, and their problematizing of the standard macro-variables of social science, including culture.

This chapter describes the complex career of the academic culture concept in one area of writing studies: second language writing (SLW). It begins with definition-oriented discussion of the two main concepts: 'culture' and 'second language writing/SLW'. It then describes historical perspectives on the culture–SLW connection. Next, it reviews critical problematizations of the culture concept in SLW, and, following that, current research on culture in the field. The chapter concludes with my personal thoughts on the future of the culture concept in SLW.

2 Definitions

Culture

As an academic concept, culture is largely the product of German–American cultural anthropology, as developed by Franz Boas and his students (Kuper 2000; Stocking 1967). The eighteenth-century German philosopher J. G. Herder had argued that each people possessed its own unique folk spirit, customs, and values, which were organically tied to its unique history and environment. As a result, there was no sense in which peoples could be judged superior or inferior – they were simply different. This nascent *cultural relativism* was developed further by the mid-to-late nineteenth-century Berlin school of ethnology, which opposed mainstream ethnology's – and contemporary mainstream society's – belief that different peoples existed at different levels of development on a universal scale of 'primitive' ← →'civilized'. Berlin school ethnologists argued instead that apparently distinct human groups were most likely hybrid amalgams, both physically/ ethnically through intermarriage and in their material products and beliefs, which were largely borrowed and adapted from others. If some societies appeared more advanced, it was primarily an accident of environment. The academic culture concept, then, in its natal form, was a counter-discourse to dominant discourses of inequality in human development and civilization: It viewed peoples as different in some ways but fundamentally equal.

This belief system travelled to the New World with Franz Boas, who emigrated to the US in 1886. There, he established 'cultural anthropology' as a leading approach in the comparative study of humankind. As the name suggests, culture was central to cultural anthropology because it explained the differences among human groups in the face of massive (pre/historical) hybridity, borrowing, and diffusion. That is, cultural groups differed primarily in the unique values and viewpoints they developed in engaging with their (human and nonhuman) environment, and the unique lifestyles and life worlds that resulted. It was through these that they asserted collective identities and established coherent communities.

This is not to suggest, however, that a single definition of culture ever existed in cultural anthropology or its precursors, as Kroeber and Kluckhohn (1952) amply demonstrated. At the same time, general tendencies can be identified: some early Boasians (e.g. Lowie 1920) emphasized the haphazard nature of cultural ingredients in keeping with their Berlin forbears; others (e.g. Sapir 1924) highlighted culture's unifying effects, foregrounding the Herderian concept of a psychologically binding 'genius of a people'. It is from this latter approach that more deterministic views of culture emerged (Stocking 1967). Thus, in her enormously influential *Patterns of Culture* (1934), Sapir's compatriot Ruth Benedict wrote:

> The life history of the individual is first and foremost an accommodation to the patterns and standards traditionally handed down in his [*sic*] community. From the moment of his birth the customs into which he is born shape his experience and his behaviour. By the time he can talk, he is the little creature of his culture, and by the time he is grown and able to take part in its activities, its habits are his habits, its beliefs his beliefs, its impossibilities his impossibilities.
>
> *(3)*

Although anthropologists continue to debate the culture concept today – to the extent, at least, that they still consider it relevant (Mazzarella 2004) – 'culturalist' views like Benedict's had spread across academia by the 1960s, especially in the US. Not coincidentally, this was exactly when and where SLW put down its first roots, as described in section 3.

Second language writing

By second language writing, I mean the field that studies writers writing in languages different to their first literate languages. Historically, the main focus of SLW was on university writers of English as a second/additional language (ESL), especially in the US. Two types of writing have typically been studied: (1) the 'general academic' (in fact often essayistic) writing elicited in US university 'first-year composition' courses, which virtually all undergraduates take; and (2) discipline-oriented writing, as taught especially to graduate students in the sciences, engineering, and medical professions. More recently, however, there has been increasing interest in SLW in K-12 settings, especially among systemic–functional linguists in Australia and literacy educators in North America and the UK.

Given SLW's applied nature, even its most theoretical products tend to concern pedagogy (e.g. Silva and Matsuda 2010). This fundamentally practical character distinguishes SLW from a main source discipline: composition studies (Santos 1992). Originally developed in the US to support first-year composition, composition studies was therefore pedagogically oriented. Over time, however, it became increasingly theoretical, due largely to its adoption of anti-foundationalist and critical philosophies (Fulkerson 2005). Some SLW scholars have followed suit, a fact directly influencing SLW's current theorization of culture, as described in sections 4 and 5 below.

3 Historical perspectives

Contrastive rhetoric

In 1966, the applied linguist Robert Kaplan published a paper entitled 'Cultural Thought Patterns in Intercultural Education'. This paper is significant because: (1) it was the first academic attempt to consider SLW issues seriously in their own right; and (2) it gave culture a central place in what eventually became the SLW field.

Kaplan hypothesized that second language (SL) writers deployed their native language's or culture's preferred rhetorical/organizational patterns when writing in English, and that, in order to help these writers adapt to US university norms, it was necessary to know what those patterns were. To find out, Kaplan extended the then-popular form of applied linguistic analysis known as *contrastive analysis* – the structural comparison of two languages to predict difficulties native speakers of one would have learning the other – to rhetorical organization, yielding a 'contrastive analysis of rhetoric' (ibid.: 15). Applying this method, Kaplan undertook a preliminary analysis of nine English texts/text-parts produced by or translated from first-language writers of non-English languages. He then summarized his findings in five self-admittedly crude and 'superficial' (ibid.: 14) diagrams – diagrams which have nonetheless been widely reproduced, cited, and critiqued.

In these diagrams, a vertical vector depicted the dominant rhetorical pattern of English – a linear/deductive organization; a set of parallel horizontal vectors connected by dashed lines characterized Semitic languages, signifying elaborate parallelism; an inward-turning vortex represented 'Oriental' languages, denoting 'approach by indirection' (ibid.: 10); a solid, vertically aligned zigzag line captured the dominant rhetoric of Romance languages, representing 'much greater freedom to digress' (ibid.: 12) than in English; and a partly solid, partly dashed vertically aligned zigzag line depicted Russian, which Kaplan characterized as digressive in a particular way: many grammatical structures were 'parenthetical amplifications of structurally related subordinate elements' (ibid.: 14).

As with much pioneering work, Kaplan's arguments were sweeping, speculative, sometimes contradictory, and lacked solid empirical support. For instance, while pointing out that his characterizations of different languages' rhetorical patterns were by no means unique or monolithic ('It is necessary to understand that these categories are in no sense meant to be mutually exclusive' (ibid.: 14)), he included the following statement: 'These paragraphs [i.e. examples] may suffice to show that each language and … culture has a paragraph order unique to itself' (ibid.). Likewise, the texts Kaplan analysed were truly miscellaneous: ESL student essays, Macaulay's *History of England*, the *King James Bible*, and English translations of a French philosophy essay and an item from a Russian periodical.

Kaplan's article was not initially popular, by his own account (personal communication 2005), but as the SLW field began to coalesce in the late 1970s it registered a modest impact. Its full force was felt only in the mid 1980s, however, probably because a distinct SLW emerged first under the banner of process writing, while Kaplan's paper was *product*-focused – exactly what the process movement was reacting against. The topic area initiated by Kaplan became known as *contrastive rhetoric* (CR).

Among CR's early proponents was John Hinds, a linguist of Japanese. In preliminary work, Hinds (1983a) described four 'major' Japanese expository prose forms, three differing substantially, in his view, from 'normal English rhetorical style' (ibid.: 80). This was followed by a more focused study (1983b), which began by critiquing Kaplan's use of SL essays to detect first language rhetorical patterns. Hinds's solution was to investigate one native rhetorical pattern – *ki-shō-ten-ketsu* – he had earlier identified in Japanese. According to Hinds, there were two major differences between 'English expository prose' and the four-part *ki-shō-ten-ketsu* pattern: (1) whereas *ki* and *shō* (roughly topic 'introduction' and 'development') resembled the dominant English pattern, *ten* ('twist' or 'turn') introduced new material providing an unexpected angle on the topic, leading to incoherence if judged by English standards; and (2) the *ketsu* ('conclusion'), while relating *ten* back to *ki* and *shō*, did not generally do so in a 'decisive' manner.

In a third paper, Hinds (1987) argued that *ki-shō-ten-ketsu* provided evidence that Japanese and English were positioned differently on a scale of 'reader versus writer responsibility'. Thus, while Japanese placed more interpretative responsibility on readers, English required writers to express themselves unambiguously, guiding their readers at every turn.

In other significant CR work in the 1980s and 1990s, Connor and Kaplan (1987) produced the first edited collection of CR-oriented papers; Mauranen (1993) highlighted genre effects on rhetorical style, finding 'culture-specific' differences in English versus Finnish academic writing; Li (1996) investigated contrasting definitions of 'good writing' in China and the US; Matsuda (1997) called for a more agentive and dynamic CR; and Connor (1996) summarized CR's findings circa 1995.

Non-CR work on culture and SLW

A fair amount of work on culture and SLW was done outside the CR paradigm in the 1980s and 1990s. This work is summarized here (see Atkinson, in press, for further details).

Shen (1989) described his struggle to respond to his US university writing teachers' encouragement to 'just be yourself' in his writing: 'In order to write good English, I knew that I had to be myself, which actually meant not to be my Chinese self. It meant that I had to create an English self and be that self' (ibid.: 461). Shen did so by resorting to such strategies as filling his compositions with 'I' and imagining himself crawling out of his old Chinese skin and into a new (presumably Western) one. Eventually, however, he made the transition, ultimately viewing it as additive growth rather than cultural imposition.

Scollon (1991) recounted his attempt to introduce process writing at a Taiwanese university. Two problems arose: (1) cultural differences in expression of self, wherein the self called for by process writing assumed a unique, creative, isolated inner being who resisted socially approved norms; and (2) an implicit essay structure differing markedly from the English deductive approach and taking its inspiration from the long-discredited Chinese *pa ku wen* form. In this approach, the author's thesis was muted, and occurred somewhere in the middle of the essay. Scollon related this directly to a deferential, socially embedded Chinese sense of self.

Carson (1992) reviewed literacy acquisition research on Japan and China that might inform SLW teaching. Findings included the centrality of memorization in learning; cooperation-building as the main purpose of group work versus group work for individual development in the US; and an emphasis on moral education. In follow-up research, Carson and Nelson (1996) studied how Chinese students perceived and performed their roles in 'peer response' groups in ESL writing classrooms, wherein the main purpose was to provide useful commentary on individual group members' drafts. These students generally avoided making critical comments.

Fox (1994), Ramanathan and Kaplan (1996), and Atkinson (1997) focused on 'critical thinking' in SLW, suggesting that the concept (properly understood) had particular cultural roots, and was thus not likely to be shared globally. Empirical studies by Atkinson and

Ramanathan (1995) among others seemed to point in a similar direction. Ramanathan and Atkinson (1999) argued that an ideology of individualism underlay major pedagogical principles/ practices of first-year composition, and might therefore prove problematic for some SL writers.

Pennycook (1996) investigated the notion of plagiarism from a cross-cultural perspective, tracing it back to the development of 'creative and possessive individualism' (212) in eighteenth-century Europe. In contrast, Chinese approaches to textual ownership, assumed by Westerners to promote plagiarism because they emphasized memorization, actually viewed memorization as the *basis* of creativity rather than its opposite. Pennycook also described informal interviews with Hong Kong university students accused of plagiarism, finding that the concept did little to explain their behaviour.

By way of concluding this section, it should be noted that virtually all the studies reviewed here either: (1) seem (albeit arguably) to have assumed a 'culturalist' understanding of culture – more or less similar to Benedict's (1932) top-down approach reviewed in section 1 above; or (2) defined it (again arguably) in explicitly 'culturalist' ways. Thus, Connor (1996) defined culture as 'a set of rules and patterns shared by a given community' (ibid.: 101), while Carson and Nelson (1996) contrasted 'individualist' and 'collectivist' cultures.

4 Critical issues and topics

Philosophical perspectives

The later 1990s marked the onset of a powerful critique of cultural research in SLW. According to Li (2008), this critique emanated from two main philosophical perspectives: the 'romantic–individualist' perspective of scholars like Zamel and Spack; and the poststructuralist and post-colonialist perspectives of scholars like Kubota, Canagarajah, and Benesch. Before reviewing research inspired by these perspectives, I will describe them, reconfiguring Li's latter category as 'anti-foundationalist, neo-Marxist, and postcolonial critical theory'. One caveat: none of the researchers mentioned here would likely accept my portrayal of their views.

'Romantic–individualist' signifies a view wherein the fundamental unit of humanity is the autonomous individual, who realizes her existence fully by striving to express a unique inner self. The romantic artist – the lone genius transforming life into art – was the likely prototype for this view, as developed by the German romantics (Berlin 2001). 'Authenticity' and 'inspiration' were this perspective's touchstones: discovering one's core self, and then expressing that self in a creative act, was the ultimate truth.

This view acquired a democratic cast in American pragmatic philosophy and progressivist education (Kalantzis and Cope 1993). It re-emerged in the 1960s as part of the writing process movement in composition studies. 'Expressivism' (Berlin 1988) was a pedagogy based on self-expression: 'Your authentic voice is that authorial voice which sets you apart from every other human being despite the common or shared experiences you have' (Stewart, in Bowden 1995: 175). As noted repeatedly since then, this supposedly pure personal expression had strong literary roots:

> If process teachers were reading what they took to be the direct and unmediated prose of personal experience, the most successful students were hard at work constructing the authorial persona of self-revelatory personal essays written in a decidedly non-academic style ... [thereby] reinstitut[ing] the rhetoric of the belletristic tradition at the centre of the writing classroom.
>
> *(Trimbur 1994: 110)*

The process writing proponents constituting SLW's first critical mass were heavily influenced by this approach (Ferris and Hedgcock 1998). How it supported cultural critique will be described in the next section.

By anti-foundationalist, neo-Marxist, and postcolonial critical theory, I mean, respectively: (1) poststructuralist and postmodernist critiques of the very foundations of modern Western civilization, particularly the notions of the rational, free-willed individual, civil societies with egalitarian power structures, and political, economic, and cultural systems proffering definitive 'regimes of truth' (e.g., democracy, science, capitalism, Marxism). Foucault's intertwined notions of *discourses* – authoritative knowledge-formations functioning as regimes of truth in modern society – and *power* – effects of discourses as internalized by individuals rather than imposed externally/from above – take precedence in this view; (2) versions of critical theory inspired by Karl Marx, but emphasizing 'superstructural' influences on human activity such as education and religion versus Marx's reliance on economic forces; and (3) postcolonial theories which rely substantially on the first two categories for their theoretical base.

Anti-foundationalist/neo-Marxist/postcolonialist-inspired critiques of culture are often combined in SLW and other fields. Edward Said's (1978) *Orientalism* is a standard bearer here, mixing Foucault's theory of discourses with Gramsci's neo-Marxist theory of hegemony to explain postcolonial conditions. But Foucault and other first-generation anti-foundationalists were implacably opposed to Marxism because it offered a single, definitive 'meta-narrative' (Lyotard 1984) of truth. Contemporary neo-Marxists have returned the favour, characterizing postmodernism as 'junk theory' (McLaren 2003: 1).

Romantic–individualist critiques of cultural research in SLW

The two most powerful romantic–individualist critiques of cultural research in SLW are Vivian Zamel's and Ruth Spack's, and they are closely related. Zamel (1997) began by questioning the cultural determinism seemingly inherent in studies of culture and SLW:

> Teachers and researchers who see students as bound by their cultures may be trapped by their own cultural tendency to reduce, categorize, and generalize … a stance that assumes that we can attribute a student's attempts in another language to that student's L1 background, and that … [that] background will be problematic and limiting.
>
> *(ibid.: 342–3)*

Zamel proceeded to critique research suggesting that critical thinking was difficult and perhaps 'inappropriate' for SL writers, likewise faulting pedagogies which substituted a 'cool, dispassionate, and rational' (ibid.: 343) form of academic writing for one wherein writers constructed their own identities and voices. On this basis she argued that 'transculturation' – 'the selective, generative and inventive nature of linguistic and cultural adaptation' (ibid.: 350) – was a better tool for understanding and teaching SL writers/writing than cultural/academic assimilation or acculturation. Zamel concluded with an important statement regarding culture:

> The reality of cultures is that they are highly unpredictable, 'elusive', even chaotic, that they are 'fictions people entertain about themselves and … other peoples' (Scheper-Hughes, 1995, p. 22). We need to remember that these fictions … are extensions of who we are … and that what we make of our students and their experiences may very well be an artifact of these influences.
>
> *(ibid.)*

Spack (1997) began her paper by suggesting that the language-focused labels commonly applied to ESL students – 'speakers of *other* languages', '*nonnative* speakers', '*limited English proficient*' – 'rhetorically construct [those students'] identities' (ibid.: 765) as deficient, and misrepresent who they really are. She then critiqued *cultural* labels because they 'ignore what anthropological theorists now identify as the 'blurred' spaces in which cultural identities are formed' (ibid.: 768). Next, Spack questioned Carson's (1992 – see above) review of literacy learning in China and Japan, arguing that she had constructed a monolithic Asian student incapable of expressing opinions, immersed in Confucian ethics, and unable to participate in classroom peer-response groups, as described above.

Spack then made a strong statement – 'Teachers and students need to view students as individuals, not as members of a cultural group, in order to understand the complexity of writing in a language they are in the process of acquiring' (ibid.: 771) – and discussed TESOL research which 'reveals the fluidity of culture' (ibid.). She concluded by arguing that SL students should be empowered to tell teachers who they are rather than having it decided for them, since such decision-making limits who they can be.

Anti-foundationalist/neo-Marxist/postcolonial critiques of cultural research in SLW

As mentioned at the beginning of this chapter, anti-foundationalist/neo-Marxist/postcolonial critical philosophies have presented the single greatest challenge to the culture concept over the last half-century. This is because they question the very idea of social and individual coherence and unity, and assert the determinative role of power and ideology in all sociocultural groups. In unpublished work, I call this a '*dis*-approach' to culture, in that it emphasizes *disunity, discrimination, difference, ideology.* and *domination*, versus a '*co*-approach', which emphasizes *coherence, community, cooperation*, and *consensus*. Ryuko Kubota is the leading scholar taking a *dis*-approach in SLW; examples of her work are reviewed next.

Kubota (1997) claimed that Hinds (as reviewed above) reduced all Japanese prose to a single rhetorical structure – *ki-shō-ten-ketsu* – thereby essentializing Japanese language and culture, which in reality are dynamic and diverse. (Note that Kubota's claim is incorrect as it stands – Hinds (1983a) originally introduced *four* Japanese *expository* prose forms, of which *ki-shō-ten-ketsu* was one, stating that they were all 'major styles' (ibid.: 79). Yet Hinds did focus almost exclusively on *ki-shō-ten-ketsu* in subsequent work, thus undoubtedly giving it more importance than it deserved.) Kubota went on to argue that the understanding of culture assumed in this view was one in which its conventions were 'unitary and homogeneous', whereas neo-Marxists (i.e. the authors cited to support this point, although not identified as such by Kubota) saw 'culture as a dynamic site of struggle in which social practices are constituted and transformed in asymmetric power relations' (ibid.: 464). Kubota next argued that Hinds had over-generalized his claim based on a single newspaper column with an entertainment function. She then introduced varying interpretations of *ki-shō-ten-ketsu* by Japanese textbook writers and rhetoricians, suggesting that written Japanese itself had been profoundly influenced by English. Kubota then concluded: by generalizing from a tiny sample to all Japanese texts, Hinds 'construct[ed] instead of discover[ed] cultural differences' (475), thereby overemphasizing difference and ignoring cultural/linguistic diversity.

Kubota (1998) empirically tested Kaplan's CR hypothesis by studying whether 46 Japanese college writers used the same or different rhetorical patterns when writing Japanese and English expository and persuasive texts. Her results showed that about half the students differed in their first-language versus SL writing in thesis placement/inclusion and overall rhetorical patterning, while about half did not. Although unable to generalize due to sample size, Kubota interpreted her results as suggesting a lack of stable first language/cultural influence, and therefore as evidence against CR. While anti-foundationalist/neo-Marxist/postcolonial arguments are not highlighted in this article, they are implicit throughout.

Kubota (1999) critically examined dichotomous representations of 'East' versus 'West' in culturally oriented SLW research, with specific reference to Japan. Taking a 'post-structuralist and post-colonial' perspective, she identified these representations with 'Orientalist discourse', as identified by Said (1978). As mentioned above, discourses are authoritative knowledges that assume the status of truth: in Said's view, virtually all Western descriptions of 'Asia' participate in Orientalist discourse, since they are based (however implicitly) on a binary contrast between creative, critical-thinking, agentive, democratic, and rational Westerners versus imitative, non-critical, passive, despotic, and emotional 'Asians'. Essentialized in this way, the stereotyped Asian becomes the Other – that which Western society defines itself as *not*. Insidiously, however, Orientalist discourse circulates back to the very peoples it others, becoming received knowledge for them also. By representing Asians in this way and then persuading them to buy into this representation, the West maintains hegemonic control.

Focusing largely on representations of Japanese education, Kubota undertook to investigate the construction of such authoritative knowledge in SLW/ESL. She pointed out that the dichotomy between educational cultures devoted to 'extending knowledge and preserving knowledge' (ibid.: 17), pervasive in SLW, did not apply unproblematically to the US versus Japan, since 'Japanese language education in the current curriculum ... strongly promotes logical thinking and self-expression' (ibid.: 18), while 'self-expression and critical thinking [in US universities] may reflect not reality but what Americans wish to achieve' (ibid.).

Kubota then argued that Orientalist representations had been internalized by Japanese people themselves via their theories of Japanese cultural uniqueness, or *nihonjinron*. Next, she reviewed educational literature throwing doubt on both SLW cultural research and *nihonjinron* – virtually identical in their characterizations of the Japanese – suggesting, for instance, that Japanese elementary education was anything but the memorization-based collectivist endeavour represented by Orientalist discourse. Kubota concluded by advocating 'critical multiculturalism' as a pedagogical alternative to assimilationist and (non-critical) pluralist approaches to ESL. In critical multiculturalism, culture and language are seen as sites of power and contestation – they must therefore be examined critically. Dominant codes and conventions should be taught, but their complicity in creating inequitable relations must be deconstructed, students must be enabled to develop their own voices, and 'fighting for the transformation of a cruel and unjust society' (Freire, in Kubota 1999: 28) must be placed on the educational agenda.

5 Current research

Relatively less SLW research has directly addressed the culture concept in the twenty-first century. This is perhaps unsurprising given the powerful critique it has undergone, both in SLW and beyond. In the very field which innovated the concept in fact – anthropology – culture has been 'half-abandoned' (Mazzarella 2004: 345). Within these limitations, current research on culture in SLW can be viewed as having two main strands: (1) continuation of the cultural critique described immediately above; and (2) counter-responses to such critique which attempt to salvage/reform the culture concept. Both areas are treated synoptically here (for more detail, see Atkinson, in press).

Cultural critique in SLW in the twenty-first century

Kubota (2002) examined competing discourses regarding Japanese cultural/linguistic uniqueness, focusing especially on writing in Japan. Her aim was to counter monolithic representations of Japanese culture, language, and rhetoric by investigating their complex and sometimes contradictory political/historical contexts. Kubota found that many Japanese scholars supported CR's claim that Japanese prose was vague and indirect, some regarding it as an essential flaw and others as an important cultural value. At the same time, the Japanese government was implementing educational policies emphasizing directness of expression, critical thinking, and debate – goals likewise reflected in Japanese-language writing handbooks. Kubota then introduced *kokusaika* ('internationalization'), a discourse designed to resolve these supposed contradictions: as simultaneously a powerhouse economy and client state of the US, Japan had to highlight its support for international trade and cooperation on an 'open-markets' model while at the same time maintaining its economic aggressiveness (including protection of its own markets – author's note). This would be done, in part, by educating its youth to articulate and defend Japan's delicate (and possibly unique) international position – a task requiring clear expression, debating ability, and critical thinking – for nationalist ends.

Kubota and Lehner (2004) proposed a 'critical contrastive rhetoric' based substantially on Kubota's earlier work. They offered nine guidelines to oppose, in their view, harmful elements of CR (see Atkinson 2012 for further details): (1) question the power of standard English, which supports assimilationism; (2) question monolithic, essentialized representations of culture and language – they are political; (3) question Orientalist representations of the exotic, inferior Other; (4) resist English-only pedagogies and celebrate students' linguistic diversity; (5) examine how powerful discourses may influence other languages to adopt English-like characteristics; (6) reject modern regimes of truth in favour of postmodernist understandings of knowledge as situated, partial, and dynamic; (7) View the classroom as a site of critical pedagogy, which disrupts the action of powerful texts and rhetorics; (8) honour students' natal languages and cultures, fostering cultural and linguistic complexity; and (9) promote students' agency in determining the role of English literacy in their lives.

In a series of publications, Suresh Canagarajah has argued for a view of multiple languages and cultures as deeply intermeshed, with this multilingual hybridity driving individuals' linguistic/rhetorical creativity. He opposes this view to the doctrine that different languages/ rhetorics are radically separate and unbridgeable, which he attributes to CR. Canagarajah's view reflects his own upbringing in the complex multilingual context of South Asia – a context doubtlessly closer to those of more of the world's population than relatively monolingual contexts like Japan's.

Canagarajah (2005) examined the writings of a Tamil Sri Lankan academic in three linguistic/ rhetorical situations: (1) writing for a local audience in Tamil; (2) writing for a local audience in English; and (3) writing for an international audience in English. He found greater commonalities between the first two texts, in which the languages were different but rhetoric similar, than between the second and third texts – both written in English but for different audiences. Canagarajah therefore concluded that multilingual writers agentively and strategically shift their rhetoric depending on context, thereby disconfirming the CR claim that each language/culture has a single, unique rhetoric. (Note that this is the same claim mistakenly attributed to Hinds by Kubota; while it was an (albeit inconsistent – see section 3 above) part of Kaplan's original formulation of CR half a century ago, I know of no one – including Kaplan himself – making this claim in recent years). The pedagogical lessons to be drawn, according to Canagarajah, are that linguistic/rhetorical conventions are negotiable, and that 'students can engage critically in the act of changing the rules and conventions to suit their values, interests, and identities' (ibid.: 603). In sum, 'a multilingual pedagogy of writing ... will treat the first language and culture as a resource, not a problem. We will try to accommodate diverse traditions – not keep them divided and separate' (ibid.).

Canagarajah (2013) presented a broader critique of CR's culture concept, using the construct of lingua franca English (LFE). Defined as English communication among 'non-native speakers', LFE problematizes the idea that English 'native speakers' own the language. Regarding culture, Canagarajah argued that: (1) the culture concept was irrelevant to most LFE interactions because speakers negotiated their own communicative norms rather than relying on those of a particular linguaculture; and (2) LFE speakers occasionally adopted the linguacultural practices of communities they were not born into. Culture was therefore not stable and static, but negotiated and emergent. In place of culture, Canagarajah proposed substituting the concept of 'cosmopolitanism', signifying the contact zone character of much linguistic interaction in the twenty-first century.

Critical responses to cultural critique in SLW

Critical responses to cultural critique in SLW have taken various forms. These include strong defences of the culture concept (e.g. Li 2005), partial reformulations of the concept based on its critique (e.g. Connor 2011), and attempts to use the concept in alternative ways or to investigate its varied incarnations (e.g. Atkinson 2004).

Atkinson (2003) suggested that one important use of culture in SLW was to turn it back on 'ourselves' – to investigate the culturally inflected practices of US university composition. The emphasis on a clear thesis stated early in the text and controlling all subsequent rhetorical elements, for instance, suggests writing that is 'in a hurry', can almost 'read itself', and is thus likely implicated in the efficient production of capital.

In a second article, Atkinson (2004) argued that culture had been left largely unconceptualized in CR, acting as an explanatory variable but not itself properly defined or investigated. He then reviewed various versions of the concept, expressed dichotomously (or in the first case trichotomously): (1) received/culturalist versus postmodernist versus cultural studies versions of culture; (2) process versus product views of culture; (3) cognitive versus social approaches to culture; and (4) big culture versus small culture (Holliday 1999). It bears restating (see section 1) that anthropologists themselves have never agreed on the meaning of the concept, and that it has been widely and variously used throughout academia in the last half-century.

Connor (2004) proposed to replace the term 'contrastive rhetoric' with 'intercultural rhetoric' (IR), partly in response to the many critiques of CR in the SLW field. To develop a broader agenda for IR, she adopted Sarangi's (2005) distinction between *cross-cultural* research, which produces useful but idealized descriptions of cultural practices, and *intercultural* research, which investigates cultural mixing and meshing. Connor called for both kinds of research in the new field of IR.

Li (2005) argued that principles of linguacultural fluidity and permeability (as foregrounded, for instance, in Canagarajah's and Kubota's work) were complementary rather than opposed to notions of fixity and borders. The flexible negotiation of discourse norms, for example, can only take place when there are norms to negotiate; and permeability cannot exist without borders. Li provided evidence from empirical studies she had conducted in China to support her argument. She also rejected the charge that cultural SLW research essentialized individuals because this 'implies that there is an essential self insulated from its context' (ibid.: 128).

Carson and Nelson (2006) acknowledged the contribution of cultural critique to SLW, while noting that culture was now apparently either being avoided in the field or replaced by concepts like identity and discourse. They also defended the use of cultural dichotomies like 'individualism versus collectivism', if treated non-deterministically and non-evaluatively, and called for research on peer review groups from critical perspectives.

Li (2008) divided SLW's cultural critics into two main camps: the romantic–individualist and the postmodernist/postcolonialist (see section 4 above). She argued that both groups' vision of a cultureless world was still based on a modernist dichotomy (i.e. culture versus no culture) and did not accord with her own research results wherein culture and globalization functioned hand in hand.

Finally, Connor (2011) attempted to rework the culture concept from an IR perspective, using the metaphor of patchwork to describe her own 'individual-cultural' (Atkinson 1999) identity. Connor's natal Finnish culture represented the largest patch, on which numerous smaller patches – e.g. her US cultural identity, her professorial identity, her experience living in Japan – were superimposed. The idea of cultural identity as patchwork accords with Canagarajah's emphasis on postcolonial hybridity, Holliday's (1999) concept of small cultures – which has influenced Connor deeply – and Boas/Lowie's initial conceptualization of culture as a disunified 'thing of shred and patches' (Lowie 1920: 441). I develop this last connection immediately below.

6 Future directions

If culture continues on its current trajectory in SLW, it seems likely to fall out of use. This is especially true if concepts like identity and power – so popular over the last ten to fifteen years in applied linguistics and SLW – continue or even grow in popularity. This is because they act as partial 'replacement concepts' for the culture concept, as argued by Brightman (1995) and others.

My own current preference, preliminarily developed in Atkinson (2012, to appear), is that we return to the roots of the anthropological culture concept – particularly the version developed by Robert Lowie, the first doctoral student and apparent mouthpiece for Boas circa 1920 (Kuper 2000). Concluding his 441-page *Primitive Society*, Lowie described 'civilization, or culture, as that planless hodgepodge, that thing of shreds and patches' (1920: 441). This was in keeping with the 'diffusionist' theory of the time, conveyed by Boas directly from his German teachers. As described at the beginning of this chapter, peoples and their cultural products and practices were seen as basically hybrid in this view: 'races' were amalgams of physical characteristics produced through intermarriage, and therefore had little biological reality; rituals, work tools, and artistic traditions were borrowed from geographical neighbours or more widely, and then indigenized. That this sounds suspiciously like certain anti-foundationalist/neo-Marxist/ postcolonial perspectives described above and elsewhere in applied linguistics is no coincidence – diffusionism directly influenced the development of world systems theory (e.g. Wallerstein 2004), an important element in the establishment of anti-foundationalist/neo-Marxist/postcolonial thought in applied linguistics (Pennycook 1994). What Boas and his students added to this picture was that exactly *in spite of* such centrifugal forces operating on human groups – or rather *in direct opposition* to them – centripetal forces were also at work: without unique bloodlines or pure traditions to base their togetherness on, social groups had to invent culture. This accords with Li's (2008) observation that today's world is hardly dissolving into a cultureless mass, but rather that a dialectic is at work – cultural conventions and hybridity are co-constitutive, working hand in hand. While this line of thinking does not (and should not) resolve all the issues with culture reviewed in this chapter, it may represent a tool for rethinking the impact of culture on SLW in the twenty-first century.

Related topics

language and culture in second language learning; language and culture in sociocultural anthropology; language, culture, and identity; language, literacy and culture; world Englishes and local cultures

Further reading

Atkinson, D. (2012). Intercultural rhetoric and intercultural communication. In J. Jackson (Ed.), *Routledge Handbook of Language and Intercultural Communication* (116–29). Abingdon, Oxon.: Routledge. (Covers the history and current status of CR/IR.)

Atkinson, D. (in press). Second language writing and culture. In R. Manchon and P. Matsuda (eds.), *Handbook of Second and Foreign Language Writing*. Berlin: De Gruyter Mouton. (Gives further detail on many of the same topics covered in the present chapter.)

Belcher, D., and Nelson, G. (eds.) (2013). *Critical and Corpus-based Approaches to Intercultural Rhetoric*. Ann Arbor, MI: University of Michigan Press. (Provides discussion of culture in SLW and CR/IR from various perspectives.)

References

Atkinson, D. (1997) 'A critical approach to critical thinking in TESOL', *TESOL Quarterly* 31: 71–94.
——(1999) 'TESOL and culture', *TESOL Quarterly* 33: 625–54.
——(2003) 'Writing and culture in the post-process era', *Journal of Second Language Writing* 12: 49–63.
——(2004) 'Contrasting rhetorics/contrasting cultures: Why contrastive rhetoric needs a better conceptualization of culture', *Journal of English for Academic Purposes* 3: 277–89.
——(2012) 'Intercultural rhetoric and intercultural communication', in J. Jackson (ed.), *Routledge Handbook of Language and Intercultural Communication*, Abingdon, Oxon.: Routledge.
——(in press) 'Second language writing and culture', in R. Manchon and P. Matsuda (eds), *Handbook of Second and Foreign Language Writing*, Berlin: De Gruyter Mouton.
Atkinson, D. and Ramanathan, V. (1995) 'Cultures of writing: An ethnographic comparison of L1 and L2 university writing/language programs', *TESOL Quarterly* 29: 539–68.
Benedict, R. (1934) *Patterns of Culture*, Boston, MA: Houghton Mifflin.
Berlin, I. (2001) *The Roots of Romanticism*, Princeton, NJ: Princeton University Press.
Berlin, J. (1987) 'Rhetoric and ideology in the writing class', *College English* 50: 477–94.
Bowden, D. (1995) 'The rise of a metaphor: "Voice" in composition pedagogy', *Rhetoric Review* 14: 173–88.
Brightman, R. (1995) 'Forget culture: Replacement, transcendence, relexification', *Cultural Anthropology* 10: 509–46.
Canagarajah, S. (2005) 'Shuttling between discourses: Textual and pedagogical possibilities for periphery scholars', in G. Cortese and A. Duszak (eds), *Identity, Community, Discourse: English in intercultural settings*, Berlin: Peter Lang.
——(2013) 'From intercultural rhetoric to cosmopolitan practice: Addressing new challenges in Lingua Franca English', in D. Belcher and G. Nelson (eds), *Critical and Corpus-based Approaches to Intercultural Rhetoric*, Ann Arbor, MI: University of Michigan Press.
Carson, J. (1992) 'Becoming biliterate: First language influences', *Journal of Second Language Writing* 1: 37–60.
Carson, J. and Nelson, G. (1996) 'Chinese students' perceptions of ESL peer response group interaction', *Journal of Second Language Writing* 5: 1–19.
Connor, U. (1996) *Contrastive Rhetoric*, Cambridge: Cambridge University Press.
——(2004) 'Introduction to the special issue on contrastive rhetoric', *Journal of English for Academic Purposes* 3: 271–6.
——(2011) *Intercultural Rhetoric in the Writing Classroom*, Ann Arbor, MI: University of Michigan Press.
Connor, U. and Kaplan, R. (eds) (1987) *Writing across Languages: Analysis of L2 text*, Reading, MA: Addison-Wesley.
Ferris, D. and Hedgcock, J. (1998) *Teaching ESL Composition*, Mahwah, NJ: Lawrence Erlbaum.
Foucault, M. (1980) *Power/Knowledge*, New York: Pantheon Books.

Fox, H. (1994) *Listening to the World*, Urbana, IL: NCTE.

Fulkerson, R. (2005) 'Composition at the turn of the 21st century', *College Composition and Communication* 56: 654–87.

Hinds, J. (1983a) 'Linguistics and written discourse in English and Japanese: A contrastive study (1978–1982)', *Annual Review of Applied Linguistics* 3: 78–84.

——(1983b) 'Contrastive rhetoric: Japanese and English', *Text* 3: 183–95.

——(1987) 'Reader versus writer responsibility: A new typology', in U. Connor and R. Kaplan (eds), *Writing across Languages: Analysis of L2 text*, Reading, MA: Addison-Wesley.

Holliday, A. (1999) 'Small cultures', *Applied Linguistics* 20: 237–64.

Kalantzis, M. and Cope, B. (1993) 'Histories of pedagogy, cultures of schooling', in B. Cope and M. Kalantzis (eds), *The Powers of Literacy: A genre approach to teaching writing*, Pittsburgh: University of Pittsburgh Press.

Kaplan, R. (1966) 'Cultural thought patterns in intercultural education', *Language Learning* 16: 1–20.

Kroeber, A. and Kluckhohn, C. (1952) *Culture: A critical review of concepts and definitions*, Cambridge, MA: Peabody Museum of American Archaeology and Ethnology, Harvard University.

Kubota, R. (1997) 'A reevaluation of the uniqueness of Japanese written discourse', *Written Communication* 14: 460–80.

——(1998) 'An investigation of L1–L2 transfer in writing among Japanese university students: Implications for contrastive rhetoric', *Journal of Second Language Writing* 7: 69–100.

——(1999) 'Japanese culture constructed by discourses: Implications for applied linguistics research and ELT', *TESOL Quarterly* 33: 9–35.

——(2002) 'Japanese identities in written communication: Politics and discourses', in R. Donahue (ed.), *Exploring Japaneseness*, Westport, CT: Ablex.

Kubota, R. and Lehner, A. (2004) 'Toward critical contrastive rhetoric', *Journal of Second Language Writing* 13: 7–27.

Kuper, A. (2000) *Culture: The anthropologist's account*, Cambridge, MA: Harvard University Press.

Li, X. (1996) *'Good Writing' in Cross-cultural Context*, Albany, NY: State University of New York Press.

——(2005) 'Composing culture in a fragmented world: The issue of representation in cross-cultural research', in P. Matsuda and T. Silva (eds), *Second Language Writing Research: Perspectives on the process of knowledge construction*, Mahwah, NJ: Erlbaum.

——(2008) 'From contrastive rhetoric to intercultural rhetoric: A search for identity', in U. Connor, E. Nagelhout, and W. Rozycki (eds), *Contrastive Rhetoric: Reaching to intercultural rhetoric*, Amsterdam: Benjamins.

Lowie, R. (1920) *Primitive Society*, New York: Boni and Liveright.

Lyotard, F. (1984) *The Postmodern Condition*, Minneapolis, MN: University of Minnesota Press.

McLaren, P. (2003) 'Introduction', in D. Hill, P. McLaren, M. Cole, and G. Rikowski (eds), *Marxism against Postmodernism in Educational Theory*, New York: Lexington.

Mauranen, A. (1993) *Cultural Differences in Academic Rhetoric*, Berlin: Peter Lang.

Mazzarella, W. (2004) 'Culture, globalization, mediation', *Annual Review of Anthropology* 33: 345–67.

Pennycook, A. (1994) *The Politics of English as an International Language*, Harlow, England: Longman.

——(1996) 'Borrowing others' words: Text, ownership, memory, and plagiarism', *TESOL Quarterly* 30: 201–30.

Ramanathan, V. and Atkinson, D. (1999), 'Individualism, academic writing, and ESL writers', *Journal of Second Language Writing* 8: 45–75.

Ramanathan, V. and Kaplan, R. (1996), 'Audience and voice in current L1 composition texts: Some implications for ESL student writers', *Journal of Second Language Writing* 5: 21–34.

Santos, T. (1992) 'Ideology in composition: L1 and ESL', *Journal of Second Language Writing* 1: 1–15.

Sapir, E. (1924) 'Culture, genuine and spurious', *American Journal of Sociology* 29: 401–429.

Sarangi, S. (1995) 'Culture', in J. Verschueren, J. Ostman, and J. Bloommaert (eds), *Handbook of Pragmatics*, Philadelphia: Benjamins.

Scollon, R. (1991) 'Eight legs and an Elbow: Stance and structure in Chinese English compositions', in *Launching the Literacy Decade: Awareness into action. Proceedings of the Second North American Conference on Adult and Adolescent Literacy: Multiculturalism and Citizenship*, Toronto: International Reading Association.

Shen, F. (1989) 'The classroom and the wider culture: Identity as a key to learning composition', *College Composition and Communication* 40: 459–66.

Silva, T. and Matsuda, P. K. (eds) (2010) *Practicing Theory in Second Language Writing*, West Lafayette, IN: Parlor Press.

Spack, R. (1997) 'The rhetorical construction of multilingual students', *TESOL Quarterly* 31: 765–74.

Stocking, G. (1967) 'Franz Boas and the culture concept in historical perspective', in G. Stocking, *Race, Culture, and Evolution: Essays in the history of anthropology*, Chicago: University of Chicago Press.

Trimbur, J. (1994) 'Taking the social turn: Teaching writing post-process', *College Composition and Communication* 45: 108–18.

Wallerstein, I. (2004) *World-systems Analysis: An introduction*, Durham, NC: Duke University Press.

Williams, R. (1983), *Keywords: A vocabulary of culture and society*, London: Oxford University Press.

Zamel, V. (1997) 'Toward a model of transculturation', *TESOL Quarterly* 31: 341–52.

29
LANGUAGE AND CULTURE IN SECOND DIALECT LEARNING

Ian G. Malcolm

Introduction

Language, like culture, is variously represented in societies. Geographical dispersion of social groups within a society can be associated with regional linguistic or dialectal differences and, within the same location, social differentiation can be expressed in social dialects. The matter is complicated by the movement of groups across cultural settings and the role of language in helping to maintain the distinctiveness of groups of different origin. The phenomenon of the 'spread of English' (Garcia and Otheguy 1989: 1) has entailed significant linguistic change worldwide, in that it has led to the emergence of new Englishes and added to the linguistic repertoires of many cultures.

The fact that language and culture within a given society are diverse is not new and the existence of bilingualism and bidialectalism is normal. However, there has been much recent concern about what has been called 'the pluralist dilemma' (May 2012: 12, citing Bullivant), or that 'balancing act' whereby modern nation states are under pressure both to recognize their component subcultures and to strengthen their sense of unity.

The path taken towards the expression of national unity has in many cases been to use education, and, in particular, language education, as May (2012: 14) has put it, 'to favour civism over pluralism'. Thus, state-sponsored education has been depended on to support proficiency in one national language and the prestige dialect of that language, while '"minoritizing" or "dialectalizing" potentially competing language varieties' (May 2012: 16).

Inherent in such policies is a linguistic and cultural problem for the groups whose language variety and culture are being subordinated to those which carry national prestige. Understandably, this often shows in educational outcomes which fall below those of the speakers of the prestige language variety. Debate over the role of dialect in education, while longstanding (Cheshire *et al.* 1989: 1), came to a head in the second half of the twentieth century as linguists increasingly asserted the parity of non-recognized varieties with those which had been standardized. The outworking of the educational implications of what the linguists were saying led to the development of principles and practices of second dialect learning, or, more particularly, the learning of a standardized variety of a language by people who speak a non-standard variety of the same language.

Second dialect learning has been practised in many parts of the world, and in a range of languages other than English. Much of the current literature is surveyed by Siegel (2010). This chapter, limiting its focus to English, will consider the early applications in the United States and the ways in which changes in linguistic research have led, and are leading, to new educational developments. Of particular relevance to 'language and culture in second dialect learning' has been the recent application of cognitive and cultural linguistics, bringing the important new insight that learning a second dialect involves not simply learning a new linguistic system but learning a new system of cultural conceptualizations.

Development of bidialectal education in the United States

The context in which the early proposals for bidialectal education arose in the United States was one in which speakers of non-standard dialects in schools, and, in particular, speakers of African-American English, were having limited success in school and their shortcomings were being attributed to their use of a 'deficient' (Dillard 1978: 298) form of English and being the 'products of language deprivation' (Shuy 1969: 120). They were sometimes consigned to special education classes (Wolfram 1999: 64) on the assumption of having 'cognitive, cultural, and/or linguistic deficiencies' (Stewart 1969: 163). In some cases, the non-standard dialect speakers' differences from standard English were ignored; in other cases, they were made the target of eradication programmes (Stewart 1969: 184).

The correlation between non-standard dialect use and reading failure, which was undeniable (Wolfram *et al.* 1979: 1), was taken by some educators as confirming the assumption that the non-standard dialect was no more than a substandard variant of standard English (Stewart 1970: 8) and an obstacle to learning, and programmes were devised to bypass the dialect in teaching reading (see further Gardiner 1977: 170ff.).

At the same time, significant advances were taking place in research into social dialectology in the United States (e.g. Labov 1972; Shuy, Wolfram and Riley 1968) and such research was being given an increasingly high profile through the Center for Applied Linguistics. Baratz (1970: 20) observed the existence of two camps with respect to dialect recognition:

> [O]ne camp, composed generally of psychologists and educators, has tended to view the language of black children as defective … The other camp, composed mainly of linguists, has viewed [it] … as a different, yet highly structured, highly developed system.

Labov (1972: 4), whose sophisticated research, involving both African-American and Anglo-American data gatherers, had confirmed the systematic nature of the dialect spoken by the African-American learners he had studied, drew attention to the problem of 'reciprocal ignorance, where teacher and student are ignorant of each other's system, and therefore of the rules needed to translate from one system to another'. One result of teacher misinformation about non-standard dialects was the perpetuation of low expectations on their part with respect to non-standard dialect speaking students. Christian (1979: 6) noted: 'According to some studies, this may well be the most significant and damaging outcome of dialect differences in the schools'.

The problem, as Labov (1970: 42) saw it, was that linguists and school-based educators and psychologists had been working independently of one another:

> At present, we have only two kinds of studies of nonstandard dialects: those carried out by linguists outside the school, and those carried out by psychologists and

432

educational researchers within the school. The teaching process itself has not yet been observed through the lenses provided by systematic sociolinguistic analysis.

Building on the knowledge generated by Labov, Shuy, Wolfram and others, linguistically informed educators progressively began to develop bidialectal education (or biloquial) programmes on the principle that the non-standard dialect should be acknowledged and 'actually be used as a basis for teaching oral and written standard English' (Stewart 1969: 184).

The grounding of such programmes was seen in the education of teachers as to the nature of their own (standard) dialect and the (non-standard) dialect of the learner. Only on the basis of such education would teachers be able to see the fact that both dialects were rule governed, but that the rules were different. In the 1960s, foreign language teaching was making extensive use of contrastive analysis between the learner's language and the target language, so that the salient differences could be concentrated on in appropriate drills and pattern practice. This seemed to some (e.g. McDavid 1969: 3; Stewart 1970: 13) to be the way to go, regarding the non-standard dialect speaker as being in a 'quasi-foreign language' situation.

Some of the kinds of drills which were advocated (Feigenbaum 1970; Gardiner 1977) included:

discrimination drills, where the student was presented orally with a non-standard and a standard form (e.g. *he work hard/he works hard*) and had to indicate whether they were the same or different;

identification drills, where the student was presented with a single item (e.g. *he work hard*) and had to identify it as standard or non-standard;

translation drills, where the student was asked to translate an item from one dialect to the other; and

response drills, where the student would be given a standard or non-standard dialect stimulus and be asked to respond to it in the appropriate dialect.

Standard language patterns could also be instilled by providing the student with games, stories and role play activities where structures could be repeated many times.

There was also a focus on making learning materials appropriate. Some reading materials were developed which related 'to the culture of the ghetto' (Wolfram and Fasold 1969: 141), but it was recognized that there was a disconnect between the context and the standard English being used by the characters being depicted. The idea of having reading materials in the dialect, which still, to many, was unthinkable, was promoted, for example by Baratz (1969: 113):

> Because of the mismatch between the child's system and that of the standard English textbook, because of the psychological consequences of denying the existence and legitimacy of the child's linguistic system, and in the light of the success of vernacular teaching around the world, it appears imperative that we teach the inner-city [African-American] child to read using his own language as the basis for the initial readers. In other words, first teach the child to read in the vernacular, and then teach him to read in standard English. Such a reading program would not only require accurate vernacular texts for the dialect speaker, but also necessitate the creation of a series of 'transition readers' that would move the child, once he had mastered reading in the vernacular, from vernacular texts to standard English texts.

As it was to eventuate, this idea was somewhat ahead of its time. Dialect readers did not prove viable to publishers and support from within the profession, in the light of community opposition, was mixed (Baugh 1983: 109; Goodman 1969: 14, 26; Stewart 1969: 173; Wolfram 1991: 256, 2001: 348).

It was considered appropriate that, in a Standard English as a Second Dialect (SESD) programme, students should be able to express themselves in their non-standard dialect, while also being given opportunities to modify their utterances in the direction of the standard dialect. It was recognized that the progress between the dialects might be gradual. For example, Stewart (1969: 185) suggested the African-American student might progress through three stages in moving from AAVE to SE structures:

> Stage 1: Charles and Michael, they out playing.
> Stage 2: Charles and Michael, they are out playing.
> Stage 3: Charles and Michael are out playing.

A five-stage development from 'John, he don't got no money' to 'John hasn't got any money' was suggested by Dillard (1978: 302). The intention was to avoid stigmatizing the student's transitional efforts on the way from one dialect to the other. In making these transitions, it was recognized that the student was not replacing one dialect with another, but developing an alternative system.

Labov (1965) suggested that six levels in the acquisition of standard English by way of the non-standard dialect be recognized, with the basic grammar and fluency in the local dialect preceding social perception on which the ability to switch to the prestige standard might be based in the adolescent years. Wolfram (1970) suggested that the order in which standard English items should be introduced to the non-standard speaker should be governed by such matters as the degree to which the corresponding non-standard forms were stigmatized (i.e. their 'social diagnosticity'), the generality of the rules involved, whether the non-standard forms were regional or of wider social significance, how frequently the forms occurred, and how crucial the sociolinguistic principles were.

Current contributions and research

Bidialectal education has been widely employed and variously adapted in educational contexts where students speak a non-standard regional or ethnic dialect or vernacular or a pidgin or creole, although monodialectal assumptions still commonly prevail in educational systems, even where published policies would suggest otherwise (Truscott and Malcolm 2011; Yiakoumetti 2012: 1). In a comprehensive review, Siegel (2010) has noted that recent studies of regional dialect speakers in Europe reveal that, there is a good deal of evidence that their specific needs are not well recognized, although their test results are below those of other students. In the UK, there is a similar pattern, with many teachers unaware of the distinction between dialect forms and errors, and some non-standard dialect speaking students experiencing alienation. In the United States, strong pressure for African-American and American-Indian students to learn standard English prevails and often little attention is paid to their existing dialects. Siegel (2010: 218) does, however, report on some cases where bidialectal education approaches were employed, to the effect that:

> the use of the students' D1 in the classroom had none of the detrimental effects predicted by educators and parents. On the contrary, the approaches in general led to higher scores in tests measuring reading, writing or oral skills in the standard D2 and in overall academic achievement. Other benefits included greater interest and motivation, and higher rates of participation.

It is clear that bidialectal education approaches have been modified as linguistic research has broadened to take greater account of sociolinguistic and cultural dimensions, and as second language learning theories have changed. Wolfram (2001: 333) has recognized the limitations of the early approaches which were dominated by interest in 'inventories of vernacular structures', and Edwards (1989: 318) noted the move in Europe away from 'heavy reliance on drills to more communicative teaching techniques: learning language by using language, especially using a thematic approach'. The matter of 'language use as cultural behaviour' (Christian and Wolfram 1979) has increasingly been in focus, drawing on the principles of the *ethnography of speaking* (Hymes 1962) which analyses the ways in which cultural groups make distinctive use of speech acts, routines, and events (Christian and Wolfram 1979: 18; Edwards 1986: 6; Wolfram 1991: 266), following implicit codes (Delpit 2006: 25), and the relevance to the curriculum of all students of the study of language diversity has been recognized (Cheshire and Stein 1997: 4, 11). Such study has, in many cases, entailed a critical awareness dimension (Siegel 2010: 229–34). Labov (1972: xiv) had noted that 'the major causes of reading failure are political and cultural conflicts in the classroom, and dialect differences are important because they are symbols of this conflict'. In the same vein, African-American educator Delpit put it, 'I ... do not believe that we should teach students passively to accept an alternate code. They must be encouraged to understand the value of the code they already possess as well as to understand the power realities in this country' (2006: 40).

It has been recognized that some of the earlier input to bidialectal education was limited by an 'obsession with maximally basilectal, stigmatized structural features' (Wolfram 2001: 334) and that this met with opposition from non-standard dialect speakers themselves (Edwards 1979: 103). There has been some objection to the use of contrastive analysis to define a person's way of speaking by contrasting it with another (Edwards 1986: 27), though to define a non-standard variety without reference to the standard was seen by Labov (1969: 37) as unachievable. Dissatisfaction has also been expressed with the outcomes of the application of sociolinguistic research findings to the second dialect classroom. As Edwards (1989: 320) put it:

> Much of the research conducted in Europe and elsewhere during the 1970s and early 1980s drew on the insights of sociolinguistics, but it promised far more than we have been able to achieve. We are forced, therefore, to ask if we have actually been addressing ourselves to the right questions.

To some extent, the questions that have not been adequately addressed might relate to the existence of what has been called the *group reference* factor (Christian 1979; Wolfram 1991: 217). Students' linguistic behaviour (other things being equal) is normed by the primary groups to which they belong, rather than by the school. As Wolfram (1991: 215–16) has noted: 'To use Standard English in the context of a roomful of vernacular-speaking peers may be an open invitation to ridicule by other students'.

There is also the problem of the gap between policy (which often recognizes the validity of the language and culture of minorities) and implementation (which continues to uphold only the standard language). It has been argued (Truscott and Malcolm 2011) that what prevails is the 'invisible' language policy, or, in another context, a policy that is publicly assented to but privately subverted (Kamwangamalu 2012: 168). This is particularly the case with respect to the way in which, despite purported policies of inclusion, standardized testing continues to be carried out without reference to non-standard dialect speakers, leading to their being assessed as if they were the same as standard dialect speakers (Delpit 2006: xv; Malcolm 2011a; Wolfram 1991: 232, 2001: 346–7).

Another possible reason for the limited success of early attempts at bidialectal education is alluded to by Taylor (1989: 73), who observes that, despite the closeness of the relationship between language, culture and social reality

> the concept of culture ... has not entered our traditional composition courses ... [R]esearchers of black English and bidialectalism focused mainly on grammar, phonology, lexicon and social variation. Relatively few studies in composition and related disciplines have investigated a culture and subliminal barriers to communication that may affect class room performance and lead to academic failure.

Similarly, Trueba (1991a: 149) observed that 'teachers are culturally unfamiliar with the children's world at home and in their ethnic community. Communication between teachers and children is defective and superficial.' Wolfram (2001: 345), likewise, expressed concern about the fact that 'progress in some areas of application [of dialect research] has been so sluggish', and observed: 'There is no doubt that cultural and social values about the role of reading in community life play an enormous role in learning to read and in developing reading proficiency' (ibid.: 348–9).

The cultural–conceptual dimension

A way towards the incorporation of cultural study into language education was to open up with the development, from the 1980s, of cognitive linguistics which, as Niemeier (2004: 95) observed, 'from its very beginning emphasized the fact that language, culture, and thought are inextricably interlinked'. Cognitive linguistics is based on the idea that language is essentially the result of human representations of the world, and that it should be understood, not as a system in its own right, but as the way in which members of a group mentally structure experience in a common way so that they are able to communicate with one another. Language, according to this view, 'represents a privileged entry point into our conceptual system' (Achard and Niemeier 2004: 4). It is based on a shared way of organizing the world. In a sense, when we learn a language, from the viewpoint of cognitive linguistics, we first learn a way of thinking – 'thinking for speaking' (Slobin 1991) – which fits the language variety we are using. It follows that, when we are learning another language, or language variety, we need to learn at the same time new linguistic forms but also new ways of conceptualizing the world.

Cognitive linguists use the term *construal* to refer to the ways in which elements of experience are mentally captured to enable them to be transformed into language. Four main ways (noted by Littlemore 2009) in which phenomena or events may be construed are:

by drawing attention to aspects deemed to be salient (e.g. *bachelor* draws attention – perhaps among other things – to the fact that the person referred to is male, adult and single);
by indicating perspective (e.g. *here* implies direction towards the speaker);
by indicating constitution (e.g. *cheveux* (in French) conceives of the hairs on a person's head as a plurality, whereas the English equivalent, *hair*, conceives of the same object as an undifferentiated whole);
by categorization (e.g. a *swallow* is a good example of a bird, whereas *pelican* is rather less prototypical).

The words speakers use are mentally arranged in networks, so that some clearly associate with others. The relevant networks will differ according to the 'frame' used (Littlemore 2009: 74). Hence, polysemous words such as *pupil* or *grave* will be interpreted according to the frame provided by the subject and situation of the discourse.

Cognitive linguists have also paid considerable attention to metaphor and metonymy, recognizing that speakers of a language actually use these processes to structure their thinking and behaving. Often conceptual metaphors or metonymies are used unconsciously by the speaker, as when we use the 'conduit' metaphor to talk about *getting something across*, or when we tell someone, on the basis of the 'PART FOR WHOLE' metonymy that we will *pencil it in* (Littlemore 2009: 97, 110).

The cultural relevance of cognitive linguistics, as well as its inherent links with the ethnography of speaking and with ethnosemantics, has been emphasized by Palmer (1996) who has developed a theory of *cultural linguistics*. Palmer has taken up many of the concepts put forward, on the basis of English language research, by cognitive linguists and applied them to other languages. He has brought these together within a framework which sees mental imagery and the management of *cultural schemas* as fundamental to conceptualization and language. Palmer accepts the concept of schemas put forward by Chafe (1990: 80–1) as '"ready made models" and "prepackaged expectations and ways of interpreting", which are, for the most part, supplied by our cultures'. His work has helped to draw attention to the schemas underlying interaction, discourse, semantics, grammar, and even phonology.

The application of linguistic research to bidialectal education has progressively moved the spotlight from questions of phonology (e.g. How do non-standard dialect (D1) speakers 'hear' the standard (D2)?) to grammar (e.g. How do D1 speakers form and interpret linguistic structures in D1 and D2?), to sociolinguistics and pragmatics (e.g. How do D1 speakers participate in D1 and D2 speech events?), to discourse (e.g. How do D1 speakers, as distinct from D2 speakers, construct discourse and genres?) and finally to cognitive and cultural linguistics (e.g. How do D1 speakers, as distinct from D2 speakers, construe the world in the way they receive and produce language?).

Application of cognitive and cultural research to bidialectal education is at an early stage of development. With respect to cognitive linguistics, there have been a number of relatively recent attempts to explore growing knowledge of construal and associated concepts to second language learning (e.g. Achard and Niemeier 2004; Littlemore 2009; Pavlenko 2011; Tyler 2012) and some of the outcomes of this exploration may be relevant to second dialect learning. A major emphasis has been on the use of naturally occurring language and the encouragement of learners to view the grammar of the target language with attention to meaning rather than form (Tyler 2012: 215). It has been strongly advocated that students should work inductively from 'usage events' to understand principles of speaker construal rather than the linguistic system (Waara 2004). This means engagement of learners with the target language speaking community to discover their 'encyclopaedic knowledge' (Littlemore 2009: 71) and cultural key words which serve as triggers or 'access nodes' to areas of cultural knowledge. It has been suggested that new words will be better retained if taught in categories, and that associated meanings of words can be explored visually though plotting them on radial category diagrams (Littlemore 2009: 41–2; Tyler 2012: 72). Since embodiment is often a part of meaning, it has been suggested that gesture be used as an aid to listening comprehension (Littlemore 2009: 141; Tyler 2012: 77). There has also been focus on the place of metaphor in second language learning. Teachers can work with metaphors to help students to see how the target language speakers structure thought and they can help them to look for hidden meanings (Niemeier 2004: 110–11) and understand idioms (Tyler 2012: 70). Teachers can also help students to find the frames that are essential to the interpretation of the language they encounter (Trueba 1991b: 50; Pavlenko 2011: 244). Fundamentally, it is important that teachers do not assume that construal is constant across the languages or varieties being taught. The assumptions of the language user need to be made explicit.

While these applications have not been made with second dialect learning in mind, they can be applied to bidialectal education to bring to it a different kind of focus on form which embraces understanding of the reasons why speakers of the D2 express themselves the way they do. Clearly, there are also implications for the teacher, in that, while on the one hand the students have to access the encyclopaedic knowledge of D2 speakers in learning the D2, the teacher, with the help of community members and support personnel, needs to access the encyclopaedic knowledge of the community to which the learners belong in order to understand and adjust to them.

Some of the early initiatives in applying cultural linguistics to language teaching are reviewed by Palmer and Sharifian (2007), who note how it has been observed that the approach of cultural linguistics (like that of cognitive linguistics, as noted above) makes language more explainable to students as it shows the motivation behind language. They report on work which advocates teaching students a cultural domain before teaching them the language use in that domain, and on helping students to understand the relevant schemas and categories in the target language or dialect which contrast with those of their L1.

Specifically in relation to second dialect acquisition, Malcolm and Sharifian (2002) have focused on cultural schema theory and its application. They observe that, while the non-standard variety Australian Aboriginal English appears to share much vocabulary with Australian English, it is informed by a distinctively Aboriginal semantic system. This is apparent in the schemas associated with lexical items, as shown in their associative chains, and in the construals they represent (for example, *long* incorporates the vertical dimension). It is also apparent at the discourse level, showing in discomfort in teacher–pupil interactions, and in the recurrence in students' oral narratives of a limited number of culturally relevant schemas (described in detail in Malcolm and Rochecouste 2000). It is apparent that certain pervasive schemas, such as that which views experience in terms of 'hunting', may be extended as conceptual metaphors when discussing other aspects of experience such as fishing and playing football (Malcolm and Sharifian 2002: 175).

Sharifian (2011) explored the conceptualizations evoked by 32 common English words among Aboriginal and non-Aboriginal students, respectively, in three primary (elementary) schools in metropolitan Perth, Western Australia. He worked with Aboriginal and non-Aboriginal research assistants and used the association–interpretation methodology, which involved presenting the stimulus words to the students in random order and inviting them to say what they brought to mind. Although the apparent linguistic differences in the English used by the participants were minimal, Sharifian (2011: 64) reports that 'viewed from a conceptual per-spective, the data suggested the operation of two distinct, but overlapping, conceptual systems among the two cultural groups'. For example, the word *family* evoked for most non-Aboriginal students the nuclear family, but for most Aboriginal students the extended family; the word *home* evoked for most non-Aboriginal students the idea of one's own allocated space and chosen activities, but for most Aboriginal students the idea of shared space associated with shared responsibilities; the word *shame* suggested guilt to most non-Aboriginal students but shyness to most Aboriginal students. Sharifian's research belied the assumed transparency that is commonly deemed to exist between culturally different speakers whose dialects seem to show little variation at the level of surface features.

Other work influenced by Cultural Linguistic theory (Malcolm 2011b) has attempted to clarify with respect to a non-standard variety with pidgin/creole antecedents (Australian Aboriginal English), what semantic continuities can be traced in ways in which distinctive conceptualizations are associated with the maintenance of linguistic forms which diverge from those of the majority culture. Six such semantic continuities were isolated as providing conceptual reasons for such linguistic features as grammatical simplification, restructuring and innovation, lexical blending and compounding, and semantic shifts. Such evidence was used to support bidialectal as opposed to monodialectal education for such students.

Sharifian and associates (Sharifian *et al.* 2004, 2012) have employed cultural schema theory in association with a system of idea unit analysis to investigate how Australian Aboriginal English speaking students and their teachers, using standard English materials, mutually interpret one another. They provided evidence of 'reschematization' whereby both parties resorted to familiar schemas associated with their respective dialects in order to make sense of what they heard in the other dialect, often significantly changing it. This work supports the need for 'rich instruction' (Littlemore 2009: 88, citing Nation), to make sure meanings are not assumed but explicitly discussed.

In classroom-based action research with teachers of Australian Aboriginal students partnered with Aboriginal teaching assistants (locally called Aboriginal/Islander Education Officers) in 15 schools across Western Australia (Malcolm *et al.* 1999), some 70 audio and video tapes of student interaction were recorded, transcribed and analysed in bi-cultural research teams. The analysis included attention to categorization (including analysis of prototypes across Aboriginal and non-Aboriginal groups), schematization and discourse conventions, leading towards a description of what (in cultural linguistic terms) Aboriginal students bring to school. The project proposed 'two-way bidialectal education' as an appropriate way of coming to terms with (and giving expression to) the Aboriginal students' distinctive linguistic and cultural background while at the same time developing research-informed ways of bridging between their dialect and that of the school.

Siegel (2010) in surveying recent approaches to bidialectal education classifies them according to whether they are instrumental, accommodation or awareness in approach. Instrumental approaches, of which most cited involve creoles, employ the students' D1 as medium of instruction at least for initial literacy and, in some cases, content subjects. Generally, findings on these programmes endorse the approach. Accommodation approaches, often used in classes with a mix of standard and non-standard dialect speaking students, accept the use of the non-standard D1 by students but do not use it as a medium of instruction. Such approaches have been used with African-American, Hawaiian, Singaporean, Australian, and Caribbean students with some success, especially with regard to strengthening students' self-esteem. Awareness approaches, while accepting the use of the non-standard dialect in the classroom, go further to use it as a resource for learning the D2. They also seek to inform students about how and why dialectal variation exists. What this threefold classification does not show is that some programmes may include elements of all three approaches.

Critical issues and topics

Legitimacy of bidialectal education

Despite consistent evidence that recognition of the vernacular in education leads to improved skills in reading and language arts (Rickford 1999: 1) as well as improved self-esteem and interest in the standard variety (Rickford 1999: 11) and improved academic performance generally (Yiakoumetti 2012: 301), '[d]ialect tolerance is still minimal' (Trudgill 1979: 21) and there is a worldwide reluctance to commit to educational change which will interfere with the exclusive use of the standard variety (Yiakoumetti 2012: 1). As Migge, L'église, and Bartens (2010: 2) have noted, '[t]he debates concerning the possibility for a language to be used in school … are always based on political and ideological arguments'. Wolfram (2001: 345) has referred to the dominance of a 'language subordination ideology' which has obstructed efforts to implement bidialectal education for African-American English speakers. Another way of referring to this is in terms of the 'standard language ideology', which Siegel (2010: 186) defines as 'the pervasive belief in the superiority of the abstracted and idealised form of language based on the spoken language of the upper middle classes – i.e. the standard dialect'. In some contexts there are other dimensions to such beliefs. For example, in some African countries an ideology of development (favouring the standard) is set against an ideology of decolonization (favouring the local vernaculars) (Kamwangamalu 2012). In traditionally English-speaking countries there is commonly a 'monoglot ideology' (Siegel 2010: 187), or a 'monolingual mindset' (McIntosh et al. 2012, citing Clyne) which regards standard language monolingualism as normal. The recognition of bidialectalism will continue to be a matter of debate because, as Taylor (1989: 156) has noted, '[b]idialectalism as a philosophical goal allows for the power of language to work to the advantage of all learners' and, as such, it may be seen as a threat by some and as a right (Wolfram 1991: 214) by others.

Factors in the implementation of bidialectal education

There remain areas of dispute with respect to how bidialectal education should be implemented. One of these is the matter of the relevance of the contrastive analysis hypothesis, dating from the 1950s. When bidialectal education was introduced, it was seen as important to recognize the areas of contrast at phonological and grammatical levels between the non-standard and standard dialects so that students, and teachers, could be alerted to the differences and overcome interference between the dialects. As language teaching approaches have changed, the idea of isolating and drilling linguistic forms and patterns has lost support. There has also been some research evidence that interference is not as significant a factor in student underachievement as was once thought. However, more recently, there has been an increased focus on 'language transfer' in second language teaching and some confidence in the relevance of contrastive analysis, within the context of language awareness teaching, has been restored. Wolfram (1991: 220–1) has noted: 'Students do not need to learn the "English language"; they need to learn Standard English correspondences for particular socially stigmatized forms … This contrastive base must be taken into account regardless of the type of instructional method used to teach Standard English.' It has also been seen that the concept of interference is relevant at sociolinguistic as well as linguistic levels (Yiakoumetti 2012: 300).

Another area of disagreement relates to the use of dialect readers. As noted earlier, dialect readers were recommended in the United States in the 1960s but, due to what Rickford (1999: 20) called 'knee-jerk negative reactions from parents and educators', not continued with (Wolfram et al. 1979: 12). However, there is evidence of the benefits of the use of dialect readers in improving student attitude and achievement (Siegel 2010: 200) and their use as a 'transitional prop' towards literacy in the standard dialect has been defended (Edwards 1989: 318, cf. Cheyney 1976: 93). The possibility of the use of dialect readers is still being pursued (Wolfram 2001: 348) and, in some cases, actualized (Königsberg, Collard, and McHugh 2012).

Much debate also surrounds issues of dialect and socio-cultural identity. Linguists may be perceived as seeing students' problems as essentially linguistic and educational, but language is always identity related. Baugh 1983 reports that '[t]he social distance between groups has been sufficient to drive perceptual wedges between blacks and whites. As a consequence of this linguistic dilemma, many street speakers remain silent when standard English is the dominant dialect.' He notes further that black people feel 'discomfort' in the presence of whites (Baugh 1983: 6, 24). The silence or inappropriate form of response may be a form of expression which has meaning in one culture but not in the other. Delpit (2006: 25) has noted: '[M]embers of any culture transmit information implicitly to co-members. However, when implicit codes are attempted across cultures, communication frequently breaks down. Each cultural group is left saying, "Why don't these people say what they mean?"' 'The conflict that arises between a teacher and children of different backgrounds generally has its roots in the cultural set each one brings to the classroom arena' Cheyney (1976: 28). The ultimate response to such conflict may be 'dis-identification with the academic exercise' (Rickford 1999: 8). In response to this recognition, there are increasing calls for community engagement on the part of educators. A bidialectal programme without community involvement would be doomed to failure (Wolfram 1991: 218).

Future directions

Bidialectal education began as an application of linguistic knowledge to an area of educational failure. As it has developed, areas of linguistic knowledge and focus have broadened, so that, progressively, the social, cultural, and cognitive dimensions which have informed linguistics have come to inform bidialectal education. At the same time, second language education has moved from a structuralist to a communicative base and has become increasingly focused on aspects of language use. As the cultural focus in bidialectal education has increased, its potential to attract opposition, especially from systems devoted a narrowing socio-political focus, has increased. It is important that the proponents of bidialectal education continue to pursue it as a means of validating the linguistic and cultural practice of non-standard dialect speakers while extending their repertoire. Increasing attention will need to be devoted to the incorporation of insights from cognitive and cultural linguistics to bidialectal education in a way which recognizes that both non-standard and standard dialect speakers can benefit from gaining insight into their respective world-views. The notion of dialect also needs to be modified to recognize its conceptual dimension. Importantly, in addition, priority will need to be given, in an era of national standardized testing, to the development of culturally and linguistically valid means of assessment of the language skills of bidialectal students as such, and not as monodialectal speakers of the standard dialect.

Related topics

cultural linguistics; language and culture in foreign language learning; language and culture in sociolinguistics; language, culture, and context; language, culture, and identity; language, culture, and prototypicality; language, literacy, and culture

Further reading

Adger, C. T., Christian, D. and Taylor, O. (eds) (1999) *Making the Connection: Language and Academic Achievement among African American Students*, McHenry, IL: Center for Applied Linguistics and Delta Systems Co. (This collection provides information on reactions to the controversy associated with the 1996 decision of the Oakland (CA) School Board to recognize African-American English (Ebonics) as the primary language of its African-American students.)

Delpit, L. (2006) *Other People's Children: Cultural Conflict in the Classroom*, New York: New Press. (This work offers significant insight on the experience of linguistic and cultural exclusion from the point of view of the African-American student and educator.)

Königsberg, P. and Collard, G. (eds) (2002) *Ways of Being, Ways of Talk*, East Perth, Western Australia: Department of Education and Training, and Königsberg, P., Collard, G. and McHugh, M. (eds) (2012) *Tracks to Two-Way Learning*, East Perth, Western Australia: Department of Education. (These constitute comprehensive training materials for two-way bidialectal education in the Australian context.)

Siegel, J. (2010) *Second Dialect Acquisition*, Cambridge: Cambridge University Press. (This provides a broad review of research and practice in second dialect acquisition in both naturalistic and classroom contexts.)

Yiakoumetti, A. (ed.) (2012) *Harnessing Linguistic Variation to Improve Education*, Oxford: Peter Lang. (This provides discussion of examples of bilingual and bidialectal initiatives worldwide.)

References

Achard, M. and Niemeier, S. (2004) 'Introduction: Cognitive linguistics, language acquisition and pedagogy', in M. Achard and S. Niemeier (eds) *Cognitive Linguistics, Second Language Acquisition and Foreign Language Teaching*, Berlin: Mouton de Gruyter.

Adger, C. T., Christian, D. and Taylor, O. (eds) (1999) *Making the Connection: Language and Academic Achievement Among African American Students*, McHenry, IL: Center for Applied Linguistics and Delta Systems Co.

Baratz, J. C. (1969) 'Teaching reading in an urban Negro school system', in J. C. Baratz and R. W. Shuy (eds) *Teaching Black Children to Read*, Washington, DC: Center for Applied Linguistics.

——(1970) 'Educational considerations for teaching standard English to Negro children', in R. W. Fasold and R. W. Shuy (eds) *Teaching Standard English in the Inner City*, Washington, DC: Center for Applied Linguistics.

Baugh, J. (1983) *Black Street Speech: Its History, Structure and Survival*, Austin, TX: University of Texas Press.

Cheshire, J., Edwards, V., Münstermann, H. and Weltens, B. (1989) 'Dialect and education in Europe: A general perspective', in J. Cheshire, V. Edwards, H. Münstermann and B. Weltens (eds) *Dialect and Education: Some European Perspectives*, Clevedon, UK: Multilingual Matters Ltd.

Cheshire, J. and Stein, D. (1997) 'The syntax of spoken language', in J. Cheshire and D. Stein (eds) *Taming the Vernacular: From Dialect to Written Standard Language*, London: Longman.

Cheyney, A. B. (1976) *Teaching Children of Different Cultures in the Classroom: A Language Approach*, 2nd edn, Columbus, OH: Charles E. Merrill.

Christian, D. (1979) *Language Arts and Dialect Differences*, Arlington, VI: Center for Applied Linguistics.

Delpit, L. (2006) *Other People's Children: Cultural Conflict in the Classroom*, New York: New Press.

Dillard, J. L. (1978) 'Bidialectal education: Black English and Standard English in the United States', in B. Spolsky and R. L. Cooper (eds) *Case Studies in Bilingual Education*, Rowley, MA: Newbury House.

Edwards, V. K. (1979) *The West Indian Language Issue in British Schools: Challenges and Responses*, London: Routledge & Kegan Paul.

Edwards, V. (1986) *Language in a Black Community*. Clevedon, UK: Multilingual Matters.

——(1989) 'Dialect and education in Europe: A postscript', in J. Cheshire, V. Edwards, H. Münstermann and B. Weltens (eds) *Dialect and Education: Some European Perspectives*, Clevedon, UK: Multilingual Matters.

Feigenbaum, I. (1970) 'The use of nonstandard English in teaching standard: Contrast and comparison', in R. W. Fasold and R. W. Shuy (eds) *Teaching Standard English in the Inner City*, Washington, DC: Center for Applied Linguistics.

García, O. and Otheguy, R. (1989) (eds) *English across Cultures, Cultures across English: A Reader in Cross-cultural Communication*, Berlin: Mouton de Gruyter.

Gardiner, J. (1977) 'Teaching standard English as a second dialect to speakers of Aboriginal English', in E. Brumby and E. Vaszolyi (eds) *Language Problems and Aboriginal Education'*, Mount Lawley, Western Australia: Aboriginal Teacher Education Program, Mount Lawley College of Advanced Education.

Goodman, K. S. (1969) 'Dialect barriers to reading comprehension', in J. C. Baratz and R. W. Shuy (eds) *Teaching Black Children to Read*, Washington, DC: Center for Applied Linguistics.

Hymes, D. (1962) 'The ethnography of speaking', in T. Gladwin and W. Sturtevant (eds) *Anthropology and Human Behavior*, Washington, DC: Anthropological Society of Washington.

Kamwangamalu, N. M. (2012) 'The medium of instruction conundrum and "minority" language development in Africa', in A. Yiakoumetti (ed.) *Harnessing Linguistic Variation to Improve Education*, Oxford: Peter Lang.

Königsberg, P. and Collard, G. (eds) (2002) *Ways of Being, Ways of Talk*, East Perth, Western Australia: Department of Education and Training.

Königsberg, P., Collard, G. and McHugh, M. (eds) (2012) *Tracks to Two-Way Learning*, East Perth, Western Australia: Department of Education.

Labov, W. (1965) 'Stages in the acquisition of standard English', in R. W. Shuy (ed.) *Social Dialects and Language Learning*, Champaign, IL: National Council of Teachers of English.

——(1969) 'Some sources of reading problems for Negro speakers of nonstandard English', in J. C. Baratz and R. W. Shuy (eds) *Teaching Black Children to Read*, Washington, DC: Center for Applied Linguistics.

——(1970) *The Study of Nonstandard English*, Champaign, IL: National Council of Teachers of English.

——(1972) *Language in the Inner City: Studies in the Black English Vernacular*, Philadelphia: University of Pennsylvania Press.

Littlemore, J. (2009) *Applying Cognitive Linguistics to Second Language Learning and Teaching*, Basingstoke, UK: Palgrave Macmillan.

McDavid, R. I. Jr (1969) 'Dialectology and the teaching of reading', in J. C. Baratz and R. W. Shuy (eds) *Teaching Black Children to Read*, Washington, DC: Center for Applied Linguistics.

McIntosh, S., O'Hanlon, R., and Angelo, D. (2012) 'The (in)visibility of "language" within Australian educational documentation: differentiating *language* from *literacy* and exploring particular ramifications for a group of "hidden" ESL/D learners', in C. Gitsaki and R. B. Baldauf Jr. (eds) *Future Directions in Applied Linguistics: Local and Global Perspectives*, Newcastle upon Tyne: Cambridge Scholars.

Malcolm, I. G. (2011a) 'Issues in English language assessment of Indigenous Australians', *Language Assessment Quarterly*, 8(2):190–9.

——(2011b) 'Learning through standard English: Cognitive implications for post-pidgin/-creole speakers', *Linguistics and Education* 22:261–72.

Malcolm, I. G., Haig, Y., Königsberg, P., Rochecouste, J., Collard, G., Hill, A. and Cahill, R. (1999) *Towards More User-Friendly Education for Speakers of Aboriginal English*, Mount Lawley, Western Australia: Centre for Applied Language and Literacy Research, Edith Cowan University and Education Department of Western Australia.

Malcolm, I. G. and Rochecouste, J. (2000) 'Event and story schemas in Australian Aboriginal English discourse', *English World-Wide* 21(2):261–89.

Malcolm, I. G. and Sharifian, F. (2002) 'Aspects of Aboriginal English oral discourse: an application of cultural schema theory', *Discourse Studies* 4(2):169–81.

May, S. (2012) 'Educational approaches to minorities: context, contest and opportunities', in A. Yiakoumetti (ed.) *Harnessing Linguistic Variation to Improve Education*, Oxford: Peter Lang.

Migge, B., L'église, I. and Bartens, A. (eds) (2010) *Creoles in Education*, Amsterdam: John Benjamins.

Niemeier, S. (2004) 'Linguistic and cultural relativity – Reconsidered for the foreign language classroom', in M. Achard and S. Niemeier (eds) *Cognitive Linguistics, Second Language Acquisition and Foreign Language Teaching*, Berlin: Mouton de Gruyter.

Palmer, G. B. (1996) *Toward a Theory of Cultural Linguistics*, Austin, TX: University of Texas Press.

Palmer, G. B. and Sharifian, F. (2007) 'Applied cultural linguistics: An emerging paradigm', in F. Sharifian and G. B. Palmer (eds) *Applied Cultural Linguistics*, Amsterdam: John Benjamins.

Pavlenko, A. (ed.) (2011) *Thinking and Speaking in Two Languages*, Bristol: Multilingual Matters.

Rickford, J. R. (1999) 'Language diversity and academic achievement in the education of African American students – an overview of the issues', in C. T. Adger, D. Christian and O. Taylor (eds) *Making the Connection: Language and Academic Achievement Among African American Students*, Washington, DC: Center for Applied Linguistics.

Sharifian, F. (2011) *Cultural Conceptualisations and Language*, Amsterdam: John Benjamins.

Sharifian, F., Rochecouste, J., Malcolm, I. G., Königsberg, P. and Collard, G. (2004) *Improving Understanding of Aboriginal Literacy: Factors in Text Comprehension*, East Perth, Western Australia: Department of Education and Training.

Sharifian, F., Truscott, A., Königsberg, P., Malcolm, I. G. and Collard, G. (2012) *'Understanding Stories my Way': Aboriginal-English Speaking Students' (Mis)understanding of School Literacy Materials in Australian English*, Leederville, Western Australia: Institute for Professional Learning, Department of Education.

Shuy, R. W. (1969) 'A linguistic background for developing beginning reading materials for Black children', in J. C. Baratz and R. W. Shuy (eds) (1969) *Teaching Black Children to Read*, Washington, DC: Center for Applied Linguistics.

Shuy, R. W., Wolfram, W. A. and Riley, W. K. (1968) *Field Techniques in an Urban Language Study*, Washington, DC: Center for Applied Linguistics.

Siegel, J. (2010) *Second Dialect Acquisition*, Cambridge: Cambridge University Press.

Slobin, D. (1991) 'Learning to think for speaking: Native language, cognition, and rhetorical style', *Pragmatics* 1:7–25.

Stewart, W. A. (1969) 'On the use of Negro dialect in the teaching of reading', in J. C. Baratz and R. W. Shuy (eds) *Teaching Black Children to Read*, Washington, DC: Center for Applied Linguistics.

——(1970) 'Foreign language teaching methods in quasi-foreign language situations', in R. W. Fasold and R. Shuy, (eds) (1970) *Teaching Standard English in the Inner City*, Washington, DC: Center for Applied Linguistics.

Taylor, H. U. (1989) *Standard English, Black English and Bidialectalism: A Controversy*, New York: Peter Lang.

Trudgill, P. (1979) 'Standard and non-standard dialects of English in the United Kingdom: Problems and policies', *International Journal of the Sociology of Language* 21:9–24.

Trueba, H. T. (1991a) 'Learning needs of minority children: contributions of ethnography to educational research', in L. M. Malavé and G. Duquette (eds) *Language, Culture and Cognition*, Clevedon, UK: Multilingual Matters.

——(1991b) 'The role of culture in bilingual instruction: linking linguistic and cognitive development to cultural knowledge', in O. García (ed.) *Bilingual Education: Focusschrift in Honour of Joshua A. Fishman on the Occasion of his 65th Birthday*, Amsterdam: John Benjamins.

Truscott, A. and Malcolm, I. G. (2011) 'Closing the policy–practice gap: Making Indigenous language policy more than empty rhetoric', in J. Hobson, K. Lowe, S. Poetsch and M. Walsh (eds) *Re-Awakening Languages: Theory and Practice in the Revitalisation of Australia's Indigenous Languages*, Sydney: Sydney University Press.

Tyler, A. (2012) *Cognitive Linguistics and Second Language Learning*, New York: Routledge.

Waara, R. (2004) 'Construal, convention and constructions in L2 speech', in M. Achard and S. Niemeier (eds) *Cognitive Linguistics, Second Language Acquisition and Foreign Language Teaching*, Berlin: Mouton de Gruyter.

Wolfram, W. (1970) 'Sociolinguistic implications for educational sequencing', in R. W. Fasold and R.W. Shuy (eds.) *Teaching Standard English in the Inner City*, Washington: Center for Applied Linguistics.

——(1991) *Dialects and American English*, Englewood Cliffs, NJ: Prentice Hall.

——(1999) 'Repercussions from the Oakland Ebonics Controversy – The Critical Role of Dialect Awareness Programs', in C. T. Adger, D. Christian and O. Taylor (eds) *Making the Connection: Language and Academic Achievement among African American Students*, Washington, DC: Center for Applied Linguistics and Delta Systems Co.

——(2001) 'Reconsidering the sociolinguistic addenda for African American English: The next generation of research and application', in S. L. Lanehart (ed.) *Sociocultural and Historical Contexts of African American English*, Amsterdam: John Benjamins.

Wolfram, W. A. and Fasold, R. W. (1969) 'Toward reading materials for speakers of Black English: three linguistically appropriate passages', in J. C. Baratz and R. W. Shuy (eds) *Teaching Black Children to Read*, Washington, DC: Center for Applied Linguistics.

Wolfram, W., Potter, L., Yanofsky, N. M. and Shuy, R. W. (1979) *Reading and Dialect Differences*, Arlington, VA.: Center for Applied Linguistics.

Yiakoumetti, A. (ed.) (2012) *Harnessing Linguistic Variation to Improve Education*, Oxford: Peter Lang.

30

LANGUAGE AND CULTURE IN INTERCULTURAL COMMUNICATION

Hans-Georg Wolf[1]

1 Introduction

Intercultural communication is a highly diverse field; it is being studied within numerous academic and para-academic disciplines and from a range of more or less interdisciplinary perspectives. Intercultural communication is of concern to researchers and practitioners in various strands of linguistics, translation studies, media and communication research, business and management, ethnography, psychology, pedagogy, sociology, philosophy, and international relations – and this list may not be exhaustive. Moreover, a conglomerate of synonymous or related terms exists, such as 'cross-cultural communication', 'intercultural training', 'intercultural competence', and 'intercultural integration'. A search on Amazon.com (conducted on 29 August 2012) for 'intercultural communication' (all searches with quotation marks) yielded 2,651 results and for 'cross-cultural communication' another 707 hits for books alone. A search conducted on the same day in the Linguistics and Language Behavior Abstracts (LLBA) database (ProQuest) turned out 17,322 results for 'intercultural communication' and 14,559 for 'cross-cultural communication' – and these hits only include the relevant works published in English. Within the framework of this chapter, it is impossible to survey the myriad of books and articles individually. Instead, the attempt is made here to trace basic orientations, theoretical positions and philosophical models towards the triangular constellation of language, culture and (intercultural) communication that, implicitly or explicitly, underlie most works and approaches, and to highlight the particular contribution cultural linguistics can make and has already made to the field.

In concurrence with the multitude of works on this subject matter, one finds nearly as many definitions of 'intercultural communication' or, for that matter, 'cross-cultural communication'. Although, in my view, these two terms are interchangeable (see Allwood 1985: 1; Gudykunst 2003: vii; Scollon *et al.* 2012: 8–10, for a differentiation), the more common and perhaps more encompassing term 'intercultural communication' is used in this chapter. Trying to define this term for the present purpose would lead into a kind of regress, because such a definition – in light of the title of this chapter – would require separate definitions of 'language', 'culture', and 'communication' as well (see Chapters 4 and 7 this volume). To avoid terminological and conceptual entanglements, it seems expedient to presuppose a certain understanding of these terms on the side of the reader and to adopt the near tautological definition of intercultural communication as 'communication between people of different cultures', proposed by Bennett (1998: 2). The generality of this definition, however, does not imply a theoretical randomness, as should become clear in the course of this chapter. At this general level, the most fundamental question informing any theory of intercultural communication is 'what do speakers (or writers) engaging in such communication try or should try to achieve?' The answer to this question is not trivial, but reveals two basic orientations: the predominant paradigm in intercultural communication, across various disciplines, focuses on successful *functioning* in intercultural encounters. The 'minority position', so to say, foregrounds intercultural *understanding*. These two positions reflect different philosophies of communication and ultimately the human existence. Successful or 'effective' functioning, at first sight, does not seem to imply more than the pragmatic tenet of reaching some kind of communicative goal; yet at a closer look, it becomes evident that this position rests on a mechanistic, more often than not market-driven worldview. The alternative position in intercultural communication, on the other hand, is heir to a humanist–hermeneutic model, in which making sense of the world – or specifically making sense of other cultures – is held supreme. Cognitive linguistics – the 'mother paradigm' of cultural linguistics (see Chapter 32 this volume) can be situated in this hermeneutic tradition (see Geeraerts 1992, 1997; Wolf and Polzenhagen 2009: ch. 3). To be sure, in actual studies of intercultural communication, these philosophies are rarely played out in pure form, and functionalist and meaning-oriented approaches need not be mutually exclusive. Moreover, in recent years, a third perspective on intercultural communication has emerged, which, in some ways, is aligned with the first paradigm, but tries to deconstruct culture (and hence intercultural communication) and replace it by a concept of globalization.

This chapter is structured as follows: in section 2, the philosophical positions indicated above are discussed further, with specific reference to the categories 'communication' and 'culture', and cultural linguistics is situated within the humanist–hermeneutic camp. Also, some light is shed on the emergence of the field of intercultural communication itself. Section 3 addresses the following questions: are groups or group membership valid factors in intercultural communication or is only the individual speaker in specific communicative situations (allowed to be) of theoretical interest? Is intercultural understanding possible at all or, in other words, how is the problem of relativism to be dealt with? Finally, how does the fact that English is the global lingua franca impact the study of intercultural communication (see Chapter 18 this volume)? In section 4, cultural–linguistic contributions to the field of intercultural communication are reviewed. These contributions have focused on cultural metaphors and conceptualizations expressed in languages and varieties of languages. Closing this chapter, section 5 points to possible theoretical extensions of the cultural–linguistic approach to intercultural communication and future directions of research.

2 Intercultural communication: historical perspectives and philosophical positions

Intercultural communication as a research paradigm emerged in the context of the US State Department's Foreign Service Institute after the Second World War, with E.T. Hall as the seminal figure (Rogers and Hart 2002: 3–4; also see Martin and Nakayama 2011: 45–8; Piller 2011: 28–33). The field was further developed by American communication scholars in the 1960s and 1970s (Rogers and Hart 2002: 4), though today, it is too multifaceted and fuzzy an area to trace the genealogy of its various strands and approaches that have fed into it (for a broader look, see Martin, Nakayama, and Carbaugh, 2012). Similar to intercultural communication, communication studies themselves are an outgrowth of cold-war efforts at psychological warfare, 'that favored a particular applied and pragmatic approach to communication research ... In this context, communication was conceptualized and investigated as an instrument for persuading or dominating target groups' (Radford 2005: 83). This paradigm understands communication, or language, for that matter, as a tool to reach a desired goal in a particular communicative situation as 'effectively' as possible, with the ultimate aim of control (see Radford 2005: 77–83). This view has gained so much popularity that by now, 'effective communication' and 'to communicate effectively' have become stock phrases in descriptions of communication and language learning programmes. It is easy to see the nexus between such an understanding of communication and the dominant, functionalist view of intercultural communication in linguistic pragmatics. There, culturally induced differences in the topical gamut of linguistic pragmatics (e.g., speech acts, politeness, forms of address, etc.) are seen as impediments to successful or 'effective' communication, i.e., the reaching of some communicative goal or the transfer of messages. A quote from the book description of Kotthoff and Spencer-Oatey's (2007) *Handbook of intercultural communication* may serve as a representative example (also see, e.g., the book description of Rogers and Steinfatt 1999 on Amazon.com n.d.):

> In today's globalized world of international contact and multicultural interaction, effective intercultural communication is increasingly seen as a pre-requisite for social harmony and organizational success. This handbook takes a 'problem-solving' approach to the various issues that arise in real-life intercultural interaction.
>
> *(retrieved from www.degruyter.com n.d.)*

Consequently, interlocutors in intercultural encounters require 'intercultural communication skills' (Martin and Nakayama 2011) to solve 'intercultural problems' and are often metaphorized as 'managers' of the communicative situation and the various factors therein. Such a take on intercultural communication expresses the essence of functionalism and buys directly into a discourse of business. The use of the term 'management' in the context of intercultural communication (for representative examples, see, e.g., Bilbow 1997; Cheng and Tsui 2009; Martin and Nakayama 2011; Neuliep 2012) is particularly revelatory of the particular kind of world-view criticized above. Consider, for example, the definitions of 'management' in the *Oxford English Dictionary* (OED online 2012) and from Wikipedia (2012):

> Organization, supervision, or direction; the application of skill or care in the manipulation, use, treatment, or control (of a thing or person), or in the conduct of something.
>
> *(OED online 2012)*

> Management in all business and organizational activities is the act of getting people together to accomplish desired goals and objectives using available resources efficiently and effectively. Management comprises planning, organizing, staffing, leading or directing, and controlling an organization (a group of one or more people or entities) or effort for the purpose of accomplishing a goal.
>
> *(Wikipedia 2012)*

These notions of management are mapped one-to-one on theories of intercultural communication; not only are language and communication reduced to serving some implicit or explicit purpose but also the interactants involved in it. Moreover, culture seems to be an *a priori* given variable in the description of communicative differences between speakers of different groups, while its 'causal' role is rarely explained (see Blommaert 2011: n.p.; Wolf and Polzenhagen 2006: 288)

Wolf and Polzenhagen (2006, 2009: ch. 3) have critiqued the functionalist view of intercultural pragmatics at length and proposed a more meaning-oriented methodological and theoretical extension of the field, based on cognitive linguistics (for concrete examples, see below) and the hermeneutic philosophy of Hans-Georg Gadamer (also see Vasilache 2003). The hermeneutic orientation foregrounds *understanding* and hence puts the human subject – not a more or less structured system – at the centre of attention. Importantly, cultural stereotypes or pre-conceptions, to use another word, are not seen as some kind of taboo to be avoided (they cannot be), but as necessary preconditions for conceptual change (on conceptual change in intercultural communication, see below). The realization of some anomaly, i.e., of some cultural difference will start the hermeneutic circle of interpretation and reinterpretation, until the partners engaged in an intercultural dialogue will, asymptotically, achieve a degree of mutual understanding, or to use Gadamer's term, a 'fusion of horizons' (Gadamer 1989: 306; see Wolf and Polzenhagen 2009: ch. 3). This process cannot be achieved in singular encounters, but requires continuous intercultural exposure (see Wolf and Polzenhagen 2009: 201–2). At a meta-level, to facilitate the process of intercultural understanding, the task is to work out the preconceptions but also the differences in the conceptualizations and their realizations in language (Wolf and Polzenhagen, 2006: 308). Methodologically, such analyses could follow the 'checklist' of criteria proposed in Wolf and Polzenhagen (2009: 180–1).

A third strand within the field of intercultural communication could be labelled 'deconstructionist' and/or 'postmodernist'. This strand is deconstructionist/postmodernist on various grounds. For one thing, it questions the assumption of a 'linear' connection between communication and culture. Similar to the functionalist approach outlined above, the focus is on actual communicative situations and 'observable linguistic behaviour' therein (see Wolf and Polzenhagen, 2006). Leaning on Gumperz, Blommaert (2011: n.p.) argues that

> 'culture' in the sense of a transcendent identity composed of values and norms and linearly related to forms of behavior is not necessarily there. What can be observed and analyzed in intercultural communication are different conventions of communication, different speech styles, narrative patterns, in short, the deployment of different communicative repertoires.

Furthermore, Blommaert (2011: n.p.), posits 'a massive overestimation of the degree and the nature of differences in speech styles' attributed to cultural differences. In short response to these claims, one could argue that (a) the (purported) identities of participants in communicative situations are not the same as the culturally embodied conceptualizations on which they act and which function as filters of understanding and (b), that the real issue of intercultural communication is not so much communicative repertoire but rather modes of understanding. Concurrent with the restriction of intercultural communication to actual communicative encounters is the denial of 'cultural groups' as a meaningful focus for intercultural studies – a point to which I will return in the following section. Another 'deconstructionist' concern is shifting attention from cultural differences to socio-political inequalities. Arguments of cultural differences, in many instances, are perceived to be merely a 'cloak' to hide issues of discrimination (Piller 2011: ch. 9; also see Blommaert 2011: n.p.). While issues of discrimination and inequality are important social concerns, the deconstructionist strand thus runs the risk of throwing out the baby with the bathwater, i.e., eliminating culture altogether from 'intercultural communication' (though authors of that leaning still make use of this marketable label). 'Culture' as a meaningful category is similarly lost in the postmodernist focus on the situationality, fluidity, and negotiability of interpersonal (to use inter 'cultural' would be a contradiction in terms in this context) encounters. The ideal is communities that are 'not based on commonalities' and the focus on communication that is 'situationally and linguistically accomplished to achieve one's changing and tentative interests and goals' (Canagarajah 2012: 111). Note that the last quote highlights the functionalist leaning of such postmodernist theorizing.

3 Critical issues and topics

This section highlights three critical issues pertaining to language and culture in intercultural communication, two of which are more of a theoretical/philosophical and one more of a practical nature: the validity of situating culture at the group level, the problem of relativism, and culture in English as lingua franca interactions.

3.1 The validity of situating culture at the group level

As mentioned above, in deconstructionist or 'poststructuralist' (Piller 2011: 84) approaches to intercultural communication, groups as bearers and sharers of culture have fallen into disrepute (see Wolf and Polzenhagen 2006: 289–91; Wolf and Polzenhagen 2009: 195–8). The reason is a fear of 'essentialism', i.e., assigning immutable traits to larger groups, such as nations (see Piller 2011). It is believed that positing certain cultural characteristics to specific groups is an act of stereotyping, and stereotyping, in turn, is regarded as a kind of taboo, both at the level of theorizing as well as at the level of actual intercultural communication. Given the multilingual and multicultural reality of most countries in the world, it would indeed be fallacious to equate a nation with a particular culture. Yet it would be equally fallacious to equate a language with a culture, as cultures, or, perhaps less reifying, cultural conceptualizations may be shared across different languages and groups of speakers, and, in turn, may differ for speakers of different varieties of a language (as in the case of English, see below). In sociolinguistics and related fields, the speech community – a group of speakers who share the attachment to a given language or variety – is still the focal point of sociolinguistic investigation, not the individual speaker. As Bennett (1998: 4) cogently argues:

> despite the problems with stereotypes, it is necessary in intercultural communication to make cultural generalizations. Without any kind of supposition or hypothesis about the cultural differences we may encounter in an intercultural situation, we may fall prey to naive individualism, where we assume that every person is acting in some completely unique way. Or we may rely inordinately on 'common sense' to direct our communication behavior. Common sense is, of course, common only to a particular culture. Its application outside of one's own culture is usually ethnocentric.

In fact, if culture is not assumed to be shared, it becomes an analytically useless concept. Sharifian's (2003) model of distributed cultural cognition, understood as 'distributed representations across the minds in cultural groups' (ibid.: 190) allows for generalizations regarding conceptualizations shared by members of a given cultural group, without assuming that all members of that group share all its cultural conceptualizations. The model also consoles the perspective of the individual mind/speaker with that of the group.

As to stereotypes, they cannot be argued away, and 'ignoring them does not mean that they disappear' (Wolf and Polzenhagen 2009: 186). On the contrary, stereotypes should be embraced as important preconditions of understanding and sociolinguistic cognition (see Chapter 18 this volume; and also Kristiansen 2003). 'Prejudices', another word for stereotypes, play an important role in the hermeneutic philosophy of Hans-Georg Gadamer, and theoretically correspond to concepts developed in cognitive linguistics, such as folk model or cultural model (see Wolf and Polzenhagen 2009: 186–7). It is only when we become aware of our own and the other's preconceptions that change, or, in Gadamer's (1989: 306) terms, a 'fusion of horizons' can become possible. Such awareness is triggered by observing 'anomalies' or conceptual divergences in the process of intercultural communication, as in the examples below. Yet awareness is not enough for conceptual change; extended cultural contact with a circle of interpretation and reinterpretation is required (see Wolf and Polzenhagen 2009: ch. 3, for a fuller explanation). With that in mind, it is not theoretically or ethically odious to generalize about cultures. A refreshingly creative example of cultural generalization is the approach by Gannon and Pillai (2010), who metonymically use a specific cultural institution or product as a heuristic to analyse (supposed) cultural characteristics, for example the German symphony, American football, and the Singapore hawker centres (though one has to admit that these – what Gannon and Pillai (2010) call – 'metaphors', may have the same reality-creating effect as reading a horoscope). Culturalist interpretations of language have been common in the nineteenth century and are, by now, an accepted dimension of linguistic discourse again. As part of this development, linguistics is moving closer to cultural studies (see Polzenhagen and Wolf 2010).

3.2 The problem of relativism

A perennial theoretical issue of studies of 'the other' – be they concerned with other cultures or, at the individual level, other minds – is the problem of relativism: for intercultural communication, it revolves around the question of whether understanding (a person from) another culture is possible at all, since 'there is no culturally neutral basis from which the conceptual systems of speakers from different cultures can be compared and described' (Wolf and Polzenhagen 2009: 202). In other words, our own conceptualizations are the lens through which we interpret another culture. This problem is less virulent for functionalist approaches to intercultural communication than it is for meaning-oriented ones, such as cultural linguistics, because the former, as explained above, highlight 'successful functioning' – by whatever standard – rather than intercultural understanding. To address this issue, Wolf and Polzenhagen (2009: 204), leaning on Gadamer, propose a 'cultural consciousness', i.e., a consciousness of our own cultural prejudices that is provoked when we encounter cultural conceptualizations different from the ones we hold. In short, becoming conscious of our own preconceptions is a prerequisite for the initiation of the hermeneutic circle, the process of interpretation and reinterpretation sketched above. While an objective understanding of 'the other' is not possible, individuals can overcome their particular cultural limitations by 'transposing' themselves into another culture. Thereby, we do not give up our own conceptualizations but take them to a higher level of universality, which leads to the abovementioned 'fusion of horizons' (see Wolf and Polzenhagen 2009: 205; and Gadamer 1989: 306). This notion is in theoretical accord with cognitive theories of cultural contact and blending, as outlined in section 5 below.

3.3 The problem of culture in English as lingua franca interactions

It is common knowledge that English is the most widely used lingua franca in the world (see Kaur 2009). While most intercultural encounters take place in English, the academic fields of intercultural communication and English as a Lingua Franca (ELF) / English as an International Language (EIL) have not yet converged in any significant way. So far, one cannot but fail to notice two neglects: On the one hand, most scholars working the field of ELF have not seriously addressed the issue of culture. To refer to two representative examples: both in a recent issue of *Intercultural Pragmatics* (2009) devoted to English as a lingua franca as well as in a collective volume featuring prominent proponents of the field (Mauranen and Ranta 2009), a discussion of 'culture' is conspicuously absent. On the other hand, the established works in intercultural communication are only beginning to realize the importance of the fact that Englishes are the main linguistic modes for intercultural encounters. Scollon *et al.*, for instance, only briefly refer to English as a global language and 'distinctive patterns of discourse ... carried within English' (Scollon *et al.* 2012: 18), though they acknowledge underlying cognitive schemata and scripts elsewhere (Scollon *et al.* 2012: 74–5). Yet, as the examples in the following section demonstrate, intercultural communication involves diverging culture-specific conceptualizations on the side of the interactants (also see Sharifian 2009). One would be deceived to restrict problems of English as a lingua franca only to phonetics, syntax, lexicon, and discourse patterns. The cognitive–sociolinguistic and cultural linguistic approaches (for a distinction, see Wolf and Polzenhagen 2009: xi) to World Englishes are ideal to systematically describe cultural conceptualizations realized in the different varieties of English. These approaches can thus make an important contribution to the study of intercultural communication and pedagogic approaches to intercultural competence (see Sharifian 2012b).

4 Cultural–linguistic and cognate contributions to 'language, culture, and intercultural communication'

A central tenet of cognitive linguistics is that 'culture ... is not an external category in linguistic investigations [but] an integral dimension of it' (Wolf & Polzenhagen 2009: 19). Hence, potentially all cognitive–linguistic studies, and especially those investigating metaphor, could contribute to intercultural understanding, as defined above. Yet the various strands and approaches within cognitive linguistics or congenial to it are far too numerous to be reviewed here. They have been classified and described in Wolf and Polzenhagen (2009: section 1.3), to which the reader may refer for further details. Instead, studies within Cultural Linguistics or those that have applied cultural–linguistic and/or cognitive–linguistic approaches explicitly to problems of intercultural communication are discussed in the following (also see Sharifian 2012a, 2012b).

A first cluster of studies has come from a research team around Ian Malcolm, from Edith Cowan University, Australia. Applying, *inter alia*, schema theory (see Chapters 18, 21, 26, and 29 this volume) to discourse analysis, these researchers elucidated how divergent cultural schemata can lead to intercultural misunderstanding, and, in a wider perspective, educational and social problems. The bulk of these studies has been on Australian Aboriginal English (see, e.g., Malcolm and Rochecouste 2000; Sharifian 2001, 2004, 2010; Sharifian *et al.* 2004) vis-à-vis 'Anglo-Australian English' (their term), but also on Chinese Australian English (Hui 2004, 2005), and Persian (e.g., Sharifian 2005, 2008; Sharifian and Jamarani 2011).

A short exchange between an Aboriginal Australian (B) and an Australian with a different (unspecified) cultural background (F) illustrates the problem:

> B: They told me my Auntie is sick, I wen' an' gave a pump to 'er heart, she was alright then.
> F: Where does she live?
> B: She lives up north.
> F: It must have been a long trip.
> B: (Puzzled) What trip?!!

(Sharifian 2011: 83)

As Sharifian (ibid.) explains, the misunderstanding is due to F's unfamiliarity with the Aboriginal speaker's conceptualization pertaining to the spiritual form of healing, which does not require physical proximity of the healer. Moreover, F was apparently unaware of the fact that B is considered to be *clever* or a *cleverman*, terms that, in Aboriginal Australian English, denote a person with 'special Spiritual powers such as healing at a distance' (ibid.). Numerous other accounts of intercultural misunderstandings between Aboriginal Australians and Anglo-Australians due to conceptualisations pertaining, e.g., to HOME, FAMILY, ANCESTORS, SPIRITS, SING, SMOKE, and MEDICINE can be found in Sharifian (2010, 2011).

Focusing on Chinese Australians, Hui concentrated on differences regarding the FAMILY schema between English speakers of this group and Anglo-Australians (Hui 2004), as well as on the Chinese cultural schema of EDUCATION in an Australian context (Hui 2005). She notes that the evocation of the FAMILY schema in interactions between these two groups of speakers can lead to misunderstandings or even communicative failure, as the example 'Talking about his family', taken from her corpus of spoken Anglo-Australian English and Chinese Australian English discourse (Hui, unpublished manuscript), demonstrates. The passage is shortened and slightly edited for the purpose of this chapter. *A* is an Anglo-Australian, *C* a Chinese speaker of English (no further information was given on the background of the speakers):

> C: I came from southern, southern China. It's a, the place where I come from is very small village … **My father** is a fisherman, but originally, he came from the farm. He is **both a farmer and a fisherman**. He is **very good** with fishing (A: laughing). He, he **always, always** goes to fishing.
>
> .
>
> A: Yeah, yeah, oh, it's good to do something
> C: that's practical work
> A: for your family, yeah
> C: A lot practical work, same as my. It's very funny, you know **my whole traditional family**, my, my fa- my grandfather, he is a woodworker. He made things. Same as my mo- as father, but **my father** leave me about, when I was about 12 years old.
>
> .
>
> C: But **my brother** is different from me. He
> A: Oh? What does he like?
> C: He likes to play sports.
>
> .
>
> C: I only enjoy playing table tennis, and I'm only good at table tennis. (A laughing). That's weird. **Everyone is different. My brother**, he loves all kinds of sports, crickets, footy, soccer, badminton, tennis, all sorts of sports.
> C: Now **my father** lives with me and my brother. He looks after both of us.
> A: So all boys are together in the family. (C: yes) So who does the cooking? Your father?
> C: **My dad is a very good cooker**.
>
> .
>
> C: I'm not a very good cooker, but **my brother**, he, he likes cooking. I don't. But one thing **my father** is not good at is the electronics and electricity, and the electricity. And that's why I want, that's one of most the things we work now. So Asian, so I want my **sons and my grandsons** knows something about electronics and electricity, that's it. That's one thing that **my grandparents** don't know about, so I'll learn about that.
> A: That's new in the world, isn't? I bet your grandparent don't.

C: Yeah, it changes the future, you know, it changes the future. So that's one of the things that that we grow up with.

A: Good. And has your father ever wanted to go back to China?

C: **He** loves to, but unfortunately, um, he doesn't have that kind of money, you know.

.

A: And so have you got family back there like

C: Oh yes! I do, I have **my two uncles, and one, three aunties**, and I've got **lots of cousins**. I've got five, oh, seven or eight in my village.

A: So it's only you and your brother, how do you get to meet girls? Do you only meet Chinese girls, or do you also meet Australian girls, or girls from school?

C: *What do you mean?*

The passages in bold face signal instantiations of the Chinese informant's FAMILY schema, in which notions of the extended family, as well as family roles and relations, are salient (also see Polzenhagen and Wolf 2010 for further empirical validation). To paraphrase Hui (unpublished manuscript), for the Chinese informant, the FAMILY domain is a conceptually 'closed' mental space, at least in this stretch of discourse, in 'that he was not prepared to talk about anyone outside his family'. Moreover, Hui (unpublished manuscript) observes vigilance and discomfort on the side of the Chinese informant.

As to speakers of English with a Persian background, Sharifian (2005, 2008) investigated the Persian cultural schema SHEKASTEH-NAFSI, 'modesty', which surfaces in interactions with Anglo-Australians, while Sharifian and Jamarani (2011) focused on the Persian schema of SHARMAN-DEGI. The occurrence of the latter in intercultural communication is briefly reviewed in the following. SHARMANDEGI is activated in instances of 'expressing gratitude', 'offering goods and services', 'requesting goods and services', 'apologizing' and 'accepting offers and refusals' (Sharifian and Jamarani 2011). In their data, they found that the English equivalents of '*sharmandam* (a short form for *sharmandeh hastam* meaning "I'm ashamed") or *sharmandam mikonid* (meaning "you make me ashamed")' (Sharifian and Jamarani 2011: 233) are frequently used by Persians in interactions with Anglo-Australians. Sharifian and Jamarani (2011) systematized and interpreted a number of communicative situations for each pragmatic function. Their example for 'expressing gratitude' may serve as an illustration:

> Mr. Anderson (Australian) and Roya (Iranian) are neighbors. Each month when mowing his lawn, Mr Anderson mows Roya's front lawn as well. She is very pleased, and one day tells him: Roya: You always make me ashamed by mowing my lawn. (Mr. Anderson stopped mowing her lawn from that date.)
>
> *(Sharifian and Jamarani 2011: 237)*

Sharifian and Jamarani (ibid.) believe that Mr. Anderson stopped mowing Roya's lawn in order to avoid making her ashamed, while Roya, whom they interviewed, finds it strange that Mr. Anderson stopped mowing her lawn after she thanked him.

Applying a mix of corpus–linguistic methods, conceptual metaphor analysis and questionnaire surveys, Wolf and Polzenhagen (2006) focused on conceptualizations pertaining to the domain(s) of FAMILY, AGE, and ANCESTORS and issues of intercultural incomprehension or misunderstanding. Their study involved L2-speakers of English from Cameroon, Hong Kong, and Germany, whose respective concepts and conceptualizations differ markedly. The point Wolf and Polzenhagen make, though, is that misunderstandings may not be apparent in actual communicative situations, when English terms, for example kinship terms like *cousin* or *sister* or the term *family* itself, are used by speakers from different cultural backgrounds. These terms are identical in form but not in meaning across the varieties in which they are used. Yet speakers may take the meaning particular to their own culture for granted. For example, a speaker with a Western background may assume that an African speaker's reference to 'my cousin' is restricted to sons and daughters of aunts and uncles (again understood here in a Western sense), while the African speaker refers to a person from, say, the same village. It is only through extended cultural exposure that speakers may become aware of a cultural 'mismatch' (Wolf and Polzenhagen 2006: 295; also see above).

Concentrating on discourse in international diplomacy, Slingerland *et al.* (2007) investigated how shared and divergent conceptual metaphors were played out in the so-called 'EP3' or 'Hainan Island Incident' – the collision of an American EP-3E surveillance plane with a Chinese F-8 fighter in 2001. The collision resulted in the death of the Chinese pilot, the unauthorized emergency landing of the American plane on China's Hainan Island, the detention of the American crew, a bilateral dispute over China's demand for a formal apology and eventually the US government's issuing of a letter in which they stated their regrets. In a corpus of media reports on the incident, Slingerland *et al.* (2007) identified seven 'coding families' (their term), i.e., sets of related conceptual metaphors expressed in the media accounts. They found that the Chinese and the American side shared the use of conceptual metaphors pertaining to WAR, ECONOMY, and JOURNEY. GAME and TECHNICAL FIX metaphors were exclusively used by the Americans; on the other hand, VICTIM and INTERNATIONAL RELATIONS AS CIVIL RELATIONS were predominant conceptualizations expressed by Chinese and nearly absent in American discourse. Importantly, Slingerland *et al.* (2007) add a hitherto neglected theoretical dimension to conceptual metaphor analysis, namely the emotive component of the metaphors – what they call 'somatic marking'. The authors find it to be no coincidence that GAME and TECHNICAL FIX metaphors are used by the Americans, since these metaphors 'are value-neutral, unemotional, impersonal, and frame a situation in which blame and apology are equally inappropriate'. In other words, they serve the purpose of averting China's insistence on a formal apology. On the other hand, VICTIM and INTERNATIONAL RELATIONS AS CIVIL RELATIONS conceptualizations, used by the Chinese side with references to 'violation, victimization, nation as home, and breach of social etiquette' (Slingerland *et al.* 2007: 68) are emotionally charged. As Slingerland *et al.* (ibid.: 69) explain:

> Someone breaking into your home and killing your son (the violation of home and family metaphor used by the Chinese) is most definitely not a game. The Chinese emphasis on violation and victimization clashes with the American emphasis on reaction to the incident as a game or puzzle in which one outmaneuvers the opponent … These competing metaphors help explain the contentious stalemate over the need for an apology. The Chinese metaphor of violation or egregious rudeness calls up a need for punishment of a perpetrator, or at least contrition on the part of the perpetrator to avoid punishment.

Slingerland *et al*.s study shows that *understanding* cultural conceptualizations can be literally vital in intercultural dealings. Moreover, it ties in with Hui's and Wolf and Polzenhagen's claims regarding the importance of family and family conceptualizations in Chinese culture, underscoring once again the value and importance of a cultural–linguistic approach to intercultural communication.

5 Future directions

As outlined in the preceding section, studies in cultural linguistics have proven to be fruitful for a deeper understanding of intercultural differences. Yet, as the brief survey of works showed, to date only a small portion of the cultures in English and a few other languages have been studied from a cultural–linguistic angle. These studies could serve as models for the investigation of all possible kinds of intercultural constellations. Yet while the methodological apparatuses of cognitive sociolinguistics and cultural linguistics applied so far has proven its worth for a more encompassing and philosophically deeper take on intercultural communication, they would benefit from theoretical and methodological extensions. For example, the conceptual effects on and changes for participants in intercultural encounters are largely unexplored (see 3.1 above). Here, one needs to distinguish between 'online' adaptations in actual communicative situations or at initial stages of intercultural encounters – pace the functionalist approaches – on the one hand, and long-term changes in the conceptual structures of individuals or speech communities at large on the other. Following Schmid *et al.* (2008: 94), one could envisage studies based on Fauconnier and Turner's (e.g. 2002) Blending Theory for the former, more discourse-oriented perspective, and the *syncretic concept* approach developed by Schmid, Ibriszimov, Zulyadaini, Gottschligg, and Kopatsch (see Ibriszimov and Zulyadaini 2005a, 2005b; Schmid *et al.*, 2008; Ibriszimov & Zulyadaini 2009; Ibriszimov & Zulyadaini 2011) for the latter. According to Fauconnier (n.d.: 1–2):

> Mental spaces are very partial assemblies constructed as we think and talk, for purposes of local understanding and action. They containin [*sic*] elements and are structured by frames and cognitive models. Mental spaces are connected to long-term schematic knowledge, such as the frame for walking along a path, and to long-term specific knowledge ... Spaces are built up from many sources. One of these is the set of conceptual domains we already know about (e.g., eating and drinking, buying and selling, social conversation in public places). A single mental space can be built up out of knowledge from many separate domains.

Forceville (n.d.: 1), accordingly, interprets input spaces to be variously constrained by 'the communicative situation in which it is used'. Moreover, 'because blends are contextualized ad-hoc structures', he sees the need 'to discuss them as intentional, discursive chunks of information' (ibid.: 4).

To the best of my knowledge, no studies exist that have applied Blending Theory to instances of intercultural communication in any systematic way – and hence no elaborated example is available that could be cited here – but one can immediately realize the explanatory power Blending Theory may have for the topic at hand. Consider the following non-linguistic example. In very simple terms, the picture below depicts the artefactual result of a conceptual blend, with WESTERN EATING UTENSILS and ASIAN EATING UTENSILS as separate input spaces.

Syncretic concepts, instead, 'are defined as the results of conceptual blending in a linguistic and cultural contact situation whose cognitive structures are different from the two (or more) input concepts to such an extent that they can be seen as emergent, qualitatively new concepts in their own right, emancipated from their sources' (Schmid *et al.* 2008: 94). To stay with the pictorial example, it can be argued that the gadgets shown there have not achieved the state of conceptual independence from their sources or, for that matter, independence in use, in that a new style of consuming food would have materialized in which their combined technical functions would be essential. In contrast, Schmid *et al*.'s (2008) nuanced study shows that in Nigerian English qualitatively new concepts have emerged in that they share the linguistic forms with native varieties of English but differ significantly from related concepts in Hausa and American English. Schmid *et al*.'s methodology, inspired by Rosch's 'attribute-listing task', would lend itself to testing cultural–conceptual change across all L2-varieties of English.

Akin to this approach would be the application of a connectionist model in which cultural schemas and conceptualizations are 'viewed as emerging from the interactions between the

Figure 30.1 The artefactual result of a conceptual blend, with Western eating utensils and Asian eating utensils as separate input spaces (Found on coolest-gadgets.com, accessed 1 September 2012)

minds that constitute the cultural group' (Sharifian 2003: 192). This model could well be extended to interactions between members of different cultural groups, from which new or hybrid conceptualizations emerge.

Long-lasting cultural contacts and their effects on languages and their speakers are also at the heart of postcolonial pragmatics, a recent new strand of pragmalinguistic studies (see Anchimbe and Janney 2011a). Postcolonial pragmatics sheds light on discourse in postcolonial communicative situations, which, more often than not, are cultural and linguistically highly complex. Importantly, postcolonial pragmatics makes clear that time-honoured concepts of pragmatics, such as politeness, face and speech acts – which were developed in Western contexts – are not always adequate or applicable in postcolonial ones; i.e., are not universal (see Anchimbe and Janney 2011b: 1452–4). While the works produced in this paradigm are of the functionalist nature described in section 2 above and lack a cognitive., i.e., cultural linguistic explanation, the examples provided in Anchimbe and Janney for 'group/collective face' in Nigerian English, for 'social roles across languages' in African societies (in terms of 'parenthood, mentorhood, and advice-giving ... performed by people who may not necessarily be related in that role-capacity to those for whom those roles are performed', for 'levels of formality and politeness across languages' as well as for 'naming and name avoidance' (ibid.: 1454–7) could all be related to the African COMMUNITY model, described, e.g., in Wolf and Polzenhagen (2009). In the future, postcolonial pragmatics may fruitfully incorporate cultural linguistic approaches and vice versa.

Finally, from a more applied perspective, the cognitively oriented approach to intercultural communication needs to seek contact with scholars working in second language teaching and pedagogy in order to transfer its insights into the development of intercultural competencies (see Sharifian 2012b).

6 Conclusion

Intercultural communication is a highly diversified and variegated field, and a multitude of approaches is surely required to capture the complexities of today's multilingual and multicultural world. Despite this diversity, two broad theoretical orientations can be discerned: one is more concerned with successful or effective functioning in instances of intercultural communication, while the other foregrounds long-term understanding. Besides, there also exist postmodernist/ deconstructionist writings on intercultural communication, which denigrate the reality of culture as a parameter in discoursal encounters. Hence, as a matter of earnestness, these writings should not come under the label 'intercultural'. This chapter highlighted cultural linguistics and cognate fields of cognitive linguistics as powerful tools to describe and come to grips with cultural conceptualizations realized in language. While a number of such studies already exists, the cultural linguistic paradigm within intercultural communication is only emerging.

Related topics

language and culture: a historical account; language, culture and prototypes/prototypicality; language, culture, and interaction; culture and kinship language; language, culture, and identity; language and culture in sociolinguistics; language and culture in cognitive anthropology; language and cultural embodiment, cultural linguistics; embodiment and culture; language and culture in second dialect learning; world Englishes and local cultures

Further reading

Christina Bratt Paulston, Scott F. Kiesling and Elizabeth S. Rangel (eds). (2012) *The handbook of intercultural discourse and communication*. Chichester, UK: Wiley-Blackwell. (This handbook looks at intercultural communication from a variety of perspectives and includes theoretical discussions of the topic as well as concrete case studies.)
Jackson, Jane (ed.). (2012) *The Routledge handbook of language and intercultural communication*, 17–36. New York/London: Routledge. (This edited volume is very broad in scope and covers a range of both theoretical and applied approaches to intercultural and communication.)

Note

1 I would like to thank Frank Polzenhagen for a critical review of the text and his comments.

References

Allwood, Jens. (1985) 'Intercultural communication. English translation of: "Tvärkulturell kommunikation"', in Allwood, J. (ed.). *Tvärkulturell kommunikation, Papers in Anthropological Linguistics 12*, University of Göteborg, Dept. of Linguistics. Available HTTP: <http://sskkii.gu.se/jens/publications/docs001-050/041E.pdf> (accessed 29 August 2012).
Amazon.com n.d. Book description of Rogers. Everett M. and Thomas M. Steinfatt (1999) *Intercultural Communication*. Prospect Heights, IL: Waveland Press. Available HTTP: <http://www.amazon.com/Intercultural-Communication-Everett-M-Rogers/dp/1577660323/ref=sr_1_1?ie=UTF8&qid=1347877 860&sr=8-1&keywords=Roger+and+Steinfatt> (accessed 17 September 2012).
Anchimbe, Eric and Richard W. Janney (2011a) 'Postcolonial pragmatics', special issue, *Journal of Pragmatics* 43.
——(2011b) 'Postcolonial pragmatics: An introduction', special issue, *Journal of Pragmatics* 43: 1451–9.
Bennett, Milton J. (1998) 'Intercultural communication: A current perspective', in Milton J. Bennett (ed.), *Basic concepts of intercultural communication: Selected readings*, 1–20. Yarmouth, ME: Intercultural Press. Available HTTP: <http://www.ikwa.eu/resources/Bennett_intercultural_communication.pdf> (accessed 29 August 2012).
Bilbow, Grahame T. (1997) 'Cross-cultural impression management in the multicultural workplace: The special case of Hong Kong', *Journal of Pragmatics* 28: 461–87.
Blommaert, Jan (2011) *Different approaches to intercultural communication: A critical survey. Plenary lecture, Lernen und Arbeiten in einer international vernetzten und multikulturellen Gesellschaft*, Expertentagung Universität Bremen, Institut für Projektmanagement und Wirtschaftsinformatik (IPMI), 27–28 February 1998. Available HTTP: <http://www.flw.ugent.be/cie/CIE/blommaert1.htm> (accessed 19 September 2012).
Canagarajah, Suresh (2012) 'Postmodernism and intercultural discourse: World Englishes', in Christina Bratt Paulston, Scott F. Kiesling, and Elizabeth S. Rangel (eds), *The handbook of intercultural discourse and communication*, 110–32. Chichester, UK: Wiley-Blackwell.

Cheng, Winnie and Amy B.M. Tsui (2009) '"ahh ((laugh)) well there is no comparison between the two I think": How do Hong Kong Chinese and native speakers of English disagree with each other?', *Journal of Pragmatics* 41: 2365–80.

degruyter.com. n.d. Produktinfo for Kotthoff, Helga and Helen Spencer-Oatey (eds) (2007) *Handbook of intercultural communication* (Handbooks of Applied Linguistics 7). Berlin/New York: Mouton de Gruyter. Available HTTP: <http://www.degruyter.com/view/product/38919?rskey=xnj3D6&result=3&q= Kotthoff> (accessed 17 September 2012).

Fauconnier, Gilles. n.d. 'Mental spaces'. Available HTTP: <http://terpconnect.umd.edu/~israel/Fauconnier-MentalSpaces.pdf> (accessed 22 November 2012).

Fauconnier, Gilles and Mark Turner (2002) *The way we think: Conceptual blending and the mind's hidden complexities*. New York: Basic Books.

Forceville, Charles (n.d.) 'A course in pictorial and multimodal metaphor. Lecture 6. Metaphor, hybrids, and blending theory'. Available HTTP: <http://projects.chass.utoronto.ca/semiotics/cyber/cforceville6.pdf> (accessed 1 September 2012).

Gadamer, Hans-Georg (1989) [1960] *Truth and method*, 2nd rev. edn. Translation rev. by Joel Weinsheimer and Donald G. Marshall. New York: Continuum.

Gannon, Martin J. and Rajnandini Pillai (2010) *Understanding global cultures: Metaphorical journeys through 29 nations, cluster of nations, continents, and diversity*, 4th edn. Thousand Oaks, CA: Sage.

Geeraerts, Dirk (1992) 'The return of hermeneutics to lexical semantics', in Martin Pütz (ed.) *Thirty years of linguistic evolution. Studies in honour of René Dirven on the occasion of his 60th birthday*, 257–82. Amsterdam/Philadelphia: John Benjamins.

——(1997) *Diachronic prototype semantics*. Oxford: Clarendon.

Gudykunst, William B. (2003) 'Foreword', in William B. Gudykunst (ed.), *Cross-cultural and intercultural communication*, vii–ix. Thousand Oaks, CA: Sage.

Hui, Leng (2003) 'The influences of cultural schemas on intercultural communication between Chinese speakers of English and Anglo-Australians', unpublished manuscript.

——(2004) 'Cultural knowledge and foreign language teaching and learning: A study of Chinese family schemas in language, culture and intercultural communication', *Hong Kong Journal of Applied Linguistics* 9(2): 17–37.

——(2005) 'Chinese cultural schema of Education: Implications for communication between Chinese students and Australian educators', *Issues in Educational Research* 15(1): 17–35.

Ibriszimow, Dymitr, Hans-Jörg Schmid, and Balarabe Zulyadaini (2005) '"My clothes are my home" or what do we really mean? A Hausa example', in Catherine Baroin, Gisela Seidensticker-Brikay and Kiyari Tijani (eds), *Man and the lake. Proceedings of the XIIth Mega-Chad conference, Centre for Trans-Saharan-Studies*, 185–95. Maiduguri: Centre for Trans-Saharan Studies.

Ibriszimow, Dymitr and Balarabe Zulyadaini (2009) 'I think what you think. An evaluation of L1 and L2 Hausa cognitive structures', in Eva Rothmaler (ed.), *Topics in Chadic linguistics V. Papers from the 4th BICCL*, 95–103. Köln: Rüdiger Köppe Verlag.

——(2011) 'Fighting friends with a scent of a bride: Wives, 'family' and 'relatives' in Hausa from a cognitive semantic point of view', in Doris Löhr and Ari Awagana (eds), *Topics in Chadic linguistics VI. Papers from the 5th BICCL*, 101–7. Köln: Rüdiger Köppe Verlag.

Kaur, Jagdish (2009) *English as a lingua franca: Co-constructing understanding*. Saarbrücken: VDM Verlag.

Kristiansen, Gitte (2003) 'How to do things with allophones: Linguistic stereotypes as cognitive reference points in social cognition', in René Dirven, Roslyn Frank, and Martin Pütz (eds), *Cognitive Models in language and thought. Ideology, metaphors and meanings*, 69–120. [Cognitive Linguistic Research 24]. Berlin – New York: Mouton de Gruyter.

Malcolm, Ian and Judith Rochecouste (2000) 'Event and story schemas in Australian Aboriginal English discourse', *English World-Wide* 21(2): 261–89.

Martin, Judith N. and Thomas K. Nakayama (2011) *Intercultural communication in contexts*, 5th edn. New York: McGraw-Hill.

Martin, Judith N., Thomas K. Nakayama and Donal Carbaugh (2012) 'The history and development of the study of intercultural communication and applied linguistics', in Jane Jackson (ed.), *The Routledge handbook of language and intercultural communication*, 17–36. New York/London: Routledge.

Mauranen, Anna and Elina Ranta (eds) (2009) *English as a lingua franca: Studies and findings*. Newcastle upon Tyne: Cambridge Scholars Publishing.

Neuliep, James W. (2012) *Intercultural communication: A contextual approach*, 5th ed. Thousand Oaks: CA: Sage.

OED Online, Oxford University Press. Available HTTP: <http://www.oed.com/view/Entry/113218> (accessed 12 November 2012).

Piller, Ingrid (2011) *Intercultural communication: A critical introduction*. Edinburgh: Edinburgh University Press.

Polzenhagen, Frank and Hans-Georg Wolf (2010) 'Investigating culture from a linguistic perspective: An exemplification with Hong Kong English', *Linguistics and cultural studies*, special issue, ed. by Christian Mair and Barbara Korte. *Zeitschrift für Anglistik und Amerikanistik (ZAA)*: 58(3): 281–303.

Radford, Gary P. (2005) *On the philosophy of communication*. Belmont, CA: Thomson Wadsworth.

Rogers, Everett M. and William B. Hart. (2002) 'The histories of intercultural, international and development communication', in Gudykunst, William B. and Bella Mody (eds), *Handbook of international and intercultural communication*, 2nd edn, 1–18. Thousand Oaks, CA: Sage.

Schmid, Hans-Jörg, Dymitr Ibriszimov, Karina Kopatsch and Peter Gottschligg (2008) 'Conceptual blending in language, cognition, and culture. Towards a methodology for the linguistic study of syncretic concepts', in Afe Adogame, Magnus Echtler and Ulf Vierke (eds), *Unpacking the new: Critical perspectives on cultural syncretization in Africa and beyond*, 93–124 (Beiträge zur Afrikaforschung 36). Zürich/Berlin: LIT Verlag.

Scollon, Ron, Suzanne Wong Scollon and Rodney H. Jones (2012) *Intercultural communication: A discourse approach*, 3rd edn, Chichester, UK: Wiley-Blackwell.

Sharifian, Farzad (2001) 'Schema-based processing in Australian speakers of Aboriginal English', *Language and Intercultural Communication* 1(2): 120–34.

——(2003) 'On cultural conceptualisations', *Journal of Cognition and Culture* 3(3): 187–207.

——(2005) 'The Persian cultural schema of *shekasteh-nafsi*: A study of complement responses in Persian and Anglo-Australian speakers', *Pragmatics & Cognition* 13(2): 337–61.

——(2008) 'Cultural schemas in L1 and L2 complement responses: A study of Persian-speaking learners of English', *Journal of Politeness Research* 4(1): 55–80.

——(2009) 'Cultural conceptualisations in English as an international language', in Farzad Sharifian (ed.), *English as an international language: Perspectives and pedagogical issues*. Bristol, UK: Multilingual Matters.

——(2010) 'Cultural conceptualizations in intercultural communication: A study of Aboriginal and non-Aboriginal Australians', *Journal of Pragmatics* 42: 3367–76.

——(2011) *Cultural conceptualisations and language: Theoretical framework and applications*. Amsterdam/Philadelphia: John Benjamins.

——(2012a) 'Cultural Linguistics and intercultural communication', in Farzad Sharifian and Maryam Jamarani (eds), *Language and intercultural communication in the new era*. Oxford: Routledge/Taylor and Francis.

——(2012b) 'World Englishes, intercultural communication, and requisite competencies', in Jane Jackson (ed.), *The Routledge handbook of language and intercultural communication*. New York/London: Routledge.

Sharifian. Farzad and Maryam Jamarani (2011) 'Cultural schemas in intercultural communication: A study of Persian cultural schema of *sharmandegi* "being ashamed"', *Intercultural Pragmatics* 8(2): 227–51.

Sharifian, F., Judith Rochecouste and Ian G. Malcolm (2004) '"It was all a bit confusing … "': Comprehending Aboriginal English texts', *Language, Culture, and Curriculum* 17(3): 203–28.

Slingerland, Edward, Eric M. Blanchard and Lyn Boyd-Judson (2007) 'Collision with China: Conceptual metaphor analysis, somatic marking, and the EP-3 Incident', *International Studies Quarterly* 51: 53–77.

Vasilache, Andreas (2003) *Interkulturelles Verstehen nach Gadamer und Foucault*. Frankfurt/M. and New York: Campus Verlag.

Wikipedia: 'Management'. Available HTTP: <http://en.wikipedia.org/wiki/Management> (accessed 19 September 2012).

Wolf, Hans-Georg and Frank Polzenhagen (2006) 'Intercultural communication in English: Arguments for a cognitive approach to intercultural pragmatics', *Intercultural Pragmatics* 3(3): 285–321.

——(2009) *World Englishes: A cognitive sociolinguistic approach*. Applications of Cognitive Linguistics 8. Berlin: Mouton de Gruyter.

31

WORLD ENGLISHES AND LOCAL CULTURES

Andy Kirkpatrick

Introduction

The relationship between language and culture is complex and the subject of several chapters in this *Handbook* (e.g. Chapters 2, 30, and 32 this volume). This chapter will consider how different varieties of English reflect the culture and pragmatic norms of their speakers. While different varieties of English can be distinguished by their distinctive use of morpho-syntactic and phonological features, although many share non-standard forms, it is the reflection of the local culture and the pragmatic norms of its speakers that really create a distinctive variety of English. This process has been called acculturation (Kachru 2005; Sridar 2012) which is the process by which a language takes on the cultural cloak of its speakers. In the case of varieties of English, acculturation is often accompanied by deculturation, where the new variety of English divests itself of cultural references to older varieties, such as British English. And when the new varieties of English are postcolonial, this typically occurs at what Schneider has called the 'nativisation' stage of a new variety of English, a stage at which ties with the country or origin are weakening and interethnic contacts are strengthening (2007, 2010: 381) Acculturation is accomplished through several means. These are presented below, along with examples.

Making words make a new variety

A common way in which a new variety of English takes on the culture of its speakers involves several processes associated with vocabulary. For example, the new variety of English will adopt words from local languages which reflect and describe local phenomena.

Australian English is characterized by the adoption of many words from different Australian Aboriginal languages. To take three 'iconic' words of Australian English as examples, *kangaroo*, *koala*, and *boomerang*, all three come from Aboriginal languages, with kangaroo coming from the Guugu Yimidhirr language of Northeast Queensland and the other two from the Dharuk language spoken around the Sydney region. Australian English's need for words from Australian Aboriginal languages is not surprising. A local variety of English needs ways of describing local flora and fauna and it is natural for the local words for these to be adopted. Words which describe Aboriginal culture have also been adopted. To give just one example, *corroboree* (also from Dharuk) describes a dance ceremony (Dixon, Ransom, and Thomas, 1990). We shall see below how Aboriginal culture has also fashioned new meanings to English words.

Many scholars of world Englishes have described the ways in which words from local languages have entered the local variety of English. Kachru, who can justifiably be called the founder of the field of world Englishes, has been the pathfinder in this respect for Indian English and has shown how the process which he terms 'hybridisation' (1983: 38) operates to create new and creative words, phrases and expressions. Examples of Hindi-English hybrids are *lathi charge* (a baton charge by police) and *tiffin carrier* (a receptacle for carrying cooked food) are two well-known examples. Suffixes from local languages can also be attached to 'English' words to create these new hybrids. *Police-wala* (policeman) is an example. Similarly, English suffixes can be attached to Hindi words. *Patelship* (being Indian) is an example.

Suffixes can be used in other creative ways. For example, both Nigerian and Ghanaian English have the words *enstool* and *enskin* to describe the official installation of a tribal chief (Ahulu 1994; Bamiro 1994). These are clearly adapted from *enthrone*, but to suit the circumstance whereby the chief is placed on a stool rather than a throne as such, and clothed in an animal skin.

This process can also be seen in currently developing varieties of English, over which there is debate about whether they can yet be classified as varieties of English. There is no doubt, however, that Chinese English, for example, has adopted many words of Chinese, some of which are now familiar in traditional varieties of English such as British English. Some of these are now so familiar that they occur in many different varieties of English. Examples include *fengshui* (a form of geomancy) and *guanxi* (relationships – usually used in the context of their importance in doing business in China). Xu (2010: 285–7) gives many other examples, such as *xiaokang* as in a *xiaokang* society, a society in which all enjoy a reasonable level of living. *Fuye* refers to a part-time job and *maodun* a contradiction or dilemma. Unlike *fengshui* and *guanxi*, these words of Chinese English require a familiarity with Chinese culture.

Local varieties also develop new vocabulary items and expressions by translating terms for the local language into English. Examples in Chinese English include *barefoot doctor, iron rice bowl*, and *work unit*. All these carry distinctive Chinese meanings. A *barefoot doctor* was a type of paramedic with minimal qualifications who were prominent during the 1950s and 1960s. *Iron rice bowl* refers to a secure job for life. Indian English has greetings which are direct translations, such as 'Bless my hovel with the good dust of your feet'. 'You goose-faced minion' is somewhat less respectful (Kachru 1983: 132).

It is also common for new varieties of English to afford different meanings to words. The Australian English *bush* is an excellent example. In Australian English bush refers to pretty much all of Australia except urban areas. Butler (2002) demonstrates its distinctive meaning in Australian English by showing that the Australian dictionary, the Macquarie, has many more listings under *bush* than do either the American Random House or the British New Oxford dictionaries. Among the many collocates of *bush* in Australian English include *bush tucker* (tucker means food), *bushranger* (outlaw) and *bush ballad* (a song about the *bush* or outback). Here it is used in a radio interview in the context of 'bush block' a parcel of undeveloped land. Adaminiby is a small town in the Snowy Mountains (Kirkpatrick 2007: 73).

Int: How are you Craig? What's your story?
Craig: I come from Cooma, a truck driver during the week and got a bit of a block up the back of Adaminaby
Int: Bit of a block?
Craig: Yeah, bit of a bush block.

This change in meaning can be referred to as semantic shift and is a common feature of all new varieties of English. In Singaporean English, for example, 'Christian' refers specifically to Protestants (Deterding 2000) and 'alphabet' refers to individual letters of the alphabet. Thus, in Singaporean English, the alphabet comprises 26 alphabets. An example of semantic shift In Bruneian English is the meaning of *konfiden* (confident), which has only a negative connotation, meaning something more like overconfident or arrogant (McLellan 2005: 39).

The adopted meaning of a word can have a highly significant cultural basis. For example, the word 'shame' in Australian Aboriginal English expresses a meaning quite distinct from its meaning in British English (Harkins 1990; Kaldor and Malcolm 1982). The concept is described by Kaldor and Malcolm as being any situation in which a person feels uncomfortable for being 'singled out for any purpose, scolding or praise or simply attention when the person loses the security and anonymity provided by the group' (1982: 99). Harkins (1990: 294) cites several descriptions of 'shame' given by Australian Aboriginal students, including this one:

> Big shame is when people get embarrassed and feel uptight, e.g. when they are called up on stage, when they are picked out of a crowd.

As Harkins explains, an understanding of this becomes crucially important in cross-cultural communication, even though the speakers may feel they share the same language, a point we develop further below.

A second example is how the word 'family' in Australian Aboriginal English refers to a much wider set of categories than it does in British English. People who form close personal bonds can be referred to by kinship terms such as 'brother' or 'cousin' and this often implies certain obligations (Sharifian 2010: 443). Similarly, Wolf has convincingly argued (2010: 208) that the frequent collocations of family, community and society in many African varieties of English indicate the importance of community and kinship in the local cultures. In this way, lexical items can carry cultural conceptualizations (Chapter 32 this volume) distinctive to the local culture.

In places where a new variety of English has developed as a medium for people who already speak other languages, a common way for people to express identity and cultural collegiality is to use code-mixing. Typically, such varieties have developed in post-colonial settings where English has been retained for important institutional functions and where it exists alongside local languages. This example of code-mixing is taken from an advertisement in Malaysian English (Hashim 2010: 525).

> *Abah*: Listen, *abah*'s got a save-petrol plan for our *balik kampong* trip

Abah means father and also note how the speaker uses the term to refer to himself. *Balik kampong* means to return to one's home village and also refers to the exodus from the cities at times of public holidays. *Kampong* is in itself, an iconic word of Malaysian English meaning the traditional Malay village. The following code-mixing examples come from Bruneian English (McLellan 2010: 431).

> Ban *pasar malam* (ban the night market)
> ... and there is no more *bangsa melayu* (and there is no more Malay race)
> When I went for *jalan jalan* (when I went for a walk around).

As McLellan also illustrates, this form of code-mixing is reflected in 'rich intrasentential alter-nation' (2010: 433) where complete texts are characterized by many switches of code. This requires high levels of proficiency in the relevant languages, not only to produce but also to understand. Such uses are therefore commonly found within speech communities where speakers are confident that all share similar linguistic resources. The final example from South Africa shows three languages – Afrikaans, English, and Zulu – being used in the same utterance. The Afrikaans is in bold, the English in italics and the Zulu in normal type.

I-*chiefs* isidle nge-*referee's optional time, otherwise* ngabe ihambe **sleg. Maar**, why benga **stopi** *this system* ye-*injury time?*

The Chiefs won owing to the referee's optional time, otherwise they could have lost. But why is this system of injury time not phased out? (Gough n.d. cited in Kirkpatrick 2007: 109).

Code-mixing of this complexity is obviously impossible for people outside the local speech community to understand what is being said. This does not matter so much as this is precisely why speakers use this type of language. It is to signal common identity and for intra-cultural, rather than intercultural communication.

However, it is important that we all recognize how local varieties of English borrow words from local languages and adapt the meanings of other words in order for the new variety of English to be able to reflect the cultures of their speakers. It is also important to stress that this process also takes place in vernacular varieties of 'traditional' Englishes. For example, in the Doric, a variety of English spoken in the Northeast of Scotland around Aberdeen, 'quine', a word borrowed from Scandinavian languages, refers to girls in general rather than the Queen, as in standard British English. African-American vernacular varieties of English contain many words from African languages. For example, 'tote' (carry, now commonly used in many varieties as in 'tote bag'), goober (peanut) and 'gumbo' (a type of stew), all come from Bantu.

New varieties of English also reflect local cultures by encoding local pragmatic norms so I now turn to a discussion of the ways in which these are represented in local varieties of English.

Pragmatic norms and new varieties

Pragmatic norms refer to the ways in which people of particular cultural background normally attend to functions such as requesting, naming and greeting, and complimenting. This is a complex field, not least because increased intercultural contact and communication means that pragmatic norms are constantly changing and developing, often under the influence of other cultures. It also means that these pragmatic norms are constantly being negotiated, as people try to act appropriately in different cultural settings. This is captured by the cartoon of an American businessman meeting his Japanese counterpart. The American is bowing and the Japanese is stretching out his hand.

Requests and the pragmatic norms associated with them are probably the most researched of these functions (e.g., Blum-Kulka, House, and Kasper 1989). Cultures modify or soften requests in different ways. Chinese prefer to offer reasons for a request prior to making it (Kirkpatrick and Xu 2002), while speakers of American English are more likely to make the request first – usually softened in some way by linguistic politeness markers such as 'I wonder if you'd mind … ' and the ever-present use of 'please'. These differences can give rise to cross-cultural misunderstanding. A Chinese may consider an American who makes a request early in the piece to be rude and abrupt. An American may consider a Chinese who prefaces a request with many reasons or justifications for it as being unsure of their ground, tentative, if not inscrutable. This preference for prefacing a request before making it has also been noted in other Asian cultures, such as Indonesian (Rusdi 1999) and Japanese (Conlan 1996).

The 'Anglo' preference for making the request early but clothing it with linguistic softeners has led to these request forms being called 'whimperatives' (Wierzbicka 2003). While they have the form of questions, the real purpose is to get someone to do something. Thus the apparent questions 'Would you open the window please?' does not actually allow for the other person to say 'No', as the question form might imply. Wierzbicka suggests that this form is used in 'Anglo'-Englishes, as autonomy is such an important cultural value in those cultures and it is important, therefore, for the requester to at least give the impression that the requestee has the option of deciding on whether to accede to the request or not. As she further points out, the use of whimperatives of this type in Slavic languages would be considered rude by the requestee, as the use of this form would imply that the person being asked might actually refuse to comply. Thus, it is more appropriate in Slavic cultures for the imperative form to be used in such circumstances. One can easily see how this might lead to cross cultural misunderstandings. A Russian apparently ordering an Australian to 'Open the window' might not be heard with complete equanimity. This is why it is so important that people become familiar with different varieties of English and learn that English now provides the conduit for many different cultures. This is of special significance in a world where the vast majority of English speakers have learned it as an additional language. They come from a wide range of cultural and linguistic backgrounds and are speakers of one of the many new varieties of English that have been established or are developing. Native speakers of English now find themselves in a minority and have some obligation to familiarize themselves with these new varieties of English and the cultures they represent.

Another function that can cause cross-cultural misunderstandings is complimenting. If you come from a culture in which complimenting is considered both polite and pleasing to the person receiving the compliment, it may come as a surprise to hear that there are cultures where compliments can cause feelings of great discomfort, not unlike the concept of 'shame' in Australian Aboriginal culture discussed above. In Japanese culture, for example, giving compliments can cause distress to the person receiving the compliment, especially if it is a compliment which praises the person's – or a member of their family's – character, intelligence or success.

Naming and greeting are apparently simple functions, but also differ considerably across cultures. For example, in cultures where hierarchies are important and where it is important to respect these hierarchies in speech, naming and greeting become important ways in which this can be done. In Japan, therefore, no undergraduate student would dream of referring to the professor by their first name. Similarly, this would be unheard of in Korea and China. In Australia, on the other hand, it is considered normal for an undergraduate student to address the professor by their first name. This can cause discomfort for international students who are invited by their professors to call them by their first names. This would so offend their own culture that they find it impossible to do this, even though they are aware that it is appropriate in the local culture. This feeling of cultural discomfort has been termed 'pragmatic dissonance' (Li 2002). And one can see potential for cross-cultural disharmony if Australian students were to call their Japanese professors by their first name.

Local cultural values can also be expressed linguistically in the sense that the form or shape of a word may be altered to reflect the speakers' cultural values. An example of this from Australian English is the way speakers often shorten words. This shortening of words, also known as clipping, reflects the Australian desire for informality. Clipping occurs regularly in Australian colloquial speech. Examples include 'arvo' for 'afternoon', 'pollie' for politician and 'cossie' for swimming costume. Names are also often clipped. Anyone who has a surname McX ... or Macx ... , such as McMillan or Macnamara, is likely to be addressed and referred to as 'Macca'. The popular Australian radio announcer, Ian Cameron, is routinely known as 'Cammo'.

Speakers naturally shape new varieties of English to reflect cultural and pragmatic norms. Persian English is a newly developing variety and Sharifian discusses a number of cultural conceptualizations in Persian English. One such is *aberu* (2010: 444), defined by a Persian-English dictionary as 'respect, credit, prestige, honour'. It is a concept closely related to 'face' – the term literally means 'water of the face', although 'face' is itself culturally distinctive (Xu 2010). Sharifian defines *aberu* as being connected with 'the social image and status of a person and/or their family, both nuclear and extended, and their associates and friends' and it is 'tied to a large number of social norms in relation to financial status, behavior, both linguistic and non-linguistic, and social relationships and networks' (2010: 445). He concludes his study by arguing the importance of studying different varieties of English from the perspective of cultural conceptualizations, a call echoed by scholars such as Wolf (2010) and Honna (2008).

To date we have discussed ways in which local cultures are reflected in varieties of English through the use of vocabulary and expressions and the ways pragmatic norms are realized. The focus has been more on the spoken variety than the written. A further way in which local cultures are reflected in varieties of English is through literature written in the variety and through the rhetorical structures that are used and it is to these that I now turn.

'Local' literature and rhetorical norms

New varieties of English are well represented by literature written in those varieties. For example, there are many internationally renowned authors from across Asia, Africa and the Caribbean writing in local varieties of English. These include the Nobel Prize winners, Wole Soyinka of Nigeria and V.S. Naipaul and Derek Walcott from the Caribbean. In their survey of Indian literature in English over the two decades between 1980–2000, Naik and Narayan review the work of no fewer than 56 authors. The authors describe the development of English in India using a rhetorical style that appears distinctively Indian, especially through their use of extended metaphor. I have cited this before (e.g., Kirkpatrick 2007: 86), but cite it again here, not least because it also captures how a local variety of English develops ways of portraying local cultures

> Years ago, a slender sapling from a foreign field was grafted by "pale hands" on the mighty and many-branched Indian banyan tree. It has kept growing vigorously and now, an organic part of its parent tree, it has spread its own probing roots into the brown soil below. Its young leaves rustle energetically in the strong winds that blow from the western horizon, but the sunshine that warms it and the rain that cools it are from Indian skies; and it continues to draw its vital sap from this earth, this realm, this India
>
> *(Naik and Narayan 2004: 253)*

The decision for authors to write in English is, of course, not one that is taken lightly. Writers have to decide whether or not writing in English rather than the local language represents some form of cultural betrayal; and if they decide to write in English, they have to be convinced that the variety of English they use can adequately reflect their own cultural experience and values. This is a complex issue and has been widely covered by a number of scholars and writers over many years (e.g., Achebe 1975; Bolton 2002; Ha Jin 2010; Kirkpatrick 2007; Omoniyi 2010). Here I shall merely cite a selection of authors who take opposed positions. The Sri Lankan poet, Lakdasa Wikkramasinha, felt that writing in English was indeed a betrayal.

To write in English is a form of cultural treason. I have had for the future to think of a way of circumventing this treason, I propose to do this by making my writing entirely immoralist and destructive.

(cited in Canagarajah 1994: 375)[1]

The Pakistani novelist, Sidhwa takes a different view. She feels that 'English … is no longer the monopoly of the British. We the excolonised have subjugated the language, beaten it on its head and made it ours' (1996: 231) and that, 'We have to stretch the language to adapt it to alien thoughts and values which have no expression in English' (ibid.: 240).

Sidhwa here is clearly stating that English can be adapted so that it can adequately reflect the local cultural experience.

The Nigerian novelist, Chinua Achebe, takes a practical position. He points out that if there is a 'national' language for sub-Saharan African, then that language is English as it is spoken in more countries than any other language. His view is that the African writer should 'aim at fashioning out an English which is at once universal and able to carry his personal experience' (2005: 170).

Achebe's fellow Nigerian, the novelist and playwright Ken Saro-Wiwa, published a novel in which he used the local vernacular variety of English throughout. In the author's note, he explains that novel was the result of my 'fascination with the adaptability of the English language and my closely observing the speech and writings of a certain segment of Nigerian society'. He called the novel 'Sozaboy: A Novel in Rotten English' (1985). Where 'Sozaboy' is the local equivalent of 'Soldier Boy'. The following excerpt gives a flavour of the novel's style:

Radio begin dey hala as 'e never hala before. Big big grammar. Long long words. Every time. Before before, the grammar was not plenty and everybody was happy. But now grammar began to be plenty and people were not happy. As grammar plenty, na so trouble plenty. And, as trouble plenty, na so plenty people were dying

(1985: 3)

This short extract illustrates, in Sidhwa's words, the 'stretching' of English and its adaptation to 'alien thoughts and values' and several of the ways in which this can be done. With regards the development of vocabulary, Saro-Wiwa uses local versions of English words. For example, *hala* is derived from 'holler' and it here describes the never-ending pronouncements coming from the (government-controlled) radio. His use of 'grammar' is an example of semantic shift, with the word referring to the many government pronouncements being 'hollered' over the radio. The local rhetorical style of repetition is also much in evidence, both with the frequent repetition of specific adjectives ('big big', 'long long'), and with the repetition of phrases as evidenced in the final two sentences, where the local discourse marker 'na' is also adopted to add further local flavour to the style.

There is only space to here to make reference to a very small selection of the wide and expanding range of 'new' literatures being created in English. But, as new Englishes develop, so are new literatures and other cultural representations being created. While some may despair at the 'stretching' of English to reflect different cultural values and experience, others see it as a contribution to English. As the Chinese-American novelist, Ha Jin, has written, 'Indeed the frontiers of English verge on foreign territories. And therefore we cannot help but sound foreign to native ears, but the frontiers are the only proper places where we claim our existence and make our contributions to this language' (2010: 469). Today, however, the frontiers are becoming more central and universally experienced as the new Englishes start to transcend borders and cultures. In the next section, I look at the rise of popular culture associated with new varieties of English and the phenomenon of 'transcultural flows' (Pennycook 2007: 6). where local cultures become, depending on one's point of view, contaminated or enriched by external cultures.

Popular culture

I gave examples above on how people use code-mixing in new varieties of English to establish their identity and membership of specific speech communities. They can also adopt code-mixing to establish a different identity, for example, one that signals they are part of an international community rather than a local one. This is a type of 'crossing' a phenomenon identified by Rampton (1995) through which one group may deliberately adopt the linguistic features and styles of another group. Thus white middle class British males may start to adopt the speech styles of black Afro-Caribbean males. People may also code mix in ways that are not found within the local culture. Pop culture is an example of where this is common (Moody 2010, 2012). People may also wish to establish some form of international urban identity as opposed to a localized identity. Maher (2005: 83) has called this 'metroethnicity' and Pennycook calls it 'metrolingualism' (2010:683). As Pennycook explains:

> As language learners move around the world in search of English or other desirable languages, or stay at home but tune in to new digital worlds through screens, mobiles and headphones, the possibilities of being something not yet culturally imagined mobilizes new identity options. And in these popular transcultural flows, languages, cultures and identities are frequently mixed. Code-mixing, sampling of sounds, genres, languages and cultures is the norm.
>
> *(2010: 683)*

An example of this type of code-mixing using transcultural flows is provided by Moody (2012), where he discusses the lyrics of the Japanese group Love Psychedelico as they mix between Japanese and English. He quotes a review (2012: 217):

> The most remarkable thing about Love Psychedelico would have to be the Sheryl Crowesque vocals of Kumi. The influences are clear, as she shifts fluently and easily from Japanese to English in mid-sentence with the strut well intact. The packaging contains lyrics that expose her almost imperceptible movements from language to language.

As Moody notes, Kumi spent five years of her early childhood in San Francisco, and Love Psychedelico are attempting to capture a specific 'returnee' style of Japanese. The impact and identity of these returnees should not be underestimated, as there are now many hundreds of thousands of, for example, Japanese, Koreans, Chinese – including from Hong Kong – who have spent a significant time overseas – primarily but not exclusively in English-speaking countries – and have returned to their home countries. They commonly use code-mixing to express their returnee identity, but their code-mixing differs from the local community's in that the English they use is heavily influenced by their overseas experience and is quite distinct from the local variety of English. The extent to which this 'returnee' code mixing is accepted or rejected by locals is debatable and depends in some cases on the setting. It would certainly repay further research. The most obvious current example of popular culture influenced by transcultural flows is the K-pop sensation 'Gangnam Style'. This is almost entirely in Korean with a few words of English – including, crucially perhaps, in the title – scattered throughout the song.

Conclusion

In this chapter I have described how speakers of a new variety of English 'stretch' it so that it can accommodate and represent the local culture. The processes involved include the adoption of words from local languages which describe local cultural items and phenomena, creativity with words and code-mixing. The speakers of new varieties of English also introduce their own pragmatic norms and cultural values into their English. This means that different Englishes encode different cultures and it is therefore important that all users of English become aware of this and, as far as practically possible, become familiar with how this encoding takes place. It would be unrealistic, of course, to ask all speakers of English of whatever variety to become familiar with the different cultures encoded by different varieties of English. But it has been proposed that speakers of English need to develop a set of skills if they wish to operate successfully within different varieties of English (Sussex and Kirkpatrick 2012: 226–9). Under the overall notion of 'communicacy', a sub-set of skills for speakers of English could include the following:

An understanding that linguistic and pragmatic variation is natural and that 'meeting and matching the centric norm is no longer the primary objective'.
An understanding that code-switching is natural among multilinguals and that speakers of new varieties of English will commonly engage in switching.
An understanding that different varieties of English encode different cultural norms and that such an understanding is crucial for successful intercultural communication.

At the same time all of us who are speakers of English need to develop strategies of repair and skills of negotiation, which includes the ability to accommodate our language to the language of our interlocutors.

How new varieties of English continue to develop and encode yet more cultures and how these complement or stand in contradiction to the new transcultural Englishes will be a major topic of future research. In any event, we shall all need to develop our communicacy skills.

Related topics

studies of language and culture; cultural linguistics

Further reading

Brut-Griffler, J. (2002). *World English: A Study of Its Development*. Clevedon: Multilingual Matters. (This presents a historical and critical account of colonial language policy in the British Empire and challenges the conventional wisdom of how English has become the world's most dominant language.)
Kachru, Braj B. (ed.) (1992) *The Other Tongue: English across Cultures*. Chicago: University of Chicago Press. (This book contains a number of seminal chapters on World Englishes and is considered a classic in the field.)
Kirkpatrick, A. (ed.) (2010). *The Routledge Handbook of World Englishes*. London: Routledge. (This handbook comprises 39 chapters in six sections and provides a comprehensive overview of the recent debates and developments in the field.)
Schneider, E.W. (2007). *Postcolonial Englishes: Varieties from around the World*. Cambridge: Cambridge University Press. (Schneider presents his dynamic theory for how Englishes have developed in postcolonial settings, arguing that their spread and the development of different varieties can be explained by one underlying process.)

Note

1 Wikkramsinha took his own life but left behind a body of work of Sri Lankan poetry in English that few could describe as 'immoralist and destructive'. Rather, it is hauntingly beautiful. Interested readers can listen to a selection of his poems being read by the Sri Lankan scholar, Thiru Kandiah, on the CD accompanying Kirkpatrick (2007).

References

Achebe, C. (1975/2005) 'The African writer and the English language', in J. Jenkins, *World Englishes*. London: Routledge, pp.169–72.

Ahulu, S. (1994) 'How Ghanaian is Ghanaian English?', *English Today* 10(2): 25–9.

Bamiro, E.O. (1994) 'Lexico-semantic variation in Nigerian English', *World Englishes* 13(1): 51–64.

Blum-Kulka, S., House, J. and Kasper, G. (1989) *Cross-cultural Pragmatics: Requests and Apologies*. Norwood, NJ: Ablex.

Bolton, K. (ed.) (2002) *Hong Kong English: Creativity and Autonomy*. Hong Kong: Hong Kong University Press.

Buchan, P. and Toulmin, D. (1989) *Buchan Claik*. Edinburgh: Gordon Wright Publishing.

Butler, S. (2002) 'Language, literature and culture – and their meeting place in the dictionary', in A. Kirkpatrick (ed.) *Englishes in Asia: Communication, Identity, Power and Education*. Melbourne: Language Australia, pp. 143–68.

Canagarajah, S. (1994) 'Competing discourses in Sri Lankan English poetry', *World Englishes*, 13(3): 361–76.

Conlan, C. (1996) 'Politeness, paradigms of family and the Japanese ESL speaker', *Language Sciences* 18, 729–42.

Deterding, D. (2000) 'Potential influences of Chinese on the written English of Singapore', in A. Brown (ed.) *English in Southeast Asia*. Singapore: National Institute of Education, pp. 201–9.

Dixon, R.M.W., Ransom W.S., and Thomas, M. (1990) *Australian Aboriginal Words in English*. Melbourne: Oxford University Press.

Ha Jin (2010) 'In defence of foreignness', in A. Kirkpatrick (ed.) *The Routledge Handbook of World Englishes*. London: Routledge, pp. 461–70.

Harkins, J. (1990) 'Shame and shyness in the aboriginal classroom: A case for "practical semantics"', *Australian Journal of Linguistics*, 10(2): 293–306.

Hashim, A. (2010) 'Englishes in advertising', in A. Kirkpatrick (ed.) *The Routledge Handbook of World Englishes*. London: Routledge, pp. 520–34.

Honna, N. (2008) *English as a Multicultural Language in Asian Contexts: Issues and ideas*. Tokyo: Kuroshio.

Kachru, Braj B. (1983) *The Indianization of English*. New Delhi: Oxford University Press.

——(2005) *Asian Englishes: Beyond the Canon*. Hong Kong: Hong Kong University Press.

Kaldor, S and Malcolm, I. (1982) 'Aboriginal English in country and remote areas', in R. Eagleson, S. Kaldor, and I. Malcolm (eds) *English and the Aboriginal Child*. Canberra: CDC, pp. 75–112.

Kirkpatrick, A. (2007) *World Englishes: Implications for International Communication and English Language Teaching*. Cambridge: Cambridge University Press.

Kirkpatrick, A. and Sussex, R. (eds) (2012) *English as an International Language in Asia: Implications for Language Education*. Dordrecht: Springer.

Kirkpatrick, A. and Xu Zhichang (2002) 'Chinese pragmatic norms and China English', *World Englishes* 21(2): 269–80.

Li, D.C.S. (2002) 'Pragmatic dissonance: The ecstasy and agony of speaking like a native speaker', in D.C.S. Li (ed.) *Discourses in Search of members: In Honor of Ron Scollon*. Lanham, MD: University Press of America, pp. 559–95.

McLellan, J. (2005) 'Malay–English Language alternation in 2 Brunei Darussalam online internet chatrooms', Ph.D. dissertation, Curtin University.

——(2010) 'Mixed codes or varieties of English?', in A. Kirkpatrick (ed.) *The Routledge Handbook of World Englishes*. London: Routledge, pp. 425–41.

Maher, J. (2005) 'Metroethnicity, language and the principle of cool', *International Journal of the Sociology of Language*, 175(6): 83–102.

Moody, A. (2010) 'The Englishes of popular cultures', in A. Kirkpatrick (ed.) *The Routledge Handbook of World Englishes*. London: Routledge, pp. 535–49.

Moody, A. (2012) 'Authenticity of English in Asian popular music', in A. Kirkpatrick and R. Sussex (eds) *English as an International Language in Asia*. Dordrecht: Springer, pp. 209–22.

Naik, M.K. and Narayan, S.A. (2004) *Indian English Literature 1980–2000: A Critical Survey*. New Delhi: Pencraft International.

Omoniyi, T. (2010) 'Writing in English(es)', in A. Kirkpatrick (ed.) *The Routledge Handbook of World Englishes*. London: Routledge, pp. 471–89.

Pennycook, A. (2007) *Global Englishes and Transcultural Flows*. London: Routledge.

——(2010) 'The future of Englishes: One, many or more?', in A. Kirkpatrick (ed.) *The Routledge Handbook of World Englishes*, London: Routledge, pp. 673–87.

Rampton, B. (1998) 'Crossing: language and ethnicity among adolescents', *Language in Society*, 27(4): 552–5.

Rusdi, T. (1999) 'Schema of group seminar presentations and rhetorical structures of seminar introductions: A cross-cultural study of Indonesian and Australian students in university settings', *Asian Englishes*, 2(1): 66–89.

Saro-Wiwa, K. (1985) *Sozaboy: A Novel in Rotten English*, Port Harcourt: Saros International.

Schneider, E.W. (2007). *Postcolonial English: Varieties around the World*. Cambridge: Cambridge University Press.

——(2010) 'Developmental patters of English: Similar or different?', in A. Kirkpatrick (ed.) *The Routledge Handbook of World Englishes*. London: Routledge, pp. 372–84.

Sharifian, F. (2010) 'Semantics and pragmatic conceptualisations within an emerging variety: Persian English', in A. Kirkpatrick (ed.) *The Routledge Handbook of World Englishes*. London: Routledge, pp. 442–56.

Sidhwa, B. (1996) 'Creative processes in Pakistani English fiction', in R.J. Baumgardner (ed.) *South Asian English: Structure, Use and Users*. Urbana, IL: University of Illinois press, pp. 231–40.

Sridar, Kamal K. (2012) 'Acculturation in World Englishes', in *The Encyclopedia of Applied Linguistics*.

Sussex, R. and Kirkpatrick, A. (2012) 'A postscript and a prolegomenon', in A. Kirkpatrick and R. Sussex (eds) *English as an International Language in Asia*. Dordrecht: Springer, pp. 223–31.

Wierzbicka, A. (2003) *Cross-cultural Pragmatics: The Semantics of Human Interaction*. Berlin: de Gruyter.

Wolf, H.-G. (2010) 'East and West African Englishes: Differences and similarities', in A. Kirkpatrick (ed.) *The Routledge Handbook of World Englishes*. London: Routledge, pp. 181–96.

Xu Zhichang (2010) 'Chinese English: A Future Power?', in A. Kirkpatrick (ed.) *The Routledge Handbook of World Englishes*. London: Routledge, pp. 282–98.

PART VII

Cultural linguistics: past, present, and future directions

32

CULTURAL LINGUISTICS

Farzad Sharifian

Introduction

Cultural Linguistics is a multidisciplinary area of research that explores the relationship between language, culture, and conceptualization. Originally, this area grew out of an interest in integrating cognitive linguistics with the three traditions present in linguistic anthropology, namely, Boasian linguistics, ethnosemantics, and the ethnography of speaking (Palmer, 1996). In the last decade, Cultural Linguistics has also found strong common ground with cognitive anthropology, since both explore cultural models, which are associated with the use of language. For Cultural Linguistics, many features of human languages are entrenched in cultural conceptualizations, including cultural models. In recent years, Cultural Linguistics has drawn on several disciplines and sub-disciplines, such as complexity science and distributed cognition, to enrich its theoretical understanding of the notion of *cultural cognition* (Sharifian, 2011). Applications of Cultural Linguistics have enabled fruitful investigations of the cultural grounding of language in several applied domains such as world Englishes, intercultural communication, and political discourse analysis. This chapter elaborates on these observations and provides illustrative examples of linguistic research from the perspective of Cultural Linguistics.

What is Cultural Linguistics?

As a sub-discipline of linguistics with a multidisciplinary origin, Cultural Linguistics explores the interface between language, culture, and conceptualization (Palmer, 1996; Sharifian, 2011). Cultural Linguistics explores, in explicit terms, *conceptualizations* that have a cultural basis and are encoded in and communicated through features of human languages. The pivotal focus on *meaning as conceptualization* in Cultural Linguistics owes its centrality to cognitive linguistics, a discipline that Cultural Linguistics drew on at its inception.

The term 'Cultural Linguistics' was perhaps first used by one of the founders of the field of cognitive linguistics, Ronald Langacker, in a statement he made emphasizing the relationship between cultural knowledge and grammar. He maintained that 'the advent of cognitive linguistics can be heralded as a return to *cultural linguistics*. Cognitive linguistic theories recognize cultural knowledge as the foundation not just of lexicon, but central facets of grammar as well' (Langacker, 1994: 31, original emphasis). Langacker (forthcoming) maintains that 'while meaning is identified as conceptualization, cognition at all levels is both embodied and culturally embedded'. In practice, however, the role of culture in shaping the conceptual level of language and the influence of culture as a system of conceptualization on all levels of language was not adequately and explicitly dealt with until the publication of *Toward a Theory of Cultural Linguistics* (1996) by Gary B. Palmer, a linguistic anthropologist from the University of Nevada, Las Vegas. In this book, Palmer argued that cognitive linguistics can be directly applied to the study of language and culture.

Central to Palmer's proposal was/is the idea that 'language is the play of verbal symbols that are based in *imagery*' (1996: 3, emphasis added), and that this imagery is culturally constructed. Palmer argued that culturally defined imagery governs narrative, figurative language, semantics, grammar, discourse, and even phonology.

Palmer's notion of imagery is not limited to visual imagery. As he puts it, '[i]magery is what we see in our mind's eye, but it is also the taste of mango, the feel of walking in a tropical downpour, the music of *Mississippi Masala*' (ibid.: 3). He adds, 'phonemes are heard as verbal images arranged in complex categories; words acquire meanings that are relative to image-schemas, scenes, and scenarios; clauses are image-based constructions; discourse emerges as a process governed by reflexive imagery of itself; and world view subsumes it all' (ibid.: 4). Since for Palmer the notion of imagery captures conceptual units such as cognitive categories and schemas, my terminological preference is the term *conceptualization* rather than imagery. I elaborate on my use of this term later in this chapter.

Palmer's proposal called for bringing three traditional approaches found in anthropological linguistic to bear on research carried out in the field of cognitive linguistics, as follows:

> Cognitive linguistics can be tied into three traditional approaches that are central to anthropological linguistics: Boasian linguistics, ethnosemantics (ethno science), and the ethnography of speaking. To the synthesis that results I have given the name *cultural linguistics*.
>
> *(ibid.: 5, original emphasis)*

Palmer's proposal is diagrammatically represented in Figure 32.1. Boasian linguistics, named after the German-American anthropologist Franz Boas, saw language as reflecting people's mental life and culture (see Chapter 2 this volume). Boas observed that languages classify

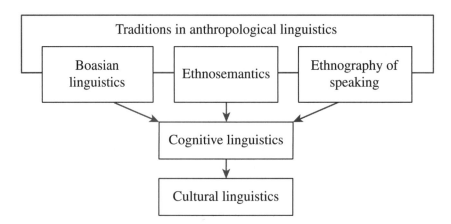

Figure 32.1 A diagrammatic representation of Palmer's (1996) proposal for Cultural Linguistics

experiences differently and that these linguistic categories tend to influence the thought patterns of their speakers (Blount, 1995[1974], 2011; Lucy, 1992). The latter theme formed the basis of later work by scholars such as Edward Sapir and Benjamin Whorf (see Chapter 2 this volume). The views of the relationship between language and culture that have been attributed to this school of thought range from the theoretical position that language and culture shape human thought to one that regards human thought as *influenced* by language and culture. It is worth noting that although the former is often attributed to scholars such as Sapir and Whorf, in recent decades others have presented much more sophisticated and much more nuanced accounts of the views held by these two researchers (see Lee, 1996; Chapter 2 this volume).

A related subfield is that of ethnosemantics, which 'is the study of the ways in which different cultures organise and categorise domains of knowledge, such as those of plants, animals, and kin' (Palmer, 1996: 19; see also Chapter 5 this volume). For example, several ethnosemanticists have extensively studied kinship classifications in the Aboriginal languages of Australia and noted their complexity relative to the kinship system classifications in varieties of English such as American English or Australian English (Chapter 11 this volume; Tonkinson, 1998). An important field of inquiry, closely related to ethnosemantics, is ethnobiology which is the study of how plants and animals are categorized and used across different cultures (Berlin, 1992).

The ethnography of speaking, or the ethnography of communication, largely associated with the work of Dell Hymes (for example, 1974) and John Gumperz (for example, Gumperz and Hymes, 1972), explores culturally distinctive means and modes of speaking, and communication in general. Hymes emphasized the role of sociocultural context in the ways in which speakers perform communicatively. He argued that the competence that is required for the conduct of social life includes more than just the type of linguistic competence Chomskian linguists had studied. He proposed that a discussion of these factors be placed under the rubric of *communicative competence*, which includes competence in 'appropriate' norms of language use in various sociocultural contexts. Generally, the three linguistic–anthropological traditions discussed so far 'share an interest in the native's point of view' (Palmer, 1996: 26) as well as an interest in the sociocultural grounding of language, although a number of anthropological linguists have simply focused on documenting, describing, and classifying lesser known languages (see Duranti, 2003 for a historical review).

Cognitive linguistics itself utilizes several analytical tools drawn from the broad field of cognitive science, notably the notion of 'schema'. The concept of 'schema' has been very widely used in several disciplines and under different rubrics, and this has led to different understandings and definitions of the term. For cognitive linguists such as Langacker, schemas are abstract representations. For example, for him, a noun instantiates the schema of [[THING]/[X]], whereas a verb instantiates the schema of [[PROCESS]/[X]]. In classical paradigms of cognitive psychology, however, schemas are considered more broadly as building blocks of cognition used for storing, organizing, and interpreting information (for example, Bartlett, 1932; Bobrow and Norman, 1975; Minsky, 1975; Rumelhart, 1980). Image schemas, on the other hand, are regarded as recurring cognitive structures which establish patterns of understanding and reasoning, often elaborated by extension from knowledge of our bodies as well as our experience of social interactions (for example, Johnson, 1987). An example of this would be to understand the body or parts of the body as 'containers'. Such an understanding is reflected in expressions like: 'with a heart *full of* happiness'. Another analytical tool used in cognitive linguistics is the 'conceptual metaphor', which is closely associated with the work of Lakoff, and to a lesser extent Johnson (for example, Lakoff and Johnson, 1980). Conceptual metaphors are defined as cognitive structures that allow us to conceptualize and understand one conceptual domain in terms of another. For instance, the

English metaphorical expressions: 'heavy-hearted and light-hearted', reflect the conceptual metaphor of HEART AS THE SEAT OF EMOTION. In proposing the framework of Cultural Linguistics, Palmer persuasively argued that it is very likely that all these conceptual structures have a cultural basis.[1] His own work is based on the analysis of cases from such diverse languages as Tagalog, Coeur d'Alene, and Shona (for example, Palmer 1996, 2003).

Although Palmer believed that the link with cognitive linguistics could provide Cultural Linguistics with a solid cognitive perspective, his proposal received criticism for *not* having a strong cognitive base, specifically, in the areas of cognitive representations, structure, and processes (for example, Peeters, 2001). The criticism, however, appears to be related to the fact that there are different interpretations of the term 'cognitive'. What makes studies associated with mainstream cognitive linguistics 'cognitive' is their emphasis on *cognitive conceptualization*, whereas studies of cognitive processing in the subfield of psycholinguistics mostly focus on non-conceptual phenomena, such as response time and strength of response.

In recent years, Cultural Linguistics has drawn on several other disciplines and sub-disciplines in the process of developing a theoretical framework that affords an integrated understanding of the notions of 'cognition' and 'culture', as they relate to language. This framework is one that may be best described as *cultural cognition and language* (Sharifian, 2008b, 2009b, 2011) in that it proposes a view of cognition that has life at the level of culture, under the concept of *cultural cognition*.

Cultural cognition draws on a multidisciplinary understanding of the collective cognition that characterizes a cultural group. Several cognitive scientists have moved beyond the level of the individual, working on cognition as a collective entity (for example, Clark and Chalmers, 1998; Sutton, 2005, 2006; Wilson, 2005). Other scholars, working in the area of complex science often under the rubric of Complex Adaptive Systems (CAS), have been seeking to explain how relationships between parts, or agents, give rise to the collective behaviours of a system or group (for example, Holland, 1995; Waldrop, 1992). A number of scholars, notably Hutchins (1994), have explored the notion of 'distributed cognition', including factors external to the human organism, such as technology and the environment, in their definition of cognition (see also Borofsky, 1994 and Palmer, 2006 for the notion of *distributed knowledge* in relation to language). Drawing on all this work, Sharifian (2008b, 2009b, 2011) offers a model of cultural cognition that establishes criteria for distinguishing between what is cognitive and what is cultural and the relationship between the two in the domain of Cultural Linguistics.

Cultural cognition embraces the cultural knowledge that emerges from the interactions between members of a cultural group across time and space. Apart from the ordinary sense of 'emergence' here, cultural cognition is emergent in the technical sense of the term (for example, Goldstein, 1999). In other words, cultural cognition is the cognition that results from the interactions between parts of the system (the members of a group) which is more than the sum of its parts (more than the sum of the cognitive systems of the individual members). Like all emergent systems, cultural cognition is *dynamic* in that it is constantly being negotiated and renegotiated within and across the generations of the relevant cultural group, as well as in response to the contact that members of that group have with other languages and cultures.

Language is a central aspect of cultural cognition as it serves, to use the term used by wa Thiong'o (1986), as a 'collective memory bank' of the cultural cognition of a group. Many aspects of language are shaped by the cultural cognition that prevailed at earlier stages in the history of a speech community. Historical cultural practices leave traces in current linguistic practice, some of which are in fossilized forms that may no longer be analysable. In this sense language can be viewed as storing and communicating cultural cognition. In other words, language acts both as a memory bank and a fluid vehicle for the (re-)transmission of cultural cognition and its component parts or *cultural conceptualizations*, a term elaborated upon later in this chapter.

Why Cultural Linguistics?

A question might be asked in relation to the need for the development of Cultural Linguistics. Scholars who have been interested in exploring the interrelationship between language and culture have faced at least two significant challenges in regards to the notion of 'culture': one is its abstractness and the other, the essentialist and reductionists implications often associated with it. These challenges have led to the avoidance of the term by many scholars. For example, as Atkinson (Chapter 28 this volume) puts it, '[i]n the very field which innovated the concept in fact – anthropology – culture has been "half-abandoned"'. Many scholars have found the notion of 'culture' to be too abstract to be useful in explicating the relationships that link beliefs and behaviour to language use. Although linguists have had rigorous analytical tools at their disposal, what has not been available to them is an analytical framework for breaking down cultures and examining their components, so that features of human languages could be explored in terms of the relationship between language and culture. Cultural Linguistics, and in particular the theoretical framework of cultural cognition and cultural conceptualizations, is an attempt to provide such an analytical framework.

First of all, this framework avoids the abstractness of the notion of 'culture' and instead focuses on exploring culturally constructed *conceptualizations*. As this chapter has shown, the framework draws on several disciplines, such as cognitive science and cognitive linguistics, for its analytical tools, such as 'cultural schemas', 'cultural categories', and 'cultural metaphors'. These analytical tools allow cultural conceptualizations to be examined systematically and rigorously. Furthermore, they enable the analysis of features of human languages in relation to the cultural conceptualizations in which they are entrenched.

As for the essentialist and reductionist tendencies associated with the notion of 'culture', the theoretical model of cultural cognition and cultural conceptualizations avoids these by, first of all, examining cultural conceptualizations rather than examining speakers and then ascribing cultures to people, or people to cultures. It also views cultural conceptualizations as *heterogeneously distributed* across the members of a group, rather than equally shared by the speakers. Both language and culture demonstrate a similar pattern of distribution across speech communities, and neither of them is homogenously held by speakers. These themes will be further expanded in the remainder of this chapter.

Cultural conceptualizations

Among the analytical tools that have proved particularly useful in examining aspects of cultural cognition and its instantiation in language are 'cultural schema', 'cultural category' (including 'cultural prototype'), and 'cultural metaphor'. I refer to these collectively as *cultural conceptualizations* (Sharifian, 2011). Consistent with the view of cultural cognition discussed earlier in this chapter, these analytical tools are seen as existing at the collective or macro level of cultural cognition, as well as that of the individual or micro level (Frank and Gontier, 2011). Cultural conceptualizations and their entrenchment in language are intrinsic to cultural cognition. This formulation of the model of cultural cognition, cultural conceptualizations, and language are summarized diagrammatically in Figure 32.2.

Figure 32.2 captures the close relationship between language, cultural conceptualizations, and cultural cognition. As reflected in Figure 32.2, various features and levels of language, from

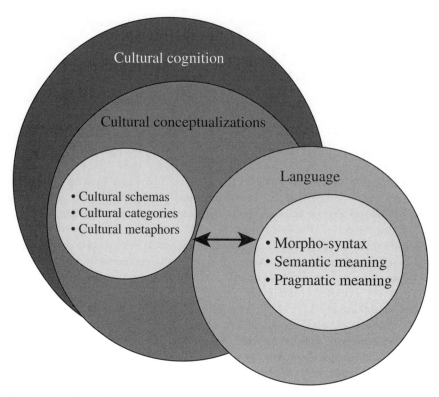

Figure 32.2 Model of cultural cognition, cultural conceptualizations, and language

morpho-syntactic features to pragmatic and semantic meanings may be embedded in cultural conceptualizations in the form of cultural schemas, cultural categories, and cultural metaphors. The following section elaborates on the interrelationship between language and each of these types of cultural conceptualizations.

Cultural schemas and language

The notions of schema and conceptual metaphor were discussed earlier in this chapter. The following section elaborates on the notion of 'cultural schema' and discusses how it relates to language. Cultural schemas are a culturally constructed sub-class of schemas; that is, they are abstracted from the collective cognitions associated with a cultural group, and therefore to some extent based on shared experiences, common to the group, as opposed to being abstracted from an individual's idiosyncratic experiences. They enable individuals to communicate cultural meanings. In terms of their development and their representation, at the macro level, cultural schemas emerge from interactions between the members of a cultural group, while they are constantly negotiated and renegotiated across time and space. At the micro level, over time each individual acquires and internalizes these macro-level schemas, albeit in a heterogeneously distributed fashion. That is, individuals who belong to the same cultural group may share some, but not all, components of a cultural schema. In other words, each person's internalization of a macro-level cultural schema is to some extent collective and to some extent idiosyncratic. This pattern is diagrammatically presented in Figure 32.3.

Figure 32.3 shows how a cultural schema may be represented in a heterogeneously distributed fashion across the minds of individuals. It schematically represents how members

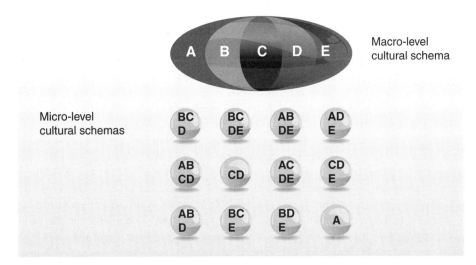

Figure 32.3 Diagrammatic representation of a cultural schema (adapted from Sharifian, 2011)

may have internalized some, but not all, components of a macro-level cultural schema. It also shows how individuals may share some, but not all the elements of a cultural schema with each other. It is to be noted that the individuals who internalize aspects of a cultural schema may not only be those who are viewed as the insiders by the cultural group. 'Outsiders' who have somehow had contact and interaction with the group can also internalize aspects of their cultural schemas.

Besides its pivotal use in Cultural Linguistics, the notion of 'cultural schema' has also been adopted as a key analytical tool in cognitive anthropology (for example, D'Andrade, 1995; Shore, 1996; Strauss and Quinn, 1997; see also Chapter 26 this volume). For cognitive anthropologists culture is a cognitive system, and thus the notion of 'cultural schema' provides a useful tool to explore cognitive schemas that are culturally constructed and maintained across different societies and cultural groups. A term that closely overlaps with cultural schema and has again received major attention in cognitive anthropology is that of the 'cultural model' (for example, D'Andrade, 1995; D'Andrade and Strauss, 1992; Holland and Quinn, 1987). This term, which was initially intended to displace the term 'folk models' (Keesing, 1987), has also been employed in the sense of 'a cognitive schema that is inter-subjectively shared by a social group (D'Andrade, 1987: 112). D'Andrade constantly refers to the notion of 'schema' in his explication of the term 'cultural model' (ibid.) and he regards models as complex cognitive schemas. Strauss and Quinn (1997: 49) also maintain that 'another term for cultural schemas (especially of the more complex sort) is 'cultural model'. Polzenhagen and Wolf (2007), however, have used the notion of 'cultural model' to represent more general, overarching conceptualizations encompassing metaphors and schemas which are minimally complex.

An example of the use of cultural models in cognitive anthropology is the exploration of the cultural model of American marriage. For example, Quinn (1987) observes that the American cultural model of marriage is based on metaphors such as MARRIAGE IS AN ONGOING JOURNEY, reflected in statements such as 'this marriage is at a dead end'.

From the outset, the notion of 'cultural schema' proved to be pivotal to Cultural Linguistics. In *Toward a Theory of Cultural Linguistics*, Palmer (1996: 63) maintained that '[i]t is likely that all native knowledge of language and culture belongs to cultural schemas and the living of culture and the speaking of language consist of schemas in action'. Cultural schemas capture encyclopaedic meaning that is culturally constructed for many lexical items of human languages. Take an example of the word 'privacy' in a variety of English such as American English. The pool of knowledge that forms a web of concepts that define 'privacy' in relation to various contexts and factors is best described as the cultural schema of PRIVACY. The cultural construction of this schema is partly reflected in complaints that some speakers make about members of some other cultural groups, such as 'they don't understand the meaning of privacy'.[2]

Cultural schemas may also provide a basis for pragmatic meanings, in the sense that, knowledge which underlies the enactment and uptake of speech acts and that is assumed to be culturally shared is largely captured in cultural schemas. In some languages, for example, the speech act of 'greeting' is closely associated with cultural schemas of 'eating' and 'food', whereas in some other languages it is associated with cultural schemas that relate to the health of the interlocutors and their family members. The available literature in the area of pragmatics makes very frequent references to 'inference' and 'shared assumptions' as the basis for the communication of pragmatic meanings. It goes without saying that inferences about the knowledge of listeners are technically based on the general assumption that shared cultural schemas are necessary for making sense of speech acts. In short, cultural schemas capture pools of knowledge that provide a basis for a significant portion of semantic and pragmatic meanings in human languages.

Cultural categories and language

Another class of cultural conceptualization is that of the *cultural category*. Categorization is one of the most fundamental human cognitive activities (see Chapter 18 this volume). It begins, albeit in an idiosyncratic way, early in life. Many studies have investigated how children engage in categorizing objects and events early in life (Mareschal, Powell, and Volein, 2003). Children usually begin by setting up their own categories but as they grow up, as part of their cognitive development, they explore and discover how their language and culture categorize events, objects, and experiences. As Glushko *et al.* (2008: 129) put it:

> Categorization research focuses on the acquisition and use of categories shared by a culture and associated with language – what we will call 'cultural categorization'. Cultural categories exist for objects, events, settings, mental states, properties, relations and other components of experience (e.g. birds, weddings, parks, serenity, blue and above). Typically, these categories are acquired through normal exposure to caregivers and culture with little explicit instruction.

The categorization of many objects, events and experiences, such as 'food', 'vegetables', 'fruit', and so on, and their prototype instances, are culturally constructed. It is to be noted that the reference to 'wedding' as a category in the above quotation is distinct from the use of this word in relation to cultural schemas. The 'wedding' as a cultural category refers to the type of event that is opposed to 'engagement' or 'dining out', for example. 'Wedding' as a cultural schema includes all the other aspects of the event, such as the procedures that need to be followed, the sequence of events, the roles played by various participants and expectations associated with those roles.

As for the relationship between cultural categories and language, many lexical items of human languages act as labels for the categories and their instances. As mentioned above, in

English the word 'food' refers to a category, and a word such as: 'steak' is an instance of that category. Usually categories form networks and hierarchies, in that instances of a category can themselves serve as categories with their own instances. For example, 'pasta' is an instance of the category of 'food' with its own instances, such as 'penne' or 'rigatoni'.

Apart from lexical items, in some languages cultural categories are marked by noun classifiers. For example, Murrinh-Patha, an Australian Aboriginal language, uses ten noun classes which are reflective of Murrinh-Patha cultural categorization (Walsh, 1993; Street, 1987). These categories are identified through noun class markers that appear before the noun. The following list from Walsh (1993: 110) includes the class markers and the definition of each category:

Kardu: Aboriginal people and human spirits
Ku: Non-Aboriginal people and all other animates and their products.
Kura: Potable fluid (i.e., 'fresh water') and collective terms for fresh water (i.e., 'rain', 'river').
mi: Flowers and fruits of plants and any vegetable foods. Also faeces.
thamul: Spears.
thu: Offensive weapons (defensive weapons belong to *nanthi*), thunder and lightning, playing cards.
thungku: Fire and things associated with fire.
da: Place and season (i.e. dry grass time).
murrinh: Speech and language and associated concepts such as song and news.
nanthi: A residual category including whatever does not fit into the other nine categories.

The above categorization also allows for multiple membership in the sense that depending on its function, a noun may be categorized into one class at one time and another class at another. For instance, a boomerang may be categorized as *nanthi* when it is used as a back-scratcher and *thu* when it is used as an offensive weapon (Walsh, 1993). Also, in the Dreamtime Creation stories, when the Ancestor beings turn into animals while engaged in their journey of creating the natural world this change is signalled by a switch from one noun class into another. This system of noun classification is entrenched in Murrinh-Patha cultural categorization, which in turn is based on the Murrinh-Patha world-view. For instance, as Walsh argues, the fact that fresh water, fire, and language are classified separately indicates that each holds a prominent place in the culture of the Murrinh-Patha.

Apart from noun classifiers, there are pronouns in many Aboriginal languages that reflect cultural categories, through marking moiety, generation level, and relationship. In Arabana, as an example, the pronoun *amanthara*, which may be glossed into English as 'kinship-we', captures the following complex category:

Arnanthara = we, who belong to the same matrilineal moiety, adjacent generation levels, and who are in the basic relationship of mother, or mothers' brother and child.
(Hercus, 1994: 117)

In Arabana, this cultural categorization of kin groups is also marked on the second plural kinship pronoun *aranthara* and the third person plural kinship pronoun *karananthara*. These examples clearly reveal how some cultural categories are encoded in the grammatical system of a language (see also Lakoff, 1987).

Cultural metaphors and language

As mentioned earlier, conceptual metaphor refers to the cognitive conceptualization of one domain in terms of another (for example, Lakoff and Johnson, 1980). Extensive research in cognitive linguistics has shown how even our basic understanding of ourselves and our surroundings is mediated by conceptual metaphors. For example, in clock-and-calendar industrial cultures time is commonly understood in terms of a commodity, money, a limited resource, and so on. This is reflected in expressions such as 'buying time', 'saving time', and the like. More importantly our understanding of ourselves is achieved through conceptual metaphors. For example we can conceptualize our thoughts, feelings, personality traits, and so on in terms of our body parts (see Chapter 16 this volume).

Research in Cultural Linguistics is interested in exploring conceptual metaphors that are culturally constructed (for example, Palmer, 1996; Sharifian, 2011; see also Chapter 16 this volume), which I refer to as *cultural metaphors*. Several studies have explored cultural schemas and models that give rise to conceptual metaphors, for example through ethnomedical or other cultural traditions (Sharifian, *et al.*, 2008; Yu, 2009a, 2009b). For example, in Indonesian it is *hati* 'the liver' that is associated with love, rather than the heart (Siahaan, 2008). Siahaan traces back such conceptualizations to the ritual of animal sacrifice, especially the interpretation of liver organ known as 'liver divination', which was practised in ancient Indonesia. In some languages, such as Tok Pisin (Muhlhausler, Dutton and Romaine, 2003), the belly is the seat of emotions. Yu (2009b) observes that many linguistic expressions in Chinese reflect the conceptualization of THE HEART IS THE RULER OF THE BODY. He maintains that the 'target-domain concept here is an important one because the heart organ is regarded as the central faculty of cognition and the site of both affective and cognitive activities in ancient Chinese philosophy' (Yu, 2007: 27). Studies of such cultural conceptualizations are currently gathering further momentum (for example, Idström and Piirainen, 2012).

It should be noted here that the cognitive processing of conceptual metaphor is a rather complex issue to explore. While the use of the term 'metaphor' here highlights the involvement of two distinct domains of experience (that is: source and target) it does not follow that every use of an expression that is associated with a conceptual metaphor involves the online cognitive process of mapping from one domain to another. Some cases of conceptual metaphors are simply 'fossilized' conceptualizations that represented active insight at some stage in the history of the cultural cognition of a group. Such metaphors do not imply current speakers of the language have any conscious awareness of the cultural roots of the expressions, or are engaged in any conceptual mapping when they use them. In such cases, the conceptual metaphors may serve rather as cultural schemas which guides thinking about and helps with understanding certain domains of experience. In some other cases, the expressions that are associated with such cultural conceptualizations may be considered simply as figures of speech.

As for the relationship between cultural conceptual metaphors and language, it is clear from the above discussion that many aspects of human languages are closely linked with cultural metaphors. In fact, Cultural Linguistics and cognitive linguistics heavily rely on linguistic data for the exploration of conceptual metaphor. As mentioned above, the language of emotion (for example, *you broke my heart*) largely reflects culturally mediated conceptualizations of emotions and feelings in terms of body parts.

In short, Cultural Linguistics explores human languages and language varieties to examine features that draw on cultural conceptualizations such as cultural schemas, cultural categories, and cultural conceptual metaphors, from the perspective of the theoretical framework of cultural cognition.

Applied Cultural Linguistics

While the ultimate aim of Cultural Linguistics is to examine the relationship between language, culture, and conceptualizations, thus far a Cultural Linguistics perspective has been used in several areas of applied linguistics. The following sections present brief summaries of how a Cultural Linguistics framework has been applied to world Englishes, intercultural communication, and political discourse analysis.

Cultural Linguistics and research into varieties of English

Cultural Linguistics has offered a ground breaking approach to the exploration of varieties of English, based on the premise that varieties of English may be distinct from each other when their respective cultural conceptualizations are taken into consideration (Sharifian, 2005, 2006). Malcolm and Rochecouste (2000) identified a number of distinctive cultural schemas in the discourse produced by a number of speakers of Australian Aboriginal English. These schemas included: travel, hunting, observing, scary things, gathering, problem solving, social relationships, and smash (an Aboriginal English word for a fight). The first four schemas were found to occur most frequently in the data.

Other researchers (Polzenhagen and Wolf, 2007; Wolf, 2008; Wolf and Polzenhagen, 2009) have explored conceptualizations of the African cultural model of community in African varieties of English. Wolf (2008, p. 368) maintains that this 'cultural model involves a cosmology and relates to such notions as the continuation of the community, the members of the community, witchcraft, the acquisition of wealth, and corruption, which find expression in African English'. For example, by examining a number of expressions in Cameroon English, e.g., 'they took bribes from their less fortunate brothers', Wolf observes that the central conceptual metaphors in that variety of English are KINSHIP IS COMMUNITY and COMMUNITY IS KINSHIP (Wolf, 2008, p. 370).

Sharifian, (2005, 2008a) examined cultural conceptualizations in the English spoken by a group of Aboriginal students who, because they sounded like speakers of Australian English, were not identified by their teachers as Aboriginal English speakers. Through a study of word association, however, he found that English words such as 'family', 'home', and 'shame' evoked cultural conceptualizations in these students that were predominantly those associated with Aboriginal English rather than Australian English. For example, for Aboriginal students the word 'family' appeared to be associated with categories in Aboriginal English that extend far beyond the 'nuclear' family, which is the central notion in Anglo-Australian culture. Consider the Table 32.1, showing data from Sharifian (2005).

The responses given by Aboriginal participants instantiate the Aboriginal cultural schema of Family as they refer to members of their extended family, such as aunts and uncles. The responses from the Anglo-Australian participants suggest that the word 'family' is, in most cases, restricted to the 'nuclear family', while sometimes house pets are also included.

Responses such as *they're there for you, when you need 'm they look after you* by Aboriginal participants reflect the responsibilities of care that are very alive between the members of an extended Aboriginal family. Uncles and aunties often play a large role in an individual's upbringing. The closeness of an Aboriginal person to a range of people in his or her extended family members is also reflected in the patterns of responses where the primary responses refer to uncles and aunties or nana and pop instead of father and mother. Responses such as *my million sixty-one thousand family* and *I've got lots of people in my family* reflect the extended coverage of the concept of 'family' in the Aboriginal conceptualization. Moreover, for them the word 'home' appeared to be mainly associated with family relationships rather than 'an attitude to a building' used as a dwelling by a nuclear family.

Table 32.1 A comparison of Aboriginal and Anglo-Australian meanings for 'family'

Aboriginal	Anglo-Australian
Stimulus word: family	Stimulus word: family
<ul><li>Love your pop, love your nan, love our mums, love our dads.</li><li>Brothers, sisters, aunnie, uncles, nan, pops, father, nephew and nieces.</li><li>They're there for you, when you need 'm they look after you, you call 'm aunie and uncle an cousins.</li><li>People, mums, dads, brother, group of families, like aunties and uncles nanas and pops.</li><li>I've got lots of people in my family, got a big family, got lots of family.</li><li>My family, you know how many family I got? One thousand millions, hundred ninety-nine million thousand thousand nine nine sixty-one ... million million, uncle, Joe, Stacy ... cousins, uncles, sisters, brothers, girlfriends and my million sixty-one thousand family</li><li>I like my family, all of my family, my aunties an' uncles and cousins, and I like Dryandra.</li><li>Just having family that is Nyungar [an Aboriginal cultural group] and meeting each other.</li></ul>	<ul><li>You got brothers and sisters in your family and your mum and dad, and you have fun with your family, have dinner with your family, you go out with your family.</li><li>Dad, mum, brother, dog.</li><li>Mum, and dad, brother and sister.</li><li>Fathers, sisters, parents, caring.</li><li>People, your mum and dad, and your sister and brother.</li><li>All my family, my brothers and sisters, my mum and my dad.</li><li>Kids, mums, dads, sisters, brothers.</li><li>Mother, sister, brother, life.</li><li>Mum, dad, my brother.</li><li>I think of all the people in my family [F: Who are they? I: My mum, my dad, an my sister]</li><li>They have a house, they have a car, they have their kitchen, their room, their toilet, their backyard, their carport, they have a dog and a cat.</li></ul>

Cultural Linguistics has also been recently used in compiling a dictionary of Hong Kong English. In a very innovative project, Cummings and Wolf (2011) have identified and included underlying cultural conceptualizations for many of the words included in the dictionary. The following is an example of an entry in the dictionary:

> **Spirit money** (also **paper money**, **hell money**, **hell bank notes**)
> Fixes expressions, n.
> Definition. Fake money burned in a ritual offering to the dead
> Text example: 'An offering of oranges may be peeled and placed on the grave, together with **paper money**. Finally, crackers are let off.'
> **Underlying conceptualisations**: A SUPERNATURAL BEING IS A HUMAN BEING, A PAPER MODEL IS A REAL OBJECT IN THE SUPERNATURAL WORLD [TARGET DOMAIN > SUPERNATURAL BEING, PAPER MODEL] [SOURCE DOMAIN > HUMAN BEING OBJECT IN THE SUPERNATURAL WORLD]
>
> *(ibid.: 163–4)*

This is a groundbreaking approach to the way dictionary entries are compiled for it allows readers to become familiar with the cultural conceptualizations underlying certain expressions in the given language or the language variety. But, of course, in many cases the underlying conceptualizations themselves have their roots in older cultural traditions, including religious and spiritual ones.

Cultural Linguistics and intercultural communication

In the past, intercultural communication has been investigated primarily from the perspective of linguistic anthropology (see also Chapter 30 this volume). For instance, some thirty years ago Gumperz (for example, 1982, 1991) introduced the notion of 'contextualization cues' as an analytical tool for exploring intercultural communication/miscommunication. He defined these cues as 'verbal and non-verbal metalinguistic signs that serve to retrieve the context-bound presuppositions in terms of which component messages are interpreted' (Gumperz, 1996: 379). Central to this notion is the importance of the 'indirect inferences' speakers make during intercultural communication as they rely on linguistic and non-linguistic cues.

From the perspective of Cultural Linguistics, making indirect inferences during intercultural communication is largely facilitated by the cultural conceptualizations shared by the interlocutors (see Chapter 30 this volume). Cultural conceptualizations provide a basis for constructing, interpreting, and negotiating intercultural meanings. These conceptualizations may be the ones that are associated with their L1, or they may be others that the individuals have had access to as a result of living in a particular cultural environment, or even new ones that they have developed from interacting with speakers from other cultures.

In recent years several studies have shown that in certain contexts, intercultural communication, and in particular miscommunication, reflect differences in the ways in which various groups of speakers conceptualize their experiences. In doing so they draw on their own cultural schemas, categories, and metaphors. Wolf and Polzenhagen (2009) observe that 'cross-cultural variation at the conceptual level calls for a strongly meaning-oriented and interpretive approach to the study of intercultural communication' and that is what Cultural Linguistics has to offer.

As an example of studies of intercultural communication carried out from the perspective of Cultural Linguistics, Sharifian (2010) analysed examples of miscommunication between speakers of Aboriginal English and non-Aboriginal English that mainly arose from non-Aboriginal speakers' unfamiliarity with Aboriginal cultural conceptualizations relating to the spiritual world. Many lexical items and linguistic expressions in Aboriginal English are associated with spiritual conceptualizations that characterize the Aboriginal world-view. These include words such as 'sing' and 'smoke'. Take the following example from a conversation between a speaker of Aboriginal English and a non-Aboriginal English speaker:

> A: My sister said, 'when you go to that country, you [are] not allowed to let 'em take your photo, they can sing you'.

According to the Aboriginal cultural schema of 'singing', 'to sing someone' is the ritual used to cast a charm on someone with potentially fatal consequences. For example, if a man falls in love with a girl he might try to obtain strands of her hair, her photo, or some such thing in order to 'sing' her. This would make the girl turn to him or, in the case of her refusal to do so, the 'singing' could result in her falling sick with a serious or even fatal illness (Luealla Eggington, p.c.). It is clear that unfamiliarity with the Aboriginal cultural conceptualizations intimately associated with the use of words such as 'singing' could well lead to miscommunication.

Another Aboriginal cultural schema associated with an English word in Aboriginal English is 'medicine' in the sense of 'spiritual power' (Arthur, 1996: 46). The following is an example of the use of the 'medicine' in this sense, from a conversation between the author of this chapter and an Aboriginal English speaker:

> That when … my mum was real crook and she … she said, 'I woke up an' it was still in my mouth … the taste of all the medicine cause they come an' give me some

medicine last night an' she always tells us that you can't move … an' you wanna sing out an' say just … sorta try an' relax. That happened to me lotta times I was about twelve.

In this narration the speaker is remembering that once her mother was ill and that she mentioned the next morning that 'they' went to her and gave her some 'medicine' that she could still taste. She also describes her mother's reaction to the 'medicine' as wanting to shout and then forcing oneself to relax. Without having the requisite schema, the audience of the above anecdote/ would be likely to think that 'they' refers to medical professionals who visited the mother after hours and gave her syrup or a tablet. However, further discussion with the speaker revealed that her mother was referring to ancestor beings using their healing power to treat her illness. It is clear from these examples how unfamiliarity with Aboriginal cultural schemas informing Aboriginal English can lead to miscommunication.

Another example of cultural schemas that are functioning cognitively in the background in such instances of intercultural communication comes from Sharifian and Jamarani (2011). The study examined how the cultural schema, called *sharmandegi* 'being ashamed', can lead to mis-communication between Persian and non-Persian speakers. This cultural schema is commonly instantiated in Persian through expressions such as *sharmand-am* (short for *sharmandeh-am* 'ashamed-be.1SG') meaning 'I am ashamed', or *sharmandeh-am mikonin* 'ashamed-ISG do.2SG' meaning 'you make me ashamed'. Such expressions are usually used in association with several speech acts, such as expressions of gratitude, offering goods and services, requesting goods and services, apologizing, accepting offers and making refusals. The following is an example of such usage, from a conversation between a student and a lecturer where the student is expressing gratitude to the lecturer for writing a letter of recommendation for her:

> Speaker A (the lecturer): *in   ham nâme-yi   ke   mikhâstin*
> This too letter-ART   that   requested.2PL[3]
> 'Here is the letter that you asked for'
>
> Speaker B (the student): *sharmandeh-am,   vâghean mamnoon*
> Ashamed-BE.1SG   really   grateful
> 'I am ashamed, I am really thankful'

Here the use of *sharmandegi* is intended as an expression of awareness that the other person has spent some time/energy in providing the speaker with goods and services they were under no obligation to supply. The speaker acknowledges this by uttering a 'shame' statement, as if guilty because of this awareness. Although the cultural schema of *sharmandegi* is very widespread and commonly drawn upon among speakers of Persian, it can lead to miscommunication during intercultural communication between speakers of Persian and non-Persian speakers. Consider the following example from Sharifian and Jamarani (2011):

> Tara's (Iranian) neighbour Lara (Australian) offered to pick up some groceries for her, when she was doing her own shopping. Tara happily accepted the offer and told Lara what she needed. When Lara brought the groceries back, Tara wanted to pay her straight away:
>
> Lara: It is okay, you can pay me later.
> Tara: No, you have made me enough ashamed already.
> Lara: But why do you say so?! I'd offered to do the shopping myself, and I had to do my own shopping anyway.

It is evident here that Lara is surprised to hear the expression, or accusation, of 'shame' on the part of Tara, as she had willingly offered to do the shopping for her. However, from the perspective of the Persian cultural schema of *sharmandegi* Tara's response is entirely appropriate, simply reflecting Tara's gratefulness to Lara. Examples such as this reveal how the process of intercultural communication involves a 'meeting place' for cultural conceptualizations, where successful intercultural communication requires a sensitivity to and an awareness of cultural differences and hence the need to recognize and negotiate meaning.

Cultural Linguistics and political discourse analysis

A number of recent studies in political discourse analysis have adopted the approaches of cognitive linguistics and Cultural Linguistics. In general, these studies are in agreement with the long-standing belief that political discourse relies heavily on conceptual metaphor and that political metaphors are often rooted in certain underlying ideologies and cultural models (Dirven, Frank, and Ilie, 2001; Dirven, Frank and Pütz, 2003). These conceptual devices are by no means incidental to political discourse but rather serve to establish or legitimize a given perspective (Sharifian and Jamarani, 2013).

George Bush, for example, repeatedly used either novel or conventional metaphors in his speeches about the Iranian government's nuclear technology. In one of his press conferences, Bush used the metaphorical expression of *house cleaning* in relation to Iran's nuclear programme and stated that *these people need to keep their house clean*. In this metaphor, nuclear technology is conceptualized as dirt, which needs to be removed from the house, the house here being the country. It is difficult to disagree with the statement that *one's house needs to be kept clean* and the use of the *clean house* metaphor appears to present the US president in the legitimate position of exhorting others to perform a socially desirable act. In other words, Bush's statement positions Iran in a very negative light, as associated with *dirt* [dirty house], while positioning himself, or the US government, very positively, as speaking from the moral high ground and putting pressure on the Iranian government to *clean Iran's house*. However, Iran construed its nuclear programme not in the negative sense of 'dirt' but as 'technology' and 'energy', both of which have positive connotations.

From the perspective of Cultural Linguistics, political discourse is not free from cultural influence and is in fact heavily entrenched in cultural conceptualizations (Sharifian, 2007, 2009a). For example, when people attempt to translate from one language into another, such as for the purpose of international negotiation (see also Baker, 2006; Cohen, 1997; Hatim and Mason, 1990), they 'are very likely to need to convey cultural conceptualisation found in one language by means of cultural conceptualisations found in another'. In other words, the process of translation or cross-cultural rendering of cultural conceptualizations can be difficult since languages encode the culturally differentiated and hence historically entrenched ways in which speakers have conceptualized their world in the past and continue to do so in the present. As a result, finding sets of words that successfully capture equivalent cultural conceptualizations in another language can become complicated, depending on the degree to which the two cultures have been in contact and, as a result, have similar although perhaps not identical cultural conceptualizations (see Avruch and Wang, 2005).

Sharifian (2007) analyses the cases of words such as 'concession' and 'compromise', which are pivotal to international political discourse, and argues that the meanings of these words lend themselves to certain culturally constructed conceptualizations. For example, the positive connotations of *compromise*, that is, arriving at a settlement by making concessions, hearken back to the secular foundations of Western democracies and, in turn, link to beliefs promulgated by nineteenth-century classical liberalism, a view that elevated the status of the individual and promoted the notion of contractual relations between 'free agents' in commerce, and so on. This conceptualization is far from a universal one, and some languages do not even have a word for this concept. Also, a historical analysis of the dictionary entries for this concept reveals a tendency towards attributing positive meanings to it rather than negative ones. In general, the approach of Cultural Linguistics can help unpack aspects of political discourse that largely draw on cultural conceptualizations. Given the importance of political discourse, and the possible consequences when misunderstandings arise, the contribution of Cultural Linguistics to this area of inquiry is undoubtedly very valuable.

Future directions

Research on Cultural Linguistics and its applications is still in its infancy. Many features of human languages can be examined for their embeddedness in cultural conceptualizations, from morphosyntactic features to semantic and pragmatic meanings and discourse structure. As discussed and exemplified above, many features of human languages can be used to index cultural conceptualizations such as schemas, categories and metaphors. The results of such analyses of language and culture will be of benefit to scholars in several disciplines, including linguistics and anthropology. Cultural Linguistics will also hopefully generate significant interest among applied linguists whose research also focuses on language and culture. As shown in this chapter, areas of applied linguistics such as world Englishes, intercultural communication, and political discourse analysis can benefit from the approach of Cultural Linguistics in that it provides them with a robust framework and sharply honed analytical tools. Cultural Linguistics has also been applied to the study of second dialect learning, in particular on the part of Aboriginal English speaking children in Australia (see Chapter 26 this volume). Also, application of Cultural Linguistics to the area of Teaching English as an International Language (TEIL) has shown significant promise. Drawing on Cultural Linguistics, Sharifian (2013) offers the notion of *metacultural competence* (Sharifian, 2013) as a target for learners, in order to succeed in the use of English as a language of international communication. This competence enables interlocutors to communicate and negotiate their cultural conceptualizations during the process of intercultural communication.

As has been demonstrated in this chapter, Cultural Linguistics has drawn on research that has been carried out in several areas of applied linguistics while, at the same time, it has already proved its ability to provide new insights into the complex relationships holding between language and culture, especially in intercultural settings. In general, it is expected that any area of inquiry that involves the interaction between culture and language will significantly benefit from adopting the framework of Cultural Linguistics.

Concluding remarks

One of the most important and at the same time challenging questions facing anthropological linguists has been the relationship between language, culture, and thought. Theoretical stances regarding this theme have ranged from a view that language shapes human thought and world-view to one that considers the three to be separate systems. Cultural Linguistics, with its multidisciplinary origin, engages with this theme by exploring features of human languages that encode culturally constructed conceptualizations of human experience. One of the basic premises in this line of inquiry is that language is a repository of cultural conceptualizations that have coalesced at different stages in the history of the speech community and these can leave traces in current linguistic practice. Similarly, interactions at the macro and micro levels of the speech community continuously can act to reshape pre-existing cultural conceptualizations and bring new ones into being. Also, while placing emphasis on the culturally constructed nature of conceptualizations, Cultural Linguistics shares with cognitive linguistics the view that meaning is conceptualization. Overall, due to the multidisciplinary nature of the analytical tools and theoretical frameworks that Cultural Linguistics draws upon, it has significant potential to continue to shed substantial light on the nature of the relationship between language, culture, and conceptualization.

Related topics

embodiment, culture, and language; language and culture in second dialect learning; world Englishes and local cultures; language and culture in cognitive anthropology

Further reading

Palmer, G. B. (1996) *Toward a Theory of Cultural Linguistics* (Austin: University of Texas Press). (This book proposes a theoretical framework for Cultural Linguistics that draws on Boasian Linguistics, ethnosemantic, ethnography of speaking, and cognitive linguistics.)

Sharifian, F. (2011). *Cultural Conceptualisations and Language: Theoretical Framework and Applications* (Amsterdam/Philadelphia: John Benjamins). (This book advances the field of Cultural Linguistics by presenting the theoretical framework of cultural conceptualizations and language, along with its applications to some areas of applied linguistics.)

Sharifian, F., R. Dirven, N. Yu, and S. Neiemier (eds) (2008) *Culture, Body, and Language: Conceptualizations of Internal Body Organs across Cultures and Languages* (Berlin/New York: Mouton DeGruyter). (This collection of essays presents research that explores cultural conceptualizations that are associated with internal body organs, in particular with the heart, in different languages and cultures.)

Yu, N. (2009) *The Chinese HEART in a Cognitive Perspective: Culture, Body, and Language* (Berlin and New York: Mouton de Gruyter). (This book focuses on cultural conceptualizations associated with the heart in Chinese and explores the grounding of such conceptualizations in Chinese traditional medicine and ancient Chinese philosophy.)

Notes

I would like to thank Professor Gary B. Palmer and Professor Roslyn M. Frank for their helpful comments on an earlier version of this chapter. I received financial support from Australian Research Council twice throughout the conduct of the research that forms part of this chapter (ARC DP and Australian Postdoctoral Fellowship [project number DP0343282], ARC DP [project number DP0877310], and ARC DP [project number DP140100353]).

1 The reader is also referred to a discussion of the cultural basis of metaphors (see Quinn, 1991), where the cognitive anthropological perspective (i.e. metaphors reflect cultural models) challenges the traditional cognitive linguistic perspective (i.e. metaphors constitute cultural models).

2 http://plato.stanford.edu/entries/privacy

3 The use of the plural in this example marks politeness/social distance.

References

Arthur, J. M. (1996) *Aboriginal English: A Cultural Study*. Melbourne: Oxford University Press.

Avruch, K. and Z. Wang (2005) 'Culture, apology, and international negotiation: The case of the Sino-U.S. "spy plane" crisis', *International Negotiation*, 10, 337–53.

Baker, M. (2006) *Translation and Conflict: A Narrative Account*. New York and London: Routledge.

Bartlett, F. C. (1932) *Remembering*. Cambridge: Cambridge University Press.

Berlin, B. (1992) *Ethnobiological Classification: Principles of Categorization of Plants and Animals in Traditional Societies*. New Jersey: Princeton University Press.

Blount, B. G. (ed.) (1974) *Language, Culture, and Society: A Book of Readings*. Cambridge, MA, Winthrop Publishers.

——(1995) *Language, Culture, and Society: A Book of Readings*. Prospect Heights, IL: Waveland Press. [expanded reissue of the 1974 book]

——(2011) 'A history of cognitive anthropology' in D. B. Kronenfeld, G. Bennardo, V. de Munck, and M. Fischer (eds) *A Companion to Cognitive Anthropology*. New York: Wiley-Blackwell.

Bobrow, D. J. and Norman D. A. (1975) 'Some principles of memory schemata' in D. G. Bobrow and A. M Collins (eds) *Representation and Understanding: Studies in Cognitive Science*. New York: Academic Press.

Borofsky, R. (1994) 'On the knowledge of knowing of cultural activities', in R. Borofsky (ed.) *Assessing Cultural Anthropology* (New York: McGraw–Hill).

Clark, A. and D. Chalmers (1998) 'The extended mind', *Analysis* 58, 10–23.

Cohen, R. (1997) *Negotiating across Cultures*. Washington, DC: US Institute for Peace.

Cummings, P. J. and H. G. Wolf (2011) *A Dictionary of Hong Kong English: Words from the Fragrant Harbor*. Hong Kong: Hong Kong University Press.

D'Andrade, R. G. (1987) 'A folk model of the mind' in D. Holland and N. Quinn (eds) *Cultural Models in Language and Thought*. New York: Cambridge University Press.

——(1995) *The Development of Cognitive Anthropology*. Cambridge: Cambridge University Press.

D'Andrade, R. G. and C. Strauss (eds) (1992) *Human Motives and Cultural Models*. Cambridge: Cambridge University Press.

Dirven, R., R. M. Frank and C. Ilie (eds) (2001) *Language and Ideology, Vol. 2: Cognitive Descriptive Approaches*. Amsterdam and Philadelphia: John Benjamins.

Dirven, R., R. Frank, and M. Pütz (eds) (2003) *Cognitive Models in Language and Thought*. Berlin and New York: Mouton de Gruyter.

Duranti, A. (2003) 'Language as Culture in U.S. Anthropology', *Current Anthropology*, 11 (3), 323–47.

Frank, R. and Gontier, N. (2011) 'On constructing a research model for historical cognitive linguistics (HCL): Some theoretical considerations', in Kathryn Allan, Päivi Koivisto-Alanko, Heli Tissari, and Margaret Winters (eds.), *Essays in Historical Cognitive Linguistics*. Berlin: Mouton de Gruyter, pp. 31–69.

Glushko, R. J., P. P. Maglio, T. Matlock and L. W. Barsalou (2008) 'Categorization in the wild', *Trends in Cognitive Science*, 12 (4), 129–35.

Goldstein J. (1999) 'Emergence as a Construct: History and Issues', *Emergence: Complexity and Organization*, 1 (1), 49–72

Gumperz, J. J. (1982). *Discourse Strategies*. Cambridge, England: Cambridge University Press.

——(1991) 'Contextualization and understanding', in A. Durand and C. Goodwin (eds) *Rethinking Context: Language as an Interactive Phenomenon*. Cambridge: Cambridge University Press.

——(1996) 'The linguistic and cultural relativity of conversational inference' in J. J. Gumperz and S. C. Levinson (eds) *Rethinking Linguistic Relativity*. Cambridge: Cambridge University Press.

Gumperz, J. J. and D. Hymes (eds) (1972) *Directions in Sociolinguistics: The Ethnography of Communication*. New York and London: Holt, Rinehart and Winston.

Hatim, B. and I. Mason (1990) *Discourse and the Translator*. London: Longman.

Hercus, L. A. (1994) *A Grammar of the Arabana-Wangkangurru Language Lake Eyre Basin, South Australia* Pacific Linguistics Series C-128. Australian National University: Canberra.

Holland, D. C. and N. Quinn (eds) (1987) *Cultural Models in Language and Thought*. Cambridge: Cambridge University Press.

Holland, J. H. (1995) *Hidden Order: How Adaptation Builds Complexity*. Reading, MA: Addison Wesley.

Hutchins, E. (1994) *Cognition in the Wild*. Cambridge, MA: MIT Press.

Hymes, D. (1974) *Foundations in Sociolinguistics: An Ethnographic Approach*. Philadelphia: University of Pennsylvania Press.

Idström, A. and E. Piirainen (2012) *Endangered Metaphors*. Amsterdam/Philadelphia: John Benjamins.

Johnson, M. (1987) *The Body in the Mind: The Bodily Basis of Meaning, Imagination, and Reason*. Chicago, IL: University of Chicago Press.

Keesing, R. M. (1987) 'Models, "folk" and 'cultural': Paradigms regained', in D. C. Holland and N. Quinn (eds) *Cultural Models in Language and Thought*. Cambridge: Cambridge University Press.

Lakoff, G. (1987) *Women, Fire, and Dangerous Things: What Categories Reveal about the Mind*. Chicago, IL: University of Chicago Press.

Lakoff, G. and M. Johnson (1980) *Metaphors We Live by*. Chicago, IL: University of Chicago Press.

Langacker, R. W. (1994) 'Culture, cognition and grammar' in M. Pütz (ed.) *Language Contact and Language Conflict*. Amsterdam/Philadelphia: John Benjamins.

——(forthcoming) 'Culture and cognition, lexicon and grammar', in M. Yamaguchi, D. Tay, B. Blount (eds.) *Towards an Integration of Language, Culture and Cognition: Language in Cognitive, Historical, and Sociocultural Contexts*. London: Palgrave Macmillan.

Lucy, J. A. (1992) *Grammatical Categories and Cognition: A Case Study of the Linguistic Relativity Hypothesis*. Cambridge: Cambridge University Press.

Malcolm, I. G. and J. Rochecouste (2000) 'Event and story schemas in Australian Aboriginal English', *English World-Wide*, 21(2), 261–89.

Mareschal, D., D. Powell, and A. Volein (2003) 'Basic level category discriminations by 7- and 9-month-olds in an object examination task', *Journal of Experimental Child Psychology*, 86, 87–107.

Minsky, M. (1975) 'A framework for representing knowledge' in P. H. Winston (ed.) *The Psychology of Computer Vision* (New York: McGraw-Hill).

Muhlhausler, P., T. E. Dutton, and S. Romaine (2003) *Tok Pisin Texts: From the Beginning to the Present*. Amsterdam/Philadelphia: John Benjamins.

Palmer, G. B. (1996) *Toward a Theory of Cultural Linguistics*. Austin, TX: University of Texas Press.

——(2003) 'Talking about thinking in Tagalog', *Cognitive Linguistics* 14(2–3), 251–80.

——(2006) 'Energy through Fusion at Last: Synergies in Cognitive Anthropology and Cognitive Linguistics' in G. Kristiansen and R. Dirven (eds.) *Cognitive Linguistics: Foundations and Fields of Application*. Berlin/New York: Mouton de Gruyter.

Peeters, B. (2001) 'Does Cognitive Linguistics live up to its name?', in R. Dirven, B. W. Hawkins and E. Sandikcioglu (eds) *Language and Ideology, Vol. 1: Cognitive Theoretical Approaches*. Amsterdam/Philadelphia: John Benjamins.

Polzenhagen, F. and H.G. Wolf. (2007) 'Culture-specific conceptualisations of corruption in African English: Linguistic analyses and pragmatic applications', in F. Sharifian and G. B. Palmer (eds) *Applied Cultural Linguistics: Implications for Second Language Learning and Intercultural Communication* (Amsterdam/Philadelphia: John Benjamins).

Quinn, N. (1987) 'Convergent evidence for a cultural model of American marriage', in D. Holland and N. Quinn (eds) *Cultural Models in Language and Thought* (Cambridge, England: Cambridge University Press).

——(1991) 'The cultural basis of metaphor', in J. W. Fernandez (ed.) *Beyond Metaphor: The Theory of Tropes in Anthropology*. Stanford, CA: Stanford University Press.

Rumelhart, D. E. (1980) 'Schemata: The building blocks of cognition', in R. and J. Spiro, B. Bruce, and W. Brewer (eds) *Theoretical Issues in Reading Comprehension: Perspectives from Cognitive Psychology Linguistics, Artificial Intelligence and Education*. Hillsdale, NJ: Lawrence Erlbaum.

Sharifian, F. (2005) 'Cultural conceptualisations in English words: A study of Aboriginal children in Perth', *Language and Education*, 19(1), 74–88.

——(2006) 'A cultural-conceptual approach to the study of World Englishes: The case of Aboriginal English', *World Englishes*, 25(1), 11–22.

——(2007) 'Politics and/of Translation: Case studies between Persian and English', *Journal of Intercultural Studies*, 28(4), 413–24.

——(2008a) 'A Cultural model of Home in Aboriginal children's English', in G. Kristiansen and R. Divern (eds) *Cognitive Sociolinguistics*. Berlin/New York: Mouton de Gruyter.

——(2008b) 'Distributed, emergent cultural cognition, conceptualisation, and language' in R. M. Frank, R. Dirven, T. Ziemke and E. Bernandez (eds) Body, Language, and Mind (Vol. 2): Sociocultural Situatedness. Berlin/New York: Mouton de Gruyter.

——(2009a) 'Figurative language in international political discourse: The case of Iran', *Journal of Language and Politics*, 8(3), 416–32.

——(2009b) 'On collective cognition and language' in H. Pishwa (ed.) *Language and Social Cognition: Expression of Social Mind*. Berlin and New York: Mouton de Gruyter.

——(2010) 'Cultural conceptualisations in intercultural communication: a study of Aboriginal and non-Aboriginal Australians', *Journal of Pragmatics*, 42, 3367–76.

——(2011) *Cultural Conceptualisations and Language: Theoretical Framework and Applications*. Amsterdam/Philadelphia: John Benjamins.

——(2013) 'Globalisation and developing metacultural competence in learning English as an international language', *Multilingual Education*, 3(7), 1–12.

Sharifian, F., R. Dirven, N. Yu, and S. Neiemier (eds) (2008) *Culture, Body, and Language: Conceptualizations of internal body organs across cultures and languages*. Berlin/New York: Mouton de Gruyter.

Sharifian, F. and Jamarani, M. (2011) 'Cultural schemas in intercultural communication: A study of Persian cultural schema of *sharmandegi* 'being ashamed'', *International Pragmatics* 8(2): 227–51.

Sharifian, F. and Jamarani, M. (2013) 'Cultural conceptualizations and translating political discourse' in A. Rojo and I. Ibarretxe-Antuñano (eds) *Cognitive Linguistics and Translation: Advances in Some Theoretical Models and Applications*. Amsterdam/Philadelphia: John Benjamins.

Shore, B. (1996) *Culture in Mind: Cognition, Culture, and the Problem of Meaning*. Oxford: Oxford University Press.

Siahaan, P. (2008) 'Did he break your *heart* or your *liver*? A contrastive study on metaphorical concepts from the source domain organ in English and in Indonesian', in F. Sharifian, R. Dirven, N. Yu, and S. Neiemier (eds) *Body, Culture, and Language: Conceptualisations of Heart and Other Internal Body Organs across Languages and Cultures*. Berlin/New York: Mouton de Gruyter.

Strauss, C. and N. Quinn (1997) *A Cognitive Theory of Cultural Meaning*. New York: Cambridge University Press.

Street, C. (1987) *An Introduction to the Language and Culture of the Murrinh-Patha*. Darwin: Summer Institute of Linguistics.

Sutton, J. (2005) 'Memory and the extended mind: Embodiment, cognition, and culture', *Cognitive Processing* 6(4), 223–6.

——(2006) 'Memory, embodied cognition, and the extended mind', *Philosophical Psychology*, special issue, 19(3), 281–9.

Tonkinson, R. (1998) 'Mardudjara kinship', in W. H. Edwards (ed.) *Traditional Aboriginal Society*, 2nd edn. Melbourne: Macmillan.

Waldrop, M. M. (1992) *Complexity: The Emerging Science at the Edge of Order and Chaos*. New York: Simon and Schuster.

Walsh, M. (1993) 'Classifying the world in an Aboriginal language', in M. Walsh and C. Yallop (eds) *Language and Culture in Aboriginal Australia*. Canberra: Aboriginal Studies Press.

wa Thiong'o, N. (1986) *Decolonising the Mind: The Politics of Language in African Literature*. London: Heinemann.

Wilson, R. A. (2005) 'Collective memory, group minds, and the extended mind thesis', *Cognitive Processing*, 6(4), 227–36.

Wolf, H. G. (2008) 'A cognitive linguistic approach to the cultures of World Englishes: The emergence of a new model', in G. Kristiansen and R. Dirven (eds) *Cognitive Sociolinguistics: Language Variation, Cultural Models, Social Systems*. Berlin: Mouton de Gruyter.

Wolf, H. G. and F. Polzenhagen (2009) *World Englishes: A Cognitive Sociolinguistic Approach*. Berlin: Mouton de Gruyter.

Yu, N. (2007) 'Heart and cognition in ancient Chinese philosophy', *Journal of Cognition and Culture*, 7(1–2), 27–47.

——(2009a) *From Body to Meaning in Culture: Papers on Cognitive Semantic Studies of Chinese*. Amsterdam and Philadelphia: John Benjamins.

——(2009b) *The Chinese HEART in a Cognitive Perspective: Culture, Body, and Language*. Berlin and New York: Mouton de Gruyter.

33

A FUTURE AGENDA FOR RESEARCH ON LANGUAGE AND CULTURE

Roslyn M. Frank

Introduction

The purpose of this chapter is to assess the future of Cultural Linguistics (see Chapter 32 this volume) as a tool for exploring a variety of linguistic phenomena along with their intra-group and inter-group cultural instantiations.[1] As a subfield of linguistics, Cultural Linguistics has the potential to bring forth a model that successfully melds together complementary approaches, e.g., viewing language as 'a complex adaptive system' and bringing to bear upon it concepts drawn from cognitive science such as 'distributed cognition' and 'multi-agent dynamic systems theory'. This will allow us to move away from essentialist models of the entity we call 'language' (Frank, 2008) and hence to adopt and build on theoretical approaches, e.g. 'enactive cognitivism', already being exploited by researchers working in related areas more characteristic of the cognitive sciences, that is, by those who no longer subscribe to the tenets of 'classic cognitivism'. The paradigm emerging from research in Cultural Linguistics draws on a highly nuanced multi-disciplinarily informed approach that allows for a greater appreciation for individual choices and the motivations behind these choices as they coalesce into and around 'cultural conceptualizations' (Sharifian, 2003, 2009a; see also Chapter 32 this volume).

The approach also allows for the role of synchronic and diachronic sociocultural context to be foregrounded. As will be shown, it is a framework that is particularly sensitive not only to the role of culture in linguistic choices and perceptions, but also to the role of language in maintaining and transmitting the cultural conceptualizations that these linguistic choices have produced over time under the influence of pre-existing cultural and linguistically entrenched schemas. In addition, it opens up an avenue for an in-depth exploration of the relationship between two conceptual entities, the term 'culture' on the one hand, and 'language' on the other, whose definitions, although often assumed in practice to be givens, have shifted radically over the past decades (Strauss and Quinn, 1997).[2] More significantly, even though until now a unified sub-discipline focusing on the relationship between language and culture has never been fully developed, the theoretical framework for such an enterprise is well underway, a topic that will be taken up in the first part of this chapter. In short, this is a framework that could create a flexible transdisciplinary umbrella for future work on language and culture.

In describing the purview of Cultural Linguistics, Sharifian (2011) refers to its transdisciplinary framework stating that it provides a disciplinary synthesis by drawing on analytical tools and theoretical notions that previously have often been explored and exploited in separation from each other. Moreover, a natural common ground exists between the various theoretical disciplines in terms of their concern with cultural conceptualization and the nexus between language and culture, e.g., applied linguistics, cognitive psychology, cognitive linguistics, sociolinguistics, cognitive anthropology and anthropological linguistics. When viewed broadly, the points of intersection between these disciplines and sub-disciplines are significant, that is, they tend to be concerned with the nature of group-level cognition while taking into account the role of both language and culture, albeit with different degrees of emphasis. Sharifian (2011) makes the case that one of the primary goals of Cultural Linguistics is to establish a framework for the study of language as it is grounded in cultural cognition and that this could provide the missing link in the interface between these disciplines.

From my perspective, the development, dissemination and acceptance of a theoretical framework that is more in consonance with the frameworks and developments taking place in the cognitive sciences could represent a major breakthrough in terms of the way that research being carried out under the transdisciplinary umbrella of Cultural Linguistics will be received and evaluated by the larger community of researchers across the disciplines. In the first sections of this chapter I will bring into clearer focus the way that the theoretical framework proposed for Cultural Linguistics dovetails with the overarching framework currently evolving across a number of disciplines which, in turn, are actively collaborating in the construction of the mega-discipline of cognitive science.

Rethinking the language–culture nexus: the role of complex adaptive systems theory

In this section we will examine an important aspect of the theoretical framework proposed for Cultural Linguistics and the way that it draws on conceptual tools from complexity science. Specifically, it will be argued, as Sharifian (2011, this volume) has done, that the construction, emergence, transmission and perpetuation of cultural conceptualizations (CC) are phenomena best understood as constituting 'a complex adaptive system' (CAS). 'CCs may be instantiated and reflected in cultural artefacts such as painting, rituals, language, and even in silence. Aspects of these conceptualizations may also be instantiated through the use of paralinguistic devices such as gesture. In fact different cultural groups may devise certain unique 'devices' for instantiating their own CCs' (Sharifian, 2011: 12). In other words, when defining cultural conceptualizations, they are inextricably linked to a wide field of social and linguistic practices and cultural cognition, a form of cognition that, in turn, is not represented simply as some sort of abstract disembodied 'between the ears' entity.

The utilization of a CAS theoretical framework allows us to understand 'language' and 'culture' from a different perspective, that of dynamic systems theory. From a CAS perspective, 'language' and 'culture' are not viewed as entities independent of one another but rather as constantly interacting systems that form networks of overlapping, mutual influence and whose overall functioning is best captured by modelling them as complex adaptive systems. However, keeping in mind the fact that CAS is a framework which may be relatively unfamiliar to many, a review of its basic characteristics is in order. In the following general discussion, the focus will be primarily on language viewed as a CAS. However, cultural conceptualizations – and more globally cultural processes – can be viewed as being instantiated in a similarly organized multi-agent system.

Complex adaptive systems are ubiquitous in nature. Typical examples include social insects, the ecosystem, the brain and the cell, the Internet, and also, in general, any human social group-based endeavour that takes place in a sociocultural system. Broadly defined, a complex adaptive system is one that is self-organizing in which there are multiple interactions between many different components while the components themselves can consist of networks that in turn operate as complex (sub)systems. Since the global and local levels of the system are coupled, this coupling also drives the system to be dynamic at the global level (Hashimoto, 1998).

A complex adaptive system is self-organizing in that it is constantly constructed and reconstructed by its users while it is characterized by distributed control in that control is exercised throughout the system. Stated differently, the system operates with no centralized mechanism of control. CAS thinking is concerned with understanding the global behaviours arising from local interactions among a large number of agents. Often this global behaviour or emergent dynamics is complex. However, it is neither specified by prior design nor subject to centralized mechanisms of control. And, consequently, it is often difficult or impossible to predict solely from knowledge of the system's constituent parts what the emergent global level properties of the system will be.

Complex systems are systems that constantly evolve over time. Thus, change is an integral element of their functioning. Complex *adaptive* systems are adaptive in that they have the capacity to evolve in response to a changing environment (also known as adaptability, cf. Conrad, 1983). Since complex adaptive systems arise in a wide range of contexts (from the individual cell to the biosphere and the Internet), this theoretical framework is rapidly gaining ground in a variety of disciplinary areas in cognitive science including as a means of modelling cultural processes, language evolution and change.

A CAS approach to language states that *global order* derives from *local* interactions. Language agents are carriers of individual linguistic knowledge which becomes overt behavior in local interactions between agents. Through these *local level* (microscopic) interactions agents construct and acquire individual ontologies, lexicons and grammars. When the latter are sufficiently entrenched within the system, they become part of the *global level* (macroscopic) properties of collective ontologies, lexicons and grammars of the speech community. Actually, the process is even non-linear in the sense that individual ontologies, lexicons and grammars continuously contribute to and, in turn, are influenced by the global level. This shift in perspective provides us with a different non-essentialist view of language: it is understood as a constantly evolving system that defies simplistic taxonomic, essentialist categorization. In short, language is understood as a multi-agent complex adaptive system in which emergent phenomena result from behaviours of embodied, socioculturally situated agents.[3]

As stated, the phenomenon of language is best viewed as a complex adaptive system that is constantly constructed and reconstructed by its users. Therefore, language should be considered an emergent phenomenon, the result of *activity*, the collective, cumulative behavior of language agents over time. These emergent phenomena have a strong causal impact on the behavior and learning of each individual language agent. Hence, there is a type of recursiveness to the system in which feedback mechanisms operate as an intrinsic component of it. The functioning of these feedback loops is referred to as 'circular' or 'recursive causality'. At the local level the individual language agent's behaviours (utterances) determine language, that is, language understood at the global level. Similarly, at the local level the resulting emergent global level structures of language co-determine the range of behaviours of the agents, that is, the range of possible interactions at the local or microscopic level.

This top-down influence is established in several ways. First, we need to keep in mind that the global level systemic structures of language are already in existence prior to the entrance of the local agents. As such, they act as a strong constraint on the linguistic behavior of individual language agents. While the latter acquire their local level understandings of this already existing system as their idiolect, these are understandings that can be renewed, restructured over and over again in the course of the individual's lifetime. Then we can see that the bottom-up influence is established in the following manner. The local level systemic structure of language constantly acts to bring about emergent structure, that is, change, from the bottom-up, so to speak. While the speaker – the individual language agent – has to abide by the structures provided by the system at the risk of not being understood, there is always a degree of flexibility to expand the existing system.[4] Although the structures are to some extent in constant flux, in communicative practice, the speaker is capable of: (1) choosing to draw, consciously or unconsciously, from among them and (2) selecting from amongst those structures that are present in the 'feature bank' of her idiolect, her microstructural 'knowledge' of the global level macrostructures. From this perspective, in the case of bilingual or multilingual language agents they can draw on additional microstructural 'knowledge' that, in turn, can act to set in motion perturbations in the emergent global level structures.

Now if we apply a wide-angled field of vision to the objects under analysis, namely, cultural conceptualizations, we find that they, too, interact with social and linguistic practices and actions, influencing them and in turn being influenced by them. Hence, if these cultural con-ceptualizations are considered collectively, the result could be perceived as another way to define of the 'culture' of a community of speakers. And as long as cultural cognition and the resulting cultural conceptualizations themselves are also framed from the point of view of complex adaptive systems theory, rather than in an essentialist fashion, we can see that both 'language' and 'culture' could be conceptualized in a similar way.

Rather than attempting to define the static 'content' of the two terms, that is, an approach that reflects a fundamentally essentialist position,[5] the CAS approach focuses on dynamic 'process' and applies the tools of analysis to real-world phenomena. For instance, in traditional frame-works 'culture' is often defined in terms of 'contents' as 'whatever it is one has to know or believe in order to operate in a manner acceptable to its members, and do so in any role that they accept for any one of themselves' (Goodenough, 1957: 167). And this definition, although certainly useful, suggests that 'culture' should be viewed as something inside the heads of the individual members of a community rather than focusing on both 'culture' and 'language' as closely intertwined, complementary complex adaptive systems. From this perspective, they must be viewed as inextricably meshed together, systems that are continuously interacting, influencing each other and consequently restructuring themselves through multiple feedback loops. In summary, whereas traditionally culture was frequently viewed as a body of content on which the cognitive processes of individuals operated, from a CAS perspective, culture shapes the cognitive processes of systems that transcend the boundaries of individuals, while the cognitive processes taking place at the micro-level feed back into the overall macro-level of the system.

It should be noted that in recent years the need to bridge the conceptual divide between 'language' and 'culture' has attracted the attention of a number of scholars. For instance, in two recent publications Silverstein has argued that what he calls the 'linguistic/cultural distinction' has already collapsed, as the titles chosen for two of his articles deftly suggest, '"Cultural" concepts and the language–culture nexus' (2004) and 'Languages/cultures are dead! Long live the linguistic-cultural!' (2005). Similarly, discussions of language as a complex adaptive system are not entirely new (Beckner *et al.*, 2009; Frank and Gontier, 2011; Holland, 2005; Steels, 1999) and in the past cognitive anthropologists have attempted to model – simulate – cultural processes by viewing them as emergent properties of systems of interacting agents (Hashimoto, 1998; Hutchins and Hazelhurst, 1991, 2002; Kronenfeld and Kaus, 1993). It should be kept in mind, however, that until now applications of CAS to cultural processes have regularly consisted of multi-agent computer simulations aided by algorithms, not research dealing with the interactions of speakers in complex real-world contexts such as those that are regularly encountered and analysed by researchers working in Cultural Linguistics. In fact, the vast majority of CAS oriented research on language evolution and change has been based on similar multi-agent computer simulations (Steels, 2012; Steels and de Boer, 2007).

Yet there are notable exceptions, for example, Ellis and Larsen-Freeman (2009) and Frank (2008) while Kronenfeld (2002, 2004) has put forward an agent-based approach to cultural (and linguistic) change. However, he approaches the notion of culture not explicitly as a CAS, but rather from a slightly different position, namely, describing it as 'a decentralized system of distributed cognition' and conceiving culture's various sub-systems not as memorized behaviours or fixed knowledge but as productive representations (based on flexible and adaptively growing knowledge systems) that are capable of generating novel responses (Kronenfeld, 2002: 430):

> Either included within culture, or standing as a major parallel learned system is language … Since culture (like language) is intrinsically social, and only exists as a social device, it cannot be what is in any single head, but has to consist of socially shared forms. But since culture has no existence outside of our individual representations of it, and since these representations are variable, there exists no single place where the whole of any culture is stored or represented. Thus culture is necessarily and intrinsically a distributed system.

In summary, the elaboration of an overarching framework capable of applying a CAS theoretical paradigm and its tools of analysis to both real-world languages and cultures should be seen as one of the goals of Cultural Linguistics and when achieved, a major advance. Moreover, as Beckner *et al.* (2009: 1) have underlined, the 'CAS approach reveals commonalities in many areas of language research, including first and second language acquisition, historical linguistics, psycholinguistics, language evolution, and computational modeling'. Finally, the adaption of a CAS approach as well as other analytical tools, such as 'distributed cognition', opens up the possibility of productive dialogue between scholars in the humanities and investigators operating in subfields of cognitive science, most particularly those engaged in research projects who have already embraced the assumptions inherent to the new cognitivism and the notion of 'enaction' that informs it.

Cultural Linguistics meets enactive cognitive science

Most researchers are familiar, at least in its general outlines, with what is referred to as classical, first-generation cognitivism, based on the Computational Theory of the Mind (CTM), a framework to which the generative linguistics of Chomsky and those who came after him belong (Stewart, Gapenne, and Di Paolo, 2011a; Stokhof and van Lambalgen, 2011). Today, however, that paradigm has been repeatedly criticized, particular by those working in the field of Artificial Intelligence and Robotics, making room for a different research paradigm, described by some as 'embodied cognitivism' and by others as 'enactive cognitive science' (Stewart, Gapenne, and Di Paolo, 2011b). It is also a paradigm that brings into play concepts such as 'distributed cognition' (Hutchins, 1995, 2001) and the 'extended mind' (Clark and Chalmers, 1998) and highlights the importance of micro-level and macro-level interactions within the system. It is an approach in which because of its focus on multi-agent and complex adaptive systems with their internalized notion of circular causality, emphasis is placed on micro-level actions and choices of individual agents that, in turn, bring about emergent structure at the macro-level of the system, guiding the choices open to the agents (Frank and Gontier, 2011; Steels, 1999, 2002).

The following comments by Tom Ziemke, one of the foremost authorities in the area of Artificial Intelligence, shed further light on the paradigmatic shift to which Cultural Linguistics is contributing. When speaking of cognitivism Ziemke is referring to the traditional model which he then contrasts with the enactivist paradigm.

> Cognitivism can be said to be 'dominated by a 'between the ears', centralised and disembodied focus on the mind'. In particular, cognitivism is based on the traditional notion of representationalism, characterised by the assumption of a stable relation between manipulable agent-internal representations ('knowledge') and agent-external entities in a pregiven external world. Hence, the cognitivist notion of cognition is that of computational, i.e. formal and implementation independent, processes manipulating the above representational knowledge internally.
>
> *(1999: 179)*

In contrast, the enactivist paradigm 'emphasises the relevance of action, embodiment and agent environment mutuality. Thus, in the enactivist framework, cognition is not considered an abstract agent-internal process, but rather embodied action, being the outcome of the dynamical interaction between agent and environment' (ibid.). In subsequent publications, Lindblom and Ziemke also bring into focus the role of social–cultural situatedness and group-level interactions as defining characteristics of cognition, underlining the complex relationship between body, language and culture (Lindblom, 2007; Lindblom and Ziemke, 2003, 2007).

This major reorientation of the dominant paradigm in cognitive science provides an opening for researchers working in Cultural Linguistics and the sub-disciplines comprised by it. Conversely, the expertise and data of those already working within this framework will contribute in significant ways to the restructuring of the overall research paradigm. The opportunity for increased cross-disciplinary dialogue is enhanced by the fact that Cultural Linguistics already incorporates conceptual frames and approaches currently being utilized in cognitive science, e. g., viewing cultural conceptualizations as the emergent product of a complex adaptive system (Sharifian, 2008) or recognizing that language itself can be understood by applying the same theoretical and methodological lens (Frank and Gontier, 2011).

The possibilities for initiating productive dialogues across the disciplines should not be underestimated, although at this stage they are just beginning to get under way. Stated differently, while many investigators whose work falls within the purview of Cultural Linguists might still view 'cognitive science' as a disciplinarily distant terrain or even an alien one, things are changing rapidly. Moreover, the far-reaching process of renewal that cognitive science is undergoing as a whole has gained the attention of researchers in a number of fields, among them anthropology.[6] Cultural Linguists need to have a seat at the same table.

Methodological and theoretical considerations

Up until now, for the most part, work in the area of language and culture has been done with an open-ended range of methodologies, theories and objects of study, as the chapters in this volume clearly attest. Among the questions that arise is whether in the future this loose articulation of methodologies and theories has the potential to form a more coherent whole or whether such a development is even desirable given the commitments of researchers to particular disciplinary traditions and the pressures brought about by institutional structures within academia (budget shortfalls and administrative downsizing).

Although there is a diversity of approaches, as attested in this volume, there are also aspects of Cultural Linguistics that already suggest avenues that could open up in the future. For instance, as Sharifian (2008, 2009a, 2011) has emphasized in his writings concerning the relationship between cultural conceptualizations and language:

> [h]uman conceptualisation is as much a cultural as it is an individual phenomenon. Members of a cultural group constantly negotiate 'templates' for their thought and behaviour in exchanging their conceptual experiences. Often complex cognitive systems emerge out of somehow concerted conceptualisations that develop among the members of a cultural group over time. Such conceptualisations give rise to the notion of *cultural cognition*.
>
> *(2011: 3)*

In describing the nature of such cultural conceptualizations and their instantiations in language and culture, Sharifian adopts a model that draws on insights from complexity science and dynamic systems theory, specifically a research model that views the processes involved in the generation, evolution and transmission of cultural conceptualizations, intra- and inter-linguistically, as a complex adaptive system (CAS). This approach can be viewed as melding language and culture together into a single dynamic system in which the cultural level of cognition is best described as consisting of cultural conceptualizations that are 'distributed' heterogeneously across the minds of members of the group constituting the community in question. Understood as a CAS, both 'language' and 'culture' can be conceptualized as forming a nexus, a complex intertwined whole, as Silverstein (2004) has suggested.

At the same time, by applying this dynamic systems approach to both of these entities, one bracketed off and called 'culture' and another referred to as 'language', allows us to appreciate the structural similarities between them and, hence, the advantages that accrue when this CAS approach is used to model both entities.[7] In this case it is important to recall that the theoretical framework under development in Cultural Linguistics equates cultural cognition with action and sees this as activity that is socially situated. Therefore, cultural conceptualizations can be viewed broadly for they encompass not merely a 'between the ears' kind of cognitive processing, but also the socially situated actions of the members of the group which give rise to such conceptualizations and, thus, cultural conceptualizations that are often expressed and hence exteriorized in non-verbal ways.

As Sharifian (2011: 20) has observed, for some, cognition is an aspect of culture in that culture influences various cognitive processes (e.g. Altarriba, 1993; Redding, 1980; Chapter 17 this volume). Sperber and Hirschfeld view the relationship between culture and cognition along two dimensions, reflected in the following statement:

> The study of culture is of relevance to cognitive sciences for two major reasons. The first is that the very existence of culture, for an essential part, is both an effect and a manifestation of human cognitive abilities. The second reason is that the human societies of today culturally frame every aspect of human life, and, in particular, of cognitive activity.
>
> *(1999: cxv)*[8]

This is a departure from the view on which 'cognition' has been associated with its focus primarily on mind and mental activity and the individual, although it is still not one that fully embraces the question of the intimate and inextricable connections between 'language' and 'culture'.

Moreover, those working on questions related to 'cognition' in various areas of cognitive science are often still operating with theoretical and methodological frames drawn from different incarnations of generative linguistics. This is an example of how the methodological and theoretical grounding of a discipline is influenced by its connections to other sciences through mechanisms that Silverstein (2005: 104–6) has called 'theoretical and methodological calques' and which consist of borrowing influences and conceptual shapes gained from familiarity with, if not real knowledge of other fields. This leads one group to begin conceptualizing their materials in a particular way so as to draw interpretative conclusions from them. In the case of theoretical calques, a similarity in the conceptual frameworks utilized to give significance to the data can be detected whereas methodological calques can give rise to data being treated much like those of another field. When there is a convergence between the epistemological positions of the fields and their objects of interest are conceptualized in a similar way, synergistic effects can take place as they did in the case of the rapid acceptance and dissemination of the writings of Noam Chomsky in other branches of inquiry quite removed from linguistics itself.

Indeed, as Stokhok and van Lambalgen (2011) have noted, because the Chomskian paradigm has functioned for more than four decades as a model for other disciplines in the humanities as well as fields within the purview of cognitive science, the relevance of the question of its appropriateness as a model extends far beyond linguistics. Furthermore, as we will see in the sections that follow, there are clear indications that this paradigm is losing its power to influence frameworks being developed in many disciplines today and, as a result, new theoretical approaches are emerging, among them the approach being put forward by Cultural Linguistics.

Yet because of the parallels holding between what happened back then in the emerging field of cognitive science – now known as 'classic cognitivism' – and what is happening now, we can turn to the recent and highly relevant analysis by Stokhof and van Lambalgen (2011)[9] entitled 'Abstractions and idealisations: The construction of modern linguistics', where the term 'modern linguistics' is a catch-all expression for the generative grammar research paradigm which they define as 'one of the most remarkable and successful scientific innovations of the twentieth century' and go on to state that

> [t]he rise of generative grammar in the fifties and sixties produced an atmosphere of intellectual excitement that seemed to be reserved for fundamental developments in the natural sciences. And the excitement was not restricted to linguistics as such, it stretched out to other disciplines, such as philosophy, the emerging disciplines of computer science and cognitive psychology, anthropology and literary studies. And to the present day modern linguistics is held up as a model of scientific innovation to other disciplines in the humanities.
>
> *(Stokhof and van Lambalgen, 2011: 1)*

The two authors then lay out the factors that led to the rapid acceptance and diffusion of this theoretical generative framework at precisely the juncture in time when this process took place. They emphasize that one of the major factors was a convergence of concerns and interests in other disciplines that dovetailed with the characterization of language put forward by Chomsky which replaced earlier understandings by a 'logical, mathematical (algebraic) concept of a language, viz., that of a potentially infinite set of well-formed expressions generated by a finite, or finitely characterisable, set of rules (i.e., a grammar) … Behind this is the fundamental assumption that in the end language and linguistic competence can be understood as phenomena that are anchored in human biology, and that it is only via the methodology of the natural sciences that we may acquire insight into their nature and function' (ibid.: 3, 5).

Nonetheless, this fundamental assumption that has persisted across many decades is now rapidly losing ground, as the questions posed by Stokhof and van Lambalgen suggest:

> These observations give rise to a fundamental question with regard to linguistics as such: Could modern linguistics perhaps be an example of a 'failed discipline'? As was already noticed above, the adoption of the models and methodologies of the natural sciences and the formal sciences was one of the keys to the success of modern linguistics. Moreover, especially in Chomsky's views a clearly naturalistic goal can be discerned: according to him linguistics studies what in the end is an aspect of human biology. Is this naturalism perhaps one of the causes of the present, confusing situation? Is it that modern linguistics, knowingly or unknowingly, follows a naturalistic approach to phenomena – language and linguistic competence – that are of a fundamentally other nature?
>
> *(ibid.: 3)*

In other words, upon reviewing the history of the construction of the central concepts and goals of the research paradigm associated with 'classic cognitivism' there is every reason to believe that it was decisively influenced by ideas and developments in other disciplines, notably the formal and the natural sciences, but also philosophy and, of course, Chomskian linguistics. Consequently, it is not surprising that a similar convergence of interests is occurring today which augurs well for the future of research in Cultural Linguistics and the theoretical framework that it is formulating. Indeed, the adoption and application of terminology and concepts not only familiar to cognitive scientists, but which act as functionally equivalent expressions is important in that they can be read as analogues across these disciplines. This allows them to resonate and contributes to another degree of convergence within the cognitive sciences where the concept of 'distributed cognition', for example, is commonplace. As will be demonstrated in the following section, these theoretical and methodological calques, understood in their positive sense, are especially salient when a concept such as 'socially distributed cognition' is brought into the picture.

Cultural Linguistics and socially distributed cognition

Writing more than a decade ago, Waloszek (2003) offered this comment about 'socially distributed cognition' which coincides with the framework of Cultural Linguistics, stating 'that the idea of socially distributed cognition, prefigured by Roberts (1964), is becoming increasingly popular. Recently, the idea has emerged that social organization is itself a form of cognitive architecture. Distributed cognition extends this notion by including interactions between people and their environment, in addition to phenomena that emerge in social interactions.' In contrast to computer-inspired models of the information-processing paradigm, for distributed cognition minds are not representational engines, 'whose primary function is to create internal models of the external world. Instead, the organization of the mind is an emergent property of interactions between internal and external resources' (Waloszek, 2003).

To obtain a better purchase on the way these theoretical paradigms are converging upon each other, concretely, that of Cultural Linguistics and the paradigm of the Enactive Cognitivism which is increasingly prevalent in the cognitive sciences, we can examine how complex systems theory allows language and cultural conceptualizations to be viewed as a form of 'distributed cognition'. Waloszek (2003) summarized the distributed cognition approach in the following manner, drawing on the recently published research of Hollan, Hutchins and Kirsh (2000):

> The first principle concerns the boundaries of the unit of analysis for cognition:
>
> Distributed cognition looks for cognitive processes in the functional relationships between elements that participate together in a process – the traditional cognitive unit of analysis is the individual.
>
> The second principle concerns the range of mechanisms that may be assumed to take part in cognitive processes:
>
> While traditional views look for cognitive events in the manipulation of symbols inside individual actors, distributed cognition looks for a broader class of cognitive events and does not expect all such events to be encompassed by the skin or skull of an individual.
>
> When one applies these principles to the observation of human activity, various distributions of cognitive processes become apparent. The following three are of particular interest [...]:
>
> > Cognitive processes may be distributed across members of a social group
> > Cognitive processes may involve coordination between internal and external (material, environment) structure
> > Cognitive processes may be distributed through time, so that the products of earlier events can transform the nature of later events.

In Table 33.1, the tenets of the traditional view are contrasted with the distributed cognition framework. As can be seen, the acceptance of the distributed cognition model by those working in fields of cognitive science is another indication of the movement away from the older information-processing paradigm.[10]

As can be appreciated from this discussion of the characteristics of 'distributed cognition', the framework is one that coincides closely with the tenets and theoretical approaches of those working in areas of Cultural Linguistics and other usage-based models of language. In short, the shared assumptions are substantial.

Table 33.1 Traditional view and distributed cognition view (adapted from Waloszek (2003); Hollan, Hutchins and Kirsh (2000))

	Traditional view	*Distributed cognition view*
Unit of Analysis	individual person	all – the system is larger than individuals, all sizes of social-group networks; speech communities
Mechanism	manipulation of symbols and linguistic artifacts by individual actors; synchronic emphasis	functional systems, groups, emphasis on space-time, diachronic dimension
Methodology	controlled experiments, emphasis on cognitive properties of individuals	language viewed as a complex adaptive system, emphasis on cognitive properties of systems, dynamical systems approach, sociocultural situatedness, ethnography

Reflections on cognitive linguistics and its experiential hypothesis

To fully appreciate the significance of integrating innovative concepts such as CAS and 'distributed cognition' into the research paradigm of Cultural Linguistics, we need to keep in mind the role played by cognitive linguistics over the past thirty years. Although there certainly have been notable exceptions and dissenting voices were often heard, for the most part cognitive linguistics went off in directions that took it away from the study of role of culture in shaping language and its influence on all levels of language, not just the lexicon but also grammatical elements that interact with cultural components.[11] This distancing of the field from culturally oriented pursuits increased as the Lakoffian theory of conceptual metaphor gradually gained ground as well as, eventually, the associated framework called 'experiential realism' or 'embodied scientific realism' (Lakoff and Johnson, 1999) which briefly stated, argued that our metaphors, and therefore our reasoning, derive from our bodies: they are *embodied*. In 1999, Lakoff and Johnson asserted that 'human concepts are not just reflections of an external reality, but … they are crucially shaped by our bodies and brains, especially by our sensorimotor system' (Lakoff and Johnson, 1999). That stance was buttressed by their earlier work on metaphor and more importantly the notion of *image schemas* which again came to be viewed, ultimately, as bodily-based entities (Grady, 1997; Johnson, 1987; Lakoff and Johnson, 1980; Lakoff and Turner, 1989).[12]

At the same time, researchers began to question 'the more theoretical question of the extent to which the metaphorical patterns to be found in the lexicon have their origins in (universal) bodily experiences, and the extent to which they are cultural and ideological constructs' (Goatly, 2007: 5). The Lakoffian view was anchored in a universalist position and spoke of the dominant or even exclusive role of bodily experience in shaping metaphor, leaving cultural influences and variations aside. However, as Goatly and others have argued, 'a considerable number of metaphor themes lack a bodily experiential correlation as their basis, suggesting non-universality, and [one] concludes that the experiential hypothesis may be a form of reductionism, a hypothesis already challenged by the idea of the body as historical and cultural as well as biological' (Goatly, 2007: 7).

With respect to the factors that contributed to the acceptance and rapid assimilation of Lakoffian theory not only within cognitive linguistics but also in fields adjacent to it, e.g., inside cognitive science itself, Goatly (2007: 276) makes the following cogent observation:

> I would like to turn our ideological lenses upon what Lakoff calls '*The* contemporary theory of metaphor'. This grew up in a particular context, among Chomskyan notions of language. Two aspects of Chomsky's theory seem to have been inherited. The emphasis on linguistic universals or universal grammar, and the notion that language is an innate genetically determined faculty, though for Chomsky's mental faculty Lakoff and his followers substitute the biological.
>
> *(Lakoff and Johnson, 1999: 476)*[13]

In contrast, early in the history of the development of cognitive linguistics as a sub-discipline there was the perception that cognitive linguists could have much in common with cognitive anthropologists, 'since both groups dealt with their main area of focus (namely, language and culture respectively) as cognitive systems. However, this perception soon faded, perhaps because many working in the field of cognitive linguistics did not fully recognize just how closely culture interacts with and shapes language and conceptualization' (Sharifian, 2011: xv). Rather than focusing on the language–culture nexus and consequently the sociocultural situatedness of language, cognitive linguistics moved off in other directions.[14]

However, in recent years, far greater attention has been placed on these ontological and epistemological issues and to reflecting on the sometimes deep-seated assumptions that have guided a significant part of the research carried out under the banner of cognitive linguistics in the past thirty years (Frank, 2013; Harder, 1999; Sinha, 1999; Sinha and Bernárdez, this volume). In other words, when looking at the larger picture, we can see that this current reassessment of the scope of the cognitive linguistics enterprise as well as its ontological and epistemological foundations reflects major shifts in emphasis not only in that field, but also the new assumptions that have been feeding into the reorientation of the larger transdisciplinary research paradigm developing in the cognitive sciences.

Looking to the future: successes and challenges

Whereas only time will tell what influence Cultural Linguistics will have on the transdisciplinary paradigm emerging in the cognitive sciences, certainly one of the major success stories of this new methodology for linguistics is the research that has been carried out in intercultural communication, multilingualism and world Englishes (Sharifian, 2009b; Sharifian and Jamarani, 2013; Sharifian and McKay, 2013; Sharifian and Palmer, 2007). While the contributions that have been made in these subfields are already substantial, given the increasing globalization brought about by the role of English as the de facto lingua franca of a myriad of technologically enabled communication acts, the interest and need for further studies in these areas will only increase, bringing into even clearer focus the importance of a methodology capable of addressing the issues raised by the 'glocalization' these diverse cultural and linguistic communicative practices (Sharifian, 2013).

Similarly, the impact of the application of approaches informed by cultural conceptualizations on cross-cultural studies of metaphor and emotion has been significant, moving discussions away from reductionist positions to more historically nuanced and entrenched approaches and, hence, to investigations of the socioculturally contingent properties of language use and, for example, away from more traditional Lakoffian accounts of conceptual metaphor. While this more culturally oriented approach to deciphering the historical entrenchment of metaphors and emotion has been underway for some time (Dirven, Frank, and Ilie, 2000; Geeraerts and Grondelaers, 1995), in the past ten years this area of Cultural Linguistics has taken on a life of its own with the publication of a significant number of in-depth studies on the subject, yet another indication of the increased interest in historically informed research initiatives that weave together linguistic, anthropological and philosophical materials to provide an explanation for the particular patterns of usage (Frank *et al.*, 2008; Kövecses, 2005; Sharifian *et al.*, 2008; Yu, 2009).

At the same time, in recent years there has been significant cross-fertilization between cognitive linguistics and critical discourse theory which has led, in turn, to the interrogation of metaphorical patterns in terms of their role in reflecting, representing and shaping social practices and beliefs, e.g., Chilton (1996) and van Dijk (1998) among others. Of late, these two traditions have begun to come together as the central focus of a significant number of researchers (Charteris-Black, 2005; Musolff, 2004; Musolff and Zinken, 2004). In a similar way, Cultural Linguistics takes up a position that builds on the belief that culture and language are inextricably intertwined, 'that language is not some transparent medium, but that it shapes our thoughts and practices' (Goatly, 2007: 4).[15] And, keeping in mind that language is a complex adaptive system and hence characterized by circular causality, speakers do not merely passively reproduce the dominant patterns of their culture and language, rather through their micro-level speech acts and related sociocultural practices they shape, transmit and alter the overall system – the macro-level of the system – albeit for the most part unreflectively (Frank and Gontier, 2011; Sharifian, 2009a; 2011: 19–44).

Consequently, developing and solidifying a methodology and theoretical framework capable of tracing the way that cultural conceptualizations, entrenched in this language–culture nexus, are created, maintained and propagated – both vertically and horizontally – within particular linguistic communities as well as across diverse linguistic communities will continue to be one of the challenges facing those producing applied research in the sub-discipline of Cultural Linguistics. However, it is clear that these goals will not be accomplished overnight or by fiat, but rather they will come about slowly, through a negotiated process of gradual accretion, resulting in a coalescence of positions and guided by the methodological approaches brought to bear by researchers working on specific topics in Cultural Linguistics and focused on concrete questions of linguistic and cultural practice.

The multidisciplinary challenge

When defining the scope of Cultural Linguistics, one of the characteristics that is often pointed out is its multidisciplinary focus: that the focus on work on language and culture brings together scholars from a variety of different disciplines, often academically isolated from each other. Until recently, disciplines by their own nature and the power structures implicit in the competition for scarce institutional resources created centripetal tendencies, where the discipline or sub-discipline in question regularly developed terminological and methodological characteristics that were usually or primarily understood only by members of the in-group, closing it off from other disciplines or sub-disciplines and giving it a unique identity.

At the same time the discipline or sub-discipline tended to develop a distinct paradigmatic tradition within the larger contested domain brought about by the need to secure funding, prestige and other resources. However, over the past twenty years, these disciplinary frontiers, although still prevalent on paper and characteristic of much of the institutional organization of the academy, are increasingly breaking down with more and more disciplinary border crossings and, in some cases, actual realignments of internal academic departments and units to accommodate research initiatives and to take advantage of funding sources that depend upon or explicitly require an interdisciplinary perspective.

In some instances, this has resulted in the creation of inter-disciplinary clusters where faculty from various departments are brought together to address problems whose very nature demand an interdisciplinary or multi-disciplinary approach. Whereas this tendency does contribute to inter- and multi-disciplinary initiatives, there is a down-side, as Clifford (2005) has noted in his reflections on these broader changes that are exerting pressures on current reconfigurations of disciplinary boundaries. There is definitely room for concern in terms of the reasons for the creation of such clusters, namely, the role placed by 'the neoliberal corporate university, with its increased emphasis on marketable outcomes, flexible research teams, and audit-driven interdisciplinarity' (Clifford, 2005: 48).

Even though Cultural Linguistics is not a unified theory of language and culture, but rather a flexible and evolving theoretical framework, for this field of research to flourish inside and outside the academy there is the need for a sense of coherence, common goals, and at least to some degree, a shared methodology and theoretical framework. These can be brought about by a variety of means, e.g., the organization of conferences, publications and handbooks such as this one that show the depth and breadth of research being carried out, the development of research projects drawing team members from different disciplines and addressing questions that require a multidisciplinary approach. Yet there are challenges to the development of collaborative research projects, including the tendency for linguists as well as anthropologists to conceptualize and carry out their investigations alone, rather than in teams. Moreover, if at some point Cultural Linguistics begins to fully interact with the evolving paradigm in cognitive science, this will involve reaching across the disciplines and engaging with problems and issues that call for collaborative effort and cross-disciplinary input (Bender, Hutchins and Medin, 2010: 377).

In recent years this sense of multidisciplinary coherence has increased in part because of the dissemination of research in areas related to Cultural Linguistics and the rise to prominence of subfield journals produced by various sectors of those working in the field of Cultural Linguistics, including the recently launched *International Journal of Language and Culture* (IJoLC). In addition, a number of substantial book-length studies have brought increased attention to Cultural Linguistics, beginning with the publication of Palmer's seminal work *Towards a Theory of Cultural Linguistics* (1999) and followed up by Sharifian's comprehensive study *Cultural Conceptualizations and Language: Theoretical Framework and Applications* (2011). And another important milestone has been the establishment in 2011 of the John Benjamins book series, *Cognitive Linguistic Studies in Cultural Contexts*, which provides a home for additional cutting-edge research in this area. Furthermore, of particular significance in this process of pedagogic accommodation to work on cultural conceptualizations and Cultural Linguistics in general has been the cross-disciplinary applicability of much of the research being carried out this area and hence its congruence with the evolving nature of these inter-departmental and institutional reconfigurations within academia.

There is every indication that in the future the sub-discipline of Cultural Linguistics will continue to draw on and take advantage of theoretical and methodological developments in other disciplines, for example, cognitive linguistics, cognitive anthropology, anthropological linguistics, cognitive psychology, cultural anthropology and areas of applied linguistics including world Englishes and intercultural communication, English as an International Language and cross-cultural pragmatics. At the same time, there is every reason to believe that it will continue to pursue flexible arrangements for knowledge production and transmission, arrangements that are fully open to dialogue with these other disciplines as well as to engaging in dialogues with other areas inside linguistics.

Concluding thoughts

At this juncture it is clear that the subfield of Cultural Linguistics along with its new journal IJoLC will create a space for these multidisciplinary endeavours by investigators and allow them to expand their horizons, taking the full implications of the linguistic–cultural nexus into account, both methodologically and theoretically, when carrying out their work. There is little doubt that in the years to come cross-disciplinary exchanges already taking place will foster multidisciplinary collaboration and joint projects that in turn will result in research initiatives and new debates which have the capacity to impact the broader field of cognitive science itself as well as other related disciplines and sub-disciplines. In turn, since Cultural Linguistics is characterized by an openness to these boundary crossings, we can expect that the resulting exchanges will contribute to further methodological and theoretical innovation within the field of Cultural Linguistics itself.

To what extent these processes of cross-fertilization will impact the larger evolving research paradigm of those working in the cognitive sciences is an open-ended question. It will depend on whether investigators with a commitment to Cultural Linguistics will also see the importance of gaining a better grounding in related areas, attending to the concerns and issues motivating researchers working, for example, from within the paradigm of Enactive Cognitive Science or those attempting to apply Bayesian approaches to modelling and comparing the content of large datasets composed of linguistic, genetic and cultural materials drawn from different populations and hence from a diversity of language–cultures (Dunn *et al.*, 2005; Holman *et al.*, in press;

LIBRARY, UNIVERSITY OF CHESTER

Russell, Silva, and Steele, 2014).[16] While there are clearly areas of overlap where insights from Cultural Linguistics could shed new light on questions that are central to these other disciplinary endeavours, for Cultural Linguists to have a real impact on these areas of cognitive science will require developing, as mentioned, new investigative models. To do so, teamwork will be necessary and this, in turn, should lead to the development of innovative collaborative initiatives which are truly transdisciplinary in nature. In conclusion, as is well recognized, established canonical traditions that have tended to separate and compartmentalize disciplines often break down in practice through interdisciplinary collaboration, articulation and re-articulation (Clifford, 2005). In this sense, Cultural Linguistics promises to serve as a bridge that brings together researchers from a variety of fields, allowing them to focus on problems of mutual concern from a new perspective and in all likelihood discover new problems (and solutions) that until now have not been visible.

Related topics

culture and emotional language; culture and translation; cultural linguistics; language and cultural history; language and culture in cognitive anthropology; language, culture and identity; linguistic relativity: precursors and transformations; world Englishes and local cultures; writing across cultures

Further reading

D'Andrade, R. (1995) *The Development of Cognitive Anthropology*. Cambridge: Cambridge University Press. (A comprehensive historical account of cognitive anthropology from its origins in the 1950s, tracing how early notions about semantics and taxonomies evolved into theories about prototypes, schemas and connectionist networks, and concluding with a review of recent scholarship on the social distribution of cultural knowledge and cultural models.)
Gentner, D. and Goldin-Meadow, S. (eds) (2003) *Language in Mind: Advances in the Study of Language and Thought*. Cambridge, Mass./London: The MIT Press. (An excellent collection of introductory essays covering a broad and representative range of topics on language and culture.)
Lucy, J. A. (1992) *Language Diversity and Thought: A Reformulation of the Linguistic Relativity Hypothesis*. Cambridge: Cambridge University Press. (One of the classic studies of the Sapir–Whorf linguistic relativity hypothesis, it surveys the various responses that the writings of Boas, Sapir and Whorf have elicited across time and puts forward a proposal emphasizing the need for further empirical research in the field so that these theories and methods can be brought to bear on empirical data, the kind of assessment that attends to both cognitive and cultural outcomes.)
Shore, B. (1966) *Culture in Mind: Cognition, Culture and the Problem of Meaning*. New York: Oxford University Press. (Covering a wide range of material, both theoretical and ethnographic, Shore delves into the more cognitive side of culture, highlighting the need to rethink culture in terms of models while placing emphasis on the interplay between 'personal' or 'mental' models and 'conventional', or socially instituted' cultural models.)

Notes

1 For discussion of the directions that future research may take with respect to the other research topics covered in this volume, the reader is referred to the sections in each chapter where these developments are treated.
2 For a discussion of the myriad ways that the word 'culture' has been defined and dissected, cf. Clifford (2005). This is a topic that many of the contributors to this volume have commented upon. For example, Eglin (see Chapter 10) states the following concerning the multifarious definitions and overall slippery nature of this concept: 'The same argument may be made about culture. No sooner is an attempt made to establish a formal definition for it (thought of as a determinate thing) – for example,

an "integrated and distinct set of rules which give meaning to activities" … or, famously, "whatever it is one has to know or believe to operate in a manner acceptable to [a society's members], and do so in any role that they accept for any one of themselves" … than it has to be admitted that in any actual case accommodation will have to be made for sub-cultures, local cultures, the cultures of particular groups of all sorts and the idea, say, that while some set of cultural practices may be "shared" by neighbouring societies one of them "owns" the cultural practices in question and the other has "copied" them … For many of its uses "culture" may be replaced with "society", "values", "customs", "mores", "the way we do things round here" without it ever being possible to pin down once and for all what that "way" is. Cultures as determinate objects are professional anthropologists' inventions, the product of "ethnographic work" in the "organization of fieldwork data".'

3 These dialectics are also pointed out at the psychological level by Clark (1996: 100–20) when he introduces his famous distinction between personal and communal common ground. And Tomasello's (2004: 4) characterization of cumulative cultural evolution as a kind of ratchet effect can also be interpreted as an attempt to capture these dynamics.

4 The close parallels holding between this CAS model and usage-based approaches to language are found in the following discussion of 'units of language' where the latter are defined as 'not fixed but dynamic, subject to creative extension and reshaping with use. Usage events are crucial to the ongoing structuring and operation of the linguistic system. Language productions are not only products of the speaker's linguistic system, but they also provide input for other speakers' systems (as well as, reflexively, for the speaker's own), not just in initial acquisition but in language use throughout life' (Kemmer and Barlow, 2000: ix).

5 Earlier definitions of culture were even more content-oriented. Indeed, one of the most influential of such definitions was Tylor's: 'Culture or Civilization, taken in its wide ethnographic sense, is that complex whole which includes knowledge, belief, art, morals, law, custom, and any other capabilities and habits acquired by man as a member of society' (Tylor, 1871, p. 1).

6 In their review paper that recapitulates 'the uneven history of the relationship between Anthropology and Cognitive Science over the past 30 years, from its promising beginnings, followed by a period of disaffection, on up to the current context', Bender, Hutchins and Medin (2010: 374) lay out the groundwork for reconsidering what anthropology and (the rest of) cognitive science might have to offer each other: 'We think that this history has important lessons to teach and has implications for contemporary efforts to restore Anthropology to its proper place within Cognitive Science. The recent upsurge of interest in the ways that thought may shape and be shaped by action, gesture, cultural experience, and language sets the stage for, but so far has not fully accomplished, the inclusion of Anthropology as an equal partner.'

7 For a related discussion of the nexus between language and culture and the concept *linguaculture*, see Chapter 6 this volume.

8 Another insightful incursion into this topic is found in Sperber and Claidière (2005).

9 See also Haspelmath (2011).

10 Perhaps one of the best-known early attempts to appropriate a theoretical framework from cognitive science is represented by the connectionist-inspired discussions of Strauss and Quinn (1997: 48–84, esp. 60–1) where the architecture of prototypical connectionist models of cognition (also sometimes referred to as 'parallel distributed processing' or 'neural network modeling') is contrasted with that of the more typical traditional model of 'symbolic processing', 'classical' or GOFAI (Good Old Fashioned Artificial Intelligence), also known collectively as 'computational' theories of mind.

11 Here I refer to syntactic devices that can interact with cultural conceptualizations, e.g., the noun-class markers in an Australian Aboriginal language like Murrinth-Patha or the use of second-person plural pronoun in Persian (Sharifian, 2011; Walsh, 1993).

12 In his critique of the experiential hypothesis, Harder (1999: 195–6) phrases it this way: 'Because the concern of cognitive linguistics has been to assert the embeddedness of language in a wider cognitive experiential context. … no sharp distinctions [are made] between cognitive and biological phenomena, because language is grounded in the human body, and because all the skills can be seen as mediated by neurological processes (which can be modeled by increasingly sophisticated connectionist simulations).'

13 Even though today in the field of cognitive linguistics conceptual categories are viewed as both embodied and culturally constructed – that such cognition is shaped by interactions of individuals with each other and their perception of the world including the cultural environment and their bodily experience – there is no question that for many years the Lakoffian experiential model of neural embodiment held sway and set the tone for many research initiatives.

14 Writing some twenty years ago, Geeraerts (1995: 111–12) provided this description of the major research interests of those working in the field of cognitive linguistics, themes that were prevalent at that time and that have not changed significantly since then: 'Because cognitive linguistics sees language as embedded in the overall cognitive capacities of man, topics of special interest for cognitive linguistics include: the structural characteristics of natural language categorization (such as proto-typicality, systematic polysemy, cognitive models, mental imagery and metaphor); the functional principles of linguistic organization (such as iconicity and naturalness); the conceptual interface between syntax and semantics (as explored by cognitive grammar and construction grammar); the experiential and pragmatic background of language-in-use; and the relationship between language and thought, including questions about relativism and conceptual universals.'

15 See Chapters 3, 4, 8, 17 and 22 this volume.

16 See Levinson and Evans (2010) for a remarkable and at times heated debate between those in the traditional cognitivist camp with their universalizing abstract frameworks and two linguists who propose an integrative, co-evolutionary model to describe the complex interaction between mind and cultural linguistic traditions. In their article entitled 'Time for a sea-change in linguistics', they argue 'that the language sciences are on the brink of major changes in primary data, methods and theory' (Levinson and Evans, 2010: 2733), a position that coincides closely with the arguments made in this chapter. See also Evans and Levinson (2009).

References

Altarriba, J. (ed.) (1993) *Cognition and Culture: A Cross-cultural Approach to Cognitive Psychology*. Amsterdam: Elsevier Science Publishers.

Beckner, C., Blythe, R., Bybee, J., Christiansen, M. H., Croft, W., Ellis, N. C., Holland, J., Ke, J., Larsen-Freeman, D., Schoenemann, T. (2009) 'Language as a complex adaptive system', in N. C. Ellis and D. Larsen-Freeman (eds), *Language as a Complex Adaptive System. Language Learning 59. Special Issue. Supplement 1*, 1–26.

Bender, A., Hutchins, E., and Medin, D. (2010) 'Anthropology in Cognitive Science', *Topics in Cognitive Science*, 2, 374–85.

Charteris-Black, J. (2005) *Politicians and Rhetoric: The Persuasive Power of Metaphor*. Basingstoke: Palgrave Macmillan.

Clark, A. and Chalmers, D. (1998) 'The extended mind', *Analysis*, 58(1), 7–19.

Clark, H. H. (1996) *Using Language*. Cambridge, MA: Cambridge University Press.

Clifford, J. (2005) 'Rearticulating anthropology', in D. A. Segal and S. J. Yanagisako (eds), *Unwrapping the Sacred Bundle: Reflections on the Disciplining of Anthropology* (pp. 24–48). Durham/London: Duke University Press.

Conrad, M. (1983) *Adaptability*. New York: Plenum.

Dirven, R., Frank, R. M., and Ilie, C. (2000) *Language and Ideology. Vol. 1. Cognitive Descriptive Approaches*. Amsterdam/Philadelphia: John Benjamins.

Dunn, M., Terrill, A., Reesink, G., Foley, R., and Levinson, S. C. (2005) 'Structural phylogenetics and the reconstruction of ancient language history', *Science*, 309, 2072–5.

Ellis, N. C. and Larsen-Freeman, D. (eds) (2009) 'Language as a complex adaptive system', *Language Learning* 59, special issue, supplement 1.

Evans, N. and Levinson, S. C. (2009) 'The myth of language universals: Language diversity and its importance for cognitive science', *Behavioral and Brain Sciences*, 32(5), 429–92.

Frank, R. M. (2008) 'The language–organism–species analogy: A complex adaptive systems approach to shifting perspectives on "language"', in R. M. Frank, R. Dirven, T. Ziemke and E. Bernárdez (eds), *Body, Language and Mind. Vol. 2. Sociocultural Situatedness* (pp. 215–62). Berlin: Mouton de Gruyter.

——(2013) 'Body and mind in Euskara: Contrasting dialogic and monologic subjectivities', in R. Caballero-Rodríguez and J. E. Díaz Vera (eds), *Sensuous Cognition. Explorations into Human Sentience: Imagination, (E)motion and Perception* (pp. 19–51). Berlin: Mouton de Gruyter.

Frank, R. M., Dirven, R., Ziemke, T., and Bernárdez, E. (eds) (2008) *Body, Language and Mind. Vol. 2. Sociocultural Situatedness*. Berlin: Mouton de Gruyter.

Frank, R. M. and Gontier, N. (2011) 'On constructing a research model for historical cognitive linguistics (HCL): Some theoretical considerations', in H. Tissari, P. Koivisto-Alanko, K. I. Allan and M. Winters (eds), *Historical Cognitive Linguistics* (pp. 31–69). Berlin: Mouton de Gruyter.

Geeraerts, D. and Grondelaers, S. (1995) 'Looking back at anger: Cultural traditions and metaphorical patterns', in J. R. Taylor and R. E. MacLaury (eds), *Language and the Cognitive Construal of the World* (pp. 153–79). Berlin/New York: Mouton de Gruyter.

Goatly, A. (2007) *Washing the Brain: Metaphor and Hidden Ideology*. Amsterdam/Philadelphia: John Benjamins.

Goodenough, W. H. (1957) 'Cultural anthropology and linguistics', in P. L. Garvin (ed.), *Report on the Seventh Annual Round Table Meeting on Linguistics and Language Study* (pp. 167–173). Monograph Series on Language and Linguistics 9. Washington, DC: Georgetown University Press.

Grady, J. E. (1997) 'Foundations of meaning: Primary metaphors and primary scenes', unpublished Ph.D. dissertation, University of California, Berkeley.

Harder, P. (1999) 'Partial autonomy: Ontology and methodology in cognitive linguistics', in T. Janssen and G. Redeker (eds), *Cognitive Linguistics: Foundations, Scope and Methodology* (pp. 195–222). Berlin/New York: Mouton de Gruyter.

Hashimoto, T. (1998) 'Dynamics of internal and global structure through linguistic interactions', in J. S. Sichman, R. Conte and N. Gilbert (eds), *Multi-agent Systems and Agent Based Simulation* (pp. 124–39). LNAI Series, vol. 1534. Berlin: Springer-Verlag.

Haspelmath, M. (2011) 'The language system is abstract but cannot be understood without its social functions (Comments on Martin Stokhof and Michiel van Lambalgen, "Abstractions and idealisations: The construction of modern linguistics")', *Theoretical Linguistics*, 37(1–2), 45–50.

Hollan, J., Hutchins, E., and Kirsh, D. (2000) 'Distributed cognition: Toward a new foundation for human–computer interaction research', *ACM Transactions on Computer–Human Interaction*, 7(2), 176–96.

Holland, J. H. (2005) 'Language acquisition as a complex adaptive system: Essays in evolutionary linguistics', in J. W. Minett and W. S.-Y. Wang (eds), *Language Acquisition, Change and Emergence: Essays in Evolutionary Linguistics* (pp. 411–35). Hong Kong: Hong Kong University Press.

Holman, E. W., Wichmann, S., Brown, C. H., and Eff, E. A. (in press) 'Diffusion and inheritance of language and culture: A comparative perspective', *Social Evolution and History*, 14(2).

Hutchins, E. (1995) *Cognition in the Wild*. Cambridge, MA: MIT Press.

——(2001) 'Distributed cognition', in N. J. Smelser and P. B. Baltos (eds), *International Encyclopedia of the Social and Behavioral Sciences* (pp. 2068–72). Amsterdam/New York: Elsevier.

Hutchins, E. and Hazelhurst, B. (1991) 'Learning in the cultural process', in C. Langton, C. Taylor, D. Farmer and S. Rasmussen (eds), *Artificial Life II: SFI Studies in the Sciences of Complexity*, vol. 10 (pp. 689–706). New York: Addison Wesley.

——(2002) 'Auto-organization and emergence of shared language structure', in A. Cangelosi and D. Parisi (eds), *Simulating the Evolution of Language* (pp. 279–305). London: Springer-Verlag.

Johnson, M. (1987) *The Body in the Mind: The Bodily Basis of Meaning, Reason and Imagination*. Chicago, IL: University of Chicago Press.

Kemmer, S. and Barlow, M. (2000) 'Introduction: Usage-based conception of language', in M. Barlow and S. Kemmer (eds), *Usage-based Models of Language* (pp. vii–xxviii). Stanford, CA: CSLI Publications.

Kövecses, Z. (2005) *Metaphor in Culture: Universality and Variation*. Cambridge: Cambridge University Press.

Kronenfeld, D. B. (2002) 'Culture and society: The role of distributed cognition', in R. Trappl (ed.), *Cybernetics and Systems*, vol. 1 (pp. 430–1). Austrian Society for Cybernetic Studies: Vienna.

——(2004) 'An agent-based approach to cultural (and linguistic) change', *Cybernetics and Systems*, 35(2/3), 211–28.

Kronenfeld, D. B. and Kaus, A. (1993) 'Starlings and other critters: Simulating society', *Journal of Quantitative Anthropology*, 4, 143–74.

Lakoff, G. and Johnson, M. (1980) *Metaphors We Live by*. Chicago; London: University of Chicago Press.

——(1999) *Philosophy in the Flesh: The Embodied Mind and Its Challenges to Western Thought*. Chicago, IL: University of Chicago Press.

Lakoff, G. and Turner, M. (1989) *More than Cool Reason: A Field Guide to Poetic Metaphor*. Chicago, IL: University of Chicago Press.

Levinson, S. C. and Evans, N. (2010) 'Time for a sea-change in linguistics: Responses to comments on "The myth of language universals"', *Lingua*, 120(12), 2733–59.

Lindblom, J. (2007) *Minding the Body: Interacting Socially through Embodied Action*. Linköping: Linköping University Institute of Technology.

Lindblom, J. and Ziemke, T. (2003) 'Social situatedness of natural and artificial intelligence: Vygotsky and beyond', *Adaptive Behavior*, 11(2), 79–96.

——(2007) 'Embodiment and social interaction: A cognitive science perspective', in T. Ziemke, J. Zlatev and R. M. Frank (eds), *Body, Language and Mind: Embodiment* (pp. 129–63). Berlin: Mouton de Gruyter.

Musolff, A. (2004) 'Metaphor and conceptual evolution', *metaphorik.de*, 7, 55–75.

Musolff, A. and Zinken, J. (2004) *Metaphor and Discourse*. London: Palgrave Macmillan.

Palmer, G. B. (1999) *Toward a Theory of Cultural Linguistics*. Austin, TX: University of Texas Press.

Redding, S. G. (1980) 'Cognition as an aspect of culture and its relation to management processes. An exploratory review of the Chinese case', *Journal of Management Studies*, 17(2), 127–48.

Roberts, J. M. (1964) 'The self-management of culture', in W. H. Goodenough (ed.), *Explorations in Cultural Anthropology: Essays in Honor of George Peter Murdock* (pp. 433–54). London: McGraw Hill.

Russell, T., Silva, F., and Steele, J. (2014) 'Modelling the spread of farming in the Bantu-speaking regions of Africa: An archaeology-based phylogeography', *PLoS ONE*, 9(1), e87854. Available at http://www.plosone.org/article/info%0087853Adoi%0087852F0087810.0081371%0087852Fjournal.pone.0087854 [accessed 04.06.14].

Sharifian, F. (2003) 'On cultural conceptualizations', *Journal of Cognition and Culture*, 3(3), 187–207.

——(2008) 'Distributed, emergent cultural cognition, conceptualisation and language', in R. M. Frank, R. Dirven, T. Ziemke and E. Bernárdez (eds), *Body, Language and Mind. Vol. II. Sociocultural Situatedness* (pp. 109–36). Berlin: Mouton de Gruyter.

——(2009a) 'On collective cognition and language', in H. Pishwa (ed.), *Social Cognition and Language: Expression of the Social Mind* (pp. 163–80). Berlin: Mouton de Gruyter.

——(ed.) (2009b) *English as an International Language: Perspectives and Pedagogical Issues*. Bristol, UK: Multilingual Matters.

——(2011) *Cultural Conceptualizations and Language: Theoretical Framework and Applications*. Amsterdam/Philadelphia: John Benjamins.

——(2013) 'Globalisation and developing metacultural competence in learning English as an international language', *Multilingual Education*, 3(7), 1–12. Available at http://www.multilingual-education.com/content/pdf/2191-5059-2193-2197.pdf [accessed 04.11.14].

Sharifian, F., Dirven, R., Yu, N., and Neiemier, S. (eds) (2008) *Culture, Body, and Language: Conceptualizations of Internal Body Organs across Cultures and Languages*. Berlin/New York: Mouton de Gruyter.

Sharifian, F. and Jamarani, M. (2013) *Language and Intercultural Communication in the New Era*. New York/London: Routledge.

Sharifian, F. and McKay, S. L. (eds) (2013) 'Globalization, localization, and language use/learning', *Multilingual Education*, special issue, 3(3).

Sharifian, F. and Palmer, G. B. (eds) (2007) *Applied Cultural Linguistics: Implications for Second Language Learning and Intercultural Communication*. Amsterdam/Philadelphia: John Benjamins.

Sharrock, W. W. (1974) 'On owning knowledge', in R. Turner (ed.), *Ethnomethodology: Selected Readings* (pp. 45–53). Harmondsworth, UK: Penguin Education.

Sharrock, W. W. and Anderson, R. J. (1982) 'On the demise of the native: Some observations on and a proposal for ethnography', *Human Studies*, 5(1), 119–35.

Silverstein, M. (2004) '"Cultural" concepts and the language–culture nexus', *Current Anthropologist*, 45(5), 621–52.

——(2005) 'Languages/cultures are dead! Long live the linguistic–cultural!', in D. A. Segal and S. J. Yanagisako (eds), *Unwrapping the Sacred Bundle: Reflections on the Disciplining of Anthropology* (pp. 99–125). Durham, NC: Duke University Press.

Sinha, C. (1999) 'Grounding, mapping and acts of meaning', in T. Janssen and G. Redeker (eds), *Cognitive Linguistics: Foundations, Scope and Methodology* (pp. 223–55). Berlin/New York: Mouton de Gruyter.

Sperber, D. and Claidière, N. (2005) 'Why modeling cultural evolution is still such a challenge', *Biological Theory*, 1(1), 20–2.

Sperber, D. and Hirschfeld, L. (1999) 'Culture, cognition and evolution', in R. Wilson and F. Keil (eds), *MIT Encyclopaedia of the Cognitive Sciences* (pp. cxi–cxxxii). Cambridge, MA: MIT Press.

Steels, L. (1999) 'The puzzle of language evolution', *Kognitionswissenschaft*, 8(4), 143–50.

——(2002) 'Language as a complex adaptive system', in F. Brisard and T. Mortelmans (eds), *Language and Evolution* (pp. 79–87). Wilrijk: UIA. Antwerp Papers in Linguistics 101.

——(ed.) (2012) *Experiments in Cultural Language Evolution*. Amsterdam/Philadelphia: John Benjamins.

Steels, L. and de Boer, B. (2007) 'Embodiment and self-organization of human categories: A case study of speech', in T. Ziemke, J. Zlatev and R. M. Frank (eds), *Body, Language and Mind. Volume 1: Embodiment* (pp. 411–30). Berlin/New York: Mouton de Gruyter.

Stewart, J., Gapenne, O., and Di Paolo, E. A. (2011a) 'Introduction', in J. Stewart, O. Gapenne and E. A. Di Paolo (eds), *Enactivism: Towards a New Paradigm in Cognitive Science* (pp. vii–xvii). Cambridge, MA: MIT Press.

——(eds) (2011b) *Enactivism: Towards a New Paradigm in Cognitive Science*. Cambridge, MA: MIT Press.

Stokhof, M. and van Lambalgen, M. (2011) 'Abstractions and idealisations: The construction of modern linguistics', *Theoretical Linguistics*, 37(1–2), 1–26.

Strauss, C. and Quinn, N. (1997) *A Cognitive Theory of Cultural Meaning*. Cambridge: Cambridge University Press.

Tomasello, M. (2004) 'The human adaptation for culture', in F. Wuketits and C. Antweiler (eds), *Handbook of Human Evolution, Vol. 1: The Evolution of Human Societies and Cultures* (pp. 1–23). Weinheim, Germany: Wiley-VCH Verlag.

Tylor, E. B. (1871) *Primitive Culture: Researches into the Development of Mythology, Philosophy, Religion, Language, Art and Customs, Vol. 1*. London: John Murray.

van Dijk, T. A. (1998) *Ideology: A Multidisciplinary Approach*. London: Sage.

Waloszek, G. (2003) 'Dissolving boundaries with distributed cognition and xApps'. Available at http://www.sapdesignguild.org/editions/edition7/print_distrib_cognition.asp [accessed 04.02.14].

Walsh, M. (1993) 'Classifying the world in an Aboriginal language', in M. Walsh and C. Yallop (eds), *Language and Culture in Aboriginal Australia* (pp. 107–22). Canberra: Aboriginal Studies Press.

Yu, N. (2009) *From Body to Meaning in Culture: Papers on Cognitive Semantic Studies of Chinese*. Amsterdam/Philadelphia: John Benjamins.

Ziemke, T. (1999) 'Rethinking grounding', in A. Riegler, M. Peschl and A. von Stein (eds), *Understanding Representation in the Cognitive Sciences* (pp. 177–90). New York: Kluwer Academic/Plenum.

INDEX